A Passion For
Opera

A Passion For
Opera

*Learning to Love It:
The Greatest Masters, Their Greatest Music*

PETER FOX SMITH

Trafalgar Square Publishing

North Pomfret, Vermont

First published in 2004 by
Trafalgar Square Publishing
North Pomfret, Vermont 05053

Printed in China

Copyright © 2004 Peter Fox Smith

Library of Congress Cataloging-in-Publication Data

Smith, Peter Fox.
    Opera : learning to love it : the greatest masters, their greatest music /
Peter Fox Smith.
            p. cm.
Includes bibliographical references and index.
ISBN 1-57076-280-5
1. Opera. I. Title.
MLLL1700.S65 2004
782.1—dc22   2204009965

A special thank you to Lebrecht Music and Arts Photo Library, the world's largest resource for music images and pictures of all the arts at www.lebrecht.co.uk. All the photographic images throughout the book are from their vast library.

Frontispiece: This Arthur Rackham image of a Rhinemaiden from Wagner's *Das Rheingold* is reproduced with the kind permission of his family.

Book design: Heather Mansfield
Cover design: Glenn Suokko
Typeface: Trump Mediaeval and Frutiger

10 9 8 7 6 5 4 3 2 1

DEDICATION

To Joanne

TABLE OF CONTENTS

ACKNOWLEDGMENTS

Many students requested I write this book as did Raymond V. Phillips, the "Father" of Vermont Public Radio. So much I regret that Ray died recently before seeing it. I am indebted to other VPR colleagues: Ray Dilley (now of Nebraska Public Radio), Betty Smith, Walter Parker, and especially Sam Sanders. For more than twenty-five years he has worked with me on the weekly production of "Saturday Afternoon at the Opera." Sam is one of the best audio technicians in the country with awards to prove it. He knows as much about music as anyone I know and I'm a constant beneficiary of this expertise.

From Helen Whybrow and Glenn Suokko I received good practical advice when starting the project and at the end Glenn, an excellent designer, produced the book's covers. Gail Vernazza meticulously entered my typed manuscript into a computer, Doris Troy's skillful copy editing improved every page, and Cristen Brooks carefully attended to all corrections.

The experienced professionals of Trafalgar Square transformed the manuscript into this beautiful book. Heather Mansfield did the interior design and Rebecca Schmidt, editorial assistant, and Martha Cook, managing editor, attended to countless details and solved numerous problems. Caroline Robbins, publisher and editor, patiently, and with remarkable perception toiled endlessly with me to improve the book. I cannot imagine working with a better and more accommodating editor, and forever will be grateful.

Also, I am very thankful for the insights and comments of Meredith and William Mayer, and Louise and Robert De Cormier.

In memoriam, I must acknowledge my dear friend, Robert Grinnell, who for years enthusiastically encouraged me in my work; my Harvard University thesis advisor, the brilliant teacher and eminent Wagnerian scholar, Jack M. Stein; my mother, Alice Johnson Smith; and my father, Ralston Fox Smith, Jr., first and best teacher always.

Finally, constant support from a loving family is so important and this I received from son Peter, his wife Grace, and their children Lauren and Andrew; and from daughter Alice, her husband Pepper, and their sons William and Peter. But above all, the presence of my wife Joanne is in every word on every page.

PREFACE

Opera! For more than four hundred years it has fascinated princes and peasants, kings and commoners, as well as gifted musicians and countless ordinary people. For them the seductive Carmen, the rakish Don Giovanni, and poor little Butterfly are more real than life itself. These vivid characters live on in words and music in the imaginations of true opera lovers who thrill with joy or weep and sob along with the heroes and heroines in this most emotional art form. This book is about them and many other equally fascinating and unforgettable personalities.

These characters will be introduced to you in the context of their famous stories and memorable songs, of course, but also within their place in the history and art of opera. In the pages that follow you will encounter operatic essentials: the greatest composers and their most notable, influential, and often performed works; an elementary vocabulary of operatic terms and names; something about great and famous singers; and how to go to an opera prepared for the fullest possible understanding and enjoyment. All of this will be accomplished in ordinary English. Even though you may be able to read music and translate some foreign languages, in writing this book I have not assumed this of every reader. I have avoided including excerpts in musical notation and throughout there are translations of the foreign words encountered. So many opera books either represent this magnificent art in the complex, technical language of one expert talking to another, or through oversimplified presentations. Emphatically, this book avoids both the jargon of aficionados and the bland commentary for rank beginners. I assume the reader is curious, intelligent, and wants to know all about opera.

All the basics, therefore, are here but they can be found in other versions of perfectly acceptable and informative operatic guides. This book is much more than a guide. The difference lies herein. Far more than just learning about opera, this book is about learning how to love it. It is about a passion for opera. My lifelong passion that inexplicably I am compelled to share with you as already I have done with thousands of others for many years: with generations of college students, undergraduate and graduate, as well as an uncountable number of listeners to my "Saturday Afternoon at the Opera" broadcasts on Vermont Public Radio for over twenty-seven years. Those students and these listeners constitute irrefutable evidence that the power of opera is such that once within you it takes hold of your head and heart and never lets go. The ultimate intention of this book is to make certain that this happens to you and because it is the music more than any other factor that achieves this, the music always is at the center of whatever I have to say.

Because the music is central, the book is for anyone and everyone. For those who know little or nothing about opera it will serve as an introduction, yet there is much to be gained by those already familiar with operas and opera history. Even those who know much may find new revelations. Clarification pertaining to Mozart's different operatic styles, for example, or the religious foundations of Wagnerian music drama, or perhaps, how and why modern music is made the way it is, and so much more.

There are various ways you may use this book. It can serve as a handy reference work. Suppose a friend invites you to attend an opera, let us say *Der Rosenkavalier* by Richard Strauss. You know nothing about it. Looking in the index you learn an introduction to this opera begins on page 600. There you find it and begin to prepare yourself for the performance. Or you can read the entire chapter on Richard Strauss, into which *Der Rosenkavalier* fits, as a means of obtaining a fuller perspective. I hope, however, this book will be more than just a reference book. I invite you to read it as you would any other story from start to finish. Within this wonderful, long story, many opera plots contain romance, comedy, ploys, schemes, mistaken identities, heartbreak, evil, goodness, tragedy, trysts, and triumphs. So often they are intriguing entertainment before a single note of the music is heard.

Also, and this is very important. The book can serve as a text for an opera course: your own private course that you administer to yourself or one offered by a school, club, literary society, music group, library, or any other such organization. This third aspect was my primary motivation for writing it. In many years of teaching about opera, I never was able to find the book that did what I wanted and what I believed was the best way to introduce the fascinating subject that has been an indispensable part of my life. (If you are impatient to commence your own conversion, go to the CD Guide, page 693, where I have a quick reference to the operas and recordings that became the first love of so many of my students.)

Finally, opera is a daunting topic for a book. More than four centuries of opera history have produced thousands of works by hundreds of composers. To select only several dozen composers and less than one hundred operas for consideration is still a huge undertaking. Numerous biographers spend decades chronicling the life and works of just one composer. The countless number of books and articles associated with this project constitute a vast reading list far beyond my ability to master. Accordingly, there will be mistakes, and those errors are mine. What I can vouch for is the music introduced to you by this book. There are no mistakes there. As a body of music, it represents much of the greatest operatic creativity. Line up the superlatives: beautiful, dramatic, enchanting, lyrical, melodic, powerful, serene, sublime, overwhelming. I cannot imagine life without this music nourishing me daily. And if only one tune gets under your skin, or if a few excerpts you cannot do without send you to buy the recordings, then you will have redeemed the cost of this book. That I promise you!

Now, having said all this, let us begin our story; but, curiously enough, not at the beginning.

1
INTRODUCTION

When the curtain rang down for the first time on Giacomo Puccini's opera *La bohème (The Bohemians)* on February 1, 1896, in Turin, Italy, opera history was a few months away from its three hundredth birthday. Today, more than a century after that world premiere, *La bohème* is one of the most often performed and most loved operas in the world, and with it our book begins.

La bohème always was one of the operas I presented to my students in introductory courses. To illustrate my lectures I used both audio and video excerpts from the world of opera and for my *La bohème* presentation the class ended with a superb video performance of the final scene of this heart-wrenching drama. I will never forget one class many years ago. No composer was a greater master of operatic melody expressing pathos than Puccini, and one of many supreme examples is in the last moments of this opera when a poor poet realizes his beloved has died in his chilly Parisian garret. When the curtain came down on this now famous scene at a performance in Palermo several weeks after the premiere, the overwhelmed audience would not leave the theater until the scene was repeated. As the curtain closed on my video presentation, I turned on the lights for a few final words to my students. Several of the young women were weeping openly, young men surreptitiously wiped their eyes, and an entire class who only several weeks before had never seen a single opera sat still, emptied and dazed! A great operatic performance will do that every time, and in later years, when a class concluded with scenes of powerful and devastating effect, I used the dimmer to turn on just enough light to end the session and to allow students to depart without stumbling over chairs.

I cannot reduce to a formula opera's power to shatter emotions even though time and again I have seen it at work. I can point to poignant poetry profoundly intensified by the capacity of music to transcend speech in going to the heart of a matter, but I cannot say what this power is, nor can I define it. But if and when this experience first happens to you, you will know it as one you have never had before and one you will seek again and again. You will be hooked on opera. The purpose of this book is to help promote such experiences.

La bohème is not the only opera with the power to move an audience but it is high on the list of those with tremendous emotional impact. Some operatic experiences consist of watching a performance and waiting for the next famous hit tune to come along because many opera plots are silly, even downright stupid. The only reason some operas survive is because a gifted composer wrote enough memorable music to transcend the story and give it life. Not so with *La bohème.* Here a good story develops with the accompaniment of marvelous music. The story in *La bohème* evolves with terrific speed and with music of remarkable melodic beauty. There is not a boring moment in the entire drama, first note to last.

The original story is by the French writer Henri Murger, who is remembered for his sketches of Parisian life in the first half of the nineteenth century. The novel *Scènes de la vie de Bohème (Scenes of Bohemian Life)*, from which Puccini derived his opera, has its basis in fact. Murger had a passionate affair with a young woman who died of consumption (tuberculosis) after they had become estranged. In Puccini's opera the Lucile of Murger's novel has become Lucia, known as Mimi, and her lover is a poet named Rodolfo. After Mimi and Rodolfo amicably agree to part, she, in the final scene, weak and wracked by consumption, returns to the garret, where love first blossomed, and dies.

I want both to tell the whole story and to indicate where within the story the most famous music is heard.

The opera is in four acts, each representing a different scene in the lives of six bohemians living in Paris about 1830. The poet

Rodolfo lives in poverty in a garret that he shares with three friends, Marcello, a painter; a philosopher named Colline; and Schaunard, who is a musician. The two women are Mimi, whom we meet in the first act, and Musetta, who first appears in Act II. As the curtain opens on Act I it is Christmas Eve in the freezing garret. Rodolfo and Marcello, with no fuel for their stove, contemplate alternatives: to burn a chair or, perhaps, Marcello's most recent painting. They settle on the manuscript of a play Rodolfo is writing, which is comfortably ablaze as Colline arrives.

Soon thereafter, the play now all but ashes, Schaunard enters with attendants carrying fuel, food, and wine. He astonishes the others by tossing on the floor money earned by giving music lessons to an Englishman; it is their policy to share all income. Schaunard rejects attempts by his friends to set the table, declaring they will dine out. They agree to a drink before departing, which is interrupted by the landlord Benoit, who insists on rent owed to him. They offer a drink, have sport with having seen him, a married man, with another woman, feign shock and disgust with such behavior, and dismiss him without a penny. As Marcello, Colline, and Schaunard depart, Rodolfo promises to follow in a few minutes—he wants to complete an article he has been writing.

Alone with pen and paper, he progresses slowly until a knock on the door interrupts work. Here commences one of the most anticipated scenes in all opera. He opens the door to find before him a beautiful, frail young woman who lives in the room below. Her candle is out and she needs it lighted. Rodolfo notices she is weak and woozy. He helps her to a chair and restores her with some wine. As she prepares to leave, she drops her key. Her candle again goes out. His, too, extinguishes and they are alone together with only the light of the moon to ease the dark. Sinking to their knees, they run their hands over the floor in search of her key. Rodolfo find it, pockets it secretly, and, as their hands chance to meet, takes hers in his. "*Che gelida manina*," he sings, which means, "Your little hand is frozen." Now, as he warms it in his own, comes one of the most famous and beautiful songs in all opera. In it Rodolfo introduces himself as a poor poet, a writer of rhymes and love songs who, nevertheless, has the soul of a millionaire. Fascinated with this neighbor he has not met before, Rodolfo concludes by asking if now she will tell him about herself. She complies in a song equally famous and beautiful: "*Si. Mi chiamano Mimi, ma il mio nome è Lucia*" ("Yes. I am always called Mimi but my real name is Lucia"), which over the years has prompted and promoted the popular opera quiz question "What is Mimi's real name?"

Her story is brief and simple. She is a seamstress who works at home, loves flowers, rarely goes to church but likes to pray, and is a neighbor who inopportunely has bothered him.

Rodolfo's friends call from the street, wondering why he is delayed and what he is doing up in the room alone to keep them waiting. Rodolfo confesses he now is not alone and urges his friends to depart for the café and to save a table. He and his new friend will follow soon—but not until they confess the mutuality of their love at first sight in a most memorable duet. "*O soave fanciulla,*" Rodolfo begins: "Oh! lovely girl, oh! sweet face bathed in the soft moonlight . . ." Rarely in opera does one famous song immediately follow another, culminating in a glorious duet, all without interruption for some plot development. Singing together the word "love" (*Amor* in Italian) over and over, they depart the cold garret to join the others as the first act ends.

The second act is swift, playing in less than twenty minutes, and often is performed in conjunction with the first act without an intermission. The scene is the square outside the Café Momus in the Parisian Latin Quarter where a large, festive crowd of adults, students, and children mill and mix with barking vendors and bustling waiters. Some people are buying gifts; others busy themselves with errands or browsing. Rodolfo and Mimi join his friends, all take their table, and Mimi is introduced. As the group order their meal and enjoy animated conversation, the toy seller, Parpignol, enters the square, producing considerable excitement among the children.

Then Musetta, obviously known to all, arrives arm-in-arm with an elderly, wealthy, obsequious admirer. Noticing the bohemians, she demands a table next to theirs. Musetta and Marcello, once lovers, are now estranged. As she tries to attract his attention, he attempts to ignore her, much to the embarrassment of Alcindoro, the sugar daddy. When Musetta gets up from her table and struts about while singing her delicious and familiar waltz, it is too much for Marcello. "Tie me to the chair," he exclaims as she, with a seductive saunter, passes him by singing *Quando me'n vo* ("When I walk alone along the street people stop and stare, head to toe, at my beauty"). "Musetta's Waltz," as it is commonly known, is the one famous tune of the second act, which otherwise is a continuous flow of melodic conversational invention virtually unprecedented in opera.

Musetta, aware that Marcello once again is in her grasp, returns to her seat. Pretending one of her shoes is hurting her, she dispatches Alcindoro on the phony errand of getting her shoe fixed, and then falls into a passionate embrace with the all too willing painter.

The waiter presents a bill far beyond the bohemians' means, but as a band and soldiers appear and intensify the general hubbub, Musetta leaves both her bill and that of her friends for presentation to Alcindoro, who returns in time to see her being carried away, feet high in the air, one shoe on and one shoe gone, on the shoulders of Marcello and Colline. The curtain falls.

I have encountered recordings of "highlights" from *La bohème* that obviously include the two famous songs and the duet from the first act, "Musetta's Waltz" from Act II, and three popular tunes from the fourth and final act—but no music from Act III. Do not buy any recording of highlights of *La bohème* that excludes music from the third act: Here are some of the most beautiful melodies in the opera, especially Mimi's song of farewell near the act's end and the extraordinary quartet that concludes this act.

Two months have passed since the festivities of Christmas Eve. The curtain parts on daybreak at one of the gates of Paris for Act III. As the gate is opened and snow is swept from the street, workers pass through on the way to their tasks. Mimi appears. She looks about, seeks directions to a certain inn, and once there summons Marcello, who comes out to speak with her. Marcello tells Mimi he and Musetta are living together at the inn, she giving music lessons, he painting houses. And Rodolfo, too, is there. In a fit of jealousy he has walked out on Mimi. Marcello advises Mimi she should part from Rodolfo if they cannot get along. She agrees, but they cannot seem to separate. Marcello comments on Mimi's terrible cough, then, as Rodolfo comes out of the inn, she hides behind a tree. Rodolfo attempts to convince both Marcello and himself that he has left Mimi because she is such a flirt but ultimately the true reason is told: Her declining health is being made even worse by his cold room where they live. Mimi, of course, overhears the conversation about the seriousness of her illness and she commences to cough uncontrollably. She is found by Rodolfo. They embrace.

Marcello, suspicious with regard to what Musetta may be up

to with a stranger within the inn, goes inside while Mimi and Rodolfo contemplate an amicable parting suggested by Mimi in her lovely song *Donde lieta uscì* ("Back to the place I left"). Rodolfo responds lovingly but what has begun as another charming duet becomes an ingenious quartet. As Mimi and Rodolfo exchange sentiments of devotion, Marcello and Musetta come out of the inn quarreling outrageously. How Puccini managed to meld four voices into one—the gentleness of Mimi and the vitriol of Musetta with the disparate emotions of Rodolfo and Marcello—in this extraordinary scene can be explained simply by acknowledging his genius for melodic beauty and appropriate accompanying orchestral expression as a manifestation of an intuitive feeling for authentic theater.

The final-act curtain opens on the garret of the first act. Rodolfo and Marcello cannot seem to work. Both are separated from the women they love and memories of happier days flood head and heart. Marcello flings his brush to the floor and Rodolfo drops his pen, and now begins one of the loveliest duets for male voices in all opera: *O Mimi, tu più non torni* ("Oh Mimi, you will return no more"). He remembers ". . . lovely days . . . tiny hands . . . sweet-smelling locks . . . that snowy neck . . ." and laments, "Ah! Mimi! My brief youth." Marcello has joined the singing. He may want to paint ". . . earth or sky . . . winter or spring . . ." but his brush, with a mind of its own, produces only Musetta's face. (I know only one other duet for male voice the equal of this in expressing meditative veneration over lost love with such beautiful melodic lines. But more about this other duet when I write about Georges Bizet.)

Schaunard enters the room, followed by Colline. The four friends begin to sing and dance in a frolicking attempt to forget poverty and unhappiness when suddenly Musetta rushes through the door with the news that Mimi is coming behind her. She is dying and wishes to return to the room where she and Rodolfo once were so happy. Rodolfo runs out, soon to return helping a pale and feeble Mimi to the bed. With a little rest she begins to feel better but the bohemian garret is devoid of food and drink. Musetta will sell her earrings for nourishment and medicine, and she departs with Marcello. Colline, in a famous song, bids farewell to his beloved coat, which he intends to pawn. He and Schaunard then leave.

Alone, Rodolfo and Mimi recall joyful days and express their limitless love in still another gem from Giacomo Puccini's miraculous pen. Schaunard, followed closely by Marcello and Musetta, return to hear Mimi coughing terribly. The frail young woman sinks into unconsciousness. Musetta murmurs a prayer as Schaunard carefully observes Mimi. Rodolfo still has hope but Schaunard whispers to Marcello ". . . she's dead" as Colline returns with money for a doctor already on the way. Rodolfo, thinking Mimi asleep, notes sun on her closed eyes and with Musetta's cloak he shades the window. "See! She is quite peaceful," he says. Encountering the blank, strange expressions of the others, he blurts "What does this mean?" *"Coraggio"* ("courage"), says Marcello, as Rodolfo runs to the bed. "Mimi! Mimi! Mimi!" he cries, and the curtain falls.

What you have just read is similar to presentations in numerous guides that tell the story of an opera and isolate the famous musical numbers. But I hope you have asked yourself, "Why does the book begin with *La bohème,* an opera not composed until opera history was entering its fourth century?" Well, several reasons. It is a good place to begin to nurture an interest in opera because its universal appeal suggests that we simply cannot go wrong with *La bohème.* It is a good place to begin because as one of the most popular, well-known, and beloved operas in the world, it is one a neophyte might be invited to see as his or her first opera. (For more, see p. 518.) And, finally—and this is quite important— beginning with such a popular and recent opera makes it easy for me to point out what has been excluded in my presentation.

The introduction, in telling the story and isolating the opera's most famous musical excerpts, does not include much other information essential to comprehending operatic art. *La bohème* did not appear as a musical wonder out of the blue. Its basic ingredients—poetry, song, set and costume design, and acting—all are part of operatic art, which in a variety of fascinating ways combines these several basic arts into a single powerful experience. But there was nothing said about what kind of opera *La bohème* is and there are, indeed, numerous different kinds of operas. Accordingly, there was no consideration of how this opera differs from other operas, those that came both before and after.

Also, I referred to the musical numbers as songs, which, of course, they are, but it is customary to call opera songs "arias" after the Italian word meaning "an elaborate composition usually for solo voice with instrumental accompaniment." There are many different types of arias. And in referring to the songs—the arias—of Rodolfo, Mimi, Musetta, or Colline, no mention was made of the voice ranges of the singers, and what constitutes a tenor or a soprano or a bass is important in opera. So is the huge and still unresolved debate on the relationship between the words and the music, a debate that has been active since opera began: "Is one more important than the other or *should* one be more important than the other?"

And what of the poets, Giuseppe Giacosa and Luigi Illica, who provided the words that Puccini set to music? The relationship between poet and composer is important, especially because very, very few composers in the long history of opera have written their own poems that they then set to music. And how does the poem tell the story as well as expressing great emotions that composers make into arias? What is the role of the orchestra? Does it simply accompany the singers or can it have an independent voice? How did Puccini utilize choral voices in his famous Act II crowd scene? And what *is* a crowd scene?

All these questions, and others, are indispensable to a basic understanding of the way an opera works. The answers constitute the means of explaining the vast difference you would hear immediately if you listened to a snatch of *La bohème* and then compared it to some operatic music by Monteverdi, Mozart, or Bartók. These are the questions this book considers as it presents the stories and celebrated musical excerpts of the most notable operas.

I wrote this book because when teaching introductory courses on opera I could not find a book that started from scratch and did all this. As you gain answers to the basic questions, your knowledge of opera will constantly grow, and with it, I predict, your appreciation as well.

⁊

So now it's time to start again—this time at the beginning. And if the first years of opera history strike you as somewhat academic, be assured it's the same for me. There are only a handful of the thousands of operas written between 1597, the year of the first opera performance as we know it, and Mozart's time, the last half of the 18th century, that I listen to regularly or am moved by. Nevertheless, much that happened during those first two hundred years of opera history is crucial information even for a beginner's understanding.

Claudio Monteverdi

MONTEVERDI TO MOZART:
THE BEGINNINGS OF OPERA

Opera is an Italian word associated with work. When used musically, opera refers to a work combining several arts—music, poetry, drama, acting, stage and costume design, and, often dance—into a single theatrical representation. Here is my working definition: An opera is a play that tells a story through words with musical accompaniment. The words are sung, at times spoken, by costumed characters who act out their story on a stage decorated with appropriate sets. For at least two important reasons this must be a working definition, one needing refinement as I progress. First, there are many different types of opera. For example, grand opera and ballad opera both are covered by the definition but they differ quite significantly, as do Handel's operas in the Italian style and Wagner's gigantic music dramas, which also fit the definition. Second, according to my working definition, Verdi's *Aïda*, an opera; *Die Fledermaus (The Bat)*, an operetta (Italian for "little opera") by Johann Strauss, Jr.; and *The Sound Of Music*, by Rodgers and Hammerstein II, a Broadway musical, would all be considered operas. I'll split those hairs later. For now it is important to remember that during the past four centuries, that which is known as opera was constantly developing, thus manifesting itself in a variety of types and styles, and even though opera, operettas, and musicals are closely related art forms, they are not exactly the same.

Dafne is considered the first opera, although most of the music has been lost. This work had its first performance in Florence, Italy, in 1597. The poet Ottavio Rinuccini and the composer Jacopo Peri belonged to a small group of literary and musical men who met periodically at the palace of Count Giovanni Barci in Florence. (These names you will not need again unless you wish to amass opera trivia.) Another member of the group was Vincenzo Galilei, father of the noted astronomer. The group became known as the Florentine Camerata (*camerata* is an Italian word meaning "friend" or "comrade" or even the little room where friends would meet). Their purpose was to discuss the possibility of creating a new musical style that imitated, as they understood it, the use of poetry and music in the ancient Greek drama. This, of course, was part of the pervasive tendency of Renaissance men to ensure the rebirth of the ancient culture that was so dominant in Europe during the fourteenth through sixteenth centuries. These men had to make educated guesses as to how the ancient Greek tragedians incorporated music into their plays because only one mutilated fragment of Greek dramatic music has survived. From the writings of ancient Greek philosophers, especially Aristotle, who produced theoretical treatises, it is clear that a chorus with musical accompaniment was an important part of ancient drama.

There can be no doubt about the intent of the Florentine Camerata to re-create their version of a play with music based on the dramatic art of the ancients. After *Dafne*, Rinuccini and Peri collaborated again in 1600 to produce *Euridice*. After the title, they placed the words *dramma per musica*, drama for music, and with these two works—*Dafne* and *Euridice*—opera was born.

Opera, however, was not born "out of the blue" by men attempting to re-create ancient Greek drama in their own time. The ancient Greeks, to be sure, had combined drama and music and so did those who made the liturgical dramas and mystery plays during the Middle Ages. Opera did not begin in a vacuum. It was developed out of a long history, both secular and religious, by artists seeking to intensify drama through the addition of music.

CLAUDIO MONTEVERDI

A "master" is one eminently skilled in something, be it masonry or music, and the first master of operatic composition was Claudio Monteverdi. He is the first composer of opera whose works are still performed and recorded. Monteverdi was born in Cremona, the town famous for its violin makers, in May of 1567 and died in Venice on November 29, 1643. We are not sure how many operas he composed. We do know that many—more than a dozen—were destroyed by invaders.

His first opera, *La favola d'Orfeo (The Fable of Orpheus)*, was presented in 1607 in Mantua. The title tells us important things about the first operas. Their subject matter came from the ancient stories of gods and heroes. A favorite was that of Orpheus, the poet and singer in Greek mythology who could charm even wild animals with the beauty of his music. Orpheus, therefore, represented the power music can have over all living things. As he was both poet and musician, Orpheus was able to create that extraordinary wonder of marvelous words combined with expressive music, which, basically, is precisely what opera is about.

"Words" and "music" are the most important of the several arts that are combined in the making of an opera. Throughout the history of opera the question "Which is more important, the words or the music?" has been asked and answered continuously, and it is still debated to this day. In the early history of opera, some deemed the words so important that the music was considered merely a supplement, while in some late-nineteenth-century operas the overwhelming power of the music produced by huge orchestras all but obliterated the words. The genius of Monteverdi was his ability to retain a balance between the words that tell the story and his music, which intensifies the drama.

It is important to understand the distinction between a story accompanied by music—film music is an example—and a story that is expressed through both words and music, which, of course, is what opera is. Monteverdi's surviving works are masterpieces upholding standards of excellence to the present day. In fact, in the twentieth century, through the considerable growth of the recording industry, Monteverdi's operas have gained their largest and most appreciative audience. Wonderful videos are available with the orchestra playing period instruments (instruments used during the time the music was written rather than more highly developed instruments that did not evolve until much later).

The myth of Orpheus, the subject of Monteverdi's *La favola d'Orfeo*, is the basis of dozens of other operas, mostly serious but some comical or satirical. Only three, however, achieved world-wide popularity. Monteverdi's is one, an opera by Gluck, *Orfeo ed Euridice*, and the third is by Offenbach, *Orphée aux enfers.*

This myth tells of Orpheus, a poet and musician who marries Euridice. When she dies, he decides to follow her to Hades, where he redeems her life through the wonder of his music on the con-dition that he not turn around to look at her as he leads her back to the world of the living. Nearing the end of the journey, he makes the fateful turn toward his beloved, only to see her whisked back to the underworld. Overcome with grief, he spurns all other women and drives them mad with his wailing until some Thra-cian women tear him to pieces. Muses collected his fragments for burial at the foot of Mt. Olympus.

Alessandro Striggio wrote the text of Monteverdi's opera and adapted the original myth into the poetic story for which Mon-teverdi composed music. The one who prepares a text for an opera (usually a poet) is called the librettist, and the text is called the libretto (the Italian word *libro* means book, a *libretto* is a little book or booklet, and the one who writes such a little book is a librettist). There are five acts and a prologue wherein Music pro-claims her powers. In the first act, shepherds and nymphs are filled with joy over the wedding of Orpheus and Euridice. The main event of the second act is the terrible news brought by a messenger: Euridice has died. In Act III, Orpheus decides to ven-ture into Hades after his beloved. In the fourth act, he almost suc-ceeds in winning back her freedom into the world but, making certain that his beloved is following him, Orpheus turns to look for her and thus loses her again. In the final act, in a variation on the original myth, his father descends from heaven to inform him that Orpheus is to be immortalized and that he will see Euridice again among the stars.

In Monteverdi's opera, the story is easily understood, for it was a principle of the Camerata that words were to be sung natu-rally so they could be comprehended. The music must not act upon the words in such a way as to distort their normal declama-tion, but rather unites with them to express their meaning and mood. Monteverdi's *Orfeo*, his first opera, reveals his genius for expressing the meaning of words without his music ever getting in their way. This was another principal articulated by the Camerata. *Orfeo* has numerous expressive solos, duets, and beautiful choral numbers. Seventeenth-century opera may sound antiquated and strange to your ears; but, with exposure to Monteverdi, they will adapt, for his musical genius is above questioning. Many of my students, who at first were put off by what they considered to be emotionless musical expression, have learned to love Monteverdi after viewing a video of one of his operas—*Orfeo*, or his final operatic masterpiece, *L'incoronazione di Poppea (The Coronation of Poppea)*.

This last masterwork of Monteverdi derived from the Annals of Tacitus. *L'incoronazione de Poppea* was the first of them. Emperor Nero (tenor) has fallen in love with Poppea (soprano) and, accordingly, wants to divorce his wife, the Empress Ottavia (mezzo-soprano). Poppea becomes suspicious of Seneca (bass), philosopher and former tutor of Nero, thinking him part of a plot against her. Nero forces him to suicide. The plot becomes even more malicious when Ottavia persuades Ottone (baritone), Poppea's former lover, to murder the woman who jilted him. But his attempt fails and he is caught. His new love, Drusilla (soprano), lady-in-waiting to Ottavia, saves him when she confesses that she also was planning to murder Poppea: a confession that ultimately reveals Ottavia's plot. Ottone and Drusilla are banished, Ottavia divorced, and Nero and Poppea are married. The opera ends with the celebration of the coronation of Poppea.

Monteverdi was seventy-five years old when he wrote his last opera. His superb music expresses true-to-life emotions of love, hate, passion, despair (the wonderful Act III lament of Ottavia), and triumph (the duet of Nero and Poppea that ends the drama). A favorite scene occurs in Act I. Poppea—in some productions she is portrayed in her bath—expresses hope that love will bind her to Nero, but her old nurse Arnalta (contralto) warns that her ambition may be her undoing or that Nero's love may grow cold. Poppea, in her great song, *Non temo di noia alcuna. Per me guerreggia Amor* ("I fear no obstacle. Love and Fortune are my allies"), shows what she is made of. In somewhat uncharacteristic fashion, she prevails in this story in which Ottavia, Ottone, and Seneca get a dirty deal and passionate, illicit love triumphs. (I say uncharacteristic because, as we will learn, the general trend in employing ancient history as an operatic source was to celebrate the triumph of justice over injustice.)

Some immediately hear the expressive power and beauty in Monteverdi's music. Others need the nurturing of more exposure to opera. Test your response, if these operas are unfamiliar to you, by borrowing a recording from a library, or rent one of the splendid videos that have been made. Or you may wish to wait until you have had ample exposure to the sounds of more "modern" operas before you sample Monteverdi. Either approach is fair and reasonable, as long as you do not leave Monteverdi untouched.

Basic Male and Female Vocal Ranges
Throughout this book, you will see that I include each character's voice range after his or her name in opera plot synopses. We all know that the natural voice is high, low, or in between. Singing voices have names, mostly Italian, to designate these differing ranges. The basic voices for men and women are:

Voices:	Male	Female
High voice:	Tenor	Soprano
Medium voice:	Baritone	Mezzo-Soprano
Low voice:	Bass	Contralto

Within these basic ranges, numerous subdivisions of different types or voice qualities exist in operatic singing, but such differences are not always precisely agreed on from country to country. It can become confusing. For example, you may hear of dramatic tenors and lyric tenors and, in Germany, *Heldentenors*. There are also distinctions for sopranos: lyric, dramatic, *spinto*, *leggiero*, *hoher*, soubrette, and more. Do not worry yourself or make a fuss over all this now. When you become an expert, you will know all these things. As you become better acquainted with the differing sounds and qualities of the operatic voices, you will not only recognize the basic ranges, high to low, but you will also begin to associate them with certain operatic characters even to the point of being able to distinguish qualities within the same range. You will hear that both Don Ottavio (in Mozart's *Don Giovanni*), and Tristan (in Wagner's *Tristan und Isolde*) are tenors but that there is a world of difference within these two types of tenors, both of whom sing in the upper range for males but with obvious variations in style, voice quality, and sound.

Becoming familiar with the six categories—three male and three female, high to low—is the important first step, one that can become quite entertaining if you begin to apply the following "rule of thumb" to which, of course, as is true with all "rules," there will be exceptions. Nonetheless, there is enough consistency in the following to be both helpful and enjoyable.

The good guy, the hero—the guy who gets the girl, or should get the girl—often is a tenor, at least the most important tenor in the opera. The girl, or the heroine, or the most important female, whatever she may be, usually is a soprano: the most important soprano when there is more than one, which often is the case.

Bad guys, or good guys who do not get the girl, or fathers or older men, tend to be baritones. Seductive women, bad girls, a sorceress or a witch, gypsies, a maid or an attendant, a girlfriend or sister of the primary soprano are frequently portrayed by mezzo-sopranos, whose vocal quality is slightly deeper and less brilliant than that of the soprano.

Basses are kings, priests, old men, servants, sometimes a military figure or a philosopher, and evil men, even the devil himself. Elderly women, old nurses or servants, and ominous women or stately women, an empress or a queen, for example, are contraltos.

But do not fret if, at times, in your listening to singers you learn you were wrong in your guess or you find yourself stumped or confused. There can be an arbitrary aspect to these basic categories of character and of voice, for a baritone capable of singing high can be confused with a tenor singing in his lower register. Other baritones are capable of singing wonderful low notes. They are called bass-baritones and therefore may be mistaken for a bass. For now high, medium, and low is what you should aspire to know. As your ear becomes increasingly familiar with the different sounds of operatic voices, you will surprise yourself by your ability to correctly identify one famous tenor from another by the sounds and qualities of their voices.

Who After Monteverdi?
If the purpose of this book is to introduce you to the most well-known composers and their most significant and popular operas, rather than attempting to present a comprehensive assessment of all of operatic history, then I am tempted to answer this question with Mozart. Mozart is the first composer of operas whose works are performed on a regular basis in opera houses around the world. Mozart was born in 1756, more than one hundred years after the death of Monteverdi, whose last opera, *The Coronation of Poppea*, appeared in 1642, the year before he died. Does this mean that there was a "dark age" of little or nothing of importance in the

history of opera from the death of Monteverdi until Mozart wrote his first operas as a teenager in the late 1760s? No! Even though thousands of operas were written between the time of Monteverdi and that of Mozart, very few of which are still performed today, there are some operas and several important events in the development of opera that we must consider before embarking on a long and important consideration of Mozart as the father of modern opera.

Operatic Development in Italy

One of the most important events in opera history was the opening, in March 1637 in Venice, of the Teatro San Cassiano opera house to the public, that is, to anyone who bought a ticket. Previously, opera had been the private province of the aristocracy. The ruling class commissioned operas to be performed at their courts. Performances might commemorate important events in their lives: births, marriages, a coronation. When, for example, a French king married an Italian countess, what could be a more appropriate way to celebrate their union than with a private production at their court of an opera written for them on the subject of the imperishable love of Orpheus for Euridice? It was natural and easy, in all their smugness, for aristocrats to identify with the noble deeds and heroic events told in ancient lore. (This helps to explain why ancient literature provided such appealing subject matter for librettists and composers who sought to please patrons by glorifying them through operas extolling the great deeds and virtuous acts of ancient gods, goddesses, heroes, and heroines. In this way, opera was self-serving for the ruling class.)

With the opening of the Teatro San Cassiano to the public, opera departed the control of the aristocracy and this event, as we shall see, will dramatically alter its development. The public filled the first opera house open to them. They thrilled to spectacles of plays told in both words and music. Soon Venice had nearly twenty opera houses. Opera as public entertainment in Italy quickly became paramount.

Opera, which began in Florence, rapidly spread to other Italian towns, including Mantua, Padua, Venice, and Rome, to cite just a few. The relationship between this new art form and Italians was a natural and cozy one. Italy's predominant religion was Roman Catholicism and thus Italians had long been conditioned to ornately costumed clergy performing ceremonies, music included, in an overtly theatrical manner in magnificent buildings. The pomp of the Catholic Church service and the grand sets and elegant costumes of the opera house went hand-in-hand. The opera house and the church were much like first cousins. Accordingly, you could expect that opera would spread first to Italy's Catholic neighbors and this it did, quickly gaining popularity in Austria and France. To the Protestant north, opera would be slower in taking hold of the public imagination. It was forty years after the opening of the first opera house in Venice before the first German opera house opened its doors.

Before continuing with a consideration of other mainstream operatic developments in Italy, I must attend an important, unique, and isolated operatic event in faraway England.

Dido and Aeneas

At Mr. Josias Priest's Boarding School for Girls, Chelsea, London, in 1698, was heard for the first time *Dido and Aeneas*, a little opera by Henry Purcell (1658–1695). Purcell wrote other compositions for the stage but *Dido* is the only one possessing the basic ingredients of opera. *Dido and Aeneas* is an opera with prologue in three acts. The music of the prologue either was never composed or has been lost. The text, by Nahum Tate, is based on Book Four of Virgil's *Aeneid*, which tells of the love of Queen Dido of Carthage and Aeneas, the hero of Troy, whose destiny it was to found Rome, according to legend.

Aeneas, as a guest in Carthage, and the Queen fall passionately in love but eventually duty calls and Aeneas tells Dido he must leave. Her stunned reaction leads him to reconsider, to say he will stay, but the proud woman no longer wants anything to do with a lover who could have thought of leaving her. "Away, away," she demands, knowing that when he departs, death will come to her. Her lament, "When I am laid in earth," is one of the supreme moments in the history of opera and it boggles the mind to know that this opera was first performed at a girls school. What young girl could possibly have performed this profound unity of words and music portraying the devastation unto death of the broken-hearted Dido?

Probably I think this way because I first heard this music sung by the Norwegian soprano Kirsten Flagstad, one of the greatest singers of the twentieth or any other century. (You will meet her again when I consider the operas of Richard Wagner.) She recorded Dido's lament several times. My favorite was made on May 29, 1948, in London. Other famous sopranos have portrayed and recorded Dido in the twentieth century but it is fascinating to note that after its performance at Josias Priest's school in 1689, this operatic masterpiece collected dust for nearly two centuries before it was rediscovered and revived by the Royal College of Music, which launched it in the twentieth century as the little gem that it is. (Little because the entire opera takes only about an hour to perform, which is less than half the length of many of Verdi's famous operas and a mere fraction of the length of Wagner's longest music-dramas, which reach nearly five hours.)

Dido's celebrated lament is followed by the chorus, "With drooping wings, ye cupids come, and scatter roses on her tomb," music of unearthly beauty and sorrow—a fitting end to the tragedy of Dido.

This opera conceived and performed in a girls' school many, many miles from opera's birthplace and where it was flourishing, is the next masterpiece after those of Monteverdi. Simply stated, it is "a must."

Now let us return to Italy to consider some more significant operatic events and operas that lie between Monteverdi and Mozart.

Early Italian Opera Style

When we learn what these early operas were like, we will know much about *how* operas were made for many years as well as *why*. Even though many thousands of operas were composed and performed between 1597 and the time of Mozart, fewer than a dozen remain today among the most significant and popular in the world. Alessandro Scarlatti (1660–1725), for example, wrote 115 operas, 70 of which have survived. Not one of them is among the one hundred most well-known and often performed operas today, yet this Italian master of many musical forms, especially oratorios and cantatas, was one of the greatest composers of his time, indeed, of any time. Many other lesser-known composers also wrote operas. These composers and their works rest in oblivion. Why?

To our ears, most of these early operas sound unnatural, stilted, and much too formal. Their subject matter, taken from myths and histories of the ancient world, was serious: undying love, heroic deeds, noble gestures.

It is in these serious operas that we find the dominant Italian operatic style. It is called *opera seria* (Italian for "serious opera"). These operas consist of a singsong form of musical speech, which tells the story and develops the plot, and songs in which the characters express their emotions. The most common form of this musical speech is called *recitativo secco*, which means, "dry recitation." The word "dry" here refers to the fact that these recitations had limited musical accompaniment. They were accompanied by only a harpsichord or a bass instrument and not by the full orchestra, which during a seventeenth-century operatic performance would have consisted of the harpsichord, some string instruments, perhaps a woodwind or two, and a brass instrument or two, all conducted from the harpsichord, sometimes by the composer. This conversational aspect of the drama would be interrupted by songs that express individual thoughts and feelings. These songs are called arias. One of the meanings of this word in Italian is "tune." These tunes could be sung solo, that is, by one character, or as duets or trios.

Choruses, dances, and orchestral interludes, which would by the end of the eighteenth century become known as *operatic sinfonia*, together with the recitativo and aria, were the basic musical components of Italian opera and would remain so until well into the nineteenth century, when distinctions between recitativo and aria would diminish as a continuous musical pattern blending words and music evolved.

In early Italian opera, however, the distinction between the recitations that told the story and the arias that expressed emotions are easy to hear. For the aria the full orchestra often was employed and these arias, as operatic composition developed, acquired strict forms. One of the most common and most famous types of aria was composed in the *da capo* form. *Da capo* is Italian and means "to the head," as in go back "to the head," that is, to the beginning of the aria. A *da capo* aria was composed of three parts, the first and the third being the same in words and music. The second part, totally different from part one and its part-three repeat, allowed the singer to express two different emotions within the same aria. Because it is important to an understanding of how these early operas were made and, accordingly, of why to our ears they sound so formal, unnatural, and unlike the manner in which people really do express their emotions, let us consider an example.

Let us assume we are listening to an opera wherein a young man has learned through a conversation (recitation) with his mother that his father has just been decapitated by a violent faction of criminals within the victorious political party opposing his dad. The outraged youth will express his emotions in a *da capo* aria. His first emotion is the awakening in his heart of the desire for revenge. Powerful words and music express this emotion, which is part one of the aria. This emotion, in the aria's second part, gives way to gentler recollections as he acknowledges support from his father's ghost—different words, of course, and contrasting music. His desire for revenge is then iterated and this repetition of the words and the music of the first part represent part three, the go-back-to-the-beginning form of the aria. This is precisely what transpires in the magnificent *da capo* aria of Sextus in George Frideric Handel's opera *Giulio Cesare (Julius Caesar)*. In *Svegliateve nel core* ("Awaken in my heart") we have ample proof that even though some music from early Italian opera may seem old-fashioned, it can be exceedingly powerful, beautiful, and exciting.

It was part of the genius of Handel, one of the greatest composers ever, that such formal constraints did not limit his creativity. Unlike Alessandro Scarlatti and other major composers who wrote what have become forgotten operas, Handel wrote six or seven operas that have survived the years and are today reaching the widest audience ever through recordings on compact discs and videos. In all, Handel composed forty operas.

GEORGE FRIDERIC HANDEL

Some of the most enduring serious operas composed before those of Mozart were written by Handel, who was born in Germany in 1685, studied in his native land, traveled to Florence and Venice, returned to Germany, and then went to London, where he settled for the rest of his life. He became an English citizen in 1726 and died in London in 1759, the year in which Mozart turned three. This consideration of Handel represents our second digression out of Italy to faraway England, but he was such a towering figure in all music history that we must go where he went.

Handel mastered opera seria composition, but *Giulo Cesare* (1724) is the only one discussed here. *Rinaldo* (1711) is an early opera of Handel's about a Christian hero, and *Rodelinda* (1725) is about a queen of Lombardy. Two of his most inspired operas appeared in 1735: *Ariodante* and *Alcina*. *Serse* (*Xerxes*) appeared in 1738. Within the overture to this opera, you will hear one of the most famous and immediately recognizable tunes, which curiously enough is known as "Handel's Largo" (an Italian tempo marking meaning "broad") even though Handel marked it *larghetto* (less broad than *largo*). *Semele* (1744) was first performed as an opera but then in concert versions as an oratorio. Semele, daughter of Cadmus, King of Thebes, sings an aria in the second act that has become the most famous of all Handel's remarkable arias: "Oh sleep, why dost thou leave me?" Its celebrity has gone beyond the opera house and the concert hall to recording studios, where it became the province of both male and female voices.

One recording, nevertheless, has put all the others to rest. It remains to this day, some seventy-five years after it was made, one of the most technically astonishing and elegant interpretations of opera singing ever recorded. It was made by the noted Irish tenor John McCormack on April 1, 1920. Fortunately, antique recordings such as this are being remastered onto compact discs. If you want to hear examples of some of the finest singing ever recorded, you must seek out some of these historic recordings, and that is why I mention them.

Handel's operas were exceedingly popular during his lifetime, but then, unlike his instrumental music and certain oratorios that never have gone out of vogue, they fell into neglect. This was due in part to an intriguing episode that would begin to erode Handel's stature as the leading composer of opera in England, and with it his finances were adversely affected.

To comprehend what happened it is essential to know that Handel's major works, for the most part, were composed and presented in the traditional Italian opera seria format, which flaunted heroic figures on a stage of exuberant decor. The music of great power and emotional intensity fit lofty words telling of great deeds and heroic acts. Such sensational dramatic representations Handel's adoring public expected of him—indeed, demanded of him—as one opera followed another year after year. Such grandiose presentations, however, could be an easy target for spoof or mockery. And thus, it was that his adoring public was challenged in 1728 by a production of a new type of opera making fun of serious Italian opera.

Handel, the leading composer in the Italian tradition, would feel the financial repercussions of a work that made a fortune for those who conceived and produced it. Instantaneously it became one of the most popular operas of its time. (Twentieth-century revivals and recordings once again have brought it before an appreciative public, especially in English-speaking lands.)

The Beggar's Opera

This ballad opera was created by John Gay, who wrote the words, and John Christopher Pepusch—like Handel a German removed to England—who collected and arranged the music. An important word in this last sentence is "collected." Pepusch, unlike Handel, did not compose the music out of his own brain. A definition of ballad opera will explain.

Ballad opera was a popular eighteenth-century English entertainment in which spoken dialogue alternates with songs. Usually the songs were made by using old melodies and writing new words for them. There is no Italian recitativo. The story is told, as in a play, in natural, normal speech without musical accompaniment. The development of the story alternates with songs the music of which, as just stated, comes from old folk tunes, ballads, and, for satirical purposes, even from arias. That is what Mr. Pepusch did. He collected and arranged these old and familiar tunes and melodies, which, in a ballad opera, almost always were fit with new words by the poet, in this case as a means of satirizing both contemporary politicians and the overly serious and excessively emotional manifestations of opera seria.

The Beggar's Opera, one of the first and ultimately the most renowned and successful ballad opera ever, may have originated in a remark made to John Gay by that incomparable Irishman, Jonathan Swift: "A Newgate jail might make an odd, pretty sort of thing" for an opera plot. Gay set to work to provide just such a story—a story about criminals, a story that makes sport of significant people in authority, specifically Sir Robert Walpole, then the prime minister, and mocks other important people in authority who might, and indeed do, yield to a bribe. Corruption is the material out of which this opera is made.

More than this, *The Beggar's Opera* mocks the traditional, serious form of the fashionable operas of the reigning king of opera in England: Handel! John Gay is said to have remarked, "I hope I may be forgiven, that I have not made my opera throughout unnatural, like those in vogue; for I have no recitative."

The Beggar's Opera was performed for the first time on January 29, 1728. It was an immediate sensation, drawing hosts from

Handel's theater to enjoy what would become one of the great satires in theater history. This ballad opera was so successful that it made a fortune for the authors and for John Rich, who managed both Lincoln's Inn Fields Theater and Covent Garden. This opera, first at one, then the other, drew great crowds, prompting a local wit of the day to say of this opera that "it made Rich gay, and Gay rich."

Gay's story immediately strikes an almost incomprehensible contrast to the opera seria based on mythological and historical gods and heroes of the ancient world. Macheath is the hero of *The Beggar's Opera*, which appropriately is introduced by the beggar, a role that is only spoken and not sung. Macheath, who leads a band of highwaymen, is betrayed by some of his women and is incarcerated in Newgate Prison, where Lockit is in charge. Lockit's daughter, Lucy, and Polly, the daughter of Peacham, a dealer in stolen property, both seek Macheath's favor to the point of a willingness to hang with him, should that be the case. The beggar, however, intercedes to resolve a happy ending in this tale of thieves, prostitutes, and other unsavory characters.

Pepusch collected and arranged sixty-nine airs or tunes, a majority of which are English, for Gay's words. The opera is a tapestry of concise and intriguing dialogue alternating with delicious melodic music.

This is an easy opera to get into, and fortunately good recordings, aural and video, leave it easily accessible. Try it. You may be delighted. And if you try it, you will be a step ahead when we consider, as part of our discussion of twentieth-century opera, *Die Dreigroschenoper* (*The Threepenny Opera*), by Weill and Brecht, a modern interpretation of *The Beggar's Opera* wherein Macheath becomes Mack the Knife, celebrated in that song we all know so well.

⁊

Long before *The Beggar's Opera* appeared as a spoof of Italian opera seria—and in doing so created a new fashion for ballad opera throughout England, Scotland, and Ireland during the eighteenth century—a second type of Italian opera had developed. A humorous form originated in the short scenes often placed at the ends of opera seria acts as a brief comic diversion. These diversions, interruptions of the action of the larger opera seria, were called *intermezzi* (Italian for "interludes"): thus the singular intermezzo, an interlude between acts. This word "intermezzo" we will encounter again in nineteenth-century opera, where it will have obtained another important meaning.

The seventeenth-century interludes naturally developed into longer episodes with an operatic identity of their own. It was thus that *opera buffa* (comic opera) was born. As early as 1639 operatic comedy, called *commedia* in Italian, existed in Rome. Whereas opera seria looked back to ancient times for heroes and extraordinary actions for its subject matter, opera buffa utilized episodes in the lives of ordinary, common, contemporary people for its humor. Of course, these people and their actions were often exaggerated for the stage. The stock figures and situations of the *commedia dell'arte* (comedy of art), a form of popular Italian comedy developed during the sixteenth, seventeenth, and eighteenth centuries, where masked entertainers improvised comic stories based on ordinary human behavior, was handily adapted into opera buffa. Opera buffa portrayed the audience to themselves, with all their aspirations, delusions, foibles, infirmities, and predicaments—especially, their conflicts and the ludicrous pickles into which people can get themselves. Opera buffa, therefore, was a portrayal of the truthfulness of life as it was lived by ordinary people, blown up, of course, for dramatic purposes, and ultimately causing them to roll in their seats as they laughed at themselves.

The most famous of these pre-Mozartian comedies—and the only one to live on through the ages—is an intermezzo in two parts by Giovanni Battista Pergolesi (1710–1736), a setting of a text by G.A. Frederico. *La serva padrona (The Maidservant Becomes the Lady of the House)* was first performed in 1733. Part One played after the first act and Part Two after the second act of Pergolesi's opera seria, *Il prigioniero superbo (The Haughty Prisoner)* now completely forgotten. In his short life, Pergolesi wrote both serious and comic works, but it took the little *La serva padrona* to secure his operatic immortality.

The plot is simple: Serpina, a maidservant to her bachelor master Uberto, lures him into marriage, thus making her the lady of the house, by pretending to depart with a ferocious soldier, who in fact is none other than one of the other servants in disguise. Again, modern productions exist for both listening and viewing. It is a charming, charming respite from the long and lofty serious opera seria manifestations.

It is also the first gem in the tiara of Italian comic opera, a crown every opera lover would proudly wear, which contains other rarities by Mozart, Rossini, Donizetti, Verdi, and Puccini— all of which still await us.

Opera Outside Italy

I have noted three isolated cases of operatic success outside of Italy in our discussion of *Dido and Aeneas*, Purcell's little master-piece; Handel's triumphs of opera seria works in London; and the popularity of *The Beggar's Opera*, all taking place in England. England, however, has a much greater reputation for importing opera than for creating and exporting it. (The operettas of Gilbert and Sullivan in the nineteenth century and operas in the twentieth century by Benjamin Britten are the two most notable exceptions to that statement.) Italy was the country of opera's birth and of its most rapid and pervasive expansion. Its two basic forms, opera seria and opera buffa, dominated stages for a long time and would remain the primary motivating forces within operatic develop-ment until late in the eighteenth century.

The French, too, were quick to incorporate opera into their theatrical life and by 1670 had made their first attempt to develop their own national art form derived from Italian examples. The French, though, would give poetry an exceedingly important place in opera: The words must be delivered so as to be comprehended. This was in accord with the original principles of the founders of Italian opera, but the subsequent development of Italian operas experienced an ever-increasing importance of music's role through the dominance of virtuoso singing. Because of their fascination for ballet, the French elevated the importance of dance in opera. The chorus also was a key component in French opera, as was instru-mental music. Both Italian and French opera shared these same basic ingredients, but there was a more obvious balance of them in French works.

Jean-Baptiste Lully (1632–1687), a native of Florence (where his name was spelled Lulli), settled in France and gave to French opera its initial form and direction. Jean-Philippe Rameau (1683–1767) continued in this tradition. Both wrote numerous sig-nificant works, and contemporary recordings exist of their most famous operas. They are not among those introduced in this "lit-tle" book, though, whose boundaries include only those operas that are the most popular, the most often performed, and the most frequently recorded. Once you have the contents of this book under your belt and are somewhat familiar with music in the various styles discussed herein, reward your ears with some Lully and Rameau. Or do it right now—perhaps Lully's *Armide* (1686) or Rameau's opera ballet *Les Indes galantes* (1735). You have nothing to lose.

The first German opera may be *Daphne*; same title and same subject of the first opera ever—and like its Italian predecessor, the music is now lost. The German *Daphne*, by the noted composer of religious music Heinrich Schütz, appeared in 1627. The history of opera in German in its formative years, however, is the story of imported Italian composers appointed to German courts. During this period of our consideration, Monteverdi to Mozart, the only German opera composer of lasting stature is Handel, whom we have already encountered in England writing famous operas in the Italian opera seria style.

The great Austrian composer Franz Joseph Haydn (1732–1809) wrote many operas in different styles: opera seria, opera buffa, and puppet opera, which is exactly what you would expect it to be. His first five operas have been lost. He never worked with a poet who provided him with adequate verses. Much wonderful operatic music by one of the greatest of all composers has become obscure because his operas have been neglected. Recent developments in the recording business are encouraging for fans of Haydn, and I am chief among those. Over half of his surviving operas—more than a dozen—have been recorded. Weak libretti notwithstanding, Haydn's music in any form is too sublime and beautiful to remain inaccessible. These operas probably will never join that inner circle of the most beloved operas but no music by Haydn should ever languish unheard.

Next, I move on to a major operatic accomplishment that took place outside Italy after Monteverdi and before Mozart: the reforms of Gluck.

CHRISTOPH WILLIBALD GLUCK

Christoph Willibald Ritter von Gluck was born in Bavaria in 1714 and died in Vienna in 1787. He was one of the most seminal thinkers in the history of opera. Gluck's ideas about what an opera ought to be and his significant compositions reshaped the art form and altered its development. The influence of his concepts remained effective for nearly a century after his death. In his operas, the musicologist discerns both Italian and French influences but it is through Gluck's serious, studious manner of composing that his German (Bohemian is more precise) genius would emerge with striking originality.

Gluck studied in Milan and settled in Vienna to compose. His standards of excellence and perfection became evident in the thoroughness of his compositions and in their preparation, which, he decreed, had to be mastered prior to the premiere in numerous rehearsals. As the conductor of his own works, Gluck's inflexible standards quickly gave him the reputation of an artistic tyrant. Educated, sophisticated, and an experienced traveler, Gluck, an aristocrat, was worldly-wise and he anticipated both the problems inherent within musical theater of his time and the solutions so desperately needed to resolve them. He saw the need to purge opera of several self-destructive excesses. An imbalance of word and music, wherein music had become the dominant part almost to the exclusion of the importance of poetry, concerned him. This was manifested in those operas primarily constructed for vocal displays of celebrated singers of the age. These singers, with their powerful and emotional voices, were given roles encouraging to their vocal capacities, often at the expense of dramatic integrity. Put another way the philosophy seemed to be: "To hell with the drama! Let the singers sing." To this Gluck responded with a radical, and reasonable, rejection. These vocal deities often had little or no comprehension of the true emotions of the characters represented; indeed, often they offered no more than a glorious vocal display of technique. No again, said Gluck.

Had he a rallying cry, it would have been the single word "simplicity." According to Gluck, singers had come to dominate opera through grand, overly formal, and unnatural *da capo* arias. These vocal triumphs may thrill the audience and "bring down the house," but they more often than not interrupt the flow, meaning, and integrity of the drama. All this Gluck sought to reform. The *da capo* aria, as we have learned, was restricted to an inexorable formula. To be sure, it could provide for vocal brilliance and emotional contrasts, but did it, perhaps, also inhibit authenticity of dramatic expression as it attempted to represent human emotions?

In his reforms, Gluck contended that opera seria was an artifice, a stultifying form of musical theater bearing little or no relationship to expressive delineation of true characters enacting a drama of human life. The drama, said Gluck, is foremost. The job of music is to serve the drama, not to overwhelm it. Drama was not set forth as the lackey of unbridled music running wild through pyrotechnics of vocal virtuosity. Singers, Gluck concluded, distorted opera when an opera allowed singers to utilize the art form for their own glorification. This sin, by the way, will happen again in opera history. And again! And again! Oh, for the wonder of the glories of the most supreme of human voices but, dammit, let them learn their place. And that is what Christoph Willibald Gluck was about.

In the now famous preface to his 1767 opera *Alceste* (a wonder that, ultimately, we cannot do without), Gluck wrote that it was his intent, in this work, to purge singers of their many abuses and "to restrict music to its true office by means of expression and by following the situations of the story." His watchwords were clarity and simplicity. His music, accordingly, in ears nurtured by vocal acrobatics of superstar opera seria singers, seemed sparse, even barren. Much of it, in fact, is of an almost unearthly, pristine, unadulterated beauty.

His reform operas were not without success. Along with the works of Handel, Gluck's operas are performed and recorded more often than any other composer after Monteverdi and before Mozart. His reform principles—and this is really important—remained influential long after his death and until Richard Wagner, that controversial German who, in following Gluck's lead, steered opera thereafter into a new, indisputable direction. But not just Wagner. Others, as well, responded to the reforms of Gluck: Berlioz and Richard Strauss, for example, whom I will discuss later.

Gluck, the father of German opera, contributed his share to what must be the most remarkable corpus of serious music ever produced by a single culture. I am always tempted to digress to recite the litany of names (and I succumb to temptation here): Bach, Beethoven, Brahms, Berg, Handel, Haydn, Mahler, Mendelssohn, Mozart, Schubert, Schoenberg, Schumann, J. Strauss, R. Strauss, Wagner, Weill, von Weber—an incomplete list, certainly, but long enough to make a point. For the moment, though, Gluck is our focus. His contributions to opera history, both as thinker and composer, are important not only in the period after Monteverdi and before Mozart but also today. As I write these words I am listening to his *Orfeo ed Euridice (Orpheus and*

Euridice) and I still, after hearing it so many times for many years, marvel at its simplicity, its beauty, and its incomparable balance between words and music. (Mozart, by the way, was six years old and had composed his first keyboard works when Gluck's most famous opera was premiered in 1762.)

In this opera, Gluck's remarkable music supports and intensifies the drama without obliterating the words. His restraint in no way detracts from the power or beauty of the music. Indeed, such restraint is part of the wonder of this opera, an irony, perhaps, of less being more.

From our account of Monteverdi's work we know the basic story. In Gluck's opera, it is not told by *recitativo.* In Gluck's version there is the twist of a happy ending. Recall that Orpheus (Orfeo in Gluck's opera) is allowed to return his beloved Euridice to the land of the living. Amor, God of Love, had decreed that he may lead her by the hand but he may not turn to gaze upon her. That he will not even glance at her is interpreted by Euridice as his no longer loving her, and without his love she prefers death. And so he lovingly looks upon her as he turns and embraces her. Instantly she dies in his arms. *Che farò senza Euridice* ("What is left without Euridice?") begins one of the most famous laments in opera literature. So moving and beautiful is his expression of grief that Amor intervenes. By touching Euridice, he restores life, and thus commences the happy ending. This famous lament has become the province of many famous sopranos and mezzo-sopranos because, in most productions of the opera, Orfeo is portrayed by a woman dressed as a man.

Castrati and Travesti

Why does a woman portray a man? The question is a good one, one that leads to an explanation of two important operatic terms that ought to be familiar even to a beginner. They are *castrati* (castrated male singers) and *travesti* (a member of one sex adopting the attire and portraying a member of the opposite sex; the most common operatic version of this is a woman portraying a male). Saint Paul declared, in 1 Corinthians, XIV, 34, "Let your women keep silence in the churches: for it is not permitted unto them to speak." Such intolerance, even in historical context, does not befit an intelligent man, and yet his injunction rang down through the ages even to our own time. For years, the Roman Catholic Church sanctioned the artificial preservation of a young male's unbroken soprano or contralto voice through a surgical operation prior to puberty. By this means, the full spectrum of the human vocal register produced by only males could be heard in church music. Of course, it was but a few short steps for the castrato from church choir to opera stage and some of the greatest and most famous opera singers of the eighteenth century were castrati. They retained soprano voices but they were "female" voices of great power and intensity, for they were driven by the male physiognomy. The heyday of the castrato was the great age of opera seria, with its *da capo* arias inviting vocal brilliance.

Though Gluck originally wrote the part of Orfeo for a male contralto, it is interesting to note that it would prove to be his own reforms that commenced the decline of the castrato's art, which did live through the early part of the nineteenth century. The last of the castrati was Alessandro Moreschi (1858–1922). Between 1902 and 1903, when the science was still in its infancy, he made ten recordings. Moreschi's records recently have been reissued on compact disc, should you wish to hear him. He did not sing opera, by the way.

Gluck was not opposed to *travesti* roles and his Orfeo became one of the most famous examples of a role in which a woman plays a male character. With Mozart, Gounod, and Richard Strauss we find other composers who also wrote enduring music for women portraying males. *Travesti* is the past participle of the Italian verb *travestir*, meaning "to disguise." Such a part in German is called *Hosenrolle*, which means "trouser role." In England, these parts are normally referred to as "breeches parts." In a later version of his *Orfeo ed Euridice*, Gluck rewrote the part of Orpheus for a tenor, but virtually all of the most famous recordings of the aria *Che farò senza Euridice* belong to the soprano voice. Many great composers have preferred to musically portray a young male—often males yet to reach full maturity—by a soprano or mezzo-soprano sound. (In my ears, because it is what I am used to, Orfeo's famous aria does not sound right unless it is sung by a woman, and I cannot think of Gluck's Orfeo as anything other than a *travesti* role.)

By the time Mozart was composing opera (Mozart and Gluck overlap; Mozart's first operas were written before Gluck's last), if a part was conceived as a *travesti* role, such is how it remained. The breeches part had entered opera and remained until into the twentieth century. Gluck's most well-known operas other than *Orfeo ed Euridice* are *Alceste, Iphigénie en Aulide,* and *Iphigénie en Tauride.*

ↄ◞

Now you are ready for Mozart. My discussion, though far from comprehensive, will be lengthy because Mozart was one of the greatest, if not the greatest, musical geniuses the world has ever known: he wrote a number of operatic masterpieces, several of which authorities and ordinary music lovers consider "the greatest opera ever written"; and, finally, because he is my favorite composer, an opinion unaltered since I was about eight years old.

Wolfgang Amadeus Mozart

He wrote his first opera in his eleventh year.

MOZART: THE FATHER OF
MODERN OPERA

When Wolfgang Amadeus Mozart died, during the night of December 5, 1791, the history of opera was almost two hundred years old. Of that long span, our book isolated for recognition only a few composers and a handful of operas and yet during those two centuries numerous composers throughout Europe wrote countless operas. Almost all the composers and nearly all of the operas are forgotten; many of their works are lost. Here and there a revival brings to the stage, or more often to the recording studio, one of these relics, and surely there rest in numerous libraries operas that if performed would delight. On a recent opera tour to Europe, an intimate theater-in-the-round production of *Orpheus* (1762) by Telemann, a work so obscure that not one note of it was known to or had ever been heard by anyone in our group, received the highest praises. The development of opera from Mozart to at least the first half of the twentieth century, by comparison, has been so fruitful and so overwhelming in its musical diversity, beauty, and intensity that many, nurtured by this more "modern" sound, find the style of most early opera to be too formal, stilted, repetitive, unnatural, and uninteresting. In short, there is much in early opera that sounds uninspired, alien, even boring.

This book has noted several works that certainly transcend all those limitations and rank with the masterpieces in opera literature. Yet it is with Mozart that the history of modern opera begins at least in one important way: He is the first composer of opera during its first two hundred years whose works remain in the repertory of the major opera houses around the world and the object of recording projects well into this century. But there is much more to Mozart's position in opera history than this.

Why Mozart is such and important figure will take more than several pages to answer because Mozart is not only one of the giants of all opera history but also the first composer of modern opera. We must consider this question carefully. First, we need a definition for "modern," for in many ways the last half of the eighteenth century—Mozart was born in 1756 and died in 1791—is usually not what we would consider modern. It was during this time in Western European history that important political, economic, and philosophical ideas were articulated, instituted, and fought for: democracy, free enterprise, the worth of every individual, and the right of every individual to determine her or his own destiny. These ideas were alive in Europe and in America when Mozart was composing the operas for which he is most well known. He could have opposed them, as did the reactionary forces of the day, which were entrenched in the Catholic Church and in the aristocracy. If born into wealth and power, he could have ignored these ideals, assuming the posture that art is above the issues of the day, or he could have become a voice for new and challenging concepts. In that he moved in the forefront of his time in opposition to the absoluteness of aristocratic and religious powers, Mozart was a modern man and a modern artist whose work often represented modern leanings. His operas were not totally "modern," though, if we force on them a dictionary definition of modern as it pertains to art: "of or pertaining to styles of art, literature, music that reject traditionally accepted or sanctioned forms and emphasize individual experimentation and sensibility." We will learn later that the German composer Richard Wagner, according to that definition, was far more "modern" than Mozart. Mozart did not reject all the traditional forms, such as opera seria and opera buffa. What he did do was to utilize them, modify them, and even combine them to fit his own art, and in doing so raised them to the highest form of perfection.

Many consider Mozart the supreme genius in the history of western music. As a four-year-old, he played keyboard pieces from his sister's music book and by the next year, according to his father, he was composing his own music. His musical proclivity having been recognized early, Mozart was performing for dignitaries in Austria and Germany by age six. Many stories and anecdotes have been told elucidating and documenting his prodigious talent. But before his thirty-sixth year Mozart was dead, leaving 626 documented compositions in virtually every significant genre.

This is the place to explain why each of Mozart's compositions has the letter "K" and a number after it, as in, for example, Mozart's *Die Entführung aus dem Serail (The Abduction from the Seraglio)*, K. 384 (or KV 384, which is the German form). This means that, according to the scholar Ludwig von Köchel, working from historical records and accounts, that particular opera chronologically was the 384th of Mozart's compositions. Mozart did not number his works in the order in which he composed them, a practice that later became standard among most composers as in, for example, Beethoven's Piano Concerto No. 1, Op. 15. Either this work was Beethoven's 15th composition ("opus" means a literary or musical work) or, as in most cases, the number refers to the order of published works. Köchel's catalogue of Mozart's works lists 626 compositions. Even though subsequent scholars have made corrections and amendments, the Köchel list ("K" for Köchel) still stands. Some Mozart aficionados love to show off their knowledge by making comments such as "Oh, my favorite Mozart is the K. 589." Avoid anyone who talks like that.

Among Mozart's works are some of the finest symphonies, concerti for a variety of instruments, masses, serenades, divertimenti, string quartets, and operas ever written. That opera was a favorite form of Mozart's is without question. His first operas—they are still performed and recorded today—were written when he was twelve and thirteen. During his short life, he would write nearly twenty works for the stage, several of which were never finished. I'll consider Mozart's seven best known and most frequently performed and recorded operas. They are *Idomeneo, Die Entführung aus dem Serail, Le nozze di Figaro (The Marriage of Figaro), Don Giovanni, Così fan tutte (All Women Do It), La clemenza di Tito (The Clemency of Titus)*, and *Die Zauberflöte (The Magic Flute)*.

Mozart's Three Operatic Styles

There are three distinct operatic forms or types into which these seven great works of Mozart can be placed:

1. Opera seria: *Idomeneo* and *La clemenza di Tito*
2. *Singspiel* (German for "song-play"): *Die Entführung aus dem Serail* and *Die Zauberflöte*

3. A synthesis of comic (*buffa*) and serious (*seria*) elements:
    Le nozze di Figaro, Don Giovanni, and *Così fan tutte.*

In barely more than a decade Mozart wrote seven of the most significant operas ever composed. You are reading this book because
you want to learn about opera, and these are seven operas that you
should know something about. Three of them retain the reputation today among many knowledgeable people—though it was not
always this way—as candidates for one of, if not the, greatest
opera ever written. These are *Le nozze di Figaro, Don Giovanni,*
and *Die Zauberflöte.* (This book will, from time to time, include
such statements to introduce the reader to a general assessment of
certain works. Ranking operas and composers, however, is not
what this book is about, though I am sure you have noticed some
of my biases shining through.) Each of these seven major operas
must be considered in turn and because the three different styles
of their composition have just been delineated, our discussion will
proceed chronologically in the order of each opera's first performance.

IDOMENEO (1781)

Even though *Idomeneo* is a superb opera of wonderful music for
solo voice, ensembles, and chorus, its international popularity
until quite recently has been limited, probably because of the
degree of formality inherited from opera seria, which was losing
its force when Mozart wrote. He did not dislike this form and it is
fascinating that Mozart, composing at the end of the age of opera
seria's dominance, wrote what may be the two supreme works in
that style: *Idomeneo* and *La clemenza di Tito.* With Mozart, opera
seria reached perfection, and thereafter slipped quietly into the
history books.

   The libretto of *Idomeneo,* by Giambattista Varesco (a name
you will not encounter again), is based on a classical plot. Both
Homer and Virgil mention King Idomeneus, which becomes
Idomeneo in Italian. The opera is in three acts and the central
characters in the drama are:

ILDOMENEO, King of Crete, *tenor*
IDAMANTE, his son, *originally castrato, later soprano,*
   recently rewritten for tenor
ILIA, a Trojan princess, *soprano*

ELECTRA, a Greek princess, *soprano*

Also in the drama are Arbace, confidant of Idomeneo,
tenor; the High Priest of Neptune, *tenor*; the Voice
of Neptune, *bass*; and people of Crete, Trojan prisoners, sailors, soldiers, priests of Neptune, and dancers.

The setting is ancient Crete.

Idomeneo, returning from the Trojan War, has sent captives before
him to his home, including Ilia, the daughter of Priam, the defeated Trojan king. She and Idamante will soon declare their love, provoking the rage of Electra, who also is in love with Idamante.
Idomeneo's ship is caught in a terrible storm. To appease the god
of the sea, Idomeneo vows to sacrifice the first living thing he
encounters once safely ashore. To his horror, it is his own son. In
an attempt to avoid the vow and to save his son, Idomeneo sends
Idamante to Argos as the escort of Electra, thus returning her to
her home.

Another storm pounds Crete, a sea monster attacks the island,
and the terrified populace conclude that someone has offended the
gods. Idomeneo confesses. Idamante prepares to fight the monster
and the people demand a sacrificial victim. After killing the monster, Idamante offers himself as the means of honoring his father's
vow but the Voice of Neptune, god of the sea, spares him, declaring that Idomeneo must abdicate in favor of his son. Idamante,
with Ilia at his side, ascends the throne as the new king.

That, in a nutshell, is the story of the opera. In writing the
music, Mozart did not bind himself to the strictest rules of the
opera seria format, but the formal, serious style he did adhere to.
Recitatives tell the story and arias express emotions. There are
wonderful ensembles and splendid choruses. This opera can be
considered the first of his works for the theater that knocked on
that door where masterpieces are housed.

As this opera becomes increasingly familiar to a large audience through several superb recordings and live performances, its
stature grows and grows. I like it more every time I hear it. Without a doubt, the opera has the indelible mark of Mozart's genius.
Nowhere in the drama is it more obvious than in the now famous
Act III quartet, which Mozart scholars cannot seem to praise
enough: One calls it the most memorable ensemble in opera
seria's long history; another considers it perhaps the most beautiful ensemble ever composed for the opera stage.

It is important to remember that Idamante's part had been written for a castrato. Today, in some performances, this part is transposed down an octave for tenor voice, which means that the part is rewritten eight notes lower so that a tenor can more realistically portray the young Idamante. Such transposing, however, alters the original vocal balance of the music Mozart composed, and this is most apparent in ensembles. It is more common today to retain that original vocal balance, and to have the original castrato part sung by a mezzo-soprano as a trouser role. This opera was heard for the first time in Munich two days after Mozart's twenty-fifth birthday.

DIE ENTFÜHRUNG AUS DEM SERAIL (1782)
The Abduction from the Seraglio

Usually this opera's German title is translated into English as above. Let us not enter into an attempt to resolve the obscure and uncertain etymology of the word "seraglio," which actually is an Italian word (serràglio in modern Italian). The English word harem will do nicely, as in *The Abduction from the Harem.* This comic opera in three acts, though certainly not the first singspiel opera, is the first of its genre to remain in repertory. A singspiel is a type of German opera wherein the musical numbers are separated by dialogue. The characters in the opera both speak and sing. (In one of my favorite recordings of this work, actors and actresses brilliantly recorded the spoken parts and opera singers the musical portions.) The spoken parts move the story along as the plot unfolds, while the songs express the human emotions, just as do the devices of recitativo and aria in Italian opera.

This opera tells of a Spanish nobleman, Belmonte, who has gone to Turkey to try to find his beloved Constanze, also of Spanish noble rank. Constanze and her English maid, Blonde, were carried off by pirates and Belmonte believes them to be housed in the harem of Pasha Selim. Belmonte's former servant Pedrillo, in love with Blonde, is now in the service of the Pasha as a gardener. He will assist Belmonte in an attempt to secure the escape of the women they love. Osmin, the Pasha's overseer of the harem, also is in love with Blonde and, accordingly, is the archenemy of Pedrillo. The plot unfolds and the attempted escape fails but with unexpected magnanimity the Pasha restores Constanze and Blonde, both unbesmirched, to their lovers and all are allowed to go free. Osmin is utterly furious.

This opera is important for reasons other than it being one of the most famous of all singspiels and the first of that genre to still "hold the boards" (remain in repertory). Pasha Selim is one of few operatic roles that have no singing part; the villain Osmin is one of the greatest comic creations in all opera, and the lighthearted, if not even somewhat silly plot, inhabited by stock comedy characters and noble counterparts, is given life, energy, and believability by the miracle of Mozart's music. All five of the singing parts have wonderful songs that are consistent with each character's nature. Many of these arias have become quite popular outside the opera house as excerpts on recordings and numbers on recital programs in the concert hall.

In the first act, Belmonte, anticipating seeing Constanze again, sings the now famous tenor aria *Constanze! Constanze! dich wiederzusehen* ("Constanze, Constanze! To see you again"). In Act II, Mozart gave to Constanze one of the most demanding soprano arias that he ever wrote, the extraordinary *Martern aller Arten* ("Tortures of all kinds"), wherein she defies the Pasha's attempt to woo her by informing him that not even tortures could make her submit to him. Blonde, in the same act, having learned from Pedrillo of the escape plan, expresses her great joy in the aria *Welche Wonne, welche Lust* ("What joy, what delight"). Pedrillo, early in the third act, signals the women that the escape is about to begin with *Im Mohrenland* ("In Moorish land"). This beautiful serenade is one of the most appealing songs for the "second tenor" in all of opera. (In this opera Belmonte, though a less interesting character than Pedrillo, is considered the first or more important tenor part.) Finally, Osmin! He has significant music in all acts, as do the other characters, but nothing could be more captivating than his gloating in Act III after he has foiled the attempted escape of the women from the Pasha's harem: *O! wie will ich triumphieren* ("O how I will triumph").

Another way in which this opera is important is that it provides a striking example of a Mozartian musical characteristic to be found in all his major operas. For nobles or characters with a serious bent Mozart writes arias that can be described as more elegant, loftier, even more demanding or musically complicated than the simple, folklike tunes he composed for peasants, servants, and others not belonging to the aristocracy. Now, this is a rule of thumb and not an absolute rule but handy enough for you to utilize as a means of getting to know some of those wonderful people who inhabit Mozart operas. As an example of this, let us consider the Act II arias of Constanze and Blonde. The arias are separated by dialogue characteristic of a singspiel.

First comes Constanze's soprano tour de force *Marten aller Arten*; later, Blonde sings her aria *Welche Wonne, welche Lust*. The contrast between the two arias is extraordinary. Mozart provides the noble lady with a long orchestral introduction to her big aria, which establishes her mood of inexorable determination not to yield to Selim's advances. The aria has sixty-six words of poetic text. From orchestral introduction to conclusion it can take about seven minutes to perform, which for an opera aria is above average in length. There are thirty-four words in Blonde's aria, which is sung in about two and a half minutes, perhaps a little less than an average opera aria. Of course, these arias ought to be different in that they are expressions of different moods by different women: Constanze's resolve and Blonde's joy. We would also expect the contrast in the music Mozart wrote: the long, drawn-out expression of resolve and the brief expression of joy.

But there is more than that. One would expect a noblewoman to be lofty and serious and a servant girl to be less restrained in her emotions. Constanze's elaborate music befits her social station; Blonde's quick, catchy little tune is appropriate to hers. This identification of social station through musical sound we will encounter again and again in Mozart as he gives to his characters music that expresses not only their emotions but also who and what they are as human beings. He always knew what all his characters should sound like and his manner of giving them voice is so distinctive that Mozart's music, his style, his sound—once you get them in your head and heart—are generally easy to recognize. Upon hearing something new by Mozart, you probably can say, "I don't know what it is but I'll bet it's Mozart."

And having just spoken of social station, I must include here reference to an episode that occurs as the second act begins. Osmin, in love with Blonde, orders her about. They are in Turkey, he reminds her, and he is the master and she the slave. She is obstinate in her refusal to capitulate. "Have you forgotten that the Pasha gave you to me as a slave?" asks Osmin, to which Blonde, one of my favorite Mozartian characters, responds, "Pasha this, Pasha that! Girls are not goods to be given away. I'm an English-woman, born to freedom!"

Mozart—such a wise man—always comes down on the side of women.

A final word about *The Abduction from the Seraglio* must emphasize the glory of two choruses and memorable ensembles. This
opera would be recognized worldwide as the greatest, most popular, and most tuneful singspiel ever written had Mozart not already
accomplished that feat nine years later with *Die Zauberflöte*.

Now, before we continue our chronological investigation of
the seven Mozart masterworks, we need to meet a poet and a playwright.

Lorenzo da Ponte

Idomeneo is opera seria. *The Abduction from the Seraglio* is a
singspiel. The third operatic style of Mozartian composition (that
I mentioned on page 38) is one he created in his collaboration with
the Italian poet Lorenzo da Ponte. The three unparalleled masterpieces they made are: *Le nozze di Figaro, Don Giovanni*, and *Così
fan tutte*. Though primarily and overtly comic operas, they contain serious ideas, serious poetry, and serious music. I call them
the "synthesis operas" between the comic (opera buffa) and the
serious (opera seria).

Da Ponte was born seven years before Mozart. Like Mozart, he
was fascinated by women. His studies in a Venetian seminary
were terminated when his amorous adventures became public,
and he was forced to leave the city. Several years later, in Vienna,
he and Mozart met. Fate made them for each other. Soon we will
discuss the manner in which their treatment of human sexual
behavior in the operas that they worked on together is both comic
and serious: the situations usually comic, their implications,
when pondered, normally serious.

First, however, I take issue with the universal assumption that
their three operas are by Mozart alone as implied in the question,
"Have you seen the film version of Mozart's *Don Giovanni*?" or
in the newspaper headline, "London critic praises new production
of Mozart's *The Marriage of Figaro*." When referring to opera it is
traditional to omit the name of the librettist and credit only the
composer of the music. One reason is that many opera libretti are
by journeyman poets; indeed, some are by hack poets who caused
many fine composers undue frustration by not delivering the lines
they wanted and needed. Another reason is that one prevailing
view of operatic composition holds that it is the function of the
poet to serve the musician or, to state it differently the words exist
to serve the music. I do not plan to contest this view or to try to

resolve what four hundred years of opera history has debated. Mozart adamantly believed it was the job of the poet to serve the music, which meant the poet's primary concern was not his or her own artistic and creative expression but rather to produce the words the musician needed to write the best and most appropriate music to intensify the drama.

Da Ponte served Mozart so well that their masterpieces are a perfect blend of words and music. Accordingly, when referring to these three operas, I always say "by Mozart and da Ponte" in the same way that we refer to the Broadway collaboration of "Rodgers and Hammerstein" or as we always say "Gilbert and Sullivan" when referring to the geniuses responsible for their incomparable operettas.

Anyway, the Mozart and da Ponte collaboration was brief, but as we have said, it produced three operas, three of the greatest ever written. This they accomplished in about five years. Soon after their final creation, Mozart was dead.

In 1805, da Ponte, escaping from creditors, sailed to America, ultimately to become a professor of Italian language and literature at New York City's Columbia University. He was also an important figure in introducing opera to this new, young country. When he died, an ocean apart and nearly half a century after Mozart, da Ponte's remains, like those of Mozart, were placed in an unmarked grave.

Pierre Augustin Caron de Beaumarchais

Figaro, one of the most popular and engaging characters in opera, was created by the Frenchman Pierre Augustin Caron de Beaumarchais, clock-maker, musician, and playwright. Figaro's fame endures because he is the title character in two different operas, both favorites everywhere opera is performed and written by different composers (thus, the understandable potential for confusion). These operas are *Le nozze di Figaro* by Mozart and da Ponte, and *Il barbiere di Siviglia (The Barber of Seville)* by Rossini. Figaro is the central figure in a trilogy, the first play of which appeared in 1775. He is a barber and factotum who lives in Seville and makes things happen. It was Figaro as servant outwitting his master—a touchy subject in those days of fomenting democratic revolutions—that became the talk of the town. It was Beaumarchais's pen that begot Figaro and made him famous, but it was through opera that Figaro achieved immortality. Beaumarchais was a brilliant and indomitable man whose life makes for fascinating reading. Our subject, however, is opera; and our concern with Beaumarchais is because two of the three plays in his trilogy have become such famous operas. Those two plays are *Le Barbier de Seville* (1775), the source of Rossini's most famous work, and *Le Mariage de Figaro* (1778), the source of Mozart and da Ponte's opera, which we will be considering in some detail soon. The third play of Beaumarchais's trilogy, *La Mère Coupable, (The Culpable Mother)* (1778), has been the source for several operas, none of which has achieved international recognition and repertory status.

Now to the source of potential confusion. Rossini was not born until one year after Mozart's death, but he chose to make his opera about the events of Beaumachais's first play. Before Rossini was even born, Mozart and da Ponte had written and produced a most successful masterpiece about the events of Beaumarchais's second play. Figaro is central to both operas. The potential for getting confused with regard to Figaro is that the operatic Figaros appeared backward, so to speak: An older Figaro about to be married appears on the opera stage thirty years before the young Figaro—barber, factotum, and man about town—makes an appearance in Rossini's opera. Were not both operas so popular, there would be no reason to confuse Figaros.

Serious Comic Opera

Certainly, Mozart and da Ponte were neither the first nor the last to create works for the stage that combine comedy with serious themes or that utilize comedy to underscore a point that is worth some serious consideration. The Italian operatic tradition, however, it is good to remember, was one of keeping seria and buffa in their separate places. Now, there can be no doubt that Mozart and da Ponte presented their operas as comic entertainment, and surely, that is how the majority of the first audiences would have received them. Yet, any seasoned operagoer in those first audiences, if he had a brain in his head, could not have missed the mix of comic and serious both in words and in music. As a child, I enjoyed the bravado of Figaro and Don Giovanni and awaited the wonderful tunes so familiar to me. As an adult, however, I have never been able to view a Mozart/da Ponte opera solely as comedy. Behind the comic facade, so much more is implied or asked. This is not always understood. Poor Beethoven—and he was no dummy—missed it altogether. He said he could never write an opera like Mozart because Mozart composed to such silly, trivial plots. (Beethoven took everything quite seriously, as will be gleaned when we come to his only opera, the extraordinary *Fidelio*.) The ways in which the Mozart and da Ponte collaborations at once are both comic and serious should become clear as we consider each work.

Now we'll continue our chronological introduction of the seven greatest of the Mozart operas, the next three of which are the celebrated Mozart and da Ponte collaborations synthesizing comic and serious elements.

LE NOZZE DI FIGARO (1786)
The Marriage of Figaro

It helps to know the background. In Beaumarchais's first play in the trilogy, *The Barber of Seville*, which in time will be the subject of Rossini's opera, Figaro outwits Dr. Bartolo, who seeks to marry his wealthy and attractive young ward, Rosina, thus promoting the successful suit of Count Almaviva. In *The Marriage of Figaro*, an opera in four acts, Count Almaviva and Rosina, now the Countess, are married. In a somewhat cynical course of events, the Count has already begun to tire of his wife's attributes and is looking for a little fun. The Count and Countess, living in a castle near Seville, are served by Figaro and by Susanna, Figaro's bride-to-be. Guess who the Count is looking at. According to the law of "the feudal right," the lord of a manor is allowed to sleep with a female serf before "losing her" in marriage to a husband. The Count recently abolished this "law" and now regrets having done so, for now if he is to get Susanna into bed it must be through seduction. Figaro is both a jealous man and one of strong, independent, and revolutionary spirit. He will have none of the Count's attentions toward Susanna. "If the Count wishes to dance, he will dance to my tune," declares Figaro, thinking aloud early in the first act in an infectious tune swaggering with bravado: *Se vuol ballare.*

The opera buffa dimensions of this opera will result in considerable intrigue and complicated situations. The plot is involved so let me first get the characters before you:

FIGARO, servant to Count Almaviva, *baritone*
SUSANNA, maid to the Countess Almaviva, *soprano*
COUNT ALMAVIVA, *baritone*
COUNTESS ALMAVIVA, *soprano*
CHERUBINO, a young page in Count Almaviva's castle,
   soprano or mezzo-soprano

DR. BARTOLO, *bass*
MARCELLINA, former housekeeper of Dr. Bartolo, *soprano*
ANTONIO, the Count's gardener and Susanna's uncle, *bass*
BARBARINA, Antonio's daughter, *soprano*
DON BASILIO, a music teacher, *tenor*
DON CURZIO, a lawyer, *tenor*

The opera is set in the Count's chateau in eighteenth-century Seville.

Act I

When I interrupted the story to introduce the characters, Figaro had just sung an aria proclaiming that if the Count wants amusement, then Figaro will give it to him, the metaphor being that the Count will dance to Figaro's tune. The political and social impact of this aria, radical when it was heard for the first time in Vienna on May 1, 1786, usually is lost on today's audience. Contemporary operagoers are far removed from servants and masters and, accordingly, much less sensitive to social distinctions and to the unheard of independence of a servant who will call the shots where his wife and his life are concerned. When Figaro first sang this aria, the American Revolution was still smoldering and the French Revolution lay just around the next corner.

The Count's desire for Susanna, however, is not the only problem disturbing Figaro's wedding plans. Dr. Bartolo wants revenge on Figaro, who, when he was the barber of Seville (in Beaumarchais's first play of the trilogy), thwarted the old man's marriage plans. Bartolo sought to marry his wealthy ward, Rosina. She was young, attractive, and enamored with one Count Almaviva, who represented himself to her in his humble suit as simply Lindoro, a poor student. The wily Figaro blocked Bartolo's schemes, enabling the young couple to elope. Now, in the second portion of the trilogy, Bartolo and his ex-housekeeper, Marcellina, have a plan to force Figaro to honor an old contract to marry her. Bartolo revels in revenge as he sings *La vendetta* ("Revenge"), a famous comic aria. This considerable intrigue is complicated further by the presence in the castle of the page Cherubino, an adolescent of noble birth who was placed in the household in order to learn good manners. Awakening sexual desire is overwhelming young Cherubino, who directs most of his attention to the Countess, though he also enjoys flirting with Susanna—much to the consternation of both the Count and Figaro.

Cherubino's is a trouser role wherein an adolescent male is portrayed by a soprano or mezzo-soprano dressed as and enacting the part of a male—who, during the intricate complications of the unfolding plot, will be called upon to appear disguised as a female in a sort of double *travesti* (if you get the meaning). Mozart wrote for Cherubino two arias that no soprano with the timbre for this part would dare be without. When properly sung, with an orchestra doing the right things, you can hear the rapid palpitations of a heart beating and the almost breathless desires of a young man in love with love; but a love, nevertheless, of which both Susanna and the Countess are much aware, and that neither has bothered to discourage. A translation into English of Cherubino's aria *Non sò più* reveals so much for those who do not understand Italian and in doing so makes the point that there is a wealth to be gained from taking the time to know the story of an opera and to be familiar with the texts of at least its famous arias:

I no longer know what I am or what I'm doing,
Now I'm burning, now I'm made of ice . . .
Every woman makes me change color,
Every woman makes me tremble.
At the very word love or beloved
My heart leaps and pounds,
And to speak of it fills me
With a longing I can't explain!
I speak of love when I'm awake,
I speak of it in my dreams,
To the stream, the shade, the mountains,
To the flowers, the grass, the fountains,
To the echo, the air, the breezes,
Which carry away with them
The sound of my fond words
And if I've none to hear me
I speak of love to myself.

The Count will solve the problems of Cherubino's disturbing presence by ordering him to depart the castle and to report as an ensign in his regiment. As the first act is ending, Figaro has another aria, as famous as his first, wherein he bids Cherubino farewell with no regrets and informs him that military life will be an end to his games with girls: *Non più andrai, farfallone amoroso* ("No more, you amorous butterfly, will you go fluttering").

I told you that the plot of this opera is complicated, and now it becomes even more so. So far we know that Figaro intends to marry Susanna, the Count hopes to sleep with her, Marcellina and Dr. Bartolo are preparing revenge on Figaro, and charging about the castle is a young man on fire with sexual desire. Sex, indeed, is the central theme in the opera. Not tawdry or titillating sex, mind you, but rather sex as an elemental force and determinant in the ways people behave. Both poet and musician, by the way, had ample familiarity and experience with the subject of their drama.

In the second and third acts, Susanna, totally unreceptive to the Count's attentions, contrives with the Countess a plan to embarrass the Count. Their plan is successful in Act IV, when the Count attempts to make love to Susanna in the garden at night. Or at least he *thinks* the woman before him is Susanna. Actually, it is his wife, the Countess, disguised in Susanna's clothes. With this culminating event, all intrigues become revealed and resolved. The humbled Count apologizes to his wife, all are reconciled, and a host of happy couples agree that after a day of such madness they ought to revel in joy all the night. With this, the opera ends.

This is but an outline of this complicated story of desires, jealousy, disguise, and mistaken identities. To gain full comprehension of any opera plot you will always benefit by reading a good synopsis of the story, act by act, and even better, to read the libretto in whatever language you can. Also, comedy places greater intellectual demands on an audience than does tragedy. To appreciate fully a comedy requires "getting it," that is, understanding what is funny. Comedy is more intellectual than tragedy. We can more easily glean the meaning of tragic events through feelings—the heart. Comedy is aimed at the head. *The Marriage of Figaro*, its serious implications notwithstanding, first and foremost is a comedy, and if you are going to get it, you must do the necessary preparations. The incessant, magical flow of Mozart's music in this opera is enhanced when you know what that music is expressing, for his opera music always is more than just catchy tunes and beautiful sounds. Mozart's operatic music is a distillation in sound of the essence of what his characters are thinking and feeling, so you really must make the effort to find out what is going on.

To those who know this opera well, all the music—first note to last—is famous. If you are just getting started, though, there are certain excerpts that have become so well known and so anticipated in the opera house that you should know about them.

The Act I excerpts already have been noted. Act by act, here are the rest of them.

Act II

Porgi, amor ("Grant, love to me"): the superb, serious aria of the Countess imploring the God of love either to restore her husband's affections or to let her die.

Voi che sapete ("Tell me, fair ladies"): another testimonial by Cherubino (who has yet to be dispatched to the military life) to the pleasures and pains of love.

The scene concluding the second act, wherein the Count, Marcellina, Bartolo, and his witness, Don Basilio, believe that their will has prevailed as Figaro, Susanna, and the Countess express their dismay over an unexpected turn of events is one of the most exhilarating finales in all opera.

Act III

Vedrò mentr'io sospiro ("Must I forgo my pleasure"): in which the Count expresses annoyance as he suspects that Susanna and Figaro, mere serfs, may be thwarting his plans.

Sua madre? Suo padre? ("His mother? His father?"): a comic sextet wherein it is revealed that in Marcellina and Bartolo our Figaro has discovered his long-lost parents.

Dove sono ("I remember days long departed"): another lament—elegant, serious, and sublime—of the Countess.

Che soave zeffiretto ("What a gentle zephyr"): one of the most anticipated "letter scenes" in all opera. A letter scene was an extremely popular episode in seventeenth-century opera. A character would read aloud a missive received or, as here, dictate one. Letter scenes survived several more centuries, often taking the twist of a character reading aloud a letter to be dispatched. Planning to envelop the Count in the trap of his own desires, the Countess dictates a letter while Susanna, repeating her words, writes to the Count agreeing to an evening assignation in the garden.

Act IV

Deh vieni, non tardar ("Come now without delay my heart's delight"): Susanna's serenade in the garden.

During the finale to the opera, all complications associated with the marriage of Figaro have been resolved into a happy ending.

The Marriage of Figaro is for many—from musicians to experts to ordinary opera lovers—the operatic masterpiece par excellence. I indicated earlier that rating operas and composers is not the point of this book, but I would be remiss not to note those works that transcend normal appreciation and popularity to such a degree that they have acquired musical immortality. *The Marriage of Figaro* is a comedy through and through. Words and music proceed rapidly in delightful conversational flow. Mozart and da Ponte have put on the stage a series of lifelike episodes involving desires from love to revenge, all exaggerated to comic proportions. Certainly, that is how the first audience in Vienna received it. Behind the comic situations, nevertheless, reside hints of something serious: Perhaps the characters in the drama are not just characters in an operatic farce but rather representations of real human beings attempting to cope with the swirl of problems and frustrations associated with sexual desire, love, and matrimonial commitment.

Another operatic miracle by Mozart and da Ponte premiered a year and a half later in Prague. Their second collaboration, *Don Giovanni*, also is about sex.

DON GIOVANNI (1787)

For a long time, beginning when I was quite young, *Don Giovanni* was my favorite opera. It was the first opera I knew thoroughly. It remains one of my favorite works, though I have admitted others into that tantalizing desert island query—I am persistent in my refusal to select only one opera to accompany me into isolation. *Don Giovanni* was not the favorite of those adolescent years because it is an opera about sex, about a ladies' man, even though these topics have a normal appeal to a young male. It was a favorite because from the first chord of the overture to the final note of the opera's epilogue I was mesmerized by the music.

Don Giovanni was the first opera of which I had a complete recording, a birthday present from my father. I still have it, over fifty years old. Through one playing after another, I learned the opera and with a teenager's ludicrous megalomania claimed that I could conduct it without a score. This preposterous nonsense, nevertheless, revealed my preoccupation with this opera, which later got me into trouble in a college course in musical appreciation.

Like all too many such courses, this one unfortunately did not serve "musical appreciation." I had to protect an already above average involvement with classical music by not paying attention, which was easy until it became opera time. The professor had selected *Don Giovanni* to "teach us about opera," and in an instant, I came alive. I poured out my passion for this work. There was not a question I could not and did not answer with an almost uncontrollable enthusiasm. This transformation of a heretofore sleepy, uninterested dolt into an expert left my professor both bewildered and with the expectation that he had found his prize student. When he was finished with *Don Giovanni*, however, and moved onto an uninspired presentation of "absolute music" compared to "program music," it was sleepy time again.

The more subtle mix of seria and buffa elements in *The Marriage of Figaro* is much less so in *Don Giovanni*. *Don Giovanni*, of course, is the Italian for that famous, or infamous, character Don Juan, the legendary seducer. How many have gone to this opera unaware it is about Don Juan, I wonder? Like *The Marriage of Figaro*, this opera represents the passage of but a few hours, a twenty-four-hour period at most. The characters are:

Don Giovanni, a young nobleman, *baritone, bass, or bass-baritone*
Leporello, his servant, *bass*
Donna Anna, betrothed to Don Ottavio, *soprano*
The Commendatore, her father, *bass*
Don Ottavio, friend of Don Giovanni, *tenor*
Donna Elvira, a lady of Burgos, *soprano*
Zerlina, peasant girl betrothed to Masetto, *soprano*
Masetto, a peasant, *baritone*

The opera is set in seventeenth-century Seville.

Act I

Don Giovanni, masked, is in the house of Donna Anna seeking to seduce her. (Whether he was successful is never specified in the libretto and thus remains an unresolved topic.) Her attempt to identify her attacker (or seducer) produces a clamour that brings forth her father, the Commendatore, who insists on dueling with Don Giovanni, who is seeking to escape. In self-defense, the Don mortally wounds the old gentleman before running off with his servant Leporello. Donna Anna and Don Ottavio discover the body and vow to take revenge on the masked intruder.

The scene changes. Don Giovanni commences to sweet-talk another woman only to discover she is Donna Elvira, a woman he loved and left. She is hot on his trail but the Don sneaks away. The scene changes again to show Don Giovanni as he happens upon the wedding party of some country folk. The pretty bride-to-be, Zerlina, the Don cannot pass by. He instructs Leporello to occupy the groom-to-be and to move the wedding party along, thus leaving him alone with Zerlina. She attempts to remain strong but yields. They walk off, arm in arm, toward Don Giovanni's villa. Donna Elvira, still hot in pursuit, bursts on to the scene to rescue the peasant girl. The scene changes.

Donna Anna recognizes in Don Giovanni's voice that of her masked visitor on the previous night and she informs Don Ottavio of this. Another scene change: Don Giovanni, with a grand seduction on his mind, will invite all his peasant friends to a party featuring wild and intoxicating dancing. All three masked, with the intent to trap Don Giovanni, Donna Anna, Don Ottavio, and Donna Elvira, also attend the party. Again, Don Giovanni tries to seduce Zerlina, whose screams save her. The masked guests then unmask and confront Don Giovanni with his crimes. Sword in hand, he escapes as the first of the two acts ends.

Act II
As the second act begins, Don Giovanni forces Leporello to exchange cloaks and to pretend to be the irresistible young nobleman escorting a naive and ever-willing Donna Elvira off into the night. Masetto and friends haunt the darkness intent on finding and killing Don Giovanni, who, now disguised as Leporello, encounters them and directs them on a goose chase. Zerlina, Masetto, Donna Anna, Don Ottavio, and Donna Elvira mistake Leporello for the Don. Before being beaten, the servant reveals himself and escapes in the nick of time.

The scene now changes to a graveyard, where Leporello and Don Giovanni have their jocular discussion about seductions interrupted by the chilling voice of the stone statue of the Commendatore (constructed, erected, and commemorated faster than any other in all history) warning Don Giovanni that his laughter will be silenced before morning. Leporello is terrified. An imperturbable Don Giovanni orders his servant to invite the statue to be his guest for dinner.

The final scene shows Don Giovanni at dinner. The statue arrives and drags a defiant, unrepentant, and heroic Don Giovanni down to hell. In an epilogue, Donna Elvira announces that she will enter a convent, Donna Anna plans to observe a year of mourning before wedding Don Ottavio, and, in perfect peasant fashion, Zerlina and Masetto intend to go home and have dinner. Leporello will seek a new master. Together they sing the moral of the opera:

> This is the evil doer's end.
> Sinners finally meet their
> just reward and always will.

As you become more familiar with the story, its diverse characters, and their music, you will see why this opera, from its sensational premiere in Prague on October 29, 1787, to this day, remains one of the most popular and highly praised of all operas. Mozart's music sets perfectly the words of da Ponte's poetry and the characters that he drew so well. They simply could not sound any other way than they do. There are numerous plays on the Don Juan legend and nearly three dozen operas. This *Don Giovanni*, by Mozart and da Ponte, puts the others to rest. Their drama, like their previous collaboration, races from event to event in an astonishing presentation of perfectly blended words and music. Beautiful arias, duets, and ensembles abound. The list of the most famous musical highlights of this opera is long.

Before we introduce them, though, it is appropriate to ask a question that, once considered, will provide a helpful introduction to the music. Wherein lies the synthesis of serious and comic elements in this opera?

The structure of *Don Giovanni* is typical of opera buffa formats with its comic songs, disguises, beatings, mistaken identities, and a big comic finale ending the first act. Furthermore, in words and music da Ponte and Mozart have created in Leporello one of the most endearing comic characters in opera. Nevertheless, they labeled their opera a *dramma giocoso*, an Italian term implying a comic opera with serious episodes, and of this mix *Don Giovanni* is the most notable example. In fact, serious episodes firmly establish themselves in the opera before a single humorous event offers the striking contrast: the somber death of the innocent Commendatore, Donna Anna's grief, and her pledge of revenge with Don Ottavio. Only then comes the first bit of comedy as Donna Elvira confronts an amazed Don Giovanni.

Mozart's music throughout the drama, of course, alternates with the serious and humorous scenes—compare Leporello's buffa catalogue aria (soon to be discussed) with the opera seria arias

Donna Anna sings to hear both comic and serious expressions. And in the Don, Mozart and da Ponte have created a character at once both reprehensible and captivating.

Beyond this are the implications within the unfolding of the drama that a sensitive and perceptive member of the audience will take home to reflect upon. Do people really behave in the manner depicted on the stage? No one sympathetic to male and female relationships could just write off Don Giovanni's treatment of women. Poor Donna Elvira, and what about Zerlina, even though no seventeenth-century nobleman would have had a qualm over attempting to seduce a peasant girl on her wedding day. Obviously, the penis of Don Giovanni had a mind of its own, and yet for all his self-centered search for pleasure there are indications that Don Giovanni had convinced himself that he was in love with all women and that his pleasure was their pleasure too.

In the second act, da Ponte has Leporello scold his master for treating women unfairly, and who could disagree? Don Giovanni, of course.

> *Don Giovanni to Leporello:*
> Are you ready to carry out my orders?
>
> *Leporello:*
> So long as you leave women alone.
>
> *Don Giovanni:*
> Leave women alone! You're mad!
> Why, they're more necessary to me
> than the bread I eat,
> than the air I breathe!
>
> *Leporello:*
> And you've the heart to deceive the lot?
>
> *Don Giovanni:*
> It's all for love!
> To be faithful to one
> is to be unfaithful to the others.
> I have so generous a heart that I love
> every single one of them: but women
> who have no head for figures,
> call my good nature deception.

Now, the self-delusion of this sham may be all too obvious. However, the astounding number of women who went to bed with the Don—women of all ages, shapes, and sizes; married and single; and of every social rank—raises the question as to the possibility of this hanky-panky being a two-way street. In short, here we are again confronting the questions of sexual desire and fidelity broached in *The Marriage of Figaro*, but in this opera, they have been intensified to frightening proportions. We all know that most people enjoy sexual intercourse and that they do not always confine their pleasure to one partner. Some yield to temptation, as Zerlina was about to do, and temptation seems always to be present. Don Giovanni's preoccupation with sexual pleasure, however exaggerated, reminds us all, male and female, that human beings are not always monogamous.

The power of sex portrayed in *The Marriage of Figaro* has exploded in *Don Giovanni* and does not go away in the third and final Mozart and de Ponte collaboration, *Così fan tutte*. In all three of these operas, comic behavior ultimately removes a shield behind which people generally hide their true thoughts. The comedy makes of human foibles a laughing matter, reminding us that we are imperfect creatures. As such, taking life too seriously— especially when manifested in inexorable judgment of others—is not funny. This is the perpetual fascination of the opera *Don Giovanni*, wherein the comic and the serious do indeed hold a mirror to reality.

I have mentioned that I was still a young boy when the musical numbers of *Don Giovanni* had become familiar to me. As soon as the first was sung I anticipated the second and so on, Mozart delivering them in such unbroken rapid fire that I was left breathless by the astonishing turmoil of the Act I finale, and there was to follow yet another act equally rich! But first, the famous music from the beginning.

Act I
Light and darkness both are sounded in the Overture, which leads seamlessly into Leporello's complaint of the hard life of a servant who just waits while his master seeks his pleasure. Seeking to identify the masked intruder, Donna Anna brings forth her father, who is killed when he attempts to prevent Don Giovanni's escape. As he dies his voice mixes with those of the Don and Leporello in a brief, haunting, and somber trio that is, when a bass sings Don

Giovanni's role, the only trio for three bass voices that I know. Don Giovanni next must escape from Donna Elvira, leaving Leporello to ". . . tell her everything" as he sneaks away. And now behold one of the most anticipated and celebrated arias in all opera, that buffa masterpiece for bass voice known as the catalogue aria: *Madamina, il catalogo* ("Little lady, this is the list"). Leporello stuns Donna Elvira by "telling her everything," namely that her name is but one in the list of the women loved by Don Giovanni that Leporello is required to catalogue in a little book. The totals to date are 640 in Italy, 231 in Germany, 100 in France, 91 in Turkey, but in Spain alone, 1003, which in Italian is *mille e tre*, a phrase reappearing throughout the aria, making certain that the point is not lost on the Spanish noble lady (or on the audience).

This aria never goes stale no matter how many times I hear it, and I have heard it many hundreds of times. As a boy I played my recordings of this aria—I had several—over and over. One of my brothers, who also loved opera, always had more catholic tastes in music than I do. (In fact, both of my brothers, and my sister, also do.) Stephen spent his own money, for which he had worked hard, to purchase a recording of "Rock Around the Clock" by Bill Haley and the Comets. He played this record over and over (around the clock) until I thought I would lose my mind. Three times I asked him to please stop playing it and three times I was ignored. I was the elder and, for a limited time, the bigger of the brothers so I took the record and threw it against the wall, shattering it into a million shards. My brother sought justice with an appeal to our father: "Dad! Peter broke my new record." "Thank God for your brother Peter," was our father's reply. It was from him that I had learned intolerance for lesser lights than Mozart.

Don Giovanni next will try his luck with Zerlina, the pretty bride-to-be in a peasant wedding party. First, he must get rid of the bridegroom, who sees what is going on but remains subservient to the will of the nobleman. Masetto sings *Ho capito, signor sì* ("Oh, yes, I understand, sir"). Understand he may, but like it he does not. Alone with Zerlina Don Giovanni commences one of the most exquisite duets in any opera with *Là ci darem la mano* ("There we'll take hands") offering to lead her away to his villa. She would like to but dares not, is her response. This represents her brief resistance before in unison they sing "Then come, oh come, my dearest" as arm in arm they move toward the villa, only to be interrupted by the fortunate or inopportune (take your choice) arrival of Donna Elvira, who saves Leporello the job of adding Zerlina's name to the list. The Don, of course, will try again. Elvira warns Zerlina in a robust aria, *Ah, fuggi il traditor* ("Ah, flee the traitor"), about Don Giovanni.

Minutes later, Donna Anna, now on the scene, recognizes Don Giovanni's voice as that of her masked visitor. Alone with Don Ottavio she sings a big opera seria-style aria, *Or sai chi l'onore* ("Now you know who sought to steal my honor"). If, by the way, she did capitulate, as some interpretations of the opera proffer, she has no intention of telling her boyfriend! Left to absorb this, Ottavio sings a most lovely aria asserting that her well-being is his sole concern: *Dalla sua pace* ("On her peace of mind").

Both Donna Anna's aria and this gem for the lyric tenor are in the opera seria tradition and offer a remarkable contrast to two arias yet to be heard in Act I. When Donna Anna and Don Ottavio sing, we hear the qualities of the ruling class. Don Giovanni also is a member of the aristocracy but more than this he is a rogue, and that is what is heard when he sings the so-called "Champagne Aria," *Finch'han dal vino* ("While from the wine"). He instructs Leporello to ensure wine and dancing and by dawn, he will have a dozen more names to write.

(I have seen *Don Giovanni* more than any other opera but one particular performance I will never forget. Don Giovanni was being sung by the handsome, self-taught Italian bass Cesare Siepi. My wife measured his sex appeal not in meters but in miles and following the performance, we were to attend a party to meet him. Now there he was, on the stage before us, ready to deliver his celebrated "Champagne Aria." He was dressed in white from his shoes to the feather in his hat. There was not a woman in the house whose eyes were not transfixed upon him. He sang the aria holding a glass of champagne, then quaffed the wine, and, as he turned on his heels to exit, he tossed the empty glass high into the air, leaving it to fall and shatter on the stage symbolically just as a woman's heart might break. Siepi gave a magnificent performance but due to exhaustion reneged on the party—much to my relief; my wife was a little too eager to meet him.)

Nor is there anything of the aristocratic in Zerlina's aria *Batti, batti, o bel Masetto* ("Beat me, beat me, dear Masetto"), knowing that she deserves what she gets. She is contrite over her momentary lapse with Don Giovanni and seeks forgiveness in a simple folklike melody in keeping with her personality and her station. This charming little song sets her far apart from the ultra-serious declarations of Donna Anna and Donna Elvira. Apart, as well, are Don Ottavio and Don Giovanni. Ottavio, Donna Anna's wimpy, puppy-dog boyfriend, is elegant, proper, and passionless when he sings; Don Giovanni is rakish and sensual. These contrasts exemplify what I mean when I say this opera is a synthesis of elements deriving from both serious and comic opera traditions. And, the buffa qualities of Leporello? They are unforgettable.

The first act ends with a tour de force. This, therefore, is an appropriate place to introduce the opera buffa traditions of *primo finale* (first finale) and *secundo finale* (second finale). Buffa operas often were in two acts or, as is the case with *The Marriage of Figaro*, two distinct parts (Acts I and II of this opera constitute the first part, Acts III and IV the second part). The comic momentum of opera buffa culminates with the end of the first act in a primo finale that expresses in actions, words, and music the confusion, madness, bewilderment, stupefaction, or whatever form of chaos prevails. I call this primo finale the finale of dissolution, a world coming apart at the seams.

Comic episodes continue throughout the opera as the second act drives toward resolution—everything coming out all right. That is why I refer to the secundo finale as the finale of resolution. When you are aware of this tradition and how it is utilized by poet and composer, enjoyment of the opera is enhanced as solo voices, chorus, and orchestra, all full tilt, express first complete disorder and then, at the opera's conclusion, a happy end.

The Marriage of Figaro follows this format even more closely than does *Don Giovanni*, the ending of which must be varied sufficiently to incorporate the serious descent into the fires of hell by the Don as well as the nonchalant and happy epilogue that ends the drama. The *Don Giovanni* primo finale must be noted, however, for it is artistry of the highest order. The Don's great party is under way and as promised there is dancing. Stage bands (musicians in costume on stage as part of the action) perform, including, simultaneously, musicians playing a minuet for the gentry, others playing a contredanse for the villagers, and still others playing a waltz. All at once? Don't ask me how Mozart did it. The answer with Mozart is always simple: He was a genius!

Don Giovanni attempts another pass at Zerlina but this time she screams instead of capitulating. The Don has been caught. His attempt to transfer blame to Leporello fails and it is with sword drawn that he escapes his now unmasked accusers. This finale is considered one of the great masterpieces of dramatic music.

Act II

There are five famous arias in the second act. Don Giovanni sings the first to the maid of Donna Elvira who is only seen; she has no vocal part. To her the Don delivers his delicious serenade *Deh, vieni alla finestra* ("Look down from out your window") accompanying himself on the mandolin. I suppose somewhere at sometime there has been the unique musician who could both sing the aria and play the mandolin, but I do not know of one. In fact, all too often it is not a mandolin at all that we hear but rather a member of the violin section in the orchestra playing pizzicato (plucking the strings of the violin) while the Don fakes strumming an instrument that bears no resemblance to a mandolin. I realize that it is too much to expect of Don Giovanni that he also be a mandolinist. But Mozart wrote this fetching accompaniment for the mandolin and that is how it ought to be played. The mandolin and violin are, indeed, first cousins instrumentally but they are not the same sounds, and there must be a mandolinist who would love to accompany Don Giovanni's serenade. Here is what you do if you wish to become a purist: When looking for a recording of *Don Giovanni*, make certain that this aria is accompanied by a mandolinist or save your money! When you apply for tickets for a performance of the opera, ask after the mandolinist. If you are told there is none, then see a different show!

The next famous aria is Zerlina's. Masetto and his band of renegades comb the dark seeking revenge against Don Giovanni, who, disguised as Leporello, scatters them into the night on a wild goose chase except for Masetto, whom he retains for a beating. Masetto's cries bring Zerlina to his side and he is the recipient of her most graceful aria: *Vedrai carino* ("You'll see, dearest").

The third of the celebrated Act II arias belongs to Don Ottavio—one even more acclaimed than his in the first act. This aria, *Il mio tesoro*, a second affirmation of his unwavering commitment to his beloved Donna Anna, has been called "the supreme test of classical song." If you wish to hear it the way it was meant to be sung, you must listen to a recording (available on compact disc) made on May 9, 1916, by the Irish tenor John McCormack, who said, "I will let my reputation as a singer stand or fall by my recording of *Il mio tesoro*." The wily Irishman knew he had nothing to worry about. His reputation, fifty years after his death, is still that of one of the finest singers of the twentieth century. His recording of this aria remains the measure of musicianship, elegance, and beauty.

Donna Elvira has the next big moment. Her aria *Mi tradì quell' alma ingrata* ("Betrayed") has an interesting history. This aria was not in the opera at its world premiere in Prague. The soprano who played Elvira when the opera had its first Vienna performance entreated Mozart to write for her another aria. She wanted to knock the socks off the Viennese audience, which heretofore had not appreciated her as did other audiences. (In the eighteenth century and early in the nineteenth it was not unusual for composers to add or subtract arias in order to fit the abilities of the singers. In this same Vienna production, for example, the Don Ottavio declared his second act aria, *Il mio tesoro*, too difficult; for him Mozart wrote the splendid Act I *Dalla sua pace*.) So for the begging soprano Mozart wrote an aria expressing Elvira's awareness of her weakness for Don Giovanni. He has done her wrong and she knows it and she should exact revenge but her heart falters. The Elvira whose mastery of vocal technique is supported by a splendid set of God-given pipes can "bring down the house" with *Mi tradì*.

Prior to the final scene, Donna Anna has an aria now equally as famous as Elvira's. *"Non mi dir"* ("Say no more"), she says to quiet Don Ottavio's hints of their forthcoming marriage. The marriage will have to wait—this is a time for grief.

There are other wonderful musical moments in this act—Leporello's *Ah! pietà, signori miei!* ("Spare me, spare my life, I pray"), for example, and the famous graveyard scene wherein a terrified Leporello is ordered to give the stone statue of the Commendatore an invitation to dinner—but I must set limits or I will end up pointing to every note start to finish.

The final scene begins with Don Giovanni at dinner in his palace. He requests music. Again, in some performances the band is actually on stage, which lends credibility to a lighthearted exchange that precedes Don Giovanni's doom. First, the band plays airs from an opera, *Cosa Rara*, by Martin y Soler, a contemporary of Mozart. While Don Giovanni gorges, he feigns not seeing Leporello sneaking food. Next the band plays a tune from an opera by Sarti. Then is heard a melody everyone was familiar with. It is Mozart's own *Non più andrai*, which Figaro sings in *The Marriage of Figaro*. Leporello has up to this point been enjoying the music but now he turns to the musicians and mutters *"Questa poi la conosco pur troppo!"* which means, "Now, that tune I know only too well," a remark never lost on an audience that comprehends Italian.

Elvira enters. She begs the man who has betrayed her and played dirty tricks on her to change his ways. The Don replies, "Do let me eat: You can join me if you wish." Furious, she departs, only to return shrieking in terror to find another exit. The stone statue has come to dinner. Now it is the statue that demands repentance of Don Giovanni. He is resolute in his refusal: "For me there is no repentance." He is consumed by the fires of hell.

Some performances end here. Especially this was so during the nineteenth century and into the early part of the twentieth century; audiences were attuned to a more tragic interpretation of the drama befitting the age of Romanticism. A moralizing epilogue, however, was the tradition for all plays based on the Don Juan legend, and Mozart provided one for his original version. This is how most of us today know the opera. After the somber, dire demise of the heroic Don, a light epilogue allows the remaining characters to gather before the footlights to moralize and to announce their plans for the future. This final back-to-back contrast of the serious and the lighthearted is an appropriate end to Mozart and da Ponte's synthesis of opera seria and opera buffa elements.

COSÌ FAN TUTTE (1790)
All Women Do It

The entire story of this opera is contained in its title, *Così fan tutte*, which means, "All Women Do It." Precisely what is it that all women do, according to this opera? They find that their affections are fickle. They may promise undying love to one man but in his absence, they find themselves capable of being affectionate with another. Let me quickly add, before women readers depart this book cursing "Just another male thing," that few male artists have been more sympathetic to women than Mozart and da Ponte, who will make it clear, indeed, already have made it quite clear in *The Marriage of Figaro* and *Don Giovanni*, that men do it, too. The sexual behavior of humans can lack both constancy and rectitude. The men in this opera become equally guilty, if that is the right word, of dalliance as the women. That is the point of the story and thus the subtitle of the opera: *Ossia la Scuola degli Amanti (The School for Lovers)*.

But before the story is told I want to tell you that this opera, the third and final Mozart and da Ponte collaboration, more than two hundred years after its world premiere in Vienna in 1790, has never obtained the popularity of the other two. Now, it would be a huge mistake to assume that the reason for this is that its poetic and musical expression is not quite up to that of the other two masterpieces. The opposite, in a sense, I think, is true. Both men were at the peak of their creative powers, which had been honed by having collaborated on two earlier masterworks. It is pertinent to note that this opera, while bearing certain operatic conventions and forms consistent with its predecessors, differs from *The Marriage of Figaro* and *Don Giovanni* in that its pace is slower and it doesn't contain a seemingly endless string of arias.

Of course, there is the famous trio early in Act I, *Soave sia il vento,* which, according to Sam Sanders (dear friend and for more than twenty-five years the technical producer of our Vermont Public Radio program *Saturday Afternoon at the Opera*), is "the most beautiful piece of music in the history of the universe." Also, there is the famous aria for soprano, *Come scoglio* ("Firm as rock"), but then go on, name some more, and you begin to encounter some difficulty. This is because *Così fan tutte* is such a beautiful ensemble opera. It does not travel with the captivating speed of *The Marriage of Figaro* or *Don Giovanni.* Its poetry and music are sophisticated and demand much of a listener, but make no mistake about it: This is a supreme creation. When you read the story you may wonder "How can this be?" for it is thought by many to be ludicrous, merely a farce, a silly little improbable plot allowing Mozart and da Ponte the opportunity to make just another comic entertainment. In fact, some people have been offended by the plot, and during the nineteenth century attempts were made to provide a more savory story as a means of salvaging the beautiful music. Of course, all such approaches quickly failed, as they ought to. Once again, behind the lighthearted story, improbable as it may seem, reside serious issues. The improbable story, by the way, is said to have derived from a real incident that became the talk of Vienna.

The opera of two acts has six characters:

> FERRANDO, an officer in love with Dorabella, *tenor*
> GUGLIELMO, an officer in love with Fiordiligi, *baritone*
> DON ALFONSO, an elderly philosopher, *bass*
> FIORDILIGI, a young lady, *soprano*
> DORABELLA, sister to Fiordiligi, *mezzo-soprano*
> DESPINA, the sisters' maid, *soprano*

The setting is Naples in the eighteenth century.

Act I

In a café, Ferrando brags that his Dorabella will be faithful to him forever. Guglielmo claims the same for his beloved Fiordiligi. To their irritation Don Alfonso, a wise old philosopher friend, says he knows better. The men strike a bet with the agreement that Alfonso may contrive any scheme of temptation to test the fidelity of the young ladies. And what a scheme he plots. He will inform the sisters that their soldier lovers have been ordered away on duty, there will be a sad farewell, and then Ferrando and Guglielmo, disguised as a pair of dashing Albanian noblemen, will return, each to court the other's fiancée.

Despina, in cahoots with Don Alfonso, as part of his scheme urges her mistresses not to despair over departed lovers but rather to take love lightly and to enjoy the courting of the Albanians. At first, the sisters are resolute and the soldiers believe their wager almost won, but Don Alfonso is confident as the remainder of his scheme unfolds. Again protesting love and again rebuffed, "the Albanians" pretend to take poison in the presence of the sisters, Alfonso, and Despina. They feign dying. Despina departs, disguises herself as a doctor, and returns to save them by waving over them a huge magnet (the invention of the famous Dr. Mesmer) to extricate the poison. All this has begun to tell on the young ladies, and as the first act ends, in a glorious sextet, the revitalized "Albanians" demand kisses as part of their miraculous recovery.

Act II

Despina suggests to the sisters that they try at least a little flirtation and the weakening girls agree, each, of course, choosing the other's lover as the object of her fun. The men recommence their wooing. Dorabella yields first, then Fiordiligi eventually. Alone, the soldiers and Alfonso all must agree that *"Così fan tutte."*

Now all is set for the final scene: the wedding of the two happy couples. Despina, in another disguise, portrays a notary with marriage contract, but the proceedings are interrupted by a repeat of the military music heard in the first act to signal the officers' departure. The Albanians exit hastily to hide but, naturally, return as Ferrando and Guglielmo. The ruse is revealed as the sisters admit that they were about to be married. Don Alfonso has won his bet and the lovers have gone to school and have learned what life is like. All is forgiven as the young lovers concede that the old philosopher has taught them a thing or two. Then Alfonso has the lovers join hands as bride and groom and all join in to sing, in another sextet, *Fortunato l'uom che prende...*

> Fortunate is the man who takes
> everything for the best,
> and in all events and trials
> allows himself to be led by reason.
> What usually makes others weep
> is, for him, a source of laughter,
> and in the midst of the world's whirlwinds
> he will find a lovely calm.[†]

Da Ponte's libretto, by the way, does not make it clear, probably purposely so, which pair of lovers join hands in the finale: the original pair or the new. Preposterous as the plot may seem, I remind you that it may have derived from a true scandal, greatly embellished by da Ponte for theatrical purposes, of course. Furthermore, I will argue against usual interpretations that find in the opera only lighthearted comedy. It is thought that the subject was dictated by Emperor Joseph II, who commissioned it. The subject was in fact one painfully close to Mozart's heart, for while writing the music he heard accounts of his wife's conduct in Baden. She had gone there for a cure and from the reports a cure was not all Mrs. Mozart was getting. In August of 1789 Mozart wrote to her:

> I am glad indeed when you have some fun—of course I am—but I do wish you would sometimes not make yourself so cheap. . . A woman must always make herself respected, or else people will begin to talk about her. My love! Forgive me for being so frank, but my peace of mind demands it as well as our mutual happiness. Remember that you yourself once admitted to me that you are inclined to comply too easily. You know the consequences of that. . ."[†]

Behind the comic facade, again in a remarkable blend of words and music, do we perhaps hear Mozart and da Ponte making a plea

---

[†] Mozart, *Così fan tutte* (Angel Recording Libretto, translation by William Weaver, 1963), p. 19

for a more enlightened and compassionate acceptance of human behavior? Human beings, however hard they may try, however much they may proclaim it, do not live unblemished lives. Human beings have weaknesses, they can yield to temptation, they can even do that which they think they do not want to do. Both Mozart and da Ponte ask for tolerance of human weaknesses. They make it quite clear that in spite of all their protestations the original pair of lovers become, through Alfonso's test case, profoundly infatuated, if not in love, with a new lover. And though the scheme may seem cruel, one that goes far, even too far, it does so safely on the opera stage in order to reveal the moral of the story: Alfonso deceived in order to undeceive. Alfonso awakens the naive young lovers to the facts of life.

The plot of this opera always makes me think of the words to a popular song from the Broadway musical *Finian's Rainbow*, "When I'm not near the one I love, I love the one I'm near." It is a fact of life that humans can be attracted to more than one person, and this can lead to temptation and beyond. Mozart and da Ponte realize this and ask their audience to be reasonable, forgiving, understanding, and loving.

This they ask in one of the most beautiful of ensemble operas. *Così fan tutte* is more notable for its concerted numbers than for the solo arias. The cast makes a perfect sextet and both the *primo* and *secundo* finales are sextets. Though not devoid of solo numbers, the opera overflows with glorious duets, trios, and quartets. The events of the opera are those of human frailties on earth; the music of the opera is that of heavenly beauty. Every time I hear the serene and sublime melodies of this opera I give my shoulders a shrug and to myself I say, "Mozart was unquestionably the peerless genius of Western music." (Actually, I say of "all music" but a friend of mine, a noted oriental scholar, suggests "it would be more politically correct" to say "Western music.")

                                       ∾

Now it is time for the helpful reminder that Mozart's operatic music is in three distinct styles of composition: traditional Italian opera seria, Germanic singspiel, and what I define as a synthesis

---

† William Glock, *Mozart's Così fan tutte* (Angel Recording Libretto, 1963), p. 2

of serious and comic elements in Italian opera. All three styles now have been discussed but there still remain two famous operas by Mozart of the seven presented in this book. One is an opera seria, the other a singspiel.

❧

There are those musicians and scholars who claim that *La clemenza di Tito* is the greatest opera seria in all opera literature and that *Die Zauberflöte* has no serious competition for the singspiel par excellence. With these works, his last operas, Mozart virtually closed the door on two basic operatic styles by taking them to their highest manifestation. After these operas, would anyone attempt to write in these styles again? What works *were* attempted have been forgotten. With these two operas, Mozart gave almost all of what was left of his weakening body and his fevered brain. *La clemenza di Tito* premiered in Prague on September 6, 1791, *Die Zauberflöte* in Vienna on September 30 of that same year. At 1:00 a.m on December 5, 1791, Mozart died. His last work, a requiem mass, was left unfinished. He was not yet thirty-six years old and he had composed a body of music unequaled in human history, even by composers who lived more than twice his number of years.

LA CLEMENZA DI TITO (1791)
The Clemency of Titus

Mozart, more in need of money than ever, was writing *Die Zauberflöte* when he received a commission to compose an opera to celebrate the coronation in Prague in 1791 of the Austrian Emperor Leopold II as King of Bohemia. Unbelievable as it may seem, *La clemenza di Tito* was composed in eighteen days, Mozart assigning to his student the writing of the recitatives. For many, many years, a ludicrous critical opinion circulated claiming that Mozart dashed off this opera only for the money, that he was quite ill when he wrote it (this much was true), and that because of the speed of composition due to illness and his deadline as stipulated by the commission *La clemenza di Tito* is an uninspired work. You only have to listen once to the music to dispel the vapidness of this evaluation. Mozart loved the opera seria form. He certainly must have had reservations about a story that glorifies benevolent despotism—his own political posture was more liberal than that—but that he composed beautiful music is beyond doubt. Obviously, there is no one-to-one relationship between speed of composition and the quality of that composition. An ingenious creation can spill off a pen as fast as it can be made to write or it can be born of almost endless agonizing labor. Music could form in Mozart's head faster than his hand could write it down.

There are six characters in this two-act drama about the Roman Emperor Titus. The time of the story: AD 79 to 81. The place: Rome. No historical claims are made for this story of his clemency. Titus (tenor), which is Tito in Italian, is planning to marry a woman other than Vitellia (soprano), who loves him dearly. Spurned, Vitellia plots revenge. Easily she is able to convince Sextus (a contralto trouser role), a young Roman patrician, to help her in the conspiracy because this young man is in love with her. Tito then changes his matrimonial mind, now favoring the sister of Sextus, Servilia (soprano). Servilia, however, tells Tito she loves Annius (a mezzo-soprano trouser role), another young Roman patrician. With still another change of heart, Tito now finally favors Vitellia and plans to wed her. She, not yet aware of this, has set her plot in motion. Tito escapes death and Sextus is caught. Ultimately a contrite Vitellia, no longer able to bear her guilt, confesses her role in the conspiracy, thus saving just in the nick of time the life of Sextus, who was about to be thrown to the lions (or some such wild beasts). In the end, the merciful emperor forgives all. By the way, the sixth character is Publius (bass), the captain of the Praetorian Guard. Plot never was the forte of opera seria, whose purpose was to make a moral satisfying to the nobility, who often commissioned the work, through a lofty story set to beautiful music. The obvious moral of *La clemenza di Tito* is shown in the mercy of the great Titus. He forgives no matter how severely wronged.

Of twenty-six musical numbers in the opera, only eleven are arias. Like *Così fan tutte,* this opera contains many extraordinary concert numbers: duets, trios, and the splendid Act I finale, for example. Two arias performed back-to-back in the second act illustrate a point made earlier in this book about the manner in which Mozart wrote in different styles for different types of characters. Servilia, the sister of Sextus, simply does not have the stature, the passion, or the complex makeup of Vitellia. For Servilia he wrote a delightful little arietta (short aria), *S'altro che lagrime* ("If you use nothing but tears") followed by a monumental recitative and aria for Vitellia, the now famous *Non più di fiori* ("No more the flowers"). The other great solo showpiece of the opera belongs to Sextus in the first act. It is the aria *Parto, parto* ("I am leaving"), Sextus being on his way to do Vitellia's bidding by setting her plot in motion. I concur, word for word, with conductor James Levine, when he said that in *La clemenza di Tito* we have some of Mozart's greatest music in a virtually unknown work for this opera has lain in obscurity for nearly two centuries. Levine was instrumental in its renaissance.

DIE ZAUBERFLÖTE (1791)
The Magic Flute

My initial experience with *Die Zauberflöte* was mildly perplexing. I was a teen when I first heard the opera. I knew it had something to do with a fairy tale and I knew it was by Mozart. Usually I would have read at least a synopsis and listened to some of the music but when I came to it for the first time one Saturday afternoon through a Metropolitan Opera radio broadcast I was unprepared. Immediately and throughout the opera, I was entranced by the music but I was puzzled because what I heard was too sublime and dignified for a fairy story. Of course, in time I was to understand that the story of this opera, which appears to be a fairy tale and indeed was derived from one, was utilized by composer and librettist as a means of expressing their representation of substantial personal philosophical issues. Even more than that, both Mozart and Emanuel Schikaneder, who adapted the story from an Oriental tale and composed most of the libretto, if not all of it, expressed their personal creed as Freemasons. Freemasonry, which began in the Middle Ages as a secret society for masons, through the centuries had grown into a brotherhood bound by shared liberal beliefs. By the end of the eighteenth century, it had spread throughout Europe and across the waters to England and beyond. Freemasonry is now an organized system of morality open to men of all creeds. Its primary commitment is to mutual assistance and the promotion of brotherly love. Its message and meanings are veiled in allegories and illustrated through symbols. Tests or trials of worthiness were part of the initiation into the brotherhood, which met in lodges. That is about as much as a nonmember such as myself would be inclined to know. Here is an official definition of Freemasonry translated from a German handbook:

> Freemasonry is the activity of closely united men who, employing symbolic forms borrowed principally from the mason's trade and from architecture,

work for the welfare of mankind, striving morally to ennoble themselves and others, and thereby to bring about a universal league of mankind, which they aspire to exhibit even now on a small scale.[†]

A definition much like this could have been part of Mozart's initiation to the order in 1785. He and Schikaneder were members of the same lodge. Knowing this, the lofty beauty of the music no longer is the least bit perplexing for a fairy story that Schikaneder expanded to infuse a Masonic message. The original story tells of a sorcerer who stole the daughter of the Queen of the Night, only to have the girl rescued by a prince and his magic. Here you may have the following question: What did Schikaneder and Mozart do with that little story?

Their opera, *The Magic Flute*, is in two acts. The characters are:

TAMINO, a prince, *tenor*
Three ladies, attendants of the Queen of the Night, *two sopranos, one mezzo-soprano*
PAPAGENO, a birdcatcher of the queen, *baritone*
Queen of the Night, *soprano*
MONOSTATOS, Sarastro's captain of the guard, *tenor*
PAMINA, daughter of the Queen of the Night, *soprano*
Three genii, *either two sopranos and one mezzo-soprano or, preferably, three superb boy sopranos*
The Speaker of the Temple, *bass*
SARASTRO, High Priest of Isis and Osiris, *bass*
Two priests of the temple, *tenor and bass*
PAPAGENA, *soprano*
Two men in armor, *tenor and bass*

The opera is set in ancient Egypt.

Act I
An overture precedes the opening of the curtains, which part to reveal Prince Tamino fainting as he attempts to escape from a huge serpent. The three ladies-in-waiting to the Queen of the Night

---

[†] Edward J. Dent, *Mozart's Operas* (Oxford University Press, London, 1947), p.230

enter, kill the snake, admire the unconscious, handsome prince, and depart. Papageno, the Queen of the Night's birdcatcher, dressed in the feathers emblematic of his trade, enters as Tamino awakens. Papageno's entrance song always is much anticipated by those who know this opera. The folklike, simple, catchy melody has become famous. The delightful *Der Vogelfänger bin ich ja* ("I am the bird-catcher"), which includes runs on pan pipes, immediately establishes Papageno as a lovable, comic character. Schikaneder was not only the librettist of the opera but he was an accomplished singer and actor as well, and he portrayed Papageno in the premiere in the theater that this multitalented man managed. (*The Magic Flute* made considerable money for this theater but not for Mozart. He would live only a few months after the September 30, 1791 opening.)

After his entrance song, Papageno, in dialogue (part of a singspiel format), credits himself as the slayer of the serpent. This fib is overheard by the three ladies. They punish him for his falsehood by putting a padlock on his mouth. Then they show Tamino a miniature of Pamina, daughter of the Queen of the Night. It is love at first sight expressed in an elegant, refined aria for tenor: *Dies Bildnis ist bezaubernd schön* ("This portrait is so beautiful"). Pamina he is told is being held captive by Sarastro, who is falsely represented to Tamino as an evil man. Tamino resolves to rescue Pamina. The Queen of the Night arrives and urges him on in the first of her two celebrated arias. *O zittre nicht, mein lieber Sohn* ("Be not afraid, my noble youth"), she says, displaying what is called coloratura singing. (*Coloratura* is an Italian word derived from the German *Koloratur* meaning to add color to a melody by embellishing it with additional notes, called grace notes. Coloratura singing utilizes elaborate ornamentation of a melody through trilling the voice or by means of other virtuoso techniques. Though any of the various vocal ranges can employ coloratura techniques, they are most common in arias for a high, brilliant soprano voice wherein these techniques are easily heard.)

A quintet follows the exit of the Queen of the Night, and what beautiful music it is! The three ladies-in-waiting, Prince Tamino, and Papageno constitute the five voices. The quintet begins comically as Papageno's locked mouth attempts to sing. "Hm hm," he begins. The padlock is removed. Then, as they sing, Tamino is given a magic flute to aid him in his journey and Papageno, who has been instructed to assist Tamino, is presented with a set of magic bells. The three genii arrive to guide their way.

A scene change shows a room in Sarastro's palace. Monostatos,

while guarding Pamina, attempts to woo her. Papageno, temporarily separated from Tamino, enters and the startled Monostatos flees.
Papageno informs Pamina that soon she will be rescued by one who
loves her; she in turn assures him that he, too, will find love. This
is expressed in the famous duet *Bei Männern, welch Liebe fühlen*
("A man filled with love"), a tune of exquisite beauty that
Beethoven in time would use in his suite of now famous variations
based on that music. (*The Magic Flute* was the opera of Mozart's
that Beethoven really liked. The seemingly frivolous and immoral
qualities of some of the other Mozart operas offended him.)

Another change of scene shows the three genii conducting
Tamino to a temple with three doors, the number three being of
considerable significance in Freemasonry lore. The first two doors
remain unopened to Tamino but from the third comes the Speaker
of the Temple, and it is through his dialogue with the Speaker that
an enlightened transformation takes place in the young prince, who
to this point has simply and mindlessly followed a course set by the
Queen and her attendants. A desire for wisdom awakens within
Tamino, as do suspicions pertaining to the Queen, as mysterious
offstage voices tell him that Pamina, the object of his quest, still
lives. Left alone, Tamino plays a tune on his magic flute, which is
heard by Papageno. Papageno answers with his pan pipes and the
two seek to reunite. But Monostatos and his lackeys intervene and
attempt to capture Papageno and Pamina. Papageno employs his
magic bells and the would-be captors are stymied as they capitulate
to the music and fall into a mesmerized dance.

Sublime music, obviously religious in nature and intent,
announces the arrival of Sarastro as the final scene change of the
first act is under way. Pamina tells Papageno that they must speak
only the truth about their attempt to escape. Sarastro informs her
that he has held her "captive" to keep her free of her mother's evil
influence. Monostatos now hopes to be rewarded for his efforts in
preventing the abduction of Pamina, but the wise and farseeing
Sarastro will have him punished instead, as all praise their noble
leader and the curtain closes on the first act.

Act II
More solemn music associated with the temple and the brotherhood opens the second act. Tamino seeks membership into their
priesthood. Sarastro is asked by the others, "Is he virtuous?" and
answers, "Virtue." When asked, "Can he keep silence?" Sarastro
responds, "Silence." But when asked, "Is he rich in good deeds?" his

answer reveals the conflict between good and evil—which is at the center of the opera:

> Of good deeds! If you deem him worthy, then
> follow my example . . .
> Sarastro gives you thanks in the name of all
> mankind. The gods have ordained the gentle,
> virtuous Pamina for this youth; it was for
> this that I took her from her mother, a woman
> who thinks too greatly of herself, and thinks
> to hoodwink her people by trickery and supersti-
> tion, and to destroy our temple. That she shall
> not! Tamino himself shall help us keep it safe.

Clearly, this is Mozart and Schikaneder's Masonic brotherhood into which Tamino seeks entry. When your history book tells you that Austria's reigning monarch was Empress Maria Theresia, who, believing Freemasonry a significant threat to Roman Catholicism, ordered lodges closed, it has become a tradition to identify Maria Theresia's intolerant religious posture with the Queen of the Night and Sarastro's benevolence with the Enlightenment virtues of wisdom, reason and nature. Mozart was born a Catholic but the creed of his last years was that of a Freemason. (For those especially interested in Freemasonry, there are other associations to be found in *The Magic Flute* but having made our point, let us move along.)

A scene change shows Monostatos infatuated with the sleeping Pamina. Mozart, who has just presented the listener with music of sublime beauty, music that George Bernard Shaw considered unequivocally religious, next contrasts the sacred with the profane with his setting of *Alles fühlt der Liebe Freuden* ("Everyone feels the joys of love"), wherein erotic desire and lascivious intent are given a unique and masterful musical expression. As Monostatos is about to touch Pamina, the Queen of the Night appears and gives to her now awakened daughter a dagger with the command to kill Sarastro. Her aria is a volcanic boiling of desire for revenge as Mozart, as always, writes music to fit the emotion. *Der Hölle Rache kocht in meinem Herzen* ("A vengeful Hell does pulse within my heart"), is her second coloratura tour de force, an even greater test of virtuosity than her Act I aria. She departs and Monostatos resumes his approach to Pamina, but she is rescued by the opportune entrance of Sarastro. She asks of him that he not take revenge on her mother. *In diesen heil'gen Hallen kennt man die Rache*

nicht ("Within these holy halls one knows nothing of vengeance"),
Sarastro answers, in another bass aria of great beauty. The back-to-
back cry of revenge by the Queen of the Night, her shrieking rage
so dominant, and the sublime calm of Sarastro's pacifisim emphasize in word and music the dichotomy of evil and good.

Tamino and Papageno are awaiting their trial, which will test
their fitness for initiation, as the scene changes. An old crone enters
and introduces herself to Papageno as his long-sought Papagena, but
he does not take her seriously. Tamino is given his flute, Papageno
his magic bells. They receive the command of a vow of silence.
When Pamina, unaware of this vow, enters and is ignored by
Tamino, she misconstrues his silence as rejection. Her breaking
heart is revealed in the impassioned lament *Ach, ich fühl's, es ist
verschwunden* ("Ah, I know it, all is gone now"), but do not worry,
for you know they are destined to be reunited. Papageno breaks his
vow of silence to sing a charming little ditty, *Ein Mädchen oder
Weibchen* ("It is for a maiden or a wife that Papageno yearns"). The
old crone reappears, extracts from him the promise of lifelong fidelity, and transforms herself into a beautiful young girl. As the astonished and delighted Papageno reaches out for her, she is whisked
away by a priest. The two men are being severely tested indeed.

We can anticipate an eventual happy resolution, for a change of
scene presents the three genii singing of dawn, the symbol of light
and a new day. They then rescue a distraught Pamina from a suicide
attempt. The beginning of the final part of the trial, an ordeal by fire
and water is announced by two men dressed in armor singing a
solemn, churchlike chorale. Pamina will be allowed to join Tamino
for his final ordeal. In fact, she will be allowed to serve as his guide,
which is a fascinating indication of the importance of the female in
this opera, where an all-male brotherhood is represented as so significant. Earlier in the opera it was said that the role of a woman is
that of meekly following the influence of the male, a masculine sentiment typical of the eighteenth century. In the culmination of the
opera, however, Mozart and Schikaneder have Pamina at Tamino's
side as his successful guide through the last ordeal.

The penultimate scene continues the swing of the pendulum
through serious and comic episodes. Papageno thinks he has lost his
Papagena. He contemplates suicide even to the point of turning to
the audience: Is there no woman who will save him? he asks. The
three genii remind him of his magic bells, which naturally, when
played upon, produce his beloved Papagena. Each is stunned in
wonder by the presence of the other. They commence a comic duet,

one of the most eagerly anticipated numbers in the entire score, of their love and the fertility expected to produce many little Papagenos and Papagenas. The duet is slow getting under way, though, because they are so stunned they can only stammer Pa-Pa-Pa-Pa on and on before they get their tongues in gear to announce the other's name.

In the last scene, good triumphs over evil as the Queen of the Night, now with the traitor Monostatos by her side, fails in her attempt to assault the temple. The stormy music of the forces of darkness is swept away by the triumphant chorus of light and beauty extolling the eternal reign of Beauty and Wisdom as the opera concludes.

❧

Mozart brought traditional operatic forms to their highest manifestation and in so doing closed the door on the history of early opera as he emerged the father of modern opera. There is no one right way to get started, but for many generations of my students we began with the Ingmar Bergman film of *The Magic Flute*, which is on video. From there, you may study *Don Giovanni*, *The Marriage of Figaro*, and *Così fan tutte*, to be followed by *The Abduction from the Seraglio*, and finally the two great opera seria works. And then you can go on to all the other operas by Mozart that were not included in this book, which now moves into opera's great age, the nineteenth century, during which many of the most popular operas were composed. We will begin with a consideration of nine *bel canto* operas. You must proceed to chapter 3 to learn what that means.

Gioacchino Rossini

Gaetano Donizetti

Vincenzo Bellini

BEL CANTO OPERAS: ROSSINI, DONIZETTI, AND BELLINI

The three masters of bel canto opera were Gioacchino Rossini, Gaetano Donizetti, and Vincenzo Bellini. Legend has it that when Gioacchino Rossini was asked to designate the requirements of an opera singer he replied, "*Voce, voce, voce*" ("Voice, voice, voice"). By voice, this composer of thirty-nine operas did not mean overwhelming vocal power but rather vocal artistry and beauty of voice. Beauty of voice, or beautiful singing, in Italian is called *bel canto.* These can be risky words to use because they not only mean beautiful singing but also carry within them numerous references to and many implications of a long history of the traditional art of Italian singing developed between the seventeenth and nineteenth centuries. This tradition, which included operatic singing, embraced art song and secular and sacred music as well. Essentially, the basis of all bel canto singing emphasizes beauty of tone and mastery of technique with considerable attention to proper phrasing called, in Italian, *legato*: singing without a perceptible interruption between the notes.

The eighteenth century was the high age of bel canto style and its development paralleled the development of opera seria, in which the emphasis was on elegance, beauty of tone, and brilliance of presentation. Mastery of vocal technique had priority over the expression of dramatic intensity and great emotions. Bel canto is the only style acceptable for Italian opera up to and including the operas of Mozart and on even into the first part of the nineteenth century.

Rossini inherited and never questioned this exceedingly demanding artistic style of singing. Almost all he wrote for voice is in the bel canto style. It is, indeed, a curious anomaly that even though many, many hundreds of operas were written in the seventeenth and eighteenth centuries and performed in the bel canto manner, "the bel canto operas" refer to those by three Italian composers who wrote in the nineteenth century. They were the last significant composers of opera to embrace this style of singing. Verdi and Wagner were just around the next operatic corner.

Rossini, Donizetti, and Bellini wrote more than 110 operas among them. Nearly one-third of Rossini's thirty-nine operas remain more or less in repertory, a dozen or so by Donizetti are well known, and already mentioned is Bellini's achievement of half a dozen major works. Of these thirty or so operas are three from each a beginning student of opera should know about: not three apiece just to keep everything even but because each wrote three works that belong in the repertory of any informed operagoer.

GIOACCHINO ROSSINI

Rossini lived a long life. He was born the year after Mozart died (1792) and lived into his seventy-sixth year. Both his parents were musicians, the father a trumpeter and the mother a singer of secondary operatic parts. They supported his musical interests and by the age of fifteen, Rossini had learned violin and harpsichord and had sung in public. He also studied music in a conservatory. Before his twentieth birthday, he had composed half a dozen operas, two of which are still performed and recorded today. By age thirty-nine, he had written thirty-nine operas, five in one year alone. Then one day he put down his operatic pen, never again to compose another note of operatic music. (More on this later.) To uninitiated ears, Rossini's music can sound like Mozart, whom he revered. More sophisticated listeners, however, hear the remarkable beauty and facility of Rossini's own unique opera voice.

The three operas *Il barbiere di Siviglia* (1816), *La Cenerentola*

(Cinderella) (1817), and *Guillaume Tell (William Tell)* (1829) are Rossini's contribution to the repertory.

IL BARBIERE DI SIVIGLIA (1816)
The Barber of Seville

In the chapter on Mozart, the background to *Il barbiere di Siviglia* already has been acknowledged. You will recall this opera derives from Beaumarchais's trilogy, as does Mozart and da Ponte's *Le nozze di Figaro*. Recall, as well, that Rossini's opera (text is by Caesare Sterbini; we do not meet him again) details events of the first play in the trilogy while *Le nozze di Figaro* portrays events of the second play. I explain this again because, as noted before, beginners can easily confuse their Figaros. Once again, this intriguing character is at the center of one of the most popular operas in the world. Rossini's Figaro is the younger Figaro, the busy barber in Seville who doubles as general factotum. Figaro is a baritone. The other characters and their voice ranges are:

COUNT ALMAVIVA, *tenor*
DR. BARTOLO, *basso-buffo—comic-bass*
DON BASILIO, a singing teacher, *bass*
FIORELLO, servant to the Count, *bass*
AMBROGIO, servant to the doctor, *bass*
ROSINA, the doctor's ward, *mezzo-soprano*
BERTA, Rosina's governess, *soprano*

The time is the seventeenth century and the place is Seville.

Act I

Before the curtain opens on the first of the acts, one of the most famous overtures in the entire operatic literature is heard. Always I am amused when I read a description of it by an opera authority who explains how Rossini perfectly expresses the spirit of the whole opera in these wonderful seven and a half musical minutes and goes on about how Rossini also delineates certain distinguishing characteristics of Figaro and Rosina. Well, the original overture, if Rossini even wrote one, was lost and he, rather than write it, or rewrite it, or compose another, simply borrowed one from an 1813 opera of his that had not succeeded: *Aureliano in Palmira*. Borrowing an overture of one's own and substituting or deleting arias to fit a singer's ability or lack thereof was still commonly practiced early in the nineteenth century. The overture, called a *sinfonia* (meaning a little operatic symphony prior to the action), usually had three parts in sonata form (ABA): A equals the statement of a theme, B its development, and A again the repetition of the original theme. Rarely, at this stage of Italian opera history, was the overture written with the intention of expressing the overall spirit of the opera or to establish the mood of the first scene. There was nothing bizarre in Rossini's substituting one of his overtures for another.

As the curtain parts on the first scene of Act I it is just before dawn at the house of Dr. Bartolo on a square in Seville. Count Almaviva, a Spanish Grandee, has prepared a serenade for Rosina, the young, beautiful, and wealthy ward of Dr. Bartolo. Almaviva has fallen in love with her at first sight and his servant, Fiorello, assembles a band of musicians to accompany Almaviva's serenade. He sings the lovely aria *Ecco ridente in cielo* ("Now smiling in the eastern sky"), which Rossini also borrowed from his unsuccessful *Aureliano*. (The aria he had originally written for Almaviva's serenade flopped in the February 20, 1816, world premiere in Rome; thus Rossini made the substitution.) It was a perfect choice. The beautiful aria fits the moment like a hand in a tailored glove as the love-smitten nobleman sings of the coming of dawn and bids "Wake! Oh, awake, my lady, Rise to the song I sing you!"

Almaviva pays the musicians, who then depart, and hides just as Figaro enters and sings his famous patter song, *Largo al factotum della città* ("I am the factotum for all this great, big town"). A patter song conveys humor to a great extent through its manner of delivery: As many words as possible are uttered as quickly as possible in a style of singing constructed so as to give the impression that the singer is actually speaking. And yet, there is beauty of tone as well as stunning virtuosity involved in this bel canto tour de force when the performance is as it should be. Does not nearly everyone know this Figaro and his "Figaro, Figaro, Figaro, Figaro"? I think so!

I remember when I was a young boy my father, a baritone who had sung this aria hundreds of times, would play our half-dozen different versions of it on 78 rpm records in those days of yore— by Lawrence Tibbett, John Charles Thomas, Reinald Werrenrath, and other favorite baritones. First, I was to try to identify the singer by the sound of his voice and the quality of his style. Second, I was to make my case for the preferred performance. All of this was fun for me and at the time I had no awareness I was being "taught" a great deal about operatic singing in these listening sessions with my father, which went on for all the years of my boyhood.

Count Almaviva, at the conclusion of Figaro's song, emerges from his hiding spot and greets the barber. Rosina then appears on her balcony and manages to drop a note to her serenader through the oppressive security of that old goat Dr. Bartolo (who guards her carefully, for it is his intention to wed his pretty, rich ward). She wants to know her admirer's name. He answers in a second serenade, not as famous as the first, but quite nice, indeed. He identifies himself simply as Lindoro. The revelation of his love is well received except that Rosina's response is cut short by the slamming of her window—presumably Dr. Bartolo's work. The Count informs Figaro he will pay handsomely if the factotum can contrive a means of introducing him into Dr. Bartolo's house so that he can meet Rosina. The young lovers adore each other by sight even before they have met. The promise of money sets Figaro's brain quickly in motion, he contrives a plan, and the deal is struck in a long, extraordinary duet.

The scene changes to a room in Dr. Bartolo's house. Rosina enters and sings one of Rossini's most brilliant arias, *Una voce poco fa* ("A little voice I heard just now"). Her mind is made up; Lindoro is her choice. Bartolo, however, has made known to his crony, Don Basilio, a cleric and music teacher, and above all, perhaps, a scandal monger, his suspicions regarding Count Almaviva, who he assumes is in town with the intention of courting Rosina. Basilio's advice comes in the celebrated buffo aria *La calunnia* ("Start a rumor"), wherein he suggests that Bartolo let slip a little fabricated scandal about Almaviva, then sit back and wait for it to grow from a whisper into a storm.

Figaro's plan is effected. The Count, disguised as a drunken soldier, forces entry into Bartolo's house but the doctor sees through the disguise and has Almaviva arrested. Upon producing evidence that he is, indeed, a grandee of Spain, he is immediately released. A significant comic finale ensues as the central characters vent their differing emotions. This finale, twelve minutes long, is a musical miracle in its expression of these varied emotions through changing tempos and voice combinations until all sing together as the mounting musical momentum culminates in a near frenzy. I adore this finale! Listen to it and your addiction to it will have commenced. That I promise.

Act II

In the second act, the Count again enters Bartolo's house in disguise, this time as a music teacher. He has been sent by Don Basilio, he says, who is ill, as a substitute. The famous "music lesson scene" begins, allowing the lovers an opportunity for whispered conversation. This scene has become notable because its music was thought to have been lost forever and Rossini is reported to have left instructions for Rosina to sing anything she wanted. The list of music utilized for the lesson, in the nineteenth and early twentieth centuries, is long and remarkable, including arias from other operas, a Strauss waltz, "Home, Sweet Home," and even "The Last Rose of Summer." In fact, the "lost" aria of legend does exist and now is sung in performances and on recordings.

The lovers use the music lesson as a surreptitious means to express their love. Figaro obtains the key to the balcony door, a midnight escape is planned, and a quick marriage contemplated. But Basilio arrives. Will this foil everything? No! In one of the wonders of the score, a quintet, the Count, Figaro, and Rosina are able to convince Basilio (with the help of a little money slipped into his hand) in the presence of Dr. Bartolo that he is, indeed, sick and ought to be home in bed. The almost endless repetition of *Buona sera* ("Good evening") culminates this wonderful number.

Figaro shaves Bartolo while the lovers plan their elopement. Bartolo becomes suspicious and, departing his chair, overhears affectionate talk. Figaro and the Count leave and now begins Bartolo's attempt to deceive Rosina. Through the manipulation of letters, innuendo, and subterfuge he is able to convince Rosina that her Lindoro has another lady love. In jealous anger she agrees to marry her guardian, but Figaro and the Count return and set her straight. Not only does her beloved Lindoro adore her, but he is also a Count and a grandee. The notary, summoned for the quick marriage of the couple, marries the young lovers. Bartolo accepts his fate and a happy finale concludes the opera.

The role of Rosina is one of the most coveted in Italian opera. The original Rosina was a contralto—rare for a heroine. Rossini much admired the warm qualities of the lower female voice, a voice that has been described as "that of the Italian woman." So popular became Rosina's part, however, that mezzo-sopranos took over and ultimately coloratura sopranos had the role transposed to fit their high register. It was these songbirds who pocketed the role and made it their own, adding their own frills, trills, and embellishments to the glory of their voice. The renowned nineteenth-century soprano Adelina Patti, the highest paid singer of her day, once sang the part in a Paris performance with an aged Rossini in attendance. She took such liberties with her own flourishes in Rosina's *Una voce poco fa* that Rossini was quoted as saying, "A very pretty song! Whose is it?" Today the part often has been restored to a lower voice, where it belongs.

Giovanni Paisiello, composer of more than one hundred now forgotten operas, in 1782 had written has own *Il barbiere di Siviglia*, which became popular throughout Italy, so much so that the public was against the young Rossini when they heard he had written his own *Barber*. Rossini, before composing his opera, had written to Paisiello a courteous letter hoping to obtain the older composer's permission to use the same subject. Paisiello agreed, it has been recorded, secretly hoping the young man's opera would fail. And fail it did on the first night, Rossini at the pianoforte conducting. One fiasco followed another until the hooting and hollering of the audience all but obliterated the music. But with the second—successful—performance, this opera began its journey on the way to becoming one of the most popular and often performed operas in the world. Rossini composed it in three weeks.

LA CENERENTOLA (1810)
Cinderella

La Cenerentola followed less than a year later, with its premiere in Rome on January 25, 1817. I cannot imagine anyone questioning my choice of *The Barber of Seville* or the remarkable *Guillaume Tell* (unless the quibble is that *Tell* is not a true bel canto opera, and that point is, of course, correct, but this work is too significant in the Rossini corpus to even think about excluding it) as two of the three Rossini operas to discuss, but why *Cinderella*?

Because this opera represents Rossini's comic and melodramatic genius at its best. Here is music to equal many sections of *The Barber of Seville* and, furthermore, during the past twenty years superb performances in this country and abroad, excellent recordings, and captivating videos (the best of which stars Frederica von Stade in the title role) have contributed to the prominent revival of this opera as one of Rossini's most intoxicating. The opera just sings, beginning to end, with arias, patter songs, buffa showpieces, choruses, and finales unsurpassed in Rossini's large output.

The opera derives from Perrault's fairy tale *Cendrillon*. The text that Rossini set to music, by Jacopo Ferretti (we will not meet him again, either), varies a little from the basic story wherein Cinderella is treated sternly by her stepmother and stepsisters. In the more well-known versions, her fairy godmother adorns her magnificently and sends her to the ball to which her sisters were invited and she was not. Cinderella and the prince fall in love at first sight. She is to leave by midnight and when the clock strikes twelve she departs in haste, leaving behind her glass slipper. The prince must find his unknown love and goes about the land trying the glass slipper on girl after girl until with Cinderella there is a perfect fit. All ends happily.

Ferretti, who based his text on a libretto of an earlier operatic version of this story, made some changes. There is no stepmother, only an unkind stepfather. There is no glass slipper routine; a pair of matching bracelets is used instead. For Rossini, who opposed operatic action being determined by supernatural forces, there is no fairy godmother; instead, Alidoro, the tutor of the prince, provides Cinderella "transportation" to the ball. Finally, the stepsisters, silly and vain in the extreme, are not, nevertheless, "ugly." Except for the prince, who is right out of fairy-tale land, the other characters are standard buffa characters.

The opera, for all its comic qualities and conventions, is called a melodrama, allowing for the shift from amusing to more dramatic events. The opera preaches at times—for example, when Cinderella states that it is respect, love, and kindness in a suitor she seeks and, later, thinking her suitor an equerry (the prince has changed roles with his valet), she says his station makes no difference to her as long as he is loving and virtuous. The tone of the drama shifts to the serious when the prince confronts Cinderella for the first time as prince, having put aside his disguise. All are shocked. The stunned stepsisters call her vile names and her stepfather, too, is most nasty. But Cinderella begs the prince to forgive them, thus the subtitle of the opera, *La bontà in trionfo* ("The Triumph of Goodness"), which, of course, ultimately is the outcome. (Ferretti recorded that he wrote the verses in twenty-two days, Rossini the music in twenty-four. Later in this book, we will encounter operas that were years in their making.)

Cinderella, in two acts, takes place in the stepfather's house and in the palace of the prince. After listing the cast of characters and their voice ranges, several of the most prominent musical excerpts will be introduced—not all the great tunes in the opera (there are so many) but enough to reveal why for much of the nineteenth century *La Cenerentola* equaled, even surpassed, *Il barbiere di Siviglia* in popularity and established quite clearly why in this last quarter of the twentieth century it experienced a triumphant revival.

ANGIOLINA (Angelina), known as Cinderella, Don Magnifico's stepdaughter, *contralto*

DON RAMIRO, Prince of Salerno, *tenor*

DANDINI, his valet, *baritone*

DON MAGNIFICO, an impoverished Baron of Montefiascone, *bass*

CLORINDA AND TISBE, his daughters, *soprano and mezzo-soprano*

ALIDORO, Don Ramiro's tutor, *bass*

Notice that the title role of Cinderella originally was for contralto voice, like that of Rosina in *Il barbiere di Siviglia*. The same singer, Geltrude Giorgi-Righetti, premiered both roles. Since the number of contraltos today trained in the production of coloratura embellishments is small, the role of Cinderella usually is sung by a mezzo-soprano.

Act I

After the sinfonia introduction, Clorinda sings while she does a little dance step and Tisbe, before her mirror, comments on the placement of a flower in her hair in a brief, catchy little number. Cinderella, immediately thereafter, sings to herself a sad song as she blows the fire with a bellows. This song, *Una volta c'era un re* ("Once there was a king"), foretells, unwittingly, of course, the whole story of the opera: This king, in seeking a wife, rejects pomp and shallow beauty and chooses innocence and goodness. There is no way, though, that Cinderella is not going to be beautiful as well as good and innocent when her prince appears.

The two sisters awaken their father, who berates them for interrupting a dream he was enjoying in a comic aria always heartily applauded when sung with the verve it calls for. When the Prince arrives at Don Magnifico's home, disguised as his own valet, he and Cinderella meet and instantly fall in love. Cinderella enters singing again her little sad song. Seeing Ramiro, she exclaims, "Ah! It's happened." He does not understand but notes to himself *"Un soave non so che in quegli occhi scintilla"* ("A sweet something sparkled in those eyes of hers"). Soon they are full of each other and they have a fine duet. The first finale begins with a patter duet between Ramiro and Dandini. The sisters enter to express their desire for the Prince, whom they take erroneously to be Dandini, and then all focus their attention on the veiled lady who has arrived at the festivities of the Prince. She sings, unveils, and astonishes all with her beauty—all but Don Magnifico and his daughters, who note the woman bears a resemblance to Cinderella.

Act II

Early in the second act, Don Magnifico has another substantial comic aria, *Sia qualunque delle figlie* ("Whichever one of you, my daughters"), telling whoever will get the Prince remember not to abandon your magnificent papa. Later in the act, when the matching bracelets verify Cinderella was meant for Ramiro, now revealed as prince and not valet, astonishment displayed in different emotions reigns over Ramiro, Cinderella, the sisters, Dandini, and Magnifico in one of the most splendid numbers in the entire score. No! Not just the entire score, but here is an ensemble to set beside any other that Rossini—indeed anyone else—ever wrote.

∾

Guillaume Tell, the third of the Rossini operas presented in this chapter (below), was premiered in Paris on August 3, 1829. Upon hearing a performance, a famous Viennese music critic claimed that it had begun a new era not just in the development of French opera but in all of European opera as well. By the early years of the nineteenth-century Paris had become the opera capital of Europe. There gathered the great composers, librettists, directors, managers, instrumentalists, and singers. There, for example, went the Italian composer Luigi Cherubini, one of the fathers of French grand opera and composer of *Médée (Medea)* in 1797—an opera of considerable significance even though its popularity remains limited. There, too, traveled another Italian composer, Gasparo Spontini, whose opera *La Vestale (The Vestal Virgin)* was a triumph in 1807. And to Paris also in November 1823, went the most famous living opera composer, Gioacchino Antonio Rossini. He was only thirty-one years old and in less than thirteen years he had written more than thirty operas. In Paris he would write several more, the last of which, *Guillaume Tell*, a work of extraordinary originality, has been called the first masterpiece of French grand opera and one of the forerunners in the development of nineteenth-century romanticism in opera.

Grand Opera

What is meant by "grand opera" and "romantic opera"? Thus far in our consideration of opera, I have designated these distinct types: serious Italian opera, *opera seria*; comic Italian opera, *opera buffa*; the Mozartian/da Ponte synthesis of these two elements, *ballad opera*; and *singspiel*. Grand opera, which developed in France in the late eighteenth and early nineteenth centuries, is still another type. The word "grand," the same in both French and English, can have subtle differences in these languages and such is the case when it pertains to opera. Whereas grand in English implies something quite magnificent, even highfalutin, the French meaning, when associated with opera, denotes big, extensive, and expensive as in elaborate sets, a large chorus, many characters, plots and subplots, many instrumentalists—in short, a work of epic proportions. Specifically, however, French grand opera is always serious with a *fully composed text*; there are no spoken parts, as in a singspiel, and no recitative with or without the accompaniment of a harpsichord or any other instrument. The entire text is sung to composed music.

The German composer Giacomo Meyerbeer (his original name was Jakob Liebmann Beer) was one of those drawn to Paris, and there he collaborated with Louis Véron, an important director and entrepreneur (we do not meet him again), and one of the most considerable librettists in opera history, Eugène Scribe. Had Scribe been an Englishman, a pun on the aptness of his last name could be made—a name to remember, for he wrote a huge number of libretti for some of the greatest composers of his age, including Rossini, Donizetti, Bellini, Gounod, Offenbach, and Verdi. The collaboration of these three men, director, librettist, and composer, was pertinent to the development of grand opera in France, and their *Robert le Diable (Robert the Devil)* is an example. Meyerbeer's major works, all to texts by Scribe, are *Les Huguenots (The Huguenots)* of 1836, called the grandest of all grand operas, with the famous "bathers chorus" sung by women on the bank of the Seine; *Le Prophète (The Prophet)*, of 1849; and *L'Africaine (The African Maid)*, of 1865, which is considered his finest work.

A complete performance of this opera could last six hours

(length was often a component of grand opera). Grand opera placed great demands on singers not only because the works were long but also because big stages in big houses with big orchestras and demanding arias meant big voices working hard and overtime. Meyerbeer loved to create effects: He relished pomp and spectacle, and he sought grandeur. For these reasons, as well as the demands placed by his music on performers, his operas have fallen somewhat out of favor, but he did write some exceedingly wonderful music—arias, choruses, ballet scenes, and ensembles.

The composition of *L'Africaine* occupied Meyerbeer off and on for more than twenty years. He considered it his masterpiece, and so totally did he give himself to its creation that he died, old, ill, and exhausted, soon after completing the score and prior to its premiere. Few great tenors would fail to include the aria *O paradis*, given to Vasco da Gama in the fourth act of this opera, in their recordings. It remains one of the most famous tenor arias in opera literature and if, for now, Meyerbeer's operas—overly grand and demanding—remain out of favor, we must not forget how the operatic pendulum swings back and forth. Meyerbeer is too important a composer to fall into permanent obscurity. The compact disc is reviving many works, and Meyerbeer will be back again. With his return, you will have a prime example of nineteenth-century French grand opera.

Romantic Opera

Romantic opera is not another type or style of opera, nor does it imply that romance is the subject of the opera. Romanticism refers to the reaction against the major tenets of literature, philosophy, and aesthetics in the eighteenth century, the primacy of intellect and reason and an adherence to strict forms in composition. The French philosopher Jean-Jacques Rousseau was a major voice of reaction as he extolled the virtues of simplicity and naturalness, and the importance of feelings, instinct, and subjectivity. Accordingly, emotional expression and freer artistic forms went hand-in-hand as part of the literary development of romanticism, a significant force in the arts by the beginning of the nineteenth century through the impact of the *Sturm und Drang* (storm and stress) movement in Germany.

Music, especially, was to feel the force of the romantic movement, and its influence already can be heard in the later compositions of Beethoven. It reached a fullness of expression in the music of Franz Schubert and the operas of Carl Maria von Weber, and six composers, all born within a few years of each other, would produce the consummation of romanticism in music: the Frenchman Berlioz; the Pole Chopin; the Hungarian Liszt; and Mendelssohn, Schumann, and Wagner, all from Germany. Berlioz will have a place in this book; and Wagner—one of the seminal figures of opera history—will get chapters unto himself.

GUILLAUME TELL (1829)
William Tell

William Tell is grand opera devoid of superficial pomp and spectacle for the sake of effect. It is a work of art, not just an artifice of operatic entertainment meant to make people applaud. Hooey on "art" like that! There is all too much of it. *Tell* is unlike anything Rossini had composed before. Primarily, he had made his fame dashing off, with the brilliance given only to the genius, captivating comic operas bubbling with intoxicating arias, patter songs, and ensembles, especially the incomparable *primo* and *secundo* finales. (The sine qua non of his buffa triumphs, these finales would have made his idol, Mozart, proud.) Along with his celebrated buffa works, Rossini composed substantial opera scria works that must not be forgotten, but nothing in the entire Rossini corpus could have prepared those in attendance at the Opera in Paris on August 3, 1829, for what they were about to hear: the world premiere of *Guillaume Tell*. This work was not only Rossini's most original but it was and remains also a composition that contributed significantly to the development of opera in its most fecund century, the nineteenth.

This opera was planned to be the first in a series of five operas composed by Rossini but it turned out to be his last operatic composition. At the young age of thirty-seven this most well-known, honored, and popular composer of opera retired to a life of wealth and fame. To this day scholars speculate and write about why Rossini composed no more opera even though he lived another thirty-nine years. Six years before he died, he did comment "retiring in time requires genius too." However this man of great wit may have meant this comment, flip or otherwise, there is within it a great clue.

With *Tell*, Rossini opened the door to contemporary operatic developments, grand and romantic, creating to date the supreme work of French grand opera. He anticipated that huge wave of romanticism soon to crash upon northern European shores to flood the entirety of musical expression—song, the literature of the piano, instrumental ensembles of all sorts, and opera. But at the same time, he closed the door on his own great operatic career. His penchant and proclivity, no doubt, lay in comic opera. Did he not tell Wagner in 1860 that he felt at home in comic opera, not in serious subjects? And less than a decade after he composed his sensational *Tell*, did he not refer to it as a work of melancholy music, music of peasants and mountains and miseries? Indeed, all this he did say. More importantly, as a musician, already he had said all he had to say of a comic nature, and often repeated himself. With *Tell*, he had said all he would have to say on the subjects of grand opera and romanticism, the two rages of the day. He had not only proved he could master the inherited traditions of Italian opera but with a single work he had proved, too, that the new directions of opera were under his thumbs. Having proved all that, he stopped. Yes, "Retiring in time requires genius too," and Rossini was a man of genius.

William Tell is a work in four acts. The legend, story, myth (take your choice) of William Tell is a familiar one. Tell leads his Swiss compatriots against the Austrians, who had dominated and ruled Switzerland for more than one hundred years. The often repeated portion of the story relates the episode—central to the third act in the opera—in which Tell and his son Jemmy refuse to bow to the hat of the Austrian tyrant Gessler. As punishment, an apple is plucked from a tree and placed on Jemmy's head. Tell is told he must shoot it off. He does. Nevertheless, Tell and Jemmy are imprisoned. Jemmy escapes and signals the insurrection. Tell, too, escapes, kills the tyrant Gessler, and the Austrian domination is dispatched.

The famous German poet and dramatist Friedrich von Schiller (we will meet this significant author later) made of this story a play to which—with a few variations—the opera is faithful.

GUILLAUME TELL, *baritone*
HEDWIGE, his wife, *soprano*
JEMMY, their son, *soprano*
GESSLER, Austrian tyrant, *bass*
MATHILDE, his daughter, *soprano*
ARNOLD, her suitor, *tenor*
MELCTHAL, Arnold's father, *bass*
RUDOLPH, captain of Gessler's guard, *tenor*

WALTER FURST, Swiss patriot, *bass*
LEUTHOLD, shepherd, *bass*
REUDI, fisherman, *tenor*
Peasant, hunters, soldiers, guards, ladies

The time of the action is the thirteenth century and the place is Switzerland.

Act I

The overture, which long has had an independent life in concert halls and on recordings, is one of the most familiar in all opera. If you are of a certain age, you know it first from radio and later from television as the music accompanying the words, "Return with us now to those thrilling days of yesteryear . . . From out of the past come the thundering hoofbeats of the great horse Silver—the Lone Ranger rides again." The quiet calm of an Alpine setting is depicted in the overture's beginning, but the calm gives way to a storm, and then heard is a *"Ranz des vaches"* (a type of Swiss mountain melody utilized by herdsmen to call their cows). The fast final section, with trumpet calls, represents a call to arms for the Swiss in their uprising against the Austrians. Much wonderful music follows the raising of the curtain on the first act, indeed, of all acts of this long opera. Here are some of the highlights.

As dawn breaks on an Alpine hamlet high above Lake Lucerne, the villagers sing, then specifically the fishermen, then the villagers again. This is a lovely musical beginning. Early in the opera Arnold (a tenor), one of the villagers, has a big aria. He once rescued Mathilde, the sister of the despised Austrian governor Gessler, from drowning. She and Arnold have fallen in love. Thinking about her, he sings, *O Mathilde, je t'aime* ("Oh Matilde, I love you"). This music asks for a tenor who can sing powerful, ringing high notes. The final fifteen minutes of the first act is quite an appealing combination of choral singing and dance music.

Acts II & III

The second act, an hour in length, has become so popular it often has been performed independently of the rest of the opera. Within this act is a notable aria for soprano: Mathilde's *Sombre forêts* ("Somber forests"). The third act contains an engaging ballet and Tell's aria *Sois immobile* ("Keep quite still") in which the baritone instructs his son for the shooting-the-apple-off-the-top-of-the-head scene. William Tell possesses flawless aim, and a joyful victory chorus follows his true shot.

Act IV
Arnold has another aria in Act IV, a song of despair when he learns his father has been murdered. (The French composer Berlioz considered this aria the most beautiful music in the score.) The prayer in this act, the storm scene, the clearing, and the awareness of the bliss of freedom constitute an impressive conclusion to the drama.

The best introduction to the opera is a recording made in 1973, which in 1988 was remastered onto compact disc. The singing is splendid on this EMI CD. It features Gabriel Bacquier in the title role with Nicolai Gedda, Montserrat Caballé, Mady Mesplé, among others, giving excellent performances.

❧

When asked which of his compositions would outlive him, Rossini cited three: Act II of *Tell*, *Otello*, and *The Barber of Seville.* He was wrong about *Otello*. Never his most popular opera, it was rendered obscure by Verdi's *Otello*, one of that composer's greatest works. He was wrong, also, in failing to name a dozen or so other operas still popular. He was correct with regard to *The Barber of Seville*, his most popular and enduring work, and he was right about Act II of *Tell.* Of *Guillaume Tell*, Donizetti would say that Acts I, III, and IV were composed by Rossini, but Act II was written by God.

GAETANO DONIZETTI

Donizetti lived from 1797 to 1848, writing approximately seventy operas. His musical aspirations were not supported by his parents, so he enlisted in the Austrian army, where he found time to compose. In his twenty-first year he had a significant operatic success. A second success soon followed. He asked for and received a discharge, and the career of one of opera's major figures was well under way. An audience of Donizetti followers developed quickly. They awaited his latest work in the same way that musical theater buffs today await the latest Kander and Ebb. Accordingly, often he wrote too fast and a significant portion of his work needs revising and polishing. Nevertheless, with nearly seventy operas under his belt by age fifty-one, you can assume—correctly—that a number of these hit the operatic nail right on its head. Late in life he became overcome by fits of melancholy. Paralysis followed, and he died soon thereafter.

Often it has been written in the history of Italian opera how Donizetti is the most important predecessor of Verdi, which means his music is closer to what Verdi would write than that of Rossini or Bellini.

Donizetti's three operatic candidates for every opera lover are, in order of their first presentation, *L'elisir d'amore (The Elixir of Love)*, 1832; *Lucia di Lammermoor (Lucy of Lammermoor)*, 1835; and *Don Pasquale*, 1843. *L'elisir*, a comedy, is the most successful opera Donizetti ever wrote. *Lucia* is the most prominent and often performed of his many significant serious operas, and *Don Pasquale*, his comic masterpiece, ranks alongside the best in the long tradition of buffa operas. All three of these works were composed in traditional formats of Italian opera, which Donizetti accepted without question. He was no innovator. His great gifts were melodic invention and an ability to make the poetry he set to music sound perfectly natural when sung. His music sets feet tapping and gives heartstrings a tug. He wrote for the populace and for a long while he had them in the palm of his operatic hand. With lightning speed, he turned out opera after opera, mostly serious, some comic, all rich in melodies.

L'ELISIR D'AMORE (1832)
The Elixir of Love

The text for the opera, in two acts, essentially is a translation of a French opera libretto into Italian by Felice Romani (another of the few first-rate poets and librettists, and one we will meet again). The characters:

ADINA, a rich, capricious, young and pretty owner of a
   farm, *soprano*
NEMORINO, a decent, simple farmer in love with Adina,
   tenor

BELCORE, an army sergeant stationed in the village, *baritone*
DULCAMARA, an itinerant, quack doctor, *bass*
GIANNETTA, a country girl, *soprano*

The time is the end of the eighteenth century, the place a
Basque village.

Act I

Adina, rich and beautiful, has sport with Nemorino's clumsy,
bashful attempts to woo her. She, by the way, has been reading the
story of Tristano (Tristan), who won the love of Isotta (Isolde) after
sipping a love potion. Belcore enters. He takes his turn at courting
Adina and seems to have some success, which causes Nemorino
grief. Dulcamara arrives. Among the wares he is peddling is—you
guessed it—a love potion; in reality, though, it's nothing more
than cheap wine in a flask. Nemorino buys some, having been told
by the quack how under its influence he will win Adina in twenty-four hours. He empties the flask and immediately feels the
effects of the wine. He commences to dance, sing, and ignore
Adina, which piques her interest but to taunt Nemorino she
seems to agree to wed Belcore (who has been called to duty) on
this very day. Nemorino fails in his attempt to dissuade her and
the act ends.

Act II

As the curtain opens on the second act the villagers are anticipating a wedding ceremony. Adina stalls, however, leaving the wedding contract yet to be signed, thereby giving a touch of hope to
Nemorino, who will try another bottle of the elixir. Meanwhile,
Giannetta learns Nemorino's rich uncle has just died, leaving him
a large inheritance. Nemorino knows nothing of this and assumes
it is the power of the elixir that has turned the attention of the
young women to him. Adina now becomes serious about Nemorino and vows to use a powerful elixir of her own to win him.
Nemorino notices her change of attitude and she, finally, admits
her love for him. Belcore rationalizes his rejection: The world is
full of girls, as he says. The villagers, having what is to them
incontrovertible evidence of the elixir's efficacy, buy out Dulcamara as all ends happily.

This is not an elaborate, complicated opera plot. It is, in fact, quite
simple: a fun little story, like a fairy tale, of no great impact. The

drama of this opera is nothing more than the utter melodic spontaneity of the music as Donizetti set Romani's poetry to one fetching tune after another. *L'elisir d'amore* had its premiere on May 12, 1832, at the Teatro della Canobbiana in Milan. It was an instantaneous hit, and has remained so. It has always been Donizetti's most successful opera. The continuously delightful music skips along, precisely as you would expect a bucolic love story built around a love potion and an itinerant quack doctor would sound.

A string of ever popular excerpts commences moments after the first parting of the curtain with Nemorino's cavatina *Quanto è bella, quanto è cará* ("How beautiful she is, how dear she is") expressing his emotions as he looks upon Adina while she is reading. (A *cavatina*, another Italian musical word, is a brief solo song that is less elaborate than an aria. Normally, there would be no repeats in a cavatina or repeats only of the basic concept expressed usually in a single sentence or so. The cavatina was common to eighteenth- and nineteenth-century opera and oratorio.)

When Nemorino does attempt to woo Adina, they find that they are speaking at cross purposes; she wishes to remain free, taking a new love every day, while he can think of nothing but her. These sentiments are expressed in the first of several memorable duets in the score: *Chiedi all'aura lusinghiera* ("Ask the fluttering breeze"). Dulcamara's cavatina, *Udite, udite, o rustici* ("Listen, listen, country folk"), introducing himself and his medicines, is a great buffo scene; his duet with Nemorino wherein the sale of the marvelous elixir takes place also is a gem. At its conclusion begins the primo finale, which in true buffa fashion is long and of various parts, two in particular now quite famous: the duet of Nemorino and Adina where she notes a definite change in his behavior, and Nemorino's heartfelt imploring that Adina not marry Belcore on this day.

In 1928, the incomparable Italian Tito Schipa—he had the sweetest tenor voice I've ever heard—recorded this lovely aria, *Adina, credimi* ("Believe me, Adina"). It is, among many recordings, still my favorite. You can find it remastered on CD.

You will like the choral introduction to the second act as villagers sing a wedding toast and then join Dulcamara and Adina as they sing "the latest song," a barcarolle the quack learned in Venice, telling of a pretty young gondolier girl who rejects the advances of a rich old man:

Io son ricco e tu sei bella,
Io ducati, e vezzi hai tu.
Perchè a me sarai rubella
Nina mia, che vuoi di più!

I am rich and you are pretty,
I have money and you have charm.
Why be so difficult with me,
My sweetheart, what more could you want?

The most familiar music in the opera is Nemorino's romanza, *Una furtiva lagrima* ("A furtive tear"). It is no exaggeration to say this tenor aria is as famous as any in all Italian opera. A *romanza* (*Romanze* in German and *romance* in French and English) is a type of aria usually amorous in nature and, sometimes, a soliloquy. In this case, it is both. A romance usually has a meditative quality to it, and accordingly lacks the virtuosity and vocal display of big arias, which usually proclaim love, declare war, or call for revenge. Nemorino has noticed a tear in Adina's eye and it dawns on him that for all her fickle behavior she does, indeed, love him: "I ask for nothing more, I would die of love."

Enrico Caruso, more than eighty years after his death, remains one of the most famous tenors who ever lived—some would even say *the* most famous. Virtually every note he recorded on the hundreds of recordings he made has been remastered onto compact disc under the title of *The Complete Caruso*. This aria was one of his staples. His 1904 rendition is the best of his four different recordings of this aria. It is one of the most famous recordings of the century, and though Caruso is not in any way my favorite tenor, I do cherish having this antique record in my collection. It was Caruso's good fortune that his career and that of the development of the gramophone coincided. He was the first significant "gramophone tenor" and it once was noted that "Caruso made the gramophone and the gramophone Caruso."

I have now, during these first three chapters, had an opportunity to mention three great tenors of yesteryear. While writing of *Don Giovanni*, I noted a recording of the Irish tenor John McCormack and during this discussion of *L'elisir d'amore* I mention two great Italian tenors, Tito Schipa and Enrico Caruso. Of course, it would be hard to be alive today and not to have heard of "The Three Tenors" through the videos and recordings made by the Spaniards Placido Domingo and José Carreras and the Italian

Luciano Pavarotti. Even those who know nothing about opera are aware of their worldwide celebrity, for their fame has burst out of the opera house and the concert hall to flood the marketplace of the general public. They are three of the greatest modern tenors, and I do hope you are familiar with at least some of their recordings.

For many years I have been on a mission, however. I want to make certain that in knowing, admiring, and supporting the great singers of today, the great singers of the past are not forgotten. The marvel of the recording industry is that we have access to both. Through ongoing efforts of remastering antique recordings with the most meticulous care we can hear—in many cases with what must be remarkable accuracy—what legendary singers of the past sounded like. Let me suggest another "Three Tenors" recording. Remastered onto compact disc on the Nimbus label are recordings from 1904 until 1937 of Enrico Caruso, Tito Schipa, and John McCormack. Of these three, I prefer McCormack and Schipa in a tie for first with Caruso third. "That, Peter, is because you never heard Caruso in person," is what my grandfather Smith used to say, to which I replied, "Neither did I ever hear McCormack or Schipa in person, unfortunately!"

The title of this boxed set is simply *Tenors*. The bel canto opera tradition is well represented. Caruso sings three Donizetti arias and included is his famous 1904 recording of *Una furtiva lagrima* mentioned above. McCormack sings four Donizetti arias including his 1910 recording of that same aria for your comparison. Schipa's disc includes six bel canto opera selections, five by Donizetti and one by Rossini. Unfortunately, no Bellini is to be heard on this set. Caruso's style would be closer to that of today's "Three Tenors": big powerful voices compared to what for me is the more elegant, sophisticated, and aristocratic singing of McCormack and Schipa. That is why I prefer them.

My daughter, having heard me play records from my huge John McCormack collection (I have been collecting his records for more than fifty-five years) while she was growing up, must have missed his voice when she established her own home, for her request, several years ago, for a Christmas present was tapes of "those recordings I heard when I was a little girl." I sent them off and later asked her what her friends thought when they dropped by and heard John McCormack, not Lyle Lovett, coming from the speakers. "They think I'm weird, Dad," she said, but her friends, of course, would never have heard of John McCormack, which to me is similar to someone living in the twentieth century admitting that he had never heard of William Butler Yeats or Ted Williams.

A final word on *L'elisir d'amore.* The word *dulcamara* in Italian means "bittersweet" and one could get from Nemorino the sense of "a little nobody." In Belcore, there is the sense of "a good-hearted one." We may be tempted to ponder the implications within the names and to probe for deeper and hidden meanings in the opera. Don't bother. As far as *L'elisir* is concerned, the music is all. When we get to the Wagnerian music drama, there will be opportunities enough for contemplating the pregnant meanings suggested by translating some of the names.

LUCIA DI LAMMERMOOR (1835)
Lucy of Lammermoor

Rossini, Bizet, Bellini, and Donizetti are the best known of those who composed to libretti deriving from the voluminous literary achievement of Sir Walter Scott. More than seventy-five operas have been composed to his stories: *Kenilworth* leads the way with twelve operas, *Ivanhoe* is second with ten—including the failed attempt at grand opera by the great composer of operetta Sir Arthur Sullivan—and *The Bride of Lammermoor* is third with seven operas. Of all the "Sir Walter Scott operas," far and away the most prominent is Donizetti's *Lucia di Lammermoor* to a libretto by Salvatore Cammarano who admirably reduced Scott's novel to focus exclusively on the effects of Lord Henry Ashton's betrayal of his sister Lucy. Cammarano, taking liberties with some names and events, distills the action into three acts of two scenes each (if a brief scene at the beginning of Act III is not counted, because it so often is excluded from performances). Here are the characters:

> LORD HENRY (Enrico) Ashton, of Lammermoor, *baritone*
> LUCY (Lucia), his sister, *soprano*
> EDGAR (Edgardo), master of Ravenswood, *tenor*
> LORD ARTHUR (Arturo) Bucklaw, *tenor*
> RAYMOND (Raimondo), chaplain at Lammermoor, *bass*
> ALICE (Alisa), companion to Lucy, *mezzo-soprano*
> NORMAN (Normanno), follower of Ashton, *tenor*

The time of the action is about 1700; the place, somewhere in Scotland.

Act I

Since I met all of the characters first in the opera, I refer to them by their Italian names. Normanno, on behalf of Enrico, orders guards to seek the identity of a stranger seen lurking in the woods before dawn near Lammermoor Castle. Enrico confesses to Raimondo his precarious financial position, from which he can be rescued by a political marriage of his sister to a man of means. Lucia, however, will have none of it. She loves Edgardo, the sworn archenemy of her brother. Enrico's men return to confirm that Edgardo is he who was lurking.

The change of scene reveals a fountain in the park of the castle of Lammermoor. Lucia enters with Alisa. Is she there to meet Edgardo? Lucia gazes into the fountain and recalls it holds the corpse of an ancestor murdered by a jealous lover. This she takes as a bad omen. Edgardo arrives with the news he must leave for France immediately. He declares his love, Lucia reciprocates, and they pledge, with an exchange of rings, their eternal fidelity.

Act II

Several months have elapsed when the curtain opens on Act II in Enrico's apartment in the castle. Here we learn that Edgardo's letters to Lucia have been intercepted and her brother has plotted the marriage of Arturo to Lucia. Her resolve weakens when Enrico shows her a forged document accusing Edgardo of unfaithfulness. Raimondo promises her a "divine reward" if she will consent. She capitulates.

The scene changes to the great castle hall for the wedding ceremony. A distraught Lucia signs the marriage contract only a moment before the surprise arrival of Edgardo, who has returned home to claim his betrothed. Seeing the signed contract, he requests the return of his ring and curses both Lucia and his own dire fate as the second act concludes.

Act III

The often omitted scene, when performed, opens Act III. Enrico has gone through a storm to a remote spot, there to find Edgardo and to challenge him to a duel. The challenge is accepted and set for sunrise in the Ravenswood graveyard. When omitted, and frankly, it adds nothing when included, there is a more uninterrupted unfolding of the plot. The third act would now begin with the continuation of wedding festivities, which are interrupted as Raimondo enters and stuns all with the news that Lucia has lost her mind and killed Arturo. In the bloodstained remains of her wedding gown, Lucia enters for one of the most anticipated scenes in all opera: the celebrated "mad scene," wherein she imagines reunion and marriage with Edgardo. Lucia is quite ill; she is dying.

In the final scene of the opera, among the tombs of Ravenswood, as Edgardo prepares for his duel and speculates on his own demise, he learns from a group of mourners the story of the madness, the murder, and the imminence of Lucia's death, which then is proclaimed by knells of the castle bell. Separated by fate on earth, he and Lucia can forever be united in heaven. He draws a dagger, stabs himself, and follows her into death.

There is much music to admire in this opera, Donizetti's finest and most popular serious work, beginning with his orchestral *pre-ludio* (prelude). Unlike the generic sinfonia that quieted audiences prior to the start of countless seventeenth- and eighteenth-century Italian operas, Donizetti's preludio to *Lucia* actually begins the opera by establishing an appropriate, ominous mood for the events to follow. Among a virtually constant flow of melodic treats, in each of the first two acts there is a major musical event you should know about. In Act III, two famous tenor arias follow the most sustained scene for coloratura soprano in opera: Lucia's "mad scene," which is almost twenty minutes long.

The finale to Act I is a long duet. Lucia, next to the fountain in the park, sees Edgardo approaching. Alisa, carefully, will keep watch over the lovers' tryst. On arrival, Edgardo explains that diplomatic obligations are sending him to France, but before departing, both as a pledge of love and as an act of making peace of the hostility raging between their families, he will ask Enrico for his sister's hand. Lucia remonstrates. Their love must remain a secret. He replies that the hatred he once felt for her family passed as his love for her grew. "Let love alone burn in your heart," she says and he puts on her finger a ring as he announces that before God they have vowed to unite their destiny. She then gives him her ring. They know they must part and here comes the most lyrical portion of this long, beautiful scene. First, Lucia sings *Verranno a te sull'aure* ("Borne by gentle breezes"). . .

> my ardent sighs will come to you.
> Hear how in the murmuring seas
> my lamentations echo.
> Think then that my nourishment

comes from sighs and suffering.
Then cry a bitter tear
upon this pledge! . . .

Edgardo repeats these lines and then together they acknowledge both their union and their parting. People who do not know Italian, swept along by the beauty of the music, completely miss the drama. A lovers oath in eighteenth-century Scotland had the validity of a wedding ceremony. Lucia is, indeed, now Edgardo's bride and when unwittingly she, in the second act—having been lied to and betrayed—signs a marriage contract with Arturo, she violates her vow.

To participate as fully as possible in the drama of opera, the reading of a synopsis is not sufficient. Too many subtleties are missed, subtleties purposely intended by a competent poet as a means of making dramatic episodes that will be intensified by the skill of the musician. There is much to be gained by reading the libretto. If you read the words of this duet, you'll have a better understanding of what transpires in the second act when, unexpectedly, Edgardo enters the great hall of Lammermoor Castle to discover before him a "wife" who has just signed a marriage contract.

He is about to explode with anger, yet asks, *Chi mi frena in tal momento?* ("Who restrains me at such a moment?") This is the opening line of what many consider to be opera's most famous and familiar sextet.

The bel canto operas often are referred to as "singer's operas," which, when spoken in a positive manner, means the story, the drama, and the orchestra all serve the beauty of the human voice. When said disparagingly the phrase condemns an opera as a superficial and undramatic vehicle for singers to show off. This celebrated sextet certainly is an opportunity for singers to show off but it is not undramatic. Even though the six characters simply stand and pour out beautiful sound for almost four minutes, there is still considerable drama. The drama is in the effect of the words and the music because no one, not even native-speaking Italians, can comprehend six people singing their different emotions simultaneously. Thus, we have yet another reason why knowing the words by having read the libretto ahead of time is important.

Notice I said *ahead of time:* few things are more annoying to an enthralled operagoer than the sound of pages being turned and the bumpity-bumpity glare of a little flashlight as the person sitting next to her in the opera house tries to read the libretto line by line while the singers sing. Nowadays subtitles and supra-titles are helping to resolve some of these problems, but they can create others. I know of those who paid dearly to go to an opera they never saw because the whole while they sat in their seats reading the story via supra-titles above the stage. But even supra-titles are not going to help much during the sextet: Too much is going on. Prepare yourself ahead of time. Starting with a good video at home is always a good solution.

Edgardo's concern is for Lucia, Enrico reveals he has betrayed his sister and feels remorse, Lucia laments that death did not come to end her torment, Alisa likens Lucia to a wilted rose, and Arturo and Raimondo comment on what an awful moment is transpiring before them. All this happens in four minutes of one of the most exhilarating ensembles ever heard.

Lucia's third-act mad scene demands more than a remarkable high voice of immense beauty and agility. Lucia enters the Great Hall. She is ghostly pale, her hair disheveled, her torn gown stained with blood, her look a fixed stare, and her periodic twitch-es adding to the unmistakable effect of a deranged being. This impression must be conveyed before she sings a note of her first line, *Il dolce suono mi colpì di sua voce!* ("The sweet sound of his voice captured me"), thinking she and Edgardo are together again and about to be married. "Lord have mercy on her," comment those gathered there.

Throughout her long scene Lucia must convey with both voice and demeanor that she is in her own little world. Greatness of voice and vocal technique alone are not enough to make the scene work in the opera house or on film. Lucia must be portrayed by a singing actress who has mastered both the art of song and that of acting. There are just a few, but when in the presence of one it is a sublime experience. Gestures are eloquent, the voice of flawless and constant pitch, especially when it sings in unison with the flute. The first Lucia so moved the audience, it was reported, dur-ing the world premiere at the Teatro San Carlo in Naples on Sep-tember 26, 1835, that sobbing was heard as the scene concluded.

Recently I was fortunate to be in a Berlin opera house as part of a tour I was leading, when a superb singing actress delivered the goods. The tenor portraying Edgardo knew a standing ovation would greet her curtain call. His two great arias dominate the short final scene and, obviously, he wanted his share of the laurels, so he took every molecule of sound in his voice box and sent it forth throughout the house. The only problem is that the meaning of the words he sings requires some restraint. It is night. He stands among the tombs of his ancestors. Anticipating the duel, he plans to throw himself on Enrico's sword, for life without Lucia has no meaning. *"Fra poco a me ricovero dàra negletto avello"* ("Soon an uncared-for tomb shall give me refuge") he sings, then, learning of subsequent events after his departure from the wedding scene and hearing the death knells, he alters his fate hastily. *"Tu che a Dio spiegasti l'ali"* ("You who have spread your wings to heaven"), the second aria begins, and concludes with "may God in heaven unite us." He draws his knife and stabs himself. There are intense dramatic moments in this scene, and the tenor gets some high notes, too, but the entire scene is not one to be bellowed as it was on the occasion of which I speak.

A young woman in our group, a serious student of piano, was immersing herself in opera for the first time. She wanted to laugh aloud as a dispirited and then dying tenor ignored the varying emotions in his lines and simply poured out sound. After the opera she asked me why. Overacting and oversinging are unfortunate faults of some opera singers, I told her, and even though great improvements have been made in training opera singers and in preparing them for their roles, there are still many who remain insensitive to the meaning of the text they are singing and give it their all when the words do not call for it. I had to explain that those with the highest parts are often most guilty because it is the sustained high note that can cause the greatest effect on an audience more interested in pyrotechnics than in accurate and subtle portrayals. That night the tenor was heartily applauded as he smiled and bowed, but Lucia needed a bushel basket to carry off the flowers thrown to her.

DON PASQUALE (1843)

Soon after Donizetti completed *Don Pasquale,* one of the three masterpieces of nineteenth-century Italian comic opera (*The Barber of Seville* and Verdi's *Falstaff* are the accompanying two), he was as mad as Lucia. Exhausted from unceasing work, despondent over his wife's death, suffering from headaches and melancholia, he would be found pounding his piano and ranting. He was taken to an asylum, where he died in 1848. Like many of his other operas, this one was composed with record-breaking speed, and it is a wonder that someone moving rapidly toward mental collapse in such a somber state of mind could produce a work so perfectly made, one replete with music so light, airy, sunny, and fresh, so totally intoxicating, so memorable, music that makes us want to hear it again and again—and music perfectly suited to the plot.

It is a fun little comic episode. There are three acts. The characters are few:

DON PASQUALE, an old bachelor, *bass*
DR. MALATESTA, his friend, *baritone*
ERNESTO, Don Pasquale's nephew, also Malatesta's friend, *tenor*
NORINA, a young widow, *soprano*
A notary, *baritone*

The time is early in the nineteenth century, Donizetti's own period, and when these characters appeared on stage in contemporary attire—an unprecedented move—the audience was, indeed, startled. The setting is Rome. Both opera seria and opera buffa had all but expired, by the way, and *Don Pasquale* is the last buffa masterpiece.

Act I
In the first act, we learn that Ernesto, because he loves Norina, has opposed the will of his rich uncle, the curmudgeonly bachelor Don Pasquale, and refuses to marry the bride selected for him by the old man. Don Pasquale will punish the insolent boy by getting married himself, thus depriving Ernesto of a promised inheritance. Doctor Malatesta, friend to both Pasquale and Ernesto, is summoned for advice by the old man. Pasquale's mind, already made up, cannot be altered, so Malatesta concurs marriage is a good idea and he will provide as bride his attractive sister Sofronia, presently in a convent.

Pasquale, an old coot of seventy, is beside himself with joy and wild with anticipation. He claims he feels twenty-one again. When Ernesto learns of Malatesta's participation in Pasquale's wedding plans he feels betrayed. Ernesto is unaware the good doctor has a plan to make a fool of the old miser. The plan requires Norina to pose as Sofronia, the bride-to-be, for both women are unknown to Pasquale. Malatesta informs Norina of his scheme as Act I concludes. Ernesto, still not privy to the ruse, has written to his beloved that he must leave the country because their love cannot be. Without an inheritance, their plans collapse.

Act II
As the second act begins, Ernesto sings of his unfortunate circumstances—cast out by his uncle and betrayed by his friend. To Pasquale Malatesta brings Norina, posing, of course, as Malatesta's sister. Pasquale is at once enchanted by her shy, obedient simplicity, by her good looks, and by her subservient, homebody attitudes. She is all he could ever want. Malatesta, always prepared, anticipated the success of his presentation and brings with him a notary, who is called in to draw up a wedding contract. Pasquale signs immediately and Norina, as Sofronia, is about to sign when unexpectedly Ernesto enters to say farewell to all. Malatesta tries hastily to clue Ernesto into the scheme. It works, and the ceremony is completed.

Instantly, the bride's attitude changes from that of a shy girl just out of the convent into that of a high-spirited woman with an agenda. Pasquale is stunned as she orders him about. Calling in the butler, she doubles the servant's wages and instructs him to increase the staff with young, healthy, good-looking men. She says she will need two carriages and that all the old furniture must be replaced. She needs a tailor, a hairdresser, a jeweler, and more, and it is hell on earth for the helpless Don Pasquale.

Act III
As the curtain opens on the final act we see Pasquale inundated with bills and surrounded by female apparel. Sofronia is set to go to the theater, alone naturally. Pasquale says no. He tries to order her about. She whacks him one. Go and don't come back, he tells her. As she leaves she lets fall a letter, which he thinks is just another bill. It turns out to be a contrived love letter, part of the overall plan, designating a tryst in the garden and signed "Your faithful lover." This is more than Pasquale can endure. He calls for Malatesta and apprises him of all that has transpired. Malatesta suggests spying on the lovers, catching them in the act, and then throwing Pasquale's wife out of the house. Pasquale concurs and in doing so is about to walk into his own trap.

There is commotion in the garden. There he finds Sofronia and accuses her of meeting someone. "No one is here, you old fool, I am just getting some night air," she claims. He tries to throw her out of the house but she reminds him he cannot because it is her house. Malatesta steps in for the rescue of both of his friends. First, he demands carte blanche from Pasquale, who, now so desperate for deliverance, grants it. Then of Pasquale he demands he agree to let Ernesto marry Norina with his inheritance restored. Pasquale again agrees. Sofronia is revealed as Norina, Pasquale realizes he has been tricked, and Malatesta succeeds in prevailing upon Pasquale to forgive and forget. The moral of the happy ending belongs to Norina:

> The moral in all this
> Is very plain to see.
> I'll tell you very quickly
> If you'll be pleased to listen:
> To marry in old age
> Is but weakness of mind;
> Only trouble and annoyance
> With wedding bells you'll find.

Did you notice I neglected to mention the name of the librettist in introducing you to this opera? This was done on purpose. There were several—and one quit—and Donizetti also contributed some lines. This matter long has engaged the attention of scholars, but it goes beyond our concerns here. The music is wonderful, fitting the story and the characters like custom-made clothes. If you will listen to the following eight excerpts, you and this opera will be friends for life.

In the first act, Pasquale learns his friend Malatesta will provide his sister as the bride he seeks. He is wild with delight. "Ah! I feel within me a strange new fire that now I can resist no longer." This is the bristling cavatina, *Ah! Un foco insolito.* Ernesto, having learned of his disinheritance, laments, "Farewell, pure, sweet dreams I've cherished for so long." One of Donizetti's finest tenor arias is this *Sogno soave e casto.* Norina is given an engaging tune, a cavatina, as we meet her reading a book about chivalry: *Quel guardo il cavaliere* ("That glance pierced the knight"). Near the act's end, Malatesta and Norina rehearse how they will behave before Pasquale when upon him they unload their ruse full force. This music bubbles like sparkling wine. It is the Act I finale, with tune running to tune and coloratura soaring, *"Pronto io son"* ("I'm ready"). It is unmistakable and unforgettable Donizetti. The act ends.

We are in Ernesto's quarters as Act II begins. Poor Ernesto laments he is facing the loss of love and the loss of his quarters (Pasquale has ejected him) in the aria, a famous one, *Cerchero lontana terra* ("I will seek some distant land"). The quartet of the principal characters, which ends the act, is notable indeed. It commences with Malatesta dictating the terms of the marriage contract: *Fra da un parte etcetera* ("The party of the first part").

In the third act Malatesta and Pasquale have a comic duet, *Cheti, cheti immantinente* ("Softly, softly now to the garden we'll go"). Pasquale begins in one of the brightest jewels in buffo literature. It is followed by another gem, Ernesto's serenading of Norina. The aria *Com' è gentil* ("How soft the night") is for those tenors of lyric voice and bel canto styling as much a part of their person as the clothes they wear. This aria, properly sung, is quintessential bel canto; it is the distillation of what bel canto is all about.

Donizetti certainly thought of himself as a craftsman. The romantic preoccupation with one's inner life as a source of creative inspiration was not his way. At his piano every morning at seven sharp, he worked tirelessly until four each afternoon. In his mind he was simply another craftsman; some made cabinets and others made shoes. He made operas and he was proud of his work, his successes, and the speed with which he turned them out. It was this indisputable accomplishment that made his younger friend Bellini jealous.

VINCENZO BELLINI

The life of the exceedingly gifted Vincenzo Bellini was all too brief. Born in Sicily in 1801, he died in his thirty-fourth year in 1835. Both his father and grandfather were composers of reputation. He showed a talent for music at an early age—this is not unusual for the child of an organist—so he was sent to a famous conservatory in Naples. There he composed two unsuccessful operas but works of sufficient merit for him to attempt a career as an opera composer at twenty-four. It lasted merely a decade, during which time he wrote eleven operas, more than half of which are quite remarkable, leaving unanswered the question of what might have emanated from his pen had he lived another ten, twenty, or forty years. His unique gift for melody influenced other important composers, and they were not just opera composers. Chopin was the most notable of them.

Donizetti had been inspired by Rossini, and Rossini also gave Bellini some encouraging shoves in the right operatic direction. However, Bellini did not possess the natural fluency of composing so striking in the other two, who dashed off operas in weeks or days to meet deadlines for getting new entertainment on the boards. Though Bellini's music also is in the bel canto vein—indeed, it is of the purest and most sustained melodic invention in the history of the Italian bel canto tradition—he worked much more slowly than Rossini and Donizetti. An opera a year was his self-subscribed pace.

Bellini revised and revised in the quest for perfection. He would make a thorough investigation of his texts, noting subtleties and nuances in the poetry. As a composer, he produced undeniable light bel canto works, but his work methods were of those adhering to creeds of romanticism, which never penetrated sunny Italy with the same force that swept Germany. (The Germanic preoccupation with a tedious, perfectionistic creating of the flawless masterpiece is best exemplified by Beethoven, to whom we will go after Bellini).

The three Bellini operas you should start with, in chronological order of their premieres, are *La sonnambula (The Sleepwalker)*, *Norma*, and *I Puritani (The Puritans)*. The texts of the first two were by Felice Romani, whom we met in our discussion of Donizetti's *L'elisir d'amore*. Romani was far and away Bellini's preferred collaborator, and together they worked on most of the composer's major operas.

LA SONNAMBULA (1831)
The Sleepwalker

This opera in two acts was presented for the first time in Milan on March 6, 1831. There are six main characters:

COUNT RODOLFO, lord of the castle, *bass*
TERESA, proprietress of the mill, *mezzo-soprano*
AMINA, her foster daughter, *soprano*
ELVINO, a young farmer engaged to Amina, *tenor*

LISA, proprietress of the inn in the village, *soprano*
ALESSIO, a young peasant who loves Lisa, *bass*
A notary and villagers

The story is set in a Swiss village early in the nineteenth century.

Act I

This is not the only opera I know without a baritone, but it is one of just a few. The orchestra establishes a festive atmosphere for a minute or so before being joined by a chorus of villagers singing happily as they anticipate the nuptials of Amina and Elvino. Lisa gets the first tune of a score that abounds with melody, *Tutto è gioia, tutto è festa* ("All is joyful, all is festive"). All except Lisa. She is not happy, for she, too, loves Elvino. Amina enters and sings of her good fortune and happiness on this day. Her recitative, to slight orchestral accompaniment and choral commentary, is followed by an aria, *Come per me sereno* ("How peacefully for me")†, which is followed by a *cabaletta* (an Italian word deriving from *cavatina*, which usually means the brief, and of quicker tempo, conclusion to an air), *Sovra il sen la man mi posa* ("Place your hand upon my heart") joined by the chorus—a most delightful scene.

Elvino arrives, the contract is signed, and one of my favorite duets, especially when sung by Tito Schipa and Amelita Galli-Curci, for tenor and soprano follows: *Prendi: l'anel ti dono* ("Here, receive this ring"). A stranger arrives, actually Rodolfo, the lord of the castle. He introduces himself in a fine aria that also has a *cabeletta: È gentil, leggiadra molto* ("She is lovely, very charming"), directed at Amina and unsettling to Elvino, naturally. Teresa urges everyone to retire, it is time, for this is a village visited by a phantom. Lisa prevails on Rodolfo to stay at the inn, and all depart except for Amina and Elvino. He is upset over the attentions of Rodolfo but they are reconciled in a second lovely duet, *Son geloso del zefiro errante* ("I envy the wandering breeze"). They part, happily. But more trouble lies ahead.

The scene changes to the inn, specifically to Rodolfo's room, where he soon finds the proprietress has come to make sure all is

---

† Vincenzo Bellini, *La sonnambula* (Centra-Soria Records Libretto, 1953, translations of this opera by William Weaver)

well with him. They begin to flirt but are interrupted by noises. Lisa hides just before Amina, dressed in white, enters Rodolfo's room. He is amazed but immediately realizes she is walking in her sleep, that she is a somnambulist. The nobleman deduces the identity of the phantom that has terrorized the naive villagers. They, having been apprised of his own identity, are now on their way to offer official welcome. But what they find sleeping on the Count's bed is Amina. Lisa has returned and makes the most of this event. Elvino, also drawing the wrong conclusions, scorns Amina though she protests her innocence. What a finale we have to end the first act. In true comic fashion, all is coming apart at the seams, dissolving in the confusion of having jumped to conclusions based on appearances.

Act II
The first scene of the second act shows a valley woods through which the villagers are passing. They are on their way to find Count Rodolfo to beg him to prevail on Amina's behalf if she is, indeed, innocent. Amina and Elvino have another encounter. She still loves him and he cannot comprehend why he does not hate her, yet for him their relationship is over and he takes back his ring.

The scene changes to show the mill. Elvino will marry Lisa instead. Lisa is happy with this but it is a happiness to be short-lived, for Rodolfo seeks to explain somnambulism to the unsophisticated Elvino. The young man remains unconvinced until, by chance, Amina unwittingly proves the point by walking about the mill in her nightdress, obviously asleep, and talking about the loss of her love and her ring. This is one of the two most famous sleep-walking scenes in opera (the other is that of Lady Macbeth in Verdi's *Macbeth*). Elvino has seen and heard enough. Amina has navigated a narrow, precarious bridge during her excursion and all are relieved she is safe. When she awakens, Elvino replaces the ring on her finger as all is forgiven. Amina's concluding *cabeletta* with chorus, *Ah! non giunge uman pensiero* ("Human thought cannot conceive of the happiness that fills me"), culminates one of Italian opera's finest scenes. It is justly famous for Bellini's extraordinary music and generations of coloratura sopranos delivering the bel canto goods as *La sonnambula* draws to its joyful close, the villagers proclaiming

> Innocent Amina, so dear to us,
> Made lovelier by your grief,

Come to the church and there,
At the altar, begin your joy.

NORMA (1831)

Many of those who attended the world premiere of *Norma* on
December 26, 1831, in Milan were not thrilled. Heretofore they had
approved what Bellini had given them, but *Norma* was different. It
is a melding of lyrical, melodic beauty and powerful, dramatic emotions. The glory of Bellini's music is here but it is serving a tragic
story, darker and deeper than any his previous operas would have
led them to anticipate. Bellini left the theater after the first performance having experienced what he deemed to be failure. He wrote
that night to a friend how the "dear Milanese" who had welcomed
so heartily three other operas—most recently their tumultuous
reception of *La sonnambula* nine months before—had been

> severe and yet I believe that I presented them with
> a worthy sister in *Norma!* I say just to you, with
> my heart in my mouth (if passion does not deceive
> me) that the introduction, the entrance and cavati-
> na of Norma *(Casta diva)*, the duet between the
> two women *(Sola, furtiva al tempio)* and the trio
> that follows *(Oh di qual sei tu vittima)*, the finale
> of the first act *(Vanne, si mi lascia, indegno)*, then
> the other duet of the two women *(Mira, o Norma)*
> and the entire second act finale from the war
> hymn *(Guerra! guerra!)* on are such musical pieces
> and please me so much (modesty) that, I confess to
> you, I would be happy to be able to make their
> counterparts for the rest of my artistic life.
> Enough!!! Of theatrical works, the public is the
> supreme judge. I hope to make an appeal against
> the judgment pronounced upon me, and if I suc-
> ceed in changing their minds, I shall have won my
> cause, and *Norma* will then be proclaimed the
> best of my operas. . .[†]

[†] Herbert Weinstock, *Norma* (London Records, Inc. New York, 1968), p. 6

That is precisely what happened. The second performance went much better and the third better still, so much so that *Norma* was well on its way to being considered not just Bellini's masterpiece but also one of the masterpieces of all nineteenth-century opera. And of course, Bellini was right in isolating the scenes that soon would become famous. Let us consider the supreme musical moments within their context of the drama.

Norma is an opera in two acts (text by Romani). There are six central characters:

NORMA, high priestess of the Druid temple, *soprano*
ADALGISA, a virgin of the temple, *soprano*
POLLIONE, Roman proconsul in Gaul, *tenor*
OROVESO, the Archdruid, Norma's father, *bass*
CLOTILDE, a confidante of Norma, *soprano*
FLAVIO, a centurion and friend of Pollione, *tenor*
(The parts of Adalgisa and Clotilde can be performed by *mezzo-sopranos* and often are. Note, too, the absence of a baritone.)

It is set during the Roman occupation of Gaul, about 50 BC.

Act I
In the sacred forest of the Druids a religious march is heard. Oroveso, leading a procession of Gallic warriors and priests, proclaims that with the rising of the moon Norma will cut the sacred mistletoe to signal the start of the Gallic uprising against Roman occupation. The Druids depart. Pollione and Flavio enter. Pollione confides to his friend that his love for Norma has died. They had kept their affair secret because it violated the vows of a priestess. Norma has borne him two sons. Pollione feels terrible remorse and fears Norma's vengeance if she learns he now loves a young, beautiful priestess of the temple who reciprocates his passion. The men depart.

The Druids return. Norma enters to make her prophecy: The time is not right for the Druids, of inferior military force, to attempt to overthrow the Romans; the occupiers will eventually perish by their own vices. She performs the mistletoe rite. This is the entrance of Norma, (mentioned in Bellini's letter), that precedes the *Casta diva* ("Chaste goddess") aria. That aria was revised by the composer eight times until he achieved perfection, its long, delicate orchestral introduction perfectly establishing the mood for:

Chaste goddess, who dost silver
these ancient sacred trees,
turn upon us thy fair face
unclouded and unveiled.

From Adalgisa, left alone, we learn the overpowering attraction she feels for Pollione has caused her to forget her vows. He
enters with the news he must go to Rome and implores her to join
him. She consents, helpless in her passion. Now we have had the
main events of the first part of the first act, and we can guess how
they will come to a boil in a second, briefer segment.

We find Norma tormented by wildly mixed emotions, an illicit love that has borne two children clashing with sacred vows and
duties. A trembling Adalgisa arrives and confesses to Norma that
her passion for a man has caused her to break her vows. Norma
reflects the while on the similarity to her own situation several
years ago. In his letter, Bellini wisely isolated this duet, too, which
begins as Adalgisa sings *Sola, furtiva al tempio* ("Secretly, alone at
the temple I often waited for him"): Link a superb mezzo with a
superb soprano here and you will shiver with delight. Norma comforts her, quieting her torment until she puts two and two together just as Pollione arrives. The great trio of revelation follows—
Norma proclaims death would be preferable for Adalgisa than to
know this man; Adalgisa quakes, fearing the magnitude of the revelation at hand; and Pollione attempts to pass the buck to the
judgment of heaven. It is with Norma's words, *Oh di qual sei tu
vittima crudo e funesto inganno* ("Oh what a cruel, infamous
deception has entrapped you") that this famous trio begins.

Pollione attempts to leave, taking Adalgisa with him. She
holds back. Norma demands his attention and Adalgisa scorns his
faithlessness. Norma, her inner rage heretofore repressed, is contained no more as the Act I finale commences: *Vanne, si mi las-
cia, indegno* ("Yes, leave me worthless man: forget your children,
your promises, your honor"). Pollione curses his fate, Adalgisa
will do anything within her power to reunite him with Norma and
their children, and the temple bells call Norma to her rites. Pollione walks away. Act I ends.

Act II

In the woods, the Gauls have gathered awaiting instructions from
Norma. The scene then changes to the temple, where Adalgisa
informs Norma she failed in her attempt to prevail on Pollione to

return to Norma and their children. Adalgisa wishes to resume her vows but Pollione has threatened to take her, by force, to Rome. Norma summons her people. There will be war, she decrees. *Guerra! guerra!* ("To battle! To battle!") is the chorus in which Bellini had such confidence.

It takes us to the long denouement of the Act II finale. Clotilde enters with news that a Roman who desecrated the temple has been caught. It is Pollione. His fate now is in Norma's hands. She demands he allow Adalgisa to return to the altar and that he take their children. Norma will not see him again. He refuses. Norma responds with a threat to kill the children and to burn Adalgisa in a sacrificial fire. "I'll strike your heart through hers," she promises.

Norma calls for the pyre to be prepared and announces there will be a new victim for the sacrifice: "a perjured priestess who has broken her vows and betrayed her nation and its gods," Norma informs them. "Who is she?" they clamor. *Son io* ("It is I") she responds. She confesses all and asks that the children be cared for. She will die in the flames. Pollione is moved by her integrity and the magnanimity of her being. His love for her is reawakened. *Il tuo rogo, o Norma, è il mio* ("Your pyre, oh Norma, is mine"), he declares, "there beyond, purer, holier, begins eternal love!" He joins her, and together they enter the flames.

Bellini's music satisfies when properly performed but such music, with its long melodic lines and its share of sustained high notes, is not easy to sing, especially when the high notes are to be delivered softly. (It is much easier to sing loudly than softly, wherein the slightest imperfections are glaring.) In the middle of the twentieth century, the American-born Greek soprano Maria Callas made Bellini more prominent than ever through her numerous recordings of his heroines. (Indeed, not just Bellini; Callas was applauded around the world for her bel canto interpretations of Rossini and Donizetti women as well.) Those who saw her claim there was nothing like her on the stage. She became the character she portrayed. Her attention to the words and their meanings set new standards for the singing actress, and many are those who used the word "love" to describe what she put into the music she sang. Her huge recorded legacy, however, reveals she had good days and not such good days. Her voice could become strident, especially in the upper register, and unsteady. When she was good, though, she stood alone, worthy of comparison only with the great Rosa Ponselle, who so often partnered Caruso and who many experts claim has had no equal.

At times I may hear something in Callas that is annoying, but perhaps you will be more tolerant. My very high standards were given to me as a young boy by Rosa Ponselle, a good friend of my Grandmother Smith (a well-respected singer in her own right), for she often sang in my grandparents' home. To have had this as a child means I was as spoiled as I was lucky.

Do consider the Callas recording of *Norma* that she made in 1953 with Mario Filippeschi, Ebe Stignani, and Nicola Rossi-Lemeni with the La Scala Orchestra and Chorus, Tullio Serafin conducting. And get yourself some Rosa Ponselle. She has been remastered onto compact disc. (But more about her later.)

After its shaky opening night, the fame of *Norma* grew steadily throughout Italy and beyond. It had reached England by 1836. *Norma* was performed in New Orleans the year before and in New York in 1841. Throughout the last century, many a baby girl was christened Norma.

I PURITANI (1835)
The Puritans

Bellini's last opera, *I Puritani,* was premiered on January 25, 1835, in Paris, where Rossini was living in celebrity and retirement. He was forceful in supporting Bellini's work. Bellini died of dysentery on September 23 that same year. (Because of his young age, a legend would develop that he, like Mozart, had been poisoned.) At this time, *I Puritani* was being presented and the singers, after a performance, left the stage and went directly to sing at his funeral. This opera is in three acts. The names of the English characters are Italianized, of course, when the opera is sung in the original language.

ELVIRA, daughter of Lord Walton, in love with Arthur, *soprano*

LORD WALTON (Valton), Governor General of the Puritans, BASS

LORD ARTHUR TALBOT (Arturo), a cavalier fighting for the Stuart restoration, *tenor*

SIR RICHARD FORTH (Riccardo), a Puritan to whom Elvira is promised, *baritone*

SIR GEORGE (Giorgio), the Puritan uncle of Elvira, *bass*

HENRIETTA OF FRANCE (Enrichetta), widow of Charles I,
  mezzo-soprano
SIR BRUNO ROBERTSON, a Puritan officer, *tenor*

The time is that of the English Civil War, about 1650, and
it is set near Plymouth, England.

Act I
Elvira learns from her uncle that he has prevailed upon her father
to allow her to marry the man she loves, Arthur, and not the man
to whom she has been promised, Richard. She is grateful and
happy. In the Great Hall of her father's castle the wedding is eagerly anticipated. Arthur arrives and is dismayed to find that Henrietta, his Queen, is held prisoner in the fortress. She is to be executed, as was her husband the king. Henrietta fiddles with Elvira's
wedding veil, and then tries it on, which gives Arthur an idea. The
veil could disguise Henrietta and he could conduct her past the
guard to an escape. As the first act ends, the escape has been made
but Elvira draws the wrong conclusion. She believes Arthur has
run off with another woman and she loses her reason.

Act II
Her madness is the focus of the second act. The "mad scene" was
quite popular in opera during the 1820s and 1830s—both Bellini
and Donizetti composed two such significant scenes for different
operas. The prototype of all operatic mad scenes is that of Ophelia
in Shakespeare's *Hamlet*. Elvira, like Donizetti's Lucia, envisions
herself at the altar marrying the man she loves. (As a brief aside, by
the way, Bellini's mad scene for Elvira premiered nine months
before Donizetti's Lucia and his mad scene for Imogene in *Il pirata (The Pirate)* beat Donizetti's *Anna Bolena (Anne Boleyn)* to the
punch by three years.) Also in this act, besides Elvira's mad wanderings about the castle, is a scene wherein Richard and George
announce their readiness to meet Arthur in battle unto his death.

Act III
In the third act, we find Arthur in a wooded area not far from the
castle. There is great danger for him but he must see Elvira. He
meets her and explains the real reason he ran off with the Queen.
Elvira is vague. Arthur notices she is not in her right mind. Puritan soldiers pursuing Arthur interrupt them, however, and the
prospect of his death at their hands is enough of a shock to restore

her sanity. Just in time a messenger arrives, announcing the defeat of the Stuarts. Amnesty prevails, Arthur is freed and the lovers are reunited.

These are the essentials of the plot; it is not a wrenching tragedy. The creation of intensely dramatic scenes was neither the intention nor the forte of Bellini, who knew his gift was melody. Throughout *I Puritani*, lyricism prevails.

I have a tape of a live performance of this opera in South America in 1961. Arias, duets, and ensembles just keep coming and after each one—because the cast was an extraordinarily good one—the audience expressed its appreciation with a mounting intensity that inspired the singers to give their all. And that they did. For *I Puritani*, all you need are the basics of the story and then you should just sit back and let Bellini's music go to work. I have read several testimonials claiming the melody of *Qui la voce sua soave* ("Hear his gentle voice"), in Elvira's Act II mad scene, one of the most beautiful ever written. It is a lovely, fragile melody: as fragile and tenuous as her psyche. Of all the mad scenes I know, this one is the most lyrical, from its first note through the *cabaletta*: *Vien, diletto, è in ciel la luna* ("Come, beloved, the moon's in heaven") with which it concludes on its soaring sustained high note on the word "love."

Vocally and melodically, this is the central piece in the opera, but also in this second act is the stirring martial duet *Suoni la tromba* ("Let the trumpet sound") of Richard and George.

In the first act there are three notable arias: Richard grieving over the loss of Elvira, *Il duol che al cor mi piomba* ("The grief that weighs upon my heart"), Arthur's romance to Elvira, *A te, o cara, amor talora* ("To you, beloved, once before"), and Elvira's *Son vergin vezzosa* ("I'm a pretty maiden"), sung as she enters the Great Hall to reveal her wedding veil.

Act III, too, has its splendid musical moments. Arthur hears Elvira singing their love song, *A una fonte affitto e solo* ("By a fountain, sad, alone"); Arthur and Elvira's passionate duet *Vieni fra queste braccia* ("Come to my arms, my love") always brings down the house; and the big ensemble that carries the opera to its conclusion, *Credeasi, misera! da ma tradita* ("The poor girl believed I had betrayed her"), has become the most anticipated and well-known musical moments of this last act of Bellini's final opera.

The passionate boy-girl episodes in Bellini's operas were part of his own "operatic" life, as well. Bellini was exceedingly good-looking, and both men and women referred to him as "a beautiful man." Almost as if it were an essential part of his preparing a new opera, there was Bellini in bed with his prima donna in another passionate, but fleeting, love affair. Few were the leading ladies who did not succumb.

With Bellini's last opera we have reached the finale of our introduction to the nineteenth-century bel canto operas. Once you are familiar with those presented in this book, more than one hundred other bel canto operas by these three composers await you. Not all of them have been recorded but many of them have, and in the lot are some very good ones. The bel canto operas carried the great tradition of Italian opera that Mozart brought to perfection on into the nineteenth century. Mozart, as we know, also created masterworks in the tradition of German opera, and we now backtrack to Vienna, Austria, Beethoven's adopted city, to resume the story of the development of the Germanic opera tradition following the death of Mozart.

Ludwig van Beethoven

Carl Maria von Weber

EARLY 19ᵀᴴ CENTURY GERMAN OPERA: BEETHOVEN AND WEBER

What happened in German opera after Mozart and before Wagner? Ludwig van Beethoven and Carl Maria von Weber happened! Beethoven wrote only one opera but it is an operatic monument, and in von Weber's three major operas, *Der Freischütz (The Free Shooter)*, *Euryanthe*, and *Oberon*, we have the creation of German Romantic opera that was brought to its ultimate expression by Richard Wagner.

LUDWIG VAN BEETHOVEN

Beethoven was born into a musical family of several generations; workmanlike musicians served the nobility by making music just as other craftsmen made bottles or boots. Beethoven will break that mold. With him, the great musician becomes a giant stalking a domain uninhabited by ordinary beings or, as Wagner later would put it, "Beethoven was a titan wrestling with the gods." With Beethoven, no more will the great musician be in the service of the aristocracy, providing them with pretty music for their amusement. With Beethoven, the great musician will expect the nobility to step aside on the street and expect, as well, that they will serve the musician and not the other way around.

Beethoven's music probes the human heart to its depths as well as the far reaches of the cosmos. The huge musical legacy of Beethoven is his affirmation of goodness, truth, and beauty as he knew it. Through his music Beethoven expresses what life at its best would be. With Beethoven, the classical pattern of definite musical forms and rational restraint will give way to the broodings and joyful ejaculations of a passionate human heart and a lofty moral sense.

His early works were composed in the classical tradition of Haydn and Mozart. They embody the basic principles of classicism: formal structure, elegance, simplicity and clarity, dignity, restraint, and rational order. Beethoven lived during the time when these principles would yield to new standards for creative expression. These aesthetics of the eighteenth century—The Age of Reason—would be replaced by less formal structures and passionate, virtually unrestrained emotional expression in literature and the arts. This new age of Romanticism no longer extolled primacy of intellect and structure. Rather, it favored idealism, imagination, "bearing of the soul," and romantic content unfettered by rigid forms and structures. Classicism's rational restraint had become the fervent ardor of Romanticism. Beethoven was the vehicle that carried Western music through this transformation. Musicologists divide his compositions into three periods: the early elegant classical works; the compositions of his middle period of pushing these inherited classical musical forms to their breaking point; and his late period of powerful emotional expressions of pure romantic music. A simple listening experiment can tell far more than can words. Consider a comparison of three of his nine famous symphonies. His first symphony, Opus 21, is in the classical tradition; the fifth symphony, Opus 67, derives from the middle period, and the ninth symphony, Opus 125, is late.

Beethoven was born in Bonn in 1770. His first published music appeared in his twelfth year. The spring of 1787 found him in Vienna, where he was to study with Mozart, and he may even have had a lesson or two before his mother's grave illness called him home. It was reported that Mozart, when he heard the young Beethoven play improvisations on the piano, said, "Keep an eye on that young man—some day he will give the world something to talk about!" Late in 1792 Beethoven, back in Vienna, had a few lessons with Haydn, but ultimately his independence of spirit prevailed. Though he had inherited the classical forms of Mozart and Haydn, he would soon fill them to the breaking point with his own dynamic, tumultuous music. When these forms fractured, the wondrous flood of romanticism in music had been set free, and Western music entered a new age.

Beethoven was committed to lofty ethical ideals such as freedom and brotherhood. He spurned the Mozart/da Ponte operas as frivolous, finding in them no redeeming moral qualities. He considered the subjects "repugnant." You, of course, know that on this subject Beethoven was shortsighted. You have read the preceding chapter and know that tolerating human weakness and offering forgiveness are important virtues, but Beethoven's aim was higher than that. Of Mozart's operas, only *The Magic Flute* appealed to him because he did not fail to note the ethical commitments intertwined with the fairy tale. Beethoven's only opera, *Fidelio* (this name of the title character is obviously suggestive of fidelity), which is made of the ingredients of a singspiel, transcends this form in its high and mighty declarations of ethical ideals. In doing so this opera is unlike any that came before it and to this day remains unusual in how this composer utilized an operatic format as a testimonial to the values and virtues of conjugal love, fidelity, and freedom. Beethoven never married but always hoped he would find the ideal woman. The true and loving wife, one of two central themes in the opera, Beethoven again gave expression in his setting of "Ode to Joy," words by Schiller, in the fourth and final movement of his ninth symphony, one of the most famous pieces of music in the world. Ultimately, for Beethoven, it was only in his creation of *Fidelio* that he found the ideal woman, although his letters to the "Immortal Beloved" make it certain that at least one mysterious young woman once was deep in his heart.

FIDELIO (1805)

The first performance of *Fidelio* was in Vienna, Beethoven's adopted city, in 1805. As it was considered a failure, he revised the work and an 1806 production was more successful. Driven by his overwhelming sense of perfection, in 1814 Beethoven revised the work again into the form now given. With that performance, *Fidelio* went into the opera annals.

Fidelio is another opera originating in what has been reported as a true story: A woman disguises herself as a male, achieves employment in a prison where her husband has been incarcerated, and liberates him. This will not be the last time in this book that we meet an opera born out of an unusual life episode (Leoncavallo's *Pagliacci* and Berg's *Wozzeck* still to come). Beethoven's only opera generally is referred to simply as *Fidelio* but the full title of the work is *Fidelio, oder die eheliche Liebe* ("Fidelio, or a married couple's love"). The love of Leonore (disguised as a man going by the name of Fidelio) for her husband, Florestan (a Spanish nobleman), is one of two central themes in the drama. Human freedom is the other. Both will be given magnificent musical expression. The often utilized theatrical device of symbolizing evil by dark and good by light (recall that Mozart used this in *The Magic Flute*) will be even more obvious in *Fidelio*, whose libretto by one man after a libretto by another man was revised by a third man, none of whom you are ever likely to hear about. The opera is in two acts. There are seven characters:

> FLORESTAN, a Spanish nobleman, *tenor*
> LEONORE, his wife, who is disguised as the man Fidelio, *soprano*
> ROCCO, head jailer of the prison, *bass*
> MARZELLINE, his daughter, *soprano*
> JACQUINO, assistant to Rocco and in love with
>   Marzelline, *tenor*
> DON PIZARRO, governor of the prison, *baritone*
> DON FERNANDO, minister of state, *bass*
> Soldiers, prisoners, and local people

The setting of the story is a fortress near Seville and the time of the action is the eighteenth century.

Act I

The *Fidelio* Overture precedes the opening of the curtain on Act I. Beethoven wrote four overtures for his opera before being satisfied. (This important and complicated matter we will come back to as we near the opera's end, because one of these four overtures has become so famous and popular that some conductors like to play it prior to the final scene.) The first scene is in the courtyard of the state prison next to the lodgings of Rocco, the head jailer. His daughter Marzelline is being courted by Rocco's assistant, Jacquino, but the young girl's attention is elsewhere, namely on Fidelio, another young man, or so she thinks. Actually, Fidelio is the assumed name of Leonore, the wife of a Spanish nobleman, Florestan, unjustly imprisoned by the evil Pizarro. Carefully disguised as Fidelio, she has succeeded in obtaining a position as Rocco's assistant as part of her plan to liberate her husband.

Marzelline stalls Jacquino's wooing and daydreams about Fidelio: *O wär' ich schon mit dir vereint* ("O were I now united with you"). Rocco and then Fidelio enter and their brief dialogue gives way to each musing on separate emotions. *Mir ist so wunderbar* ("I feel so strange"), Marzelline begins in an extraordinary quartet wherein each character inhabits his own world and reveals no connection to any other in his reflections. The stage direction for this quartet is *Für sich*, which means everything is sung as an "aside." Marzelline is aware of a new and strange feeling in her heart. Fidelio, aware of Marzelline's fixation, notes the futility of it in an important phrase, one that will represent the reunion with her husband near the opera's end with the change of just one word. The phrase she now sings is *O namenlose Pein* ("O nameless pain"). Rocco will accept his daughter's desire for the new assistant, and Jacquino finds that the reversal of Marzelline's affection and Rocco's approval, have made his hair stand on end. This quartet is one of the most beautiful and famous ensembles in German opera.

Another brief dialogue, typical of a singspiel, follows. Then Rocco pronounces that there is more to marriage than love and with good middle-class stability delivers his aria on money. *Hat man nicht auch Gold daneben* ("If you don't have money") certainly could be part of a singspeil, which so far *Fidelio* seems to resemble. But as Leonore's plan is set in motion, Beethoven's music more and more responds to the conflict of good and evil and increasingly this opera becomes unlike any opera preceding it. The libretto, though not brilliant, represents the triumph of ethical concepts greatly appealing to Beethoven and he responded by creating a hymn to human freedom, love, and fidelity in marriage. *Fidelio* wears its ethical maxims on its sleeve. Already we have had the good burgher's testimonial to the importance of money in marriage, and more lofty and spiritual ethical conceptions are soon to come.

Leonore, noting that Rocco is a tired old man, offers to help him in the prison cells, thereby hoping to ascertain whether one of them contains Florestan. His affirmative reply raises her hopes but, "there is one dungeon where I am not allowed to take you," he says, and continues by explaining that Pizarro has ordered him to deprive that prisoner of virtually everything until he dies. Leonore is quite willing to help him and in a trio, Rocco advises his new assistant, "Always have courage, then you will achieve your ends." Leonore responds, "Love can endure terrible suffering," and poor Marzelline misconstrues Leonore's words as meant for her.

A situation to test these virtues of courage and love arrives with Pizarro. The scene changes to martial music as he and his platoon of sentries are let through the gates. Pizarro learns the minister of state soon will be arriving to inspect the prison. He knows Don Fernando must not find out that he has unjustly and cruelly incarcerated a prisoner who now must quickly be killed and buried. *Ha! Welch ein Augenblick* ("Ha! What a moment!") is a powerful, difficult aria for bass voice. It is followed by a duet with Rocco wherein the governor tries to bribe the jailer to murder the wretched man. "No, sir. To take a life is not my duty," Rocco replies. Then Pizarro will do it. He orders Rocco to descend and dig a grave. Leonore has overheard. When Rocco and Pizarro depart, she steps forward to vent her rage in one of the monumental soprano solos in German opera, the mighty outburst *Abscheulicher!* ("Monster!"). It is an aria of two moods. Her expression of fury gives way to an affirmation of hope, still another of those virtues that make one think of *Fidelio* as "*the* ethical opera." Here are her words:

> Come, Hope, let the last star
> not forsake the weary!
> Brighten my goal; be it ever so far,
> love will reach it.
>
> I follow an inner compulsion,
> I do not falter,
> strengthened by the duty
> of faithful married love!
>
> O you, for whom I bore everything,
> could I but penetrate the place
> where evil threw you in chains,
> and bring you sweet comfort!
>
> I follow an inner compulsion,
> I do not falter,

> strengthened by the duty
> of faithful married love.

Were I to retranslate the final stanza, taking a few liberties in order to represent the original rhyme scheme, it is obvious Beethoven did not have before him inspiring verse to move him to great music.

> I follow an inner drive,
> I will not digress,
> strengthened by my marriage oath, I press
> on to keep my love alive!

This is not great poetry, but oh! the music Beethoven wrought out of it. Such was his genius!

Now, no one can fault Rocco for beholding the practical importance of money in a marriage; it makes things go more smoothly. But notice the list of traditional, classical virtues so far unearthed in this opera: courage, hope, and love. "Providence" soon makes an appearance. Fidelio has successfully encouraged Rocco to let out the prisoners into the warmth of sunshine and light. Beethoven is the one who does not falter. "The Prisoners' Chorus" is another great tune—subdued, restrained, melodic, and harmonically beautiful:

> With trust we will
> build on God's help.
> Hope whispers gently to me:
> We shall be free, we shall find rest!

Freedom and God have entered the scene. I am not making light of this. Rather, I call on you to notice how traditional virtue is piled on traditional virtue to the point where there is barely room for more. Rocco tells Fidelio he needs his help in the dungeon below in digging a grave, the prisoners are returned to their cold, dark cells, and the first act is over.

Act II

This act opens on the dark, subterranean dungeon of Florestan. He is held by a long chain secured to the wall. There is no waiting for his big aria, *Gott! Welch' Dunkel hier!* ("God! What darkness here!"), wherein he seems to accept his fate knowing "I have done my duty" (the exposing of Pizarro's wrongs). With a reverie, a mystical premonition for the audience, and an anticipation of death, Florestan ends his song:

> Do I not feel a gentle, soft-stirring breeze?
> And is not my tomb illumined?
> I see in the rosy air as it were an angel
> moving to my side in pity.
> An angel, so like my wife Leonore,
> who leads me to freedom in the Heavenly
> Kingdom!

Exhausted, Florestan sinks down on the stones, his face hidden in his hands. Rocco and Leonore descend the steps into this dungeon carrying pick, shovel, lantern, and jug. The door they have left open allows some light into the darkness. With their arrival on stage we have the beginning of a "melodrama and duet" within the opera.

An operatic melodrama presents a mix of pantomime, words, and music. Music can accompany the gestures and words or alternate with the words. Not many repertory operas present extended melodrama. The grave-digging scene in *Fidelio* is one of the most well known. Today the word *melodrama* implies an intensification of sentiment and exaggerated emotion, which is precisely what this scene would represent were it not rescued by Beethoven's marvelous music.

Rocco and Leonore begin to dig. The prisoner, hidden in the dark, stirs. Rocco points to him. Leonore cannot make out his features. They continue to dig. Rocco, now waist deep in the hole, needs help with a stone. Together they move it. Leonore tries to watch the prisoner and in an aside says, "Whoever you are, I will save you, by God!" The prisoner awakens and speaks. Leonore, recognizing the voice, swoons, then, as Rocco and Florestan converse, she regains consciousness. A trio ensues: Rocco believing the prisoner's suffering soon will end, Florestan expressing appreciation for a refreshing draught given to him by the jailer, and Leonore offering him bread, her heart pounding in anticipation of the moment soon to arrive when it is either death or deliverance. Pizarro enters, has Rocco unlock Florestan's chain at the wall, and draws a dagger: "Let him die! But first he shall know who hacks his proud heart from him." Florestan replies, "A common murderer stands before me." Leonore jumps between them: "Stab this heart first you must!" Pizarro pushes her away. She steps back to shield Florestan. "First kill his wife!"

> *Pizarro*: His wife?
> *Rocco*: His wife?
> *Florestan*: My wife?
> *Leonore*: Yes, behold here Leonore!

Pizarro is furious. "Shall I tremble before a woman? I will sacrifice them both to my fury!" Leonore pulls a pistol from her coat: "One more sound and you are dead!" What a moment! Then, right on cue, the trumpet sounds the arrival of the minister of state for the prison inspection. Jacquino and soldiers arrive. Rocco and Pizarro leave with them to meet him. A liberated Florestan and Leonore embrace and sing of their joy in a superb duet, one of the phrases being *O namenlose Freude* ("O nameless joy"). Recall earlier how Leonore, in the Act I quartet, remarked on the nameless pain of her having to deceive Marzelline. This scene ends with their overwhelming happiness. Now it is nameless joy.

The end of this duet should lead directly to the Act II finale but a practice of long standing has introduced a tradition now followed, by many conductors, of playing the celebrated Leonore Overture No. 3 as an orchestral interlude prior to the finale. Beethoven wrote four overtures before being satisfied. It was his habit to carry with him wherever he went sketchbooks and a pencil. Home or away, he always was writing down new ideas and revising those already conceived. He worked slowly and meticulously. His initial sketches for what would become some of the grandest moments in this remarkable opera, for example, were so trivial, attests one commentary, "it would be impossible to admit that they were Beethoven's if they were not in his own handwriting." One of the great arias is found in eighteen variants before Beethoven was satisfied. His sketchbooks show ten revisions of the opera's concluding chorus and, as mentioned above, he left four overtures. The overture that now begins the opera is known as the *Fidelio Overture*. The others are Leonore Overture Nos. 1, 2, and 3. The order of the composition of the four overtures has been debated, a subject we need not attempt to settle here.

Of the four, number three is the pièce de résistance, an orchestral masterpiece that builds to a thrilling climax, subsides, and climaxes again, all in an exhilarating fifteen minutes. Audiences love it. And the conductor and the orchestra love it too, because they become the star of the show as the entire house is whipped into an intoxicating musical frenzy.

The problem with all this is that musically it is not dramatically right. At this point in the drama it is inappropriate. First, it invades the flow of dramatic action. The minister of state has arrived and Florestan has been rescued. We need to get him out of darkness into warm sunlight. His chains need to be removed from his wrists. We need to get on to the triumphant hymn to freedom and married love that closes the drama (the chorus Beethoven rewrote ten times before getting it the way he wanted it). The Leonore Overture No. 3, magnificent as it is, is a musical intrusion. It also contains some of the great musical themes Beethoven utilized in the finale for the triumph of freedom and married love; thus, playing this overture at this point of the drama lets the musical cat out of the bag. I know of one scholar who does not like this magnificent overture played as part of the opera. His solution: Play it after the opera. This, also, is silly. The proper solution is to go to the store, purchase a recording of the Leonore Overtures by your favorite orchestra and conductor, and play them to your heart's content. Of this, Beethoven surely would approve.

For the finale, the scene changes to the parade grounds of the fortress. Prisoners and townspeople have gathered. Don Fernando is there, as are Don Pizarro, Rocco, Jacquino, and Marzelline, too. Indeed, everyone is here. The themes of the joys of a loving marriage and of brotherhood, "brother seeking brother and helping if he can" (the same themes to which Beethoven will return in the celebrated fourth and final movement of his last symphony), are proclaimed by all. Don Fernando greets his old friend Florestan, whose chains are removed by Leonore; Don Pizarro is arrested and led away; and Marzelline and Jacquino are reunited as Leonore exclaims, "Love guided my efforts, true love fears nothing." This triumphant hymn to freedom, brotherhood, and conjugal love is one of the most splendid musical outpourings in Beethoven's large legacy.

Beethoven, who composed some of the most affirming music ever written, loved to pun—and the worse the pun, the better. He enjoyed practical jokes, as long as he was not the butt, and he played them out on his friends incessantly. His dress and his person could be unkempt, his manners frequently crude, even rude, and he was outspoken. At the home of a certain Count, Beethoven, adored by the music-loving nobility of Vienna, often was a special guest. Once, he and a friend were playing a duet on the piano. A young nobleman, refusing to acknowledge several requests not to talk during the music, continued conversing with a young woman. Beethoven abruptly stopped playing, stopped his friend from playing, and in a loud voice announced, "I play no longer for pigs."

His playful nature also loved nicknames, some made up and others adapted from other sources. A friend named Linke (which is the German word for "left") he dubbed, *Liebe linke und rechts* ("Love left and right"), and another friend he referred to always as Papageno, the beloved character in Mozart's *The Magic Flute*. Beethoven thoroughly disliked the wife, and soon to be widow, of his brother Carl. He considered her a bad woman and he would do all in his power to keep Carl's son from her after his brother's death. Beethoven referred to her as the Queen of the Night.

Surely you must have noticed similarities between Mozart's *The Magic Flute* and Beethoven's *Fidelio:* The evil queen in the one and the evil Pizarro in the other, representing the powers of darkness, are overcome by good and light; and though the concept of brotherhood dominates Mozart's opera, it also has a place in Beethoven's, even though it is married love in his work that holds center stage. Often I have wondered if Beethoven, like Mozart, had any connection with Freemasons. I have found no evidence that he was ever a Mason but his close association with various Freemasons is known. *The Magic Flute*, already I have noted, is the opera of Mozart that Beethoven liked best. He knew the work well. He wrote a famous theme and variations on the duet *Bei Männern*, he utilized characters in the opera for nicknaming, and, most of all, the high ethical posture of Mozart's opera resounds in Beethoven's masterpiece, his single contribution to operatic literature. Numerous are the composers who wrote many operas and contributed much less than did Beethoven with this one mighty drama.

Finally, there is this story associated with Beethoven's death on Monday night, March 26, 1827, in his fifty-sixth year. A late-winter storm raged outside the house where he lay dying. Snow and hail fell, lightning tore the sky, and a huge thunder clap awakened Beethoven, who opened his eyes, made a fist, and raised it above him to shake it at the heavens. His hand then fell and this man who so loved nature in all its beauty and elemental force, this man whose genius so often transformed thunder in the universe into magnificent music, was dead.

CARL MARIA VON WEBER

Beethoven was born almost fourteen years before Carl Maria von Weber and lived almost a year longer, von Weber attaining only forty years. Von Weber's musical life was varied. He was a composer of works in numerous genres, a conductor, a pianist, and a music critic. Most would remember him as the creator of German Romantic opera. He wrote nine operas, the three most enduring being *Der Freischütz* (1821), *Euryanthe* (1823), and *Oberon* (1826).

DER FREISCHÜTZ (1821)
The Free Shooter

The first of these is the only German opera after *Fidelio* and before the operas of Richard Wagner to have secured a prominent and permanent place on the opera stages of the world. Therefore, it has a place in this book, which, accordingly, passes over the other two but not without noting that they are something for you to come back to another time. One preoccupation of German Romanticism was its increasing interest in the irrational that found expression in both literature and music through a fascination with supernatural effects, events, and powers. *Der Freischütz* is a good example, especially if we begin with the untranslatable title. *Der Freischütz* literally means "The Free Shooter," but what does that mean? The "free shooter" of the opera is a forester who makes a pact with a demon in the wild as a means of obtaining magic bullets to allow him to win an important shooting contest. The supernatural element is implied right from the start when we "translate" the title into words that tell what is meant by *free shooter*, namely, *A Marksman and His Magic Bullets*. Writing to his fiancée, Carl Maria von Weber elaborates as he tells her about the opera he is writing:

> An old hunter in the service of a Prince wants to give his loyal assistant, Max, the hand of his

daughter and also appoint him as his successor. The Prince agrees to this, but there exists an old law, which requires the young man to undergo a severe shooting test. Another malicious and dissolute hunter's assistant, Kaspar, also has his eye on the girl but has sold himself, half and half, to the Devil. Max, who is otherwise an excellent shot, misses everything during the time immediately preceding the shooting test and, in his despair, is enticed by Kaspar into making so-called "free bullets," of which six invariably find their way home, but in return for which, the seventh belongs to the Devil.[†]

Germanic Romanticism is rich in tales and legends of yesteryear, stories with long oral and, subsequently, written traditions about supernatural powers, good and evil, demonic forces, divine intervention, elves, trolls, mysterious places, dark forests, and on and on. The text of this opera is by Johann Friedrich Kind (whom we do not meet again). The two basic elements in the story are eighteenth-century rural hunting life in a German principality and demonic powers. Weber noted, "To my mind the most important passage was represented by Max's line 'I am being ensnared by dark powers' for it gave me an indication as to what was to be the opera's principal characteristic." To create music for rustic hunting scenes and forest life he utilized the horns of the orchestra, writing for them simple tunes and at times adapting phrases from popular hunting melodies for authenticity. To express the somber and ominous quality of dark powers, repeatedly heard throughout the score, Weber utilized the lowest register of the string section of the orchestra, clarinets, the bassoon, and strokes and rolls on the kettle drum.

Der Freischütz was produced in Berlin on June 18, 1821, seven years after the success of Beethoven's final version of Fidelio and twenty-two years before the premiere of Wagner's first major work, Der fliegende Holländer (The Flying Dutchman). Spoken dialogue carries along the plot and set musical numbers (songs, ensembles, and choruses) express emotions and portray local

---

[†] Carl Maria von Weber, *Letter to his Fiancé* (New York: Seraphim Records Liner Notes, translation by Peggy Cockrane, 1960), p. 2

color. Above, in his letter to his fiancée, Weber provided a skeleton of much of the plot, but his account is not sufficient for one who wants to understand how the story develops in relation to the main musical numbers, and it is important for you to understand that it is those musical numbers that have kept this opera alive, well, and on the boards all these years. The story's childlike depiction of a haunted glen and conflicting supernatural forces could not have lived alone and long endured. The music is wonderful. The opera is in three acts. Nine characters have a part:

PRINCE OTTOKAR, *bass*
CUNO, the head forest ranger, *bass*
AGATHE, his daughter, *soprano*
MAX, an assistant forest ranger in love with Agathe, *tenor*
AENNCHEN, Agathe's cousin, *soprano*
KILIAN, a rich peasant, *baritone*
CASPAR (or Kaspar), another young forester, *bass*
SAMIEL, the demonic, wild huntsman, *speaking part*
A hermit, *bass*

It takes place in Bohemia in the middle of the seventeenth century.

Act I

The now very famous overture opens the opera. This overture is one of the first, if not the first, in opera history intentionally to have been made from melodies used in the opera. Recall how some music preceded seventeenth-century operas as a means of quieting the audience. Later, Mozart's overtures establish a mood. Rossini exchanged overtures, one for the other as needed just as he might change a shirt. Beethoven utilized a theme from an air in the opera for the *Fidelio* overture, but Weber includes complete melodies from the score in writing the overture to *Der Freischütz*, melodies associated with music primarily for the two central characters, the young lovers. Many composers were to copy this approach of waiting until the score was complete and then determining what melodies summarized or told the story or predicting what melodies were likely to become the most popular and then making from them the overture. Some operettas and many musicals have an overture entirely made by segueing one major tune after the other.

As the opera begins, Kilian defeats Max in a shooting contest.

Delightful music accompanies the teasing of Max. Cuno enters, worried: His daughter has been promised to Max, whose performance suggests it is unlikely he will win the big contest on the following day before Prince Ottakar. According to custom, victory would give Max eventual succession to Cuno's position. Alone, Max expresses his concern in the aria *Durch die Wälder* ("Through the forests"), wherein a beautiful melody yields to a darker expression as Samiel, unseen by Max, haunts the background. Caspar appears with evil on his mind. He plies Max with wine, hands him a gun, points to an eagle high in the sky, and bids Max to shoot. Max fires, and from a great height, the eagle falls at his feet.

I remember one performance of this scene that greatly amused an audience. We were attending a presentation by an opera company devoted to little gimmicks (much too distracting for my taste). On this occasion Max aimed at the dome of the opera house, BANG went the gun, and from the dome plummeted a moth-eaten bird, looking more crow than eagle, kerplunk onto the stage. Max and Caspar had to pause while the audience applauded this "dramatic" special effect.

Caspar explains the bullet was a magic bullet. They always hit their mark. If Max will meet him at midnight in the haunted Wolf's Glen, together they can cast some magic bullets. At first Max waivers, then he capitulates, promising to be there at the stroke of midnight. The first act ends.

The drinking song of this scene has become quite popular. In fact, for many German-speaking people, the songs and tunes of this opera are an inherited part of their culture. I know a German woman who sings, one after the other, the tunes of this opera in the same way that Americans raised on the musicals of Rodgers and Hammerstein sing all the songs of *Oklahoma*, *Carousel*, and the other collaborations.

Act II

The second act opens on Agathe's room, where she and her cousin, Aennchen, are in a playful mood. Their little duet is another of those irresistible tunes of the Germanic heritage. Agathe's mood alters, however, as she is left alone. She opens a window. The light of the moon fills the room. *Leise, leise, fromme Weise!* ("Gently, gently, tranquil melody") begins her prayer in this extraordinary scene for soprano. Listen to it and then listen to Amina's *La sonnambula* "Sleepwalking Scene" or Lucia's "Mad Scene," from operas written within ten and fifteen years of Weber's. What contrasts I hear, beyond the obvious differences of melody and language, are contained in the word *artifice* (and I do not mean this to be disparaging when applied to the bel canto scenes of which I am fond).

In the Weber scene, I hear the voice used as a means to express deeply felt emotions. Now, of course, I realize mental derangement and walking in one's sleep are hardly rational human activities and the atmosphere for these scenes ought to convey a sense of the abnormal. I could have directed you to a scene when Amina is awake or Lucia is not mad but selected these because they show the Italian penchant for vocal display, for the voice used as an end in itself. That is what I mean when I say there is an artificial quality, however lyrical and delightful, when bel canto is contrasted to this scene for soprano written by Weber. In this assessment I am secure, for when we consider Verdi, who followed the bel canto composers, the intensification of drama through music is apparent. There is more drama in the music for the voice in Weber's scene for Agathe than in bel canto scenes that glorify vocal display as an end in itself. My point is not that you should like one more than the other because it is better but rather to encourage you to listen for subtle differences between composers and between operatic traditions. Listen for yourself and you will find your own cup of tea.

Back to Agathe. Her prayer asking for protection finished, she rises from her prayer stool and sees Max approaching in the distance. A passionate outburst of joy accompanies her waving to him. She interprets his arrival as the answer to her prayer. Max enters. Aennchen, too, returns. Max explains, in a ruse he has had to contrive to hide his real reason for going to the daunting haunted glen, that he must depart to get a deer he shot. Max must go. The women wish him to stay longer. These are the sentiments of the tuneful trio ending this first of the two scenes of Act II.

The Wolf's Glen is an eerie place high in the mountains. It is the domain of Samiel, the demonic, wild huntsman. To him Caspar sold his soul and now he hopes to exchange Max for himself as the devil's victim. This famous scene is a high point in the history of romantic opera. Weber's marvelous music has been called the most authentic expression of the macabre ever composed. Invisible spirits chant while Caspar makes a circle of boulders. A skull next to him is pierced by his sword and raised into the air as a clock (where is a clock in this wild, remote place?) strikes twelve.

He summons Samiel and strikes the deal: Give me a respite of three more years and I will deliver a new victim to you. A terrified Max appears in the distance. Caspar urges him on but visions of his mother and Agathe thwart his descent into the haunted realm. Finally, Max negotiates the rocky cliffs and enters the circle, there with lots of hocus-pocus, to cast the magic bullets in a crucible into which ghastly ingredients are placed. With the casting of each of the seven bullets, something gruesome transpires: Frightening night birds appear, a black boar runs by, a hurricane carries off treetops, fiery wheels roll across the stage, mystical forms flash through the air, then total darkness followed by meteors and fire. Caspar falls to the ground in a convulsion. Max, too, faints. Samiel enters and stands above the two forest rangers as the act ends. We know six bullets will hit their mark but the seventh belongs to Samiel.

This scene is one over which set designers and special-effects people lick their chops. It can be quite theatrical. But it can, unfortunately, be a bit much for late-twentieth-century theater when not done well. Today, some prefer concert versions of the opera where singers and choir all elegantly dressed in formal attire sit onstage above the orchestra and stand to sing their part when it is their turn. In Florence, Italy, I attended a superb concert version of this opera, but unless the staging is too stupid, I still like to go to the Wolf's Glen hoping to find it made real by Weber's music and the genius of some designer's inventive use of lights.

Act III

A brief orchestral introduction anticipates the third and final act. The curtain opens on Agathe dressed in her white wedding gown. She sings, *Und ob die Wolke sie verhülle* ("And though the cloud obscures the sky") with cello solo. This aria and the one in the second act ("Leise, leise") already cited constitute not only Weber's two finest melodies but two of the most beautiful arias in all opera.

Though many sopranos have recorded them, the perfect rendition for me is by the German soprano Tiana Lemnitz, who died in 1995 nearing her one-hundredth birthday. She was one of the greatest singers of the twentieth century. She mastered technique and sang Mozart, Verdi, Wagner, Richard Strauss, and others with remarkable authenticity and versatility. She possessed a voice of utter beauty and rendered pianissimo (notes sung very softly) unlike any other singer I have ever heard. Those who know about the art of singing are aware that it all starts with breathing properly. As Lemnitz said, "Nothing should flutter, everything must blossom out quietly, and that can be done only with proper breathing"—the perfect statement of her own accomplishments. Recordings made by Tiana Lemnitz in the 1930s and 1940s on 78 rpm shellac records were remastered onto 33 1/3 rpm long-playing records in the 1950s. Thereafter and recently, from the original 78s, a new remastering onto compact disc has made the voice of this unique singer available through the most modern technology. All this in half a century, for I remember vividly the wonder expressed by my father early in the 1940s on that day he first brought home two Tiana Lemnitz RCA Victor shellac records. He played them over and over, exclaiming all the while, "I have never ever heard singing like this in my life." Those recordings were of "The Willow Song" and the "Ave Maria" from Verdi's *Otello*. Both, along with her Weber recordings, belong in the collection of anyone interested in hearing some of the most exquisite singing ever.

Agathe's second great aria, like her first, is an expression of her faith in a benevolent Holy Will ruling the world. She is, nevertheless, distraught as she finishes her song; her cousin, on entering the room, finds Agathe in tears. Agathe has had a disturbing, morbid dream. She was a white dove. Max aimed at the dove and fired. The dove fell, then disappeared. Aennchen, in her aria *Einst träumte meiner sel'gen Base* ("My deceased cousin once dreamt"), attempts to restore the spirits of her who will be a bride on this day if Max can win the shoot. The bridesmaids enter to sing a wedding song for Agathe—one of the melodic gems of opera choral music. As they sing, a box containing the bridal wreath is presented to Agathe, who is stunned on opening it to find a funeral wreath. She takes this as still another ill omen. Aennchen claims that the half-blind old lady who delivers boxes obviously has mixed them up, but there is a subdued quality to the conclusion of this chorus.

The scene changes to a lovely opening for the shooting contest. Prince Ottokar and his men have gathered after hunting, which they praise in a jaunty chorus equally as melodious as the one the women sang for Agathe: *Was gleicht wohl auf Erden dem Jägervergnügen* ("What pleasure on earth equals that of the hunter"). Max is having success in the early rounds of the contest. One bullet remains of those cast with Caspar in the demonic realm of Samiel. It is the bullet belonging to the devil. Prince

Ottokar orders Max to shoot at a white dove in a tree. The moment Max aims, Agathe and her bridesmaids emerge from the trees next to where the dove is perched. Agathe exhorts, *Schiess nicht, Max! Ich bin die Taube...*("Don't shoot, Max! I am the dove"), but it is too late. The gun fires, and Agathe falls. So does the evil Caspar, now revealed as having been hiding in the trees. The hermit lifts Agathe to her feet. She is alive. It is Caspar who was hit by the seventh bullet. Samiel, visible only to Caspar, appears and disappears as Caspar expires. Prince Ottokar demands of Max an explanation of the perplexing events. Max confesses his participation in the forging of magic bullets in the demonic realm. Ottokar banishes Max forever. The men and women appeal to their prince for mercy. He is resolute until the holy hermit intervenes in an aria of religious dimensions, successfully prevailing on the ruler to renege. The Prince is hailed, the wedding will take place, a general chorus praises the benevolence of the Heavenly Father, and with joyful music the opera concludes.

The contrasting musical colors of *Der Freischütz*—the happy rusticity of huntsmen, rangers, and women and the darker force of evil—Weber portrayed with lasting authenticity. This explains why the opera has remained ever popular despite its dated plot.

The young Richard Wagner instantly became spellbound by Weber's music. He was eight years old, in Dresden, when the sensational popularity of this opera swept the city in which Weber almost single-handedly established German Romantic opera. The tunes of *Der Freischütz* were among the first young Richard learned to play on the piano, often teaching himself, as the story goes, from his sisters' music books, because his mother did not wish to encourage in him a fascination for the theater. Wagner's father, a police actuary, had not fooled his wife with stories of "detained at the office" as he courted celebrated actresses of the day with talk and flowers at the stage door. Ironically for several reasons, Wagner's mother married the Jewish actor Ludwig Geyer when her husband died only eight months after Richard's birth—close enough to have left unresolved all these years the absolute certainty of Richard Wagner's parentage. Had Mrs. Wagner also, perhaps, been having her fling with an actor during the last months of her husband's life? This is not gossip into which I have fallen. It is significant that there is the possibility, however remote, of a Jew being sire to one whose unsavory, spurious anti-Semitic views would eventually be widely published.

Wagner's mother and Geyer lived in Dresden, where Weber was at work creating and establishing German Romantic opera. Weber lived near them and young Richard Wagner often saw the great composer on the street and as a visitor in his home. Weber, both as a composer and as a man, made a tremendous impression on the boy, whose passion for his music became overwhelming. He sought out a man who could play the piano version of the *Der Freischütz* overture so that he, too, could learn it and please himself by playing it. With age and accomplishment, Wagner's ego would grow and grow, allowing him to believe his genius owed little or nothing to those who went before him, his love for Weber's music and his rare open acknowledgment of the incomparable genius of Beethoven being two of few exceptions.

With the advantage of retrospection, which, indeed, is the position upon which this entire book is based, we can unmistakably see and hear the uninterrupted and direct operatic connection among three heroines of three German operas in the first half of the nineteenth century: Beethoven's Leonore, Weber's Agathe, and Senta, in Wagner's *Der fliegende Holländer*, the first of his many masterpieces. In one sense it is with these three women that German Romantic opera was created. As we move from the purported historical basis of *Fidelio* into Weber's eerie world and from there into the one created by Wagner, supernatural events and a variety of religious elements increasingly commence to find stage center to distinguish, both in intent and in audience participation, the contrasting experiences of nineteenth-century Italian and German opera.

Already we have learned how opera spread rapidly in Italy after its inception because of an affinity between the theatrical aspects of a Catholic religious service and those of the opera stage. The gods figuring in operas in the Italian tradition are the gods of ancient classical lore or of the Old and New Testament tradition. Composers of Italian opera, primarily Italians and primarily Catholics, rarely put their living God, the God in whom they ardently believed and to whom they prayed, if they were religious men, on the opera stage. That God remained in church. Gods of the opera house were gods of literature. They certainly introduced religious scenes into their operas but they did not turn opera into a form of religious music. Romanticism, which seized the Germanic imagination, brought God into the opera house. The God whom Beethoven so magnificently proclaims in the music concluding *Fidelio* is the same living deity heard in the fourth and final movement of his symphonic masterpiece, the Symphony No. 9 in D major, Opus 125, "The Choral," a setting of Schiller's "Ode to Joy" and to brotherhood. It is a real, living God Beethoven summons into the symphonic hall as he set music to the final words:

> Brothers—above the canopy of stars
> A loving Father surely dwells.
> Millions, do you fall upon your knees?
> Do you sense the Creator, world?
> Seek him above the canopy of stars!
> Surely He dwells above the stars.

None other than the same God praised so powerfully by Leonore, Florestan, Marzelline, Don Fernando, Rocco, and chorus in the final moments of his opera *Fidelio*:

> Oh, God! what a moment!
> Oh, inexpressibly sweet happiness!
> Righteous, Oh, God, is Thy judgment.
> Thou dost try, but not forsake us.

And what is sung at the end of *Der Freischütz*? More joyful praise for God:

> He, who is pure of heart and leads a blameless life,
> should put his trust, like a child, in the
> benevolence of the Heavenly Father!

∽

Weber's God, too, is the living, intervening God of German Protestantism. But it remained for Wilhelm Richard Wagner to make a synthesis of religion and opera, to transform the opera house into a temple. For the templelike opera house Ludwig II, King of Bavaria, built exclusively for him Wagner wrote *Parsifal*, called by the composer a "Consecrational Festival Play," during which, by the composer's decree, the audience was forbidden to applaud. Whereas Italian opera has always remained theater, romanticism introduced into German opera the conviction that art was the source of religious truth in an age when organized religion had become ineffective. Wagner believed he lived in such an age, bereft of an authentic organized religion, so he introduced the religious experience into the opera house. This explains that essential difference we hear in the overt theatrical qualities of Italian opera written to entertain and the solemn, serious, and religious dimensions entering German opera that reached their most perplexing, intriguing, and monumental form in the dramas of Wagner. Perhaps the greatest megalomaniac in Western art, unquestionably he was one of the greatest geniuses in the history of all art.

As a boy, I read a book about Wagner titled *He Followed a Star.* Wagner did much more than follow a star. He attempted to remake both heaven and earth in his own image. It is to his story we must go next. But with this important reservation: Our concern will be limited to explaining the operatic masterpieces of Richard Wagner in the order in which he wrote them, venturing as little as possible into the exceedingly controversial life of this complex man about whom more has been written than any other Western artist. If you are interested, tons of books and articles await you in libraries and bookstores.

Richard Wagner was "the father" of the most famous—some would say infamous—family in all opera history. Wagner's son, Siegfried, wrote fifteen operas; his grandchildren inherited the administrative and artistic leadership of the famous annual Bayreuth (a town in Franconia, Germany) Festival presenting the operas of Richard Wagner in the theater King Ludwig built for Wagner and his operas. One grandson rules over that festival now. Finally, this very day Wagner's great-grandson Gottfried Wagner has a worldwide reputation as a musicologist, scholar, opera director, multimedia director, lecturer, and humanitarian.

As a humanitarian, Gottfried Wagner dedicates considerable time and energy working to ensure that his son will grow up in a world with "a freer life beyond the bonds of silence which permits Nazism to regain holds in Germany." Two generations of Gottfried's family were intimately involved with Hitler and at the center of Gottfried's being is his never-ending effort to build bridges of love and understanding with the Jews, and the families of those Jews, who suffered under Adolf Hitler the greatest atrocity in human history. He tells his story in *Wagnerdämmerung (Twilight of the Wagners)* now translated into English, and it is from Gottfried, my dear friend and colleague of numerous eventful musical collaborations, that I have learned through long conversations so much about his extraordinary influential and controversial family. I have had to repress every urge to digress into such intriguing material, for the object of this book, as far as Richard Wagner is concerned, is limited to introducing you to the unique operas of this composer who not only changed the course of opera history, but also altered the entire direction of Western music.

The young Richard Wagner

WAGNER I:
THREE EARLY MASTERPIECES

What is so different about the operas of Richard Wagner? To answer this question we must begin with another question. Different from what other operas? Different from virtually all of the other operas of all the other composers found in this book, even those of Richard Strauss, who was so obviously influenced by Wagner. (More on that influence when we get to Strauss in chapter 13.) Monteverdi and Mozart are different and Handel and Bellini are different; indeed, there are individual differences separating all the great composers in this book. Obviously, these differences mark their unique genius or special abilities and give to their creations something unusual, thus ranking them among the less than one hundred masterpieces of umpteen thousand operas written during the past four hundred years.

But there is an operatic thread of continuity connecting Monteverdi, Mozart, Handel, and Bellini, to cite four that will enable a listener to hear similarities of form and intent. Randomly, listen to fifteen or twenty continuous minutes of any opera discussed in this book so far, then switch immediately to fifteen or twenty continuous minutes from any major opera by Richard Wagner. Your ears will know you have entered a wholly different operatic realm. Now before me there is a choice to make. I can proceed by attempting to isolate and articulate in a 1-2-3 manner what those differences are or I can reveal those differences as part of the integrated whole as I tell Wagner's story. The latter I will do. It's a more sensible approach.

The complexity of Wagner's creative genius is manifested in ten volumes of books, poetry, and articles published during his life-time as well as ten operatic masterpieces. All this does not go well with the simplicity of a 1-2-3 approach. Wagner could not create anything artistic without first working through his intentions and justifications in essays and articles. To understand fully a Wagner-ian opera requires an understanding of what he was doing and why. Never was he at a loss for words in this regard. This trait of such extensive philosophizing, so to speak—an unusual trait for the creative imagination—means we must approach Wagnerian operas in a way that would be ludicrous if applied to, for example, those of Donizetti, who in a few weeks dashed off memorable tunes to the poetic lines of standard stories. Wagner, almost unique in opera history because he was both librettist and com-poser, would take three or four years to create one of his monu-mental dramas. The word *monumental* here implies no value judgment; it means "big." As I take you through Wagner's story it will become evident from the way I write how his powerful and, at times, extremely beautiful music has had a hold on me since before I can remember. However, it is important for you to under-stand that my intent is to introduce Wagner to you, not to sell you Wagner. Your reaction to his art is in your hands, your head, your heart, and ultimately your ears.

I have had to post this warning because Wagner was such a towering and complex giant in the history of art even more than a century after his death. Even with a mountain of scholarship, his complete story continues to elude all attempts to comprehend and explain who and what he was. This story, like all approaches to Wagner, is but a partial tale, a part of a whole eluding every attempt to solve the enigma of his life and work. My purpose in this book is to introduce you to this complex figure, to introduce you to his ten major operas, and to provide you with the means of entering his artistic world with enough comprehension to avoid becoming overwhelmed and bewildered. That has happened to many who then turn tail and run to the security of the lilting, singable melodies of Verdi and Puccini. This chapter gives you "tools" to work on a Wagner opera as unintimidated as you would be to undertake a more traditional opera.

Romanticism

Let us now proceed to another question. When answered, it provides an entrée to finding and understanding the basic idea behind every one of Wagner's operatic masterpieces. What motivated Wagner's creative impulse? Romanticism was not only a philosophical reaction to an overemphasis on rational thought at the expense of an underemphasis on the worth of our feelings in directing the course of human behavior; it also repudiated institutions of failed expectations. Christian churches, both Protestant and Catholic, were judged thusly. For many Romantics the Christian religion had failed its calling by becoming still another institution committed to politics, prestige, wealth, and power. Furthermore, a fundamental conviction of Romantics was that art (which they wrote as Art) was the ultimate expression of existence and the means by which religious truths and feelings were expressed. In an age when traditional religious forms and institutions had become artificial and hypocritical, art—for many Romantics—became the final religious rite.

Every facet of Wagner's life was dominated by this conviction and he articulated it throughout voluminous prose writings as well as in the poetry and music of his operas. Wagner's operas cannot be understood or experienced as he conceived them if his unwavering belief in the centrality of art as a religious rite expressing ultimate truth is ignored. Now, of course, ultimate truth is the relative truth of those proclaiming it. Wagner was consistent in the fundamentals of his Romantic posture but his understanding of religious truth altered as he aged, read, thought, and experienced life's vicissitudes. Accordingly, his operas represent expressions of ever-changing religious convictions including mysticism, paganism, Buddhistic leanings, and his own version of Christianity.

Though his formal education—academically and artistically—was limited, Wagner was an autodidact of impressive accomplishments, and because he was an inveterate writer of anything and everything on his mind, he left an extraordinary record of his intellectual development. In a remarkable book, *Richard Wagner: His Life and His Work*, author Paul Bekker brilliantly demonstrates precisely the connection between Wagner's life and his thought; how Wagner at one and the same time became what he wrote and wrote what he became and how his life and work interacted and reinforced each other, becoming virtually an inseparable synthesis.

Numerous eighteenth-century composers had created works of great genius fulfilling commissions and simply doing their job as court composers. Wagner traveled a different road, experiencing poverty, ridicule, humiliation, threats of imprisonment, and much more, but never altering his course of serving no master other than his art.

As we will explain in pages to come, even a young king of Bavaria will subordinate all other concerns of his brief and highly unorthodox reign to serving and financing Richard Wagner's artistic vision. To understand what this vision was, and the whys of its various transformations, we must know the essentials of Wagner's thoughts, those results of his laborious self-education, which could be at times, especially in his younger years, quite shallow and tendentious.

Wagner's ideas on a variety of subjects—from ancient history, medieval Germanic literary masterworks, Christianity, and Buddhism to nineteenth-century politics, economics, and religion generally—have little and limited value in and of themselves. Their great worth is in allowing us to follow the creative process of one who made some of the most individual and remarkable creations in the history of opera.

Reminiscences of his youth as we read them in his autobiography, *My Life*, indicate an early sensitivity to art as a sacred experience. He remembers having had certain "mystical" feelings as a boy when listening to music and was thus convinced some musical sounds possessed supernatural qualities capable of transporting him to a transcendental state. These experiences occurred hand-in-hand with an early rejection of the forms of Protestant orthodoxy normally expected of a boy his age in the Wagner family. Very little in his childhood and adolescent experiences, however, even as he later recalls them, alerts us to the extraordinary developments in store.

The first real discussions coupling religion and art appear in those articles, musical reviews, and news items written during days of extreme poverty while Wagner made an unsuccessful attempt to break into the operatic world of Paris during the early 1840s. In a series of pieces collected under the title *A German Musician in Paris*, Wagner writes of the moral and religious dimensions of German music, and remarks as well on its redemptive powers. In another essay, a highly chauvinistic article entitled "On German Music" (1842) he claims for music "the holiest precinct in life." Through biased, transparent argumentation he enlarges on the theme touched on in his very first publication, in which he had implied that for Bach and Handel the Passion and the Oratorio were the proper forms for great religious music, for Beethoven it was the symphony, and for Richard Wagner, the heir to this mighty tradition, it would be the opera.

His experience in Paris, where so many artists migrated to make a name, was frustrating. He failed to achieve any significant recognition as a musician, suffering there the humiliation of having to copy and arrange other men's music to eke out a living. He despised the Grand Opera in Paris, with its superficial plots, its emphasis on spectacle and display, and its presentation as a social event to which some came late, made certain they were seen, talked, and often left early. In these early prose writings, Wagner adumbrates a new operatic form. From our vantage point, we see it to be the first germ of his music drama (to differentiate his creations from traditional opera, Wagner will call them music dramas) as a religious rite.

In 1842, Wagner took the first important step of his career when, at the age of twenty-nine, he accepted the position of Royal Kapellmeister (conductor) in Dresden. For the next eight years he proceeded to make history with triumphant performances of his opera *Rienzi*, the composition of three more operas, and finally his involvement in the revolutionary uprising of 1848–49. As a result of this he had to flee Germany with a price on his head. The opera *Rienzi* (the name of the title character in an opera about a fourteenth-century Roman tribune) Wagner considered derivative, though I happen to hear in it music both fine and original. For him his career as a composer of new, original works began with the world premiere of *Der fliegende Holländer* in Dresden on January 2, 1843.

To give you a context for what has been discussed in chapter 2, this was the day before Donizetti's *Don Pasquale* had its debut in Paris. Wagner's new opera was not particularly well received. The audience was disappointed not to hear a more traditional work like *Rienzi*, so heartily applauded the previous year. In time, however, *The Flying Dutchman* would become for some their favorite of Wagner's operas: Of his major works it is, indeed, the most traditional and the most Italianate. In this opera the melodies, frequent and quite catchy at times, are expressed through set pieces—arias, duets, choruses, and ensembles—in the Italian operatic tradition. Increasingly, in the monumental works yet to come, Wagner would do away with these conventions. An entire act in these later works, often lasting an hour or more, would constitute a musical continuum of what Wagner called "endless melody," he having done away with all arias and recitative.

To get to these works, first we must introduce the three great Dresden operas of the years 1842–50, for not only are they the means to his music dramas to come, but they also are in and of themselves masterworks. The first of them, *The Flying Dutchman*, is both a direction through Weber back to Beethoven as part of the creation of German romantic opera and the first significant step forward to the great Wagnerian music dramas. *Tannhäuser* and *Lohengrin* followed *The Flying Dutchman*. Then with *Der Ring des Nibelungen (The Nibelung's Ring)*, *Tristan und Isolde*, *Die Meistersinger von Nürnberg (The Mastersingers of Nuremberg)*, and *Parsifal* the face of opera history was altered forever.

DER FLIEGENDE HOLLÄNDER (1843)
The Flying Dutchman

Already mentioned is Wagner as a rare opera composer in setting his own poems. In the history of opera there are fewer than fifteen world-famous operas wherein poetry and music are by the same person. Most of them are by Wagner. This is another important aspect distinguishing his operas from others. Wagner was a good poet, no Goethe or Schiller, to be sure, but better than countless hacks who made a living pumping out libretti for one opera after another. Who better than Wagner could know what he wanted and needed by way of a text?

For *The Flying Dutchman* he went to Heinrich Heine's story of the legend associated with a Dutch sea captain who, attempting to round a cape in a terrible storm, swears he will succeed even if he has to sail forever. Hearing his oath, the devil puts on him a curse condemning him to sail until he can find a woman who will release him by loving him faithfully until death. The Dutchman is permitted to come ashore once every seven years to seek such a woman.

As the opera begins, a term of seven years has expired and the Dutchman will anchor and come ashore. But first, you need to know the characters and something of the overture. The characters are:

DALAND, a Norwegian sea captain, *bass*
SENTA, his daughter, *soprano*

ERIK, a hunter betrothed to Senta, *tenor*
MARY, Senta's old nurse, *contralto*
Steersman on Daland's ship, *tenor*
The Dutchman, *baritone*
Dutch sailors, Norwegian sailors, and Norwegian girls

The setting is a remote Norwegian fishing village; the time is the eighteenth century.

Wagner's original intention was for the opera to be played in one act without intermission—another of his breaks with tradition. But people must go to the potty and to have a refreshment, so in spite of Wagner's intent, normally the opera is performed in three acts. I will tell the story as Wagner wanted it, pausing only long enough for a parenthetical interjection noting act breaks of most performances. It is, I assure you, a rewarding undertaking, either as neophyte or when you have some Wagner mileage on you, to borrow, rent, or buy a video of *The Flying Dutchman*, familiarize yourself with the story, and play the opera nonstop the way Wagner wanted you to experience it.

It is a little masterpiece, less long than many movies you have watched without even thinking about it, of about two and a half hours. Had you been in the house in Dresden the night of January 2, 1843, Wagner, not yet thirty years old, in the orchestra pit conducting, you would have heard some of the most melodic, original, and dramatic opera music ever written during what then was nearing the two hundred and fiftieth anniversary of this art form's beginnings. To this day *The Flying Dutchman* has not lost a note of its splendid originality. Wagner's genius bloomed much, much later than Mozart's, but when the operatic flowers came out they appeared in an extraordinary array.

This opera is a bonanza. Such is apparent from the first notes of the overture. More than one hundred and fifty years after it first was heard it remains one of the most familiar and popular operatic orchestral pieces in concert halls and on recordings heard even by millions who know not one other note of this opera.

In his compositions Wagner, increasingly, will utilize musical themes—he called them motifs—to represent or to identify characters, concepts, and animate or inanimate things. In *The Flying Dutchman*, the Dutch sea captain has a musical theme and Wagner uses it several times in this famous overture, whose depiction of a storm at sea has no equal in operatic literature. Then, as the storm subsides, the Dutchman's theme again is heard but in a quieter manifestation. Peace and resolution follow and Wagner has condensed his entire opera into less than twelve minutes of a magnificent overture, all without a note having been sung.

"Leave it at that," the anti-Wagnerians or those who like their Wagner better without words will plead, but if you buy into such nonsense you will bypass one of the original treats in opera history.

Act I

Following the overture, called by one esteemed Wagner scholar the first and by far the best sea-picture ever portrayed in music, the curtain parts to reveal Daland's ship not far from his home port at anchor in a snug harbor where he put in during the storm. The music of the overture and the opening scene—indeed, much of the conception for the entire opera—came to Wagner aboard a ship taking him and his wife from Riga to London. He was fleeing creditors. During the voyage, a violent storm forced the captain to seek refuge in a Norwegian fjord. Wagner became familiar with life at sea during this voyage, and he represents sailors' tasks and chants in the "Hojohe! Halloho!" chorus heard after the overture.

Daland has gone ashore to get his bearings. He is surprised to find he can see his own home from atop the cliff. Returning to his ship, he orders his fatigued crew below to rest, calls the steersman to his watch, and goes below to his cabin. The steersman, too, is tired and he fights the desire to sleep by singing about the woman he loves and soon will see: *Mit Gewitter und Sturm aus fernem Meer* ("Through thunder and storm from distant seas"). It is a lovely song set to an enchanting tune, but the exhausted sailor is asleep before he can finish it.

The storm intensifies again, the wind whistling and blowing in the orchestra. A second ship enters the harbor, steers next to Daland's ship, and anchors there. Daland's is a normal ship of a Norwegian captain who makes his living at sea. The second ship is not in any way normal. The masts are black, the sails red as blood, the crew spectral, and the sinister-looking captain, dressed all in black, sings of his fate forever to sail until he finds a woman eternally faithful. It is the Flying Dutchman and he sings, *Die Frist ist um* ("The term is passed"). Every seven years (seven years being "the term") the Dutchman is allowed ashore to look for the faithful woman. Goethe had sparked considerable interest among German poets during the first half of the nineteenth century when he introduced his *Ewig-weibliche* ("an idealization of a woman who with understanding, love, and self-sacrifice brings purpose and peace to the man in her life"). Wagner, the wandering compos- er fleeing creditors and unable to find a lasting home, obviously identified himself with his opera about a woman whose self-sacri- fice and eternal love redeem a doomed man roaming meaningless- ly forever.

Daland comes on deck. The two captains acknowledge each other and meet on shore. The Dutchman tells of his wanderings, requests shelter in return for a casket of refulgent jewels, and, hav- ing learned that Daland has a daughter, asks permission to wed her. Mystified, Daland yields nevertheless, to the promise of jew- els and more treasures to come. The captains have a fine duet, Daland anticipating the pleasures of great riches and the Dutch- man longing for peace. They return to their ships. The storm now having abated, the Norwegians weigh anchor, the Dutchman promising soon to follow. The scene ends with various tunes depicting the ocean and life at sea. When the opera is divided into three acts, this is the end of Act I.

Act II

When played in a single act, this music accompanies a change of scene showing a room in Daland's house. Senta sits transfixed, staring at a picture on the wall of a bearded man dressed all in black while her friends sit at spinning wheels and join Mary in song as they spin. Few melodies by Wagner have had more univer- sal appeal than the spinning song, *Summ' und brumm', du gutes Rädchen* ("Whirl, whirl, good wheel"). Already in this opera, Wag- ner has captured an ocean tempest in music. Now we actually hear spinning wheels spin. (His friend Franz Liszt, years later, would make a piano transcription of this music, contributing to its enormous popularity as it spread through Europe and then abroad.)

Mary chides Senta for not spinning and all express concern over her preoccupation with a man in a picture. Does not Senta already have a man to love? She is betrothed to the hunter Erik. Senta asks Mary to sing the legend of the poor, fated man in the picture. Mary refuses so Senta sings *Johohoe! Johohohoe!* (Yoho- hoe! Yohohohoe! etcetera), her celebrated ballad telling the woeful tale of the black-masted ship with blood red sails captained by a ghostly man and ghostly crew relentlessly sailing forever. The pale captain can be saved from this dreadful fate only by "a woman who will be faithful to him unto death." Senta turns again toward the portrait and continues, "O pitiable captain, when will you find her? Pray to heaven, that God may send him a woman who will be ever faithful." As her great ballad ends Senta proclaims:

> I am that woman! My love shall save you.
> May God's angel guide you to me.
> I shall be your salvation.[†]

Erik, who has entered at this moment, asks Senta if she is going to betray him, then announces the arrival of Daland's ship. The young women run off to greet the men, leaving Erik and Senta alone to sing a duet.

He reaffirms his love for her, to evasive responses. Erik departs in despair. Alone, Senta iterates a fragment from her ballad as the door opens and there with her father stands the Dutchman. Senta stares at the doomed sailor, ignoring for the first time in her life her father, who praises his guest, asks her to consider him for her husband, and departs perplexed by his beloved child's inexplicable silence. Daland gleans nothing in the reciprocating stares of the Dutchman and Senta. Equally entranced by this remarkable fulfillment of their dreams, the Dutchman and Senta proclaim their awakening love in a duet beginning with the sea captain's recollection of a vision from long ago: *Wie aus Ferne längst vergang'ner Zeiten* ("A vision remembered from the distant past"). When Daland returns, it is clear to him that he may announce their betrothal at a feast already in preparation. When divided into three acts, Act II ends with this scene.

Act III
When played in a single act, there is here a change of scene to the merrymaking aboard the Norwegian ship. The music separating these scenes comprises numerous themes, both of land and of sea, now familiar to the audience. The two ships lie at anchor in the harbor in front of Daland's house, the Norwegian ship gaily lighted, the Dutchman's dark, silent, and ghostlike. Norwegian sailors sing a jaunty chorus and dance a hornpipe, some of the most tuneful music in the entire score. Women bring food and drink from

---

[†] Richard Wagner, *The Flying Dutchman* (Decca Records Libretto, translation by Ulric Kaskell), p. 21

Daland's house. An offer to share made to the unseen crew of the other ship is answered only by eerie silence.

The Norwegians call again, then commence to taunt the invisible crew. Suddenly wind and water begin to stir in ominous activity around this strange vessel. Blue flames flash in its rigging and the weird and wild crew reveal themselves as they sing a chorus striking fear into the hearts of the Norwegians. The women flee, and the men—making the sign of the cross—go below, themselves now taunted by mocking laughs of the Dutchman's crew.

Senta comes out of her father's house, Erik following. All has become calm again except Erik, agitated and heartbroken having learned of Senta's new love. Senta wishes not to talk but Erik insists reminding her of the day they, with her father's approval, pledged undying love. The Dutchman, present and hidden, overhears these words and misconstrues them. Again to sea he will go, nevermore to set foot on earth. He steps forth to chastise Senta for mocking him with promises of eternal fidelity. She throws herself before him vowing never to let him go. The Dutchman declares there is "no faithful love on earth" and hails his crew. Senta reveals that she knows his story. She throws herself in his path. Her love will save him. Thinking her doomed, Erik calls for help, bringing forth sailors and women. The Dutchman departs, boards his ship, and sails for the open sea, his now familiar magnificent music all but overwhelming us. Senta runs to the cliff and calls to the Dutchman, "Give thanks to your angel who spoke. Here I am, faithful unto death." She leaps into the sea. Immediately the Dutchman's ship splinters and sinks. In the first rays of the rising sun, transfigured forms of Senta and the Dutchman are seen embracing as they rise from the wreck toward heaven and music of great calm and beauty ends the opera.

∽

The Flying Dutchman is a good start with Wagner. My wife, whose love of the overt melodic sweep of Verdi and Puccini captured her at an early age, immediately took to this opera when she saw it for the first time. I recall both my wife's pleasure with this tuneful work and the bizarre behavior of the woman sitting behind us. Beginning with the first scene, she commenced to talk incessantly. First, I turned in my seat and glared piercingly, to no avail. A subsequent "Shhh" also failed to quiet her. Finally, fit to be tied by her rude, improper behavior, I turned and forcefully said, "Will you please be quiet?" She was quiet until the end of act one when she rose, put on her coat, and loudly made it clear to her companions that she was headed for home, concluding with "I really do not understand why that man is so upset! Doesn't he know he can buy the recording?" Unfortunately, she was not the only ill-mannered idiot I have encountered in an opera house.

It was not just the tuneful quality of this opera my wife responded to. Wagner's music supports the unfolding of the action with themes representing the ocean, life at sea, and the central characters. When we consider his huge tetrology, the four operas of *Der Ring des Nibelungen*, commonly known simply as *The Ring Cycle* or just *The Ring*, more will be said about Wagner's use of musical themes meticulously melded with his poetry into a unique synthesis.

Here let me note only the two most dominant themes in the score of *The Flying Dutchman*, the one associated with the Dutchman, the other with Senta. The motif depicting the doomed, wandering seafarer is made from three different notes, repeated and made of long and short duration until twelve notes have been sounded. Six notes, using this same process of repetition of long and shorter values, and extending them through more than one octave and using seventeen notes in all, is the theme representing Senta. The strings make the first sounds, immediately followed by bassoons and horns representing the stark theme associated with the Dutchman heard first in the overture. Senta's music is that of the ballad she sings early in Act II.

Starting with such simple musical skeletons, Wagner is able to portray the despair and hope of the Dutchman as well as Senta's preoccupation with saving him. His genius for orchestration gives to these few notes an astonishing variety of colors and intensities. Their repetition at appropriate moments of the drama knit the story into a remarkable musical tapestry. That which is sung, that which we see on stage, and that which we hear in the orchestra make an extraordinary dramatic synthesis of the arts. The orchestra—and more about this will be noted later—becomes for Wagner one of the central characters. His orchestra is not merely an accompaniment to songs. It is a living force with a language of its own expressed through musical themes.

If you do begin your introduction to Wagner with *The Flying Dutchman*, as I hope you will, let me caution you not to run out and buy the first recording you come to. Even though the role of Senta has fewer demands than Wagner places on sopranos in his monumental music dramas, hers is not an easy part. Wagnerian sopranos must have a big voice, one rich in the lower register moving smoothly and consistently up to and through the highest notes, where never should there be screeching.

Several years ago, I was with a small group of opera friends enjoying a fine dinner in an excellent restaurant. We were celebrating the same-day birthdays of a gentleman in the party and an internationally acclaimed soprano who sings Wagnerian soprano roles as they ought to be sung. A new recording of *The Flying Dutchman* became the subject for discussion, specifically the interpretation another soprano gave to Senta for which she had received considerable recognition. Seldom at a loss for an opinion, I expressed bewilderment, claiming, "She screeches her high notes." A kind man in the group defended the soprano: "Well, yes, she does have trouble in the upper register but she is a superb actress." The soprano in our group, a woman of great tact and humility, was pushed into a corner as the group pressed for her opinion. After a pause she said, simply, "Since she is such a good actress perhaps she ought to have limited her career to the legitimate stage."

Opera is awful when sung badly. If our introduction to opera is through a screeching soprano or a baritone grating on the ears, is it a wonder that we are put off? The operatic voice is not given to everyone. Nature must have ordained a wondrous set of pipes, and many years of practice and study go into their development. Once in an opera house you can always close your eyes to poor acting, but how do you close your ears to bad singing? Of course, the glorious performance happens only when those who have mastered singing *and* acting come together. The great singing actor or actress is a rare find but fortunately, today many young opera singers, attending to both arts, are working endlessly with talented coaches to achieve the lofty goal, and they will if they do not get greedy and attempt too often too many roles in too many different places around the globe.

∽

By now I am sure you have asked yourself, "What is religious about Wagner's first masterwork?" This good question requires a careful reply. The religious quality is other than those few references to God in the poem. Too often many limit their understanding of what is religious to beliefs and creeds associated with only the world's great religions, usually in their institutional forms, the least tolerant limiting religious authenticity to their own exclusive tradition. Any student of religion ought to know of the need for a broader definition, one that includes not only adherents to the most prominent of the world's religions, Jews, Christians, Hindus, Buddhists, Moslems, for example, but admits as well those whose religious beliefs differ: Indians of the Americas; tribal Africans; Aborigines of the Australian outback; Eskimos of the frozen tundra; thousands of natives of Pacific lands and islands; and many more.

An inclusive definition of *religious* must allow for the grand variety of attempts to gain some understanding of what, if anything, exists beyond the visible world and to comprehend our relationship to a power or those powers, if such exist, above or beyond nature, a power or powers being for some the source of all life and giving unto it its ultimate purpose and meaning.

An all-inclusive definition of *religious* even permits a place to those who follow no system of beliefs but who on their own seek to know their place in whatever aspect of the human experience seems to transcend the world as it is known to science and to reason. Many nineteenth-century romantics who followed no traditional religious road thought of themselves as exceedingly religious in their intellectual and emotional efforts to make sense of the human experience and to find some meaning to life's swirl through what often seemed a bombardment of random, purposeless events. Romantics sought redemption from the confusions of everyday life.

Wagner effortlessly identified with the wandering Dutchman who is mysteriously redeemed by Senta's love. This was the first but not the last redemption of man by a woman's self-sacrifice and love treated operatically by Wagner. Indeed, redemption through love will be the central theme, taking different forms, of most of his operatic creations. This theme of redemption gives to *The Flying Dutchman* a religious dimension, Wagner's initial step toward the transformation of opera into music drama as a manifestation of art perpetuating religious truth in an age when valuable religious experiences no longer dwelled in traditional, institutional religious expressions.

Romantics loved to catholicize. They were nurtured by Catholic ritual, longed for Catholic community, were turned away by sober, colorless Protestantism, and used Catholic symbols but—more often than not—all without becoming believing Catholics. Wagner's next opera, after *The Flying Dutchman*, is an excellent example of this. That opera is *Tannhäuser*. Here the religious dimension is even more apparent. On October 19, 1845, again under Wagner's direction, this work had its world premiere in Dresden.

TANNHÄUSER (1845)

After *The Flying Dutchman*, all of Wagner's operas are born of his intense immersion in the study and contemplation of medieval mythology and history, the obvious Catholic trappings of *Tannhäuser* deriving from such sources. The Catholic context of the opera is so apparent that critics attacked Wagner, after the world premiere, for his glorification of Catholicism.

There was at the time an active liberal movement in German Catholicism and Wagner was accused of having accepted a bribe from its party to write an opera supporting its cause. Only through the passage of time, persistent denial, and an authentic involvement in pagan and heathen legends was Wagner able to convince press and public that his *Tannhäuser* was not an opera about Catholicism. The opera looked to be Catholic because its setting allowed for numerous Catholic elements, and the pope and Catholic pilgrims figure prominently in the story. Behind the Catholic facade, however, is Wagner's real concern: the conflict of sacred and profane love and, again, a man's redemption through a woman's love.

There was a historical Tannhäuser. He was a knight and *minnesinger* (lyric poets of Germany, twelfth to fourteenth centuries, who sang their songs) from Salzburg, born about 1200, whose surviving poems picture him as one more interested in poetry, music, and—quoting a line of his verse—"fair women, good wine, dainty meats, and baths twice a week", than in the pursuits of a knight.

Wagner's opera is based on legend, prominent and popular in medieval Germany, and an actual event, a "Contest of Song at the Wartburg" during the reign of Landgrave Hermann of Thuringia about 1207. The legend tells of the time Tannhäuser spent with Venus, goddess of love, on her mountain of pleasure, where, with the goddess and her court of beautiful women, he reveled in the delights of the flesh. Song contests were common and much anticipated events in the Middle Ages, especially during the reign of one so committed to the arts as was the landgrave Hermann. Tannhäuser was a small boy, less than ten years of age, when a famous Contest of Song at the Wartburg (Hermann's castle) actually took place, but here Wagner bends history to fit his own needs. His Tannhäuser is a mix of legend and history, melded into one: the Tannhäuser who leaves the Venusberg (the mountainous realm of the goddess of love) to return to the real world, where he shocks all who have gathered at the Wartburg for the song contest by singing not of courtly and saintly love, as expected of him, but rather of the joys of sensual and profane love in the Venusberg.

There exist two versions of this opera. The original, called the Dresden Version, had its premiere, as I have mentioned, in Dresden in October 1845. The second version Wagner prepared later for a special performance in Paris in 1861. (What he altered and added for what is known as the Paris Version and why, though interesting, is a subject outside the purpose of this book.) In portions of the later version, we hear a more sophisticated and more mature Wagner; his revision was made fifteen years after significant further developments as an artist. Our concern is with the original version, and be assured that you are not missing anything, for all the great tunes are there.

The opera is in three acts and the central characters are:

VENUS, goddess of love, *soprano*
TANNHÄUSER, knight and minstrel, *tenor*
HERMANN, landgrave (ruler) of Thuringia, *bass*
ELISABETH, niece of the landgrave, *soprano*
A shepherd boy, *soprano*
Minstrel knights:
    WALTHER VON DER VOGELWEIDE, *tenor*
    BITEROLF, *bass*
    WOLFRAM VON ESCHENBACH, *baritone*
    HEINRICH DER SCHREIBER, *tenor*
    REINMAR VON ZWETER, *bass*
Sirens, pilgrims, Thuringian knights, nobles and their ladies, pages.

The scene is Thuringia at the beginning of the thirteenth century.

The overture, preceding the opening of the first curtain, is one of Wagner's most memorable compositions, so much so that it lives independently of the opera in countless concert performances and recordings. Another way of saying this is to acknowledge how a multitude of classical music lovers who know their concerti and symphonies but do not go to the opera know and love this music from concert performances. A friend of mine of many years, who does, by the way, go to the opera, once said to me, "Peter, when I die all I want for a service is to have a recording of the Overture and Venusberg music from *Tannhäuser* played at my funeral."

In this music, Wagner says it all. As he did with that of *The Flying Dutchman* overture, Wagner summarizes his opera by utilizing prominent themes in the drama. Increasingly, throughout his career, Wagner will rely on stating, developing, and mixing musical motifs as his means of creating remarkable orchestral sounds. They became the trademark of his genius and made him world famous. Wagner's use of these musical themes, or motifs, will undergo a transformation during his career as an opera composer, and this book will outline basic aspects of that transformation.

In earlier works, his motifs are brief musical phrases used in a literal and consistent manner to depict a character or designate a place or thing. For example, there are musical motifs, created by Wagner, to represent the feverish, seductive revelry and bacchanal of the Venusberg just as the coming and going of pilgrims has its distinctive music. When we hear these themes in the drama their association is immediately evident once we have become familiar with them.

Tannhäuser makes a more sophisticated use of these musical motifs than does *The Flying Dutchman*, more than three dozen having been identified. I used the word "identified" because Wagner certainly did not make a little pamphlet wherein he wrote out all his motifs and put names to them. Scholars and musicians studying Wagner's writings and compositions soon and easily noted how poet and composer increasingly were working within him hand in hand and how magnificent was becoming his synthesis of word and tone. *Tannhäuser* is a giant step in this direction. In this work, his fifth opera, we hear for the first time something of what in time would become Wagner's new operatic form.

The overture makes use of the most prominent thematic material in the opera. These themes have, of course, through time, become exceedingly well-known melodies. None to me is more beautiful than the theme of the song of the pilgrims, its two different strains sounding in the orchestra to portray the motion of their coming out of the distance and their passing on their way. Then the Venusberg music takes over, announced first by the violas suggesting feverish sexual pleasures. In the orchestra, before the curtain rises, Wagner has set forth the tension between the sacred and the profane and the source of conflict in Tannhäuser's soul from which he will be released and redeemed by Elisabeth's love.

Act I

The curtain opens on the mountain grotto of Venus showing a waterfall, bathing naiads, dancing nymphs, and reclining pairs of lovers as supine sirens rest on the bank. Venus, on her couch, and Tannhäuser, his harp by his side and his head on her lap, are absorbed in the uninhibited sensuality of the setting. This first scene is the Venusberg Bacchanal. Soon it is apparent that Tannhäuser's mind is shifting elsewhere. Venus probes the cause and asks him to sing to her. *Dir töne Lob!* ("May praise resound to you") begins their duet as he thanks her for pleasures but reveals his mortal desire to return to the human world. She remonstrates and attempts seductively to retain him. He seeks salvation for his sins. She declares that atonement for him will never be possible. He departs.

As the scene is transformed, he awakens in a beautiful valley below the castle of the Wartburg. We hear sheep bells in far-off hills, a shepherd sings his song, pilgrims on their way to Rome sing theirs, and Tannhäuser offers a brief prayer as the other voices fade into the distance. It is a beautiful scene. The final episode of this first act now finds Tannhäuser alone. We hear sounds of huntsmen, and soon he is greeted by the landgrave of Thuringia and minstrel knights, who except for Wolfram do not at first recognize him. The group welcomes him and invites him to rejoin them. Tannhäuser, however, feeling the terrible burden of his transgressions, cannot resume his past with them until Wolfram reveals that Elisabeth, the landgrave's niece, has pined for him since he went away (this an interesting bit of information coming from Wolfram, who, we will learn, is himself in love with Elisabeth). This revelation changes Tannhäuser's head and heart and the act ends with a chorus joyfully praising their reunion.

Act II

In the orchestral introduction to Act II, Wagner anticipates both Elisabeth's joy over Tannhäuser's return to the Hall of Song, where in the past he so often triumphed, and the joy of the minstrel who has returned to the mortal's world. All is not without some fore-boding, however, for into this happy tone poem intrudes a brief reference to the wrath of Venus.

The curtain opens on an empty Hall of Song in the Wartburg. Elisabeth enters and when she is portrayed by a great Wagnerian soprano her celebrated greeting, *Dich, teure Halle* ("You, dear Hall, I greet again"), can lift us out of our seats and onto our feet to commit the unpardonable Wagnerian sin of applauding while an act is playing. (This I know, for it is precisely what one of my opera-loving great-uncles did after the wonderful Norwegian soprano Kirsten Flagstad had sung this exhilarating greeting. As Flagstad finished singing, my rotund Uncle Alec spontaneously soared to his feet, applauding, but soon was shushed back down into his seat with equal alacrity.).

In this second act of *Tannhäuser*, with the advantage of hind-sight we can see how Wagner's creative urge to make a perfect synthesis of words and music is beginning to take opera in a new direction. Wagner always avoided Italian recitativo or German singspiel dialogue to carry forth a plot with pauses for emotions to be expressed or contemplated in set pieces: arias, duets, ensembles. Elisabeth's greeting, nevertheless, has every manifestation of a traditional aria, and as the act progresses other now famous excerpts are heard, a duet and a chorus, for example. But once the landgrave enters, greets the guests, and the song contest is under way, an unbroken musical continuum has begun and carries to the end of the act without what we would recognize as a traditional operatic excerpt.

Every word for Wagner had its counterpart in tone, none to be differentiated from another as more important. Such a musical con-tinuum is an early manifestation of what would become designated "endless melody," an approach to composing Wagner will develop to the point where each act of an opera, first note to the last, is an integrated, unbroken whole wherein all aspects of a drama—words, music, action, sets, and costumes—are conceived as a perfect syn-thesis, a single artistic expression. That is why we do not clap dur-ing an act. Applause would be a meaningless and intolerable inter-ruption of Wagner's unified, unfolding dramatic action. There is ample time to clap after the curtain falls, as my uncle learned.

After Elisabeth's greeting Wolfram and Tannhäuser appear in the hall. Elisabeth urges them in but Wolfram remains in the background. Does he love Elisabeth so much that he will restore her happiness by reintroducing Tannhäuser (whom Elisabeth also refers to by his other name, Heinrich) into her life, thus destroy-ing any hope of her reciprocating his own love for her? After vague responses to her wondering where has he been, a long declaration of love between Tannhäuser and Elisabeth finally is made, Wol-fram in the background commenting succinctly on the hope now vanishing from his life. The two minstrel knights then depart.

The landgrave enters and greets his niece, then, trumpets her-ald the arrival of guests for the Contest of Song. Here begins a scene of extraordinary splendor, with one of Wagner's all-time most appealing choruses: *Freudig begrüssen wir die edle Halle* ("Joyfully we greet the noble Hall"). The landgrave announces that the subject of the song contest will be the true nature of love. From a cup Elisabeth draws the name of the first contestant. It is Wolfram, who sings eloquently of a pure, ethereal love, alluding vaguely to Elisabeth as his inspiration. Another testimonial to vir-tuous love is sung by Walther, the second contestant.

Significant approbation from the guests has honored both, but Tannhäuser responds to their songs with a reawakening of the uninhibited pleasures of endless, erotic passion in the Venusberg. He sings of this, shocking everyone. Biterolf intercedes and chal-lenges him to a duel, but the landgrave and Wolfram restore order and Tannhäuser continues with his evocative outburst, this time directly in praise of Venus: *Dir, Göttin der Liebe, soll mein Lied ertönen!*

> To you goddess of love, shall my song resound!
> With loud voice I sing your praises!
> Your sweet charm is the source of all beauty,
> and every gracious miracle comes from you.
> He who in passion closed his arms about you
> knows what love is, and he alone—
> wretched are you who never enjoyed her love;
> go down there, go into the Venusberg!

Enraged knights and nobles draw their swords. The women flee, except for Elisabeth, who stands before Tannhäuser pleading he be spared and allowed to seek salvation. A lengthy ensemble ensues, Tannhäuser praying, Elisabeth pleading. The others, believing him accursed, nevertheless agree to spare him. The landgrave proclaims that Tannhäuser's only hope for salvation lies in his joining a second wave of pilgrims, now heard in the dis-tance, on their way to Rome to seek papal absolution.

Tannhäuser cries out *Nach Rom!* ("To Rome") and hurries after them as the act concludes.

Act III
The orchestral introduction to the third act, representing the pilgrimage of Tannhäuser, is made from motifs associated with the pilgrims' song, Elisabeth's pleading, and Tannhäuser's wretchedness, among others. The curtain parts on a valley below the Wartburg. It is an autumn afternoon. Elisabeth, kneeling before a shrine of the Virgin Mary, awaits Tannhäuser's return. Wolfram stands nearby. Pilgrims sing as they approach, then continue on, Tannhäuser not among them. Elisabeth prays, politely declines Wolfram's invitation to walk her home, and departs. Wolfram sings a song comparing Elisabeth's beauty to the Evening Star. It is one of Wagner's most serene musical inspirations.

A ragged pilgrim then strays into Wolfram's midst. It is, of course, Tannhäuser, who recounts his adventure. In Rome, even though thousands were granted forgiveness by the pope, he was denied. Forgiveness could no more be granted him than could the pope's barren staff bloom with flowers. Reviving, Tannhäuser announces he will return to the Venusberg. He envisions the goddess of love, whose voice is heard proclaiming a welcome to her "unfaithful husband." Wolfram, attempting to restrain him, mentions Elisabeth's name. Tannhäuser, enraptured, repeats it as the vision of Venus disappears with the goddess's words, "I have lost him."

Wolfram explains to Tannhäuser that he has just been absolved through Elisabeth's intercession. For him she died. As her funeral cortege approaches, Wolfram guides Tannhäuser to her bier. There, beside her, he falls dead. Dawn is breaking, a new wave of pilgrims passes proclaiming the miracle of the pope's staff; it has borne flowers. Tannhäuser, indeed, has been saved. All sing praises to God as the opera ends.

To me the music of this act is a continuum from the orchestral introduction through the final chorus, but partly this is due to my knowing it so well. There are unquestionably the set pieces of traditional opera. They will be found on any compilation of highlights of this opera and each in its own right has become a famous Wagnerian excerpt. They are the choruses of the pilgrims, Elisabeth's prayer, *Allmächt'ge Jungfrau, hör mein Flehen!* ("Almighty Virgin, hear my prayer"), Wolfram's lovely song to the Evening

Star, Tannhäuser's long narration of his unsuccessful pilgrimage, and the conclusion of the opera. These excerpts, isolated from the remarkable continuum of music in this act, represent some of Wagner's most well-known and popular music. Even though it is not in the vein of the singable, popular hit tunes that Italian opera audiences of this era expected, *Tannhäuser's* fame soon spread far and wide, for there are few who could remain untouched by the power and beauty of these melodies. Wagner's serious dramatic intent—the victory of the sacred over the profane—is missed by many who become absorbed in the beautiful music. Tannhäuser is redeemed, freed forever from the hold of Venus, by the mystical, religious intercession of Elisabeth's love.

Tannhäuser is an exceedingly personal operatic experience for me. It is the first opera I ever saw. My father took me. I was eight or nine and he had prepared me for the occasion, as he would many other times in the years to follow, by telling me the story of the opera and playing excerpts from his record collection. In relating the story he had emphasized those aspects he assumed (correctly) would have greatest appeal for a young boy: minstrel knights, swords, harps, and pilgrims. One excerpt I knew every note of and even could recite some of the words. It was Wolfram's "Song to the Evening Star." My father had sung this for me many times in his beautiful, warm, rich baritone. This song and those of the pilgrims were my first favorites from this opera. My response to the beauty of these melodies was immediate and intuitive. It would be many years before I gained any aesthetic understanding of what Wagner was doing and why.

Now, of course, the remarkable synthesis of words and music is obvious to me and I can appreciate each as a separate entity almost as much as when melded. All these years later when I see the Evening Star, Wagner's words come to mind. What a beautiful scene this is. Wolfram has asked Elisabeth whether he might depart with her. Her simple gesture both thanks him for offering and declines. What must next be done must be done alone. Wolfram understands. He has heard her prayer to the Virgin asking for release from the world. He watches her depart, sits, and begins to play his harp in the twilight. In the orchestra we hear strains of his Act II song praising spiritual love. Darkness descends and horns in the orchestra suggest doom. Wolfram improvises and begins to sing: *Wie Todesahnung Dämmerung deckt die Lande.* We do not need to believe in the mystical qualities of the poem to recognize its beauty:

Like a portent of death, twilight shrouds the earth
and envelops the valley in its sable robe;
the soul, that yearns for those heights,
dreads to take its dark and awful flight.

 The lovely orchestral accompaniment to the beginning of this song now becomes the softest pianissimo in the strings as Wolfram's words become almost spoken dialogue as he continues, after a pause, by addressing the Evening Star, which has come into view:

There you shine, o fairest of the stars,
and shed your gentle light from afar;
your friendly beam penetrates the twilight gloom
and points the way out from the valley.

The beautiful melody of the star then is sung first in the orchestra, then by Wolfram:

O my fair evening star,
I always gladly greeted thee:
from a heart that never betrayed its faith
greet her when she passes,
when she soars about this mortal vale
to become a blessed angel out there.

An orchestral coda plays on as Wolfram resumes his musing.
 During the performance to which my father took me, I recall being quite perplexed as I anticipated Wolfram's song. I had no idea at that age what a medieval shrine of the Virgin Mary was. There was Elisabeth, kneeling with hands folded in prayer, singing to this box on a stake. Having been well schooled by my father on opera house etiquette, I waited until after the performance to ask, "Why did Elisabeth sing a prayer to a birdhouse?"
 Tannhäuser, also, was the last opera my father and I ever talked about together. He was visiting me and my family in Vermont. "You have studied Wagner in school. I wish you would tell me what you learned about *Tannhäuser*," he said. "You know it is my favorite of his operas." On and on I talked, my father listening and asking questions.
 Returning to his home, strong, happy, and seemingly healthy, he died suddenly from heart complications soon thereafter. Sorting

through sheet music and scores in his music room I came across the score to *Tannhäuser*. Inscribed inside on the well-worn front cover was my paternal grandmother's name, below it that of my father. Throughout the score, in his hand so familiar to me, were many pencilings and notes made throughout the years and I realized that even to the very end of his life, there still was much he could have taught me about his favorite Wagner opera.

LOHENGRIN (1850)

Three months before the first production of *Tannhäuser*, in October 1845, Wagner had made a sketch of *Lohengrin*. Unlike *The Flying Dutchman* and *Tannhäuser*, this was not to be yet another opera of a doomed man's redemption through the sacrificial love and death of a woman. The answer to the questions "What is *Lohengrin* about?" and "What is religious about it?" are not as easily provided as was the case with its immediate predecessors. To this day, the opera remains open to a variety of interpretations. Though the setting of *Lohengrin* is medieval Christianity, Wagner's prose writings tell the reader it is not an opera of Christian testimony. Wagner considered it a psychological tragedy in which love and faith are destroyed by doubt. He conceived it as a Germanic counterpart of the Zeus and Semele myth from ancient Greece. Zeus appeared before Semele, who asked to see him in all his majesty as god of lightning. Zeus complied and Semele was destroyed.

Increasingly, Wagner was becoming fascinated by classical Greek antiquity. Wagner's grandson Wieland, a prominent stage director, made his interpretation of this drama before he died in 1966, a version I happened to see. Wieland Wagner was the driving force of revolutionizing his grandfather's dramas through modern, abstract productions. He de-emphasized the traditional approach of naturalism to focus on mythic and psychological dimensions. Realistic scenery was replaced by simple, abstract forms, the most powerful scenic effects being created by a masterful use of lighting.

In 1996, Wagner's great-grandson Gottfried staged his intriguing and controversial interpretation in Dessau, and though I missed the performance, I have seen film clips and even before the production enjoyed a morning in Gottfried's study going over the text, pictures, sketches, and the entirety of his interpretation from the original conception through his rehearsal of the cast.

Perhaps there is no final answer as to what *Lohengrin* is about.

Perhaps it is as Wieland Wagner once said of his work, "Every new production is a step on the way to an unknown goal." Nevertheless, we can know much of what Wagner intended when we place the opera within the context of what was happening in his life during the time he created it and take careful note of anything offering clues as to what the opera is about and wherein are to be found its religious dimensions. More than anywhere else, our resolve is rewarded in an event pertaining to Wagner's duties as appointed court conductor.

On the fifth of April 1846, Palm Sunday, Wagner presented Beethoven's last symphony to the Dresden public. His choice was determined not only by the fact that the symphony was almost totally unknown there but also for personal reasons. The winter of 1845–46 had not gone well for him. Repeated attempts to break out of the unimaginative routine of the court's artistic life had been frustrated at every turn by complacency and conservatism. Failure in frivolous Paris had been one thing, but to be scorned and rejected on his own soil was another. He plunged into the preparation of the Ninth Symphony as an escape from an imperfect real world into the ideal.

Beethoven's Ninth was thought by some to be the work of a deaf madman. Seventeen years after Beethoven's death this great symphony still had not been given a comprehensible performance, but for Wagner this music was a mystical region he understood and where he could be alone. In presenting such a formidable work as Beethoven's Ninth, Wagner was aware he was breaking comfortable tradition and challenging the musical understanding of both his musicians and their public. To assist their comprehension of the symphony, he prepared explanatory program notes making use of carefully selected passages from Goethe's *Faust* that he thought approximated in words what Beethoven said more fully with tones. In the short preface to these notes he wrote, "Though it must be admitted that the essence of higher instrumental music rests in its uttering in tones a thing inexpressible in words, we believe we may distantly approach the solution of an essentially impossible task by calling certain lines of our great poet Goethe to our aid . . . " By the use of these excerpts, Wagner developed the themes of struggle, the quest for joy and happiness, and universal brotherhood. Referring to the close of the first movement, he says a gloomy mood expands "to take possession of a world that God had made for *joy*" but in the final movement happiness and universal brotherhood win out: "With God to consecrate our *universal love*, we now dare taste the *purest* joy."

The religious foundation of these themes is obvious and this alleged capacity of music to express the ineffable is a more advanced form of Wagner's musical mysticism. Beethoven's final symphony is neither church music nor sacred music in any traditional sense, yet in Wagner's mind what Beethoven had done was to consecrate the symphonic form. To him this made infinitely more sense than trying to express religious content in the older musical forms of Bach and Handel. Music was for him a mystical religion in which he heard and grasped the eternal truths lying beyond the reach of human speech.

Wagner's performance, by the way, was a resounding success: the first truly intelligent rendering of that magnificent symphony.

Just as he had heard the eternal speak through Beethoven's Ninth, he was now impelled to try his own hand at priestly mediation in *Lohengrin*. There is an easily recognized religious quality to the opera: Elsa, charged with the murder of her brother, asserts her innocence and agrees to accept the judgment of God; King Henry arranges for a trial by combat and Elsa chooses a knight seen in her dreams. She prays to God to send her champion; to the amazement of those gathered for the combat, he arrives in a small boat pulled by a swan. Men sing of the miracle while ladies offer thanks to God. In the end, the knight reveals he is Lohengrin, son of Parsifal, a servant of the Holy Grail.

This use of a Christian setting as the foundation for his opera is one of three ways in which religion and art come together in *Lohengrin*. Wagner, however, never spoke of this side of the opera as having any important religious significance for him. The setting is Christian but Wagner's concern is not limited to this one historical religion. He considered, as already noted, his opera the Germanic version of the Zeus and Semele myth. *Lohengrin* is a psychological tragedy, not Christian testimony. As we can see in *Tannhäuser* the conflict between the demands of the spirit and those of the flesh, *Lohengrin* deals with the destruction of love and faith by doubt. The tragic consequences that doubt has on love and faith are not Christian alone. This example of mythical truth appears in many cultural forms and is not the insight of a single tradition. Wagner was becoming increasingly interested in the idea that through the myths of the people the ultimate truths of the human situation are revealed. This is the second way religion and art come together in the opera. The third way is the most fascinating and for our purposes the most significant.

Wagner prepared a programmatic guide for the now famous prelude to the opera. Repeating for his own work what he had recently done for Beethoven's Ninth, he tried to approximate with words what only music can fully express:

> Out of the clear blue ether of the sky there seems to condense a wonderful yet at first hardly perceptible vision; and out of this there gradually emerges, ever more and more clearly, an angel host bearing in its midst the sacred Grail. As it approaches earth it pours out exquisite odors, like streams of gold, ravishing the senses of the beholder.

The vision draws near, climaxing in the revelation of the Grail. The beholder drops to his knees. The Grail covers him with light and

> consecrates him to its service; then the flames gradually die away, and the angel host soars up again to the ethereal heights in tender joy, having made pure once more the hearts of men by the sacred blessing of the Grail.†

How are we to interpret this? Is there room for a position between two extremes, in which these words are either a statement about the art of music with no religious significance or an expression of the Catholic faith? Indeed there is. Wagner had only recently claimed (in his program notes on Beethoven) that the essence of instrumental music was its ability to utter the inexpressible through tones. The music of his prelude, therefore, expresses more than he can say with the words of his programmatic elucidation.

He was beginning to see, as was just noted, cross-cultural truths in the myths and folktales of all people. By his use of mythical materials and through the practice of his theory of music, Wagner was presenting in his opera a statement of certain human

---

† Ernest Newman, *The Wagner Operas* (Alfred A. Knopf, New York, 1963), p. 127

truths as he understood them, truths not limited to this or that historical tradition or institution but expressible through them—in this instance, medieval Christianity. The vision of the Grail in the prelude is a historical manifestation of the Catholic faith, but mystical experiences are not owned by Catholics alone. Music, Wagner was convinced, does not express a particular thought, feeling, or belief. Music expresses the eternal idea, not its historical manifestations. This is moving in the direction of the more sophisticated developments in Wagner's thinking, which we will observe after his study of Schopenhauer in 1854, when his latent Platonism comes forth.

I do not want to be guilty of reading future refinements of his thought into these observations on his prelude to *Lohengrin*, yet I do believe that at this time Wagner was making the distinction between the eternal idea and particular expressions of it. The joy that is sounded so magnificently in Beethoven's Ninth Symphony is not, for Wagner, an expression of Protestant Christian joy. It is the sound of joy itself: joy residing in the structures of the universe and available to all people in all times regardless of faith or race. The words Wagner used to point to a mystical experience are limited by the German language and his choice of Christian terminology. The tones he uses in the prelude to *Lohengrin* have no such limitations. Through them Wagner expresses all he can about the mystical experience. From his program notes, we know the prelude is about a purifying power from beyond the pedestrian world that appears in our midst as a vision to remind us of our size and our finite place in the eternal arrangement of things. Enlightened by this vision, one can rise and serve a higher calling. Ultimately, *Lohengrin* is about religious mysticism.

Wagner completed *Lohengrin* in 1848. The opera had its premiere in Weimar on August 26, 1850, in an impressive performance produced and conducted by his friend Franz Liszt, but Wagner was not there to hear it. The year before, well disguised and with forged documents, he had snuck out of Germany and gone to Switzerland in self-imposed exile, a political revolutionary with a price on his head (more later on this fascinating episode when we consider *The Ring Cycle*). It would be fourteen more years until Wagner could hear this beautiful masterpiece of his early years, the opera many consider the most lyrical he ever wrote.

The story, again, links legend and history. The legend pertains to the Holy Grail and the knights of the Grail, who keep it.

Though the Holy Grail commonly is associated with the chalice (or cup) drunk from at the Last Supper, according to medieval legend it is "the platter used by Our Savior at the Last Supper, in which Joseph of Arimathea received the Savior's blood at the cross." Wagner's confusion is evident. Lohengrin is a knight of the Grail. King Heinrich I of German is historical: He is Henry the Fowler (876?–936), who fought the Hungarians. The characters are:

LOHENGRIN, *tenor*
KING HEINRICH, *bass*
ELSA, daughter of the late Duke of Brabant, *soprano*
FRIEDRICH VON TELRAMUND, a noble of Brabant, *bass or baritone*
ORTRUD, a sorceress and the wife of Telramund, *mezzo-soprano*
HERALD, *bass*
Nobles, pages, Saxons, Brabantians, and Gottfried, Elsa's brother, a brief silent part.

The scene is Antwerp; the time is the first half of the tenth century.

We quoted Wagner's doctrinal elucidation of his now famous prelude played prior to the opening of the curtain on the first act. Unlike the prelude to *The Flying Dutchman* and the overture to *Tannhäuser*, both made from prominent tunes in the opera and both being an orchestral expression of the essential events of the opera, this prelude, though thematically related to music in the drama, depicts the mystical appearance of the Holy Grail, its radiance, and its disappearance. Nothing written by Wagner before this and little, if anything, after approaches the sheer lyrical beauty of this music. There should never be applause following this prelude!

Act I
The curtain parts. Near Antwerp, on the bank of the Scheldt River, the people of Brabant are called together by King Heinrich's herald. The king intends to resolve a local matter before raising an army to fight the Hungarians. Telramund accuses Elsa of having murdered her brother Gottfried in order to inherit the dukedom of her late uncle. Telramund, as we will learn, driven by his wife,

Ortrud, wants the job. All are horrified by the accusation. Elsa is summoned by the King. She comes. Her behavior is of one physically present but mentally and emotionally elsewhere. She responds to the King's questions by relating a dream. Known simply as "Elsa's Dream," *Einsam in trüben Tagen* ("Alone in troubled days"), is a beloved gem for soprano voice in all Wagnerian literature.

How strange all this is, a knight sent from heaven in a dream to champion her cause. It is determined that God will judge through mortal combat between Telramund and Elsa's mysterious knight. Trumpets sound the challenge but no knight appears. Elsa pleads, "Oh Lord, tell my knight now to help me in my need," and as women pray and men wait, before their eyes a miracle happens. In the distance, a boat towed by a swan with a golden chain in its beak has come into view carrying in it a knight in silver armor. The boat arrives at the bank, the knight debarks, bids the swan farewell and to return to whence they came, and announces to the King his readiness to defend the maid against the false accusations. To Elsa he then asks, "If I am successful in combat, will you marry me?" She agrees. He then states his bizarre terms (reminiscent of Semele, who was not to get too close to Zeus):

> You must never ask me
> nor try to discover
> where I come from
> nor what is my name and heritage!

Elsa vows she will never ask. The combat is arranged, the trumpets sound, the mysterious knight fells Telramund but spares his life for repentance. Ortrud fears all her hopes have vanished, and as Telramund faints at her feet all else proclaim the victory of Elsa and her knight and the act ends. In the entire act there is but one famous aria, in the traditional sense, "Elsa's Dream," but throughout there is much music of great lyric beauty. The chorus of nobles, knights, and their ladies has a significant role in this act. Although often there is little action, with a multitude standing and commenting on the unprecedented happenings, who cares? What they have to sing is glorious, a perfect lyrical musical manifestation of the medieval pageantry depicted before our eyes. So good is this music that everyone, no matter how jaded one may be, soon is swept into accepting all the pomp, the proclamations, the combat—indeed, as some would have it, the "whole nine yards" of having been transported into the Middle Ages, with its accoutrements of sword and spear and shield. Death to the producer that gets it into her or his head to make a twentieth-century remake of this opera. Can people not learn to leave well enough alone? (I will have more on this touchy subject.)

Act II
The second act opens on the citadel of Antwerp at night. Telramund and Ortrud sit on a step next to the cathedral gate, he wondering why he stays with a woman who cost him his reputation, she rebuking him. He reveals that she inveigled him into marrying her and into concocting a story accusing Elsa. She taunts his cowardice by which he succumbed to the mysterious knight. She will have her way through her own powers, she says. Again, Telramund falls under her spell as she explains how the mysterious knight, who is under some spell of his own, will be rendered powerless if forced to disclose his name and lineage. Elsa, she asserts, must be induced to pose the forbidden questions and Telramund must charge the knight with sorcery. Together they will have vengeance.

Elsa appears on the balcony and sings her second famous aria of the opera: *Euch Lüften, die mein Klagen* ("You breezes, which my laments often so sadly filled, now I must tell of my happiness"). Ortrud dispatches Telramund to the background, calls to Elsa, and begins to unfold her scheme by asking what she did to deserve being reduced to such a hapless state. Elsa goes inside to descend and join Ortrud, who, momentarily alone, cries out to her pagan gods to aid her sweet revenge. Elsa appears, feels sorry for Ortrud, asks forgiveness, and promises to help restore her and her husband to respectability. Ortrud plants the evil seed, warning Elsa not to trust too blindly in her happiness—it may disperse as quickly as it came. Elsa vows trust in her knight; Ortrud, in an aside, vows to undermine it. The two women go inside. Telramund reappears, exclaiming confidence of being avenged through his wife's cunning.

Dawn now is breaking. The herald announces that Telramund is banished and the mysterious knight, the new Protector of Brabant, and Elsa that day are to be married. From among the many people four nobles, cohorts of Telramund, isolate themselves. They do not want to follow the new knight and when Telramund reveals himself to them they conceal him. A procession begins, preceding the now magnificently attired Elsa. Ortrud steps forth and stops everything, claiming Elsa has usurped her rightful place. She begins to taunt Elsa, who cannot even call her husband-to-be by his name. She chides her for knowing nothing of this champion of hers, insinuating all has been hidden because he is a traitor.

The mysterious knight appears, as does the King, then Telramund, who demands from the knight his identity as proof against evil magic as the source of his powers. The knight reveals nothing. Only Elsa can compel him to speak.

Here begins an extraordinary ensemble: Ortrud and Telramund rejoicing over doubt on Elsa's face, Elsa wanting now to know the secret, and the knight praying to heaven to protect Elsa as the King and his followers proclaim their confidence. Telramund confides to Elsa that he will help her learn what she wants to know, but the mysterious knight takes her, trembling, to the cathedral, she avoiding Ortrud's look of triumph as the second act ends.

Again, we have been treated to wonderful music, but music not easily packaged in little chunks of excerpts with obvious neat beginnings and clean, crisp ends. Elsa has her aria and Ortrud her pagan outburst, but much of the act flows in a unified, unbroken dramatic unfolding. Wagner has moved even closer to what will be, six years later in his next opera, *Das Rheingold (The Rhine Gold)*, a complete break with opera's long-standing format of alternating conversational episodes with set musical numbers. As Franz Liszt was at work preparing *Lohengrin* for its premiere in Weimar, Wagner wrote to him from exile, "Nowhere, in the score of *Lohengrin*, have I written the word 'recitative'; the singers are not to know there are recitatives in it. On the contrary, I have made an effort to calculate the speech rhythm so exactly and sharply that the singers need only sing the notes exactly in accordance with their note values and the rhythm will be correct." What Wagner was intending was the creation of a drama wherein all words have a musical counterpart, where words and music are linked, and where, thus, each supplements the other and enforces the other in an uninterrupted expression of dramatic situations intensified through music.

As Wagner moves closer to his goal in *Lohengrin*, it becomes harder to distinguish what are known as opera excerpts or highlights. All this notwithstanding, *Lohengrin* has its highlights, the most famous of which are heard at the beginning of the third act.

Wagner did not always work start to finish. With *Lohengrin* the music of Act III came first, Acts I and II thereafter. Act III, accordingly, is the most traditional in structure.

Act III

The prelude to the final act, brilliant and brief, portraying the wedding festivities, is an orchestral *tour de force* of immense worldwide popularity second only, in this opera, to the music following it: the "Bridal March" and "Bridal Chorus." Rare is the bride who does not know this music—music known even to those who will never hear the name Wagner in their lifetime. Left alone in their bridal chamber, Elsa and her husband, in a significant duet, declare their love. This long scene normally is referred to as the "Bridal Chamber Scene." The mysterious knight is able to call his beloved by her name but she knows not his, and she wants to know it so she can say it. He begs her not to ask but she believes she sees his swan boat in the near future arriving to take him from her and she blurts out the dreaded questions just as Telramund and his followers break into the room with swords drawn. In time, the knight is warned by Elsa. He quickly draws his sword from its scabbard and in one speedy thrust kills Telramund. His terrified friends drop their swords and obey the command to take the deceased to the King. Elsa, who has fainted, is lifted to a couch by her husband.

For the finale, the scene changes to a meadow by the riverbank. Nobles arrive, trumpets sound, the King and his forces enter, and Heinrich proffers a bit of chauvinism about Germany ready for the foe. Telramund's compatriots enter and disclose his body as decreed by the mysterious knight, the Protector of Brabant. Elsa, looking confused and distraught, enters. Then comes the knight, attired in silver, as he was in the first act, to explain the reason for Telramund's death. Then he tells of Elsa's betrayal. Even though she was misled by miscreants, he must answer her—she has posed the forbidden questions. Then he must depart, for his special power will have dispersed. *In fernem Land* ("In a distant land") begins this superb narrative wherein the mysterious knight tells of the Holy Grail and those who serve it, he being one of them:

> I was sent here by the Grail:
> my father Parsifal wears its crown;
> I am his knight and Lohengrin is my name.

He must now go. His swan, summoned, has appeared and is greet-ed by him in more famous music for the tenor: *Mein lieber Schwan!* ("My beloved Swan"). Lohengrin grieves at having to leave Elsa and falls to his knees in prayer. Above him appears a dove. The swan sinks beneath the swirling waters, and resurfaces as Gottfried who will now rule Brabant. Ortrud's last hope is dashed and she rages. Lohengrin departs, his boat now towed by the dove; Elsa calls after him, then lifelessly sinks to the ground in her brother's arms as the opera ends.

The words, Wagner has made it clear, tell of love destroyed by doubt. The music, Wagner tells us, takes over where the commu-nicative power of words leaves off to express the inexpressible, a mystical something or other affecting human lives. Interpreta-tions of *Lohengrin* continue to this day. Obviously, Telramund and Ortrud represent evil in their dishonest and ambitious quest for power. Equally apparent is the religious purity of Lohengrin, in the service of the Grail, God, and Goodness. By alerting us to his use of the Zeus and Semele myth, Wagner's Lohengrin, like Zeus, is of a divine realm beyond the limits of rational thought. Ulti-mately, their being must remain a mystery.

Elsa, like Semele (whose name is the Phrygian word for "earth"), is of the human world. Things human and things divine are different and must remain separate. When humans take the initiative to trespass from their realm into the other, they bring about their own self-destruction. The divine mysteriously may manifest itself on earth but this is the only way it can be experi-enced by human beings.

Of all Wagner's operas, I find the story of Lohengrin the most troubling, never fully satisfying. I think poor Elsa got a raw deal, but always there is the seductive beauty of the lyrical music to win us over into listening again and again, and in this way Wagner—unusu-al because he wrote both the words and the music—has his day. No matter what we think of the story, *Lohengrin* is a masterpiece.

One more item about this opera must be known, for its promi-ncnt place in opera lore demands it. The much loved Austrian tenor Leo Slezak, a fine singing actor who possessed an extraordi-nary sense of humor, was waiting in the wings, as Lohengrin, for his Act I entrance as the noble silver knight carried on in a boat pulled by a swan. But before he could get into the boat, it com-menced its journey, empty, across the stage. A stagehand had missed his cue and Lohengrin missed his boat. Slezak turned to the person next to him behind the curtain and asked, *Wann geht der nächste Schwan?* "What time is the next swan?"

∾

Wagner's story with his big music dramas will continue after the three early masterpieces of Giuseppe Verdi have been placed properly within the context of the history of nineteenth-century opera.

Verdi, unlike Wagner—who once he wrote *The Flying Dutchman* had no failures—had operatic ups and downs. Accordingly, no attempt will be made here to be comprehensive with Verdi's operatic corpus. Doing so would mean a book on Verdi within a book; furthermore, such a book on Verdi has been written in three comprehensive and extensive volumes by Julian Budden. It is the intent of this book only to introduce you to the six most famous of Verdi's many operas.

Giuseppe Verdi

VERDI I: THE FIRST MASTERWORKS

In 1836, Verdi wrote his first opera, *Rocester*, eventually lost. Despairing over the deaths of his wife and two daughters, all within a brief period, Verdi swore he would write no more, having completed by then three more works, but fate intervened to decree he would compose *Nabucco* in 1842, the year of Wagner's successful early work *Rienzi*. *Nabucco* brought Verdi significant attention. It is interesting that the two dominant figures in nineteenth-century opera history both had their first real success in 1842, and were both born in 1813.

Verdi followed with *I Lombardi* in 1843 and *Ernani* in 1844, the same year in which *I due Foscari* appeared. The year 1845 saw *Giovanna d'Arco* and *Alzira*, 1846 brought *Attila*, and 1847 *Macbeth*, Verdi's first expression of his lifelong fascination for Shakespeare, and *I masnadieri*. *Il corsaro* appeared in 1848 and *La battaglia di Legnano* and *Luisa Miller* in 1849. Early in 1850 *Stiffelio* appeared. *Nabucco* (an abbreviation for Nubucodonosor Italian for Nebuchadnezzar) is notable for being one of few operas in repertory on a biblical subject, for its superb second-act prayer for bass voice, *Tu sull' labbro*, but primarily for the most celebrated of Verdi's many famous choruses, *Va, pensiero*, a lament of the Hebrew slaves for their lost fatherland. *Nabucco* also is notable because it was Verdi's first great success, establishing his career as a composer. The lament of the Hebrew slaves had for many

Italians considerable political significance and, accordingly, is known as the first of his "patriotic choruses." Those Italians living under Austrian rule heard in its words and music their own desire for independence.

During Verdi's life, this beautiful music became known to countless numbers of his countrymen. After he died in Milan in January 1901, in his eighty-eighth year, his remains were to be interred the following month next to those of his wife. The city of Milan, naturally, had expected to give him a great public funeral but Verdi's will was explicit in his desire for a simple remembrance. His body was to be taken from a chapel to its final resting place. There would be music. The chorus and orchestra of the famous La Scala opera house (scene of many Verdian triumphs) was augmented by a Municipal Band conducted by the young and not yet world-famous Arturo Toscanini, all waiting in an ice cold wind. Then, as the cortege exited the chapel, Toscanini gave the downbeat and quiet chords sounded the beginning of *Va, pensiero* sung by the choristers of La Scala, who were joined quite quickly and spontaneously by the thousands lining the way. All knew this music by heart. For so many years it had expressed their own longings and hopes for freedom:

> Fly, O thought, on golden wings:
> To rest on those slopes and hills
> Where the fragrant wind blows soft and warm,
> Sweet breezes of my native land.

This could happen in Italy, the land that gave birth to opera and nurtured it with the same love expended on a child. This could happen in Italy, a land where opera is as much a part of the inhabitants' lives as the air they breathe and the wine they drink. This could have happened only in Italy. It is unthinkable in these United States, unfortunately. However, in my more than twenty-seven years of producing a weekly opera program on radio, this chorus is the second most often requested excerpt on those occasions when "listener's choice" determines the programming—some measure of its international renown. The most popular request, far and away? I will answer this question when we discuss Georges Bizet (and, no! it is not from *Carmen*).

Critics have tended to rank both *I Lombardi* and *Ernani* below *Nabucco*. I have no interest in choosing a favorite among them, for remarkable tunes inhabit all three of these engaging early Verdi operas. They do lack the profound dramatic intensity of Verdi's most mature works but they are operas you should eventually know. *I Lombardi* has several wonderful prayers and two "patriotic choruses" almost as famous as "Va, pensiero" and in *Ernani*, along with many other stirring vocal excerpts, is one of Verdi's most inspired creations for soprano voice, Elvira's aria *Ernani, involami* ("Ernani, fly with me"). *Macbeth*, too, has captivating and poignant political choruses. Verdi knew how to stir the Italian soul. The *Nabucco* chorus, and those of *I Lombardi* and *Macbeth*, wrenched the hearts of his audiences, wittingly or unwittingly serving the political end of patriotism. These operas remain known as Verdi's "patriotic operas."

It would be, however, three operas of a highly personal content written in succession between 1850 and 1853 that brought international acclaim to Verdi. These three have become among the most popular and often performed and recorded operas in the world. In 1851, Verdi shook the operatic world with his first overwhelming work of genius, *Rigoletto*, followed in 1853 by *Il trovatore (The Troubador)* and *La traviata (The Woman Led Astray)*. These three and three other operas written late in his career, *Aïda*, *Otello* (based on Shakespeare's *Othello*) and *Falstaff* (based on Shakespeare's *The Merry Wives of Windsor*), constitute the six of Verdi's more than two dozen operas you must know about first. Many other Verdian treats can follow, but these six are an indispensable start.

We now defer to the first three of these written in an astonishingly short period; the same time during which Wagner would be absorbed in beginning the colossal undertaking of composing the poetry and music of his huge *Ring Cycle*, a work that would alter operatic history.

As we commenced our introduction to Giuseppe Verdi in one of my beginning courses on opera, I recall reassuring an intimidated class of students—concerned because they could neither read music nor understand Italian—that they needed to know only six words of Italian to understand Verdi's operas: *maledizione* (curse), *sangue* (blood), *morte* (death), *bàcio* (kiss), *amore* (love), and *addio* (good-bye).

After reading the previous chapter, in which it was essential for us to consider carefully important events in Wagner's life and to explore excerpts from his voluminous writing even to begin to make some sense of the many layers of meaning in his operas, you may conclude my reduction of Verdi to six basic words a flippant revelation of my lower opinion of his place in the world of opera. Absolutely not! My purpose is not to compare Verdi and Wagner, to claim superiority for one. Incontrovertibly, they remain the German and the Italian Shakespeares of opera, and with that I have no quibble. Like yours, my moods vacillate day to day; sometimes I need Verdi, other times Wagner.

My purpose, then, is to establish important differences between these two giants, who were the most significant composers of opera in the nineteenth century and two of the most revered and influential in opera history. In common, above all, was a preoccupation with opera as their destiny. Each contributed to music literature only a few non-operatic compositions of great significance. They were born to compose operas. Other commonalties—an interest in politics and a direct involvement with the course of their country's destiny, for example—briefly will be noted as we proceed. The intriguing differences, however, are both more interesting and more important.

Through Verdi's long career, Italian opera experienced, as a result of his work, a thorough revision. *The Barber of Seville* (1816) of Rossini and Verdi's *Falstaff* (1893), both nineteenth-century masterpieces of comic opera, are miles apart in the evolution of Italian opera, and *evolution* is the critical word when Verdi is concerned. Whereas Wagner's impact on opera was revolutionary, an overt denial of much of the past and a creation of new forms for the future, Verdi worked within inherited structures. Through his great genius, his finest works are those operas many consider the unequaled pinnacle of all Italian opera. I love my Mozart and Puccini too much to go out on that limb, but you get my point, I'm sure.

For Verdi and Wagner the drama was everything, and though they had differing conceptions of how to create dramatic impact, both knew that the essence of opera is the intensification of drama through music. Verdi, however, was far more straightforward than was Wagner. Verdi's operas do not probe layers of philosophical implication requiring hours of exposition. With Verdi, what you see and hear is what you get. Verdi's operas move along quickly, getting right to the point. Of him often it has been written that his most distinguishing characteristic is "getting on with it." Seldom does Verdi keep the listener waiting. He inherited the operatic form of the bel canto giants, its basic ingredients being, you'll remember, brilliant arias for all major voices, love duets, great choruses, and, above all, the expectancy of a string of hit tunes. However, the voices of Verdi's creations would not sing just to display vocal agility and versatility. For Verdi, the human voice was a means to the end of dramatic intensity, not an end in itself. *Rigoletto* is his first masterwork of this sort.

RIGOLETTO (1851)

Of the six Italian words mentioned above, *maledizione* is the word at the heart of *Rigoletto*. Before settling on *Rigoletto* as their opera's title, Verdi and his librettist Francesco Maria Piave called it *La maledizione* ("The Curse"). Eventually, however, they settled on *Rigoletto*, a name derived from the French verb *rigoler*, meaning to laugh, to have fun, to joke; the perfect name for a jester. Piave, by the way, is a significant librettist who would collaborate ten times with Verdi, as well as providing libretti for other composers. In April 1850 Verdi wrote to his friend Piave enthusiastically about a new subject he was considering:

> The subject is grand, immense, and there's a character who is one of the greatest creations that the theater of all countries and all times can boast.

and, a few days later, to his publisher

> *Le Roi s'amuse* ("The King Amuses Himself") is the greatest subject and perhaps the greatest drama of modern times . . . it came to me like a flash of lightning, an inspiration and I said to myself . . . Yes, by God, that one can't go wrong.[†]

Verdi was writing about Victor Hugo's play *Le Roi s'amuse*, based on François I of France, who became for Verdi and Piave, due to the intervention of a censor, the Duke of Mantua. It was not the character of the king, however, that so captivated Verdi's imagination but rather the sharp-tongued, deformed court jester of the king, Triboulet, transformed by Verdi and Piave into Rigoletto.

Verdi boiled over with inspiration, for he composed the

[†] Julian Budden, *The Operas of Verdi* (Oxford University Press, New York, 1978), Vol. I, p. 477

entire score in forty days. The ominous brief prelude, less than three minutes long, introduces music throughout the opera associated with a curse on Rigoletto: the curse at the core of the entire drama. It is intriguing to me how a cultured man like Verdi, educated and well read, and one of the most liberal and progressive artists of his age, would in several of his operas give so much dramatic validity to curses. It is the curse of Count Monterone on the head of Rigoletto that drives this opera to its gruesome conclusion.

The basics of the opera's plot can be summarized quickly. Disguised as a student, the licentious Duke of Mantua has been paying court to Gilda, who, unknown to him, is the daughter of his jester Rigoletto. Unwittingly, the jester is tricked into aiding courtiers in the abduction of a woman. He is unaware that it is his daughter Gilda who is being taken to the Duke. When Rigoletto learns Gilda has been seduced by the Duke, he plots to have him killed by a professional assassin, Sparafucile. When the Duke turns his attention to a new conquest, Sparafucile's sister Maddalena, she pleads for the Duke's life. Sparafucile agrees to sacrifice the next person through his door as victim. Gilda, having overheard this, makes the sacrifice, to the eventual horror of her father. Now, where is there a curse in all of that?

Early in the first act, as the Duke pursues the beautiful Countess Ceprano during one of his many festive parties, Rigoletto taunts her husband until the gay mood instantly is changed by the unwelcome entrance of Count Monterone, whose daughter the Duke has recently dishonored. He has come to the court demanding to be heard. Rigoletto, who hates nobles because they are nobles, ceases mocking Count Ceprano to jeer instead Count Monterone. First Rigoletto imitates him, then, with mock dignity, continues:

> You have plotted against us, Sir, though we in
> true clemency pardon you. It is obviously mad-
> ness that causes you to try to reclaim your
> daughter's honor at such a time.

The insulted Monterone is furious. He turns from Rigoletto to the Duke and says:

> I shall break down your orgies in the end; then I

> shall hear your cries. I shall avenge the insulted
> and blemished honor of my house! Call your exe-
> cutioner if you will: My ghost shall haunt you,
> holding in its hand its severed head, to call down
> vengeance upon you from heaven and earth alike.

Annoyed beyond endurance, the Duke orders his guard to arrest the intruder—Rigoletto, meanwhile, asserting aloud Monterone's madness. Monterone stares at the Duke and his jester, curses them both, then upon Rigoletto's head places the famous curse:

> As for you, serpent,
> You who can laugh
> At a father's anguish,
> A father's curse be on your head![†]

Rigoletto is instantly horrified. Gilda, his beloved daughter, is all that is meaningful and loving in his otherwise demeaning existence as the Duke's acid-tongued buffoon. What portends such a curse?

We can become intoxicated with the melodies in this opera having only a superficial sense of the story, but we cannot participate fully in the drama unaware of Rigoletto's fear of Monterone's curse.

The opera, which lasts less than two hours, is in three acts, though I do know of performances and recordings in a four-act format. Monterone's curse concludes the first scene of Act I, when performed in the original three-act version, or ends Act I when presented in the unusual four-act version. The opera had its first performance at Teatro la Fenice, Venice, on March 11, 1851. It was popular from the start. Many, including exceedingly gifted and sophisticated musicians, consider *Rigoletto* Verdi's greatest accomplishment.

You will find in this opera the perfect beginning for your introduction to Verdi as well as an introduction to a new state of development in the evolution of Italian opera. It has been argued convincingly that with *Rigoletto* the door closes on *bel canto*

[†] G. Verdi, *Rigoletto* (RCA Records Libretto, New York, 1970), p. 5

tendencies of displaying wonders of the human voice as an end in itself and another opens to reveal drama as opera's reason for being. To put this another way, let me record a simple observation: With Verdi's *Rigoletto*, and thereafter in Italian opera, the vocal display of Lucia's "Mad Scene" in Donizetti's *Lucia di Lammermoor*, a vocal recital within the opera, would be unthinkable. The voice now will serve the drama, and the orchestra—once an accompaniment to the voice—becomes another "voice" in the drama. Already it has been noted that the orchestra introduces the curse in the brief prelude to *Rigoletto*.

Verdi and Wagner, though their music can sound as if they were from different planets, were not so far apart in certain basic aesthetic considerations as some may think: For both, a continuous intense dramatic expression became the ultimate goal. The big difference on this account is Verdi's inclination to just do it and Wagner's need to write about it before, and often after, doing it. I will continue to point out similarities and differences between these two contemporary giants of all nineteenth-century opera.

It is Verdi's music that significantly intensifies the dramatic action of *Rigoletto's* story. I have never seen a performance of either Victor Hugo's *Le Roi s'amuse* or the English adaptation, *The Fool's Revenge*. Portraying the court jester in the latter was one of the famous roles of nineteenth-century actor Edwin Booth, brother of Abraham Lincoln's assassin. Probably neither version is on the boards anymore. How could they be, given the success of *Rigoletto*? They wouldn't stand the comparison, for I can't imagine, having felt Verdi's impeccable score course through me hundreds of times, anything more dramatically satisfying on this subject than the opera made from the play. Only curiosity could send me to the play. To answer the above question, you will need to know the characters in the opera, their voice ranges, and the songs they sing.

> THE DUKE OF MANTUA, *tenor*
> BORSA, a courtier, *tenor*
> COUNTESS CEPRANO, *mezzo-soprano*
> MARULLO, a courtier, *baritone*
> RIGOLETTO, the Duke's jester, a hunchback, *baritone*
> COUNT CEPRANO, a nobleman of Mantua, *bass*
> COUNT MONTERONE, a nobleman of Mantua, *baritone*
> SPARAFUCILE, a professional assassin, *bass*
> GILDA, Rigoletto's daughter, *soprano*

GIOVANNA, her attendant, *mezzo-soprano*
A page, *mezzo-soprano*
An usher, *baritone*
MADDALENA, Sparafucile's sister, *mezzo-soprano*
Chorus of courtiers, servants, etc.

The scene is laid in Mantua in the sixteenth century.

Act I

The brief prelude, it has been noted above, anticipates the denouement propelled by the curse's eventual transformation from words into horrible reality. As the curtain parts, the Duke and Borsa are entering a resplendent room in the ducal palace to a little tune establishing the lighthearted merrymaking of courtiers and ladies enjoying a sumptuous party. As pages bustle about among those eating, drinking, and dancing, the Duke and Borsa move forward, the dissolute Duke commenting on his progress with a young woman he has been following to church daily. We do not yet know that she is Gilda, Rigoletto's daughter.

The sight of the beautiful Countess Ceprano diverts the conversation to the Duke's testimonial of free love in the first of his three famous arias in this opera: *Questa o quella* ("This one or that one"). There is so much beauty around him. He gives his heart to no one woman, remaining oblivious to jealous husbands and angry lovers. As the Countess crosses the room, the Duke intercepts her and commences wooing in the presence of her husband while dancing a minuet not unlike one heard in *Don Giovanni*. (There is, of course, considerable similarity in the Don's and the Duke's attitude toward women.) Arm and arm the Countess and the Duke depart, Count Ceprano watching all the while, Rigoletto taunting him before exiting. The music throughout this scene continues to establish a mood of frivolity.

Marullo enters. Unaware that Gilda is Rigoletto's daughter, he announces he has discovered that the ugly, sharp-tongued, deformed buffoon has a mistress, to the delight of all. Rigoletto and the Duke reenter, discussing the Duke's desire for the Countess Ceprano. Unmercifully, the jester mocks Count Ceprano, who, boiling with rage, declares he will have revenge, the other courtiers agreeing to aid him. Rigoletto remains untouched by the threats and all join in proclaiming desire for pleasure.

Two moods, so far, have been established by Verdi's music: the ominous prelude, in sharp contrast with the bubbling, lighthearted tunes associated with the party—even as it is interrupted by Monterone's unwelcome appearance, his demand to be heard, and the curse that strikes horror into Rigoletto's heart as the first scene ends. Will words become flesh?

The change of scene reveals Rigoletto's street. It is night. Rigoletto, ruminating on the curse, unknowingly is being followed by Sparafucile. In less than a minute, before Rigoletto utters a word, the orchestra establishes a foreboding mood in a stalking rhythm. Rigoletto is concerned about the curse. The assassin approaches to offer his services. Rigoletto, not interested at this moment, nevertheless ascertains the man's name and whereabouts. Departing, Sparafucile repeats his name twice, the second time holding the *fucile* portion of his name on a low, long resonate note for a deep bass voice. I can still recall how this moment impressed me as a young boy the first time I heard this opera, and to this day I anticipate it every time *Rigoletto* and I get together.

A great soliloquy for baritone voice follows Sparafucile's exit as Rigoletto is left alone to muse on how similar are he and the assassin: Rigoletto the tongue, Sparafucile the dagger, both cutting; the one making mockery, the other death. Once again the old man's curse insinuates itself into his thoughts. Rigoletto then comments on his awful fate as a jester, the torment of being a clown, and his loathing of the courtiers. A growing preoccupation with the curse returns at the end of this famous *Pari siamo!* ("How alike we are!") monologue. Verdi, in his melody for the Duke's *Questa o quella*, perfectly captured the carefree, self-centered personality of the handsome young nobleman; in the musical theme associated with the curse, a terrifying mood is struck, and equally perfect is the meditative dimension to Rigoletto's great monologue. Verdi, throughout his life, was fascinated with Shakespeare (more on this later), and the *Pari siamo* has all the identifying marks of a great Shakespearean soliloquy. As do Shakespeare's words, so too does Verdi's music suddenly announce a new emotion. In the opera, the music conveys the overwhelming joy of father and daughter as Rigoletto enters his garden and Gilda runs out of the house and throws herself into her father's arms. In other operas, Verdi would compose memorable music for father and daughter scenes, but none more special than this duet beginning *Figlia!* ("My daughter") *Mio padre!* ("My father").

The curse preying much on his mind, Rigoletto cautions her about going out and charges Giovanna to guard Gilda carefully. This duet is supremely beautiful and expressive of father and daughter affection. You need not understand a single word to hear love blending in a warm baritone and youthful soprano, all the more intensifying the anxiety in an audience fully aware of Rigoletto's growing fixation on Monterone's curse.

As Rigoletto goes out into the street, the Duke disguised as a poor student, slips into the garden and hides behind a bush. Rigoletto returns and as he exchanges farewells with his daughter, the Duke overhears and learns of their relationship. Rigoletto departs, Gilda confesses her love to Giovanna, and from behind the bush steps the Duke to declare his passion. He begins their famous duet with *È il sol dell'anima* ("Love is the flame that fires our souls"). Gilda wants to know his name. Claiming to be a poor student, the Duke answers "Gaultier Maldé." Giovanna returns to warn of someone approaching, the Duke departs, and in one of the most celebrated soprano solos in all Italian opera, *Caro nome* ("Beloved name"), Gilda reflects on her love.

Meanwhile, Ceprano, with fellow courtiers, has entered the street preparing to enact his revenge on Rigoletto, who returns, lost in his concern over Monterone's curse until he encounters the masked courtiers. They fool him into believing they are on his street as part of a plan to abduct Count Ceprano's wife, who lives nearby. Rigoletto will join in the prank. They mask him with a bandage. It allows him no sight and little sound, and against his own house, unwittingly he holds the ladder by which the others enter, grab and gag Gilda, and carry her off. Rigoletto, removing the bandage, is stunned to find himself before his own house, a terrified Giovanna in front of him. To music of increasing agitation, he finally utters his daughter's name four times and then exclaims, as the orchestra pounds out the demonic theme of the curse, *Ah! ah! ah! la maledizione!*

He faints as the first act ends.

Act II

The second act opens on a room in the ducal palace where the Duke has another nugget for tenor voice, singing first of his despair over having returned to Rigoletto's house and finding Gilda gone, *Ella mi fu rapita!* ("They have stolen her from me"), then of his passion, *Parmi veder le lagrime* ("I seem to see the tear"). His courtiers enter to reveal in a fetching chorus the abduction of the woman whom they believe to be Rigoletto's mistress and that she is now cloistered in the palace. A knowing and pleased Duke goes off to console her.

Rigoletto enters and here two important voices are at work: Rigoletto feigning levity and the orchestra revealing the jester's anxiety. Unable to contain himself, Rigoletto demands they return his daughter. They are bewildered by this revelation. *Cortigiani, vil razza dannata* ("Courtiers! Vile race"), he denounces them in anger, but when they bar the way to the Duke's apartment, Rigoletto falls to the floor weeping, begging them to restore to him his beloved daughter. With this magnificent music, representing first Rigoletto's hatred and then his begging, a great singer-actor puts an audience in the palm of his hand. Gilda enters, the courtiers leave them alone, and she tells him almost all, and pleads that he forgive. In another fine father and daughter duet to end the act, Rigoletto will have revenge.

Act III
The final-act curtain opens on Sparafucile's dilapidated inn on a deserted riverbank. Gilda is confessing her love for the Duke to her father, whose mind is on revenge and on proving the young man's perfidiousness. Disguised as a cavalry officer, the Duke arrives at the inn, enters, orders wine and a room, and commences to sing the biggest hit tune of the score, *La donna è mobile*, an ironic declaration of the fickle and inconstant nature of women. Sparafucile comes out and walks off. As the Duke pursues Sparafucile's sister, Maddalena, an unseen Gilda and Rigoletto observe and hear all.

The varying emotions of these four characters, simultaneously expressed in one of the most anticipated quartets in Italian opera, begins with the Duke's wooing: *Bella figlia dell' amore* ("Lovely daughter of love"). He addresses Maddalena, coquettish in her reaction; Gilda, with a breaking heart, comments; and Rigoletto anticipates revenge.

Rigoletto, at the quartet's end, instructs Gilda to go home, assume the attire of a young male, and make her way to Verona, where he will meet her. Sparafucile returns and with him Rigoletto strikes a contract on the Duke's life, vowing to return at midnight to claim the corpse and pitch it into the river.

Now the two famous set numbers of this act are behind you, the Duke's aria and the quartet. As you listen to the rest of the act, consider Verdi's achievement. From his deal with Sparafucile through the storm scene to the heartbreaking denouement, the music and words blend in an unbroken miracle of reciprocal expression: What the words say, the music sounds. It is hard to find a finer example of opera's ultimate power: the intensification of drama through music.

The storm begins. Fascinating is Verdi's use of behind-the-scene human voices in a chorus as a wordless musical instrument contributing to the eerie effects. In *Rigoletto*, Verdi has at times made of the orchestra a "human" voice (for example, "speaking" the curse) and here of human voices makes an orchestral instrument.

The Duke takes a room and soon falls sound asleep. Gilda, who left as her father requested, now has returned. Rigoletto has gone, prepared to return at midnight. As Gilda, undisclosed, listens, Maddelena attempts to dissuade her brother from murdering the Duke, who has, for all his obvious insincere declarations, nevertheless entered her heart. Kill Rigoletto instead, she requests. Gilda, overhearing, shudders. Sparafucile will not do this: He has a contract to honor. He is an honor-among-thieves assassin whose clients have his fidelity. But should any other innocent victim pass through his door before midnight, he would be willing to make a substitution in order to spare the Duke for his sister. This, too, Gilda overhears and the idea she derives from it is all too obvious: "Although he is faithless, I will die for him." She raps on the door, enters, and immediately is dispatched as the storm subsides.

Rigoletto returns as a clock strikes midnight. He pays Sparafucile the remaining portion of their deal and collects his booty sewed into a sack. This he lugs alone toward the edge of the riverbank, having refused Sparafucile's offer to help. As he pulls and tugs he hears off in the distance the Duke's song, *La donna è mobile*, at first concluding it to be an oral mirage of sorts. But then, in a terrible fright, he tears open the sack to see in a lightning flash the torn body of his beloved daughter. Gilda begs forgiveness for what she has willingly done, then dies. The opera concludes as Rigoletto utters again the same menacing words with which he concluded Act I, *Ah! la maledizione!*

For years the opera's biggest number was the Act III quartet, but in 1903 Enrico Caruso made his heralded Metropolitan Opera debut as the Duke of Mantua, and so acclaimed was his portrayal, especially for his *La donna è mobile* aria, that he made this tune into the number one hit of the opera even though sophisticated critics deemed the aria "too plebeian," too popular, too this, too that. In fact, it is a perfect tune, fitting the 'I am the only thing that matters' attitude of the young, self-centered duke like a custom-made glove. Years ago I recall reading an account of how Verdi anticipated that *La donna è mobile* would be the hit of the score, and to keep the music secret, he accordingly until the last minute withheld it from the tenor who was to portray the duke, to the poor singer's great consternation. And it was a hit from the start, for I recall also the account claiming that this music was sung by gondoliers throughout the canals of Venice within minutes after the premiere. Fact or fable, I do not know. But it makes for a fine story.

Verdi, unlike Wagner, did not leave volumes of prose explaining his artistic intentions. I have noted for you, nevertheless, how the last portion of the final act moves seamlessly from one event to another without our feeling as if specified set musical numbers are being performed. Verdi's next work after *Rigoletto is* an opera of set musical numbers, a string of one hit tune after the other, making *Il trovatore* forever among the most popular operas in the world.

IL TROVATORE (1853)
The Troubadour

My introduction to this opera differs in form significantly from my *Rigoletto* presentation, wherein my purpose was to demonstrate the importance of Verdi's music to the drama. Consider a little experiment. Sit in silence and read the libretto of *Rigoletto*, then reread it as you listen to Verdi's music. In which is the drama more intense? But with *Il trovatore*, Verdi's genius is not so much in intensifying drama through music. Because the story is somewhat of a preposterous jumble, we look elsewhere and ask, "Wherein lies the undying phenomenal success of *Il trovatore*?"

This question, unlike some others we have asked, has an easy, quick answer: in its string of memorable hit tunes. The complicated and absurd story has been rescued by a succession of hit tunes almost unprecedented in any other opera. Verdi, of course, was perfectly pleased to write another work with great public appeal, but as he contemplated the *Il trovatore* subject with his librettist Salvatore Cammarano (recall him as the librettist of *Lucia di Lammermoor*), he wrote to him: "If only in opera there could be no cavatinas, no duets, no trios, no choruses, no finales, etc., and if only the whole opera could be, so to speak, all one number, I should find that sensible and right." This is precisely what Richard Wagner was working on at that very moment several hundred miles north in Germany (more on this in the next chapter).

Cammarano, who would write more than fifty opera libretti during his career, already had produced three texts for Verdi: *Alzira* in 1845, *La battaglia di Legnano* in 1848, and *Luisa Miller* in 1849. His conceptions were traditional, however, and his skill was in producing a libretto that allowed a composer ample opportunity to provide an audience with its expectations: cavatinas, duets, trios, choruses, and finales. With *Trovatore* he delivered the goods. Since its premiere in Rome on January 19, 1853, this opera has had immense popularity. In many countries it is the most popular of all operas. This worldwide acclaim has been achieved in spite of repeated harsh critiques of the story as being absolutely ludicrous. *Il trovatore* lives through Verdi's irresistible tunes.

As a young boy, I was immune to the complexities and silliness of the tale. It had gypsies and any story with gypsies or pirates appealed to me. I knew the opera well. I knew all the tunes and the order in which they came throughout the four acts. I was much more familiar with all the music than was my father, who loved to sing the beautiful baritone aria of Count di Luna in the second act. He knew the most well-known other tunes, too, but his preoccupation with Verdi was not *Il trovatore*. He took me to see it, knowing what a favorite of mine it was. "Peter," he said, as we fit ourselves into our seats, "just nudge me in the ribs with your elbow the moment before one of the big tunes comes so I will know all the tunes you love so much." This I did. Walking out along the aisle after the performance, my father encountered an old friend. "Fox, how are you?" the man inquired. "Fine, thank you," my father replied, "except my ribs are black and blue."

Innumerable band students who have never seen, nor never will see, an opera have played a tune or three from *Il trovatore*, and countless are the nineteenth-century music boxes having in their mix of melodies one from *Il trovatore*. For others, the only music from this opera they have ever heard, probably without any idea of what it was they were hearing, came to them from the organ grinder's box as they gave a little monkey, attired in red vest and matching cap, coins for his cup. Perhaps you recall the lines from the poem "The Barrel-Organ" by Alfred Noyes:

> Yes: as the music changes,
>   Like a prismatic glass,
> It takes the light and ranges
>   Through all the moods that pass;
> Dissects the common carnival
>   Of passions and regrets,
> And gives the world a glimpse of all
>   The colors it forgets.
>
> And there *La traviata* sighs
>   Another sadder song;
> And there *Il trovatore* cries
>   A tale of deeper wrong . . .
>
> Go down to Kew in lilac-time, in lilac-time, in
>   lilac-time;
>   Go down to Kew in lilac-time (it isn't far from
>   London!)
> And you shall wander hand in hand with love in
>   summer's wonderland;
>   Go down to Kew in lilac-time (it isn't far from
>   London!)

With *Rigoletto* I suggested you read the libretto, then listen to the music to experience how Verdi's art *intensifies* the drama. Do the same with *Il trovatore* to experience how the music *is* the drama and you will understand in a moment what opera expert Gustave Kobbé, writing years ago, meant when he said, "*Il trovatore* is the Verdi of forty working at white heat." For me the vibrancy, beauty, and passion of this music has never become stale even after hundreds of hearings—mostly because the music is so wonderfully melodic and exciting and, in part, because in certain performances the conductor's heart is pounding, the orchestra is on the edge of its seat, and superb voices are on fire, surging as they pour out sounds of gold and silver.

Only music as stirring as this could salvage the drama that Cammarano derived from *El Travador* (1836) by the Spanish playwright Antonio Garcia Gutiérrez. First, let us sort out the complicated and much maligned plot, then we'll attend to the music. The opera is more easily comprehended when one is aware of significant events that transpired long before the curtain opens on the first act. Basically, these events are the subject of Ferrando's

Act I, Scene 1, narration but they make much more sense when you have done your homework ahead of time, beginning with the characters:

> MANRICO, chieftain under Prince of Biscay, reputed son
>   of Azucena, in love with Leonora, archenemy of
>   di Luna, and a troubadour, *tenor*
> AZUCENA, a gypsy, *mezzo-soprano*
> RUIZ, a soldier in Manrico's service, *tenor*
> LEONORA, a noble lady in the court of the
>   Princess of Aragon, *soprano*
> INEZ, Leonora's confidante and maid, *soprano; sometimes
>   mezzo*
> COUNT DI LUNA, young nobleman in love with Leonora,
>   *baritone*
> FERRANDO, di Luna's captain of the guard, *bass*
> An old gypsy, *baritone*
> Followers of di Luna and Manrico, a messenger, a jailer,
>   soldiers, nuns, gypsies, and unseen monks who sing

The time is the fifteenth century, the place Spain.

Act I

Now what are the events of the past, the story Ferrando relates in the first scene, that you need to know? Count di Luna's father had two sons of almost the same age. When the health of the younger mysteriously began to decline, a meddling old gypsy woman was blamed and burned at the stake. Her daughter Azucena herself the mother of an infant boy, vowed revenge. She snuck the next night into the castle and stole the Count's youngest child. She returned to the spot of her mother's demise, where intense coals still burned, and proceeded to burn the Count's son. What Ferrando does not know, and we will soon learn, is that a distraught and bewildered Azucena mistakenly threw her own infant into the fire. She raised the infant Count as her own son, Manrico, never revealing to anyone her secret, her desire being eventually to have even more revenge, perhaps through Manrico.

Ferrando is entertaining soldiers and retainers with his narration while they are on guard. Count di Luna, obsessed with his love for Leonora, his tale continues, is intent on catching his troubadour rival, who has periodically come to serenade Leonora at the palace. *Il trovatore* is an opera in four acts, each act having two scenes. Ferrando's narrative is the first scene of the first act.

Scene 2 changes to the palace gardens, where Leonora confides her story to Inez about the night she crowned the victor at a tournament. During years of civil strife he disappeared, then returned to realize all her dreams by breaking the silence of a lovely moonlit night with his serenade, sung to the accompaniment of his lute, beneath her balcony. Seized by foreboding, Inez admonishes Leonora to forget this "mysterious man" but Leonora's love is far too deep:

> Either I shall live for him,
> or for him I shall die!

Leonora and Inez go into the palace. To the garden comes Count di Luna. In the stillness of the night he appeals to Leonora to come to him. He is consumed by love for her. He moves toward the steps, but the distant sound of a lute stops him. He knows it is the troubadour. Jealous rage burns within him as the song of the troubadour is heard from afar. The Count closes himself in his cloak, Leonora races down the steps toward him, thinking he is Manrico. She claims he is late. Then, hearing Manrico's voice as he enters, she throws herself at his feet, contrite over the mistaken identity. The Count descries his fury while Manrico and Leonora pledge their love over and over. Sworn political enemies and rivals for the love of the same woman, the two men will fight a duel until death. They run off. Leonora faints, ending the act.

Act II
Each of the four acts has a title. Act I is called "The Duel." Act II is called "The Gypsy," and the first of the two scenes shows a gypsy camp in Biscay. It is almost sunrise on a new day. Azucena and Manrico sit by a fire as gypsies awaken and prepare to go to work. As their famous chorus subsides, Azucena, as if possessed, relates the story of her mother's death and her avowal of revenge to Manrico, who now has learned of the catastrophe of mixing up the babies. Whatever doubts this may have provoked regarding his parentage are stilled by Azucena's assurances that she always has taken care of him. She wants to know why Manrico did not kill the Count during his recent duel. Manrico replies that he does not know. About to run the Count through with his sword, having defeated him, he says, ". . . suddenly I felt a chill run sharply through my body, and I heard a voice from heaven cry out, 'Do not

strike.'" Azucena makes him promise not to falter if fate should allow him a second opportunity to kill the Count.

Ruiz enters. He brings news to Manrico of fighting. The troubadour is to take a command. Ruiz also tells Manrico that Leonora, believing him dead, is about to take the veil at a convent near the castle.

The scene changes to the convent where the Count, with Ferrando and retainers, hover in their cloaks. The Count will abduct Leonora before she takes her vows, but his plan is foiled by Manrico, who, with Ruiz and followers, prevents the abduction. Leonora is hardly able to believe her eyes that Manrico still lives. An impassioned scene ends the act.

Act III

This act is titled "The Gypsy's Son." Scene 1 is the camp of Count di Luna near the fortress of Castellor. It is here that Manrico has taken Leonora to safety. The Count's soldiers capture a gypsy woman whom Ferrando recognizes as the one who in revenge threw the infant "brother" of the Count into the flames. The gypsy cries out to Manrico, as her son, to come to her rescue. More enraged than ever, the Count orders her imprisonment. She is to be burned at the stake.

The change of scene is to a room next to the Castellor chapel. Leonora, Manrico, and Ruiz are there. The lovers are about to be married. Ruiz departs, leaving them a private moment, only to return in great agitation; Azucena has been captured and soon is to be burned. "I was a son before I was your lover," Manrico announces to Leonora, and dashes out with Ruiz and soldiers following to go to Azucena.

Act IV

The act is titled "The Ordeal." Scene 1 shows the ramparts of the Act I palace. There, where Azucena is chained, also is Manrico, whose attempt to rescue his mother has failed. Ruiz shows Leonora the portion of the palace where her beloved Manrico is imprisoned. She wears a ring with a large jewel, beneath which, we will learn, rests a vial filled with poison. We recall her Act II vow to Inez regarding the troubadour who sings beneath her window:

> Either I shall live for him,
> or for him I shall die!

Leonora is found alone with the Count. To his astonishment, she promises to become his wife if he will free Manrico. So overwhelming is his passion for her that he agrees.

The scene changes to the prison tower where Manrico and Azucena are confined. They reminisce about their life in the mountains. Leonora enters, pleading with Manrico to escape. He wonders at what price his freedom has been bought. First, he incorrectly assumes she yielded to the Count, only to realize the truth when the poison she has taken to foil the Count takes effect more quickly than anticipated. She dies in Manrico's arms. The Count, seeking her, finds them and orders Manrico's immediate death. He forces Azucena to watch from the window the execution of her "son." The executioner wastes no time, di Luna exclaims, "It is over!" and Azucena cries out, "He was your brother. . . .You are avenged, O mother." The opera ends on the Count's words uttered in horror, *E vivo ancor!* ("Yet I must live!").

If it's hit tunes you want in your opera, and that's precisely what an Italian opera of Verdi's time was supposed to provide, no other opera of his, on this account, has been more successful than *Il trovatore*. Any creditable opera guide would isolate for a reader no fewer than nine or ten of them. Having made sense of the story for you, the tunes now can be integrated into the action, scene by scene, but I will differentiate more than twenty of them; no wonder my father's ribs were black and blue. This will not be done solely in a "Name That Tune" approach. Many of the *Trovatore* tunes are known to opera lovers in this way, and as you become familiar with the opera you, too, will be able to say, "Oh, I know that! It's *Di quella pira*." Some of the marvelous melodic music, however, will be identified only by scene or episode, and such it is with the first one. By the way, as I list these tunes, if there is an asterisk before the number, as in *6, for example, it means this tune has achieved worldwide hit-parade popularity:

Act I, Scene 1

1. Quite simply it is the entire Scene 1 of the first act already described in detail. This is Ferrando's narration of events. Most guidebooks will list the first big tune as Leonora's famous aria at the beginning of the second scene of this act, but the scene of Ferrando's narration, ten minutes long, is wonderful. It begins immediately. For the first time, Verdi did not write an overture or a prelude to open an opera. Ferrando tells his story, soldiers and

retainers comment, and Verdi's music bounces along just as a good story should. Listen to a recording and follow the words and you will agree with me on counting this the first hit of the score.

Act I, Scene 2

2. *Tacea la notte placida* ("The peaceful night lay silent"). This is Leonora's story about the troubadour who came one night to sing to her. It is among Verdi's most famous arias for soprano.

3. *Tace la notte* ("The night is silent"). Count di Luna has entered the palace garden intent on seeing Leonora: "Ah, love's fire burns in every vein." But this musing is interrupted by the strains of a lute. He knows it is the troubadour coming and he trembles with rage.

4. *Deserto sulla terra* ("Alone upon this earth"). The troubadour's song is brief, less than a minute and a half, but one of the loveliest tunes in the opera and a significant one, also, for it is heard again, with different words, at an important moment in the fourth act. In this tune, Verdi has caught for me the spirit of a medieval troubadour and it is this tune more than any other from this opera that I hear myself humming or singing mindlessly as I finish a chore, or look for a book, or take a walk.

5. The trio of the Count, Leonora, and Manrico that ends this first act is thrilling, the word *love* finding repeated expression because both men love the same woman, who loves only one of them. The word *maledizione* is at the center of the *Rigoletto* drama and the word *amore* is critical to *Il trovatore*, nowhere more so than in this trio, but because it is love mixed with rivalry and jealous rage, Verdi's music blazes with a passionate fire. This is not love of tender sentiment. Leonora has openly and repeatedly proclaimed her love for Manrico, who asserts through such love that he is invincible, while the Count rages *Di geloso amor sprezzato arde in me tremendo il foco!* ("The fire of jealous love burns in me with a terrible flame!"). This trio is on fire.

Act II, Scene 2

*6. Everyone knows the tune at the start of the second act. It is the "Anvil Chorus," one of the most popular tunes Verdi ever wrote. As the gypsies awaken and prepare for work, they sing, pick up their tools, and ask:

> Who brightens the life of the gypsy?
> The gypsy maiden!

The women pour the men a drink of wine and they all sing, several members beating out the time of this hearty metallic tune with hammer blows on their anvils. You'll love it! Everybody does, except, of course, for a few silly snobs who are above anything so lilting, infectious, and popular, as this chorus. These stuffy aficionados deem this "too plebian." My wife wishes me not to tell you what I say to them when I encounter pomposity such as that.

7. The last note of the chorus leads right into Azucena's *Stride la vampa!* ("The flames are roaring!"), her sad song with obscure references to the burning of her mother at the stake. It is followed by a refrain of the "Anvil Chorus" as the gypsies go to work. Alone with Manrico, she is willing to agree to his request to tell her story.

8. Azucena continues her story in another aria, *E tu la ignori* ("To think that you know it not"), not as famous as *Stride la vampa!* Her story elaborates on the events of Ferrando's narration from her own experience.

9. *Mal reggendo* begins Manrico's explanation as to why he did not kill the Count, having defeated him in the duel: "He was helpless under my savage attack . . ." This becomes a fine mother-and-son duet.

10. Another mother/son duet, pulsing and jaunty and less than two minutes long, ends the first scene. Manrico is as determined to be with Leonora as Azucena is to detain him.

Act II, Scene 2

11. The Count, planning to prevent Leonora from taking holy orders by abducting her, enters the courtyard of the convent with Ferrando and retainers, aware that he is undertaking a dangerous task but one that "mad love and injured pride have set for me." He sings the big baritone aria of the score, the aria my father so much loved to sing. It is one of Verdi's loveliest for the middle male voice but also one of his most difficult, ranging widely from low to high—so lovely, one almost is persuaded not to dislike di Luna so much. Cammerano gave Verdi a nice little poem to set:

> *Il balen del suo sorriso*
> *d'una stella vince il raggio!*
> *Il fulgor del suo bel viso*
> *nuovo infonde a me coraggio*
> *Ah, l'amor, l'amore ond'ardo*

le favelli in mio favor.
Sperda il sole d'un suo sguardo
la tempesta del mio cor.

The light of her smile
makes the light of the stars seem pale
The beauty of her face
inspires new courage within me.
Ah, may the love that burns in me
speak to her for me.
May the light of her gaze drive off
the tempest raging in my heart.[†]

12. The Count, certain Leonora soon will be his, exults in the terse, convincing cabaletta, *Per me ora fatale* ("Fatal hour of my life"), nuns sing in the convent, and, calling on courage, Ferrando and retainers prepare to follow orders.

13. Leonora, believing Manrico dead, enters the courtyard with Inez, explaining why she is taking holy orders. The Count emerges from the darkness and announces, "Never," when, all of a sudden, to the astonishment of all, who appears at precisely the right moment to intervene? Manrico and his followers. The act ends with wonderful agitated music in which the Count and his followers, Manrico and his, and Leonora, Inez, plus nuns are all part of this melodic commotion.

Act III, Scene 1

14. We are in Count di Luna's camp where a famous "Soldiers Chorus" opens the act—one of Verdi's most appreciated tunes, by the way.

15. The Count, left alone, is tormented by the thought of Leonora in the arms of his rival. Ferrando enters, telling him a gypsy woman has been caught and Azucena is brought in. She reveals that Manrico is her son, Ferrando recognizes her as the gypsy he knew long ago, and the Count revels in this good news. There is lively music throughout this scene, especially for Azucena. This entire episode, almost hypnotic, is another sizzler from the pen of Verdi.

---

† G. Verdi, *Il trovatore* (RCA Records, New York, 1970, translation by Dale McAcloo), p. 9

Act III, Scene 2

16. Manrico has two famous back-to-back arias in this scene. The first, *Ah, sì ben mio* ("Ah, yes my love"), is a love song for his soon-to-be-bride, Leonora.

*17. But the wedding ceremony is interrupted by news of Azucena's capture and di Luna's plan to have her burned at the stake. Manrico pauses long enough before rushing off to her to sing *Di quella pira* ("The horrid flames of that pyre"), the other tune in the opera snobby types consider "too much." Actually, it is perfectly fitting to explosive power. It is Manrico, beloved son, heart and core, and the aria concludes in a call to arms on the words *all'armi* with one of the most famous high C's for tenor voice in all Italian opera. A high C is almost the highest note, and thus the most dramatic, in the tenor range. The high C on which this aria concludes is famous for two reasons: First, because in spite of all the other exhilarating music Manrico gets to sing in the opera, this ringing and prolonged high note is the one everyone seems to anticipate and appreciate more than any other; and second, because Verdi did not write it. Various attempts to identify the tenor who first took it on himself to raise Verdi's concluding note to a stirring high C have not resolved the question, but after it had become an established tradition, handed from one generation of tenors to the next, Verdi is reported to have sanctioned it, exclaiming, "Far be it from me to deny the public what it wants; put in the high C if you like provided it is a good one." When it is a good one, the curtain falls on the third act to tumultuous applause.

Act IV, Scene 1

18. After a brief recitativo, to orchestral accompaniment, Leonora has another famous aria: *D'amor sull'ali rosee* ("On the rosy wings of love"). This is reminiscent of her first-act aria, *Tacea la notte placida*, except now her hopes for union with an imprisoned Manrico seem doomed and sorrow fills her heart.

*19. From the tower she hears, first, monks singing a hymn, then, soaring over the solemn song of the monks, the well-known melody of her troubadour as he bids Leonora farewell. This little episode, almost five minutes long, is called simply the "Miserere" (a prayer chanted asking the Lord for mercy on the soul of one about to begin the journey of no return). I have an old opera book claiming this is "the most famous scene in Italian opera," and certainly it is the *Trovatore* tune you would have heard the organ grinder play.

20. Leonora and the Count have the duet in which she makes the deal: let Manrico escape and I will be yours. It begins with her pleading *Mira, di acerbe lagrime* ("See the bitter tears I shed"). The Count is naive, desperate for her, and about to be duped.

Act IV, Scene 2

21. The opera's final scene, set in the prison of the fortress, begins with Manrico's *Madre, non dormi* ("Mother, you're not asleep?"). Within this splendid mother-and-son episode is the gem of a duet, *Ai nostri monti* ("Again to our mountains we shall return"): hope expressed by Azucena. This music goes right to the heart.

22. The last bump into my father's ribs came about eight minutes before the dire end when Manrico sees Leonora enter his cell. He exclaims in utter bewilderment *Che! Non m'inganno!* ("Heaven! Can it be!"), and from here to the grisly end one is swept irresistibly along by Verdi's music.

However absurd you may find the story, it will live forever through its unforgettable tunes. While isolating them for an introduction to you, I thought again of Verdi's words, quoted above, to his librettist: ". . . if only the whole opera could be so to speak, all one number." I thought about this and concluded *Il trovatore* is for me just that. The individual arias, duets, trios, choruses, and finales of the old Italian opera tradition all are there, but so magical and marvelous are the innumerable melodies and the manner in which so often they segue one into the other that *Il trovatore* for me, in a sense, has fulfilled Verdi's desire of having made a "one-number" opera. I hope some day, when these tunes have become familiar to you, too, that you will hear what I mean.

Unlike some artists who create primarily for themselves or esoteric and highly sophisticated (small) audiences, Verdi was not ashamed to give his fellow Italians precisely what they expected of him—hit tunes. There is a good story about *Il trovatore* and it goes something like this: Verdi and a famous music critic were discussing this opera as it was being made ready for its 1853 world premiere in Rome. This particular critic's self-esteem was as a most sophisticated gentleman of the arts. Verdi played the "Anvil Chorus" and asked an opinion. It was scorned by the critic as a commonplace. Verdi played the aria *Di quella pira*. The critic denounced it as an appeal to base emotions. Finally, Verdi played the "Miserere" fully anticipating it, too, would not appeal to one of such lofty artistic standards. It did not. Verdi got up from his piano, and, to the utter astonishment of the critic, thanked him and gave him a big hug. "Why?" the critic asked. Verdi enlightened him: "I wrote the opera for the people, not for critics like you. Knowing you do not like it assures me it soon is to be a triumph and will be sung all over Italy." It was! And still is!

Late in life Verdi, always of an extremely independent and individualistic temperament, often altered autobiographical facts to perpetuate his preferred self-made image as the "peasant from Roncole," which is how he liked to refer to himself. He was, however, not peasant born but rather of the middle class. He did not suffer deprivation or poverty, but many believing biographers unwittingly perpetuated Verdi's image of himself until scholarship of the second half of the twentieth century established facts.

He was born sometime between October 9 and 11 in 1813, the exact moment being uncertain because in those days parish priests, recording births, reckoned a new day as beginning with sundown and the Giuseppe Verdi entry remains open to some deliberation. His own story claims he discovered, at a very young age, the ability to play notes on a spinet, later written down, as if his entire musical beginning was his own gift to himself. In fact, his extraordinary gift for music was discovered quite early by his family and nurtured. He began lessons in his third year and experienced virtually no significant interruption in his musical education thereafter, even though his peculiar fancy was the promulgation of being self-taught. He exaggerated his origins to fit a humble, genius self-image.

A dislike of nobility and clergy was not exaggerated, however, and I am sure Rigoletto's denunciations of the nobility had some autobiography in them. In other Verdi operas the clergy will not fare so well, either. Verdi, like Wagner, had little use for inherited power and privilege, the manna that nourished and perpetuated the Church and the aristocracy. Nor did the clergy condone Verdi "living in sin" for eleven years with the soprano Giuseppina Strepponi before they married. Clearly, Verdi's sympathies will lie with the unconventional heroine of his next opera, *La traviata*, the final opera of the three unparalleled early masterworks of the years 1851–53.

The diversity of these operas is remarkable, Verdi's music fitting perfectly the diverse moods and situations: the intensification

of drama through music in *Rigoletto*, the unbroken, unprecedented string of singable tunes in *Il trovatore*, and those frail,
diaphanous, shimmering, delicate melodies of life's brief joy in *La
traviata*, an opera quite unlike any he had ever written before or
would write again.

Rare is the day when I make such a categorical personal
admission as this but *La traviata* is my favorite of many wonderful Verdi operas, a confession somewhat intimidating and daunting from one who now must write about it.

LA TRAVIATA (1853)
The Woman Led Astray

Only a few people, I think, could identify Marie Duplessis; more,
especially those who know theater and film, will have heard of
Marguerite Gautier. However, every opera lover knows Violetta
Valéry. Answering the question—"Who are these ladies?"—will
provide an informed introduction to Verdi's *La traviata*, for they
are, in a sense, one and the same.

In the late 1830s, a peasant girl from Normandy, Alphonsine
Plessis, arrived in Paris seeking work. She was impoverished, fam-
ished, and approximately fourteen years old. When she died of
consumption in 1847, Marie Duplessis, the name assumed by
Alphonsine, was a wealthy celebrity. As her vast acquisitions
were auctioned in her apartment after her death, Charles Dickens
was there with many others to gawk at the luxury and to speculate on the fabulous and unconventional life she had obviously
led. She had lived but a brief few years, but eventually enjoyed a
luxury known to only a few women in Paris. Her childhood in
Normandy had been scarred by a family wherein begging, excessive drink, and debauchery were common—as was abandonment
of children, Alphonsine possibly having been sold by her father to
gypsies.

In Paris, as a seamstress, she earned a meager existence until
her rare beauty overwhelmed a wealthy young nobleman and in an
instant her career as one of history's most celebrated courtesans
began. A succession of rich lovers and patrons provided for every
need, namely all things expensive. One particular obsession was
for the camellias she wore every day (white ones except on days of
her menstrual cycle, when she wore red to signal unavailability)
because she loved them, because they were costly, and because
they had no scent; flowers of strong scent evidently made her

swoon. Obviously, she was an extraordinary person. When she arrived in Paris, an ignorant peasant, she could only write her name. In no time, she learned to read, to write, and to play the piano, and acquired all the manners essential to the underworld high society. It was not just her beauty and sexual permissiveness that enchanted men. She was a wonderful conversationalist. The famous pianist and composer Franz Liszt was fascinated with her. They quickly became good friends. And more.

In 1844, Marie now twenty, the talk of Paris, and a trendsetter in fashion and style, met another twenty-year-old. He was an unpublished writer son of a famous father, Alexandre Dumas. Dumas *fils* and Marie fell passionately in love and the story of their affair Dumas *fils* told in his novel, *La dame aux Camélias (The Lady of the Camellias)*, published shortly after her death. Several years later Dumas made a play of the same title from the novel, a sensational success when it premiered in Paris in 1852. In both the novel and the play Dumas has become Armand Duval and Marie Duplessis is now Marguerite Gautier, a role remaining to this day a remarkable challenge for a great dramatic actress on the stage and in film: Sarah Bernhardt, Eleanora Duse, and Greta Garbo were all famous interpreters. Film versions continue to be made (as recently as the 1980s), in all about two dozen.

From this play, urged on by Giuseppe Verdi's extraordinary enthusiasm, the poet Francesco Maria Piave (collaborator with Verdi on ten operas, most recently *Rigoletto*) made the libretto for their *La traviata* wherein Dumas/Armand Duval becomes Alfredo Germont and Marie Duplessis/Marguerite Gautier becomes Violetta Valéry. *La traviata* had its world premiere on March 6, 1853, in Venice. It failed the first night. Within a few years, however, it had begun to rival *Il trovatore* as the most popular of Verdi's operas. Because he so creatively accomplished certain personal aesthetic goals in *Rigoletto*, Verdi often referred to it as his favorite, but there is no doubt about the deep affinity he had for *La traviata*.

Maric, Marguerite, and Violetta, nevertheless, have not always been so loved by everyone. Censors and legions of moralists and religious do-gooders have denounced this trio as permissive and immoral. It was the special sensitivity of Dumas *fils* to perceive in his lover those qualities of a unique, fascinating, sensitive, and intelligent woman and to tell her story. Oh, yes, she swore and drank alcohol and had numerous liasons, but many other women do, too. In telling her story and in dramatizing the life of a courtesan, he created sympathy for women bought by men, at times mistreated by them, who otherwise were doomed to a life of poverty and drudgery. For many such women prostitution was the only hope for escape from a wretched existence. Alexandre Dumas may have been the first male feminist: Certainly, he was the first writer to use the word *feministe* (1872). Later in life, some of his views regarding women would be less enlightened. Nevertheless, his literary sources, and their historical origins, out of which *La traviata* was born, make a fascinating story.

Different translations of the Italian *La traviata* are commonplace. It is important to get it right, for therein is the poignant meaning of the drama. Getting it right requires making a precise translation as well as comprehending fully all implications of the phrase when it is used for the only time in the opera in the third act. We will withhold both our translation and exegesis until we get to this critical moment. For now, it is sufficient to note that of the common translations—"The Wayward Woman," "The Fallen Woman," and "The Woman Gone Astray"—the latter is the best. The woman, of course, is Violetta Valéry, a courtesan. A courtesan of mid-nineteenth-century Paris society, unlike an ordinary prostitute, usually gave herself to be kept by one man at a time, they partaking together of all the social pleasures of an unconventional underworld (*demimonde*) unattached to normal married society.

The opera of her story is in four parts, usually given as three acts with two distinct parts to the second act.

Verdi adamantly intended the action of this controversial and highly personal dramatic exploration of an unconventional lifestyle to be one hundred percent contemporaneous. At the time of its creation he was being chastised for living unmarried and openly with the singer Giuseppina Strepponi; the historical model for Violetta, Marie Duplessis, only recently had died; and Alexander Dumas was, indeed, much alive. Good old censorship, however, that great protector of our minds, our manners, and our morals, stepped in and moved the time back to circa 1700. Most productions today push the time ahead to Verdi's desired period of decor and attire, Paris of the early 1850s. For several generations there existed the curious tradition of "Violetta" dressing in the gowns in the vogue of the time of the soprano portraying her, be it 1860 or 1900.

The following cast will seem larger than it really is because the elemental thrust of the entire story involves only the interrelationships of three characters: Violetta; Alfredo Germont, the young man who adores her; and Giorgio Germont, the provincial self-righteous father of Alfredo. For a performance to be at all successful, by the way, all three of the above must know how to sing and act. No one knew this better than Verdi. (More later on this interesting aspect of the opera.) Perhaps nowhere else in Italian opera is the simplistic stereotype of girl in love (soprano), boy in love (tenor), and insensitive nemesis (baritone) more evident than in these three characters, upon whom the entire drama of *La traviata* rests. Here is a list of all the characters and their relationships as well as their voice ranges:

VIOLETTA Valéry, a courtesan, *soprano*
FLORA BERVOIX, her friend, *mezzo-soprano*
ANNINA, her maid, *soprano*
GIUSEPPE, her servant, *tenor*
DOCTOR GRENVIL, her doctor, *bass*
ALFREDO GERMONT, who loves her, *tenor*
GIORGIO GERMONT, Alfredo's father, *baritone*
GASTONE, young nobleman about town, *tenor*
BARON DOUPHOL, a lover of Violetta, *baritone*
MARCHESE D'OBIGNY, *bass*
Ladies and gentlemen, servants and masks, and dancers and guests

The time should be 1850, the place in and about Paris.

Act I

The prelude played before the parting of the first curtain employs music associated with the two basic themes of the opera, love and death. The first part of the prelude is music taken from the last act of the opera when Violetta is dying, followed by music that accompanies her impassioned Act II plea, "Love me, Alfredo, love me as I love you." The strings, especially the violins, give to *La traviata* throughout its distinctive fragile, shimmering quality, and anyone who has heard Arturo Toscanini's recording of the prelude with his own NBC Symphony Orchestra has heard the quintessential articulation of the sad, passionate beauty of this opera so perfectly condensed in such brief music.

The curtain opens on a luxurious, sumptuous room in Paris

in the apartment of Violetta. Guests are arriving late for her party;
they had lost track of time playing cards at Flora's but now are
ready to revel until dawn. All, especially Violetta, proclaim pleasure as the zest of life. Gaston introduces Alfredo to Violetta as an
admirer of hers and an esteemed friend of his. All take their seats
about a table, Violetta between Gaston and Alfredo. Gaston, *sotto
voce* ("soft voice"—that is, in an aside), says to Violetta "Alfredo
thinks of nobody but you." She deems this but a joke. Gaston continues informing her how Alfredo inquired daily about her health
during her recent illness. Violetta gives Gaston a "Shush," confidant she is nothing to Alfredo, but Gaston counters. Alfredo,
eventually drawn into the discussions, is called on to make a
toast. Violetta entreats, "I'll be Hebe [goddess of youth and spring
and, for a while, cupbearer of the gods], who pours the wine."
Interesting, because this first act takes place in August, fall soon
to show itself, and not spring. Subsequent acts take place in the
depth of winter, January and February, hardly seasonally symbolic of youth and the return of new life. Alfredo reponds, "May you
be as immortal as she."

Obviously, long before we know what is to take place, the
poetry has portrayed the impending doom both literally and figuratively. Alfredo, full of Violetta, is inspired to respond to the invitation to offer a drinking song. His toast, the famous *Brindisi*
("Drinking Song") to love and to wine, obviously is aimed at Violetta, as his eyes reveal. Violetta rises and takes up a second verse:

> Everything is folly in the world
> That does not give us pleasure . . .
>
> For the pleasures of love are swift and fleeting
> As a flower that lives and dies
> And can be enjoyed no more.

Along with the names Violetta and Flora, this is the first of many
references to flowers in the opera, all of which I will note because
a flower is the consummate symbol of the entire drama: To grasp
and feel the ephemeral beauty of the life of a flower is to have the
entirety of the meaning of *La traviata* in head and heart. In Alfredo's toast to love and Violetta's retort to pleasure are the two elemental forces of the drama. One will win. This wondrous song,
the lilting melody a perfect match for the words and mood, often
is referred to simply as *Libiamo* ("Let's drink"). Following the

toast Violetta, to Alfredo, reasserts that life is just pleasure, to which he responds, "But what if one waits for love?" She answers, "I know nothing of that—don't tell me . . ." but Alfredo persists: "Therein lies my destiny."

Music from another room is heard. It is time to dance. As all the guests, except Alfredo, start to go, Violetta, suddenly weak and pale, falters. Coughing deeply, she sits a moment, then urges her friends on to the dance, promising to rejoin them in a moment. Unaware that Alfredo is behind her, she sees in a mirror how pale she is. Then she sees Alfredo, who cautions her to take better care of herself, suggesting that, if allowed, he would guard her carefully because—and here he declares his love. Violetta laughs, but then, taking her first small serious step toward responding to his devotion, asks, if he is serious, just how long has he loved her? In his response beginning *Ah sì, da un anno. Un dì felice . . .* ("For more than a year. One happy day . . .") are words and music that throughout the opera will symbolize the love he has declared and Violetta is about to reciprocate, even though she as yet is not aware of it. After Alfredo sings an impassioned

Di quell' amor ch'è palpito
Dell'universo intero,
Misterioso, altero,
Croce e delizia al cor.

Of that unspoken love,
The pulse of the whole universe,
Mysterious, unattainable,
The torment and delight of my heart

to some of Verdi's most glorious music, Violetta, as she had done in the toast, takes up the melody and responds by admonishing him to leave if what he says is true, for friendship is all she can offer him:

I don't know how to love,
I couldn't feel so great an emotion . . .
You should look for someone else
Then you wouldn't find it hard
To forget me.

But then, as their voices join together, Violetta repeating the above and Alfredo singing again of love's mystery, we hear in the music beyond her warning and his declaration the coming together of their mutual affection.

Gaston interrupts them. "What the devil are you up to?" he wonders. To Gaston she replies, "We're talking nonsense," but to Alfredo she says, "Promise to say no more about love." Alone again, Alfredo tells her he will leave. Violetta takes a flower from her breast, saying, "Take this flower." When Alfredo wonders why, she replies, "So you can bring it back to me." He wants to know when. "When it is withered." Delirious with joy, Alfredo takes the flower, again declares his passion, and departs knowing he'll return tomorrow. This is the second significant use of a flower as symbolic of their love. Violetta, as yet, has admitted nothing, neither to herself nor to Alfredo, but why else bring him back the very next day? Indeed, love's pleasures are swift and fleeting "as a flower that lives and dies," for this already she has proclaimed in the *Brindisi* and now she ensures that he will return to her soon. All that remains is for her to put in words what her heart already knows.

Dawn has lightened the night's sky and the dancing is done. Violetta's friends thank her for the wonderful party and they, too, depart, leaving her alone with rushing thoughts and mixed emotions. Now is one of the most anticipated moments in all Italian opera. Classic and traditional is the aesthetic pattern, recitativo and aria followed by another brief recitativo followed by a second aria, but Verdi's music transforms Violetta from a person in a play into a real human being coming to terms with clashing emotions right before our eyes—yet eyes far removed, for it is only from afar that we are allowed to watch what Alfredo's declaration has done to this frail young woman, wracked by disease, in one of opera's greatest monologues.

È strano! È strano! ("How strange! How strange!") begins her recitativo. This is the first of three appearances of this expression in the opera, once in each act and with differing implications each time. In this instance what are strange are feelings Violetta has never before felt for a man. "To love and be loved!" Does she dare forgo a life of pleasure for such as this? *Ah, fors' è lui* ("Was this the man . . . ") begins the first of the two celebrated back-to-back arias wherein Violetta wonders if love, for her up to now only a fantasy, has at last found her and she finds herself repeating Alfredo's very words about love as the mysterious force palpitating throughout the universe. This dreamy reverie—and a good actress must portray this—is interrupted by a second recitativo as Violetta returns to reality, declaring, *Follie!* ("It's madness"). Pleasure is her calling, not love, and with a rapid, surging tempo the second aria begins with the assertion of freedom and pleasure, *Sempre libera* ("Always free"), which, however, breaks off into a shudder when through the window she hears the distant, departing voice of Alfredo walking down the street singing again his now famous palpitation phrase. Violetta collects herself and reasserts the folly of love and the need to remain ever free for pleasure as the curtain falls, but is there anyone in the house who does not already know otherwise? If so, then he has not been paying attention—unthinkable, in the presence of this music!

Act II
The first scene of the second act shows the ground-floor room of a country house near Paris. The first act took place in August. It now is January and Violetta and Alfredo have been living together. Alfredo enters, attired in hunting clothes. A brief, quick orchestral piece precedes his depiction of mixed moods: happiness with Violetta and anxiousness when not at her side expressed in the prominent tenor solo of the score. A recitativo precedes this aria of reflection *De' miei bollenti spiriti* ("My passionate spirit"). It concludes:

> Since the day when she told me
> "I want to live, faithful to you alone!"
> I have forgotten the world
> And lived like one in heaven.

His reverie is interrupted by the entrance of an agitated Annina who explains that she has been sent by Violetta to Paris to sell horses and carriages to raise money to cover expenses of their country idyll. Alfredo, asking why he was not informed, is told it was the wish of Violetta it be kept from him. He will go to Paris. Violetta is not to be told why. He dismisses Annina. Alfredo is remorseful. Intent on washing away this infamy, he leaves. Violetta, papers in hand, enters with Annina, who tells her mistress that Alfredo has gone to Paris for the day. *È strano!* ("It's strange").

Recall that I have mentioned she will say this in each of the three acts with different implications. In Act I, "*È strano,*" as you now know, launched one of the most famous scenes for soprano in all opera as she reflected on the effect Alfredo's declaration of love was having upon her. Here it is said in passing and would be missed by those who do not know the opera and know it will be said again in the final act. Accordingly, even though in the second act it is but a passing phrase, it leaps out, for we know what Alfredo is up to and we must anticipate threats to the idyll. Here "It's strange!" said in passing would imply nothing more than "Oh, I wonder why? or "Oh, that's unusual; I wonder what he's up to?" but her phrases, uttered with no musical accompaniment, are followed by eight ominous orchestral thumps.

A letter has come from Flora inviting Violetta to a party in which she has no interest and Giuseppe announces the arrival of a gentleman calling. With the arrival of Alfredo's father, Giorgio Germont, to most disturbing music, a long duet, over fifteen minutes, begins between him and Violetta. Not only is it the core of the second act but it is also the axis on which the drama revolves. Verdi knew this scene was one of his most successful creations, and one hundred and fifty years and thousands of performances have not dulled this miracle among many in Italian opera.

After an exchange of unpleasantries, Germont reveals the reason for his visit: He has come to ask for a sacrifice now already anticipated by Violetta. His daughter's fiancé refuses to consummate their marriage as long as Alfredo lives in sin with Violetta. His plea, *Pura siccome un angelo* ("God gave me a daughter as pure as an angel"), is lovely music for baritone. At first, Violetta consents, having misconstrued the request to mean only a temporary sacrifice of leaving Alfredo for a short while. "Not enough," he insists. It is necessary that it be forever. No, never, is her frantic response, "I would rather die . . ." Germont persists. In time, she will age. Her beauty gone, Alfredo may become unfaithful or leave her; they are not even married. His venom commences to work. She grants this may be true. He implores her to become the consoling angel of his family, and Violetta—foreseeing a possible hopeless future—capitulates with a request in what for me is one of the most touching and hauntingly beautiful strains in opera. Weeping, Violetta sings, *Dite alla giovine*,

> Say to your daughter, pure and fair,
> That there's a victim of misfortune
> Whose one ray of happiness
> Before she dies
> Is a sacrifice made for her.

Germont comprehends. Violetta has confided the seriousness of her illness. She asks that he embrace her like a daughter to give her strength for what she must now do. How can he repay her? Germont asks. Violetta, acknowledging that she soon will be dead, asks Germont to tell Alfredo how much she suffered in making the sacrifice and how much she loved him. Germont leaves. Violetta rings for Annina and instructs her to deliver a hastily written note. Violetta writes a letter to Alfredo and seals and hides it as he enters. She is visibly upset and Alfredo also is worried, for his father has written him a stern letter.

For me one of the most chilling moments in the world of opera is about to happen. It is not a famous aria or part of a big duet. It is, in fact, Verdi's setting of just a few words, but I know of nothing else like it, nothing else in all opera possessing the power to stand my hair on end and to make me tremble all over.

Alfredo knows nothing of what has transpired, nothing of what sacrifice has been made. He hopes that his father, once he meets Violetta, will weaken his resolve and accept her. Violetta knows she is about to leave the one man she has ever loved and who dearly loves her. She looks toward the garden and tells Alfredo she'll be there among the flowers always near to him. Then the words:

> *Amami, Alfredo,*
> *amami quant'io t'amo.*
> *Addio.*

> Love me, Alfredo,
> love me as much as I do you!
> Farewell!

and she runs off. Alfredo sees someone in the garden. A messenger delivers Violetta's letter. Alfredo reads, is stunned, and turns to find himself face to face with his father. He falls into his father's arms, then in despair sinks into a chair, his face in his hands, as his father sings one of Verdi's most well-known arias for baritone voice, asking his son to return with him to Provence: *Di Provenza il mar, il suol.* Seeing Flora's invitation and suspecting Douphol, Alfredo repulses his father and races to have revenge as the first scene of the second act concludes.

Gay music opens the second of this act's two scenes, showing a big room in Flora's house. Party small talk ceases as women dressed as gypsies enter to entertain with dance and song. They are followed by a second *divertissement*, Gaston and friends dressed as bullfighters. Alfredo surprises all when he enters. Rumor allowed anticipating Violetta and Douphol, but not Alfredo. Gambling at cards commences. Alfredo plays. Violetta, escorted by the baron, arrives and is dismayed to learn from Flora of Alfredo's presence. The two women sit and chat. Alfredo begins to win at cards. Violetta's agitation increases. The baron, too, will play. Alfredo continues winning. As all break for supper, Violetta summons Alfredo to warn him of the baron's anger, bidding him to leave. He's no coward but if she will follow, he will go. She will not. She lies: She professes to love the baron. Alfredo calls all before him, announces he is repaying Violetta for all she squandered on him, and at her feet, in a furious rage, throws his winnings. Violetta faints. Giorgio Germont had entered just in time to see this insult and denounces his son. To himself, Alfredo confesses the shame he feels as his father, also to himself, deals with the problem of knowing the truth but being unwilling to reveal it. The baron challenges Alfredo to a duel, Violetta revives, but she is weak and overcome with emotion. The act ends as these varied feelings are expressed in words and music.

In the entire second scene there is not one of those famous excerpts or highlights opera lovers know and anticipate, yet from the brilliant party music to the gaming to the insult through to the end of many mixed emotions Verdi's music sounds exactly what you see. Verdi, in this scene, is close to his goal of no individual numbers, just words and music. A goal, by the way, he shared with Wagner, as I've said before. Much more on this after *La traviata*, Act III. But finally for the second act, only two references to flowers: In asking Violetta for the sacrifice, Germont, referring to his daughter and her betrothed, pleads, ". . . do not turn to bitter thorns the roses of their love," and already noted was Violetta's promise to Alfredo. Knowing she is leaving him, "I shall be there amongst the flowers, always near to you." Flowers, the prominent symbol of the opera, figure more evocatively in the final act.

Act III
An all-pervasive sadness is expressed in the beautiful, slow prelude to the third and final act, the violins carrying the lovely, fragile melody above intermittent hints of melancholy from the wind instruments. Like the prelude to the first act, it tells the entire

story. Violetta is dying of consumption. About a month has expired since the events of Act II. Over the final, forlorn notes dying away softly in the violins can be heard her coughing. She awakens and calls to Annina, dozing by the fire, for a sip of water. Annina serves her, opens the shutters to let in the morning light, assists the frail woman from her bed to her couch, and lets in Dr. Grenvil, who asks routine questions, promises convalescence soon, and presses her hand to indicate he will soon return to see her again. Violetta knows better and as the doctor departs he confides to Annina, "She has only a few hours to live."

It is carnival time in Paris but Violetta feels the suffering of the poor. She instructs Annina to go for the mail and to take half of her money from the drawer for alms. From under lace covering her breast Violetta, now alone, takes a letter she knows by heart to read again. Letter scenes in opera, both long before and long after Verdi, have been a popular, commonplace convention but this one has a poignant individuality. Violetta does not sing the letter. As reflections of her past love shimmer in the strings, she reads it in a scene of great effect. *"Teneste la promessa,"* the letter begins:

> You kept your promise.
> The duel took place;
> the Baron was wounded
> but is recovering.
> Alfredo has gone abroad.
> I have let him know
> of your great sacrifice.
> He will come back to ask
> for your forgiveness.
> I shall come too.
> Take care of your health;
> you deserve a better future.
>
> —Giorgio Germont

As she looks upon her reflection in a mirror, the recitativo preceding her famous aria of farewell tells all: *È tardi!* ("It's too late"). She has waited but they have not come. The doctor has tried to give her hope but with this disease she knows all hope is dead. *Addio, del passato bei sogni ridenti* is the first line of the aria and it is important to translate it correctly. Too often, it is abbreviated to simply, *Addio, del passato* ("Farewell to the past"), which is not correct. It is a farewell to dreams of happiness now past, for she sees ". . . the roses in my cheeks already have faded," again the ephemeral life of flowers symbolizing her own fate. Nor is Alfredo there to sustain her weary spirit. Then comes the famous line of which we must make something:

Ah, della traviata sorridi al desio . . .

There is the word of the opera's title, *traviata*, in a phrase translated numerous ways. What Violetta asks is a last wish to be granted to . . . "a lost woman," "an erring soul," "a fallen woman," "a woman gone astray." As a courtesan, Violetta sees herself as "a woman gone astray." This is what *traviata* means. But if left at that, one misses the critical subtlety at the center of the whole drama. The Italian verb *traviare* means "to go astray or to lead astray." Violetta may have gone astray into the life of a courtesan, but of far more importance is the fact of her having been led astray from the one, true, meaningful, loving relationship of her all-too-brief life by the provincial, self-righteous Giorgio Germont, whose letter above clearly reveals that he has at least begun to comprehend the suffering he caused. For me *La traviata* can never be other than "The Woman *Led* Astray." Her last wish, knowing "All is over now," is that God may forgive and receive her.

Her reverie is over. Outside in the street Mardi Gras revelers sing as Annina bursts into the room greatly excited. She has seen Alfredo, who is coming to see Violetta and, in an instant, right on Annina's heels there he is in the room. Violetta is in his arms, rapid proclamations of love spilling over them, then, suddenly, a pause of some silence is followed by another lilting melody, which could belong only to *La traviata*. It is the *Parigi, o cara* ("We shall leave Paris, my dearest") duet in which both utilize the metaphor "bloom again" to mean regaining of health by Violetta. She suggests going to church to give thanks but is too weak to move. She tries to dress but falters and falls back on her couch. Alfredo now sees how dire the situation is and directs Annina to go for the doctor. Violetta wants now to live, for Alfredo is at her side, but she is not deluding herself. With what little strength remains she sings of her despair: ". . . that I should die so young." Annina and the doctor enter, followed by Giorgio Germont. He will accept her as a daughter, but she informs him it is too late. Alfredo confirms this and the elder Germont, heretofore stoic and heartless, comprehends what he has done. To Alfredo he says:

Don't torture me more,
Remorse devours my soul.
Her words strike me like lightning.
Ah, foolish old man!
All the harm that I did
I see only now.

Yes, Giorgio Germont. You did lead Violetta astray from the only love of her life, and now restored to that love she is about to die. Giorgio Germont asks for forgiveness. Violetta gives a medallion portrait to Alfredo. All are distraught. Then, for the third time, once in each act, Violetta says *È strano* ("How strange"). Is a miracle taking place before them? All her pain is gone. She feels new strength surge through her. Within her life seems renewed. Her final words are *Oh gioia!* ("Oh joy!"). She falls back on her sofa. Sorrow overwhelms the others as the curtain comes down.

The premiere of *La traviata* was a failure. Verdi feared it might be. For months he had urged management at Teatro la Fenice, the opera house in Venice where the premiere would take place, to obtain only the most competent singers, even suggesting names to consider or not consider. He was not confident with the choices and after the unsuccessful opening, he wrote to the manager what now some consider his most famous letter:

7 March 1853

Dear Emanuel Muzio,
    La traviata last night a fiasco. Was the fault mine or the singers? Time will decide.

Always yours,
G. Verdi

The singers were indeed the problem. The tenor (Alfredo) was hoarse, the baritone (Giorgio Germont) considered his role unheroic and beneath him, and poor Fanny Salvini-Donatelli (Violetta) was so stout the audience laughed aloud when she died of consumption. Furthermore, Verdi had insisted there be no "singers abuses," singers taking liberties with the score to show off their voice. Verdi was insistent the music serve the drama and not the ego of the singers. Time, indeed, has told. Subsequent performances were sensationally successful and soon *La traviata* rivaled *Il trovatore* as Verdi's most popular creation.

He had written the opera in remarkably short time, between January and March, while also at work on finishing touches for *Trovatore* in rehearsal. Imagine working back and forth on two operas so unalike in all ways. It's mind-boggling.

There are two interesting ways in which opera and reality differ in *La traviata*, a drama born out of a real love affair. Dumas *fils* was not present when Marie Duplessis died and Dumas *père* and Giorgio Germont had absolutely nothing in common.

℘

Some intellectuals refer to the three operas presented in this chapter as "Verdi potboilers." Their astounding popularity has led to this. They are the three great operas of Verdi's middle period of composition. You should start with them and pay no attention to those who disdain them because of an overwhelming universal appeal. When we resume Verdi's story, we will consider masterpieces from his final period: *Aida*, *Otello*, and *Falstaff*. Once familiar with these operas, other delights from Verdi's late years as well as those from his early period await you.

It now is 1853 and Rigoletto has been foiled in revenge, a troubadour's death ironically has avenged an earlier murder, and Violetta has joined Wagnerian heroines in self-sacrifice, one of the popular conventions of nineteenth-century romantic opera. It is now 1853 and while Verdi has astonished the Italian opera world with three triumphs in less than three years, Richard Wagner has written no opera music since the completion of *Lohengrin* in 1848. But he has been busy at work on the most momentous operatic conception in history, his *Ring Cycle*. With this, Wagner's story resumes.

Richard Wagner

WAGNER II: THE BIG MUSIC DRAMAS

The only way to understand what Wagner's major music-dramas are about is to know of the synthesis he made between art and religion. At the end of chapter 4, I mentioned that "... it remained for Wilhelm Richard Wagner to make a synthesis of religion and opera, to transform the opera house into a temple." How and why he did so is a fascinating story, but more than that, to repeat, it is the only way to understand *The Ring Cycle*, *Tristan and Isolde*, *The Mastersingers*, and *Parsifal*. Throughout his life, Wagner adhered to the essentially Romantic conviction that art was the source of religious truth in an age when religion had become ineffective because of aberrance and hypocrisy. It is therefore quite remarkable that in the mountain of literature on Wagner, very little has been written on the role religion played in his creative life and almost nothing that attempts to focus on the connection between religion and art as he understood it.

Early in his life, Wagner found in the *Oresteia* of Aeschylus what he considered to be the archetype of religious art: great dramatic tragedy built upon mythical truths. In the Attic theater, Wagner believed, great poetry, music, action, and scenery combined to reveal to the audiences the most profound truths of the human experience. When his own dramas are viewed as nineteenth-century versions of Greek tragedy, which he was convinced was a religious occasion, they take on a new dimension, and it is precisely this religious dimension in Wagner's art that this chapter explores. His synthesis of religion and art took varying forms that can be traced by studying the interrelationships among his life, his thoughts (expressed in many volumes of collected writings), and his dramas. But you don't need to do this. I will do it for you.

Earlier works, *Tannhäuser* and *Lohengrin*, for example, are expressions of his special understanding of redemption through art and musical mysticism. In 1848–49 Wagner was so markedly influenced by Feuerbach's writings on religion that they led him to a serious consideration of the New Testament. It was the "purely human" side of Jesus that moved him to produce an elaborate plan for a drama entitled *Jesus of Nazareth*. Wagner never completed the drama, but the revolutionary qualities that he found in the New Testament were incorporated into *The Ring of the Nibelung* tetrology, in which his Siegfried, especially in the first drafts, bears a striking resemblance to his conception of Jesus as a political and religious reformer. *The Ring Cycle*, as the tetrology is commonly known, changed during the course of its long composition, however, to reflect a pessimistic resignation within an evil world mainly because in 1854 Wagner came under the spell of Arthur Schopenhauer's philosophy. More on him later in this chapter. This proved to be the most significant intellectual influence he was ever to experience.

Schopenhauer's penchant for Indian thought spurred Wagner to study Buddhism, and his *Tristan and Isolde* reflects the impact of Indian religion on his art. In the period that followed this, Wagner developed still further a conception of spiritual music (as opposed to secular music), claiming that whenever great music revealed essential truths about life to the listener, it was therefore spiritual or religious. There is in *The Mastersingers* a manifestation of this conception of art as religious revelation, but it was not until his final work, *Parsifal*, that he achieved a full expression of an artistic-religious synthesis wherein opera becomes consecrational drama—indeed, a religious rite.

Parsifal is a dramatization of Schopenhauer's philosophy and, as an opera, must be considered according to its creator's intentions as a Christian ceremony and as the final religio-artistic rite of one of the leading figures of nineteenth-century Romanticism. What follows is the most difficult chapter in the book—both for me to have written and for you to grasp—because Wagner was not just another great opera composer like Mozart or Verdi. He was a megalomaniacal genius who believed he could change the world through his art. What follows will explain this. We begin with *The Ring Cycle*, the most colossal undertaking in the history of operatic composition.

The Ring Cycle

Richard Wagner was not in the business of accepting contracts from theaters to produce one hit after another brimming with captivating tunes. Wagner's art was a religious mission and to comprehend his operas is to understand the religious and philosophical concepts sustaining them. The steps Wagner took after completing *Lohengrin* were giant steps through the most turbulent time of his life. By March 1848, Wagner was nearing his thirty-fifth birthday and *Lohengrin* was finished. He became profoundly involved in studying ancient Greek and medieval German literature. Lacking a formal education, Wagner nevertheless was a voracious reader. He sought to escape from a society he considered decadent and superficial into books, where he found an ideal world. The more he withdrew into this world of his own imagination, the more intense became his desire to remake his contemporary world into something good, true, and beautiful. For some, obviously, this zeal could be but a baby step away from revolutionary activity.

Wagner became preoccupied with the *Oresteia* of Aeschylus and the Germanic Nibelungen myth and its hero Siegfried. The *Oresteia* Wagner interpreted as religious drama built upon the unification of mythical poetry, acting, music, and stage design into a single artistic impression aimed at the spiritual and moral edification of the audience. The ancient Greek poets were the teachers of the people in a society of neither organized church nor priestly class. Observing great dramas in their theater was where ancient Greeks learned how they ought to live their lives.

Wagner's own *Ring Cycle*, now stirring within him, clearly had its origins in this idea: Indeed, all of Wagner's operas after *Lohengrin* can be seen as his attempt to create German dramas on Greek models. And so his study of ancient sources, which began as an effort to disassociate himself as much as possible from the business of the day and from the unbearable social and cultural routine of Dresden, turned out to be the source of his hope for a reconstituted theater. Accordingly, Wagner, who held an official position as a state-appointed *Kapellemeister* (conductor), recorded his vision in his "Plan for the Organization of a National German

Theater for the Kingdom of Saxony." Nothing came of this plan, and the resulting sense of frustration moved him even closer to a revolutionary stance—a posture that included reading radical literature, publishing controversial articles, and meeting with revolutionaries.

His varied readings convinced him that myth, not history, was the proper material out of which dramas are made. History records only specific happenings of particular times; myths penetrate through the bewildering maze of historical events to reveal what has remained constant in the human experience. What Wagner found in myth was the way toward making an interpretation of world history. In one essay, an amazing pastiche of historical, political, and mythical elements, Wagner succeeds, to his own satisfaction at least, in interweaving Roman and Germanic historical threads in order to arrive at the equation of Germanic god Wotan + Siegfried = Christian God and Savior. This led to another essay, "The Nibelungen Myth as Subject for a Drama," which became the source of his gigantic *Ring Cycle*. It must be read as a religious allegory couched in myth, attacking the contemporary materialistic establishment that cared not at all for art, truth, beauty, love, the sacred, or the good.

The world represented in Wagner's sketch has become so wicked by the lust for gold and the power it brings that even the gods have become contaminated. Nothing short of beginning anew can set things right. This means revolution. But revolutionary activity, already widespread in France in 1848, had not as yet reached Dresden.

Next Wagner wrote the dramatic poem "Siegfried's Death," in which he develops the theme of world salvation through a heroic, sacrificial death and an intensifying of his identification of Siegfried of Germanic myth with Jesus of Nazareth. However specious his arguments, he had arrived at the subject of his next drama: either Siegfried or Jesus. Both despised earthly treasures, both came into the world to atone for its sins through a sacrificial death, and both were resurrected. Wagner produced an elaborate plan for a huge drama. *Jesus of Nazareth: a rough draft for a drama* was not published until four years after his death. Wagner's Jesus is not the gentle savior of Christian tradition. His Jesus is a revolutionary who intends to save the world. Wagner makes much of New Testament passages such as Matt. 10:34–35, where Jesus says

You must think that I have come to

> Bring peace to the earth; I have
> Not come to bring peace, but a sword . . .

And Luke 12:49, "I have come to set fire to the earth," which in quite a literal sense is precisely what Siegfried does at the end of *The Ring Cycle*. In the New Testament, Wagner found the revolutionary impulse to change the world but he abandoned the plan in favor of Germanic myth, fearing that too much of Western history was tied up with interpretations of the New Testament story for his presentation of Jesus to be understood and accepted as he intended.

During his final days in Dresden, Wagner had become steeped in the philosophy of the left-wing Hegelian philosopher Ludwig Feuerbach, and he was meeting on a regular basis with a group of revolutionaries that included the ubiquitous Russian anarchist Mikhail Bakunin. It was in these meetings that Wagner first became acquainted with the thinking of Karl Marx, and when the revolutionary activity spreading throughout Europe reached Dresden in the spring of 1849, Wagner participated openly. The uprising failed and Wagner, with a price on his head, assumed a disguise, pocketed fraudulent papers, and by night slipped across the border into Switzerland, where he lived as a political exile for nearly a dozen years. It was there that he answered his new calling: the creation of the new art, the music drama, in the service of his reconstituted religious convictions. As was his way, the articulation of his theories preceded or was at least coetaneous with the creation of his operas.

Three of his major prose works derive from this fecund period of his life, in addition to *The Ring Cycle* poems. Though Wagner's *Ring Cycle* can be appreciated for its bigness, for its power, and for considerable remarkable music, it cannot be comprehended as Wagner intended without some knowledge of the theoretical writings through which it came to be. The three major prose works written between 1849 and 1851 are two essays, "Art and Revolution" and "The Art-Work of the Future," and a book, *Opera and Drama*. Unlike two of the most dominant minds of the nineteenth century, Hegel and Darwin, both of whom held an evolutionary view of the development of life and history from simpler to higher complex forms, Wagner believed his age had fallen away from a once golden period when life was good. All three of these works refine and elaborate on his basic theme asserting that nineteenth-century culture is irreligious, materialistic, loveless, hypocritical, and decadent. The art of the time, particularly that of the theater, because it mirrors the economic and social order out of which it was created, reflects these conditions. He called for a revolution to raze the existing order and for a new art and a new religion to ensure the purity of the new social order to be built upon the ruins.

In revolution, religion, and art the hope for social and spiritual redemption resides. The new art of the future will be music dramas created by one who is both poet and musician. Myths containing universal truths are dramatized by the poet, who also creates music to intensify the drama and to express truths that transcend the limitations of human speech. Out of the ashes of a rotten world, destroyed by revolution, a new order is established in which love rules the world. It is the artwork of the future showing the way, and guess who Wagner had in mind as the progenitor of the new art extolling the religion of love?

In case you are thinking that already there was a Christian church committed to a religion of love, let me make it clear that Wagner believed Christianity, too, had fallen from its original pure state. He saw in nineteenth-century Christianity a commitment only to power and money. Indeed, for Wagner every dimension of life in the nineteenth century had made gold its god. That is what *The Ring Cycle* is about.

DER RING DES NIBELUNGEN
The Ring of the Nibelung

The Ring Cycle is a common diminutive for *Der Ring des Nibelungen (The Nibelung's Ring* or *The Ring of the Nibelung)*, the title of four operas—oops, music dramas—based on Germanic myths in which Wagner reveals both what is wrong with the world and the way to redemption. These music dramas, also referred to as Wagner's tetrology, are *Das Rheingold (The Rhine Gold); Die Walküre (The Valkyrie); Siegfried;* and *Götterdämmerung (Twilight of the Gods)*. Wagner had begun writing the poems, his librettos, in 1848. The poems were written in reverse order of the composition of the music and of a performance of the cycle. "The Death of Siegfried" was written first and in revision became *Götterdämmerung,* then *Siegfried, The Valkyrie,* and *The Rhine Gold.* They were privately printed in 1853 with the title *The Ring of the Nibelung,* the same year Wagner began to compose the music of *The Rhine Gold.*

In this chapter you will learn why the cycle was not completed until 1874 and how it was first presented to the world in 1876 in the Festival Theater, conceived by Wagner and built for him by King Ludwig II of Bavaria in the town of Bayreuth. To help you to see the big picture and to get to the point of each drama, consider the following guide that I give to my students:

Part One: *The Rhine Gold* is about the Problem; evil deriving from a lust for gold.

Part Two: *The Valkyrie* is about the Promise; a hero will come unto the world.

Part Three: *Siegfried* is about the Hero; Siegfried, of course, being that hero.

Part Four: *Twilight of the Gods* is about Redemption; salvation through love.

The story and an interpretation of each drama will be followed by a discussion of its music.

DAS RHEINGOLD (1876)
The Rhine Gold

The drama plays in one uninterrupted act of four distinct scenes. The characters and their voice ranges are:

The Gods
WOTAN, ruler of the gods, *bass baritone*
DONNER, god of thunder, *bass baritone*
FROH, god of youth and joy, *tenor*
LOGE, god of fire and trickery, *tenor*

The Goddesses
FRICKA, wife of Wotan and goddess of marriage, *mezzo-soprano*
FREIA, her sister and goddess of love and spring, *soprano*
ERDA, the wise earth goddess, *contralto*

The Giants
FASOLT, *bass baritone*
FAFNER, his brother, *bass*

The Rhinemaidens
WOGLINDE, *soprano*
WELLGUNDE, *soprano*
FLOSSHILDE, *mezzo-soprano*

The Nibelungs (dwarfs living in Nibelheim within the
   earth's depths)
ALBERICH, *bass baritone*
MIME, his brother, *tenor*

The drama is set in a legendary past. The scenes take place
in the depths of the Rhine River, atop a mountain near the
river, and in the caverns beneath the earth where dwell
the dwarfs.

Scene 1

The first scene takes place in the depths of the Rhine. There, three
Rhinemaidens frolic as they guard the river's great treasure, the
Rhinegold. Alberich, an ugly dwarf, watches them swim about.
Mesmerized by their seductive beauty, he desires desperately to
possess one of them. They take turns tantalizing him, swimming
always just out of his reach, until the glowing light from a lump
of gold diverts his attention. The Rhinemaidens explain its miraculous powers: Anyone who possesses it, makes a golden ring, and
renounces love will obtain immeasurable power. Frustrated by his
failure to experience the pleasures of the flesh, Alberich renounces
love forever and steals the gold from the stunned Rhinemaidens.

Scene 2

The scene changes to reveal a wondrous castle high in the mountains above the river. This is the new home of the gods. The giants
Fasolt and Fafner built it for Wotan, who in return promised to
give them Freia, goddess of youth and beauty, as recompense.
Wotan and Fricka, sleeping near the castle, awaken. Fricka scolds
her husband for offering her sister as payment. Wotan explains
that his promise was merely a ruse to get the giants to work. He
is counting on the wily Loge to think of an even more enticing
reward as a means of getting him out of the contract. Freia, distraught because the giants are after her, enters. The giants soon
thereafter appear to demand payment. Wotan stalls. Donner and
Froh, Freia's brothers, arrive to protect her. Finally, Loge is also on
the scene. Though he has not as yet conceived a more tempting

payment, his mind is working. Loge tells of Alberich's theft of the gold and how the Rhinemaidens hope Wotan will assist in its recovery. His story, of course, begins to tempt the dull giants, who now want gold more than they want Freia. Hearing Loge's tale, however, arouses in Wotan his own desire for the gold. The giants give Wotan until evening to decide, and they take Freia away. With her absence, the gods begin to tire and age, for she is the goddess of eternal youth. Wotan will descend deep into the caverns of the earth to Nibelheim, where the Nibelungs dwell. Loge will accompany him.

Scene 3

The scene changes to Nibelheim. Alberich has made his ring of gold, and his brother Mime, also from the gold, has made a magic helmet called the Tarnhelm. When wearing it, one can be transformed into anything one wants to be, or even can become invisible. Alberich puts it on, becomes invisible, beats his brother, enslaves all other Nibelungs, and extracts from them a hoard of gold and silver. Oh, what power derives from this gold! Alberich is ecstatic with his newly won wealth.

Much of this episode Wotan and Loge have observed. Alberich, so sure of himself and convinced of the eventual fall of the gods from power and his inevitable rule over all, commences to brag of his might. It is Loge's intent to trick the dwarf into submission. He feigns disbelief in the Tarnhelm's magic. To prove otherwise, Alberich transforms himself into a huge dragon. Loge, continuing to pretend disbelief, asks if he can become something small, and when Alberich naively makes himself into a toad, Loge tells Wotan to put him underfoot. Once Alberich is contained and his magic helmet removed, the gods bind him, once again in his dwarfish form to drag him along as they ascend to their mountaintop for the final scene of the drama.

Wotan and Loge mock the dwarf, who agrees to exchange his hoard for freedom and calls upon his Nibelungs to deliver it. The gods want it all. Loge takes the Tarnhelm and Wotan demands the ring. Alberich refuses and Wotan pulls it off his finger. Raging with hate, the dwarf curses the ring and anyone who possesses it:

> As the ring came to me through a curse
> I now curse this ring!
> Its gold gave to me power
> without measure

now let its magic
bear only death . . .

There is no escape
from my curse!

Scene 4

Alberich departs. The giants are seen approaching with Freia. Donner, Froh, and Fricka arrive, as do the giants. They want the ran-
som of gold in exchange for Freia's release: every last tidbit of it,
including Tarnhelm and the ring. Wotan balks, acquiescing only
after Erda has appeared to admonish him to give it up. Instantly
upon acquiring the hoard, the giants quarrel over its division, the
ring being the object of greatest dispute. Fafner kills his brother and
takes the ring. Already Alberich's curse is at work—a fact not lost
on Wotan, who becomes seized by foreboding.

Fricka urges that they go to their new home, which Wotan
calls Valhalla. Donner summons a thunderstorm, disperses it, and
reveals a radiant rainbow bridge leading to the castle. It is a glorious sight. Wotan turns to Fricka, takes her hand, and leads her to
the bridge. Donner, Froh, and Freia follow. Loge remains, watching them, and to himself says: The great gods who think themselves immortal are hastening to their end. At this point, one cannot help but think of the fourth drama's title: *Twilight of the
Gods*. As the gods cross the beautiful rainbow bridge leading to
their magnificent castle in the clouds, from far below can be heard
the wailing of the Rhinemaidens, lamenting the loss of their gold.

Anyone informed about Wagner's revolutionary activities and
familiar with his prose writings of the late 1840s and early 1850s
can easily interpret the allegory of *Das Rheingold*. Evil pervades
the world. From the gods above who rule to the subterranean
laborers below, greed prevails. The lusts of Alberich are no worse
than those of the god Wotan. Their all-consuming desire for
wealth and the power that is part and parcel of it, of course, is
symbolized by the gold of the Rhine, especially the power contained in a little ring made from it. Won by a renunciation of love,
the ring carries a dreaded curse. Thus does Wagner rework
medieval Germanic mythology to characterize his assessment of
the sins of his own time wherein all political, economic, and religious institutions are infected by a disease incubated in greed.
The words he gives to Loge, the god of fire, as the drama nears its

conclusion, are extremely significant and must not be missed. Accordingly, I isolate them again, this time translating almost word for word. As the gods set forth for Valhalla, Loge, remaining behind, watching them, speculates aloud:

> They hasten to their end
> thinking themselves invincible.
> I feel shame
> sharing in their actions.
> I feel tempted to destroy
> them in my fire . . .

The entire social order, from dwarfs to the great gods themselves, appears doomed. *Twilight of the Gods* has been anticipated and articulated while the telling final words of the drama are left to the wailing Rhinemaidens far below in the waters of their river:

> Rhine gold! Rhine gold!
> Once purest gold!
> O gleaming gift
> glimmer again
> in our water's depths.
> Only here is there
> trust and truth.
> Above, the god's joy
> is false and full of fear!

From the instant Donner swings his hammer to create a storm, to the gods' journey over the rainbow to Valhalla, to the Rhinemaidens lamenting below, to the dying away of the final chord in the orchestra—more than twelve minutes in all—this unequivocally is a unique and overwhelming operatic episode wherein words, gestures, costumes, and sets all become one with powerful music of unfaltering descriptive authenticity and beauty in a grand synthesis of the arts.

This synthesis is precisely what Wagner intended. The experience, when properly performed in a theater, is spellbinding. Many nineteenth-century Romantics yearned for such a theatrical presentation in which independent arts combined into a single unfolding artistic experience. The Germans, whose interest in the concept was intense, called this idea a *Gesamtkunstwerk:* a synthesis of the arts. Poets, musicians, and writers contemplated it and longed for it. They wrote about it. But it was Richard Wagner who gave to the world its definitive manifestation both in theory, in his book *Opera and Drama,* and in practice, *The Ring Cycle. Das Rheingold* more than any other drama in the cycle is a realization of Wagner's theories.

Other influences soon to bear heavily on Wagner's artistic development will produce changes—some subtle, others overt—in his composition of the rest of the cycle. Such a synthesis assumes an equality of the arts as they meld in a single artistic expression. In theory, music must be merely a part of the mix. The age-old operatic question "Which is more important, the words or the music?" in a *Gesamtkunstwerk* is answered thus: "They are equally important." As are acting and artistic design. There is no question about how serious Wagner considered his role as poet. He was fastidiously concerned with poetic techniques of rhyme, meter, alliteration, and onomatopoeia, to stipulate four aspects so aptly demonstrated by the very first words of the drama sung by Woglinde, one of the Rhinemaidens, as she swims around a rock in the deep waters:

> *Weia! Waga!*
> *Woge, du Welle!*
> *Walle zur Wiege!*
> *Wagalaweia!*
> *Wallala weiala weia!*

Let us not even attempt a translation. The poetic alliteration of nonsense words and meaningful words, all beginning with the letter *W,* together represent the lulling, billowing, flowing waters cradling the Rhinemaidens, and when heard with Wagner's music depicting same, the synthesis of word and tone is unmistakable in its watery effect.

Wagner was no ordinary librettist. He was one of the best in the long history of opera. Books and articles discussing and explaining his poetic creations await those wishing to delve into an intriguing and esoteric subject that, among other things, reveals how Wagner quite consciously sought to re-create medieval poetic devices to lend authenticity to his verses telling of legendary times. Wagner, more musician than poet, nevertheless, will find it impossible to sustain a balance between word and tone. Much more on this later.

The facade of every operatic production is that of a synthesis of the arts, but when Lucia delivers her "Mad Scene" or when the four central characters of the quartet in the last act of *Rigoletto* stand, look at the audience, and just sing, all other arts are subordinate to music. Indeed, such it is in virtually all opera, no matter how calculated the attempt to give words their due, and music soon will unbalance Wagner's own synthesis of the arts. Accordingly, *The Rhine Gold* is the opera more than any other of his creations born out of his *Opera and Drama* theories.

Having introduced the story and a brief interpretation, it remains to comment on the music.

What, if anything, is unusual about the music of *Das Rheingold?* Here you might try an interesting little experiment, allowing your ears the first attempt to answer this question. From *La traviata*, listen to the concluding twelve to fourteen minutes, beginning with the lovely, lilting duet *Parigi, o cara*. Next, listen to the end of *Lohengrin*, the opera written by Wagner before starting his cycle. Finally, beginning with Donner's summoning the storm, listen to the conclusion of *The Rhine Gold*. Though Verdi and Wagner do not sound alike, there is, nevertheless, in *Traviata* and *Lohengrin* the similarity of structure, be it duet or aria, preceding the obvious finale. You can hear set numbers. Not so with *The Rhine Gold*. The final moments of this opera have become the most often excerpted but they are not those of a set number, even though over time they have become so popular as to become known simply as "The Entrance of the Gods into Valhalla." In reality, they are part of a musical continuation that began with the opening chord of the prelude. The musical gap between *Lohengrin* and *The Rhine Gold* is huge. You can hear the difference.

There are some easily understood reasons for this, and for purposes of this book you need comprehend only three basic concepts to realize what Wagner has done to reconstitute traditional opera as music drama. The first, that of a *Gesamtkunstwerk*—the creation of an artistic synthesis out of various arts all deemed equal in importance—you are already familiar with. The second is the concept of "endless melody." The third is that of *Leitmotifs* (leading motifs). Quite intentionally, Wagner has eliminated set numbers of operatic tradition: recitativo preceding an aria, for example. As the words of the poem unfold in an uninterrupted recitation, the music too moves through one long, uninterrupted act of four scenes segueing one into the other. This is "endless melody."

Clap your little heart out after the beautiful melody of your favorite Bellini has been sung. The singer wants it, and the conductor and orchestra stop the performance to allow you to do so.

Clap before *Das Rheingold* when the conductor enters the orchestra pit and clap again when the final curtain has fallen some two and a half hours later, but do not ever interrupt the "endless melody" of the drama with applause. This conception of "endless melody" obviously makes it much more difficult to direct you to some of the supreme musical moments of the drama, especially when the concept of *Leitmotifs*—let us call them themes or motifs—also is introduced.

The music of *The Ring Cycle* is made from more than one hundred musical themes. Virtually everything in the cycle, from natural phenomena to characters, from things to even ideas and emotions, has a musical counterpart in themes associated with each. No example is more immediately apparent or more easily comprehended than one that has remained for me a favorite since I was a little boy: the entrance of the giants in Scene 2. Freia pleads with her brothers to protect her from the giants who follow her to claim her as payment for building the castle. Fricka reprimands the gods for allowing this to happen to her sister. Then the orchestra says in gigantic, stalking tones

> *brump, bur –ump –ump*
> *brump, bur –ump –ump*

The giants, Fasolt and Fafner, both armed with great clubs, have arrived. Before they say a word, their theme, the motif that will stay with them throughout the drama, has announced and identified them in music inappropriate to anything other than awkward giants clomping onto the scene. The musical miracle of the cycle is how the genius of Wagner was able to make music so perfectly expressive. He transformed billowing water into music and made a rainbow of music, too. Things have their musical themes—the Tarnhelm and the gold ring, for example—and none is more magnificent than the theme associated with Valhalla. Concepts, such as the curse, also have their musical manifestation. Most of them are quite brief, lasting only a few seconds and made from just a handful of notes, but when passed around to different instruments for varying expressions or with tempos altered or when blended with other themes, the possibilities for creating a brilliant tapestry of "endless melody" is seemingly limitless.

The episode beginning with Donner's summoning of the thunderstorm is the most extraordinary example in the opera. Wagner makes music for thunder, lightning, a rainbow; the Valhalla motif resounds, as does Wotan's music and the shimmering fire of Loge. And there are the motifs of the ring, the curse, and the lamenting Rhinemaidens. Wagner weaves together these threads in the orchestra to create a musical depiction never before heard in opera.

Wagner did not write down all his themes and name them. Scholars and musicologists have done this over time. Not all agree in every respect, but as far as the most obvious, major motifs in *Das Rheingold* are concerned, the river, its gold, Valhalla, to name only three, there is no argument. You do not need to look up and memorize each theme and then attempt to identify its every appearance in the drama unless you are preparing for a Wagner quiz program or studying to become a musicologist. To begin, it is enough to listen to the music as you follow the story on a video or with libretto and recording. You will get to know the most often utilized motifs through osmosis. As the musical continuum takes you from the depths of the Rhine into the clouds for your first view of the castle, there is no mistaking that noble theme. Nor can one forget the clamoring anvils in the descent into Nibelheim.

In spite of Wagner's attempt at creating an endless melody, some music is more interesting and captivating. The final scene I have dwelled on. This "Entrance of the Gods into Valhalla" makes me go nuts every time I hear it. Also wonderful is the opening scene with the Rhinemaidens and their tomfoolery with Alberich, then, of a sudden, the flowing gold and its theft. The Scene 2 awakening of Wotan and Fricka is notable, as are the descent into the earth and the ascent back up to the realm of the gods.

It is helpful, also, to understand that a Wagnerian music drama orchestra has a life of its own. Its function is not to play a pretty melody as accompaniment to the singer. The orchestra has become a central character in the drama, expressing what words cannot fully say or substantiating more forcefully what is being said. When Alberich puts his curse on the ring, *verflucht sei dieser Ring!* ("cursed be this ring"), the orchestra sounds the motifs of hatred and the curse. And when you first meet Alberich, Wagner does not give him an enchanting melody because he is not an appealing fellow. Wagner has transformed opera from a story told in recitativo and expressed emotionally in one catchy or memorable tune after another into a drama told in both words and music. With the Wagnerian music drama, you have entered a new and different operatic world.

Wagner's plan was for *The Rhine Gold* to play as the preliminary drama on the eve of a three-day festival, the remaining three music dramas to be performed in order, one each day. The other dramas are much longer than *The Rhine Gold*, each more than four and a half hours long. A continuous performance of all four— and this has been done on radio and in other manifestations (more on this later)—would last nearly sixteen hours for the music alone. Add intermissions for time to eat and you will need to block out a day on your calendar. *The Ring Cycle* unquestionably is the most colossal creation in all opera. Unfortunately, some are intimidated by its size and its remove from reality into a world of gods and dwarfs and, accordingly, miss countless joys and stimulating experiences awaiting them in one of the wonders in all art history. The story alone is intriguing, and despite some long passages (usually narratives, some of which are needlessly repetitive), Wagner's music at times achieves overwhelming and glorious expression. Devoted Wagnerians, of which there are many, consider it transcendent. You, too, may become seduced by it. You too may become a "Wagnerian." It has happened to numerous students in my classes who knew nothing before the course began. Or you may find it is not your cup of musical tea. But you cannot avoid it altogether and consider yourself operatically informed or literate. *Die Walküre* follows *The Rhine Gold* and plays the first day of the festival.

DIE WALKÜRE (1876)
The Valkyrie

The Valkyrie of the drama's title is Brünnhilde. She is the favorite of nine daughters, collectively known as the Valkyries, produced by Wotan and Erda during the years that have lapsed between the end of *The Rhine Gold* and the beginning of *The Valkyrie*. These warrior maidens rescue heroes felled in battle and return them to Valhalla, where they, as an army, defend the castle of the gods after they recover. Like his Greek counterpart, Zeus, Wotan was exceedingly active sexually, except maybe with his wife, Fricka, with whom he had no known child. With a mortal woman, however, and disguised as a mortal himself under the assumed name of Wälse, he had fathered twins, a boy and girl, Siegmund and

Sieglinde. Here is where Wagner made the connection with Christian mythology that fascinated him so much. Jesus, of divine origin, is born of mortal woman and comes into the world to atone for the sins of the world.

In the third act of *The Valkyrie,* Brünnhilde assures the safety of Sieglinde:

> Know and protect this:
> the noblest hero ever
> grows in your womb and
> shall be born . . .

which is why I refer to *Die Walküre* as the Promise. This hero, like Jesus, has both divine and mortal parentage. Through Siegmund and Sieglinde and their hero offspring, Wotan seeks protection from alien forces and perhaps even the means to regain the ring.

The drama is in three acts. The characters and their voice ranges are:

SIEGMUND, twin son of Wotan and a mortal woman, *tenor*
SIEGLINDE, twin daughter of Wotan and a mortal woman, *soprano*
HUNDING, Sieglinde's husband, *bass*
WOTAN, ruler of the gods, *bass baritone*
BRÜNNHILDE, a Valkyrie born to Wotan and Erda, goddess of earth and wisdom, *soprano*
FRICKA, goddess of marriage and Wotan's wife, *mezzo-soprano*

The Valkyries (sisters of Brünnhilde also born of Wotan and Erda)
GERHILDE, *soprano*
HELMWIGE, *soprano*
WALTRAUTE, *mezzo-soprano*
SCHWERTLEITE, *contralto*
ORTLINDE, *soprano*
SIEGRUNE, *mezzo-soprano*
GRIMGERDE, *mezzo-soprano*
ROSSWEISSE, *mezzo-soprano*

The time again is legendary, about one generation after the events of *The Rhine Gold*, set in Hunding's hut in a forest, then on a high rocky place, and on a mountain peak.

Act I

A storm, raging in the orchestral prelude, subsides as the curtain opens for the first act on the interior of Hunding's hut, a humble dwelling in the woods, built around a huge ash tree rising through its middle and out the roof. The hut has a large hearth, a door to the outside, and an inner door to a second room. Through the outer door comes an exhausted young man running from enemies and seeking refuge from the storm. As the hut appears empty, he lies upon the hearth. He is Siegmund. In the other room, Sieglinde, thinking she has heard the return of her husband, opens the inner door and enters the main room. She approaches the stranger with growing curiosity, for at this time their sibling relationship is not known to her. He revives and requests water, which she serves in a drinking horn. They converse and she offers him mead, and then she tenders an invitation to remain as a guest. An intense mutual attraction has begun and they gaze profoundly upon one another.

Her husband, Hunding, returns. Armed and looking inhospitable, he directs Sieglinde to prepare a meal and invites Siegmund to remain. Hunding, already having observed the striking resemblance between guest and wife, asks who he is and what is his story. Siegmund explains why he calls himself Wehwalt ("Woeful"). He is the son of Wolfe. Parted from his mother and twin sister when quite young, and from his father soon thereafter, he has wandered endlessly to avoid his enemies, for now he has no weapons. Siegmund's story reveals to Hunding that he is harboring an enemy of his race, one who once killed kinsmen. He informs his guest that he may safely stay the night but in the morning, custom requires they meet in combat. Hunding sends Sieglinde to the other room and follows, leaving Siegmund alone with his thoughts.

Siegmund muses upon a promise made to him long ago by his father, who assured him he would provide him with a sword when in dire need. At this moment, the fire collapses, causing embers to glow brightly, and Siegmund sees a sword buried to its hilt in the ash tree. Sieglinde, attired in nightdress, returns having drugged Hunding's night drink. She assures Siegmund that her husband sleeps soundly in the other room and urges the young man to make his escape while he can. She relates to him, also, the story of the sword buried in the tree. During the wedding feast of her forced marriage to a man she does not love, a stranger appeared who frightened all. He swung the sword and drove it into the tree's trunk. Ever since, no one has had strength enough to remove it but she awaits with great anticipation for the man who can do so and will lead her from her sorrow to freedom. Overcome, Siegmund embraces her ardently.

The outer door swings open by itself and the resplendent spring night is illumined by the moon. The pair are in love and sing it passionately, ultimately recollecting their past and discovering their mutual destiny—brother and sister reunited at last, for he is Siegmund, the Volsung (Wälsung), and she Sieglinde, also a Volsung. He approaches the tree and with one mighty tug extricates the sword. He names it Nothung ("Needful" . . . it will play an important part in the rest of the story), and promises to lead her away:

> Bride and sister
> be to your brother:
> let Volsung blood bloom!

They embrace passionately as the curtain falls (on what evidently is not incest as long as half of one's blood is divine).

Traditional designations divide this act into three scenes: Siegmund and Sieglinde, Hunding's arrival home and departure to bed, and the love scene. Here the story has been told as one event because there is no actual change of scenery. Because the three dramas of the cycle after *The Rhine Gold* are so long, I have decided to write about the music act by act rather than after telling the whole story.

The Rhine Gold is the first opera presented in this book with no human beings as characters. Wagner had to find appropriate music to portray gods and giants, dwarfs and a dragon, even a toad, and he did. In his attempt to create a synthesis between words and tones, there is actually an imbalance favoring the words in spite of some exceedingly innovative musical passages. It is otherwise with *The Valkyrie*. Many who know Wagner's music hear in this drama the perfect balance of words and music. It is for them the crown jewel of *The Ring Cycle*. I cannot go quite so far.

Each drama of the cycle has its own individuality, reflecting as it does a different period in Wagner's development as an artist. Recall that the cycle took almost thirty years from conception to completion. Each contains musical wonders but there is no question about *The Valkyrie* being one of the most sublime of all musical masterpieces.

In the first act, important new motifs, those associated with Siegfried, Hunding, and the sword, to list three, are heard but it is the beautiful love theme that dominates the act. Recall Paul Bekker's thesis cited in chapter 5 of the reciprocal relationship between Wagner's life and work where experiences in his life and his artistic creations become one and the same, each reinforcing and inspiring the other. The love music of the first act is a perfect example. Wagner's autograph score for this act contains little messages in private code jotted in the margins. One reads "I.l.d.gr.!" It stands for *Ich liebe dich grenzenlos!* ("I love you boundlessly"). In Switzerland, Wagner, his own marriage beginning to deteriorate, met Otto Wesendonck, a wealthy silk merchant, and his young, beautiful wife, Mathilde. Otto Wesendonck befriended the composer and even helped him financially. Wagner and Mathilde, deeply attracted to each other, spent much time together and embarked on a love affair that reached its most passionate proportions in the late 1850s during Wagner's writing of *Tristan und Isolde*. The note in code was meant for her. Their growing passion is reflected in the beautiful love music dominating the first act.

Obviously, there are no set numbers in the drama. Nevertheless, two back-to-back passages of the third scene, the love scene, are so rapturously lovely that "an excerpt" has been forced upon them. The outer door has swung open on a glorious spring night and the lovers are illuminated in moonlight. Siegmund's love song begins, *Winterstürme wichen dem Wonnemond* ("The storms of winter have yielded to the bliss of spring"). Sieglinde answers him with *Du bist der Lenz* ("You are the spring for which I have longed").

On February 2, 1935, a thirty-five-year-old Norwegian soprano, unknown in the United States and contemplating retirement after a career in Europe, made her Metropolitan Opera debut on short notice when the Sieglinde of the day canceled. Those fortunate enough to be in the audience heard history being made early in the act, and by the time she had sung *Du bist der Lenz*, the power and beauty of her monumental voice had overwhelmed both audience and critics. From obscurity to instant fame it was for Kirsten

Flagstad, who is still acclaimed as the greatest Wagnerian soprano of the twentieth century—probably ever! Many of her famous recordings have been remastered onto compact discs. Flagstad's most renowned Wagnerian roles became those of Brünnhilde and Isolde. Listen to her recordings and in an instant hear the demands the big Wagnerian roles place on the human voice. Some passages require sustained singing for many minutes at a time, and to be heard over the huge Wagnerian orchestra requires a voice of great strength and stamina. Many soprano voices can be trained to sing lyrical and dramatic roles in Italian opera. The big Wagnerian roles of some *Ring Cycle* parts and of *Tristan and Isolde* can be portrayed adequately only by those few singers whose natural vocal endowments allowed for sufficient growth and development in their voice to handle the unusual demands of these creations. This is why so much excitement surrounds the discovery of one of those voices and why, when it happens, a singer can have instant fame heaped upon her. In our consideration of *Tristan und Isolde,* there will be more to be said about singing the big Wagnerian roles, but the sensational debut of Kirsten Flagstad is a fitting place to introduce the subject of still another characteristic distinguishing Wagnerian music drama from traditional operas.

Act II

Though the scenery of the second act, like that of the first, does not change, five distinct episodes comprise this act's five scenes. In the first, Wotan dispatches Brünnhilde to the place of combat between Hunding and Siegfried, promising that the latter will prevail. As Brünnhilde departs, she sees Fricka hurrying forth. There is a bitter confrontation with her husband as she points out his frequent infidelities, one of which resulted in the birth of Siegmund. If Siegmund—guilty of both incest and adultery—defeats Hunding, she, as goddess of marriage, will be the subject of mockery and humiliation. Wotan must give his oath to her that such will not be. Siegmund must die. Wotan's arguments and explanations fail and he, defeated and dejected, capitulates.

Scene 2: Fricka leaves and Brünnhilde returns to find her father brooding. She asks why. In a long narrative he tells of the theft of the gold and the ring, of Erda's warning, and of his attempt to avert the desmise of the gods through an army of fallen heroes brought to Valhalla by the Valkyries and through the intercession of his own half-god/half-mortal children, Sigmund and Sieglinde. He is sad because now Sicgmund must die. Brünnhilde begs her father to go back on his oath but he remains steadfast and commands her to obey his will. Troubled, she departs. Wotan goes his own way, too.

The third episode, Scene 3, begins with the arrival of Siegmund and Sieglinde as they flee from Hunding. They pause to rest, they embrace, and then Sieglinde becomes remorseful and urges Siegmund to leave her. He is too good for one who, in his arms, became a deceitful wife. In the distance, she hears howling from Hunding's dogs and the sound of his hunting horn. Again, she urges Siegmund to flee, then faints from fear in his arms.

In Scene 4, Brünnhilde returns and explains to Siegmund that the gods have decided he must die. With her he will go to Valhalla, but when he learns Sieglinde will not be there with him, he refuses. Brünnhilde promises she will protect the pregnant Sieglinde and the unborn child but Siegmund will not die leaving his beloved defenseless. Rather, he will kill her while she sleeps. As he draws his sword an emotional Brünnhilde stops him, explaining that her will is her own and she will see to it that he does not fall. She departs to the sounds of howling dogs and a horn, closer now.

The final scene, Scene 5, of the second act opens with Siegmund's farewell to Sieglinde. With her still deep in sleep, he has placed her safely on a rock. He departs to meet Hunding. Violent thunder and lightning awaken Sieglinde. In the distance the fight begins, Brünnhilde protecting Siegmund, who is about to kill Hunding, when out of a glowing red light Wotan materializes. Upon his intervening spear, Siegmund's sword shatters, thus leaving him defenseless. Hunding kills Siegmund. Brünnhilde takes Sieglinde with her on her horse to safety. In great sorrow Wotan looks upon the corpse of his son, contemptuously waves a hand at Hunding, who instantly falls to the ground dead, and, raging, warns that Brünnhilde will be in for it because she disobeyed his command. The curtain falls.

Remember that Erda has foretold the dire fate of the gods because Wotan once possessed the cursed golden ring, and that in an attempt to protect the gods Wotan with her has sired the nine Valkyrie sisters, whose job it is to build from fallen heroes an army to protect Valhalla. And with a mortal woman Wotan sired the Wälsungs, Siegmund and Sieglinde, free and independent of his will, to withstand the threat of the Nibelungs' hateful desire for revenge. But because the Wälsungs violated a marriage vow,

Fricka insisted Siegmund die in combat. Nothing was going Wotan's way and, worse, his favorite daughter disobeyed him. At least Sieglinde, with child, appears to be safe. This, as we soon discover in Act III, is of great significance for the unfolding of the rest of the cycle. So is Brünnhilde's disobedience. The consequences of these two factors will culminate in the third act of *Siegfried* and form the basis of the action for *Twilight of the Gods*.

The events of *The Valkyrie*, Act II, described above, are given notable musical expression by Wagner. As with the first act, the music remains more prominent than it was in *The Rhine Gold*, establishing Wagner's finest achievement of a synthesis of the arts (remember *Gesamtkunstwerk*). This has been noted but is repeated because for important reasons, which will be articulated at the end of our *Valkyrie* presentation, music will become increasingly dominant in all the remaining Wagnerian dramas, from *Siegfried* through *Tristan und Isolde*, *The Mastersingers*, *Twilight of the Gods*, and *Parsifal*. Music's growing importance can be heard especially in the role of the orchestra. Wagner's orchestra was big and often he asked from it a huge sound that has led some to say, "Wagner's operas are too heavy." This is an interesting comment because it is in his orchestral sound that many find Wagner's greatest achievement as a musician.

The prelude to Act II is a good example. The orchestra introduces, among others, one of the most immediately recognized of all Wagnerian themes, the celebrated "Ride of the Valkyries," which returns in its fullest manifestation at the beginning of the third act. This music is followed almost immediately by a hit tune extricated from Wagner's "endless melody" because it has become so famous. Brünnhilde answers Wotan's command to arms with her "Battle Cry":

> Hoyotoho! Hoyotoho!
> Heiaha! Heiaha
> Hoyotoho! Heiaha!

There is good music in Wotan's encounter with Fricka and more in his narrative with Brünnhilde after Fricka's departure. As Wotan tells his story, motifs by now familiar to you return in the orchestra. It is the fourth scene, however, of this long act (it is more than one and a half hours) wherein the longest sustained lyrical passage of this act is heard. A slow, somber, solemn orchestral introduction leading to a muted version of the Valhalla motif

commences what is known as *Todesverkündigung* ("Announcement of Death"): Siegmund, soon to die, will follow Brünnhilde to
Valhalla but he, without Sieglinde, has no interest in its wonders.
This hauntingly beautiful passage is one of Wagner's supreme
achievements of a poetic and musical synthesis. Those who
become addicted to Wagner point to it as an example of why. The
fifth and final scene of this act culminates in the return of the
tempestuous music of storm and battle.

Act III

Act III is in three scenes, all on the summit of a mountain. The
Valkyries, minus Brünnhilde, are returning fallen warriors to Valhalla. This rocky summit is their congregating place. They wait
for their sister, who finally arrives on her horse with an unconscious Sieglinde. Brünnhilde knows her father is pursuing her and
he is spied approaching in the distance. She calls on her sisters to
rescue Sieglinde and herself from Wotan's wrath, but they are
unwilling to thwart their father's will. Sieglinde awakens and
expresses a desire to join her beloved Siegmund in death; however, Brünnhilde urges her, "Rescue the son who will grow from
your love." Brünnhilde, who will stay behind to face her father's
fury, tells a willing Sieglinde to head eastward to the large forest
where looms Fafner hiding with his hoard. She will be safe there,
for Wotan shuns it.

A storm rages closer as Wotan nears. From beneath her saddle
Brünnhilde removes the broken fragments of Siegmund's sword
and gives them to Sieglinde, telling her that her son will need to
reforge it:

> His name, now learn it from me:
> Siegfried—victorious and free!

In *The Rhine Gold* we learned of the plague of greed from which the
world suffers and in *The Valkyrie* we learn of him who will be the
noblest hero, bringing victory unto the world. Now motivated to
live, Sieglinde slips away as Wotan's voice, nearer still, calls to
Brünnhilde to stay put. The Valkyries scamper up the rocks as the
scene ends.

Scene 2 begins with the arrival of a furious Wotan demanding
the presence of Brünnhilde. As her sisters unsuccessfully attempt
to assuage his anger, Brünnhilde steps forth and asks for her sentence. No more will she ride to and from Valhalla, her father tells

her. He will banish her from his life. She will be put to sleep, to remain so until some man awakens her and takes her for his wife, for she is to be stripped of godhood. Brünnhilde's sisters are horrified at the severity of the punishment and beg their father to retract it. He is resolute. As Brünnhilde sinks to the ground at his feet, Wotan orders her sisters to leave her alone, henceforth without consolation. He dismisses them. As they ride swiftly off on their horses, the threatening storm arrives, then subsides as twilight fades into darkness.

Here begins Scene 3. It is a father-and-daughter scene lasting nearly forty-five minutes, one of the greatest scenes in opera. Wotan and Brünnhilde are alone in a long silence. Slowly she looks up to ask if what she did was so terrible as to deserve such harsh retribution. She admits disobeying his command but points out that in doing so, she actually followed the true desire in her father's heart. Throughout their dialogue his wrath diminishes. Nevertheless, the punishment stands. He will place her in a deep sleep upon a rock until a man comes to awaken and claim her. She asks for some sort of resistance guard her so she will not be vulnerable to just any man. Wotan declines until, inspired, she hits upon the idea of his surrounding her by fire so only the bravest of heroes will penetrate, one who has no fear. Wotan submits. He bids his favorite, beloved daughter an emotional farewell and promises the fire. Father and daughter embrace. As he kisses her godhood away she sinks into his arms, unconscious. Wotan carries her to a mossy bank, lays her down, gazes longingly and lovingly, closes her helmet over her face, and covers her with her shield. Moving slowly away, he points his spear at the rocks around her and summons Loge to make fire. The flames flicker, ever higher and higher. With his spear, Wotan directs them to encircle his beloved daughter. Then, overcome by sorrow, Wotan disappears and the curtain falls.

The Ring Cycle, always open to various interpretations (mythical, political, socioeconomic, psychological, and more), does not offer a huge challenge in Act III. The literal meanings, with implications, are not complicated. The title of the opera is *The Valkyrie* and this is Brünnhilde's act with her sisters; but it is also Wotan's act. In the first scene the Valkyries dominate, the pivotal episode being Brünnhilde's making certain that Sieglinde will be safe. The second scene, appropriately, is of Wotan and his Valkyrie daughters toward the end of isolating Brünnhilde for punishment. Scene 3, with Wotan and Brünnhilde alone, is a high-point in opera history. Here Brünnhilde's punishment actually becomes an elemental ingredient in the Promise: Put to sleep on a rock encircled by fire, where only a fearless hero will dare penetrate, can there be any question as to who this hero will be? I think not. Brünnhilde herself has already foretold his name in informing Sieglinde that her son will be the noblest of heroes. Siegfried, of course! Time, on a divine plane in the world of immortals, ticks away in its own dimension.

Die Walküre is Wagner's supreme musical achievement so far. Oh, it will be transcended by *Tristan und Isolde*, but it will remain one of his most beloved, admired, and popular compositions primarily because of the love scene of the first act, the anticipation of death in the second, and the assorted gems of the third, beginning with the full-fledged version of "The Ride of the Valkyries," one of the most astonishing excerpts in all opera. This music has gone far beyond the opera stage into the concert hall, to commercials on TV, and to movie cartoons.

When he was a small boy, our son had the most wonderful hobbyhorse with enlarged nostrils, flying mane, and fire in its eyes. It was suspended in space except for sturdy springs emanating from each of the four legs to a support stand. He would mount it, in full cowboy regalia, and ride with the Valkyries, their battle cries resounding from my record player and his making certain a little sister didn't miss the action.

If the opening of this act is one you can sit through bored or unmoved, then Wagner probably is not for you. The wondrous music of this act simply does not let up. Exciting, too, are Brünnhilde's arrival, Sieglinde's awakening, and the scene of Wotan and his Valkyrie daughters. But the supreme achievement of the act—perhaps, the supreme achievement in all Wagner has composed to date—is the final scene between father and favorite daughter, a beautiful balance of poetry and music, as his wrath abates and he bids her a loving farewell. "Wotan's Farewell" and "The Magic Fire Music" which follows, some of Wagner's most well-known and appreciated music, bring the final act of this remarkable drama to a close.

When I was a graduate student, a Boston radio station honored a Wagnerian anniversary by suspending regular programming to air a complete *Ring Cycle*. I did my homework and went to my study for the event with libretti and scores: *The Rhine Gold* in the morning, *The Valkyrie* in the afternoon, *Siegfried* followed, and it was in the wee hours of the morning when *Twilight of the Gods* ended. I took no phone calls and offered only my best friend an invitation. David appeared for one hour in the middle of *Siegfried*, showed considerable curiosity over what I was doing and why, but then left, dismissing me as "crazy."

Something took. Years later, Dr. David H. Crook, a professor of history at Dalhousie University in Halifax, Nova Scotia, invited me to join him in an experiment. He would give students academic credit for being exposed to something they otherwise would more than likely never experience. What they had to do was attend a complete audio performance of *The Ring Cycle* in a large empty room with a big speaker in each corner and three large screens. On one screen, still photographs of any and everything having to do with the cycle followed the story. On the second screen, a translation of the story was synchronized with the music. A machine associated with the third screen allowed me to write instructive comments to the students who had been introduced to Wagner and his cycle by my lectures prior to the event. The students could follow what was transpiring, they could read a book, they could even curl up in a sleeping bag and sleep, but they could not talk or make a disturbance, and to get full credit they had to stick it out. After each drama we took an hour's intermission for a meal.

From the beginning of "Wotan's Farewell" to its last note is more than eighteen minutes, and as Wotan began I went to the machine and wrote "'Wotan's Farewell' is one of the most famous conclusions in all opera." After four and a half hours of *The Valkyrie*, the students were ready to eat, and having seen the word *conclusion*, they were anticipating their next meal. Quietly and respectfully, they moved to the door and formed a long line. The music went on. And on. And on. Finally, David walked over to the machine and wrote "Wagner's conclusions are long!"

On another occasion, as a visiting professor at Trinity College in Burlington, Vermont, I was teaching a course on Wagner with Dr. Nancy B. Holland and I told her of the Dalhousie experiment. Intrigued, she suggested we take our students through an all-day, all-night video presentation of the *Ring*. We did and it was a huge success.

Our introduction to *The Valkyrie* completed, we now must consider why Wagner, slowly but surely, will abandon his interest in a synthesis of the arts to allow the musician in him to prevail and why he will lose interest in the optimistic idea of revolution and art building a better world. Only then is his art more fully comprehensible.

Arthur Schopenhauer

In 1854, a friend of Wagner's suggested he read a book by a German philosopher: Arthur Schopenhauer's *The World as Will and Idea*. Wagner read the book three times within six months. Schopenhauer would remain for the rest of his life the most powerful and pervasive intellectual influence Wagner would ever know. Schopenhauer reversed the direction of Wagner's thinking and, accordingly, of his art. This must be explained if you want to understand his dramas after *The Valkyrie*, if you want to understand why he set aside his *Ring Cycle* after completing only two of the three acts of *Siegfried*, and why, when he did return to the cycle to complete it, he had transformed the intent of the dramas from their political partnership with radical revolutionary activity to an expression of religious resignation.

When Wagner first read Schopenhauer's book he was in the most conducive state of mind possible for absorbing this philosopher's pessimistic, tragic view of the human experience. The revolution Wagner so much anticipated had come, failed, and left him in exile. Deeply in debt, he was forced to beg and borrow money. He was unhappy in marriage. He was despondent. His artistic intuition had always inclined toward a mystical, pessimistic worldview. Recall that the Dutchman sought release from an imperfect world and Tannhaüser struggled for salvation. *The Ring Cycle*, however, was conceived while Wagner was exposed to intense intellectual stimulation by thinkers committed to a rationalistic and optimistic worldview. Reading and rereading Schopenhauer's book made Wagner realize that his own artistic intuition had arrived at a tragic view of life long ago, for what else is the unhappy ending of *Lohengrin* about? Two of Schopenhauer's concepts in particular hit Wagner like bolts out of the blue: the philosopher's central thesis and his views on music.

The thesis of Schopenhauer's long, demanding philosophical treatise attributes the ever-present evil in the world to "the Will," the elemental, irrational, and relentless force in the universe. For Schopenhauer there is no God, nor any ultimate source of cosmic Goodness to sustain an optimistic view of life. The insatiable Will rules the world, greedily driving individuals and nations to strive for more wealth and power. There is no curbing the Will. It can never be satisfied. It is the source of all evil in the world and the evil in the world is irredeemable. Now nearing the midpoint of his *Ring Cycle*, Wagner realized that the life, death, and resurrection of his hero Siegfried would not save the world from evil. Wagner had to face a long and arduous artistic struggle to resolve this problem, which is the consequence of his greatly altered view of life that Schopenhauer so provocatively and convincingly put into words for him.

And Schopenhauer's unique views on music struck Wagner with no less force. Schopenhauer did not believe in an equality of the arts, nor was his fascination with a synthesis of the arts. Among all the arts, Schopenhauer claimed supremacy for music. The sounds of great music, he asserted, are direct expressions of eternal truths. Music reveals more about the nature of the human experience and the nature of the universe than any other source of knowledge except for the deepest insights attainable only in the contemplative life of mystics. Never mind what all this means or how it works. For our purposes, it is sufficient to know Wagner was convinced by Schopenhauer's pessimistic view of the human experience and agreed with his belief in music as the highest art.

ᴄ୦

Before he had written one note of *Siegfried*, Wagner had begun to think about the sorrowful story of Tristan and Isolde as the subject for a drama about escaping from the evils of the world. So powerful this idea soon became that Wagner would set aside his *Ring Cycle* without finishing *Siegfried* to compose what many consider his greatest artistic achievement and indeed one of the greatest works of art in human history: *Tristan und Isolde*.

SIEGFRIED (1876)
Acts I and II

The opera is in three acts. As I've just mentioned, Wagner wrote the first two acts then set the opera aside. He did not complete it until many years later after he composed *Tristan und Isolde* and *Die Meistersinger*. For reasons that I explain later in this chapter, I will discuss these operas in the manner in which he wrote them. My discussion of the third act of Siegfried, therefore, can be found on page 293.

Years have transpired since Brünnhilde was put to sleep upon the rock. Sieglinde, found by Mime, died giving birth to Siegfried, who has been raised by the dwarf in a cave in the woods near where Fafner, transformed into a dragon, guards the hoard. The characters and voice ranges are:

SIEGFRIED, *tenor*
MIME, *tenor*
WOTAN, in disguise as the Wanderer, *bass baritone*
ALBERICH, *bass baritone*
FAFNER, disguised as a dragon, *bass*
ERDA, *contralto*
The voice of the forest bird, *soprano*
BRÜNNHILDE, *soprano*

The action takes place in Mime's cave, in the forest, and on a rocky mountain in legendary times.

Act I
There are three scenes to the first act, which opens on Mime, frustrated because he cannot forge a sword Siegfried cannot easily shatter—a suggestion of the hero's power. Only the sword Nothung could serve Siegfried, but it is too much sword for the dwarf to forge. Mime hopes to use the boy's power to regain the ring by having him slaughter Fafner. The lust for gold is insatiable. Siegfried enters leading a bear, which terrifies Mime. He frees the bear to run off. Mime shows his latest effort at a sword. Siegfried rudely disdains it. Mime rebukes him, claiming to be both father and mother to him, and chastening the boy for his hateful attitude and lack of appreciation for years of nurturing and loving care. Siegfried responds with loathing and forces Mime to reveal his true parenthood; Sieglinde was his mother, his father, Siegmund, died in battle; and the sword fragments were given to Mime as payment. Siegfried orders Mime to forge the sword. He will take it and make his own way, never to return to the dwarf he despises. He departs, leaving Mime more frustrated than ever.

Scene 2 begins with the entrance of Wotan, disguised as the Wanderer, who asks for hospitality. Mime refuses. In a long dialogue, they enter into a test of wits, the loser to forfeit his head. Mime poses three questions. What race dwells in the earth? Wotan answers, "The Nibelungs." What race roams the earth's surface? Wotan answers, "The Giants." What race inhabits the cloudy heights? Wotan answers, correctly, "The Gods." Wotan's turn. What race is most dear to Wotan? "Volsungs," Mime replies correctly. What sword must Siegfried wield in killing Fafner? "Siegmund's sword," Mime responds correctly. He is stymied, however, when Wotan asks, "Who will wield the sturdy splinters of the sword Nothung?" Mime is terrified. The Wanderer responds. Only he who has never known fear can forge the sword, the same one who will have the head I leave you, Wotan declares. He departs.

The final scene of the act begins with Siegfried's return to acquire the sword. Mime explains that he could not manage it. Only one who has never felt fear is capable of forging such a sword. Siegfried, who has never experienced fear, does not comprehend and orders Mime to teach him about the new emotion. Mime consents: "Fafner will teach you fear." Siegfried will forge the sword himself before they depart for the dragon's lair. Mime's concern over the Wanderer's prophecy grows as he watches the boy succeeding at the forge. He foresees the slaying of the dragon and Siegfried getting the ring he covets, but with cunning and brains Mime will save his own head and gain the hoard. He will brew a potion to render Siegfried unconscious after he has killed the dragon. In one of the most intense scenes in all opera, Mime concocts his brew while Siegfried forges the sword, with which he shatters an anvil as the first act comes to its conclusion.

In each of the three acts of *Siegfried* is heard some of Wagner's most memorable music. The famous "Forging Scene," which concludes the first act, is dominated by a magnificent orchestral voice. To what extent Wagner consciously intended this or to what extent Schopenhauer's metaphysics of music was at this point unconsciously at work within him is, for us, academic. The power and expressiveness of the orchestra, more than with *The Rhine Gold* or *The Valkyrie*, is obvious. Wagner's synthesis of the arts is becoming decidedly unbalanced as the orchestra takes charge.

While Siegfried ecstatically forges the parts of the sword into one indomitable weapon and Mime maliciously brews both his evil plot and his deadly potion, the orchestra resounds with the dwarf's lustful scheming and the hero's jubilant satisfaction of having remade his father's sword. Siegfried, now armed with his own might and his sword's awesome power, is ready to go out into the world, but he is naively unaware of the full range of all that awaits him: Nibelung hatred, a giant's treasure crowned by an accursed ring, the faltering gods, and a beautiful, mortal woman sleeping on a rock waiting to be awakened by a fearless hero brave enough to penetrate the curtain of fire protecting her.

Act II

The second act is also in three scenes. Wagner had an extraordinary sense of dramatic balance and his dramatic forms often were built of three acts of three scenes each. The second act takes place outside Fafner's cave deep in the forest. As the curtain opens, Alberich is seen waiting and watching the cave, hoping through some turn of events to retrieve his treasure. Wotan, still in disguise as the Wanderer, appears and is recognized by Alberich. In the ensuing conversation, the angry dwarf exclaims he will obtain the ring when Fafner dies. With its power, he says, he will conquer Valhalla and become master of the world. Wotan exhorts Alberich to be aware of Mime's plot to use the young hero to gain the treasure. Then Wotan, who will not enter into the quest for the golden ring, awakens Fafner so they can warn him that a valiant hero is coming to test the dragon's strength. I love Fafner's response:

Mich hungert sein.

Me be hungry.

Alberich attempts to cajole the ring out of Fafner but the huge dragon wants only to sleep undisturbed. Wotan laughs, warns Alberich of his brother's intentions, and departs. A confident Alberich resumes his hiding place and waits to strike.

Scene 2 reveals Siegfried and Mime arriving with the dawn. Mime points to Fafner's cave. It is there, he proclaims, that Siegfried will learn fear from the dragon, who can eat him whole, whose venom can shrivel body and bone, and whose tail can crush him to death. Siegfried is unmoved. He wants to get the ordeal over with so he can be free and rid himself of Mime forever. As Mime goes off to a stream to refresh himself, hoping hero and dragon each will kill the other, Siegfried reclines beneath a lime tree and falls into a reverie. He thinks of his mother, reflects on the beauties of nature, and, enjoying the song of a bird, he wishes he could understand what it sings. Perhaps if he mimics the bird he can learn its tongue. He goes to a stream, cuts a reed, and attempts, unsuccessfully, to imitate the bird's song. Perhaps his horn will do better. He sounds some notes and these arouse the slumbering dragon, who appears. Can you, perhaps, teach me fear? Siegfried wonders. Fafner shows his great teeth, thrashes his tail, and spits venom. Then the dragon attacks. In the fray, Siegfried wounds the dragon's tail, dodges, and thrusts his sword into Fafner's heart. Dying, the dragon tells the story of the gold and admonishes the boy to beware of the one who put him up to this deed, for he has also planned the youth's demise. As Siegfried retrieves his sword he touches Fafner's blood. It burns his fingers. Putting his hand to his mouth to lick his fingers, he is amazed to discover that he now is able to comprehend the song of the forest bird, who tells of the treasure in the cave and of Tarnhelm and the golden ring:

> "Should Siegfried obtain the Tarnhelm
> great deeds he will perform;
> Should he discover the ring
> he will become master of the world."

Siegfried enters the cave.

Meanwhile, in this act's Scene 3, Alberich and Mime arrive together, quarreling furiously over the hoard and who gets what. For Alberich it will be all or nothing. They hide as Siegfried exits the cave with helmet and ring. Alberich departs, confident he eventually will regain the ring. This is Mime's big moment, but it is spoiled by the bird, who reveals to Siegfried what Mime is really thinking as the dwarf pretends to offer the boy a refreshing drink. Siegfried kills Mime, throws his corpse into the cave, and, with a huge effort, covers the entrance with Fafner's body. Again, he reclines beneath the lime tree to rest. Communing with the bird, the young hero notes that he is alone in the world and seeks a friend. The bird tells him about Brünnhilde sleeping on the rock waiting for a fearless hero to awaken her to be his bride. Siegfried now comprehends his destiny. The bird leads him out of the forest and on toward the sleeping maid as the second act curtain falls.

Following the story, surely you have put one and one together to get two. Siegfried and Brünnhilde—the mortal hero and his mortal bride-to-be—ready to encounter a world in dire need of redemption from an elemental evil raging from the greed of a god whose race is subsequently doomed by the desire for revenge of a savage dwarf.

The most famous music in this second act is the orchestral interlude now known as "The Forest Murmurs," an expression of nature's incomparable beauty as reflected upon by Siegfried sitting under the lime tree. It is another reason why I do so love this opera, and never have I been able to understand why many think less of it than *The Valkyrie* or *Twilight of the Gods*.

Lovely, also, is the conclusion to the act. Siegfried, having disposed of Fafner and Mime, returns to sit under the lime tree. There he realizes that he is alone and wishes for a friend. The forest bird sings her song of love, telling of Brünnhilde, and leads him forth.

When Wagner finished composing this act, he set aside *The Ring Cycle* for almost twelve years. When he took it up again to its conclusion, he was not the same composer. Much had happened to his life and, accordingly, to his art. Two monumental dramas, of necessity, intervened: *Tristan und Isolde* and *The Mastersingers of Nuremburg*. For important reasons, I have decided to do what Wagner did—namely, to put aside *The Ring Cycle* to discuss these two operas within the context of Wagner's life and work. It is, I think, a more informative and a more interesting approach. If you cannot wait, however, and are dying to know the outcome of *The Ring Cycle*, leap ahead for *Siegfried*'s third and final act (p. 293), followed by *Twilight of the Gods*. But if you do this and then fail to come back to *Tristan* and *The Mastersingers*, you will have passed by two of the greatest dramas in the history of opera.

The Wagnerian dramas are the most difficult to explain in the standard operatic repertory for several reasons. First, Wagner was exceedingly unusual in being both poet and musician. There are a few limited instances where a musician has set his own libretto, but no other major composer in all opera history was *always* both poet and musician in the creation of an entire corpus. Second, the works are quite long. Even Wagner's shortest operas are longer than many other standard works. Third, these dramas, starting with *The Flying Dutchman*, are based on Wagner's use of myths, which he revised as a means of portraying his own external and internal experiences. Fourth, Wagner was the most significant revolutionary in the long history of operatic development, and an understanding of such concepts as "music drama," "endless melody," "motifs," and "synthesis of the arts" contributes much to appreciating the dramas. Finally, we must not forget that his ultimate intent was not just to make opera for entertainment but rather to create religious music dramas in order to enlighten his audience and influence their behavior accordingly.

To believers of traditional religious forms, *The Ring Cycle* certainly does not appear religious, but when one knows of Wagner's detailed sketch for a drama on Jesus of Nazareth and how he envisioned Siegfried as the counterpart in Germanic myth—indeed, as already I have noted, how for Wagner one was born out of the other—*The Ring Cycle's* religious dimensions become immediately more evident.

Having reestablished how and why Wagner presents the beginning student of opera with far and away the greatest challenge, we arrive at that drama by Wagner deemed by many to be his ultimate masterpiece and his most creative, most impenetrable work: *Tristan und Isolde*. But do not cower. You can progress from beginner to expert if you are patient enough to be part of asking and answering a few basic questions, the most revealing of them pertaining to the Act I "love potion" incident, night/day symbolism in the second act, and, also in this act, the introduction of the concept of "love-death," which reaches its full manifestation in the final act.

Why did Wagner set *The Ring Cycle* aside?

We must isolate five interrelated aspects to answer this question. First, Wagner had been thinking about the story of Tristan and Isolde as a subject for a drama for several years; their sad fate held immense appeal for him as he brooded in political exile, separated from homeland and friends. Second, while in this unhappy state of mind he had become mesmerized by the pessimistic philosophy of Arthur Schopenhauer, whom he had encountered simultaneously with his infatuation with the Tristan subject. Both served as an antidote to their own gloom by vividly and brilliantly articulating a tragic view of life. Third, obviously Wagner vicariously read into Tristan and Isolde's illicit, all-consuming love story his own passionate affair with Mrs. Wesendonck. As he left Siegfried following the woodland bird (Act II of *Siegfried*), he began and quickly completed a prose sketch of the Tristan subject and soon thereafter wrote his *Tristan und Isolde* poem.

Fourth, a romantic to the core, Wagner's Romanticism, nevertheless, was of the two-feet-on-solid ground and hardheaded practicality variety. He had not had a new opera performed in more than seven years and so incomprehensibly huge a conception did his incomplete *Ring Cycle* appear to theater managers that none exhibited interest. He needed to get something on the boards. Finally, always short of funds, he had convinced himself, innocently but erroneously as we shall see, that because of the few characters and simple sets, an opera on the Tristan and Isolde story would be easy and inexpensive to mount, thus providing him with some much needed money. But the "simple" conception had a life of its own, and it grew and grew into one of the longest and most demanding dramas in the history of operatic composition.

By the time he had finished composing *Tristan*, in the summer of 1859, Wagner was beginning to realize the price he would have to pay to see this monumental work performed. One theater accepted it, only to drop it when both singers and orchestral players agreed it was too difficult. Then a second theater—after more than two dozen rehearsals—reneged, having determined the work unsingable. The press mocked Wagner for having created an "unproducible" drama. But on June 10, 1865, when the work for the first time finally was performed, it was a triumph. So it has remained unto this day. More on this to come.

A series of far more involved questions next confronts us. What is the basic feature of the original Tristan and Isolde story? How and why did Wagner use this legend? What is so unusual about the music? These three questions, which will be given one long answer, can be condensed into one question. What do you need to know about Wagner's Tristan und Isolde?

TRISTAN UND ISOLDE (1865)
Tristan and Isolde

The origins of this, one of the most famous of all love stories, is lost in a distant past. Wagner based his drama on Gottfried von Strassburg's version of the epic written about 1210 and left incomplete at his death. It tells of the orphaned Tristan raised to knighthood by his uncle, King Marke of Cornwall. In an adventure to Ireland, Tristan is wounded while killing in mortal combat the uncle of Isolt, the beautiful Irish princess. Though hating him for killing her kinsman, she heals his wound. Tristan, who returns to Cornwall, tells his uncle of Isolt's incomparable beauty. King Marke dispatches Tristan back to Ireland to bring Isolt to him to become his bride. During the sea voyage to Cornwall, Tristan and Isolt accidentally drink a love potion, which causes them to fall so passionately in love that they will use every imaginable trick to deceive Marke. Tristan, trying to forget Isolt, finally leaves and marries another—Isolt of the White Hands—though all the while still loving Isolt of Ireland. Gottfried's version ended here with his death.

Two other poets finished the story: Tristan receives a second wound only Isolt of Ireland can heal. She is summoned, but Isolt of the White Hands lies to him, saying Isolt of Ireland has refused to come. Tristan dies. When the Irish Isolt arrives, she dies from grief over her dead lover.

The medieval version makes much of the various tricks and deceptions employed by the lovers during their affair at Marke's castle. Wagner, on the other hand, has a different and far more profound philosophical and religious intent. With his customary dramatic deftness, he trims all that is superfluous to his purpose of representing a love so overwhelmingly powerful it must defy all conventional codes of morality and of life, to find consummation only in death. Trying to understand *Tristan und Isolde* without some knowledge of Wagner's own love affair with Mathilde, his fascination with and absorption of Schopenhauer's philosophy, and his immersion in Buddhist philosophy, all part and parcel with the composition of this drama, is like trying to bake bread with no ingredients. One can, of course, understand the story and even appreciate the music, but one cannot, without some knowledge of the above, experience in full measure those layers of meaning lying beneath a mere exposition of the plot.

The following synopsis presents the plot of Wagner's poem, probes the deeper meanings, and isolates musical sections of the drama in order to point out how and why this work was, and remains, such a revolutionary drama.

The opera is in three acts. The characters and their voices are:

TRISTAN, a heroic Cornish knight, and nephew of King
   Marke, *tenor*
KING MARKE, King of Cornwall, *bass*
KURWENAL, friend and retainer of Tristan, *baritone*
MELOT, a courtier, *tenor*
ISOLDE, an Irish princess, *soprano*
BRANGÄNE, Isolde's maidservant, *soprano*
A sailor, *tenor*
A helmsman, *baritone*

A shepherd, *tenor*
Sailors, knights, and attendants

The opera takes place in legendary times on a ship at sea, outside King Marke's castle in Cornwall, and at Tristan's castle in Brittany.

Act I

The prelude to the first act has become one of the most loved and famous pieces of music in the entire world of opera. Wagner called it a continuously developing expression of "the first timidest lament of inappeasable longing, the tenderest shudder, to the most terrible outpouring of an avowal of hopeless love . . . traversing all phases of the vain struggle against the inner ardor, until this, sinking back powerless upon itself, seems to be extinguished in death."[†] The story of *Tristan und Isolde* is one of a mutual love and longing so overwhelming and yet forbidden that only in death can it be fulfilled and redeemed. This is what Wagner is "saying" without words in his famous prelude to the first act.

It is music of incomparable beauty, but Eduard Hanslick, a Viennese music critic who hated Wagner, didn't think so. He said the prelude reminded him of an old Italian painting of a martyr whose intestines were slowly being unwound from his body on a large reel. (More on Hanslick with Wagner's *The Mastersingers*.) The prelude has no formal ending but, with the parting of the curtain for Scene 1, connects with the brief, unaccompanied song of a sailor on a ship on its voyage from Ireland to Cornwall. It is Tristan's ship. Isolde, her face buried in cushions, sits on a couch within a tent on the foredeck. Brangäne holds back a curtain and stares over the side of the ship across the sea. The young sailor is in the masthead singing a melancholy farewell to the wild Irish maid he has left behind. In this wonderful, terse song are four lines T. S. Eliot quoted in the opening section of his poem "The Waste Land":

> *Frisch weht der Wind*
> *der Heimat zu:*
> *mein irisch Kind,*
> *wo weilest du?*

[†] Ernest Newman, *The Wagner Operas* (Alfred A. Knopf, New York, 1963), p. 205

> The fresh wind
> blows toward home:
> my Irish lass,
> where do you abide?

Work this into your next conversation on either this opera or Eliot's celebrated poem and you will be impressive! Isolde, listening to the sailor's farewell to the girl he left behind, incorrectly hears in the reference to an Irish maid a mocking reference to herself. She looks up, agitated, asks Brangäne where they are, and is told they will land in Cornwall by dark. "Nevermore! Not today nor tomorrow," Isolde responds, commencing a dialogue in which we learn she is very upset and that her attendant is concerned for her.

Isolde calls upon the winds to destroy the ship. Brangäne pleads that she reveal the reasons for her wrath but Isolde asks for more air. Her maidservant pulls back the curtains of their compartment to reveal the ship's deck, sailors busy with their tasks and Tristan in command. Wagner designates this as the change to Scene 2.

Again we hear the sailor's lonely song from on high as Isolde stares at Tristan. He will not even look at her. She sends Brangäne to summon him but in his polite refusal he claims he must remain at the helm while Kurwenal loudly sings in praise of the great knight.

Brangäne's return to her mistress with Tristan's answer is the beginning of Scene 3, wherein Isolde, enraged by his attitude, tells Brangäne of Tristan's previous visit to Ireland to collect taxes for his lord, how he was wounded in the combat in which he killed her affianced, Morold, and how she found him in a boat, dying. He falsely represented himself to her as Tantris but she knew who he was—he who had killed her bethrothed. Her initial desire was for revenge but as she raised a sword above his head, he looked not at the sword but into her eyes. "His eyes met mine directly," she says in the most revealing phrase in the long narrative. She dropped the sword and with care and healing potions nursed him back to health. Now he who owes her his life is taking her as a vassal to be the bride of his old, weary uncle. She is furious. Brangäne, commenting on the good match Tristan has made for her, attempts unsuccessfully to console Isolde, who wants no part of an arranged, political marriage of convenience with an aged monarch who will not even love her. Brangäne, who still has not

caught on to what really is troubling her mistress, assures Isolde
that even an old, cold king can be made ardent by the potions in
the casket of magic arts packed for her by her mother. Isolde stuns
Brangäne by isolating the vial of poison, exclaiming, "The drink
here serves my turn."

Scene 4: Kurwenal enters their compartment. Land has been
sighted so he instructs them to ready themselves for debarking.
Isolde, who has composed herself, with dignity informs Kurwenal
to tell Tristan she will not be escorted by him to King Marke
unless first he comes to her to atone for his offense. Kurwenal
departs.

Scene 5: Isolde insists a horrified Brangäne prepare a drink
from the potion she has picked out. Tristan enters. Isolde wants to
know why he has ignored her. It is customary to keep away from
another man's bride-to-be, he explains. Isolde reminds him of their
past and of her unfulfilled revenge on him for his murder of her
bethrothed. Gallantly he offers her his sword, but she instead proposes a drink of friendship. He is not fooled. Tristan drinks half
the contents of the golden goblet before Isolde seizes the cup and
drinks the rest. Thus begins one of the most magnificent scenes in
all opera. Wagner's stage directions are as follows:

> She drinks, then throws away the cup. Both seized
> with shuddering, gaze with deepest emotion, but
> without changing their position, while their
> death-defiant expression changes to the glow of
> passion. Trembling seizes them; they convulsively
> clutch their hearts and pass their hands over their
> brows. Their glances again seek to meet, sink in
> confusion, and once more turn with growing long-
> ing upon each other.[†]

Then, with a trembling voice Isolde utters his name: "Tristan!"
He replies with an outburst of "Isolde!"

The rapturous, passionate music accompanying this scene is
unusual and some of the most beautiful and evocative sounds
Wagner, or anybody else, for that matter, ever wrote. Lost in a
mystical world of their own, Tristan and Isolde release their long

---

† Richard Wagner, *Tristan and Isolde* (E.P. Dutton & Co. Inc., New York,
1965, translation by Stewart Robb), p. 47

repressed and overwhelming love for each other. The ship has arrived and dropped anchor, trumpets sound from the shore, the sailors hail Cornwall, and Isolde faints upon Tristan's breast as the first act comes to its conclusion.

Tristan and Isolde, lost in surging, heaving bewilderment of their now acknowledged love for each other, had caused considerable confusion and consternation for their servants, who attempted to ready them to properly greet King Marke. Brangäne, trying to steady her mistress, asserts:

> Isolde! Mistress!
> Be calm!

Isolde, in a tizzy, responds:

> Where am I? Am I alive?
> Oh! What drink was that?

Brangäne's desperate reply is:

> *Der Liebestrank.*
>
> The love potion.

Brangäne surreptitiously substituted a love potion for the death potion Isolde requested because she loves her mistress and could not contemplate preparing a poisonous drink.

Here Wagner has made an innovation on the legend of Tristan and Isolde. In the medieval story, it is the love potion that causes them to fall in love. The love potion, in Wagner's version, merely releases the profound passion Tristan and Isolde have sublimated; the eventual revelation of their love, poetically and musically, is what this long act is about. The dialogue, narrations, and stage directions, without explicitly saying it, establish the origin of their mutual passion in the meeting of their eyes when Isolde attempted unsuccessfully to avenge the death of Morold. Tristan's aloofness during the sea voyage and Isolde's agitation over his neglect of her are superficial manifestations of their deep longing for each other, which is set free when they drink the love potion. Wagner's psychological insight regarding the love drink is brilliant. Thinking they have drunk poison, Tristan and Isolde now are free to disregard all moral conventions and to admit to the passion raging within them that caused their fussy and formal behavior toward each other during the crossing from Ireland to Cornwall. They could have drunk water with the same result. At first, they are spellbound and cannot speak, but the orchestra takes over to express the release of their intense longing in the most astounding music of this act (after that of the prelude).

Now, here is an important warning: You must be wary of opera guides giving names to the motifs out of which Wagner constructed this magnificent music. Indeed, the same holds true throughout the opera. The orchestral score of the drama is symphonic and this is one of Wagner's major revolutionary contributions to operatic development. Often the orchestra has a life of its own, independent of what is being sung, or, as is the case while the lovers are too overcome to say anything, it is the expressive voice portraying the release of an overwhelming longing and a profound and abiding love.

The orchestra is a central character in this drama. It can fully express what mere words are able to articulate only partially. Its symphonic score is constructed out of numerous musical themes that over the years have been isolated and given names. This popular undertaking is quite misleading. Wagner continues to make his "endless melody" by weaving motifs into a unified whole but no longer is he doing it in the same literal manner he employed in the early stages of *The Ring Cycle,* where, for example, a certain motif always means giants or Valhalla. Scholars have given names to the approximately thirty motifs out of which Wagner wove the glorious tapestry of the *Tristan und Isolde* score: "love glance," "ecstasy," "anguish," "love potion," to cite a few. For the preparation of my doctoral thesis, my professor, Jack M. Stein,[†] an internationally recognized Wagner expert, made certain that I understood the pointlessness of naming, isolating, and trying to identify motifs in this opera. In his revelatory book, *Richard Wagner and the Synthesis of the Arts*, he wrote the following:

> The approximately thirty motifs which occur in Tristan are so thoroughly musical and symphonic in character that it is not only irrelevant, but virtually impossible, to give them accurate names.[†]

[†] Jack M. Stein, *Richard Wagner & The Synthesis of the Arts* (Detroit: Wayne State University Press, 1960), p. 145

So, do not busy yourself trying to identify all the motifs by name when you hear them played. Doing so will be to miss what the music is really saying. Just listen. You will hear the longing, love, and expiration into death, which is what the opera is about.

An explanation of Wagner's philosophical implications latent within such words, however, is essential to comprehending all of what he had in mind. The first act has established the reality of the hidden and then revealed overpowering love of Tristan and Isolde for each other. These philosophical implications are found in their long Act II love duet, the longest and most penetrating and perplexing love duet in all opera—some would add, the most magnificent, too.

Act II

The first scene of the second act, a dialogue between Isolde and Brangäne, is introduced by a musical depiction of a lovely summer night, a perfect night for lovers. The horns of King Marke's hunting party are heard fading in the distance. The setting is a garden before Isolde's chamber. A torch burns by the open door. When extinguished it signals that the coast is clear for the waiting Tristan to come to his beloved. So helpless are he and Isolde against their passion that they have contrived to meet at night in defiance of all codes of morality and convention, deceiving Marke and exploring and fulfilling mutual yearnings. Melot, posing as a true friend to Tristan, has arranged the hunting party that takes Marke away from his castle, but Brangäne suspects that Melot intends to trick Tristan by disclosing the infidelity and thus stepping over Tristan as Marke's heir. She warns and warns again but Isolde, blind to all but the fulfillment of her desire to be with Tristan, against Brangäne's urging throws down the torch, extinguishing it, and soon, with Brangäne now on the parapet as a lookout, the ecstatic lovers are in each other's arms as the Scene 2 love duet begins with passionate exclamations of greeting:

Tristan:
Isolde! Beloved!

Isolde:
Tristan! Beloved!
Are you mine?

But here I must comment on the use of the words "love duet," for what transpires between Tristan and Isolde in this lengthy episode resembles in no way other, typical love duets in opera wherein, in essence, one says to another, "I love you." The marriage of King Marke was a "marriage of convenience" (heirs, money, political alliances) commonplace in the upper class at this time. Hopelessly drawn together by an inexorable longing for each other, Tristan and Isolde will defy such a marriage to consummate their love. Numerous are the lovers in literature of this genre who do just that, employing a "watch" to ensure the secrecy of their clandestine trysts. So far nothing atypical is at work here—that is, until the actual love duet is launched.

The couple's mutual attestations of love go far beyond their physical attraction to explore their innermost feelings, repudiating the day that keeps them apart and resolving to find fulfillment of their longings in a mystical union forever sealed in death. This famous scene is more than half an hour in length and it is never "cut." Cuts, by the way, are not uncommon, especially in long operas (Wagner is a favorite target) and are made, usually at the discretion of the conductor or theater manager, as a means of shortening the performance and/or tightening the dramatic action. Because this love scene is so long and unusual in its language, often abstruse in its philosophical implications, I will consider it arbitrarily in four separate sections even though it is, of course, a miraculous musical continuum of differing moods, speculations, and the interspersed warnings of Brangäne.

The first begins with their joyful greetings, both in words and fervent music. It is the longest single portion of the duet and includes, after their greetings and an embrace, a spontaneous outburst of words and phrases expressing their happiness—"joy exalting," "desire quivering," "mine," "yours," "forever one," etcetera—which settles down into a denunciation of daytime, which separates them: *Dem Tage! Dem Tage! Dem tückischen Tage!* ("Daylight! Daylight! Spiteful light of day!") and they proceed to express the perplexing mix of deep emotions embodied in their relationship, from first meeting, to their drinking the wondrous potion that set free their love, to this blessed moment in the protective darkness of blessed night. Tristan expresses a summation of their feelings in the final lines of the first part of their rendezvous:

> In daytime's idle fancies
> a single yearning to him remains—
> the yearning

for blessed night,
where forever
one truth alone,
love's rapture,
to him rejoices!

With these words, the ardent music of the first part of the duet has become quieter and more gentle as Tristan draws Isolde to him and they sink upon a flowery bank.

Here begins what I am designating the beautiful second part. Before continuing, however, let us note Wagner's fascinating reversal of traditional symbols in the opening portion. Recall that in both *The Magic Flute* and *Fidelio*, and in countless other works of art, the light of day is a symbol of positive attributes such as goodness, freedom, and truth; darkness symbolizes evil, falsehood, imprisonment. Under the impulse of a radical revolutionary, Wagner, too, used them in this fashion, for in his original conception of *The Ring Cycle* Siegfried is the light of the world overcoming dark, evil forces. Already noted is Wagner's intellectual transformation during the 1850s from the optimism of a revolutionary to a position of religious resignation, and with this comes the extraordinary altering of poetic symbols wherein in *Tristan und Isolde* day is evil and night is holy. The implications of all of this are made more clear when we isolate the central poetic idea of the drama found in the exceedingly beautiful opening portion of the second part of the love scene.

On the flowery bank, to strains of exquisitely beautiful music, the lovers sing to blessed night:

O sink about us
night of love,
make me forget
that I'm alive,
take me up
into your breast:
from the world
set me free.

Their hymn to the night continues, to conclude with:

Isolde:
Heart on heart

mouth on mouth;

Tristan:
Together bound
by one breath . . .

Both:
I, myself,
I am the world:
holiest love is life . . .

What kind of talk is this? Certainly this is not the language of
your normal operatic love duet. It is language partially derived
from Wagner's immersion in Schopenhauerian and Buddhist studies. But *Tristan und Isolde* is more than the philosophy of
Schopenhauer and elements of Buddhism presented operatically.
Wagner's personal melancholy, his isolation, and his world-weariness were the wellspring from which he drew most heavily for
this work. The central poetic idea of the drama is sublime extinction wherein one becomes free of all earthly delusions: *löse von
der Welt mich los* ("from the world set me free"). This concept
comprises the interrelated ideas of the world's harsh realities,
life's unfulfilled desires, and the unavoidable suffering of the
human experience.

Wagner found a philosophical articulation of this in the writings of Schopenhauer and the Buddhist materials he was reading.
The lovers' release from life's agonies into the all-encompassing
cosmic oneness is also Buddhist. Wagner employed a reversal of
the standard symbolic use of day and night to represent for the
lovers the Schopenhauerian-Buddhist rejection of unfulfilled ordinary existence and the longing for salvation. "Spiteful light of
day" represents all sufferings, illusions, yearnings, separations,
and unrequited strivings. In their hymn to the night Tristan and
Isolde extol an intellectual and emotional enlightenment, peace
and quiet, love fulfilled, freedom and the release from suffering
that it brings. What a contrast to Wagner's original conception of
Siegfried as "the light of the world" who defeats those who "rule
in darkness." As we shall discover when we return to *The Ring
Cycle*, this switching of symbolic meanings for light and darkness
will cause Wagner problems as he attempts to complete his tetrology, nurtured originally by an optimism he no longer possesses.
Now it is blessed night that nurtures.

As blessed night encompasses Tristan and Isolde, they feel themselves becoming one—indeed, even more than this, they feel they are one with the world—and, as we shall find in the concluding portions of the duet, they will long for eternal togetherness in death through the power of love. Woven into the fabric of this love scene is "Brangäne's Warning" bidding them to beware. She has a premonition that woe will come with the light of day.

The so-called third segment, which is very brief, follows. It introduces an exploration of the relationship between love and death, beginning with Isolde's *Lausch, Geliebter!* ("Listen, beloved!"). Then commences the conclusion to this long love scene, the music of which is a miracle in music history. For devoted Wagnerians there is nothing like it. Brangäne's iterated warnings fall on deaf ears and are swallowed in the increasing intensity of the lovers' mystical transfiguration into death-in-love (or love-in-death). The German world is *Liebestod*. It is one of Wagner's most important concepts and its literal translation is "love death." Tristan begins, soon to be joined by Isolde,

> So let us die,
> unseparated,
> forever united
> without end,
> without waking,
> without fearing,
> namelessly
> bound in love,
> completely each to other given
> living only in our love.

Readily apparent is the similarity between Wagner's love death and the Buddhist concept of nirvana, a perfectly blessed state achieved through the extinction of one's individual existence or by the extinction of yearning and passion. In other words, in the negation of life one can find eternal rest, void of all striving and suffering. Wagner's knowledge of Buddhism, though less than scholarly, was sufficient for him to see in its central tenet another version of Schopenhauer's thesis: Only through negation and resignation are the evils of the world avoidable. He describes nirvana as "the land of being no more." His penchant for mysticism, so dominant prior to 1848, has returned full force. Schopenhauer and Buddhism did not cause these reconsiderations in Wagner's philosophical and religious thinking, which is culminating in the creative outpourings of *Tristan und Isolde*. Rather, they provided him with a vocabulary and arguments and gave him reasons to support and defend the pessimistic view of life long alive in the unconsciousness of his artistic intuitions and now welling up to his conscious mind.

In the culmination of the love scene, the sung words of Tristan and Isolde become one with the symphonic voice of the orchestra, all three reaching an intensity beyond which it is almost inconceivable that they could go on when, all of a sudden, just as the lovers sing of love's greatest pleasure, a huge dissonance is heard in the orchestra. Brangäne shrieks and Kurwenal, sword drawn, bursts upon the entranced lovers to warn his beloved Tristan to save himself. Brangäne was right! Melot, with the dawn of a new day, has brought the hunting party to this very spot to expose the infidelity. The third and final scene of the second act has begun.

Melot asks his King if his accusations are now justified, a stunned Marke acknowledges he has been betrayed, and Tristan curses the new day. Then comes Marke's monologue on despair. Do not be misguided by common references to this famous episode as "King Marke's soliloquy." It is not. He is not talking to himself or talking as if no one else was there. Yes, he may, in his state of shock and mounting grief, appear as if he is oblivious to all else, but his is not a private, Hamlet-like soliloquy. His expression of innermost thoughts, to wrenchingly beautiful sad strains in the orchestra, is primarily a series of poignant questions directed to Tristan.

> You have done this to me?
> If Tristan is false, where can truth be found?
> Where have faith and truth gone?
> Where has virtue fled?
> Do you think so little of all I have done for you?

And on they continue to his two final interrogative reproaches: "Why must I suffer this unatonable shame?" "Who can explain this profound, unfathomable mystery to me?" Tristan, who had lowered his head to gaze at the ground during Marke's agony, lifts his eyes and looks at his uncle with great sympathy and says, literally:

> O King, that
> I cannot say;

and what you ask,
you can never know.

The literal translation, however, is insufficient. Tristan is declaring his absolute inability to express in words answers to Marke's questions. The answers are buried in the experience he is sharing with Isolde of utter helplessness against overpowering desires that hold them in their sway. A now familiar plaintive theme is sounded in the orchestra by oboe and English horn after Tristan's words to Marke. The inexpressible sounds only in the music. Then, turning to Isolde, Tristan asks if she will follow him where now he must go—to the land of only darkness, where no light of sun ever shines. Wherever Tristan goes, she too will follow. Tristan kisses her forehead. Furiously, Melot urges Marke to seek revenge. Tristan challenges Melot, who draws his sword and thrusts. But Tristan drops his sword and, struck, falls wounded into Kurwenal's arms. Isolde throws herself on his breast, exactly where she was when the first act ended. Quickly, the curtain closes.

Act III
A mood of absolute isolation, loneliness, and desolation is explored in the orchestral prelude to the third act as violins segue into the haunting sound of a shepherd piping a lamentation. For this captivating tune, Wagner attempted unsuccessfully to invent a wind instrument with a unique sound all its own. Today the tune normally is played on an English horn (*cor anglais*), sometimes on a reedy-sounding wooden clarinet of Hungarian origin (called a *tarogato*), and other times, God forbid, on a trumpet. Once heard, the penetrating poignancy of this music, unlike anything I have ever heard before, can never be mistaken for anything else.

The curtain opens on an overgrown garden at Tristan's unkempt castle in Brittany. He is revealed sleeping on a couch beneath a huge lime tree; Kurwenal sits by his head. Beyond rocky cliffs lies the sea. Having piped his sad tune, the shepherd asks Kurwenal if Tristan is awake. He sleeps, waiting for the only one who can heal him, Kurwenal replies, and then inquires if a ship as yet has been sighted. The shepherd tells him that a more merry tune than what he just played will signal the sighting of a ship but for now *Öd und leer das Meer!* ("Desolate and empty the sea"— another line quoted by Eliot in his famous poem) and he pipes himself off to his sheep.

The tune has aroused Tristan, who, slowly gaining consciousness, wonders where he is and with whom he speaks. Kurwenal explains that he has returned Tristan to Kareol, his castle in Brittany, to recover. Tristan, in a long narration, speaks again in arcane words of endless night, oblivion, and Isolde, for whom he waits. Kurwenal offers hope. He has sent for her. She is expected soon, perhaps this very day, once again to heal Tristan. Upon hearing this, Tristan is beside himself with joy. In a second long monologue, he praises Kurwenal for his loyalty and friendship in what may be the most moving ode to comradeship in song literature, and then commences to hallucinate Isolde's ship sailing on the sea. Kurwenal, dejectedly, must inform him there is as yet no ship to be seen.

Tristan's next response is even longer than the previous ones. Is it any wonder, then, after singing a duet in the second act of more than half an hour, followed in the third act by long, demanding monologues, one after the other, that there are so few tenors possessing voice and stamina sufficient to perform this role adequately? In this tremendous monologue, Tristan grows melancholy as he reminisces on the deaths of his father and mother in his infancy and how he was thus born to a fate of unrequited yearning. He becomes agitated and impassioned when his recollections turn to Isolde and he remembers their meeting, her healing, the love potion, and the subsequent torment of his aching for her. For Tristan there is in life no release.

Throughout this recollection, the shepherd's plaintive tune is woven into the orchestral score, for this is the tune Tristan has associated with sorrow and sadness throughout his life. I wonder if Tristan's name is by chance or by intent a variant of the French word for sad *(triste)*, for so perfectly does it fit him and his impelling recollections that leave him exhausted.

Kurwenal fears for his friend. Tristan revives to hallucinate again, describing Isolde's approach. Lo and behold, Kurwenal, having gone to the watchtower as instructed, joyfully shouts, "The ship! I see it coming from the north!" Excitedly, Tristan and Kurwenal discuss the ship's approach until, safely beyond the reef, it lies in port. Kurwenal goes for Isolde as the first scene ends.

A reborn Tristan, overjoyed, has torn off his bandages and feebly awaits Isolde's arrival. He hears her call him, and she enters. Weak but with wild excitement, he rushes to her, they embrace, and he sinks to the ground in her arms. She speaks his name. "Isolde," he replies, and dies in an orchestral tapestry of motifs associated with the beginning of the Act I prelude and the quaffing of the love potion. Isolde begs him to awaken to her, even for a moment, for she has come to die with him. It is in vain, however, and she falls unconscious upon his body.

The shepherd warns Kurwenal of a second ship. Kurwenal calls for help, as he has recognized Melot and Marke. Brangäne comes for Isolde. Kurwenal kills Melot, but, severely wounded, he dies at Tristan's feet. Marke, in despair, bends over the bodies and sobs. Brangäne had told him of the potion and the good King had come in peace to forgive and to unite the lovers. Brangäne revives Isolde. Marke expresses to her his intent but Isolde is now in another sphere.

Transfixed, she looks upon Tristan and here, depending again on the tempo of the conductor, begin six or seven of the most famous minutes in all opera literature. To many this music is known only in its orchestral version, where it is performed with the Act I prelude. This was acceptable to Wagner, who referred to it as *Liebestod* ("Love-Death") and *Verklärung* ("Transfiguration"). Often it is performed this way in the concert hall and more often on recordings. Now, it is usually known as "Prelude and Liebestod."

The poetry of Isolde's *Liebestod*, her mystical vision of eternal reunification with her beloved Tristan, is not easily translated. Tristan, of course, is dead but she does not see this. To Isolde he is quietly and gently smiling and she asks, to cite only a few lines,

> Friends?
> Don't you see?
> How he shines
> ever brighter
> high above
> among the stars?
> Don't you see?
> How his heart,
> full and sublime,
> valiantly swells,
> throbbing in his breast?

She wonders if she alone is aware of Tristan, of his breathing, and of the wondrous, all-encompassing melody resounding from within him and throughout her entire being, a vast ringing wave of the world's breath into which she sinks and drowns in supreme bliss. She falls into Brangäne's arms and sinks onto Tristan's breast, the same place she was when the first and second acts concluded.

A profound emotion and grief grip the bystanders as Marke makes the sign of the cross over the dead. Wagner wrote of the opera's conclusion in these words:

> . . . what fate divided in life now springs into trans-figured life in death: the gates of union are thrown open. Over Tristan's body the dying Isolde receives the blessed fulfillment of ardent longing, eternal union in measureless space, without barriers, without fetters, inseparable.

I cannot comment further on Isolde's *Liebestod*. I have had students who wondered what all the fuss was about; others openly have wept in class as we listened to it, the orchestra concluding the drama as the music of Tristan and Isolde's yearning fades into silence.

Very little stage action transpires in this long opera. The story reaches fullest expression in the music of the most symphonic dramatic score Wagner ever wrote: During some of the most dramatic moments in the opera—portions of the love duet, Tristan's monologues, and in the culminating *Liebestod* of Isolde—there is a loss of verbal comprehension as the words become one in soaring with the instruments of the orchestra in a symphony of sound. Thus, this vast orchestral score must be supplemented in the title roles by voices of tremendous power and beauty. Such vocal combinations are rare; accordingly, few are the superb stage productions and cherished recordings of this opera. To sing even the most dramatic roles in Italian opera is one thing; to sing the biggest of the Wagnerian roles, the Brünnhildes, Siegfrieds, Tristan, and Isolde, is another matter.

For the triumphant June 10, 1865, world premiere of *Tristan und Isolde,* the title roles were sung by man and wife: Ludwig Schnorr von Carolsfeld and Malvina Schnorr von Carolsfeld. Ludwig Schnorr, to this day, is considered the greatest of all Tristans even though he died suddenly after only the third performance. How can this be? He passed the supreme test. He satisfied the ultimate critic: Richard Wagner was enthralled by Schnorr's singing and was devastated by his death. Then, as now, a great Tristan or Isolde is irreplaceable.

Tristan und Isolde is Wagner's most tragic work, born out of troubles and anxieties represented in his pessimistic view of life, which, ironically, both reached its depths and came to an end with this drama. The world premiere was made possible through the financial generosity of King Ludwig II of Bavaria. This young king's dreamy, idealized world throughout his adolescence had been nurtured and nourished by Wagner's writings and music. As soon as he ascended to the throne, in March 1864, he sent for Wagner and thereafter opened great stores of the Bavarian treasury for the composer. Never again would Wagner have difficulty getting a work on the stage. In fact, for him Ludwig would build the famous opera house in Bayreuth, the Festspielhaus (Festival House), where the annual performance of Wagner's operas to this day is an international operatic event. Ludwig also built for the composer a beautiful home and made certain Wagner never again had financial worries. Wagner's dreams and those of the idealistic king were joined in one of the most unusual and productive collaborations in music history. Wagner's autobiography, *Mein Leben* (*My Life*), purposely does not relate the events of the last nineteen years of his life. He ends telling his own story with Ludwig's rescue. The final words of this book are

> . . . I was never again to feel the weight of the everyday hardships of existence under the protection of my exalted friend.[†]

DIE MEISTERSINGER VON NÜRNBERG (1868)
The Mastersingers of Nuremberg

After the success of *Tristan und Isolde* and Ludwig's rescue, did Wagner resume work on *Siegfried* and *The Ring Cycle*? No! *Tristan und Isolde*, completed in August 1859, would be nearly six years in reaching the stage and already in December 1861 Wagner had begun—and finished during the next month—the poem for a new drama: *Die Meistersinger von Nürnberg*. He finished composing the music in 1867. Schopenhauer and the composition of this new opera inspired within him a revision of his aesthetic theories, which he would publish in the 1870s. Wagner swallowed whole

---

[†] Richard Wagner, *My Life* (New York: Dodd, Mead & Company, authorized translation from the German, 1939), p. 887

Schopenhauer's view on the metaphysics of music; music is the objective expression of the true essence of the universe. Do not labor in an attempt to figure out what this means. It is enough to know that Wagner bought into the idea of music's capacity to express the eternal truths of life as well as ultimate reality, all of which elude expression in human speech. Thus, the idea of a synthesis of the arts is gone forever in Wagner's work. Music, he will write in essays now germinating within his head, is the supreme art.

After completing *The Mastersingers*, he wrote in an essay: "I would almost like to call my dramas acts of music become visible . . . The music sounds, and what it sounds you may see on the stage before you." The important words tell the story and create the characters but, ultimately, the drama's meaning is revealed in what the music "says" and in what the characters do. The actions of the actors, as they portray what the music sounds, is of great importance, and of all of Wagner's operas written to this point, *The Mastersingers* is an actor's opera.

When you see it, either on stage or by video, you will need to know the story and to pay attention to the lively actions of the central characters, but most important you will need to concentrate on the music and the manner in which it comments on those actions and expresses emotions. This is an important distinction, for in many operas the role of the orchestra is to provide an accompaniment for the singers. Wagner's operatic orchestra, increasingly, is having the final say as to what his dramas are all about. Because the Wagnerian orchestra is big and powerful, and has such a dominant voice, there are those who refer to his music as "heavy," usually meant as a pejorative. If and when some of those great orchestral excerpts get inside you and take hold, however, you will not think this way. The prelude to the first act of *The Mastersingers* is a notable example, and more on this soon.

Like *Parsifal*, Wagner's final work, and *Lohengrin*, too, *The Mastersingers* was first conceived in the spring of 1845. Having just completed *Tannhäuser*, the idea came to him to make his next work a comic opera. It was the ancient theater of Athens once again that gave his plan justification, for in those days a happy satyr play followed the somber tragedies. We have already seen that this concept had been incorporated earlier in Italian opera: Pergolesi's masterful comedy *La serva padrona (The Maidservant Turned Mistress)*, written to follow his now forgotten tragedy, for example. In the same manner, Wagner wanted to follow his serious

Tannhäuser, in which a song contest plays such an important role in the drama, with a comic opera on the Mastersingers of Nuremberg, wherein, as we are about to explain, another song contest is critical.

More than twenty years passed between conception and completion, twenty years during which Wagner experienced his grandest hopes for a new and better world and suffered his deepest depression. In 1845, he set aside The Mastersingers idea almost as soon as it was born. In the early 1860s, the project was revived, and though there remains a comic quality to *The Mastersingers* as we know it, the work is hardly the merry satyr play of his first intentions.

First of all, a performance of *Tannhäuser* would last a little more than three hours, plus intermissions, of course. A complete performance of *The Mastersingers*, originally conceived as the small comic satyr play to follow it, without adding time for intermissions, is nearly four and a half hours. The final act alone is almost two hours. Second, like most great comedy, as opposed to farce, *The Mastersingers* format is Wagner's means of dealing with serious matters, such as his profound antipathy for pedantry, creative traditionalism, and formalism in the arts, as well as other sober subjects.

The composition of *The Mastersingers* spans the years just before Wagner was called into King Ludwig's life and several years thereafter. There is in this work both a sense of resignation over the utter madness of the human experience and a joyous affirmation when the particular human situation presented in the opera resolves according to all that is right and good. Prior to this ultimate happy resolution there is considerable doubt expressed by Hans Sachs, the protagonist of the drama, as to whether there is reason to hope for something sane to come about in the midst of overwhelming human folly. In the beginning of the third act, in a long, reflective monologue, he presents the operatic version of a theme Wagner sent to Ludwig in the form of an essay: All is delusion and folly. Alone, head in hand, lost in thought, Sachs speculates on "Madness! Madness! Madness everywhere!" His thoughts continue. He has searched everywhere, in vain, for the answer to why people torment and hurt each other. No one benefits, but on and on it goes, this ancient human folly. It is the brilliantly clever Hans Sachs who will exploit this madness and transform it into a joyous resolution in the happiest and most human drama Wagner ever wrote.

↝

What is *The Mastersingers* about? You now know enough about Wagner to realize the seriousness of his mind. Thus, to repeat what I just indicated above, you ought not be surprised to find in his only comic masterpiece some serious messages. *The Mastersingers* is the story of a young knight who seeks entrance into the Guild of Master Singers in Nuremberg. Normally, an applicant must proceed gradually through many steps before he can present himself as a contestant: apprenticeship, general schooling, training with a master, and entry in a song contest, there to be measured to ascertain whether he has mastered the many canons and rules of the "Tabulature," the irrevocable list of do's and don'ts. The knight chooses to bypass these customary preliminaries and arranges to sing a trial song before the guild. He is quickly tutored by an apprentice friend until he no longer can endure the pedantic nonsense of the many rules that supposedly constitute masterful singing. Before the guild, he sings a song of his own composition, one violating virtually every canon of what is considered proper rhyme and melody. His creative, artistic powers startle the members of the guild, who are swayed to oppose him by their most pedantic and inflexible perfectionist. This is Beckmesser, who is astute enough to recognize in the young knight his chief rival for the hand of the lovely Eva, who has agreed to become the bride of the winner of the Contest of Song to take place on the following day, the Feast of St. John. Beckmesser and the other members of the guild condemn the knight and reject him. The only one to recognize the knight's genius and originality is the good cobbler Hans Sachs, who fails in his efforts to win for him a full hearing.

All this is autobiographical. The Hungarian composer Franz Liszt, a close friend of Wagner's, was with Wagner the leader of the New German School of Music. Music, it was their contention, was capable of communicating profound truths in a language unknown to human reason. Those who followed their thinking considered themselves liberated from traditional formulas and rules long utilized in writing Western classical music. Those who opposed Wagner's views on music looked to Eduard Hanslick, a Viennese music critic, as their spokesman and to Johannes Brahms as their exemplar of a great contemporary composer. In 1854, Hanslick had published his book *The Beautiful in Music*, now recognized as the classic attack on those who believed music capable of expressing truths and informing the emotions. Richard

Wagner was at the center of his criticism. Here is a summary, in Hanslick's own words, from his book, of his case against Wagner:

> What I have reproached him with is the violation of music by words, the unnaturalness and exaggeration of the expression, the annihilation of the singer and the art of singing by unvocal writing and orchestral din, the displacement of the melody of song by declamatory recitation, enervating monotony and measureless expansion, and finally, the unnatural stilted progression of his diction, a diction which offends every feeling for speech.[†]

The Nuremberg masters could have said that about the knight's song. Indeed, Beckmesser does charge the knight with, among other things, the following:

> Is this rubbish to shock us?
> Surely he means to mock us!
> Every fault from grave to slight
> I have marked down quite right:
> "Faulty verses," "Unsingable phrases"
> "Incomprehensible melody,"
> A hotch-potch made of every tone that is . . .

The similarity between Wagner, who is introducing a revolutionary approach to the creation of operas, and the Franconian knight who composes his own songs and allows his poetic and musical imagination to dictate their shape, is almost as undeniable as the identification of the unimaginative, behind-the-times Sixtus Beckmesser with Eduard Hanslick. In 1862, Wagner invited Hanslick, whom he knew, to attend a small gathering to hear his reading of *The Mastersingers* poem, then in second draft. In this particular version, he who becomes Beckmesser in the final incarnation is here called Hanslich. Hanslich is the town clerk of Nuremberg and the marker who notes any mistakes when aspirants for admittance to the guild sing their trial song. Wagner uses

---

[†] Eduard Hanslick, *The Beautiful in Music* (New York: The Bobbs-Merrill Company, translation by Gustav Cohen, 1957), p. viii

the character to draw a harsh yet humorous satire of one who is incapable of understanding or accepting anything new in music. Because he is so pedantically bound to the traditional standards of the guild, Hanslich cannot accept the new and beautiful song of the young knight. As Wagner's reading that night increasingly made Hanslich look ridiculous, Eduard Hanslick, unamused, walked out. Though Wagner often was inclined to play jokes on people, knowledge of another side of his temperament suggests he was not joking with Hanslick, for the issue of his art was not a laughing matter.

The eventual outcome of the opera, greatly expedited by the insights and compassion of the wise cobbler Hans Sachs, presents the victory of the knight in the big contest of song. As a great new creative power of expression is recognized in the song of the Franconian knight, Wagner will soon claim the same for his hero Beethoven and, immodestly, for his own work in an essay on Beethoven. Wagner believed there was a tradition of great German musical masters that, in his century, was represented first by Beethoven, then by himself. Hans Sachs, at the conclusion of the drama, takes the victorious knight by the hand and counsels him before the multitude, concluding:

> Therefore I say to you:
> honor your German Masters!
> Then you will conjure up good spirits;
> and if you favor their endeavors,
> even should the
> Holy Roman Empire dissolve in mist,
> for us there would yet remain
> holy German Art!

Lighthearted comic episodes notwithstanding, Wagner's *The Mastersingers* attacks small-minded artistic pedantry. He depicts rampant human folly, ultimately overcome by recognizing and honoring basic truths passed age to age through the tradition of great German music masters, the most recent being Beethoven and, by implication, of course, then Wagner. Such thinking is not as innocent as it may at first seem, and I will comment on this after telling the story of the opera and indicating musical excerpts.

This opera, like most of Wagner's dramas, is in three acts. Unlike its predecessor *Tristan und Isolde*, there are many characters.

Those who like to stump people with opera trivia may ask one to name all the Mastersingers and to give their occupations, in the same way that they ask one to identify all the Valkyries in *Die Walküre*. I do not play such games; in case you do, though, I have alerted you as to where you should commence your memorization.

The Mastersingers are historical. They are important in Germany during the fourteenth, fifteenth, and sixteenth centuries. They were of the burgher class, unlike the aristocratic minstrels portrayed by Wagner in his *Tannhäuser*, and did much to preserve and perpetuate a love for art, especially throughout the middle class. The protagonist of the opera was a real cobbler and a poet who wrote several thousand poems. Hans Sachs lived and worked in Nuremberg from 1494 to 1576. Wagner set some words from one of his poems for the great chorus in Act III when the populace praises Hans Sachs.

Even though this huge, magnificent drama plays in a seamless unfolding, Wagner did designate scenes and so for your benefit I will note them. The characters of the drama and their voice ranges are:

HANS SACHS, a cobbler, *bass*
VEIT POGNER, a goldsmith, *bass*
KUNZ VOGELGESANG, a furrier, *tenor*
KONRAD NACHTIGALL, a buckle maker, *bass*
SIXTUS BECKMESSER, the town clerk, *baritone*
FRITZ KOTHNER, a baker, *bass*
BALTHASAR ZORN, a pewterer, *tenor*
ULRICH EISSLINGER, a grocer, *tenor*
AUGUSTIN MOSER, a tailor, *tenor*
HERMANN ORTEL, a soap boiler, *bass*
HANS SCHWARZ, a stocking weaver, *bass*
HANS FOLTZ, a coppersmith, *bass*
WALTHER VON STOLZING, a young Franconian knight, *tenor*
DAVID, apprentice to Hans Sachs, *tenor*
EVA, Pogner's daughter, *soprano*
MAGDALENA, Eva's maid and companion, *mezzo-soprano*
A night watchman, *bass*

The time of the drama is the middle of the sixteenth century, the place is Nuremberg, and much local color is provided by burghers, journeymen, apprentices, and women.

Act I

The prelude to the first act is one of the most familiar and often performed operatic excerpts. It appears frequently in the concert hall and can be heard on an endless number of recordings. Wagner did not object to the music being played as a concert excerpt. For the concert hall, he provided a version that has an ending, whereas in a performance this prelude flows without interruption into the music of the opening scene. But he objected vehemently—verbally and in an essay on conducting—when his music was not played properly. He objected to conductors of instrumental music who had no knowledge of his operas including in their repertoire excerpts without knowing how the music relates to the dramatic action. He was especially emphatic about the correct tempo, and once said there was not a conductor in Germany who could find the right tempo without Wagner standing by his elbow.

The Mastersingers prelude is a good example. It opens with a statement of the noble theme of the Mastersingers: an expression of what is best in their art, their tradition, and their love for and pride in their city. This prelude also presents music associated with Walther and his passion for Eva Pogner and its ultimate expression in his winning "Prize Song." The apprentices also are represented. Finally, having introduced several splendid themes, Wagner, at the prelude's conclusion, in a masterful stroke of counterpoint (the playing of several distinct melodies simultaneously) combines several themes that segue, as the curtain parts, to a magnificent chorale sung by the congregation in the Church of St. Catherine.

All too often, especially in the United States, this remarkable musical transition from prelude to chorale is never heard because of the ludicrous tradition of applauding the end of a prelude or an overture as the curtain opens. *Do not applaud here!* And when you buy your recording of this prelude, make sure to get one in which all the wonderful subtleties, loud and soft, can be heard. All too often, again, too many conductors aiming for the obvious potential of a huge, stately sound miss the nuances Wagner wrote into the score. How do you know? Easy. If all you hear is bombast, you have the wrong conductor. Wagner intended the instruments to sing, not shout!

The sublime chorale is the final hymn of the church service. Walther von Stolzing, a recently arrived visitor in Nuremberg, on the preceding day met Eva Pogner, daughter of the town's goldsmith. During the singing of the hymn's verses, they carry on a little flirtation through an exchange of gestures and glances. Eva is in the congregation with Magdalena, Walther off to the side. As the service ends and the congregation departs, Eva and Walther make their way to each other. Walther must have an answer to a life-or-death question he cannot quite pose because of Magdalena. Eva, sensing this, sends her maid to fetch forgotten items from where they were sitting, but the maid's inopportune return again prevents the question.

Eva finally blurts it out. He wants to know, am I bethrothed? Magdalena explains with a yes and a no. Eva may agree to be betrothed to the winner of tomorrow's song contest. David and several apprentices arrive to prepare for some singing trials on this day before the big competition. Magdalena suggests David school Walther so he can enter the contest. Eva and Walther briefly exchange a confession of affection before she is led away to her home. The first scene ends.

David puts the other apprentices to work and then begins a long explanation about the Mastersingers Guild and its endless rules, which constitute the art of making and singing properly a song of one's own composition and then in a contest winning the approval of the masters. As a contestant sings, one of the masters, the appointed marker, notes any faults upon a board with chalk. Too many faults and the singer is rejected. All this to poor young Walther is quite daunting. With this, the second scene concludes.

Pogner and Beckmesser enter, then other masters follow and assemble for the trials. Beckmesser is worried he may not win the contest of the next day and thus will fail to win Eva. Walther presents himself to Pogner as one desiring to become a master. Beckmesser instantly forms a disliking for the young man so warmly received by Pogner, who informs Walther that the rules of the guild hold but he will propose him as a trial applicant. Fritz Kothner calls the roll and Pogner asks to speak. Pogner's address, *Nun hört* ("Now hear"), is an excellent opportunity for a bass with a deep rich voice to please any ear. He reminds the other masters of the song contest on the following day, Johannistag (St. John's Day, the traditional beginning of summer) and with great generosity offers as the prize his wealth and his daughter's hand—but only if she accepts—to the winner. The masters debate details and then accept Pogner's proposal that Walther be given an opportunity today, in a trial, to earn the right to compete tomorrow.

Walther is called forth and his qualifications are questioned: Who was his teacher and where did he study? He responds in three impressive, but highly unusual, lyrical verses of *Am stillen Herd in Winterszeit* ("At the quiet hearth in wintertime"), and succeeds at least in arousing sufficient curiosity to be invited to present a trial song.

Beckmesser is dispatched to the marker's box. He is intent, of course, on finding more than the seven disqualifying faults to eliminate him who he already senses is a rival for Eva's hand. Kothner informs Walther his song must conform to the rules of the *Tabulatur*, the do's and don'ts of poetry and song. Walther is told to begin. Unfamiliar and unpracticed with these rules, his trial song can only be an improvisation of the moment. *So rief der Lenz in den Wald* ("Thus spring called to the forest") is a lovely, passionate, and majestic love song but repeated scratching from the marker's box during its delivery tell of countless infractions of the rules. At the end of the first verse, Beckmesser, to loud laughter from the other masters, reveals a board covered with chalk marks. He enumerates the mistakes in rhyme, meter, meaning, tempo, melody—indeed, those very same things leveled against Wagner by critics and professors. All agree except Sachs, who admits that the novelty of what he heard does not agree with the rules of the *Tabulatur* but perhaps, he suggests, the song represents a new art, with rules of its own, that is worthy of investigation. Beckmesser quarrels with him, Sachs doubting the objectivity of the town clerk as marker, for he knows well of Beckmesser's longing for Eva. Sachs invites Walther to finish his song. He does so, his phrases soaring above the babble of the disapproving masters. Sachs thinks the song an inspiration and the apprentices exhibit their pleasure in what they have heard. The masters, however, motivated by Beckmesser, announce *Versungen und vertan!* ("Sung out and undone") as the curtain falls before a meditative Hans Sachs surrounded by the bustle of busy apprentices and departing masters.

Act II

The entire second act is one of Wagner's greatest artistic and dramatic achievements. It is the shortest of the three acts, about an hour long (the first lasts more than an hour and a quarter and the third approaches two hours). Start to finish the action moves swiftly through various episodes, each seamlessly connected with what has gone before and what comes after. A detailed study of the relationships of poetry, stage action, and music (far outside the boundaries of this book) reveals Wagner's splendid craftsmanship, especially the ever-present wonder of the orchestral voice, constant in establishing moods, enhancing characterizations, and commenting on the action.

A prelude, depicting the joyful anticipation of a holiday, precedes the opening of the curtain on a lovely summer eve in Nuremberg, where apprentices are closing the shutters of their masters' shops, singing and dancing all the while in happy expectation of the morrow. The many episodes of this act, joined like an elegant piece of cabinetry, beginning with the closing of shutters, continues as Magdalena appears and learns from David of Walther's failure. Sachs arrives and puts David to work in his shop.

Scene 2: Pogner and Eva sit on a bench talking. Magdalena admits to her mistress that she learned from David of Walther's plight. Perhaps Sachs can provide details.

Scene 3: Sachs returns, David in tow, dismisses his apprentice, prepares to do some work outside his shop, lays down his tools, sits back on his stool, and, the street now empty, sings the celebrated Flieder Monologue. *Was duftet doch der Flieder* ("How mild, strong, and full of the elder's scent"), one of the supreme moments in the drama, is Sachs's reflection on the beauty of Walther's song, which he cannot get out of his head. As he sings, the orchestra plays strains from Walther's song still incomprehensible to him, for it fits no rules yet by its own measure is faultless.

Sachs finishes his meditation and does not even notice that Eva has arrived before Scene 4 begins. She sits next to him as they converse. Sachs learns she wants nothing to do with Beckmesser. She would prefer the widower Sachs, who is touched but acknowledges he is much too old. Furthermore, the subject having turned to the trial song, the perceptive cobbler gleans from Eva's growing agitation her love for the rejected knight. As Eva gets up to leave, summoned by Magdalena to go to her father, Sachs nods his head and says, "Just as I thought. Now to find a way!" He goes into his shop. Magdalena informs her mistress she has learned Beckmesser intends to serenade her this very night. Eva asks Magdalena to assume a disguise and switch places with her.

Scene 5: Walther comes, Eva rushes to him, they declare their love. With no hope of becoming a master, Walther suggests they elope, the night watchman sounds his horn and sings his song, and Eva leaves to exchange places with Magdalena. Having overheard the elopement plans discussed outside his door, Sachs considers them foolish. He shines his light onto the street to prevent their clandestine rendezvous. Magdalena then appears as Eva, just as Eva, dressed as Magdalena, appears and joins Walther. Sachs's light foils their attempt to flee.

Beckmesser comes down the street lute in hand, this being Scene 6. The lovers hide in the bushes by the lime tree. Sachs turns his light on his last and begins to hammer loudly just before Beckmesser starts his song. In wondrous exchanges, we hear Beckmesser complain, Sachs talks to himself, and the lovers converse in the bushes. Magdalena, impersonating Eva, appears at the window. Beckmesser wants to sing his serenade but Sachs, who obviously has had an idea, is relentless in tormenting the town clerk with his incessant hammering. Beckmesser begs him to stop but Sachs says he cannot, for the shoes he works on are those Beckmesser has ordered and wants immediately. A compromise is reached. Beckmesser will sing and Sachs will be quiet unless the town clerk errs in his art. Such faults the cobbler will be allowed to mark with a hammer blow.

Beckmesser begins but soon one blow of the hammer follows another with quick repetition. Louder and louder sings the town clerk, attempting to drown out the hammer. Townspeople are aroused and come to their windows. David is one of them. Seeing his beloved being serenaded, he runs into the street and beats Beckmesser with a cudgel as the street fills with a tumultuous melee, musically expressed as only Wagner's genius could portray such pandemonium. Sachs manages to direct all to their respective homes, shoves Eva into her father's arms, and pulls Walther into his shop. All becomes quiet. The night watchman makes his rounds, chanting his song, and turns up an alley, leaving the empty street flooded with beautiful moonlight as Wagner's extraordinary music brings this remarkable act to an end.

Wagner, by the way, in his autobiography tells of a wild street fracas he was involved in as a young man. As was so often the case, he once again has turned life into art in the creation of the tumult that ends this act.

Act III
The third act belongs to Hans Sachs. His perception of Walther's unique talent in the first act and his growing awareness of the significance of the young knight's art in Act II, of course, suggests to an aware audience his important role in the drama, but it is in the final act that he becomes fully one of the most admired and humane characters in opera literature. Wagner prepares the listener for this development with his prelude to the third act. It is made mostly

from music in this act associated with the wise old cobbler-poet: primarily themes from his famous "all is madness" monologue and the magnificent choral tribute to Hans Sachs wherein Wagner actually sets a portion of a poem the historical Hans Sachs wrote in praise of Martin Luther and the Protestant Reformation.

The curtain rises on the interior of the workshop of Hans Sachs, who is shown seated and reading from a large folio in the morning sunlight. It is the morning after the fracas. David, fearing reproaches for his behavior the night before, enters with trepidation, and with apologies on his lips, but after a long and disconcerting silence Sachs responds in a warm and friendly manner. As David sings of the day, Johannistag (St. John's Day), it occurs to him it is his master's name day (Hans being the diminutive of Johannes; John in English). David departs. Sachs, lost in thought, sings the now famous monologue *Wahn! Wahn! Überall Wahn!* ("Madness! Madness! Everywhere Madness!" . . . meaning craziness, not fury).

As Sachs concludes his speculations about the follies of human behavior, Walther, who has spent the night in the cobbler's house, enters from an adjoining room. While he slept, a song came to him in a dream, he tells Sachs, but one that certainly will not fit the masters' rules. "Then make rules of your own and sing away," replies Sachs, obviously speaking for Richard Wagner. In this important second scene of the act Sachs tutors the young knight, who, without knowing it, is formulating the first two verses of what will be the Prize Song, on which the entire denouement rests: a song to win heart, head, and hand of the woman he loves. As Walther sings, Sachs writes the stanzas on a piece of paper. Obviously, the good cobbler has something up his sleeve. The lesson over, he takes Walther into another room to dress for the Johannistag celebration.

Scene 3: Beckmesser, already attired resplendently, peers into the shop. Finding it empty, he lets himself in. Nursing wounds from his drubbing the previous night, he attempts to sit but is too sore. He looks about, and happens to see the page upon which Sachs wrote Walther's verses. Beckmesser reads them intently, then exclaims:

> A wooing-song! By Sachs? It's true?
> Ah, ha! Now I understand everything!

On hearing a door open, he pockets the poem.

Sachs enters. Quickly, Beckmesser turns their conversation into an accusation and charges Sachs with duplicity. Deliberately he ruined his serenade and ordered David's beating of him, Beckmesser contends, because Sachs, too, intends to woo Eva in the song contest. When Sachs denies that he will be singing a wooing song, Beckmesser produces the poem in Sachs's hand as proof. To prove his point, Sachs tells him to keep it and sing it if he wants to. Beckmesser, overjoyed to have a poem by the famous Nuremberg poet, makes the cobbler promise never, ever to reveal he wrote the poem and, with fulsome appreciations and farewells, departs to work on "his" song.

Scene 4: Eva arrives, on the pretext that a shoe is pinching her foot. Obviously, however, Walther is what is on her mind. The knight enters magnificently attired. The lovers are transfixed, each staring at the other, as Sachs feigns fixing the shoe at his workbench. Spontaneously Walther sings a third and final verse of his love song. It is the perfect resolution. Overcome with joy, Eva falls against Sachs and weeps. Sachs passes her on to Walther's arms and sings his song of the many tribulations of a cobbler, one of which is a vague reference to young women and a widower. Yes, old Sachs does, indeed, love Eva, so much so that all his present efforts are to bring about her happiness with the young knight. Sachs, his song finished, attempts to leave to look for David. Eva, in a flood of emotion (expressed in words, action, and orchestra), tries to find words to thank the old cobbler, whom she would happily have for her husband were she free.

With the recent triumph of *Tristan und Isolde* fresh on Germanic musical minds Wagner, at this point, quotes a theme from the beginning of that opera's Act 1 prelude as Sachs replies to her:

My child,
I know of the sad story
of Tristan and Isolde.
Wise Hans Sachs did not
want to suffer King Marke's
painful fate
so he found the right man for you
before it was too late. . . .

An ingenious little touch.

David enters from the next room just as Magdalena enters from the street, both dressed for the occasion. Sachs reminds all of the custom of christening before witnesses a new mastersong with the name by which it thereafter will be known. Because an apprentice cannot be a witness, Sachs, approving of David, has him kneel before him for the box on the ear as he raises his status from apprentice to journeyman. They all witness the naming of Walther's song: "The Blessed Morning's Dream Interpretation." Perhaps the greatest quintet in all opera follows. *Selig, wie die Sonne* ("Blessed, as the sun") begins Eva, as she sings of the joy that has come with this day. Sachs hides his love for Eva behind a mask of happiness, Walther hopes his dream of winning Eva with a mastersong is coming true, and Magdalena and David, dizzy with delight, together sing of their future.

Now, I love every note of this marvelous opera, but the beginning of the quintet signals for me the start of more than fifty flawless consecutive operatic minutes. There is no more anticipation of a famous aria, no waiting for a hit tune, no waiting for something special. From the beginning of the quintet through the dying away of the opera's final note, one experiences a nonstop miracle of musical theater.

We now go to the fifth and final scene, the only one in the drama wherein scenery actually is changed. It takes place while an orchestral interlude plays music associated with Nuremberg. This last scene is set in a large meadow outside Nuremberg on the bank of the Pegnitz River, with the town in the background. By boats come men, women, and children in festive dress to the site of the great song contest. Flags are flying above the singers' platform. Marvelous processions of guilds enter and place their banners in the appropriate places. First are the shoemakers, followed by pipers, luthiers, and journeymen displaying toy trumpets. Tailors are next and close behind come the bakers, their two separate songs blending. Delighted by the arrival of a boat filled with young girls, the apprentices shout, sing, and dance, then suddenly call for absolute silence. The Mastersingers are about to enter.

Most everyone knows their familiar majestic music that Wagner made from a tune fragment he found in a centuries-old music book. It accompanies them to their places on the platform—Eva, of course, seated with her father.

Sachs steps forward to address the people, who, to Wagner's heroic setting of a portion of a poem by the historical Hans Sachs, hail the cobbler-poet in a mighty chorus: *Wach auf, es nahet gen den Tag* ("Awake! The dawning of day is near"). Sachs addresses the multitude to detail the terms of the contest. Pogner thanks him and a befuddled Beckmesser takes a last look at the words he will sing as Kothner calls on him to be the first contestant. To his own tune, Beckmesser attempts to sing what little he can recall of Walther's lovely poem, but his faulty memory makes a mishmash of the verses and his tune is awful. No one can comprehend what he is saying. He continues with a second attempt. It is even worse. The Mastersingers are perplexed and the crowd laughs and mocks the ludicrous performance. Stymied, Beckmesser furiously declares Sachs to be the author of the poem and rushes off, becoming lost in the crowd. Sachs, asked to explain the charge, disclaims authorship of a song more beautiful than he could compose. All believe he is joking until he calls on anyone who can sing it properly to prove him right. Walther steps forth, Sachs hands the verses left behind by Beckmesser to Kothner, and Walther begins to sing the song heard earlier in this act.

Wagner's remarkable instinct for theater, however, knows a repeat would be anticlimactic so he makes Kothner, enchanted by the beauty of the song, let the leaf of verses fall from his hand by the sixth line of the first stanza, signaling to an attentive Walther that he is free to improvise. Thus does the "Blessed Morning Dream Interpretation" become a different song, the Prize Song.

Morgenlich leuchtend im rosigen Schein ("Shining in the rosy light of morning") is one of the loveliest songs in the German language. Both Wagner's words and his music are worthy of a master's song. There are three verses. In the first Walther tells of a revelation that came to him in the morning sunlight as he stood daydreaming in a beautiful garden: Only the most beautiful woman, "Eva in paradise" could fulfill his longing. Between first and second verse both masters and multitude comment briefly on what a difference it makes when a song is sung correctly. Sachs asks him to continue. In the second verse, twilight falls as Walther, approaching a spring, has a vision of the most wonderful woman, his "Muse of Parnassus," beneath the shining stars. Again, the masters and the people comment on the beauty of the song, words, and music. Sachs asks Walther to finish his song. The final verse proclaims the awakening of the dream and victory in song, winning both "Parnassus and Paradise."

Walther does win the prize and is crowned by Eva, but when Pogner offers the golden chain of a master, he bitterly rejects it. Eva is all he wants, but Sachs takes his hand and admonishes Walther not to insult his masters, the keepers "of holy German

Art." In a great chorus all proclaim

> Hail, Sachs!
> Nuremberg's beloved Sachs!

Recall our original premise: To understand the operas of Wagner as he meant them to be requires identifying the ongoing development of the religious concepts that motivated his art. King Ludwig has rescued Wagner from the profound, otherworldly, pessimistic mysticism of *Tristan und Isolde*. Through Ludwig's generosity, Wagner foresees the regeneration of a degenerate German theater. In essays written during this time of his life Wagner says again that ultimate truth comes not from rational insight but rather through moments of intense contemplation while listening to great music. This music is spiritual. Through this great music, which just happens to reside in a tradition of German masters, modern culture stands to be revitalized by a German renaissance.

However tendentious this may seem to us, it is nevertheless what Hans Sachs's "holy German art" is about in *The Mastersingers*. Beethoven, in Wagner's prose writings, is the most recent in the long line of German masters, and Wagner is, by implication, his successor. As a great new creative power of expression is recognized in the song of the Franconian knight, so did Richard Wagner find the same in his hero Beethoven and in his own continuation of this tradition of "German masters." In his advice to Walther, Sachs said that indispensable German masters pass on the heritage of German culture from generation to generation, and even if foreigners should invade or should the sacred heritage of "Holy Rome" expire, there would remain the more viable religious experience of "holy German art." This is the religious theme that Wagner develops in *The Mastersingers:* an intense religious chauvinism that, in the wrong hands, could become exceedingly dangerous.

Within weeks of having completed *The Mastersingers*, Wagner made the acquaintance of a young German philosopher, also fascinated with Schopenhauer, who was equally as intense as Wagner with ideas for a revitalization of German culture, and who found in Wagner a mentor until their vital friendship eventually ruptured. The interrelationship of Richard Wagner and Friedrich Nietzsche is a fascinating story (sadly, outside the boundaries of this book). Nietzsche's ideas on cultural regeneration, if misunderstood, were also potentially exceedingly dangerous. It is the everlasting horror of history in the twentieth century that Wagner's art and Nietzsche's philosophy became the inspirations of the madman who led Germany into the greatest atrocities in human history and all of Europe and America into a devastating world war.

Wagner's Return to *The Ring*

Wagner completed *The Mastersingers* before November 1868 and by February 1869 he was working again on *Siegfried*. Remember Wagner has left his hero following the forest bird, who revealed to him that there is a beautiful woman sleeping on a rock encircled by fire who can be awakened only by a man who knows no fear. Siegfried realizes he is that man. With him goes the Tarnhelm and the fated golden ring. During the nearly twelve-year hiatus between the completion of the second act of *Siegfried* and resumption of Act III, Wagner's aesthetic theories were undergoing significant revisions.

The two monumental dramas written after he set aside *The Ring Cycle* were not composed as a synthesis of the arts, Wagner's guiding theoretical concept of the 1850s. Under the spell of Schopenhauer, music was becoming much more important than poetry and, especially in *The Mastersingers*, acting, gestures, and mime play an increasingly important part. The extraordinary artist in Wagner was able to recapture the general style of *The Ring Cycle* in completing *Siegfried* but he was not able to return to yesteryear void of the artistic growth represented in *Tristan* and *The Mastersingers*. Those who know *Tristan und Isolde* will hear in the famous Act III love duet in *Siegfried* some familiar touches. In the short, marvelous prelude to the third act of this opera, Wagner's free use of many motifs woven into a rich orchestral elaboration is reminiscent of his use of themes in *The Mastersingers*. Like both dramas written during the interval between *Siegfried's* Acts II and III, Wagner's orchestra throughout the third act becomes a dominant voice expressing a wondrous mix of motifs no longer simply there to recall past events or to introduce a sword or giants. This tendency toward a dominant orchestral tapestry of sound will continue in *Götterdämmerung*, the cycle's final drama, and will culminate in *Parsifal*, the last and most symphonic of all Wagner's operas.

Wagner's themes now flow in and out of a gigantic symphonic sound. Any musicologist or scholar who attempts to disassemble them, label them, and establish a one-to-one relationship between motif and text throughout the rest of the cycle has not understood the drastic aesthetic revision in Wagner's manner of working and thus is doomed to fail, as many have and, indeed, still do. The orchestra, more than ever, has become its own voice often independent of the storyline in its employment of motifs. The musician in Wagner has superseded the poet. This explains the increasing magnitude and significance of Wagner's orchestral sound in his late dramas. It can be heard immediately in the short prelude to *Siegfried's* third act (I interrupted the story of the opera at the end of Act II, on p. 256), wherein as many as nine identifiable motifs already heard at varying times in the cycle come and go and mix together in the richest symphonic expression of any prelude in the cycle up to this point. This stormy orchestral introduction establishes the mood of the first of the last act's three scenes.

SIEGFRIED
Act III

The curtain opens on a desolate, rocky region at the base of a mountain. Wotan, once again disguised as the Wanderer, is calling Erda, the earth goddess (also called Wala by him), from a deep sleep to come forth and advise him on how to forestall the relentless force of fate moving to end the reign of the gods. In their discussion of past events, we learn little that is new until Wotan finally acknowledges that time has come for power to pass from the gods to humans: to Siegfried, void of greed and thus free of the ring's curse, and to Brünnhilde, whom soon he will awaken. Let them redeem the world.

Erda returns to sleep deep in the earth as the Wanderer awaits Siegfried, who, as dawn breaks, arrives following the forest bird. This is the second scene. It takes place in the same rocky region. Again, there is a repetition of previous events in this episode. These become a test of wills between the old god, pleased with the youth's answers to his questions but angered by his insolence, and Siegfried, who is eager to continue up the mountain to where the beautiful woman sleeps within a ring of fire. Wotan, in a last act of will, holds his spear in front of himself to bar the way. Siegfried, with one blow of his sword, shatters Wotan's spear. The old god retrieves the fragments and departs. The new age has begun. The gods have been defeated. They do not appear again in *The Ring Cycle*. Will things improve in human hands? For that answer, we must wait until *Twilight of the Gods*.

Siegfried makes his way up the mountain to the ring of fire:

Scene 3. A wonderful orchestral interlude depicts his horn calls, his ascent to the ring of fire, and his fearless penetration of the flames to arrive at the same scene that concluded the *Valkyrie*. First, he sees a horse standing asleep, then the sleeping form of what he assumes is a man dressed in armor. Slowly, he approaches. He lifts the helmet off the head and Brünnhilde's long, wavy hair falls free. Then with his sword he cuts the rings fastening the breastplate, removes it, and gazes upon what he has never seen before in his life: a woman, her breast heaving with the deep breaths of slumber. Startled, he steps back to utter some of my favorite lines in the entire cycle. I've translated them not to be sung but rather to convey the humor:

> This is not a man!
> Fiery fascination
> quivers in my heart:
> ardent anguish
> grips my eyes:
> my tottering senses swoon!
> Who can I call
> for help to cure me?
> Mother! Mother!
> Remember me!

He muses in silence, overcome with desire, paralyzed with fright:

> . . . Oh Mother! Mother!
> your brave child!
> A woman lying in sleep
> has taught him fear!

Psychologists can have their fun explaining why, at this decisive moment in his life, Siegfried calls for his mother.

He bids the sleeping woman to awaken but she does not stir until he kisses her lips, long and passionately. One of the most anticipated excerpts in all Wagnerian drama has begun: the declaration of love by Siegfried and Brünnhilde. In length their duet rivals that of Tristan and Isolde, but for dramatic intensity and sheer beauty of music, even though it is one of Wagner's most notable artistic achievements, in my ears Siegfried and Brünnhilde do not quite equal the other lovers. But no others do, either! Brünnhilde awakens with the kiss and rises to a sitting position.

Heil dir, Sonne! ("Hail to thee, oh sun!"), she begins, then asks who is the hero who has awakened her. Siegfried names himself. Instantly, they are smitten with each other but as Brünnhilde sees her horse, Grane, and her armor and weapons, she grows sad with the recollection of the loss of her godhood. Overcome with shame, she becomes agitated in anticipation of the loss of maidenhood, too, and asks Siegfried to leave her. With loving tenderness, he takes her in his arms. All other emotions give way to the intensity of their love and the drama ends with their passionate embrace.

Franz Liszt was Wagner's close friend. Liszt's daughter, Cosima von Bülow, was married to another of Wagner's close friends, the conductor Hans von Bülow. Wagner's wife left him in 1861 during his affair with Mathilde Wesendonck but it was not long thereafter before Wagner and Cosima became lovers. During the *Tristan* years she bore him a daughter they named Isolde. The next year she left her husband to live with Wagner. During the *Mastersinger* years a second daughter, appropriately named Eva, was born. While Wagner was working on Act III of *Siegfried* their son, Siegfried, was born (he would grow up to write more than a dozen operas and other music). Wagner and Cosima were married in 1870. For her birthday that year—she was born on Christmas—Wagner composed one of the most beautiful pieces of music ever written. The "Siegfried Idyll" is an absolute necessity in everyone's library of recorded classical music. The love music of Siegfried and Brünnhilde in both *Siegfried* and *Twilight of the Gods* was an opportunity for Wagner secretly to express his and Cosima's emotions musically. As he put the finishing touches on *Siegfried*, Wagner already had been hard at work on the final drama of his gigantic cycle: *Götterdämmerung*.

GÖTTERDÄMMERUNG (1876)
Twilight of the Gods

Begun in the 1850s under the impulse of radical revolutionary activities, Wagner's *Ring Cycle*, which he completed more than twenty-five years later, ends on a note of religious resignation. Given amnesty, made financially secure by King Ludwig's favoritism, older, and now husband and father, his zeal to remake an evil world has passed. From Schopenhauer he learned that the world's evils are irredeemable. Whatever redemption there may be for the human condition, Wagner the poet left it for Wagner the musician to express as *Götterdämmerung* completes his tetrology. This long drama begins with a prologue and is followed by three acts. The characters and their voices are:

> The three Norns, foretellers of fate and destiny, *soprano, mezzo-soprano, and contralto*
> BRÜNNHILDE, *soprano*
> SIEGFRIED, *tenor*
> GUNTHER, lord of the Gibichungs, *baritone*
> GUTRUNE, his sister, *soprano*
> ALBERICH, a Nibelung, *bass-baritone*
> HAGEN, his son and half brother of Gunther and Gutrune, *bass*
> WALTRAUTE, a Valkyrie, *mezzo-soprano*
> WOGLINDE, Rhinemaiden, *soprano*
> WELLGUNDE, Rhinemaiden, *soprano*
> FLOSSHILDE, Rhinemaiden, *mezzo-soprano*
> Gibich vassals and women

> Time is legendary and the scenes are a rocky mountain area, a castle on the Rhine, and a wooded area next to the river.

You will notice that there are no gods in the list of characters and already you have asked, "Why, if no gods, is the drama titled 'Twilight of the Gods' (not '*The* Twilight of the Gods,' as often it is mistranslated)?" Because even the gods, as representations of the highest order in a hierarchy that includes a race of subterranean dwarfs and earth-inhabiting humans, must perish as part of the evil rampant throughout the world that has corrupted them all. With the all-consuming fire and flooding waters of the drama's conclusion, everything is burned and cleansed. It is the end of the old order. As flames ultimately destroy Valhalla, casting a glow on the distant darkening sky, it is, indeed, the twilight of the gods.

Prologue

A brief prelude precedes the curtain's rising to reveal Brünnhilde's rock. It is night. Three gloomily clad women, the Norns, spin and toss the rope of fate as they sing of the end of the reign of the gods, then disappear forever into the earth. A longer orchestral interlude accompanies the breaking of dawn as Brünnhilde and Siegfried become visible emerging from a cave. They declare their love: Siegfried removes from his finger Alberich's gold ring and puts it

on Brünnhilde's finger to seal their bond. Brünnhilde gives
Siegfried her horse for his journey. As a hero he must set forth and
perform great deeds. Brünnhilde will remain on her rock protected by the flames impenetrable to all but Siegfried. The curtains
close.

The orchestral transition from the prologue to the first act,
depicting Siegfried's departure, his trek down the mountainside to
the Rhine, and his passage on the river in a boat, has become
world famous in concert-hall performances and on recordings as
"Siegfried's Rhine Journey." It is a masterful example of Wagner's
ability to portray in music the transition from one physical and
mental state to another, the transition from the love of Siegfried
and Brünnhilde to the beginning of the drama's tragedy as devised
by the evil Hagen's plot.

Act I

The curtain reopens for the beginning of Act I in the great hall of
the Gibichung castle on the Rhine. Gunther and Gutrune sit on
their thrones drinking. Before them, seated at a table, also with a
drinking vessel, is Hagen. Hagen tells of the treasure Siegfried
won when he slew the dragon. Gunther is enticed by prospects for
power: enough to become lord of the world, Hagen asserts. If
Siegfried could be drugged and tricked into bringing Brünnhilde to
the castle to wed Gunther, and Siegfried then married Gutrune,
Hagen continues to scheme, then the power of the gold ring would
be theirs. If they could get Siegfried to consume some of their
magic potion of love's forgetfulness, all memories of Brünnhilde
would vanish. Gunther and Gutrune agree to Hagen's plot.

A horn sounding from the distance is heard. Hagen runs to the
river and recognizes Siegfried, who is welcomed ashore and into
the great hall. After appropriate greetings, Hagen cleverly introduces a discussion of the Nibelung's hoard, now rumored to be in
Siegfried's possession. Siegfried says that it meant nothing to him.
He left it in the dragon's cave, except for the cap of chain now
hanging from his belt. Hagen explains the magical powers of the
Tarnhelm, then asks "You took nothing more?" Only a ring of
gold now worn by the world's most wondrous woman, Siegfried
replies.

Gutrune offers Siegfried a drinking horn brimming with the
potion she has prepared. He toasts Brünnhilde, his true love,
drinks heartily, and instantly forgets her, seized now by a passion
for Gutrune. Bewitched by the magic brew, he offers himself to

her. Then, learning of Gunther's ardent longing for a wondrous woman living high on a rock protected by fire, offers to help his new friend win his bride. Siegfried will help Gunther win Brünnhilde in exchange for Gutrune's hand. The bargain is struck, a ceremony of blood brotherhood enacted, and Siegfried and Gunther depart.

Hagen remains to guard the castle. He sits with shield and spear before the hall watching the two comrades disappear in the distance on their boat. *Hier sitz' ich zur Wacht* ("Here I sit to watch") begins one of the cycle's greatest monologues, Hagen's brief, dark speculation over how unwittingly Gunther and Siegfried are serving Alberich's son in the Nibelung's return to power.

The orchestral interlude following the monologue, a Rhine journey in reverse, of sorts, returns us to Brünnhilde's rock for the second scene of the first act. Brünnhilde joyfully contemplates her ring, the symbol of Siegfried's love, until she hears someone approaching in the distance. It is her sister, Waltraute. Brünnhilde hopes she brings news of Wotan's forgiveness. She comes, instead, in great anxiety over the declining power of the gods. In a lengthy monologue containing numerous remarkable musical passages, she asks her sister on behalf of Wotan and all the other gods to return the ring to the Rhinemaidens, thus freeing both gods and the rest of the world from its awful curse. Of course, Brünnhilde is horrified at the thought of relinquishing the symbol of her love and sends her sister away. Night falls. Flames brighten the sky. A horn is heard.

Brünnhilde, wild with anticipation for Siegfried's return, is stunned when a stranger appears, having conquered the frightening protective flames. It is Siegfried now transformed by Tarnhelm into Gunther's form, and with simulated voice he commences to woo her. Holding her ringed finger before his face, she repulses him in the name of her beloved. He seizes the finger, wrestles from it the ring, the symbol of her power, and they enter the cave for the night as the curtain falls.

Act II

"The tremendous second act," the eminent Wagnerian scholar Ernest Newman wrote," is in some ways Wagner's supreme achievement in music drama," and this assessment of more than one hour of treachery, falsehood, and sinister plotting to the ever-increasing prominence of the orchestral voice is right on the money. The somber events of this act are anticipated in the darkening tones of the brief orchestral prelude prior to the curtain's rise on an open space outside the great hall of the Gibichung castle at night. Hagen sits sleeping where we left him in the first act. His father, Alberich, kneels before him. Hagen opens his eyes but talks without moving. Father and son speak of their despised enemy and anticipate revenge with promises of regaining the ring. Alberich departs.

As dawn breaks, Hagen stares at the Rhine. He is startled by a horn call and Siegfried's sudden appearance. Hagen is told of the successful venture: Gunther soon will arrive by boat with Brünnhilde, who will become his bride. Hagen summons Gutrune. Happy with her fate, she instructs Hagen to summon the Gibichung vassals and their women, for Brünnhilde must receive a warm welcome. She and Siegfried enter the hall as Hagen steps onto a nearby rock and bellows through his cow horn. His voice rings out everywhere:

> Hoiho! Hoihoho!
> Ihr Gibichsmannen,
> machet euch auf!

> Hoiho! Hoihoho!
> Gibich men,
> make ready!

He calls them to arms. Their cow horns answer from various directions and soon they arrive to gather in front of the hall. As they respond with questions: Why does the horn call? Why call us to arms? What is the danger?" the first chorus in the entire *Ring Cycle* has begun, and it comes well into the next to last act of the fourth and final drama. And what a chorus it is! It is nothing less than one of the most exhilarating and inventive choruses in any language as well as more evidence of how far behind Wagner has left his aesthetic ideas of the 1850s, when he explained why operatic choral singing after *Lohengrin* was inconsistent with his new theories.

As you become familiar with the music in *The Ring Cycle*, you will find excerpts that become for you favorite musical episodes you await with considerable anticipation. Such is, and for as long as I can remember has always been, this "Chorus of the Gibichung Vassals" for me. I love it!

Hagen explains that their weapons will be needed not for battle but to slaughter a steer, a boar, a goat, and a sheep in honor of the gods and in preparation for a great wedding festivity, for Gunther is arriving with Brünnhilde. When the vassals then ask what else they are to do, Hagen tells them to have their wives fill drinking horns with mead and wine, as they are to drink until drunk, all in honor of the gods that they may bless this marriage. The vassals roar with delight at the prospect and in finding "grim Hagen" so merry.

Gunther's boat arrives and the vassals welcome their King and his bride. Gunther leads Brünnhilde to the hall, where he greets his sister and Siegfried. Brünnhilde, quite naturally, is dumbstruck to see Siegfried with another woman. Fury replaces bewilderment until Siegfried announces that Gutrune will be his bride. Brünnhilde nearly faints. Caught by Siegfried, who holds her up, she looks at him wondering, "Does he not recognize me?" Then, seeing the ring on his finger, she says it is hers. Telling the story of his conquest of the ring, Siegfried disagrees. She calls him a betrayer. Both Brünnhilde and Siegfried, of course, during this long, perplexing, and embarrassing encounter, are unaware of his memory loss caused by the magic potion. On the point of Hagen's spear, Siegfried swears to the truth of his story and on the same point Brünnhilde vows the spear's ultimate destruction.

Siegfried and Gutrune head for the wedding feast. Hagen, Gunther, and Brünnhilde remain behind. She struggles violently with conflicting emotions of love and hate, Gunther wonders if Siegfried can be trusted, and Hagen—always willing to help—promotes a malicious plot to take care of any and all concerns regarding Siegfried.

Tomorrow a hunting party will be arranged and when Siegfried steps forth for a kill, Hagen will plunge his spear in the hero's back, the one spot he has learned from Brünnhilde where Siegfried is vulnerable. Gutrune and others will be told a lie, that Siegfried was gored by a wild boar. A furious Brünnhilde and a malleable Gunther, putty in Hagen's hands, agree with the plot in a formidable trio as Hagen invokes the aid of his father, Alberich, and the other two that of Wotan. Alberich and Wotan! Notice how the course of the *Ring* derives from their mutual passion for the gold by which one rules the world. Gunther and Brünnhilde now join the bridal procession that ends the act.

Act III
A brief orchestral prelude, commencing with the resounding call

of a hunting horn, precedes the curtain opening on *The Ring Cycle's* final act in three scenes, the first being a remote, wild, wooded, rocky valley of the Rhine. It is a lovely scene. The Rhine-maidens swim, as if in a dance, on the surface of the river, lamenting still the loss of their gold. They hear Siegfried's horn in the distance, dive, surface again, and greet him. He has become separated from his hunting party. They see the gold ring on his finger and ask for its return, laughing and teasing the hero. At first Siegfried refuses, then relents, only to be told to keep it at the cost of losing his life to the curse this very day. He believes this to be a ruse. They swim off merrily, and Siegfried, hearing horn calls, is reunited with the hunters. They pause for food and drink, and ask to hear from him his story.

Scene 2. And thus it is told, from dwarf, to sword, to dragon slaying, to forest bird. At this point Hagen adds an herb to Siegfried's drink. It begins to revive his memory of Brünnhilde. Gunther becomes concerned. As two black ravens fly out of a bush—omens of Siegfried's impending death—he turns his back to watch their flight over the Rhine. Hagen buries his spear in Siegfried's back and as the hero falls upon his shield, mortally wounded, Hagen calmly claims he has avenged perjury and nonchalantly walks away. Dusk turns to darkness; Siegfried briefly recalls Brünnhilde, then dies. Gunther signals the men to lift Siegfried and carry him off. Slowly he follows as the second scene ends with one of the most popular and impressive orchestral interludes in the entire cycle: "Siegfried's Funeral Music." As the procession moves out of sight, heavy mists envelop the stage and a moon shines in the dark, then the mists disperse to reveal the Gibichung castle as seen in the first act.

And now, the third scene of the third act of the final drama in the *Ring Cycle*. Gutrune, fretting over nightmares and Brünnhilde's presence, hears the call of a distant horn. It is Hagen arriving ahead of the rest of the hunting party, which arrives soon thereafter in a procession and sets down the corpse of Siegfried. A stunned Gutrune is told the fib of the wild boar by Hagen, but she accuses her brother of Siegfried's slaughter. Gunther says it was Hagen, who admits his crime and claims the ring. Gunther repulses him, Hagen draws his sword, and in the ensuing fight Gunther is killed. As Hagen approaches Siegfried to take the ring, the hero's dead hand miraculously rises threateningly, which drives Hagen back. The women shriek, the vassals cower, and an enlightened Brünnhilde enters. The rest of the drama is hers in one of Wagner's crowning achievements: "Brünnhilde's Immolation." It is a humdinger when performed by a great orchestra and a soprano with a powerful, rich, controlled voice that never screeches.

Brünnhilde denounces their treacherous scheme. She will have vengeance. Gutrune protests: "Brünnhilde! Soured by jealousy! You brought on this tragedy." Brünnhilde responds,

> Armselige, schweig!
> Sein Eheweib warst du nie . . .

> Be quiet, wretched woman!
> You were never his true wife . . .

Gutrune curses Hagen for recommending the drug that has caused such misery. She bends over the body of her brother and there remains, in deep sorrow, until the end. Brünnhilde looks long upon Siegfried's face. Shock gives way to melancholy, and then, solemnly and authoritatively, she commands the vassals to collect hefty logs, pile them into a great funeral pyre on the bank of the Rhine, and bring her horse to her. As the young men build the pyre and women bring rugs, set them down, sprinkle herbs upon them, and cover them with flowers, Brünnhilde again looks at Siegfried's corpse—so reminiscent of Isolde beholding her dead Tristan except that Isolde was transcendent in her mystical vision and Brünnhilde, her feet very much on the ground, has a mission before her. She has comprehended all. Siegfried's betrayal was ultimately brought about by Wotan in his attempt to avert the dire consequences of the all-consuming curse on the little gold ring he stole. Now, though, the twilight of the gods has commenced. Brünnhilde signals the vassals to lift Siegfried's body onto the pyre, takes from his finger the "terrible ring," and calls to the Rhinemaidens, promising its return with her death:

> The fire that burns me
> will cleanse the curse from the ring.
> You of the waters
> wash it away
> and ever guard the gleaming gold
> whose theft
> caused such evil.

Brünnhilde puts the ring on her finger. She takes a torch in her

hand and directs the ravens—those omens of doom from Wotan—
to her rock to lead Loge back to Valhalla with news of the
approaching end of the gods. She then throws the torch onto the
pyre, igniting it instantly. The ravens fly away. Grane, her horse,
has been brought to her and she greets the beloved steed with her
desire to be united with Siegfried forever by the power of love:

> Siegfried! Siegfried! Behold!
> In joyful bliss your wife greets you!

She mounts her horse and they leap into the flames. Fire con-
sumes the pyre and the Rhine starts to flood. By fire and water, an
evil world is being cleansed of sin. The Rhinemaidens appear
swimming about and Hagen, still lusting for the ring and its
power, calls to them, "Get away from the ring!"—the last words
of the *Cycle*—and dives into the flood to retrieve it. Woglinde and
Wellgunde seize him and drag him into the depth of the river as
Flosshilde with jubilation swims about holding high the ring she
has recovered.

The fire has spread far. Distant flames light up the entire sky.
Bewildered vassals and their women look upon the ruins of their
castle and watch as the flames consume Valhalla and all the gods.

Throughout this magnificent scene, the orchestral voice sings
its miraculous mix of motifs associated with the gods, Siegfried,
the Rhine, the Rhinemaidens, Valhalla, and, ultimately, the
serene motif of salvation through love that spreads softly over the
cataclysmic episode as the curtain falls.

We are left with two all-consuming, awesome, unanswered questions: Has Brünnhilde's expiation atoned for the sins of the world
and redeemed mankind by ushering in the new age of peace through
goodness and love? Or, as Wagner's great-grandson Gottfried once
asked our students in a course we were teaching, "Is there no hope
for the human race?" Wagner will answer that very question with
his final creation, *Parsifal*.

In his book, *The Perfect Wagnerite*, George Bernard Shaw is
entertaining but wrong when he interprets Wagner's *The Ring of
the Nibelung* as a socialist tract set to music—wrong because he
failed to see beyond the obvious political symbolism to the philosophical and religious foundations of the work. The almost endless difficulty Wagner had in trying to resolve problems pertaining
to the close of his tetrology shows more than political concerns.

In 1848, when Wagner wrote his first sketch for a drama based on the Nibelungen myth, he had made Siegfried the central figure. His sacrificial death is understood by Brünnhilde, his wife, who immolates herself. Then a light shows her leading Siegfried into the distance as Hagen, representative of greed and evil, perishes. As his name indicates (*Sieg* means victory and *Fried* means peace), it is Siegfried who has brought peace through the victory of good over evil. "Siegfried's Death," the poem Wagner fashioned out of his sketch, changed this ending only slightly and it in no way altered the victory of light (Siegfried) over darkness (Hagen). In fact, the poem intensifies the struggle between good and evil. There are detailed studies of Wagner's *The Ring of the Nibelung* that trace its varying forms and many revisions during the quarter of a century that passed from inception to completion. Finding the right ending, especially after his change of view on the nature of the world, was Wagner's major problem, for the ethical and religious fabric had to be patched up to fit his shift from the salvation of the world through revolution to the belief that the evils of human life are irredeemable.

This problem is far too complex to rehash here beyond the mention of one example. Wagner changed the title of the final drama in the tetrology from "Siegfried's Death" to "Twilight of the Gods." Wotan's guilt and wrongdoing, representative of the evil structure inherent within the order of all things, has become the central theme. Siegfried dies with neither a resurrection nor a victory over the evil forces. In his final revision, Wagner makes Brünnhilde take her own life by riding into her lover's funeral pyre. Remember, about fifteen hours ago, in *Das Rheingold*, Alberich foreswore love and stole the gold that became the object of all desire and the cause of so much evil. Setting the world on fire, including Valhalla and all the gods, is Brünnhilde's revenge for the cursed greed that killed her beloved Siegfried. No light shows them hand-in-hand rising in the distance. She longs only to be joined in eternal love with her Siegfried. She sings, in her famous immolation scene,

> Feel how my bosom
> so hotly burns.
> Radiant fire
> takes hold of my heart.
> On to embrace him,
> to live in his arms

> thus wedded to him
> in mightiest love!

Brünnhilde joining Siegfried in death and love is remarkably similar to the final scene in *Tristan* and certainly a long way from Wagner's original conception of world salvation. In his final version, there is no redemption of the world from evil. Rather, as the love motif is heard in the orchestra, two basic elements—fire and water—consume heaven and earth. It often is argued, quite plausibly, that Wagner proclaims salvation through love in music transcending the literalness of words, but this remains just an interpretation of the cycle's conclusion, now vastly different from the original, conceived before Wagner discovered the philosophy of Arthur Schopenhauer and swallowed it whole.

The Ring was completed in 1874 and performed for the first time in the theater built by King Ludwig II in Bayreuth. After you have listened to or viewed *The Ring Cycle* once, before your second encounter make sure to obtain a copy of Anna Russell's analysis of *The Ring of the Nibelung*. Recordings and videos are still available. The introduction to Wagner's monumental masterpiece by this famous British comedian is hilarious and must not be missed by anyone with sufficient fortitude to become familiar with the largest, by far, and most complex, by far, operatic undertaking in human history. As you laugh yourself silly, you also will learn something.

Parsifal, Wagner's last drama, completed a year before he died, is next. Here Schopenhauer's influence is most prominent. Wagner called this drama "A Consecrational Festival Play." It is his most overtly religious work.

PARSIFAL (1882)

When in 1864 the eighteen-year-old King rescued Wagner from creditors and exiled wanderings, it undoubtedly occurred to the composer, in whom romantic dreams and hardheaded practicality were uniquely coupled, that the realization of his lifelong artistic ideal, to see his religious dramas produced under festival conditions in his own theater, might at last be at hand. *Parsifal* would become the closest bond between the King and Wagner. This culminating work had been latent within him since he had first read Wolfram's poem *Parzifal* at Marienbad in 1845. But it was not until 1857 that he did something about his idea.

His autobiography tells of a strange event in that year. He awoke one beautiful spring morning overlooking a garden filled with sunshine. Birds sang and he enjoyed one of those periods of peace and rest so infrequent in his life. A personal message had brought him good news, and while enjoying the moment he suddenly remembered it was Good Friday, a day Wagner had already connected with good omens and with Wolfram's poem. All this worked in such a way as to immediately put before him the idea of a great drama, which he quickly sketched in three acts. Wagner did virtually nothing more with the idea for years, but as soon as Ludwig learned of it, he kept at Wagner to carry out his plan, so great was the boy's impatience at the prospect of this work.

In 1865, Wagner began a rough draft of the poem. There are undoubted parallels between Parsifal and Ludwig neither the author nor the King could have missed. Ludwig's fate, it must have occurred to them both, was closely similar to that of Parsifal. Ludwig's father, a king, died and was mourned on Good Friday; Titurel, the Grail King in Wagner's opera, dies and his funeral service is on Good Friday. Ludwig ascends to the throne; Parsifal is chosen the new King of the Grail. Both had to assume great responsibility at the expense of much personal sacrifice.

With the premiere of his great cycle behind him, Wagner wrote the *Parsifal* poem in January 1877. The music was finished five years later. While composing the music, Wagner also was writing articles in conjunction with his lifelong compulsion to theorize as part of the creative act. The central theme of his intellectual life had become the issue of a synthesis of art and religion. *Parsifal* is that synthesis. It is Wagner's only opera written after the festival house was finished, and it was written expressly for what he called a temple for the glorification of the eternal god.

Wagner conceived a sunken orchestra pit hidden from the audience so they could not see the musicians. What he called a "mystic gulf" separates the proscenium from the first row of seats to set off the real world from the ideal world represented on stage. In one of his last articles, Wagner wrote that the music in *Parsifal* makes a "mysterious" entry into the opera house because the musicians are invisible to the audience. Wagner died before he was able to finish a series of articles entitled "Religion and Art." The opening sentence of the first essay, without mentioning *Parsifal*, alerts the reader what to look for in this drama:

One might say that where religion becomes artificial, it is reserved for art to save the spirit of religion by recognizing the figurative value of the mythic symbols which religion would have us believe in their literal sense, and revealing their deep and hidden truth through an ideal presentation.[†]

Parsifal is Wagner's final presentation of what he considered to be the "deep and hidden truth" in myths revealed operatically. Borrowing directly from Schopenhauer's philosophy, Wagner argues that music has an advantage over the other arts when it comes to expressing something religious: Painting and poetry can only point to or represent the religious essence, whereas music is a direct expression of eternal ideas. And as Wagner, now deeply involved with *Parsifal* and the legend of the Holy Grail, comes closer to Christianity than at any other time in his life, he adds the extraordinary statement ". . . the only art that fully corresponds with Christian belief is music."

Parsifal is Wagner's Christian drama. The religious atmosphere is unmistakably Christian and Wagner forbade the audience to applaud. At the drama's conclusion, they were to file out of the festival house in silence as if exiting an intensely sacred service or ceremony. This tradition, at least in his festival house, is honored to this day. Wagner also requested his *Parsifal* never be performed anywhere other than in his festival house. This request was honored until December 24, 1903, when it was staged in the Metropolitan Opera House in New York City—causing quite a stir in the press. Now the opera has been produced in numerous theaters.

There have always been those who love *Parsifal*, those who return again and again to this music as Wagner's most poetic creation. Others, right from its start, condemn it for a variety of reasons: musical, poetic, religious, and philosophical. Gottfried Wagner, the composer's great-grandson, recently wrote disdainfully of the work "for its attitudes toward Jews and women," which he finds implicitly contained in the poem. *Parsifal* was partially responsible for the rupture in the once close friendship between Richard Wagner and the young anti-Christ philosopher Friedrich Nietzsche. He

---

† Richard Wagner, *Prose Works, Vol. V* (Broude Brothers, New York, translation by William Ashton Ellis, 1966), p. 213

published a denunciation calling the drama evidence of Wagner's "reversion to sickly Christianity" and his capitulation before the cross.

But it often happens with Wagner that no matter how unacceptable some of his ideas may be, the intoxicating power of his music can cause one to overlook, even to forget. Nietzsche had made a point of not attending the first performances of *Parsifal* when it had its premiere in the summer of 1882. It was not until 1887, four years after Wagner's death, that Nietzsche first heard music from Wagner's final work. His public denunciations notwithstanding, to his sister, privately in a letter, he wrote, "I cannot think of it without feeling violently shaken, so elevated was I by it, so deeply moved."

We must, here, recall the purpose of this book: to introduce you to the major creations of the greatest composers. *Parsifal* is such a work. For penetrating and controversial evaluations of Wagner's dramatic exposition of "the religion of pity," you will need to go elsewhere.

Parsifal is a drama in three acts. The characters and their voice ranges are:

> AMFORTAS, King of the Knights of the Holy Grail and
>   Keeper of the Grail, *baritone*
> TITUREL, father of Amfortas and formerly Grail King,
>   *bass*
> GURNEMANZ, an old Knight of the Grail, *bass*
> KLINGSOR, a wizard, *bass*
> KUNDRY, a strange creature, in bondage to Klingsor, but
>   at times a servant of the Grail, *soprano*
> PARSIFAL, the young, innocent fool who becomes the King
>   of the Grail, *tenor*
> Knights, esquires, youths, flower-maidens

> The time is the tenth century and the settings, all in
> Spain, are the castle of the Knights of the Grail, its sur-
> rounding territory, and the nearby domain of Klingsor.

Act I

The prelude to the first act has become famous and quite popular. Linked with beautiful music from the third act known as "the Good Friday Spell," the two often are heard over the radio and in concert halls around Easter time. Wagner provided King Ludwig with an explanation of its meaning as a musical expression of the three great Christian virtues of love, faith, and hope, in that order. The prelude is made of motifs heard variously during the drama. Essentially, it depicts a wondrous mystical world disassociated from mundane life. One theme would be immediately familiar to literate Germans: The "Dresden Amen" is an ancient theme that Mendelssohn used in 1830 in his Reformation Symphony. As the prelude mystically ends, the curtain opens on Monsalvat (Mount Salvagge) in Spain, the domain of the Knights of the Grail. Dawn is breaking as Wagner's version of the story begins.

A solemn reveille awakens Gurnemanz and two squires who have been sleeping beneath a tree. They arise, pray, and, as directed by the vigorous old knight, depart to attend to the King's morning bath in the lake. King Amfortas suffers greatly from a wound that will not heal. Two knights arrive in advance of his train with word of his continuing pain. Sadly, Gurnemanz remarks there are no potions to ease his agony. He makes an evasive remark about "only the one man" but changes the subject when asked for an explanation by the knights. Returning, the squires see a wild horsewoman approaching in the distance. It is Kundry, who, to an extraordinary orchestral dissonance, appears on the stage disheveled, wild both in looks and in attire. Stumbling forward, she offers a balm to Gurnemanz that she acquired for Amfortas. Exhausted, she falls to the ground.

Thus the first appearance of one of Wagner's greatest creations, which is what he, too, considered Kundry, of all his female characters. With Senta, Elisabeth, Elsa, Brünnhilde, Isolde, and Eva now behind him, this is quite an admission. This bizarre woman suffers a curse for once mocking Christ. She cannot die, and lives forever divided between good deeds and bad, sometimes serving the Knights of the Grail, at other times in servitude to the vengeful, evil Klingsor.

Carried on a litter by squires, Amfortas and his retinue of knights enter. Though a bath in the cool waters of the lake will temporarily ease his pain, Amfortas knows lasting relief will come, as a mystical voice once promised him, only through one *Durch Mitleid wissend* ("enlightened by compassion"). This phrase, *Durch Mitleid wissend*, is the central philosophical and religious concept of the drama. It is Wagner's variation on the elemental operational concept behind Greek tragedy that throughout his artistic life was so influential to his development as a dramatist.

Knowledge, or enlightenment, in Attic tragedy, eventually

comes through suffering. In Wagner's drama of the religion of pity, knowledge or enlightenment, the understanding of the nature of the human condition, comes through compassion: a sympathetic love wherein one is able to comprehend and respond to the pain and suffering of another. Amfortas awaits the promised one made wise through sympathetic love. The promised one: *der reine Tor* ("the pure fool"), Amfortas reflects. He thanks Kundry for the balm and is carried off to his bath.

Kundry, squires, and Gurnemanz remain, the squires briefly taunting the wild woman before the old knight explains she means well and in her own way serves the knights without ever accepting a word of appreciation, perhaps because she is atoning for some ancient and as yet unforgiven sin. A squire breaks in with the question of whether she may be the source of the woe that pervades the domain of the knights. The lengthy monologues of Gurnemanz that follow are Wagner's adroit way of giving the audience necessary background information as well as preparing the stage, so to speak, for the arrival of Parsifal.

Amfortas, Gurnemanz informs the squires, had been seduced by a woman of fierce beauty and while under her spell he dropped his guard, letting fall the other sacred relic of the drama, the holy spear that dealt Christ the wound when he was on the cross. It was also guarded by the knights. The evil magician Klingsor seized the spear, delivered in the side of Amfortas the wound that will not heal, mocked him, and disappeared. Gurnemanz, who had observed from afar most of this episode, rushed in to save Amfortas. Through the long narration of Gurnemanz, the youthful squires acquire an understanding of their own history. They learn how the sacred cup and spear came to Monsalvat during the reign of King Titurel, father of Amfortas, who gathered about him knights of pure heart to protect the relics and through their power to purify a sinful world.

Klingsor, because he could not control his lusts, was excluded. Angered, he sought revenge. By castrating himself he became privy to evil magical powers that he employed to transform a nearby desert into an intoxicating garden inhabited by women of irresistible beauty. In his power they were to lure good Grail knights into joyful sin and, thus preoccupied, allow the evil magician to enact his revenge. When the aged Titurel abdicated in favor of his son, Amfortas, the new King set out to put an end to such sorcery, but we now know what happened to him. As Amfortas fervently prayed for help and some sign of salvation in the holy sanctuary that once kept the spear, Gurnemanz concludes,

> a blessed radiance emanated from the Grail;
> a holy vision
> clearly spoke to him
> this message in words of fire:
> "Wait for the pure fool,
> enlightened by compassion,
> whom I have ordained."

Since the close of the beautiful prelude of nearly fifteen minutes, the curtain on this act has been up for more than thirty-five minutes and the audience has not heard what would be considered a normal operatic highlight—one of those compact excerpts from an opera that have become so popular that they are eagerly anticipated. Nevertheless, throughout the limited action of the long narrative that sets the stage for the arrival of the "ordained one," Wagner's orchestra weaves a blend of remarkable musical themes corresponding in an uncanny manner to what is seen, and, of course, to what is being sung, but corresponding not as traditional accompaniment. Rather, what you see is what you hear and vice versa—this being the ultimate aesthetic development in Wagner's career. In an essay on the meaning of the term *music drama*, which is what he called his operas, Wagner had written, "The music sounds, and what it sounds, you see on the stage." This applies perfectly to *Parsifal*.

Though I have numerous books naming all the motifs and pinpointing their appearances—"Klingsor's magic," "the pain of Amfortas," "the spear," etcetera—to follow them is just looking for trouble. As you know from our *Ring Cycle* exposition, Wagner, by the 1860s and '70s, had to a great extent abandoned the use of motifs in an exact literal manner and was employing them more abstractly to create a symphonic tapestry expressing the stage action. The symphonic dimensions of *Parsifal* immediately will be obvious to you if you refuse to play the "name that motif" game and simply listen to the manner in which Wagner employs his many musical themes. Accordingly, characters in the drama may be singing one melodic line while the orchestra, depicting the actions or emotions of the characters, sounds a totally independent but always appropriate melody of its own. There are, however, segments of the drama that have become popular highlights or excerpts, and as they arrive they will be noted as such.

Deeply moved by the recitation of the holy vision, the squires repeat the words,

Durch Mitleid wissend,
Der reine Tor . . .

Enlightened by compassion,
the pure fool . . .

to music of ethereal beauty, which after a mystical pause is shattered by a frantic orchestral voice and cries of "Woe is me" from
squires on the lakeshore.

All animals and birds, it is known, within the domain of the
knights are sacred, yet a wandering youth has entered their realm
and shot and killed a swan flying above the lake. The dead bird lies
upon the shore. There the boy is brought to Gurnemanz, who
questions him. The lad is unable to explain why he killed the
swan, where he is from, who his father is, and who sent him. Of
even his own name he is ignorant. All he knows is that his mother is Herzeleide (Heart's Sorrow), they lived in woods and wild
moors, and he made his own crude weapons.

Kundry, alert again, fills in details. She explains that because
the youth's father was killed in battle, his mother raised him free
of arms in the innocence of the wilderness hoping to avoid for her
son his father's fate, to Kundry this being foolishness. As she continues to relate more of the boy's history, it begins to occur to
Gurnemanz that the one for whom they all have been waiting
may be this youth, for he is indeed innocent, lacking wisdom, and
yet he twice in a few minutes has been moved to pity: first, when
called to gaze upon the swan he killed, and second when he
learned from Kundry of his mother's death.

By now the sun is high. Amfortas has finished his bath and
Gurnemanz invites the youth to the pious abode in the castle of
the Grail, where if he is found to be pure he will be nourished by
the Grail. "Who is the Grail?" the bewildered youth asks. This
cannot be told, Gurnemanz informs him, but if you are chosen,
you will know. He concludes by saying he has been guided to this
place by the Grail, for only the chosen find their way.

The journey from the forest scene to the interior of the Castle
of the Grail in some major modern opera houses is accomplished by
a rotating stage where the set changes before the eyes of the audience as the old knight and the young boy depart the woods, cross
rocky terrain, and enter the castle. It is magical. The accompanying
music has become well known and does appear on recordings as an

excerpt. This famous scene is known as the Transformation Scene, and with it we are slowly taken into the great hall of the castle of the Knights of the Grail for the final scene of Act I.

This scene is of great beauty. What is represented is a dramatic and musical portrayal of the most sacred Christian mystery, Holy Communion. There were those of the devout that protested and rebuked Wagner for creating an operatic portrayal of the most holy ceremony of the Christian religion. But what will be the reaction of the naive boy when he experiences this most meaningful act of faithful Christians? When at the close of the scene Gurnemanz wrongly concludes that the youth is but a dolt, the form of the drama Wagner created will tell us otherwise. More on this soon.

A procession of knights and squires sing about the love feast that renews and sustains them daily. It is a captivating chorus. Amfortas is brought in and placed on a couch, and before him is set the Holy Grail. He agonizingly laments his never-ending pain, cries for atonement, and wishes to die, but the voice of his father, Titurel, commands that he uncover the Grail and serve. As the suffering Amfortas sinks back on his couch, however, the voices of boys and young men sing the ethereal *Durch Mitleid wissend, der reine Tor,* which the squires had sung when told by Gurnemanz of the divine sign once given to Amfortas as he knelt imploring God for release from his suffering. By the dramatic structure of this scene, the tortured pleading of Amfortas, followed immediately by the soft reiteration of the mystical promise, Wagner forces us to notice the boy, who is watching the proceedings in silence. The knights tell Amfortas to have faith in the promise and to perform his office and again the voice of Titurel commands, "Uncover the Grail." This time Amfortas obeys. As an increasing darkness spreads throughout the room, Amfortas kneels in silent prayer before the chalice. From the dome, boys' voices sing, "Take my body, take my blood in token of our love!" A bright ray of light descends from above shining on the vessel now flowing with a purple tinge, and Amfortas, transfigured, raises the Grail. All are kneeling. The voice of Titurel is heard again:

> *O, heilige Wonne!*
> *Wie hell grüsst uns heute der Herr!*
>
> Oh! Sacred joy!
> How brightly the Lord greets us today!

Amfortas sets down the Grail and it is covered. The room again is filled with daylight. All except the boy sit down for the sacred meal. Gurnemanz has a place for him and motions him to come, but the youth remains standing motionless and mute.

As the love feast takes place, boys' voices sing of "Salvation in love" and "Salvation through faith." During the meal Amfortas, who has not participated, falls back exhausted. His head sinks and he presses his hand to his wound. It has started to bleed again. Knights and squires attend to him, lift him onto his litter, and carry him out of the hall. Once out of sight a last, painful cry is uttered by Amfortas and at this very moment the youth grabs his heart. This is the only movement he makes in the entire scene, and for this reason, it stands out so clearly in its simplicity.

"Do you know what you have seen?" asks Gurnemanz. When the stunned boy remains silent, shaking his head, the old knight declares, "You are just a fool," pushes him outside, and slams the door behind him. Gurnemanz did not perceive the significance of the boy's clutching his heart at the cry of Amfortas's agony. We know what Gurnemanz does not.

This is the third time, within the few hours that he has been at Monsalvat, that the boy who wandered into the realm of the castle of the Grail has exhibited empathy. Something in the cry of Amfortas moved him to reach for his heart. The evolutionary process wherein a fool becomes wise through the power of empathic love is well under way. When the boy looked carefully at the swan, he was moved to destroy his weapons. He was moved even more when Kundry told him of his mother's death. And now, in this third instance, by clutching his breast he shows a response to the suffering of Amfortas with his heart, though so far he does not comprehend with his intellect. Again, the form of the drama makes the meaning clear. Recall that the youth first entered the action precisely at the moment when the squires sang the ethereal refrain of the Grail's mystical promise.

As the boy makes his exit under the forceful hands of a disappointed Gurnemanz, to end the action of this first act an alto voice sings, *Durch Mitleid wissend, der reine Tor*, and the chorus sings "Salvation in the faith," words made for the impatient Gurnemanz, who expected a naive youth to become enlightened in a matter of minutes. The curtains close on the astonishing sacredness of Act I. When they open again on the first scene of the second act, we will be in a realm of sorcery and evil intentions.

Act II

The act opens on Klingsor's magic castle, located on the same mountain. The rejected youth, who can be seen approaching in the distance, has been lured there and Klingsor anticipates entrapping him as once he did Amfortas. Klingsor awakens Kundry to serve him. Hers is a divided nature, serving at times the knights yet periodically under the sway of Klingsor's evil powers. Though she remonstrates, Kundry eventually must serve the will of her master, who, as she shakes off the remains of her deep sleep, accounts aloud how the brave, handsome youth shows no fear as he wounds, disarms, and drives off Klingsor's guards.

The evil magician, nevertheless, is convinced the intruder is doomed and again, right before our eyes, another miraculous scenery transformation has Klingsor's castle sink out of sight as a beautiful magical garden arises, teeming with tropical vegetation and luxurious flowers. As the boy enters the garden, it fills with lovely, fetching maidens who dance about in agitated fury and reproach him for routing their protecting lovers. But soon they become immensely attracted to the comely youth, who even acknowledges that they are, indeed, quite fair even though he shows no indication of falling under the spell of their attempts to seduce him. The maidens now have adorned themselves with flowers, the opera's famous Flower Maidens, and each wants the boy for herself. Nothing in the entire drama is more enchanting than this episode, which concludes when the handsome youth, tired of their gaiety, is prepared to leave. But a hidden voice stops him in his tracks and prompts the Flower Maidens to cower and scatter in fear: "Parsifal, stay!"

I love the music accompanying the attempts of the maidens to seduce Parsifal, for we now know that is who he is, and to dissolve his resolute refusal to capitulate before their obvious wiles. And so did Wagner. As this scene was being rehearsed, several members of the production staff sat in the unlit Festival House watching. At its conclusion, a vigorous clapping issued from behind them. They turned and shushed the culprit who so flagrantly had violated Wagner's rule of no applause during or after his sacred festival play—only to look upon Wagner himself as the lights went on. It was none other than the composer who had broken his own precept in a moment of great enthusiasm. After all, it was only a rehearsal.

Of course, all along we've known that it is Parsifal who wandered into the sacred domain, shot a swan, and speechlessly observed the knight's sacred supper but here we are more than halfway through one of the longest operas ever written before his name is uttered. The Flower Maidens disperse as the voice bids them to depart and Parsifal to remain. The stunned youth turns toward the source of the voice and there, through an opening in banks of blossoms, reclining on a couch of flowers is Kundry, now transformed into a young and exceedingly beautiful woman.

"Did you call me, the one without a name?" he asks. Kundry reveals that the name Parsifal means "the pure and innocent foolish one" and was given to him by his dying father before his birth. By *der reine Tor* ("the pure fool") Wagner does not mean an empty-headed person but rather an innocent person who as yet has not become enlightened as to the elemental nature of the human condition—one still lacking the wisdom of how humans ought to live their life and how they ought to relate to one another. *Ich sah das Kind* ("I saw the child") begins the long and famous monologue of Kundry wherein she tells Parsifal about his youth. His mother, fearing her son could experience the same terrible fate of his father, death in battle, sheltered him from all weapons and the constant strife that prevails in the real world. Of this she kept him ignorant but one day, when older, he wandered off and disappeared without a trace. When he did not return, his mother died of a broken heart. Learning this, Parsifal reproaches himself for insensitive neglect, denounces himself as a fool, and grieves visibly. Kundry, under the spell of Klingsor's sorcery, commences to console Parsifal with comforting words as she puts her arms lovingly around his neck. She claims to bear his mother's blessing in this "first kiss of love" and on his lips she gives him a long, passionate kiss. She will convince him that sexual love is the source of consolation.

Suddenly Parsifal, as if stricken, frees himself, presses both hands over his heart, as he had done in the Grail temple, and in anguish cries out

> Amfortas!—
> The wound! The wound!
> It burns here in my side!

He has made the connection. For the Romantic mind the heart is the most valid source of knowledge and understanding. Parsifal has felt pity in his heart for the unending pain Amfortas suffers. He has seen the light. He almost succumbed, as did Amfortas, to the demonic; in him, however, a divine force prevailed. The nature of his spiritual mission has been revealed. He is the one to end the agony of Amfortas.

But if he can feel pity for Amfortas, cannot he also pity she who lives divided within herself and under a terrible curse? Kundry asks. She is on fire with desire. Cannot he also be the one who saves her by making love with her? He will save her, too, but not by uniting with her. But she is ecstatic with passion for him. If it was her kiss that brought revelation, would not making love with her make him a god? She persists, but unsuccessfully. It will be by other means that he will be the source of her salvation if she will lead him to Amfortas. She declines and again attempts to embrace him. Thwarted, she calls for help and suddenly Klingsor, brandishing a spear, appears and flings the weapon at Parsifal. Miraculously, it hangs suspended over Parsifal's head. He clutches it and makes the sign of the cross, and, in doing so, the entire domain of Klingsor withers and disappears. Kundry screams. As Parsifal begins to depart, he stops. He turns toward the prostrate woman and says, "You know where you can find me again." The curtains close.

Act III

The preludes preceding the action of Acts I and II represent in sound two different worlds and the two different forces vying for power within the drama. The musical prelude to the first act, remember, is constructed of musical themes called "Love," "Faith," and "Hope" by Wagner and the sound, it has been noted, is serene, sublime, and celestial: a fitting introduction to the realm of the Holy Grail. Equally appropriate are the cacophonous sounds introducing us to Klingsor's domain. The music heard at the outset of the final act expresses a weariness that reflects years of aimless wandering by Parsifal in search of the Grail castle.

As Act III opens, we are back in the realm of the Grail, this time on the edge of the forest. Years have passed since the events of the second act. A meadow full of flowers is in view and so is an anchorite's hut. As in the first act, it is still early morning, but not just any morning: It is Good Friday. Gurnemanz, now greatly aged and dressed only in a tunic of the Knights of the Grail, emerges from the hut, hears moaning, walks to a tangled thicket, separates dense undergrowth, and discovers that Kundry has returned. She appears dead, but, having heard her moan, Gurnemanz extricates the seemingly lifeless form, drags it into the open, and carries her to a grassy mound where he commences to revive her. Eventually she awakens. Attired as in Act I, she nevertheless looks less wild and more pale. Is she not grateful to him for awakening her from a deadly sleep? Gurnemanz asks. Kundry will not leave the stage in this final act but she responds with the only word she will utter. *Dienen* ("Service"), she says, then repeats it. She wants to serve and Gurnemanz agrees. From his hut she procures a water pitcher, fills it at the spring, returns to the hut, and becomes busy.

A knight dressed in black armor, his visor lowered, and carrying a spear appears in this sacred realm. Gurnemanz bids him disarm on this the holiest day of the year. The knight puts the spear upright in the ground, removes helmet, sword, and shield, then kneels before the spear to pray. Gurnemanz summons Kundry. Both recognize that the foolish boy who shot the swan and was rudely dismissed by Gurnemanz has returned as a man. Parsifal says he believes himself chosen to end the agony of Amfortas but that countless obstacles have long delayed his return to Monsalvat. Finally, he is here, the sacred spear with him.

How desperately he is needed, cries a joyous Gurnemanz, who relates that Amfortas has refused to do his sacred duty because of his suffering. Denied the sustaining power of the sacred meal, the knights have become weak and weary, Titurel has died, and a hopeless, woeful mood prevails. Parsifal blames himself. Deeply affected by the despair, he nearly faints. Gurnemanz and Kundry lead him to the sacred spring, there to cleanse him in preparation for the holy office that the old knight now knows Parsifal will soon serve. They remove his greaves and the rest of his armor. Gurnemanz sprinkles holy water on Parsifal while Kundry bathes his feet, anoints them with ointment, and dries them with her long hair in an enactment of the Jesus and Mary verse (John 11: 2) of the New Testament that is too obvious to miss. Parsifal cups his hand and scoops up some water from the spring and with it baptizes Kundry in his first sacred duty, thus freeing her from her awful curse. Then, looking across the meadow, he comments on how lovely it is on this day and here begins what many consider to be the most beautiful segment in all of Wagner's operas: "The Good Friday Spell." (Some who love this music but who do not know the opera think it an orchestral interlude because often it is linked with the Act I prelude and played in the concert hall or on recordings without the words that go with it.) Gurnemanz tells Parsifal that the beauty he sees is the magic of Good Friday, but Parsifal protests that everything should weep and mourn on this day of greatest suffering. Again, I will translate with no intention that it could be sung:

> *Du siehst, das is nicht so.*

You see that it is not so,

exclaims Gurnemanz, and he explains why:

> Today the sinner's remorseful tears
> are a holy dew
> covering the flowery meadow
> and causing it to flourish.
> Now all creatures rejoice
> at the evident presence of the Redeemer,
> and dedicate their prayers to him.
> They cannot see the cross
> so they look up upon a redeemed mankind,
> freed from all sin and dread,
> cleansed and saved by God's loving sacrifice.
> Every blade and flower in the meadow senses this,
> for today all men walk gently
> just as God, with infinite patience,
> took pity on them and suffered for them.
> On this day in piety
> Man spares the flower with gentle step.
> All creation give thanks,
> all that blooms and is mortal,
> for today nature is absolved
> and gains its innocence.

Here is a magic unlike anything Klingsor ever knew. God, man, and nature are all one in a mystical unity. To the major themes in the drama—suffering, service, and salvation—is now added this concept of a mystical unity and the interrelationship of all creation. Redemption has been visited upon all that lives through God's love, the sacrifice of his own son.

The pealing of bells is heard in the distance, and at this point Parsifal makes, if one remembers the second act, a revelatory gesture. Kundry had remained all this time on the ground at Parsifal's feet. At Gurnemanz's final words she has again lifted her head. Parsifal, having spoken—Look! the meadow is smiling"—gently kisses her on the forehead. The kiss in Act II symbolized sexual love and seduction to evil. In Act III, a different kind of love has just been revealed: first by Gurnemanz's monologue but most of all by this symbolic kiss. This is love as compassion, forgiving and redeeming love, divine love.

The bells are ringing at noon. After Parsifal is invested with the mantle of the Knights of the Grail, he and Kundry follow Gurnemanz as the scene, reminiscent of Act I, gradually changes to the dimly lit great hall of the castle.

There are many parallel episodes in Acts I and III. Again, processions of knights enter the hall from different sides, one carrying the shrine sheltering the Grail followed by Amfortas on a litter, the other bearing the body of Titurel in a coffin. Their antiphonal singing (singing in alternating choruses) is striking. Litter and coffin are placed before the altar as the knights implore Amfortas to uncover the Grail and serve his office for his father's sake. He refuses. Tearing open his garment to expose the terrible wound that will not heal, he begs them to end his agony by burying their swords in his side up to the hilt. The horrified knights shrink away from him.

Parsifal, who with Gurnemanz and Kundry, has entered the hall unobserved, steps forward and with the tip of the sacred spear touches the wound. "Only the spear that smote you can heal your wound," he proclaims. Amfortas glows with ecstasy. Parsifal commands that the Grail be uncovered. There is a beautiful synthesis between sight and sound as the drama comes to its end. Music of incomparable beauty blends perfectly with the deliberate, restrained gestures of the actors to express the final revelation. The altar boys open the shrine. Parsifal takes the Grail and kneels in silent prayer. The Grail glows, casting a glorious radiance over all. Titurel, reanimated momentarily, rises in his coffin to make the sign of the cross. From the dome, a white dove descends and hovers over the head of Parsifal, who gently waves the Grail back and forth over the brotherhood. All have their eyes on the sacred relic. Kundry, looking at Parsifal, sinks slowly to the floor, lifeless. Amfortas and Gurnemanz pay homage to the new King of the Holy Grail. The great hall fills with ethereal voices, barely audible, singing "Salvation! The greatest miracle! Salvation to the Savior!" The curtain closes.

Finally and importantly, what philosophical concepts of Schopenhauer did Wagner make use of in *Parsifal*? The answer is, most of them. *Parsifal* is a dramatization of Schopenhauer's preoccupation with suffering and salvation. Virtually every character and almost any situation in the opera correlates to concepts Schopenhauer articulated in his masterwork *Die Welt als Wille und Vorstellung (The World as Will and Idea)*, published in 1819. To trace the one-to-one relationships is a fascinating undertaking, one that would fill another two dozen pages: I know, because elsewhere I have done so. Consider this one example. In his book, Schopenhauer devotes a long and important segment to human ethical behavior. With great detail he characterizes goodness and evil. Act II of *Parsifal* is the confrontation of the good man, Parsifal, with an evil man, Klingsor. All attributes of what to Schopenhauer constitute good and bad behaviors are wrapped up in these two characters, especially Parsifal's sympathy for the suffering of Amfortas and the sinister machinations of Klingsor's vengeance aimed at the Knights of the Grail.

Schopenhauer was an anomaly in nineteenth-century German philosophy. He not only rejected a predominate Idealism purporting God or some other form of Goodness as the ultimate positive power and reality of the universe, but he also reasserted an unpopular realism wherein an untamed willfulness, a relentless unsatisfied striving, and passionate, never-satisfied appetite constitute the ultimate force not only in the universe but dwelling also in every human heart. This perverse, pervasive, dominating Will motivates the actions of humans and nations, thus causing constant conflict and driving one and all blindly to their doom. This unrestrained Will is why human history is the story of endless wars, the reason why hatred and greed are rampant, and why there is so much pain, suffering, unhappiness, and misery. Schopenhauer claimed in one of his most famous evocative statements that "the evil in the world is irredeemable." This, of course, is the concept that reversed the direction of Wagner's *Ring Cycle* away from radical revolution toward religious resignation, thus leaving us, at the end of the great tetrology, with a question we've already posed: "Is there any hope for the human condition?" Now, recall that when this question was posed, I wrote that Wagner would answer it with *Parsifal*, his final creation. So, in a sentence, what is the answer? Except for an enlightened few who experience the taming of the raging will, there is no hope.

While famous nineteenth-century intellectuals proposed one optimistic interpretation after another of the onward and upward direction in the continuing development of human history (Hegel, Marx, Darwin, for example), Schopenhauer countered with a profoundly pessimistic interpretation. But he does not slam the door on all hope. Though most never will experience sufficient enlightenment to be able to quiet and control the awful Will, for a few there is hope for some salvation amid terrible suffering. An escape from the raging, blind madness of the rest of the world comes with a revelation and with living according to Schopenhauer's aesthetic, ethical, and ascetic conceptions. If I ask and then briefly answer three questions, the core of Schopenhauer's philosophy as well as the meaning of Wagner's *Parsifal* will be clear.

Is the Act I Transformation scene merely an innovative change of scenery? When Kundry attempts to seduce Parsifal with a long, passionate kiss in Act II, why does he pull away from her embrace, clasp his heart, and cry, "Amfortas!"? And in "The Good Friday Spell" of the third act, why does Parsifal sit and contemplate the beauty of nature and all living things rather than race to heal Amfortas now that his mission as "the promised one" is clear to him?

Much more than the scenery is being transformed in this famous scene. According to Schopenhauer's aesthetics, certain experiences can bring on a temporary quieting of the relentless will, thus affording what he calls "relative salvation." Extremely beautiful aspects of the natural world—wondrous mountains, vast marvelous architectural spaces, interiors of great churches, for example, and magnificent music—can fill one with such awe as to cause a temporary cessation of striving and yearning as well as providing an insight into our actual place in time and space: We are not all that matters in the universe. As Parsifal walks with Gurnemanz out of the forest through the wild mountains and into the great hall of the Grail Castle, filling with the procession of knights and reverberating with their magnificent choral ode, he becomes exalted and so spellbound that he cannot even speak when later Gurnemanz asks him if he understands what he has seen transpire before him. Parsifal can only clutch his heart and Gurnemanz, missing the significance of this all-important gesture, dismisses him as a dolt. It was not just scenery being transformed but Parsifal, also, for literally and figuratively he has taken the first steps away from his innocent and uninformed childhood toward enlightenment. Gurnemanz does not know what you know: In an overwhelming ecstatic mystical state induced by the unbelievable beauty surrounding him, Parsifal has experienced the initial aesthetic transformation leading from suffering to salvation.

According to Schopenhauer, ethical enlightenment results in the abnegation of the will's relentless pursuit to satisfy its constantly unsatiated yearnings. This willfulness is the source of suffering and its passionate, incessant yearning is the blind, dominant driving force of human behavior—its most potent manifestation, and therefore the most dangerous one, being the sexual drive. To recognize this intuitively in oneself and to acknowledge that it is the same with all others constitutes an enlightenment only a few achieve. Kundry's passionate kiss very nearly placed Parsifal in thrall to her seductive beauty, but in the nick of time he realizes intuitively how his own fate and certain suffering is connected to that of Amfortas because we all share the same human nature. That is why Parsifal once again clutches his heart and cries "Amfortas!" after Kundry's kiss. He is one of those rare human beings who have experienced, in the words of Schopenhauer, the ethical enlightenment of his will. An enlightened will, unlike the unending strivings of a blind and unenlightened will, can be tamed. With an enlightened will comes salvation and the end of suffering. This is Parsifal.

Schopenhauer's aesthetic and ethical concepts, dramatically appropriated by Wagner, allowed Parsifal to experience the temporary, relative salvation of an intense mystical experience (Act I) followed by complete salvation derived from an enlightened will (Act II). So what has Schopenhauer's asceticism to do with "The Good Friday Spell" of the final act? Most humans, according to Schopenhauer, never experience the release from bondage to their relentless strivings as did Parsifal in the temple of the Grail. Only a very few directly and intuitively grasp a full understanding of the nature of the world and through such enlightenment are able to free themselves from powerful urges as did Parsifal after Kundry's kiss, and far fewer than this are they who are able to permanently repress all yearning and thus achieve an abnegation of the will as does Parsifal in the third act. During "The Good Friday Spell" in the peaceful contemplation of the beauty of nature, he is fully aware of a totally different type of love from the commonplace urge for sexual gratification raging within us. This is love as sympathy for all that lives. This is the compassionate love of the pure fool made wise through pity, a love that transcends all appearances of individual differences to connect all that lives in a wondrous, loving harmony. Wagner's Parsifal is the promised one made wise through the insight that All is One and that the end of suffering comes with manifesting love as empathy with all that lives. Before Parsifal can heal Amfortas, it must be established beyond all doubt that he is the ordained one—that Parsifal is, indeed, Schopenhauer's ascetic holy man.

Parsifal can be and has been deeply appreciated by many who have never even heard of Arthur Schopenhauer. Thus, they have no inkling that the opera is a dramatization of Western civilization's most pessimistic philosopher, who claimed only music of all the arts could penetrate, grasp, and express ultimate reality. No wonder Wagner was so smitten. Because he was so indebted to Schopenhauer, years ago I desperately wanted to know what the philosopher said about suffering and salvation that became the single most intellectual influence of Wagner's life and the basis for so much in his creative work. My profound love for Wagner's *Parsifal* owes much to my often experiencing the drama with Schopenhauer at my side.

Willful and striving relentlessly as a younger man, Wagner finally in his last years has found peace and quiet with the care, protection, and virtually unlimited beneficence of his patron King Ludwig. You will hear this in the beautiful music of his last masterpiece. He said that in *Parsifal* he sought to compose music that was like the commingling of clouds, their separating, and their coming together again. No one has ever bettered Wagner in describing the sublime and serene music of his *Parsifal*.

∾

Often in this book, I note the elemental question of operatic composition throughout its long history: Words or music, which is more important? Wagner provided two different answers. Early in his career he claimed, in a book and admirably demonstrated in operas, that poet and musician are equal; one should not dominate the other even though in *Lohengrin* and *Das Rheingold* the words, at times, do dominate. Once under the spell of Schopenhauer's mesmerizing theory of music as the supreme art, the musician in Wagner begins its ascent over Wagner the poet and reaches its climax in *Parsifal*. Here much action proceeds without words in his longest drama and by far his shortest poem. *Parsifal* is Wagner's most symphonic opera. After *Parsifal* he contemplated no more dramas. He intended to write pure music, a symphony devoid of pictorial or poetic ideas.

It was not to be. Wagner died in Venice on February 13, 1883.

He was sixty-nine. Verdi, also sixty-nine, was at his home in Bus-seto. At this time, though less than one hundred miles separated these two men, the towering geniuses of nineteenth-century opera in so many ways were worlds apart.

Giuseppe Verdi

VERDI II:
AÏDA, OTELLO, AND FALSTAFF

When Wagner died, Giuseppe Verdi had been retired from operatic composing for more than a decade, a retirement from which he would emerge with unprecedented power as an old man to create two of his greatest masterpieces, *Otello* and *Falstaff*. Both, obviously, are based on plays of Shakespeare, whom he revered. Verdi was living merely a few hours away, but, as I have noted, the two greatest and most influential composers of opera in the nineteenth century (some would say ever) never met, never corresponded, and, publicly, hardly even acknowledged the other's existence. The one exception I have read about is the rage with which Verdi reacted when once accused of having become "an imitator of Wagner."

Verdi's last opera, or so he had thought, was a sensational triumph. It was *Aïda*, an opera about ancient Egypt, which premiered in Cairo in 1871. These three final masterworks of the great Verdi, *Aïda*, *Otello*, and *Falstaff*, are operas you must know about, but between *La traviata* and *Aïda* are seven other Verdi operas with considerable famous music to be aware of for exploring later. For various reasons, these "in-between operas" (meaning they were composed after the three masterpieces presented in chapter 6 and before the late masterworks of this chapter) generally enjoy fewer performances and less attention than his six most well-known operas. That they are not represented in detail in this book is not to diminish their worth. To discuss all the Verdi corpus, more than two dozen operas, is a book unto itself.

Verdi scholars mark the close of his intimate, domestic Italian opera period with the completion of *La traviata*. His next opera, *Les vêpres siciliennes (The Sicilian Vespers)*, was written in the style of French grand opera in response to a commission for the Paris Great Exhibition of 1855. You easily could encounter references to this opera as *I Vespri Siciliani*, its Italian version. The time of the story is 1282 in Palermo. Sicily is occupied by French troops and the Sicilians will attempt to run them out. The excellent overture often is heard in concert performances. The most famous excerpt comes from the second act. It is a superb aria for bass voice. A banished Sicilian leader has returned. Lovingly, he greets his homeland and then urges a small core of compatriots to join him in rising against the oppressors. *O patria . . . O tu Palermo* ("Oh, Fatherland . . . Oh you Palermo"), he sings in the Italian version. Many fine basses have recorded this aria, Ruggero Raimondi in the 1974 first complete stereo version of this opera and the 1927 model performance by Ezio Pinza having a special place in my collection with Samuel Ramey's 1989 version.

Stiffelio, an opera about a Protestant clergyman who forgives his wife's infidelity, an unusual subject for a Catholic culture, was first written in 1850 and soon thereafter revised as *Aroldo*. It appeared in 1857. *Aroldo* never had much of a hold on audiences until the 1990's Metropolitan Opera revivals, then again as *Stiffelio*, with Placido Domingo. *Simon Boccanegra* followed in 1857 but was not successful, probably because of an exceedingly complicated plot based on a real fourteenth-century Genoese doge. This dark and powerful work was revised by Verdi and Arrigo Boito—composer, poet, and collaborator with Verdi on *Otello* and *Falstaff*. Though Boito made the drama less complex, *Simon Boccanegra* still is subjected to attempts to bring clarity and precision to the story. For several reasons it is, despite these ongoing problems of plot, a dramatic tour de force. The title role of *Boccanegra* is one of Verdi's greatest creations and one of his finest roles for baritone. His daughter Amelia shares with her father some of Verdi's most sensitive writing for the father/daughter relationship he often so movingly articulated in music. Another supreme aria for bass voice is one of the most memorable excerpts from the score. Fiesco, a patrician, laments his daughter's death. *A te l'estremo addio,* ("To you a last farewell, proud palace, cold tomb of my angel!") begins the recitativo. The aria, *Il lacerato spirito del mesto genitore* ("The lacerated spirit of the sad father") is Verdi at his best.

I grew up on Pinza's 1951 recording and play over and over Ramey's 1989 rendition from his *Opera Arias* compact disc, one no opera-loving home should be without. Amelia's first-act aria, *Come in quest'ora bruna* ("How in this morning light"), is a significant aria for soprano, but the best of Act I is yet to come, first in the father and daughter recognition scene and then with the finale as completely revised by Boito. Quite simply, it is one of the best scenes in any opera by Verdi. Simon's exhortation *Plebe! Patrizi! Popolo dalla feroce storia!* ("Plebeians! Patricians! People of a fierce history!) commences the culmination of this magnificent episode. Very fine, too, is the trio concluding the second act, as well as the quartet that ends an opera of great force and intensity but one lacking the string of hit tunes so anticipated in an Italian opera house.

Un ballo in maschera (A Masked Ball) premiered in 1859, the year Verdi married the soprano Giuseppina Strepponi. She was the most significant person in his life. They had met in the late 1830s when Verdi, young, married, and the father of two children, would soon experience the paralyzing loss of his daughter, son, and wife in short succession. Strepponi helped to ensure the modest success of Verdi's first opera, *Oberto*, at La Scala in 1839 and she sang Abigaille in the 1842 premiere of *Nabucco*. In 1846, she met Verdi again. They became lovers and lived together. She would prove to be a calming and positive influence on the composer's proud, independent, and, at times, fiery spirit driven by his dramatic genius, the monumental amount of marvelous music within him seeking expression, and the desire for both success and recognition. Giuseppina would urge him not to work so hard, to accept fewer commissions, to retire to the country where they could live inexpensively, and, most important, to compose only for himself. By 1859, they were settled in seclusion in the Italian countryside.

Un ballo in maschera has an interesting history. The opera is based on the assassination of King Gustavus III of Sweden. During a masked ball in Stockholm, on March 18, 1792, the King was shot in the back. Verdi's opera was to premiere during the 1858 Naples carnival season but was postponed during rehearsals when an Italian revolutionary attempted to assassinate Napoleon III. An opera about an assassinated king was a little too close to home, and governmental censors required changes. For the Rome 1859 premiere, a year later, Stockholm had become Boston and King Gustavus III was now the Count of Warwick. The events of the opera, totally ludicrous to puritanical Boston, now were acceptable to censors. During the mid-twentieth century, the original Swedish version was reinstated for a performance in Stockholm and it is in that form that the opera generally is now performed and recorded.

Vigorous ensembles, spirited choruses, and popular arias notwithstanding, *A Masked Ball* has never achieved the popularity of Verdi's most beloved works. I don't know why. I love this opera. There is much fine music for tenor, for sopranos, and for the baritone, who has the great and extremely difficult Act III aria *Eri, tu* ("It was you"), one I seem to have known all my life because it was a favorite of my father, who sang it often in our home.

Gustavus III is in love with Amelia, wife of his friend and secretary, who is equally smitten but will remain, nevertheless, faithful to her husband. Believing her false, Anckarstroem, the secretary, murders Gustavus during a masked ball. The role of Gustavus is one of the finest Verdi ever wrote for tenor voice. It includes the ever-popular aria *Di' tu se fedele* ("Tell me, if truthful"). Amelia's most well-known aria occurs at the beginning of the third act. Her husband, convinced of her infidelity, is threatening to kill her. All attestations of innocence having been ignored, she pleads to be allowed to see their son one last time: *Morrò, ma prima in grazia* ("I shall die—but one last wish"). Oscar, the King's page, is a breeches part for soprano voice, probably the finest and most musical page in operatic literature. "He" has several spritely tunes, none more notable than the Act III *Saper vorreste*, his refusal to disclose to the revenge-minded Anckarstroem what costume the King will wear to the masked ball.

Finally, Ulrica, the black fortune-teller, needs paragraphs of her own because of the American contralto Marian Anderson's historic portrayal. Ulrica's big scene is in the first act, when she predicts to the King, disguised as a fisherman, his death by the hands of a friend. On January 7, 1955, Anderson, then nearing sixty, and with her once unique voice now in decline, made her first operatic appearance as Ulrica. The first black person ever to sing on the stage of the Metropolitan Opera house, she opened the door to a long line of black singers unto this day, thus ending one of the most shameful segregations in the history of American art.

Artistic segregation was not new to Anderson. As a young woman she was refused voice lessons at a Philadelphia music school because, she was told, "we don't take colored." In 1939, her magnificent voice, now famous in Europe and America, could not be heard in concert at Constitution Hall in Washington, D.C. Ironically, the Daughters of the American Revolution refused to make Constitution Hall available to her. Mrs. Franklin Delano Roosevelt immediately resigned membership and joined other citizens in changing the site to the steps of Lincoln Memorial. There, on April 9, 1939, seventy-five thousand or more gathered to hear her sing. Because she was black, her career had been limited to the concert stage.

When Toscanini heard her in a Salzburg recital in 1935, he declared during intermission that hers was a voice heard only once every hundred years, a comment that sped around the globe, ensuring her fame. Marian Anderson's voice is among the most extraordinary instruments I have ever heard. Though she thought of herself as a contralto, her compass extended from low, rich chest tones to an ethereal high soprano. I have most of her recordings. Never pass one by should you come across it, especially any made in the 1930s, when her voice was its fullest, most versatile and vibrant. The recordings dating from this time, which she made with her Finnish accompanist, Kosti Vehanen, are treasures—Schubert's *Der Tod und das Mädchen* ("Death and the Maiden,") and "Ave Maria" of 1936 are unlike anything else I have ever heard. Many of her recordings have been remastered onto compact discs. Hers is a voice you cannot afford not to hear, and once heard you will know there is no other like it.

True, her recordings as Ulrica are those of a woman no longer in possession of the incomparable instrument of her youth, but she had by then become a symbol of freedom and equality. Listen to her spirituals, always sung with eyes closed and hands clasped, and you will hear more than glorious sounds. You will behold what our human existence could be were it void of racial hatred, prejudice, and intolerance. You will hear the song of a better world than ours.

In 1861, Verdi became involved in politics. He greatly admired the Italian statesman Camillo Cavour, a leader for the unification of Italy. Cavour had persuaded Verdi to become a member of the recently formed Italian parliament. When Cavour died soon thereafter, Verdi's political enthusiasm waned. He resigned his seat in 1865. Though the cornerstones of his politics were freedom, goodness, and a tolerant and humane social order, Verdi could not foresee them happening in a country where reigned both pope and king. For years, Verdi had been seen as an artistic revolutionary associated with the *Risorgimento*, the movement of Italian liberation and unification. "Viva Verdi," often shouted in the streets and chanted at rallies, was an acrostic political slogan standing for the unification of Italy under the king. "Viva Verdi" meant *"Viva Vittorio Emanuele, Re D'Italia"* ("Long live Victor Emanuel, King of Italy). Verdi completed only one opera between *A Masked Ball*, 1859, and *Don Carlos*, 1867. *La forza del destino* premiered in 1862.

LA FORZA DEL DESTINO (1862)
The Force of Destiny

The first three thumping chords of the prelude, which are immediately repeated (perhaps the most popular, well-known, and often performed of Verdi's overtures in concert halls and on recordings), must be three of the most familiar notes the composer ever penned. They have been called the "fate motif." They may represent the fate or destiny of the title but they do not constitute a motif because they do not recur throughout the opera as a symbolic or unifying theme. There is, however, an authentic motif of unearthly beauty—a frail, haunting theme expressed primarily in the strings, heard in the prelude and throughout the opera in association with the dire destiny of Leonora, the drama's dominating character. It is the theme I think of first whenever *La forza del destino* is mentioned.

The opera overflows with wonderful tunes but once again, Verdi had to make something from a complicated libretto. The story is a period piece of Spain and Italy in the 1750s: rival lovers, warring noble families, political intrigue, revenge, disguises, a wondrous gypsy, religious involvements, and on it goes. The "destiny" of the title turns out to be more a matter of bizarre, even unlikely, coincidences, or, perhaps, contrived circumstances to make a story. I do not look forward to unraveling this plot synopsis on those occasions when I schedule the opera on my Vermont Public Radio "Saturday Afternoon at the Opera" broadcasts, but then the music takes over. And what unforgettable music it is. Verdi's inspiration salvages a story that, without the music, would today hold minimal interest.

Excerpted from a wonderful score, the following scenes are the most familiar highlights. The role of the gypsy girl Preziosilla asks for a brilliant mezzo-soprano voice and her aria early in Act II, in spite of two notable Act I arias and a duet, often is the first "bring-down-the-house" number. People are dancing and singing in an inn located in the mountains of Spain. Preziosilla enters and after a comment or two she sings, with choral responses, *Al suon del tamburo* ("At the sound of the drum"). When the scene changes in this act to a gate of a mountain monastery, Leonora, the noble lady loved by the Don inadvertently responsible for her father's death, has a famous aria for a big soprano voice. Zinka Milanov and Leontyne Price come to mind; some experts claim the most electrifying performance of Leonora ever on record is by Maria Callas, a recording made at La Scala in August 1954 when her at times troublesome voice was deemed to be at its best. The aria following a recitativo is *Madre, Madre, pietosa Vergine, perdona al mio peccato* ("O Mother of God, Holy Virgin, forgive my sin"). The climax to this magnificent prayer is to music also heard in the overture. This second act culminates in my favorite scene in the opera because the music throughout is so beautiful. One does not need to be a believer to appreciate it. Verdi, known for his animosity toward the clergy, portrays a service in the monastery in solemn, lovely music ending with a melodic chant of holy men. Leonora is among them disguised as a monk, her voice soaring high above the others as they pray in *La Vergine degli angeli* ("The Virgin of the Angels").

The Act III duet for tenor and baritone, one of the most often recorded excerpts for this combination of voices in Italian opera, is *Solenne in quest'ora* ("In this solemn hour"). Two other famous excerpts are heard near the end of this act. In an army camp, soldiers and the women who follow them sing a happy tarantella (a rapid Neapolitan dance). Friar Melitone enters, is swept up in the dance, stops, and delivers a tongue-in-cheek sermon. Its series of extraordinary puns (you are far more concerned with bottles than with battles, for example) are fully comprehensible only to those knowing every word of the Italian. How he is having fun with the language! The comic musicality, nevertheless, can be enjoyed by all. Verdi's characterization of Friar Melitone anticipates his greatest comic delineation in Sir John Falstaff yet to come. Preziosilla's *Rataplan* ends the act. A *rataplan* is the imitation of the sound of a drum. She beats upon a drum to divert the soldiers intent on drubbing Melitone, and all join in her song in praise of a soldier's calling.

Tenor and baritone have another fine duet in the fourth and final act, where the most famous excerpt belongs again to Leonora.

It is another prayer: *Pace, pace, mio Dio* ("Peace, peace, my God"). If the plot of *The Force of Destiny* was not so preposterous, if the score was not at times uneven, and if the opera had twice as many catchy tunes, then it, like *Il trovatore*, would be ranked among the most popular of Verdi's creations. As it is, it comes close.

DON CARLOS (1867)

Verdi's *Macbeth* was revised in 1864–65. *Don Carlos* was his next opera. Written in French for the Paris Opéra, it is a long, powerful, and highly dramatic work. Because of its length, this opera is often subjected to cuts and shorter versions, one made by the composer. The original five acts sometimes are four and the original French version, *Don Carlos*, can appear in Italian as *Don Carlo*, adding to the confusion. With a *Don Carlos* opera and a Don Carlos character in *La forza del destino*, another Don Carlos in *Ernani*, a Leonora in both *La Forza* and *Il trovatore*, an Amelia in *Boccanegra* and in *Ballo*, and Emilia in *Otello*, anyone in the land of Verdi can find his or her head in a whirl.

Verdi's *Don Carlos* libretto was made from a play by Schiller, who had whitewashed the historical Don Carlos, son of King Philip II of Spain, representing him as a better and saner man than he really was. The time is the middle of the sixteenth century; the events involve struggles between liberal and tyrannical forces in France and Spain. Because the opera was composed for the l'Opéra, its complete version includes a ballet, virtually a requirement of this house during this time. Billowing passions are expressed in words and music. The most familiar music includes another inspired duet for tenor and baritone. Don Carlos (tenor) begins: *Je l'ai perdue!* ("Io l'ho perduta"; "I have lost her!")! He and his father, King Philip II of Spain, both love Elisabeth of Valois, daughter of the French king. His lament is briefly interrupted by a friar, then Rodrigo enters, and soon a duet soars to consummate beauty as the friends swear eternal comradeship in the libertarian cause while chanting monks are heard beneath the perfect blend of tenor and baritone singing in unison.

No recording of this sublime music compares to the one made in 1950 by two men of disparate backgrounds. In portraying close friends on the stage there developed an abiding friendship offstage for the Swedish tenor Jussi Björling, who loved to fish the beautiful lakes of his homeland, and Robert Merrill, an American from

Brooklyn, New York, who had held dreams of being a professional baseball player.

If you have read this far and still have not made a purchase of a recording, *stop*! Get to your nearest music store and buy the RCA Victor recording titled *Jussi Björling: Operatic Duets with Robert Merrill*. You will forever thank me. The theme of this duet, ever so beautiful, fortunately is heard often in the drama.

In the second act, the lady-in-waiting to Elisabeth, Princess Eboli, sings her now famous veil song *(Chant sarrasin du voile;* "Canzone del velo"), an exceedingly demanding aria for mezzo-soprano for various musical reasons. Act III opens with a masked ball (another Verdian masked ball) in progress. When the ballet music is not cut to ensure an abbreviated version of this very long opera, it is heard here. The first scene of the fourth act many consider one of the greatest Verdi ever composed. King Philip, in a masterpiece monologue for bass voice, laments because he knows Elisabeth, now his wife, really does not love him: *Elle ne m'aime pas* ("Ella giammai m'amò"; "She never loved me!")! Philip is Verdi's par excellence role for a basso. The blind, aged Grand Inquisitor, another bass, enters Philip's chamber at the end of the soliloquy. Their conversation, to a perfectly matched orchestral accompaniment, is musical sophistication at its best. Princess Eboli, adulterous with the king, is chastised by Elisabeth who has been told of the relationship. Left alone, Eboli sings one of the most celebrated arias of the score, *O don fatal* ("O don fatale"; "O fatal beauty"), cursing the gift of good looks bestowed upon her by fate. In the final scene of this remarkable act, Rodrigo, along with Carlo, anticipates his final hour in an aria of great beauty: *O mon Carlos* ("O mio Carlo"; "Ah, my Carlo"). Two men intrude. The one armed with a musket fires and mortally wounds Rodrigo, who sings farewell to his dear friend: *O Carlos* ("O Carlo, ascolta"; "O Carlo, listen"). The big number of the fifth and final act belongs to Elisabeth, as the curtain rises on a moonlit night. Slowly, she enters the cloister of the Saint Just Monastery, kneels before the tomb of the emperor Charles V, and addresses him:

> *Toi qui connais la vanité du monde . . .*

> *Tu che le vanità conoscesti del mondo . . .*

> You left the vanities of worldly life behind
> And found eternal peace in your tomb enshrined!

There is marvelous music other than the excerpts I have isolated in this atypical Italian opera, where the lower voices, bass and mezzo-soprano, are more prominent than the higher voices, tenor and soprano. My presentation of the highlights has assumed the complete five acts of the original version. Versions with cuts and the four-act version can jumble what I have outlined.

AÏDA (1871)

For many lovers of Verdi's music, his greatest masterworks followed *Don Carlos*: *Aïda*, *Otello*, and *Falstaff*. *Aïda* premiered on December 24, 1871. It is the first of these last three masterpieces by Verdi.

The triumphant world premiere of *Aïda* in the Italian Theatre in Cairo is only one example of Italian opera's boundless popularity encircling the globe as the nineteenth century neared its end. This opera had been commissioned by Egypt's Khedive. Other triumphs followed at La Scala in February 1872, and in New York City in November 1873, and it was at a performance in Rio de Janeiro in June 1886 that the conducting career of Arturo Toscanini had its unanticipated beginning. The young cellist was called from his chair in the orchestra to the podium to save a performance threatened by the conductor's last-minute resignation and his second's refusal to continue through the hisses and boos of the audience. The young Toscanini—he was nineteen—took over, quieted the house, and delivered the goods. One account of this now popular story has him slamming shut the score in a dramatic bit of bravado before conducting the opera from memory. Another account claims this is an embellishment. In either case, Toscanini's memory of music would prove to be phenomenal and it was on that day in June that he took his first step from cellist chair to the position of one of the greatest and most respected conductors in history.

Verdi did not choose his own subject. The Khedive gave it to the composer. It was the idea of a famous Egyptologist of the time whose knowledge was then utilized to give to costumes, sets, and atmosphere a rare authenticity. *Aïda* plays in four acts and seven scenes. Antonio Ghislanzoni provided the libretto, far and away his most famous of over eighty others, from a French text of Camille du Locle (names not encountered again in this book). Ghislanzoni turned writer when he lost his singing voice. He had sung Don Carlo in Verdi's *Ernani* in Paris in 1851. His *Aïda* libretto is one of few Verdi set to music that was thoroughly acceptable to the composer. The six main characters are:

AïDA, Ethiopian princess, daughter of Amonasro, and
    slave of Amneris, *soprano*
AMONASRO, King of Ethiopia and father of Aïda, *baritone*
KING OF EGYPT, *bass*
AMNERIS, daughter of the King of Egypt, *mezzo-soprano*
RADAMES, captain of the Egyptian guard, *tenor*
RAMFIS, high priest of Egypt, *bass*
Rounding out the cast are a messenger, a high priestess,
    priests and priestesses, soldiers, slaves, dancers, Egyptian people, and Ethiopian prisoners.

The story takes place during the time of the pharaohs in ancient Memphis and Thebes.

Act I

A brief, lovely prelude is heard before the opening of the curtain in a hall in the King's palace in Memphis. Ramfis informs Radames of encroaching Ethiopian troops soon to be met by Egyptian armies led by a warrior to be chosen by the goddess Isis. He departs and Radames daydreams of glory: If selected by the goddess and victorious, could he not be united with Aïda? He contemplates her over-powering beauty in *Celeste Aïda* ("Heavenly Aïda"), an aria as famous as any other Verdi ever wrote. The composer stipulated the aria's concluding ascent to the high note be sung softly, the voice "dying away." It is unlikely you will hear it thus sung because it is difficult to do, and trumpeted high notes are big crowd pleasers.

During this romance of Radames, Amneris has entered the room. She loves him, and it will be her uncontrollable jealousy that drives the story to its tragic end. Aïda has exchanged with Radames glances of devoted longing detected by Amneris, who feigns dearest friendship with her slave as she tries to discover her heart's secret. In a splendid duet, *Vieni, O diletta* ("Come, O dear friend") Aïda expresses concern over war between Egypt and Ethiopia while Amneris probes the secret. When Radames joins them, anticipating the woe of disclosure, a fine dramatic trio ensues. At this time, he is unaware both of Aïda's royal lineage and of the love Amneris bears him.

The King, Ramfis, and subordinates enter. A messenger

reports on the Ethiopian invasion being led by the fierce and fearless King Amonasro. "*Mio padre!*" Aïda exclaims in an aside. The King reveals Radames as the choice of Isis and orders all to the Temple of Vulcan, where the leader will be invested in consecrated armor. Amneris, giving a banner to Radames, instructs him to "return victorious." Aïda remains as all others depart. She iterates the words of Amneris, *Ritorna vincitor*, beginning the first of her celebrated arias. In the grip of powerful conflicting emotions, with an unquenchable love for Radames, who leads a formidable army against her people's force commanded by her father, Aïda contemplates her dilemma. The dramatic, poetic lines of the text inspired in Verdi music of considerable power and beauty to end the first scene.

The short second and final scene of this act is justly famous. Here the magic of Verdi's music transports the listener back through centuries to a sacred ceremony in the interior of the Temple of Vulcan. Dominated by columns, mystical lights, and shadows, a religious service includes chanting, a dance, the installation of Radames with sacred armor and sword, an invocation, and a prayer to the great god for Egypt's preservation. Little happens to advance the plot, but when performed as conceived this exotic representation portrays what life in ancient Egypt may well have been like. Soaring strains of the high priestess, hushed chanting of the priests, and strums on a harp do it for me every time I hear the opening of this magnificent scene, made authentic by the input of a famous Egyptologist, the rich poetry of the librettist, and Verdi's use of real Oriental tonal arrangements.

Act II

The second act opens in the apartments of Amneris. Female slaves are dressing her for a triumphal feast. The Egyptian troops, commanded by Radames, have routed the Ethiopian force and, presently, are marching on the road toward home with captives and spoils of war. This scene is dominated by female voices. Only briefly, toward its end, do the distant shouts of returning troops and jubilant people intervene into a most intense moment. First heard are female slaves in a lovely chorus as they dress Amneris, who expresses hope Radames will "restore joy to my heart." Moorish slaves dance for her but all are quickly dismissed by the Princess, who has spotted Aïda entering the hall. At the mere sight of her Ethiopian servant, she instantly is filled with doubt. Amneris must discover if her suspicions of hidden love between Aïda and

Radames are true. She plots to extract the secret from her. Again feigning friendship, Aïda is offered consolation for the defeat of her people. Time and love's power will heal all anguish, promises Amneris, who then unloads her terrible trick by telling Aïda her people have killed Radames. The girl's distraught reaction reveals all, Amneris confesses her deception, "I have deceived you— Radames lives!"and the duped Aïda has been caught. Openly now, they are rivals—Aïda begging for compassion, Amneris heartless in return: *Trema, vil schiava, spezza il tuo core . . .*

> Tremble before me, slave.
> Let your heart break.
> This love can mean your death:
> I hold you in my power
> As hatred and vengeance
> burn in my heart.

Next, we hear victorious voices from afar joining the threatening of the powerful mezzo and the soprano's supplications. Aïda's sense of utter hopelessness is expressed in a most pregnant couplet:

> *Questo amore che t'irrita*
> *Nella tomba spegnerò.*

> This love that irritates you
> Will expire with me in the tomb.

This premonition, as we shall see, becomes more portentous than this moment of swirling, conflicting, passionate emotions could ever have foreseen. The scene ends with Aïda's chilling

> *Numi, pietà del mio martir,*
> *Speme non v'ha pel mio dolor!*

> Oh gods, have pity on my misery!
> There is no hope for my sorrow!

Perhaps no scene in Italian opera produces more anticipation or provides greater spectacle than the last scene of Act II. If you want to know what is meant by the term "grand opera," then this is it, a far better definition than any I could give. The setting is the avenue by the Gate of Thebes. Trumpets resound, the orchestra answers, the multitudes sing *Gloria all'Egitto* ("Glory to Egypt"), and sometimes I attempt to imagine what national pride swelled in Egyptian hearts and heads during the 1871 Cairo premiere. A trumpet tune, perhaps now more famous than any other for this instrument, initiates the Grand March (generally known in concert halls and on recordings as "The Triumphal March from Aïda"), a procession of soldiers, dancing girls carrying spoils, more soldiers, banner carriers, chariots of war, and more, all passing before the King upon his throne at the base of a towering obelisk. If you have heard of elephants on an opera stage, this is where you will find them.

Radames, carried beneath a canopy conveyed by a dozen officers, concludes the procession. Radames comes before his sovereign and Amneris is instructed by her father to crown him with a laurel wreath. The King promises to grant whatever the victorious leader asks.

We know what Radames desires, but he postpones his request and calls forth the prisoners, the last being Amonasro, attired not as king but rather as soldier. Aïda recognizes him aloud as her father. "Her father!" the crowd exclaims, and from here to the end of the act, varying powerful emotions develop into a tempestuous melee of conflicting desires. If the role of music in opera is to intensify the drama, then Verdi has mastered it here. Amonasro requests mercy for his people, Ramfis and the priests call for an execution, the Egyptian people ask their king to be forgiving, and Amneris, having seen Radames and Aïda exchange loving glances, contemplates revenge. The King will be merciful and the hero, dwelling on his beloved's beauty, submits his request: Free the Ethiopians. Again priests demand death, Ramfis speculating live prisoners will only seek retaliations. Then, the King issues a stunning announcement:

> Radames, the country owes everything to you.
> The hand of Amneris shall be your reward.
> One day, with her, you shall rule over Egypt.

Amneris is ecstatic, Aïda without hope, Radames bewildered, the prisoners grateful, and Amonasro deliberates reprisal as the populace, just as this stupendous scene began, ends it with a *Gloria all'Egitto* refrain.

Listen to the music as you follow the libretto. If this does not addict you to Italian opera (though this is unlikely), there is no need to fret: Puccini's youthful masterpiece *Manon Lescaut* is only a dozen years hence. No one escapes Puccini! And to those of a so highly developed musical sophistication as to reproach Verdi's overt intent to stir emotions, I can only hope they choke on their own flapdoodle.

Act III

The third act plays in one tremendous scene. The curtain opens on a moonlit night by the banks of the Nile. Voices of priests and priestesses from the nearby Temple of Isis are heard as Amneris, Ramfis, and their entourage arrive by boat, debark, and head for the temple to invoke the goddess to bless the marriage the following day. Aïda emerges from shadowed palm trees, looking forward to a tryst with Radames (certainly not the best meeting place, with Amneris hanging around). She fears his intent will be to tell her farewell forever. If this be so, she speculates, the Nile will be her grave, and she begins to meditate on consequences: *O patria mia, mai più ti rivedrò* ("O homeland, never, ever to see you again!") Recall here Verdi's letter to his *Il trovatore* librettist, Salvatore Cammarano, during their collaboration, in which he expressed a desire to create an opera of words and music flowing together without specific set numbers. In *Aïda* he is approaching that goal. After *Ritorna vincitor!*, Act I, scene 2, we have experienced to this point a magnificent musical continuity of intrigue, pomp, and local color without one world-famous aria until *O patria mia*. Aïda laments, having assumed she will never again see the cool valleys, verdant hills, and fragrant streams of her home. For many, this aria for dramatic soprano is preeminent in Italian opera literature.

He who afterward enters into this clandestine meeting is not Radames, however. It is Amonasro. Should you by now know enough of Verdi's work to foresee another prominent father/daughter duet, you have anticipated correctly. But it is not a duet of simply intense emoting. With an economy of power and precision, it advances the plot to its turn toward the denouement of ultimate misfortune for Radames and the rivals who love him. Amonasro explains his unsuspected presence. Of the intense love triangle he is fully aware, and he curses Amneris: "Princess of a hatred race, our deadly enemy." Aïda feels helpless, a slave in the power of the daughter of Egypt's king, but the wily Amonasro commences to activate a plan to defeat his foes. He tells Aïda she can defeat her rival, return to the beauty of her homeland, and sit upon the Ethiopian's throne with the man she loves. If only he knew what road the Egyptian troops were marching, they could be ambushed and defeated, just retribution for the terrible destruction already inflicted and soon to resume unless thwarted. Naively, Aïda ponders who might discover such a priceless military secret. Her father offers enlightenment: "You could! Radames loves you and will tell you." Aïda is horrified, but Amonasro persists in painting a brutal picture of the sacking, burning, raping, and killing awaiting their homeland all because Aïda will not cooperate. His calculated enunciation is devastating but it works:

> A horrid spectre
> Rises in the shadows before us.
> Tremble, for over your head
> It lifts its bony arms.
> It is your mother—see her,
> She is cursing you! . . .
>
> You are not my daughter!
> You are the slave of the pharaohs!

A contrite Aïda capitulates and as Radames approaches, Amonasro conceals himself in the palms. Verdi was a mature and experienced composer when he created music for this unusual duet. It is one of his finest. The immense popularity of this opera (for more than 130 years) allows a certain amount of taking things for granted, a blasé response from some who have heard it many times. The trick is to try to hear it afresh if it is so familiar. It is always intense and new for me, thankfully, and if you are coming to it for the first time, so it will be for you. This entire act is a flawless, flowing musical miracle, from one great duet to another.

Aïda reproaches Radames for talking to her of love. Does not another love of a wife-to-be await him? No! He loves only her and she will be his. After he again defeats the invading Ethiopians, he will beseech the King to crown his glory with Aïda's love. Aïda, fearing Amneris would foil this plan, offers the enticing alternative of escaping to a beautiful new country. Rapturously, they contemplate their passionate love fulfilled in a free and distant land where "virgin forests rise." Then comes the ace from the sleeve. By what road can we avoid your troops? she asks. Radames reveals their whereabouts. Amanasro leaps from hiding, ecstatic with the knowledge. Radames, dumbstruck by his revelation, is reassured by Aïda and Amonasro that all will be well, but it is too late. Amneris and Ramfis, now on the scene, have heard and denounce the traitor. Amonasro threatens Amneris with a knife; Radames intercedes. As guards arrive and arrest him he urges Aïda and her father to flee as the curtain falls on this cataclysmic act.

Act IV

The last act, in two scenes, begins in a hall of the King's palace, where Amneris reflects on Aïda's escape and the dire fate awaiting Radames. So desperate is her love for him that she summons guards to bring him forth, and behold still another splendid duet! Both know a military secret escaped his lips but that his intent was not traitorous. Nevertheless, he will not attempt to defend himself before judges. Of greater concern to him than his own life is his despair over the loss of Aïda. Amneris acknowledges Amanasro was killed in flight but that somehow Aïda escaped. If Radames will vow never again to see Aïda, she will save him. He declines, turning her love into hatred as the culmination of their duet throbs to a close with intense, unmitigated emotion.

Radames is removed by guards to the judges' chamber, where Ramfis calls upon him to defend himself. To each of the three charges he remains silent and thus is condemned on all accounts a traitor. Amneris agonizes as she overhears the verdict: The man she loves so passionately will be placed in a vault beneath the altar of Isis, there to die by suffocation. She rages at Ramfis and the priests when they bring this news to her, denouncing Radames as a traitor. Grievously upset, she vilifies them, pleads for mercy, and concludes with a curse as the curtain falls.

The stage is divided into two floors for the final scene, which takes place inside the Temple of Vulcan. This unusual scenic conception was suggested by Verdi. The upper level represents the interior of the temple, the lower level a crypt wherein Radames sits as two priests put in place the huge stone enclosing him in his tomb. He sings of never seeing daylight or Aïda again, hoping, at least, that she may live happily and never learn of his fate, when, all of a sudden, like a vision, she appears before him. Having anticipated the verdict, stealthily she has crept, unseen, into the tomb to die with him. Voices of priests and priestesses sing a hymn of death as an attempt by Radames to budge the stone is futile. Resolved to their fate, the ultimate duet, as famous as any other in Italian opera, begins with *O terra addio* ("O earth, farewell"). As the orchestral strings fade away, Aïda slumps senselessly into the arms of Radames. Amneris, seen above prostrating herself on the stone that seals the vault, supplicates as choral voices proclaim the magnitude of the great god Phtha in the ethereal end to one of Verdi's most eloquent scores.

More than any other previous opera of his, *Aïda*, from start to finish, is motivated by the dramatic force of a single idea: in this case, a powerful, irresolvable love triangle. Here, to be sure, Verdi had been given all the manifestations of commonplace, traditional grand opera—opportunities for spectacle, a good story easy to follow, and stereotypical characters. Through his remarkable music, however, what in lesser hands may have been ordinary or mundane is a masterpiece.

The first time I saw *Aïda* I did not experience its dramatic conclusion. I was ten years old and was being taken to a performance by an aunt primarily to hear the great American baritone Lawrence Tibbett as Amonasro. His magnificent instrument had by this time begun its lamentable decline, but he was a long-time close friend of our family and though he had sung in my grandparents' home, I had never seen him perform on stage. Alas, by the final act the stuffy air in the opera house was closing in on my balcony seat. I went from too warm to hot. Red in the face, I became nauseated and then ill. My poor aunt sped me off into the night. Such a miserable, embarrassing episode a child never forgets, and the mention of *Aïda* to this day can chill me with that frightful memory. Tibbett's great recordings have been remastered on to CDs.

∾

A magnificent string quartet issued from Verdi's pen in 1873, a rare excursion outside the realm of opera for him, and on May 22, 1874, the first performance was held of the *Manzoni Requiem*, his musical tribute to the novelist and poet he so much admired. This requiem mass, now so very popular, had detractors from the start. Criticisms fault the operatic dimensions of what is supposed to be sacred music. I come to it with no religious commitment, preconceptions, or expectations, so all I hear is the glorious music. Opera singers love this score and, accordingly, it is recorded often. Gather together four first-rate singers—soprano, mezzo-soprano, tenor, and bass—supplemented by an impeccable choir, a great orchestra and sensitive conductor, and a spellbinding performance is guaranteed. Over many years I have managed to acquire more than half-a-dozen different versions. That says all you need to know of what I feel about this work.

Had Verdi ended his career as an opera composer with the sensational success of *Aïda*? For years it appeared so, even though a major revision of *Simon Boccanegra* was followed by an abridgement of *Don Carlo*. Fermenting within his head all the while, however, was an *Otello* (Italian for Shakespeare's *Othello*) libretto by Arrigo Boito, which was put in his hands in 1879.

Arrigo Boito

Boito was a composer, librettist, and a writer of novels under the anagram Tobio Gorria, derived from his given name. Padua, in 1842, was the place of his birth. He died in 1928, almost to the year a contemporary of Thomas Hardy, to put his life in another context. Boito's father was a painter of portrait miniatures, his mother a Polish countess who was left alone to raise her children when her husband abandoned his family. It was the mother who recognized quite early her son's facility for music, words, and language. She encouraged and supported him in a good education, one vastly supplemented by Boito's voracious reading appetite. Beethoven and Goethe he much admired, and Wagner, too. He was twenty-six when he wrote both the words and the music of his operatic masterpiece *Mefistofele* (Italian for Mephistopheles, one of the seven chief devils in medieval demonology, a central character of which is Faust. It is from Goethe's *Faust* that this opera derives). It was his first opera. His second, and last, *Nerone*, was unfinished when he died. In between, among numerous other accomplishments, he was the most gifted collaborator with whom Verdi ever worked, first on rescuing *Simon Boccanegra* with pertinent revisions; second, by providing the composer with two brilliant libretti for the penultimate and ultimate masterpieces, *Otello* and *Falstaff*. Verdi's adoration of Shakespeare and Boito's flawless libretti combined to inspire two operas you must know, for they compare favorably with the very best works written during a long life of unflagging creativity. Before we consider them, however, this is the appropriate place for a few sentences on Boito's opera, *Mefistofele*.

After the failure of the premiere, *Mefistofele* became and remains popular in Italy. Not so in France, probably because Gallic taste and pride prefer the two most famous of all operatic versions of the *Faust* legend by two Frenchmen: Gounod's *Faust* and *The Damnation of Faust* by Hector Berlioz (see chapter 9). Elsewhere the opera has its friends, and certainly, it is played and has been recorded several times. I love the opera, and even if its world-wide appeal does not warrant inclusion in this book, whose aim is to introduce the most popular and well-known works, I cannot proceed without a few more words. In my ears, the following constitute some of Italian opera's most intriguing and wonderful musical episodes.

The entire prologue is superb. Other notable excerpts are: Faust's arias, *Dai campi, dai prati* ("From the fields, from the meadows") in Act I and *Giunto sul passo estremo* ("Having reached the final verge") in the epilogue; Margherita's Act III lament *L'altra notte in fondo al mare* ("The other night into the bottom of the sea"); Mefistofele's Act II mockery *Ecco il mondo* ("Here is the world"); Act III's hauntingly beautiful duet of Margherita and Faust, *Lontano, lontano, lontano* ("Far, far, away"); and the remarkable choruses, especially those involving witches and sorcerers. My favorite recording is an old one featuring Cesare Siepi in the title role with Mario del Monaco as Faust and Renata Tebaldi as Margherita. Tullio Serafin conducts the Chorus and Orchestra of the Accademia di Santa Cecilia. If you ever come across it, do buy it!

Often in reading about Boito or about Verdi's last two operatic compositions, I find the opinion that the libretti for *Otello* and *Falstaff* are the two best in all Italian operatic literature. Much has been written about Boito's ingenious poetic abridgement of Shakespeare's *Othello* for Verdi's *Otello*. In my reading, also I have found opinions praising the operatic version as the superior drama. For me this is too much of an apples and oranges comparison to warrant any attempt at ranking. Both within their own genres are masterworks for me. Nevertheless, some studies comparing them are informative, interesting, and richly rewarding, and once a graduate student of mine wrote one of the most insightful and articulate essays I've received on this subject.

Shakespeare's play, almost 3,500 lines long, becomes 700-plus lines in Boito's condensation. One of the most noble of all Shakespearian speeches, Othello's last before he takes his own life, "Soft you: a word or two, before you go, . . ." is one of many of Boito's excisions, whereas, ironically, one of the opera's most intensely dramatic excerpts is Verdi's setting of a powerfully iconoclastic monologue not in Shakespeare but invented by Boito, himself a distinguished poet. More on this when we come to it.

OTELLO (1887)

Many there are who consider *Otello* Verdi's greatest achievement. It has been called "the perfect opera." That it came to be at all is an interesting story. Verdi and Boito, opposites by nature, represented the old and the new in the arts of the final quarter of the nineteenth century: Boito, the brilliant intellectual associated with avant-garde ideas and Giuseppe Verdi, the grand old man of Italian opera. They first met years before the *Otello* collaboration; Boito had produced the text for a "Hymn of the Nations" set by Verdi. Later Boito would poke fun at *La donna è mobile*, the most popular of tunes in *Rigoletto*, by making a polka version, and another time cast aspersions on the state of Italian music at the time it was dominated by Verdi, stopping just short of naming the composer. Their relationship was hardly hunky-dory. It was not with an open-armed embrace that Verdi contemplated *Otello* with Boito. Rather, he dragged his feet. He was sixty-six years old when the project was proposed to him. He had written no opera in almost a decade. His last opera, *Aïda*, was a triumph. He was famous and rich. Did he dare again to try his hand at Shakespeare? *Macbeth*, his first opera on a play by his favorite playwright, had failed at first. His several sporadic attempts to make an opera of *King Lear* had come to nothing. Wagnerianism was fast gaining adherents throughout operatic Europe. Why risk it? he may have thought. And perhaps Rossini's *Otello*, composed when Verdi was an infant but still quite popular, made him reluctant.

Obviously, it was Boito's libretto that proved irresistible to him—its clarity, swift action, and powerful, beautiful poetry. Nevertheless, once having agreed to the project, Verdi's feet continued to drag. He proceeded hesitantly, first fussing over *Simon Boccanegra* and *Don Carlos* and getting them right through revisions and abridgement. Five years passed and no score, Boito all the while, sensitive and extremely subtle in applying pressure. Then in secret, shutting himself off from the busy world, Verdi commenced the composition in 1884. He finished it in 1885, although orchestration would take about another year.

Verdi set strict conditions for rehearsals and production. Rehearsals would be closed to all and at any time if absolutely anything displeased him or he deemed something not right, even once into dress rehearsals, he reserved the right to cancel the production. Eventually, this collaboration produced a close friendship between composer and librettist. *Otello* premiered at La Scala on

February 5, 1887, before an audience, bursting with anticipation, who had paid dearly for the privilege of being there. Critics came from all major European cities and from America. When the final curtain fell, tumultuous acclaim prevailed deep into the night.

The story, if you know your Shakespeare, tells of Othello's baseless jealousy, nurtured by the sinister Iago, culminating in the murder of his innocent wife, Desdemona, and his suicide. In spite of massive cuts by Boito, this essential theme prevails in the opera, driving it, void of digressions, quickly from the moment of Otello's victorious homecoming to his tragic end. The evil Iago, without conscience or remorse, fascinated both composer and librettist. Verdi even temporarily considered *Iago* as the opera's title. Here are the characters, their relationships, and their voice range:

> OTELLO, a Moor, general in the Venetian army, and Governor of Cyprus, *tenor*
> DESDEMONA, his wife, *soprano*
> IAGO, his ensign, *baritone*
> EMILIA, Iago's wife and lady-in-waiting to Desdemona, *mezzo-soprano*
> CASSIO, Otello's lieutenant, *tenor*
> MONTANO, Otello's predecessor as governor of Cyprus, *bass*
> RODERIGO, a Venetian gentleman, *tenor*
> LODOVICO, a Venetian ambassador, *baritone*
> A herald, *bass*
> Soldiers and Sailors of the Venetian Republic, Venetian ladies and gentlemen, Cypriot men and women

> The time of the story is the end of the fifteenth century; the place, a Cyprus seaport. This island then was under Venetian rule. There are four acts.

Act I

No orchestral prelude precedes the opening of the curtain upon a terrible storm. At quayside, a crowd has gathered near the governor's castle to greet Otello returning from battle. His sail has been sighted in lightning flashes as the raging storm threatens the ship's safety. Fear races through the crowd as the ship, its mainsail broken, is driven toward rocks by wind and waves. Surreptiously, in an aside to Roderigo, Iago bids the ship go down to a watery grave. He is smarting, we are soon to learn, because Otello promoted Cassio to captain over Iago, who believes himself far more deserving. The ship reaches port safely, the crowd cheers, and Otello, stepping onto the quay, greets them with the brief yet thrilling *Esultate!* ("Rejoice!"), informing all of the victory over the Turks. As the Cypriots exult over the great victory, the storm subsides. Otello, followed by Cassio, Montano, and soldiers, walks toward his castle.

Roderigo and Iago speak privately. We learn of Roderigo's hopeless passion for Desdemona, to which Iago responds with biding patience and the promise that she soon will tire of the Moor. Iago confesses that his hatred of Otello is the result of Cassio's promotion. Nevertheless, he will continue to serve Otello and will feign friendship while plotting his revenge.

Meanwhile, a bonfire has been built and lighted by members of the crowd. Many dance about the flames singing the stirring chorus *Fuoco di gioia* ("Fire of rejoicing"). Cassio arrives and joins Iago and Roderigo at a nearby table, where they sit drinking wine. Iago calls for a toast to Desdemona and Otello, one Cassio cannot rightly refuse even though he says he no longer drinks. The intrigue of revenge already is working in Iago's brain. In an aside he warns Roderigo to be wary of Cassio, his insinuation being that Desdemona has taken a shine to the handsome young officer.

Iago then begins a drinking song, *Inaffia l'ugola* ("Then wet your whistle"). His intent is to get Cassio drunk. He does so. Needled by Roderigo, Cassio starts a fight. Swords are drawn, Montano is wounded while attempting to stop it, and Otello responds to the rioting by coming on the run. He stops the brawl, dismisses Cassio from his service (just what Iago intended), and instructs Iago to restore order throughout the city. Iago departs, gloating about his triumph. The crowd disperses and Otello is alone with Desdemona, who has joined him. *Già nella notte densa* ("Now in the dark night"), he begins their now famous love duet. It is a long expression of affection through recollections of happy days together and assurances of their love intensifying in days to come. Otello, finally overcome, leans against the parapet of the quay, exclaiming:

> Ah! this joy will overwhelm me.
> It is too much, it stops me here—
> I stagger—
> A kiss—

Desdemona speaks his name. Again, he says:

A kiss—And yet a kiss!

Don't forget these last words! Arm in arm, under a starry sky, they make their way to the castle as the act ends.

Purposely, I included no comments on the music during this Act I synopsis. My observations will be more pertinent in retrospect. Certain conventions of Italian opera—a *brindisi* (drinking song), melodic choruses, a love duet—are discernible, but they transpire in such a subtle and smooth manner, as one musical event segues seamlessly into another, so as to come and go unnoticed. In no previous opera has Verdi's writing come closer to the goal of eliminating set pieces in constructing unbroken musical events. In no previous opera is his orchestra as symphonic in expressing the action, in providing constantly changing colors, delineations of character, and contrasting musical contours. The storm, the joyful homecoming, Iago's villany, the drinking bout, the row, the night of love, they are all there in the orchestra. Traditional recitatives have almost vanished as one conversational episode—both verbally and orchestrally—moves in a natural way into another, as the story unfolds. This will be true throughout the drama as Boito's words and Verdi's music become one in telling the tragic tale.

Otello, therefore, is harder to excerpt than, for example, is *Rigoletto*. The brief *Esultate*! is famous, as is the *Fuoco di gioia*, and the duet ending the act for many who love Verdi's music is not only his most mature and beautiful articulation of intimate feeling between man and woman but also one of the most serene musical expressions of love ever written. Yet these "excerpts" are all part of one complete musical fabric. This flowing in *Otello* did, of course, prompt some critics to charge Verdi with imitating Wagner, a critique he naturally resented. Wagner was Wagner and Verdi was Verdi is the way he would have it. Nevertheless, *Otello* is much closer to Wagner's conception of "endless melody" than it is a manifestation of traditional Italian operatic conventions.

Act II
The second act opens in a hall on the ground floor of the castle next to a large garden. Iago, furthering his treachery, fakes concern over Cassio's dismissal by urging him to ask Desdemona to intercede on his behalf in appealing to Otello to pardon him. After all,

the villain notes, she is the leader behind our leader. Cassio is told that Desdemona and Emilia rest in the shade of these garden trees daily at noon: "Wait for her here." As Iago dismisses Cassio, those who know the opera feel their own heart begin to thump in anticipation of perhaps the most powerful and chilling declamation of the demonic in music literature.

It is known simply as "Iago's Creed." Neither the conception nor the words of this monologue are from Shakespeare. This heresy from Boito's pen is this poet's own brilliant characterization of pure evil. Iago, as I have mentioned, fascinated the creative imaginations of both Verdi and his librettist and it is in this world-famous speech that their artistic powers peak. You must know all the words. Then follow them as they are sung. And be certain to have only the greatest interpreters of Iago in your ears: Lawrence Tibbett (his 1939 recording) and Tito Gobbi, for example. A magnificent opera like *Otello*, probing the compass of human emotions, endures only through magnificent singer-actors, and they are not always easy to find. This is why you must select recordings carefully if you want only the best. A wimpy or elegantly light baritone won't do for Iago, nor will a high, lyrical baritone or one with lots of honey in the tone. The malice must be there. Darkness must prevail. Here is a good translation of Iago's Creed, the famous *Credo in un Dio crudel*:

> I believe in a cruel God, who has created me
> in his image and whom, in hate, I name.
> From some vile germ or base
> atom am I born.
> I am evil
> because I am a man;
> and I feel the primeval slime in me.
> Yes! This is my creed!
> I believe with a firm heart, as ever does
> the young widow praying before the altar,
> that whatever evil I think or do
> was decreed for me by fate.
> I believe that the honest man is but a poor actor,
> both in face and heart,
> that everything in him is a lie:
> tears, kisses, looks,
> sacrifices and honor.
> And I believe man to be the sport of an unjust fate

from the germ of the cradle
to the worm of the grave.
After all this mockery comes Death.
And then? Death is nothingness
And Heaven an old wives' tale.

This wrenching cynicism must be heard in the voice or it is not Iago's creed. *Otello* demands first-rate singing actors. Desdemona is innocent, pure, and angelic and her high notes must be impeccable. Otello's part is so demanding and difficult that many tenors, exercising good judgment, do not attempt the role. With marvelous music throughout, the Moor was given little by way of those traditional sumptuous melodic arias for Italian tenors to bring down the house or include on their recordings of highlights. The love duet is beautiful, the finale tragic, the duet with Iago at the end of Act II chilling as Otello's naiveté blindly has drawn him into an evil scheme, and Act III has its own demands. But this is not a role that slides easily up and down an Italian throat. Tenors, interestingly, accustomed to heavier roles—Tristan, for example—will take to *Otello*. Lauritz Melchior, a Dane, was one; the Canadian Jon Vickers was another. The American James McCracken was notable in the role, as was the Spaniard Placido Domingo. The Chilean Ramón Vinay, too, was a distinguished Otello, as was the Italian Mario del Monaco. They will get you started. The Domingo video I used in my opera class is an excellent introduction.

As Desdemona and Emilia enter the garden, Iago, his creed spent, hurries to Cassio, bidding him go to her, which he does. Then, pretending not to have seen Otello coming toward him, Iago speaks aloud to himself, "I do not like that." The Moor overhears this as he views Cassio walking and talking with his wife. In their ensuing conversation, Iago plants in Otello's mind seeds of terrifying suspicion, which he nourishes by admonishing him to beware of Cassio. Desdemona, returning, is greeted by inhabitants of the island who give her garlands and gifts in an enchanting episode. It is a light, lyrical, lovely break in mounting treachery.

Emilia joins her and they approach Otello. Desdemona's first words to her husband after Iago has just cautioned him to consider carefully all his wife says regarding Cassio is to request he pardon Cassio. Rebuffed, she pleads a second time. His second refusal reveals significant perturbation and his wife asks him what is wrong. He claims his head hurts. She offers to bind it with her handkerchief. He dashes it to the ground. Emilia recovers it and in a great quartet of differing emotions, Desdemona proclaims her love for Otello, who feels certain his days of joy are over. Iago demands of Emilia she hand over to him the handkerchief; she, suspicious, declines. Thwarted, he snatches it.

Desdemona renews her request but Otello asks her to go. As the women depart, Emilia is warned by her husband to speak not a word. Otello, contemplating the thought of Desdemona having been unfaithful to him, is in despair. Iago's poison is at work. Frantic, Otello fiercely demands of his ensign some proof, assaulting him in the process. Iago continues his calculated tormenting with lies, Verdi's music all the while intensifying the emotional gravity of this tremendous scene, by telling Otello he heard Cassio speaking in his sleep. In part he was heard to say,

> Sweet Desdemona! We must hide our love.
> Let us be wary! I am drowning in heavenly
>   ecstacy . . .
> I curse the fate that gave you to the Moor.

Otello is beside himself. Craftily, Iago dismisses it as only a dream but it is fact to Otello. Now Iago applies the clincher: the handkerchief given by Otello to Desdemona as the first pledge of their love. This handerchief, now hiding in Iago's pockct, he claims was yesterday seen by him in Cassio's hand. Otello rages. The act ends, Otello having called for blood, with the two men on their knees, hands raised to the heavens, swearing revenge.

Act III

Act III opens on the great hall of the castle with a herald informing Otello of the docking of ambassadors from Venice. Iago, about to depart, vows he will produce Cassio and prove perfidy. Desdemona enters. She and her husband exchange pleasantries before, unwittingly, the issue of pardoning Cassio is resumed. Otello, once again claiming his head hurts, requests its binding but rejects the handkerchief she produces. Only the one given to her by him will do, but she, of course, cannot produce it. As she fixates on the pardon and Otello on the handkerchief, they are one conversing past the other until he demands testimony of her faithfulness, which she offers but he refuses to believe. His obvious fury is incomprehensible to the innocent woman. He counters her avowal of purity with a vicious "Vile whore," leading a bewildered, shaken woman to the door, there dismissing her. Alone and abject,

Otello's monologue is a muted, restrained pondering aloud, the orchestra matching perfectly his anguished sentiments, which, as Iago enters, finally explode with a terrifying threat:

> Oh! Damnation!
> She shall confess her sin and then die!
> Confession! Confession!
> The proof!

Iago points to Cassio appearing at the entrance and bids Otello control himself and hide. It is Cassio's intent to find Desdemona to inquire if his pardon is likely. Concealed behind a pillar, Otello hears Cassio mention his wife's name in the dialogue manipulated by Iago and gleans only what to him are incriminating fragments of a juicy conversation with jesting. In reality, the two men, unknown to Otello, speak not of Desdemona but rather of Bianca, a lover of Cassio's. Cassio, then becoming serious, confides his desire to know what woman left an embroidered handkerchief in his lodging. It was planted by Iago, of course, who has maneuvered this conversation out of Otello's hearing until Cassio removes it from his doublet for Iago's inspection. Iago has repositioned himself now so that his waving of the handkerchief behind his back is in full view of the hidden Otello. This is the proof the Moor required. As Cassio admires the handkerchief and Iago warns him not to become trapped in a web of rapturous emotion, Otello, in an aside, utters *Tradimento* ("Treason").

Trumpets sounding outside are followed by a firing of the castle's cannon. Iago suggests Cassio leave to avoid encountering Otello. Distant Cypriots cheer the arrival of the dignitaries as Otello declares he will poison Desdemona. Iago advises strangling her in her bed where she has sinned, promising he will take care of Cassio. Otello makes him his captain, and Iago departs to fetch Desdemona and Emilia, as the visitors arrive accompanied by ladies and gentlemen, Lodovico and Roderigo among them. A ballet is performed for the occasion. Unlike ballets in some other operas, which have little or no bearing on the plot and are seemingly tacked on as a diversion, an opportunity to give the *corps de ballet* their time before the footlights, this ballet releases, momentarily, the tension of the plot, as did the presentation of garlands and gifts to Desdemona in a previous act.

At its conclusion, Otello receives an official letter from the doge recalling him to Venice and appointing Cassio governor of

Cyprus. Desdemona commences to explain Cassio's absence from the present company to Lodovico. Otello loses control and throws his wife to the floor before the horrified crowd. Here begins an episode, unto the act's end, of unforgettable tension, slowly uncoiling like a huge, venomous serpent readying to strike. Desdemona sings of her loss of happiness, Emilia comments on the awful events, Cassio, now present, muses on this fate-filled moment, and Lodovico and Roderigo express their concerns, as a chorus of ladies and gentlemen compassionately comment on this strange event. Otello orders all to leave. Then, overcome by the thought of Desdemona and Cassio intimate, he faints. As Cypriots cheer offstage *"Evviva Otello! Gloria al Leon di Venezia!"* ("Long live Otello! Glory to the Lion of Venice!") Iago, placing the heel of his boot on the chest of his General's unconscious, prostrate form, triumphantly proclaims *Ecco il Leone!* ("Behold the Lion! . . .") and the curtain falls.

Act IV

The tragic end to the drama, Act IV, is set in Desdemona's bedroom. It is night. A candle flickers. As she prepares for bed, Desdemona informs Emilia of her unhappiness. She recalls her mother's maid, Barbara, who, forsaken by her lover, sang a sad, sad song of a weeping willow *(salce)*. She sings "The Willow Song." Emilia embraces her as Desdemona offers a heartwrenching and foreboding *Emilia, addio!* ("Emilia, farewell!"), kneels before an image of the Madonna, and sings her prayer, *Ave Maria*. Two of the most hauntingly beautiful soprano arias in opera literature have been sung back to back. Desdemona gets into her bed and falls asleep.

Otello enters. He places his scimitar on a table, looks down upon his wife with profound emotion, and kisses her three times. She awakens. He asks if she has prayed, for now she must die for her sin of loving Cassio. Steadfastly, Desdemona protests that she loves only her husband. She asks that Cassio be brought to testify to her innocence but, thinking it so, Otello proclaims him dead. Desdemona, pleading in vain, is smothered under a pillow. Emilia knocks and is admitted. She informs Otello of Roderigo's murder by Cassio, who is very much alive. Hearing faint words, Emilia runs to the dying Desdemona, who proclaims, "I die innocent!" "Who has done this?" Emilia asks. Implicating only herself, Desdemona dies. Otello confesses, explaining the infidelity and citing Iago as confirmation. Emilia tells him he is a fool to believe Iago. The Moor seizes her but she writhes free, calling for help. Lodovico, Iago, and Cassio respond, then Montano with guards. Emilia exposes her husband's scheme, backed by Cassio and Montano, who was told of Iago's villainy by the dying Roderigo. Otello demands of Iago a refutation. Refusing to respond, Iago races out, pursuing soldiers quick on his heels. Lodovico intervenes when Otello reaches for his scimitar.

The impact of his crime consuming him, Otello goes to the bed, looks again upon his wife, addresses her chaste beauty, and, quickly removing a dagger from his doublet, stabs himself. He falls upon the bed by her side. To music from his kiss at the close of the Act I love duet Otello kisses Desdemona again, dying as he speaks those now famous final words given to the repentant Moor:

> A kiss . . . another kiss . . .
> ah . . . another kiss . . .

Otello's realization of his terrible crime and his subsequent suicide, when portrayed by a great singing actor, is music theater of the highest order: Boito, Verdi, and Shakespeare in collaboration. It doesn't get any better than this.

The opera has always been popular but it is not the easy popularity of *Trovatore*'s humble tunes or of *Traviata*'s pathetic love story. *Otello* demands much of performers and audiences, draining both. Few who know the Verdi corpus are they who do not experience *Otello* as Verdi's greatest dramatic achievement.

I remember well a fall afternoon in the 1940s. I was a young lover of opera learning my lessons from a father whose addiction began with his parents at an equally young age, when the Tiana Lemnitz records came to our home. My father told me I may never hear singing more beautiful than her "Willow Song" and "Ave Maria" from Verdi's *Otello*. He played them. And again. And again. He was right. Tiana Lemnitz acquired perfect breath control, the foundation for all proper tone production, and she could sing exceedingly difficult pianissimo (very soft) phrases unlike any other soprano I have ever heard. You, too, can hear these 1938 recordings remastered onto compact discs. Every recording of hers I could find I have bought except one used record priced at forty-nine dollars in a New York City shop over forty years ago; it was too dear for a poor graduate student. I would be kicking myself still for that decision had not fate placed before me a second chance years later at a steal.

Verdi's Comic Masterpiece

After the production of Donizetti's *Don Pasquale* in 1843 (see chapter 3), the essential comic ingredient in Italian opera, opera buffa, seems to have disappeared beneath widespread manifestations of romanticism and realism (operatic realism, *verismo*, will be thoroughly considered in the chapter on Puccini). One finds, nevertheless, in Verdi's many tragedies comic touches that refute an all too common argument purporting that he did not discover humor until he was an old man. His *Un giorno di regno* ("A King for a Day"), 1840, though certainly no masterpiece, is opera buffa worthy of the recording I own and periodically listen to. Oscar, the page, in *A Masked Ball*, is not without "his" (his is a breeches part) amusing moments, and numerous Verdi scholars have found in Brother Melitone, the funny Franciscan monk in *La forza del destino*, the prototype of Falstaff, perhaps the greatest comic invention in Italian opera.

FALSTAFF (1893)

When *Falstaff* premiered on February 9, 1893, opera buffa was reborn fifty-five years after its last triumph, *Don Pasquale*, in a new guise. Verdi and Boito subtitled their latest, and last, collaboration a *Lyric Comedy*, meaning a comedy expressed in songs. Comedy, in the theater, we know, presents an audience with problems generally absent from tragedy. I know numerous instances in which a tragic outcome is comprehensible to an audience even when revealed in a foreign tongue. Tragedy often speaks directly to the heart, to the emotions. Comedy, and I am excluding slapstick, appeals not to the inarticulate heart but rather to the comprehending intellect. There are jokes, and either you get them or you don't. Comic episodes generally involve intrigues, pranks, escapades, and complex misunderstandings, all of which are lost on one who does not understand the language in which they are contrived. A lyric comedy compounds the matter. One must contend with words and music, jokes abounding in both, jokes that are being sung. You can enjoy *Falstaff* by reading a plot synopsis and listening to the music. You will enjoy it more if you read a synopsis and then, as you listen to the opera, follow the libretto line by line, gathering in not only the meaning of the words but also the humor in the music working brilliantly in conjunction with the dialogue. An easier approach, and a fine one, naturally, is to rent or buy a good video with English subtitles, of which there are several.

Like *Otello*, the story of how *Falstaff* came to be is interesting and can be briefly told. Verdi was seventy-six years old when in July 1889 Boito presented him a sketch for an opera on Falstaff, Shakespeare's jovial, brazen, and unscrupulous fat knight of *Henry IV, Parts 1 and 2*, and *The Merry Wives of Windsor*. The latter, for more than a hundred years, served numerous composers an operatic opportunity, the most notable and enduring being, in 1849, Otto Nicolai's *Die lustigen Weiber von Windsor (The Merry Wives of Windsor)*. After Verdi and Boito's *Falstaff*, the one successful opera on the subject I know is *Sir John in Love*, by Vaughan Williams (1929), the only composer I am aware of who utilized a rendition of the song "Greensleeves" operatically. Perhaps as a matter of principle, Verdi never accepted a libretto without tinkering, and so it was with Boito's new plan. Yet the composer could not successfully conceal his boundless enthusiasm behind the facade of "But I am so old" and "What if I can't finish it?" the likes of which are found in his letters to the poet. The ensuing libretto was Boito at his best.

Othello is a greater play than *The Merry Wives of Windsor*. In producing a libretto, the task for the former essentially was reduction of the long play. With the latter, it was otherwise. The *Falstaff* libretto was derived from both Shakespearean plays in which the bold, broad knight appears. Boito took this, discarded that, condensed, altered, added, and invented—in short, he created a new, fully proportioned drama of the portly rascal, his colleagues, and their mischief articulated through his remarkable words. The secrecy insisted upon by the composer while setting the libretto was even more so than what surrounded the composition of *Otello*.

The characters and their voices are:

SIR JOHN FALSTAFF, *baritone*
BARDOLFO, follower of Falstaff, *tenor*
PISTOLA, follower of Falstaff, *bass*
FORD, a wealthy man, *baritone*
ALICE FORD, his wife, *soprano*
NANNETTA, their daughter, who is in love with Fenton, *soprano*
FENTON, a young man (tenor)
MISTRESS PAGE (Meg), *mezzo-soprano*
MISTRESS QUICKLY, *mezzo-soprano, sometimes a contralto*
DR. CAIUS, *tenor*
Servants and townspeople.

The time is during the reign of Henry IV, King of England
(1399–1413); the place is Windsor.

The musical nature of Verdi's final work requires some consideration before we enter the first of the three acts. I have read articles
pointing to the Mozartian elements in the score, for it is well
known how much Verdi admired the Austrian genius. Igor
Stravinsky's ascerbic thrust claiming *Falstaff* might be Wagner's
best work but not Verdi's best is familiar to readers of his *Poetics
of Music.* Because the opera ends with a fugue, it has been asserted—erroneously—that Verdi musically came home to Bach at the
end of his career (but there is a fugue in *Macbeth*, his first adaptation of Shakespeare, written nearly fifty years before). A famous
opera scholar, Francis Toye, heard hints of Beethoven in *Falstaff*,
especially during the opening moments. Others point back to
Rossini. Resolving this popular form of musical detective work
holds no interest for me and, at least here, probably is of little
value to you. Verdi is Verdi and no one else.

More important are the ensemble dimension of the opera, the
nature of the songs, and the speed of the orchestral score.
Throughout *Falstaff*, the most common tempo markings indicate
quickness and movement as one conversation flows into another,
as one episode hurriedly concludes, a new one taking its place
with equal alacrity. An audience not only is never kept waiting
but more often than not is also left behind, absolutely incapable of
keeping pace with Boito's speedy repartee and Verdi's nimble
tunes. Do not make your conclusive judgment after only one
encounter, unless, of course, you were instantly smitten. It is
more normal for *Falstaff* imperceptively to seep under your skin
with repetition than to win you over all at once. The easily
hummed tunes of *Il trovatore* seem to be missing as the orchestra
skips along breathlessly. Oh, there are songs, quite lovely ones,
too, especially the tunes for the young lovers, and memorable
monologues as well for Sir John and Ford, but little you would
take into the shower with you to sing.

Traditional formats of aria, preceded by recitativo or followed
by a cabeletta, would interrupt the conversational dimensions of
the work by isolating emotions with melodic pauses in the action.
Falstaff does not play in this manner. It is an opera on the run and
you'd better be in good condition if you want to keep up with it.
With a few exceptions, it is not an easily excerpted opera with
numerous well-known highlights having taken on a life of their

own in concert halls and recording studios. One of the most familiar tunes lasts barely a minute before it is gone, the orchestra and voice having moved on elsewhere as one dialogue blends into another. Perhaps it is because of this lack of clear, sustained, developed, and identifiable melody that other Verdi operas have always been more popular, and, perhaps, the intellectual demands of its comic brilliance intimidate those for whom operatic popularity resides in hurdy-gurdy tunes and glorious high notes.

Falstaff's individuality notwithstanding, of this fact no serious doubt can be raised: When the final curtain closed on the world premiere, few were they who did not marvel at what they had just seen and heard, and unto today it remains that only a brave soul or a fool publicly would proclaim *Falstaff* anything less than a consummate masterpiece.

Act I

Part One: Falstaff, having sealed two letters just written, reclines in a big chair to enjoy another bottle of sherry in the hall of the Garter Inn. Dr. Caius, entering boisterously, reproaches him for beating his servants, breaking and entering into his house, and then, having been made drunk by Bardolfo and Pistola, being robbed by them. Denying none of this, Falstaff admonishes him not to drink so much and dismisses him.

Presented with the innkeeper's bill, immediately it is evident to them that the contents of all their pockets will not pay for six chickens, three turkeys and two pheasants washed down with thirty bottles of sherry. Falstaff, accordingly, orders another bottle, affectionately pats his immense girth, as though it was the embodiment of all his seductive powers, and discloses his intent to seduce both Alice Ford and Meg Page, two beautiful women holding the coffer keys of their wealthy husbands. When Pistola and Bardolfo refuse his order to deliver a letter to each of the women, the former adamant he will not be a pander and the latter fearing loss of honor, Falstaff dispatches his epistles by a page and delivers his Honor Monologue *(L'Onore!)*.

Reading it, with Iago's Creed fresh in memory, you see easily how it is the irreverent, comic counterpart. Falstaff debunks honor as generally useless. It cannot fill your belly or mend a broken bone. Honor is nonsense; it is humbug.

> What is it, then? A word.
> What is there in this word?

> There's some air that floats away . . .
> I'll have none of it, no, no, no!

Disgusted with the knaves who endlessly will eat and drink at his expense yet refuse to serve, Falstaff, grabbing and swinging a broom, drives them from the room. Many great baritones, who are fine actors as well, covet the opportunity to play this splendid scene upon the stage.

Part Two: In her garden, next to the Ford house, Alice and her daughter, Nannetta, are joined by Mistress Quickly and Meg Page. They are, the orchestra tells us, in a merry mood. Mistress Page and Mistress Ford, confiding, share the love letter each has just received. Everything is the same except the name of the addressee: the seal, the handwriting, the effusions of love, the proposed assignation, and, to their astonished delight, the signature, "Sir John Falstaff, Knight." Their reactions direct the course of the remainder of the play. They are bemused but they will have revenge. They will play a trick on him. They will make a fool of him over this pair of absolutely identical, ludicrous proposals of love making, all affirmed in a delightful ensemble. The women remove to the back of stage left.

Enter, stage right, Dr. Caius, Fenton, then Ford, followed by Falstaff's recently dismissed minions Bardolfo and Pistola, who reveal to Ford the amorous contents of the knight's letter to his wife. Ford, too, will have revenge, a busy male ensemble periodically vying pleasantly with the women's singing as they return to center stage left. Alice, in an aside to Meg (and to pique her husband's intensely jealous nature), implies a need for secrecy. Of the women, all but Nannetta depart; of the men, all but Fenton leave. They kiss hastily. Fenton begs for more but the young woman knows why their forbidden love must remain hidden. Their tiny love duet is a gem.

The women return hatching revenge but, spotting Fenton and fearing they will be heard, run off again, thus allowing the young man briefly to resume his kissing.

The men return hatching revenge in their huddle. The women also huddle, having returned again, plotting as well. Only Fenton's singular thoughts of love shared simply with himself in an aside are not part of the conspiracies as Verdi brings together the ensembles—each, however, with a different tempo. The effect of this remarkably sophisticated music is extraordinary, its complex, speedy, conversational quality being the essence, so to speak, of

Falstaff in a nutshell: music so wonderful yet over almost as soon as it began.

The men leave, the women remaining briefly to iterate revenge on the obese, risible Falstaff before the curtain falls.

Act II

Part One: In the hall of the Garter Inn, Falstaff drinks heartily while seated in his great chair as Bardolfo and Pistola fake contrition for their disobedience and offer to serve again.

Mrs. Quickly arrives. She wants a private word with Falstaff, who, accordingly, waves off his lackeys. Alice Ford, she says, speaking quietly, succumbed to the passionate love letter and requests a rendezvous at her home between two and three, when her jealous husband is always out. Meg Page, however, she continues, whose husband is never away from home, cannot extend a similar invitation. Assuring her that Alice Ford will be met as planned, Falstaff, with a coin and a kind word, dismisses Mrs. Quickly. Alone, he relishes the thought:

> *Alice è mia!*
> *Va, vecchio John, va, va per la tua via.*
> *Questa tua vecchia carne ancora spreme*
> *qualche dolcezza a te.*

> Alice is mine!
> Go, old John, go, go your way
> For this old hide still holds
> Some sweetness for you.

The orchestra confidently expresses the anticipated pleasures. Don't miss this succinct bit of braggadocio.

Bardolfo returns to announce a gentleman caller bearing a demijohn and wishing to meet the knight. It is Ford in disguise. Bardolfo and Pistola, lurking in the background, anticipate some sport. Now in the service of Ford, here in the guise of one Fontana, they are in the know. But only the audience knows that the nearly concurrent arrivals of Mrs. Quickly and Ford represent the initiation of two separate plots by the men and the women, each, of course, unknown to the other. Ford, as Fontana, tells Falstaff that every attempt he has made, at great expense, to court Alice Ford has failed. He is mad for her. Offering Falstaff a bag of gold, he requests Falstaff to woo her, the idea being that the knight will

wear out her resistance and one sin may lead to another. Falstaff
assures Fontano of success, explaining he was about to dress for a
secret meeting with Alice Ford while her husband is out. He
accepts the money and goes off to make himself ready. Venting
jealous rage in a much anticipated soliloquy, having heard much
more than he had expected, Ford plans to catch his wanton wife
with the rake (another comic counterpart to *Otello*, where jeal-
ously led to tragedy). This "cuckold" monologue is one of the
most sustained arias of the score. It begins *È sogno? o realtà* . . .

> Is this a dream? Or reality? Two enormous horns
> Are sprouting on my head . . .

and as Ford sings this, the orchestra, too, sprouts a crescendo. Falstaff returns in elegant finery and out the door they go.

Part Two: In a room in Ford's house, where the women await
Falstaff to a merry little tune skipping through the orchestra, Mrs.
Quickly offers another of her grand imitations of Falstaff as she
recounts her visit to the inn where he resides. Now two o'clock,
the women are ready for fun—all except a troubled Nannetta, who
has been told by her father that she is to marry Dr. Caius. The
women sympathize, calling him unattractive names. Alice Ford
tells her daughter "never fear" and the happy mood is restored as
servants enter carrying a huge basket of soiled laundry. Props are
readied: a screen, a chair, and a lute. Alice sings the *Merry Wives
of Windsor* song as the comedy is about to begin, for Falstaff has
been seen approaching.

Alice is playing her lute as Sir John enters the room, breaking
into song: "At last I pluck you, radiant flower. I pluck you."
(You'll miss the humor if you don't follow all the words.) Seizing
her around the waist, he presses his suit as Alice parries. His
petite song *Quand'ero paggio* ("When I was page to the Duke of
Norfolk . . ."), about his dashing, slender youth, is as charming as
any other tune in the score. It comes and goes in thirty-five seconds, an exemplary example of the speed with which the drama
moves.

Mrs. Quickly interrupts to inform Alice of the imminent
arrival of a most agitated Meg Page. Falstaff hides behind the
screen as he hears of an enraged Ford, believing his wife to be hiding her lover in the house, heading home on the run. And there he
is, in the room, followed by Dr. Caius, Fenton, Bardolfo, and Pistola, all searching everywhere. Thespian, verbal, and musical

activity is of a maddening intensity. Ford empties the basket, scattering the clothes, then departs to investigate another room. Meg suggests Falstaff hide in the basket. The terrified knight does quickly, the dirty laundry forced over him. Nannetta and Fenton enter, hide behind the screen, and embrace. The men return, peering frantically into each cupboard and every corner as the sound of a kiss, through a rare moment of silence, rings out. Ford is certain it is his wife and Falstaff soon to be unmasked.

Meanwhile, Meg and Mrs. Quickly attempt to retain the suffocating knight beneath laundry and the young lovers continue their business until the screen is thrown aside, exposing them. Ford is stunned yet no less happy about finding his daughter and Fenton. Furious, he resumes his search elsewhere. Alice has the servants empty the contents of the basket through the window into the river below. When the men return, Alice leads her husband by the arm to the window. All howl with laughter at the sight of Falstaff bobbing in the Thames as the curtain falls.

Act III

Part One: Falstaff sits on a bench in a square next to the inn. Soaking wet, he calls a waiter for mulled wine and utters invectives against a world allowing such a great knight the indignity of having been tossed with dirty clothing into the river. He resumes his "Go, old John, your way" song, his mood brightening with the wine.

Mrs. Quickly appears to offer another tryst outlined in a letter from Alice. Hiding nearby are Alice, Ford, Meg, Nannetta, Dr. Caius, and Fenton. At first Falstaff refuses, the dunking he received too near in the past, but, of course, the temptation overwhelms him. He agrees to meet her by Herne's Oak in the Royal Park at midnight disguised as the Black Huntsman of legend. Mollified, he escorts Mrs. Quickly to the inn while the spies inch forward, Alice relating the spooky tale of how ghosts and spirits appear at midnight as the huntsman enters the park.

Complicated plotting begins. Nannetta will be clad in white, dressed as the Queen of the Fairies. Meg will be a wood nymph, Mrs. Quickly, a witch; and Alice will dress a host of children as spirits, imps, bats, demons, and fairies. Ford secretly tells Dr. Caius to dress as a monk, for he has a plan to wed him to Nannetta.

Part Two: The first to arrive in the park is Fenton singing a love song. It dissolves in kisses as Nannetta arrives, followed by the other women who dress Fenton as a monk as part of their plan to foil Ford's favoring Dr. Caius. All hide.

As the clock begins to toll midnight, Falstaff enters. Covered by a massive black cloak with a set of antlers upon his head, he boasts, "Love changes man into a beast, . . ." bellowing like a bull as Alice arrives. Immediately he tries to embrace her. She eludes him. A distant scream is heard. It is Meg warning of the approaching goblins. Alice runs off. The Fairy Queen, with helpers by her side, now appears among the foliage. Falstaff is terrified. To see the fairies face-to-face means death. He drops to the ground face-down as they emerge to circle the great oak. The music of this scene is so strikingly original that it has been the subject of thorough study by musicologists. As the fairies dance and sing, the others enter, the women dressed as planned, Ford undisguised, townspeople masked and carrying lanterns. Pistola is attired as a satyr and Dr. Caius wears the gray robe of a monk.

Bardolfo, who is concealed, all except his great red nose, in a red cape with hood, stumbles on the body of Falstaff. While he is frozen by fear, Falstaff's great bulk is prodded, poked, and pinched as evil spirits play their parts. He is raised to his knees and assaulted with nasty names while Bardolfo strikes him with a stick until he repents, admitting to being a rascal, cheater, braggart, drunkard, cuckold, etcetera. He then recognizes Bardolfo by his nose, rises, and vents himself. Ford approaches him and is mistaken for Fontana. Alice introduces Fontana as her husband and joins Meg and Mrs. Quickly in their own brand of insults aimed at "the fat and dirty old man." Seeing himself for what he is, Falstaff accepts all as a good sport.

Assuming the prank is now over, Ford suggests crowning the masquerade with the wedding of the Fairy Queen. For the women, however, the little play within a play has a final scene. They have attired Bardolfo as the Fairy Queen, entering now with Dr. Caius hand in hand. Alice introduces a second couple, a woman behind a blue veil and a man in cape and mask. Ford marries both couples, blesses them, calls on them to unmask and is stunned to see that he has married Bardolfo to Caius and Fenton to his daughter.

Vittoria ("Victory"), shout the women, as Falstaff asks Ford who now is the fool. It is agreed that of fools there are several as all is forgiven and happily resolved. To finish the play Sir John Falstaff suggests a chorus. He leads all in a fugue putting forth the moral:

The whole world is but a joke.
Mankind is born a clown.
Within our addled heads
Our brains are in a churn.
We are all fools! And each
Laughs at the other's folly.
But the best laugh is to
The one with the last laugh.

With the finale to his final opera, Giuseppe Verdi achieved a supreme end to a long career as one of the uncompromising masters in the history of composing for musical theater. Boito attempted unsuccessfully to interest him in more Shakespeare. Old and tired, Verdi had no more operas in him. He died in Milan, appropriately, on Mozart's birthday, January 27, 1901. With his wealth he established Casa Verdi, a retirement home for opera singers who had fallen on hard times. It continues to meet their needs to this day.

Hector Berlioz

Charles-François Gounod

Georges Bizet

Camille Saint-Saëns

Jacques Offenbach

Jules Massenet

19TH CENTURY FRENCH OPERA: SIX FAVORITES

During the first half of the nineteenth century, Paris was the operatic center of the world. I have referred, in a previous chapter, to the arrival in the capital, in the 1640s, of the Italian Giovanni Battista Lulli when he was about twelve years old. There his remarkable musical gift flourished. He wrote nearly two dozen operas and today is known to the world as Jean-Baptiste Lully. In 1735 appeared an opera-ballet of sublime beauty, *Les Indes galantes*, by Jean-Philipe Rameau. Gluck came to Paris, as did many other composers during this period: Rossini, Meyerbeer, Wagner, and Verdi, to cite the most famous in the world of opera, but Franz Liszt and Frédéric Chopin came, too.

Because French opera has had a long history prior to the great days of Paris in the nineteenth century, its important terms can be confusing. One encounters *grand opera, comic opera,* and *lyrical opera*. Definitions alter with the passing of time and historical development. Nevertheless, I can make it quite simple for you.

The distinctions between the two most basic terms are of elemental significance. These two terms are *grand opera* and *comic opera*. During the nineteenth century, grand opera, you will remember from my consideration of Rossini's *William Tell* (in chapter 3), meant serious, big, epic, or historical opera, often of four or five acts. The chorus had a prominent role, an Act II ballet was virtually mandatory, and all dialogue was forbidden. Spectacle and great effects were essential—they were expected by a broadening, wealthy middle class flocking to the Opéra, where these performances took place. Comic opera *(opéra-comique)* in nineteenth-century French opera terminology is a misleading concept because the operas produced at the Opéra-Comique, a different opera house, certainly were not all comedies. Here spoken dialogue, banned at the Paris Opéra, was allowed, and this is the basic distinction between the two traditional Parisian theaters. The third term, *lyric opera (opéra-lyrique)*, will be discussed later in this chapter.

Most of the great operas in French before this time were composed by foreigners who came to Paris because of its cultural and financial importance. I just mentioned the importance of *William Tell*. I also mentioned Meyerbeer, whose most well-known operas are *Les Huguenots*, and *L'Africaine* even though these operas are not included in this book. Also omitted are operas once popular but now rarely revived: Auber's *Fra Diavolo*, Adam's *Le Postillon de Lonjumeau (The Coachman of Longjumeau)*, and Halévy's *La Juive (The Jewess)*. The French composers of the nineteenth century whose operas remain on the boards and in recording studios are Berlioz, Gounod, Bizet, Saint-Saëns, Offenbach, and Massenet. Finally, we have arrived at enduring French operas composed by Frenchmen. Of the six composers just named, only Offenbach was not a native Frenchman, but Paris was his operatic home. This chapter introduces one opera of each. They are: *La damnation de Faust (The Damnation of Faust)* (1846), by Berlioz; *Faust* (1859), by Gounod; *Carmen* (1875), by Bizet; *Samson et Dalila* (1877), by Saint-Saëns; *Les Contes d'Hoffmann (The Tales of Hoffman)* (1881), by Offenbach; and *Manon* (1884), by Massenet.

HECTOR BERLIOZ

Experts on opera will quibble with my first selection, arguing for *Les Troyens (The Trojans)*, the text drawn from Virgil's *Aeneid*. I can hear them say that *La damnation de Faust* was conceived as a concert opera, to be sung in a concert hall without staging, sets, costumes, or action and thus is not really an opera. All true, yet

Berlioz meant to revise his concert version for a staged version. Even though he did not realize his intent, this work often has been given on the stage and has, accordingly, become an opera. And true, too, is the great value of *Les Troyens*, a huge opera of five acts lasting over four and a half hours. Completed in 1858, this opera did not have a full performance until 1890, more than twenty years after Berlioz died. In its extraordinary breadth we can hear some of the finest and most original music Berlioz ever wrote: the Trojan March, the immolation chorus, soliloquies for Aeneas and Dido, a nocturne-duet for them, and the sailors' song, to mention only what first come to mind. Of himself, Berlioz said he would have to live 150 years to experience the popular acceptance of his music. That which poured forth from his powerful and original mind was startling, new, and, to many of his contemporaries, incomprehensible. Not only were critics severe in their appraisals but the composer Mendelssohn also harshly declared that Berlioz, "without a shadow of talent," groped about in the dark.

The prognostication of 150 years proved true. From that perspective, and beyond, Berlioz is looked on as one of the giants of the nineteenth century. There must be a place for him in this book. *Les Troyens* is a more supportable choice than either *Benvenuto Cellini* or *Béatrice et Bénédict*, two other Berlioz operas, but I am selecting *La damnation de Faust* for your introduction to the unusual and infectious sounds of this composer, who was blessed with an extraordinary gift for evocative, dramatic music. Furthermore, this choice allows us to consider the three most familiar operatic presentations of the Faust legend: You have met already Boito's *Mefistofele,* and following Berlioz comes Gounod's *Faust.*

LA DAMNATION DE FAUST (1846)
The Damnation of Faust

There probably was, in sixteenth-century Germany, a historical Faust (circa 1488–1541), the source of a huge body of imaginary stories about a magician who, according to some accounts, had supernatural powers and who, some believed, was in cahoots with Satan. History evolved into legend, legend into literature, and literature inspired opera. Contemporaries of Faust judged him a quack and their accounts are most unflattering. The first Faust book appeared in 1587. It begat others, several of which became quite famous, including Christopher Marlowe's play *The Tragical*

History of Dr. Faustus (1604, a posthumous publication) and Goethe's masterpiece, *Faust*, upon which he worked throughout his long life. Part One appeared in 1808 and Part Two in 1832.

Faust, the legend maintains, entered into a pact with the devil wherein he sold his soul for the restoration of his youth. There are more than a dozen operas based on the legend. The three most well-known and often performed operas derive from Goethe. Boito utilizes both Goethe parts; Berlioz and Gounod draw only from the first. Berlioz called his work a "dramatic legend in four parts." He produced his own text from de Nerval's French version of Goethe's play with assistance from de Nerval and de Gandonnière (two names not encountered in this book again). The characters are:

MARGUERITE, a young woman, *soprano*
FAUST, an old philosopher-magician, *tenor*
MÉPHISTOPHÉLÈS (hereafter in English as Mephistopheles),
  one of the seven chief devils, *bass*
BRANDER, a drunk, *bass*
Students, soldiers, citizens, gnomes, sylphs, angels, and
  heavenly spirits

The settings vary in this surrealist drama from the plains of Hungary, to Leipzig, to the banks of the Elbe River, to a mountain range, to hell and back, and, ultimately, to heaven. No date is designated but late Middle Ages is assumed. There are four parts in nineteen scenes plus an epilogue of two episodes.

This chronicle of Faust's unhappy boredom, his temptations, his love affair with Marguerite, her abandonment, death, and atonement, and the damnation of Faust elucidate a basic thesis of Goethe's Faust:

Er irrt der Mensch so lang er streht . . .

Man errs as long as he strives.

His vast, profound, philosophical play in verse, probing elemental human experiences, presents possibilities for differing interpretive studies: This opera of Berlioz, accordingly, is not a simple story. Philosophical and religious implications abound with each scene as Faust makes a final attempt to experience lasting contentment. Time passes and places change abstractly. The story is told in a meditative manner. Real and visionary situations pass from one to the other. Brilliant musical characterizations evoke the personality of the dreamy, restless Faust, satiated by life and yet tempted one more time to learn its secret, and of the pretty, innocent, and simple Marguerite, their fates cupped in the hands of an evil force, Mephistopheles. The music, a perfect fit for the poetry, portrays soldiers marching, sots gambling, devils dancing, and so much more. I think it difficult to say no to this music that premiered at the Opéra-Comique on December 6, 1846.

Part One
Faust, seated in a chair, books on a table by his side, meditates as day breaks. The pleasures of solitude and the beauties of nature are not enough to bring him happiness. As peasants arrive, singing and dancing, he is envious of their joy. The peasants move on and Faust sees the Hungarian army approach, marching to the famous Racoczy war hymn. Berlioz employed a theme from this ancient tune and developed it, and the piece has become quite popular. The sight of the soldiers advancing to rousing music produces in Faust speculations on heroism and dreams of glory, but as the army passes on, they are empty dreams.

Part Two
In his study in Germany, Faust, now more despairing than ever, contemplates drinking poison to end his grief, caused by an inability to know what is lacking in his life. As he raises the cup to his lips he hears an Easter hymn, and his room transforms into the interior of a church. Dashing the cup violently to the floor, he remembers his childhood days of unquestioned piety. Temporarily comforted, Faust finds himself alone again as the church vanishes and Mephistopheles miraculously materializes before him, promising a cure for the doctor's lethargy and despair if he will neglect his books and follow him. The theater becomes completely dark as they vanish together. The orchestra plays through moments of darkness when suddenly a light reveals the cellar of Auerbach's Tavern in Leipzig. Brander sits on a table. A swarm of sots gamble and drink. Mephistopheles says,

> *Voici, Faust, un séjour de folle compagnie,*
> *Ici vins et chansons réjouissent la vie.*

> Faust, here's a place of mad company
> Where wine and song bring joy to life.

A chorus praises wine before Brander is called upon to sing a story. He is drunk. He sings the "Song of the Rat," which recounts the animal's death when inadvertently roasted in an oven by a serving maid. His inebriated friends, staggering and clutching their mugs, proffer mocking grief as they sing a *Requiescat in pace* ("Rest in Peace") to which a most inventive fugue on the word *Amen* is added. Anticipating a potential sacrilegious effrontery with his drunken fugal improvisation, Berlioz penned this note in his autograph score:

> If one is afraid of wounding the feelings of a pious audience, or an audience that admires scholastic fugues on the word "Amen," a cut of the following ten pages may be made.

Mephistopheles takes the floor to sing the "Song of the Flea," about a flea so loved by a prince that the nobleman has had his tailor measure the insect for a fine suit. It is one of the most popular numbers in the score. The pleasures of gambling, drink, and song fail to entice Faust, who vanishes suddenly with Mephistopheles through a supernatural burst of fire as the drinkers recoil in terror.

With a lovely symphonic prelude, the scene changes into a bucolic paradise of roses on the banks of the Elbe. Faust, restored to youth, lies by a bed of the flowers while Mephistopheles sings the beautiful song of the roses: *Voici des roses*. In a drama of many extraordinary scenes, this one never fails to enchant. As a chorus of gnomes and sylphs sings Faust to sleep, the roses are transformed into semi-nude dancers. Covered only by rose-colored veils, they assume erotic postures as they move about the sleeping man. The devil conjures a dream in which Faust envisions Marguerite. She will love him, he is told. Her vision vanishes, Faust utters her name in his sleep, and Mephistopheles is satisfied his evil charm is working. "The Ballet of the Sylphs" is for many the most beautiful music of the opera. Faust, awakening, is told by Mephistopheles to follow him once again.

Instantly soldiers and students fill a marketplace. They sing in turn of the pleasures of physical love. The chorus of students, of course, is cleverly set in Latin. Is there any doubt as to what is in store for Doctor Faust as the second part concludes?

Part Three

Faust is led to Marguerite's house by his companion who then leaves him alone. Faust sings *Merci, doux crépuscule* ("Thank you, sweet twilight") in joyful anticipation. When Marguerite comes, he hides. She sings her now famous ballad "The King of Thule," about a nobleman faithful to his love through death and beyond. It is a representation of a folk ballad sung by a young woman looking at nothing as she combs and braids her hair. Marguerite falls asleep. Mephistopheles summons his will-o'-the wisp spirits to aid him in charming the girl with a vision of Faust. Together they sing an entertaining minuet in which the ruination of the innocent Marguerite is ensured.

When she awakens, having had her vision of Faust, he enters her room and it is love before first sight: a love fated through the machinations of the embodiment of evil evoked separately in their dreams. Their immediate and total love is expressed in a duet. Mephistopheles finds them in an embrace as he enters the room and insists they part until tomorrow. In a trio that ends the third part, the lovers exclaim, "Love has taken possession of my ravished soul," while the devil, urging them apart, derides them: "Love will elate you and double your folly."

Part Four

Alone, Marguerite sings a beautiful aria about love, *D'amour, l'ardente flamme* ("The ardent flame of love"). Drums and trumpets resound with refrains from the songs of the soldiers and students as she departs, fearing Faust will not come. He, a scene change reveals, is invoking the power and beauty of nature in a rocky, wooded wilderness. It is with these two songs that the doomed lovers expose their most intense feelings. Mephistopheles barges in on Faust's reverie with the news that Marguerite has been arrested and condemned to die for matricide. She was unaware of the mild, poisonous nature of the drink Faust left for her to administer to her mother as a sleeping potion each night prior to their lovemaking. Faust is horrified. Mephistopheles assures him she can be saved in an instant if Faust will sign a parchment swearing to serve him. The devil calls forth two black horses, and Faust, naturally, assumes they will gallop to the jail to free Marguerite.

"The Ride to the Abyss," Faust and Mephistopheles galloping on two black horses, is the first music I remember hearing from *La damnation de Faust*. Its appeal to young and old alike is immediate, but I was young when I first heard it and was swept away. I remain so to this day after hundreds of hearings.

Praying peasants are scattered by the flying hooves of the hors-es, and Faust fears he is being followed by a monster and attack-ing birds. As they charge by dancing skeletons, the orchestra vir-tually gallops from one horror to the next until the earth heaves, raining blood, and they enter the abyss, Mephistopheles exulting over his victory.

The next scene, with no interruption, is titled "Pandemoni-um." A chorus of demons and the damned sing triumphantly, in a language made up by Berlioz, as they dance about Mephistopheles before triumphantly carrying him off as Part Four ends with Faust consumed in flames.

Epilogue

This magnificent music of demonic forces is contrasted by the Epilogue. First, on earth, a voice from the depths proclaiming hell's terror is heard, then, the stage brightening, rooftops of the village are revealed in outline against the sky beyond. Angels appear, descend, gather up the body of Marguerite, and ascend to heaven as a beautiful ethereal chorus of spirits ensures forgiveness for the guileless soul led astray by the plottings of an evil power.

‿

Many excerpts from *La damnation de Faust* have become well known and quite popular, but if you are willing to follow the numerous scenes with a libretto, allowing all the music to work its wonders, you may just learn to love all of this "dramatic leg-end in four parts" as I do. In his *Memoirs* Berlioz wrote, "The pre-vailing characteristics of my music are passionate expression, inner ardor, rhythmic impulse, and the unexpected." No one knew better than he. Berlioz was overwhelmed by Goethe's *Faust* ever since discovering it in his late teens. It dwelled within him for years, emerging musically first in the form of eight episodes, all of which eventually, in revisions, were incorporated into his own *Faust* masterpiece. Boito's version certainly possesses its many marvelous musical moments and Gounod's, as we are about to learn, due to one popular tune after another, remains of the three the most frequently performed. It was Berlioz, however, who best condensed the spirit of Goethe's masterpiece into music, expressing life's many-faceted experiences, from temptation, to terror, to atonement. You may never have an opportunity to see a staged version of *La damnation de Faust*, unless on a video, so do not pass up a concert version if voices and the orchestra are good. And by all means, at least listen once to a complete recording.

CHARLES-FRANÇOIS GOUNOD

FAUST (1859)

Gounod's *Faust* is based on the Marguerite episode, Part One of Goethe's play. It is more of a story in the traditional operatic sense, living famously year after year through its familiar catchy tunes. Gounod's *Faust* is not a work probing, as is that of Berlioz, profound sentiments through sudden contrasts, flamboyant and evocative musical colors blurring demarcations of reality and fantasy, and philosophical considerations. It is a story set to music and embellished by a parade of wonderful tunes. Both composers, however—and this generally will be true throughout consideration of French opera—respect the words of the drama. Ballet is one tradition of French opera; the importance of the words telling the story is another. Spoken dialogue of the Opéra-Comique greatly facilitated comprehending the story line, but even in those operas written for the Paris Opéra, where dialogue was forbidden, the sung recitations generally were clear and easy to follow. To that elemental operatic issue "What is more important, the words or the music?" the French answered that they are equally important. The words for Gounod's *Faust* were provided by librettists Jules Barbier and Michel Carré, collaborators on numerous excellent operas. We will meet them again in *The Tales of Hoffmann*, by Offenbach.

Charles-François Gounod (1818–1893) was born in Paris five years after the births of Verdi and Wagner. He became an accomplished organist and conductor as well as a prolific composer of operas, oratorios, other church music, and songs, the most famous of which is an Ave Maria setting appropriated from the first prelude of Johann Sebastian Bach's "Well Tempered Clavier." I know you have heard it at Christmastime. *Faust*'s premiere took place at Théâtre-Lyrique (Lyric Theater) in Paris on March 19, 1859. Earlier in this chapter, I promised a definition of a third term, important to nineteenth-century French opera. Opéra-lyrique, in conception, tended to be shorter than grand opera and certainly less spectacular. It avoided use of spoken dialogue, permitted at the Opéra-Comique, and was, accordingly, an in-between sort of drama meeting prerequisites of neither grand nor comic opera performances. Its subject matter usually was of romantic episodes clearly depicted in uncomplicated plots and set to elegant, melodic music. Gounod was a founder of this tradition, brought to a consummation by Jules Massenet before the end of the century. Gounod's *Faust*, as stated above, is the love story of Faust and Marguerite (called Gretchen in Goethe's play). Marguerite, or, more accurately, Gretchen, is not found in the Faust legend but rather was invented by Goethe. Because both Goethe and Gounod are immensely popular in Germany and because Gounod's opera derives from only a portion of the first part of Goethe's play, you will find the opera under the name *Margarethe* in Germany.

Under whatever name, it remains the most successful music Gounod ever wrote and one of the most popular operas of all time. Its worldwide appeal, which declined somewhat by the 1950s, seems to have been only temporary. You should have no trouble finding a performance in a major opera house or on good recordings.

Faust developed through several versions and attentive revisions before achieving the final form in which it is performed today, without spoken dialogue and with, often, a long Act V ballet. One of the most famous arias, Valentin's "Farewell," was added in 1863 for a London production. The characters of the drama are:

DOCTOR FAUST, a learned man, *tenor*
MEPHISTOPHELES, *bass*
MARGUERITE, a pretty young woman, *soprano*
VALENTIN, her brother and a soldier, *baritone*
SIEBEL, a village youth in love with Marguerite, *soprano or mezzo-soprano; a trouser-role*
MARTHE, Marguerite's neighbor, *soprano or mezzo-soprano*
Students, soldiers, villagers, angels, and demons

The action is set in Germany in the late sixteenth century.

Act I

A musical prelude to the first act begins with a loud chord. This followed by a mix of little ominous and mysterious themes. The big chord returns and the themes mix and mount to a pitch, then diminish as they yield to one of the most familiar melodies in the score, that of Valentin's "Farewell." The prelude resolves with music anticipating Faust's gloom as expressed in his opening monologue, which is interrupted by the lovely theme of the arrival of dawn.

Anticipating still another day in a life unfulfilled, he prepares a poisonous draft. Interruptions, however, intervene. First, the distant song of peasant girls greeting the day is heard, then a chorus blessing God offered by reapers heading for the fields. Faust, putting down his drink, slumps into his chair, doubts what God can do for him, and exclaims, "Satan, come to me!"

In a magical theatrical entrance, Mephistopheles materializes, answering *Me voici!* ("Here I am!"), and offers to lead the disconsolate old philosopher to riches or glory. Faust desires only the restoration of his youth and the return of passion. Mephistopheles makes a bargain: On earth, he will serve Faust's desires but in the world below, Faust will serve him. Faust is hesitant to sign the contract until the vision of a beautiful young woman sitting by her spinning wheel is conjured before him. This is Marguerite.

The poison now turned magic potion is drunk, Faust is transformed into a glamorous youth again, and together he and the devil set forth on the road to pleasure.

Their duet ending the act, a robust and virile tune, has been a favorite of mine since I was a young boy, for *Faust* was one of the first operas I came to know well and that is because one wonderful tune follows another. Perhaps only Verdi's *Il trovatore* equals *Faust* for operatic "hits." I have no compunctions over admitting how much I have always loved a good, catchy opera tune, one I could hum riding my bike to school or sing in the car while driving to the store.

Act II

This act begins with a parade of such tunes. The jaunty *Vin ou bière* ("Wine or Beer") chorus, Valentin's "Farewell," and the derisive "Calf of Gold" aria of Mephistopheles represent an almost uninterrupted succession of three of this opera's most familiar melodies.

The curtain opens on a tavern where a spirited crowd of students, soldiers, and townsfolk have gathered on the Easter Festival *(Kermesse)* grounds. They celebrate with a drinking chorus. Valentin, one of the soldiers who is about to go to war, expresses concern over leaving his sister, Marguerite, alone and unprotected, in a famous aria composed by Gounod for the celebrated English baritone Sir Charles Santly. It was added to the score for an 1863 production of the opera in London and was sung in an English translation made by Henry Fothergill Chorley, a critic whose reviews include vitriolic attacks on both Wagner and Verdi. So much for some music critics. His translation of Valentin's beautiful aria *Avant de quitter ces lieux* as "Even the bravest heart may swell" is a pitiful misrepresentation, and regrettably is how it has become known in English-speaking countries: First, the French:

> *Avant de quitter ces lieux,*
> *Sol natal de mes aïeux,*
> *A toi, Seigneur et Roi des cieux,*
> *Ma soeur je confie.*

Here is Chorley's infamous translation of the first four lines:

> Even the bravest heart may swell
> In the moment of farewell.
> Loving smile of sister kind,
> Quiet home I leave behind.

And, here is my literal translation of what the French text really says:

> Before leaving this place,
> Native soil of my ancestors,
> To you, Lord and King of heaven,
> I entrust my sister.

Fortunately, most translators, in attempting to retain the rhyme scheme of the original, do not take such liberties. If you know the original language of an opera or are learning it, a fun and linguistically profitable exercise is to compare the translation to the original. And remember, in all fairness to a translator, it is more than just a matter of reproducing the meaning of words in another language when the translation is meant to be sung. The translated words then must also fit the music.

Wagner (do not confuse this character with the famous composer) calls for more drinks and begins to sing about a rat. Mephistopheles interrupts with a song praising the golden calf worshiped the world around. Next, he predicts dire fortunes for Wagner, Siebel, and Valentin, disdains the wine, and, by magic, produces a rare vintage and bids all to drink their fill. When Mephistopheles toasts Marguerite, Valentin attacks him but his sword inexplicably is rent into pieces. All are now aware that they are in the presence of a demonic force. As the soldiers hold high the hilts of their swords, forming an army of crosses, Mephistopheles steps back and the crowd leaves the stage.

Faust enters. He implores Mephistopheles to take him to Marguerite but is told that she soon will come to this very place. The stage is flooded by couples waltzing to one of Gounod's most lilting melodies. Siebel, who has been awaiting Marguerite's arrival, when she appears is kept apart from her by Mephistopheles. When Faust offers the young girl his arm, she refuses him so gracefully that love strikes him with an immediate force. Mephistopheles promises to assist his wooing. The act ends as all join in a waltz song praising pleasure, music so resplendent that *Faust's* popularity remains secure. This waltz alone, one of the most familiar in the world, ensured Gounod's immortality.

Act III

Act III opens on Marguerite's garden next to her cottage, where Siebel is singing of his love for her. A flower he picks, as predicted by Mephistopheles, withers in his hand; when he dips his fingers in a font of holy water, however, the devil's spell is broken. Siebel departs briefly as Faust and his companion enter. They quickly hide as Siebel returns to affix a bouquet to the latch of the cottage door. He leaves. So does Mephistopheles, who will obtain a treasure for Faust to employ in countering Siebel's suit.

Now alone before the cottage of the beautiful young Marguerite, Faust sings his romance, one of the most anticipated arias for tenor in the literature of French opera. *Salut! demeure chaste et pure* ("Hail, chaste and pure dwelling"). Mephistopheles returns with a casket of jewels and a mirror, sets them on the cottage threshold, and pulls Faust away into the garden to observe. Marguerite appears, musing aloud upon the handsome young stranger who approached her at the festival. Sitting absent-mindedly by her spinning wheel, she sings a simple folk ballad about the King of Thule. Before she can finish her song, thoughts have strayed again to contemplate the fascinating young man. She rises, heads for the cottage door, and sees first the bouquet of flowers and then the casket of jewels. She adorns herself, expressing admiration as she gazes upon her reflection in the mirror. This is the celebrated "Jewel Song," a lyric soprano showpiece and an extraordinary contrast, spilling over with technically difficult vocal embellishments as she fondles the ornaments, to the folk ballad she had just sung.

Her neighbor, Marthe, enters, comments on the jewels, and reveals only temporary distress when she learns of her husband's death at war from Mephistopheles, now back on the scene with Faust. She quite willingly accepts his condolences as they, arm in arm, remove into the garden. In a quartet, separately strolling about the flowers, the two sets of couples get to know each other. Then, when Marthe departs, Mephistopheles summons powers of darkness to help him obliterate Marguerite's scruples before he, too, leaves.

Alone, Marguerite and Faust proclaim their mutual passion in wonderful back-to-back love duets: *Laisse-moi contempler ton visage* ("Let me look upon your face") and *O nuit d'amour, ciel radieux* ("O night of love, radiant sky"). They part, having promised to meet tomorrow. Faust heads for the garden but is detained by Mephistopheles as Marguerite enters her cottage and, believing herself to be alone, through a window sings of her love into the night. Beside himself, Faust rushes to her. As they passionately embrace, the mocking laughter of Mephistopheles resounds before the rapturous strains of love played by the orchestra die away and the curtain closes.

Act IV

The fourth-act curtain opens for a brief scene in Marguerite's room. Some time has elapsed. She has borne Faust's child but has been deserted by him. A faithful Siebel again offers love. She declines, still hoping Faust will return to her.

In some performances and on some recordings this scene is cut in favor of the act opening on one of the opera's most remarkable episodes, "the Church Scene." In the interior of a church Marguerite prays for forgiveness. Quite an organist, Gounod masterfully employs this grand instrument to evoke a reverent mood broken by the mysterious voices of Mephistopheles and demons condemning her to eternal perdition for her sin. Shrieking with terror, as a chorus of boys and priests chant *Dies Irae* ("Day of Anger"), she faints and falls upon the flagstones. This famous scene, which lasts only ten minutes, is one of tremendous intensity as soprano, bass, choruses, organ, and orchestra mix, match, blend, contrast, and unite in chilling authenticity.

Another change of scene, to the street in front of Marguerite's cottage, sharply alters the mood as soldiers returning from war sing a chorus made famous by this opera: The well-known "Soldier's Chorus" was taken from an unfinished opera, *Ivan the Terrible*, by Gounod and used here to great effect. Among the soldiers is Valentin, who, seeing Siebel, embraces his old friend and asks about his sister. The tentative response hinting all is not well sends Valentin running into the house.

Faust and Mephistopheles come sauntering down the street. Stopping at the house, Mephistopheles accompanies himself on a guitar while singing *Vous qui faites l'endormie* ("You who sleep"), a cynical serenade admonishing maidens not to relent until "the ring is on your finger." It is aimed at the guilty Marguerite as a means of coaxing her from the house because now Faust does wish to see her again. Instead, it is a furious Valentin who bursts out into the street with drawn sword. He shatters the guitar, demanding satisfaction from whomever seduced his sister. In a vigorous trio, the men express themselves: Valentin's outrage, an affronted Faust, and Mephistopheles bemused. In a duel between Valentin and Faust, the latter, with the devil's help, mortally wounds the former. As Faust and Mephistopheles run off, Marthe and other neighbors come running to the side of Valentin, hearing him curse his sister with his final breath as the act ends.

I have a recording of Faust in which the long fifth-act ballet is omitted. When performed or recorded without the ballet, the story often is rearranged into four acts. Do not spend your money on a *Faust* whose ballet is cut. The Act II *Kermesse* dance scene was not substantial enough to meet the Paris Opera ballet requirement, so when, ten years after the opera's premiere at the Théâtre-Lyrique in 1859, Gounod revised his opera for this house, he added an extended ballet of more than twenty minutes to open Act V.

Yes, it does interrupt the dramatic flow of Mephistopheles' malicious manipulation of the ill-fated love of Marguerite and Faust, but you don't want to miss this music. For me, Gounod's *Faust* is not Gounod's *Faust* without it! To provide a plot for the ballet, librettists Barbier and Carré dipped into Part Two of Goethe's drama and extricated from it the Walpurgis Night (eve of

May first) episode wherein witches and demons hold a sabbath high in the Harz Mountains invoked by a will-o'-the wisp chorus. Faust and Mepistopheles are present. Famed courtesans of antiquity, in one enticing dance after the other, appear. Faust and the devil drink pleasurably until, all of a sudden, a vision of Marguerite in a prison cell confronts the young man, who sees a thin red line around her neck. Is it a ribbon or is it a wound? He demands to be taken immediately to her and a brief orchestral intermezzo accompanies the change of scenery to a prison cell. Marguerite is asleep. In an insane moment, she killed her child and has been condemned to die.

Upon entering the cell, Faust dismisses Mephistopheles and awakens Marguerite. Though she recognizes him, as their animated duet recounts their meeting and falling in love, her mind wanders, thus foiling Faust's plan to implement her escape. Mephistopheles returns and attempts to aid Faust, but Marguerite, having entered another world, prays for her salvation. The climax is my favorite trio in all French opera. Marguerite ecstatically implores an angelic host to help her, repulsing both Faust and Mephistopheles as her lover cries out her name and the devil proclaims her damned. A great angelic *Sauvée* ("Saved") refutes him. As Faust falls to his knees and Mephistopheles cowers beneath the sword of the archangel, the soul of Marguerite is carried up into heaven as a chorus of angels sings the Easter hymn of Christ's resurrection and the curtain falls.

The religious substance of this scene has nothing to do with its great appeal for me. It is solely the glorious music. In the final trio, the central voices of the drama combine with chorus and orchestra in a miracle of sound. In Gounod's *Faust* the Marguerite is a lyric soprano of pure, unwaveringly beautiful tone; Faust's tenor, impassioned and radiant throughout; and the demonic bass of Mephistopheles—devious, derisive, and malicious—must be a powerful voice encompassing various moods, at times biting or sneering, at others bold and beautiful. I hear all the above on the remastered compact disc of the famous 1959 recording featuring the Spanish soprano Victoria de los Angeles, the Swedish tenor of Russian origin Nicolai Gedda, and the Bulgarian basso Boris Christoff.

❧

The underlying theme of the opera, the triumph of Christianity over satanic forces, is too obvious to warrant elaboration. With

Faust under your feet, consider also Gounod's *Romeo et Juliette*. The music is lovely: Some even prefer it to the more famous *Faust*.

GEORGES BIZET

CARMEN (1875)

How do I write about *Carmen*, to many the best opera there is? Even the beginner, thinking he or she knows nothing about opera, must have heard about the seductive gypsy girl who is the central character in what may be the most popular opera in the world. Popularity usually does not jibe with excellence. Taste in food, clothes, literature, movies, and music of popular culture often offends those who spend a lifetime trying to fathom the wonders of great art in any of its many forms. And, as already noted in this book, popularity in opera sometimes is pooh-poohed by aficionados whose level of acceptance generally is far above common appreciation. Bizet's *Carmen*, however, continues to receive high praise from experts, even from numerous great composers sharing little or nothing else in common—Brahms, Wagner, Puccini, and Stravinsky being four who expressed unrestricted approval (or envy). And, of course, there is the universal public that never tires of this captivating, tune-filled masterpiece.

The entire score, from the opening note, the cymbals resounding, to the twice-repeated tragic chord that closes the final curtain before the lifeless body of Carmen, has been a basic ingredient throughout my life. My father had multiple recordings of the famous arias by different singers both for enjoyment and for comparative study, and he and his colleagues often rehearsed these arias in our music room. If the next few pages help you to share Carmen's swirling, fiery world of fickle passions with an increasing fascination, I will be a happy man.

A few words pertaining to proper pronunciation is a good place to start. I know how intimidating correct operatic pronunciation can be, but with some help and practice you can master it. *Carmen* is so popular an opera that you can't avoid talking about it. In English the title character almost always is called CAR-mun, even by the experts. Listening carefully to a recording, you will hear her name is CAR-MEN, the two syllables at the least receiving equal accentuation, if not slightly favoring the second. Try it, and if you can roll the *r* a little, all the better. One of my favorite recordings of this opera is by native French singers of the famous L'Opéra-Comique de Paris (with the spoken dialogue that I much prefer to the recitatives version . . . more on this below. If any company would get it right, they would. In Act II, after the "Toreador Song," Escamillo asks Carmen what her name is. "CAR-MEN, or CAR-MEN-SEE-TUH," she replies. There is no CAR-mun. Distinguish yourself by pronouncing her name correctly. Do not those immortal operatic women Carmen, Tosca, Brünnhilde, Aïda, and so many others deserve to have their names pronounced properly? The tenor lead, who loves Carmen uncontrollably, is Don José and his name is pronounced DON JOE-ZAY, not DON HOSE-AY, because, even though he is Spanish, the opera was written in French.

Here are all the characters and their voices:

> CARMEN, a seductive Gypsy girl, *mezzo-soprano*; the role,
> however, has such great appeal that many sopranos
> have made it their own
> DON JOSÉ, a corporal from Navarre in love with Carmen,
> *tenor*
> MICAELA, a peasant girl from Navarre, *soprano*
> ESCAMILLO, a matador, *baritone*
> ZUNIGA, an officer, *bass*
> MORALES, an officer, *baritone*
> EL DANCAIRO, a smuggler, *baritone*
> EL REMENDADO, a smuggler, *tenor*
> FRASQUITA, a gypsy, *soprano*
> MERCÉDÈS, a gypsy, *soprano*
> An innkeeper, soldiers, boys, cigarette girls, townspeople

The setting is in and around Seville in 1920.

Bizet's *Carmen* is based on Prosper Mérimée's novella of the same title. The libretto, by Henri Meilhac and Ludovic Halévy (related to Bizet by marriage), is regarded as one of the finest ever produced. Meilhac and Halévy had sought to soften the baseness of a lowlife world of lying, cheating, and casual love affairs but Bizet firmly insisted on retaining *Carmen's* uninhibited, antisocial, hedonistic instincts in which even death is preferable to the loss of freedom. Mérimée's novella could not be adapted to the stage without alterations and additions. It was here the librettists contributed so much to establishing the opera's extraordinary dramatic balance, a balance achieved in giving to the four central characters obvious similarities or vivid contrasts. They were to collaborate successfully for other composers, especially Offenbach, but nothing matches the brilliance of this text.

Because they wrote the story for the Opéra-Comique (remember, this does not imply comic opera but rather an opera with spoken words), the dialogue is of critical importance. This is how Bizet intended his work to be performed. His pupil and friend Ernest Guiraud, nevertheless, accepted the request of an Austrian opera house to make a version with recitatives to musical accompaniment of his own invention after Bizet died. Beyond the world of French opera houses it was this version, for more than seventy-five years, by which *Carmen* came to be known and loved by the world. During the last half century, Bizet's original intent finally has been honored more and more, both on recordings and in the opera house. Today it's a toss-up as to which version you'll get. Even though Guiraud's well-intended 1875 version opened the door to universal acceptance and popularity, the version with spoken dialogue is superior and is the form in which you should meet the opera.

On the night of the thirty-first performance of his opera, Bizet, only thirty-six years old, died. On March 3, 1875, *Carmen* had been presented to a public accustomed to the family-oriented productions of the Opéra-Comique, Paris. The lurid, amoral vulgarity of this opera shocked the audience and fueled a hostile press. Almost no one had anything positive to say. No one, that is, except Tchaikovsky, who attended a performance after Bizet's death and predicted that within ten years *Carmen* would be the best-known opera in the world, a judgment nearly right on the money.

Each of the four characters has at least one aria wherein his or her essential nature is revealed in words and music. Carmen, in her famous entrance song (here Bizet wrote both words and music), warns all of her seductive, wild, and true-only-to-her-own-whims morality. "Micaela's Air" in the third act is the pious, pure resolve of a peasant girl in love with Don José. She was not in Mérimée's story, but rather was created by the librettists in order to place José in the middle between Micaela's rational, traditional values of fidelity, family, and home and the irrational, irresistible appeal of the alluring, provocative Carmen. In his second-act "Flower Song," José relates the extent of her inexorable hold on his helpless emotions. Escamillo's "Toreador Song" may be the most universally known tune in the opera. In this "entrance song," we meet the handsome, sexy bullfighter, the sensual masculine counterpart to Carmen and, accordingly, the inevitable threat to José's happiness. Meilhac and Halévy gave him a far more prominent part than that given by Mérimée to Lucas, the matador of the original story.

Carmen is in four acts. When lecturing to my classes I would say that the entire story can be told by simply stating the significant event of each act: Boy meets girl, boy gets girl, girl jilts boy, and boy kills girl. My students knew I could not leave it at that, of course.

Act I

The brief musical prelude, perhaps now the most familiar in all operatic literature, begins with a joyful section of carefree, exotic spontaneity that includes the swaggering melody of the "Toreador's Song," followed by a tense foreboding and, finally, in a third segment, a theme associated with immutable destiny. Seamlessly, the music becomes the first chorus sung by soldiers standing in front of a guardhouse, aimlessly commenting on those strolling about a square in Seville.

Opposite the guardhouse is a tobacco factory. A pretty young woman, looking for Don José, asks Morales where to find him. The officer explains he will soon arrive with the changing of the guard and invites her to pass the time with him. She declines, saying she will return later, and hastily departs. Trumpets announce the change of guard, which arrives followed by a marching corps of ragamuffins proudly imitating the soldiers. Morales speaks of a visitor to José, who deduces it was Micaela. As the guard changes, the boys file away with the old guard singing their trumpetlike *ta ra-ta tas*.

Zuniga, new to the post and alone with José, asks about the tobacco factory and the girls who work there. José explains that several hundred of them roll cigars. He pays no attention to them, however, because of the pretty, teenage orphan girl, taken in by his mother in Navarre, who came looking for him. Zuniga understands.

The factory bell rings recess, the square fills with people, and the cigarette girls, each smoking a cigarette, arrive singing of the pleasures of smoking and of how "the sweet talk of lovers" also is only "smoke." The first audiences attending *Carmen* were shocked by this scene. Bizet's music "sounds" like smoke swirling into a hazy cloud above the heads of the seductive women flitting from man to man until Carmen, the last to come out, appears. Upon her all men, except José, who pays no attention to what is transpiring, rivet rapt attention and ask in unison, "On which day will you love us?" Carmen responds, "When will I love you? God knows but I do not. Perhaps never! Perhaps tomorrow! But not today, that's for sure." With chorus she sings her entrance song (a habanera) as she whirls past the men in a tantalizing dance focusing her allure on the still unresponsive Don José.

A habanera is a Cuban dance in moderate tempo of Spanish origin. Not often danced today, it is an ancestor of the Argentine tango and was popular in Europe during Bizet's time. Bizet's habanera, the most well-known version of this dance, was his adaptation of a song by a Spanish-American composer, Sebastián Yradier, who would be forgotten had not Bizet's version so vastly improved the original, thus according him some sort of immortality by association. In acknowledging his indebtedness, Bizet used the word "imitated" in his score.

Bizet knew precisely what first impression *Carmen* must make in both words and music. The song not only forcefully makes that impression but it also prompts one to wonder what might happen to one who becomes smitten with Carmen.

The Habanera (*"L'amour est un oiseau rebelle"*), Carmen with chorus:

> Love is a rebellious bird
> no one can tame
> and you'll call in vain
> if it says no!
> Nothing, neither threats nor prayer, will help;
> one man's eloquent, another silent
> and he's the one I prefer:
> he says nothing but he pleases me.
> Love . . . love . . .
> Love is a gypsy child
> who knows no laws;
> if you don't love me, I love you,
> if I love you, then you better beware!
> The bird you thought you caught
> flapped its wings and flew away . . .
> When love is far away you must wait for it,
> then, when you wait no more, there it is . . .

> All around you so fast
> it comes, departs, and returns again
> and when you think you have it, it is gone
> but when you believe it gone, it holds you tight.
> Love . . . love . . .
> Love is a gypsy child [etcetera]

In her song on the nature of love, Carmen has revealed herself as fickle, rebellious, knowing no laws, ultimately unobtainable, and preferring a man who keeps his mouth shut. Nevertheless, the adoring men gather about her, pressing for an answer. She struts from one to another, gazing into their eyes. She stops in front of Don José, takes a flower from her corsage, throws it at him, and, as the factory bell rings the end of the work break, is the first to run into the building. The crowd disperses, the soldiers remove to the guardhouse, and José, alone now, comments as he stares at the flower, "All that because I wasn't paying attention to her . . ." He picks up the flower, saying, "With what skill she threw this at me, right between the eyes, hitting me like a bullet." He smells the flower: "The scent . . . Ah, if there is a sorceress, this girl is one." The scene can be comprehended and José's future anticipated even if not one word of French is understood, but this libretto is so well conceived it would be a shame to neglect it.

Enter, Micaela! Right upon Carmen's heels—her absolute opposite except, of course, that she too is quite pretty in a "girl-next-door" sort of way. José hides the flower as she appears. She has been sent by his mother. Their lovely, long duet, *Parle-moi de ma mère* ("Tell me about my mother") begins. Micaela has been sent with a letter, some extra money, and . . . demurely, she pauses. José presses her to continue. His mother had given Micaela a kiss to give to her son. The kiss, innocent and maternal, stirs within José memories of his home and how even now, from afar, his mother protects him from falling prey to a demon. Micaela does not understand but we do! José asks her to tell his mother of his love for her and he gives the girl a kiss for his mother. He then begins to read aloud the letter. When it introduces the subject of marriage, suggesting, of course, the virtuous young girl as the perfect choice, Micaela begs off to go to the store. She will return later for his answer. Finishing the letter, José acknowledges compliance with his mother's wishes but as he is dismissing the bewitchment of the flower-throwing gypsy, a frightening commotion within the tobacco factory interrupts him.

Cigarette girls exit the factory to confront the soldiers with conflicting stories of a savage fight prompted by an exchange of base insults between Carmen and another worker. Zuniga sends José and two soldiers to investigate while other soldiers attempt to control the agitated girls. As they clear the square, restoring order, José returns with Carmen to report that she cut a cross in the face of another girl with a knife. Carmen protests that it was in "self-defense," but when asked by Zuniga for an explanation she replies, with brazen musical brilliance and effrontery, "Tra la la la la la la, I'll tell you nothing." José is ordered to bind her hands while Zuniga goes to write a warrant for her arrest. For the first time she is alone with the corporal from Navarre.

Boldly, Carmen suggests he let her escape, offering a bribe and predicting it will be because he loves her. He stammers. I know you kept the flower, she says, and its spell is working. When he forbids her to speak to him, she pretends to sing a gypsy song to herself, but it is intended to seduce José. This is her famous *Seguidilla*. (A seguidilla is a dance of southern Spain, particularly Seville, of which Bizet's is an atypical example.) Nonetheless, it is Carmen's second world famous aria of the first act. Dancing, she begins to sing *Près des ramparts de Séville* ("Near the ramparts of Seville"). Her erotic motions, penetrating glances, and provocative words are too much for poor José. She will now take a new lover, the song goes on, perhaps an officer in love with her, and

> near the ramparts of Seville
> at the tavern of my friend Lillas Pastia
> I will dance the seguidilla
> and drink manzanilla . . .

José, by now captured by her evocative spell, unties the cord so as to leave the impression it is fast. Zuniga returns with a warrant and instructions to take her to jail and to guard her carefully. In an aside to José, Carmen quickly outlines her escape. As she is being led away, Carmen, face to face mocks Zuniga with the "Love is a gypsy child" stanza from her *Habanera*. Then, as she reaches the outskirts of the square, she throws off the cord, shoves José, who feigns a fall, and races to freedom as cigarette girls rush from the reassembled crowd to swarm about Zuniga with shouts of laughter. The curtain closes on the first act.

Act II

Two months have passed when the curtain rises after a brief orchestral prelude establishing the mood for late-night cama-raderie in the tavern of Lillas Pastia. There, Carmen, as promised, awaits Don José. With her friends Frasquita and Mercédès *tra la la*-ing at appropriate moments, she performs yet another beguiling dance song, the tantalizing *Les tringles des sistres tintaient* ("The bars of the sistrum jingle") known as the "Gypsy Song." It rises to a pitch of excitement as the gypsy girls whirl, Carmen clicking her castanets. (I had never seen anyone dance to clicking castanets before I went to *Carmen* the first time so many years ago. I was mesmerized by Rïse Stevens's performance with the Metropolitan Opera Company and years later when I had an opportunity to meet this great American mezzo-soprano, told her so. Her remas-tered performances are on CD.)

Lillas Pastia warns the soldiers of closing time. Before depart-ing, Zuniga mentions to Carmen that Don José, imprisoned for allowing her to escape, was freed yesterday. Hearty cheers offstage interrupt the closing of the tavern. It is a torchlight parade honor-ing the famous matador Escamillo, who over the innkeeper's remonstrations is invited for a drink. The bullfighter returns their toast with one of his own: *Votre toast, je peux vous rendre* ("I can return your toast"), he sings in the celebrated "Toreador Song." Combat is the business of both soldiers and bullfighters; his song describes the events of the bullfight. The first verse ends with "two dark eyes promising love" watch the matador. Carmen refills his glass. The second verse anticipates the kill as Escamil-lo's fancy footwork beneath his huge, scarlet cape re-creates the atmosphere of the ring. Lillas insists on closing and the song ends with a repeat of the chorus "two dark eyes promising love," the voices of the bullfighter and the gypsy girl rising above the others as they iterate and reiterate the word *love.*

Uh-oh! While waiting for her tryst with José, Carmen and Escamillo, two sides of the same coin, by chance—or call it des-tiny—find themselves standing side by side. He asks her name, promising to utter it the next time he kills a bull. She tells him. He certainly is not shy. His second question wonders if they might become lovers. To her "Not now" he responds, "I'll wait." Zuni-ga also makes his pitch and promises, against Carmen's protesta-tions, to return in an hour to see her.

When I consider operatic quintets, the first two in my mind are from Act III of Wagner's *Die Meistersinger* and Act II of Bizet's

Carmen: the first for its serene beauty, the second for its unique melodic, comic ingenuity. Pastia's inn, now closed to the public, is headquarters for a rendezvous of gypsy smugglers. El Dancairo and El Remendado attempt to enlist help from Frasquita, Mercédès, and Carmen: "When it comes to cheating, cozening, thieving, it is good to have women along; without them nothing good is ever done." But Carmen, uncharacteristically, refuses reluctantly, confessing that she waits for a soldier with whom she is now in love, and love has priority over duty. She will join them the next day.

We hear Don José singing in the distance. They meet, he declares his love, and she begins to dance for him erotically, humming and clicking her castanets. Bugles sound retreat, first far away, then outside the inn. José interrupts this seductive private performance by informing Carmen that he must report to quarters for roll call. She is livid. She mocks him, imitating the bugle call, and denounces his love for her as false. Denying this, José insists she listen to him as he sings the "Flower Song." *La fleur que tu m'avais jetée* ("The flower that you threw me") he has kept while in prison. In this passionate revelation José, caressing the flower, tells Carmen he is helpless in his love for her. If you love me, she tempts in her reply, you will go away with me to the exhilarating life of freedom in the mountains.

He cannot contemplate desertion and is attempting to leave her forever when Zuniga barges in, asks Carmen if she would prefer an officer to a common soldier, and orders José to his barracks. A fight commences but Carmen steps between the rivals as her renegade friends, now on the scene, disarm Zuniga and take him away at pistol point. Realizing he now is one of them, José joins Carmen and her gypsy smugglers, whose song caroling the intoxicating lure of a life of liberty in the mountains ends the second act.

All music in *Carmen* is wonderful but the second act . . . WOW! "The Gypsy Song," the "Toreador's Song," the quintet, Carmen's dance, the "Flower Song," and more—is it any wonder why this opera remains as popular and often performed and recorded as any other opera in the world?

Act III

A lovely prelude precedes Act III, which is set in a wild, remote, rocky place where smugglers transporting their contraband sing a lilting chorus in anticipation of their riches. It is night and they rest. José and Carmen have a spat. His possessiveness irks her and when she suggests they part, a most critical exchange occurs:

> *Don José*: If you speak to me again of us
> separating . . .
> *Carmen*: . . . you'd kill me, perhaps?

Carmen leaves him to join her friends Frasquita and Mercédès. She tells their future with cards by the light of a warming fire. This card scene is one of Bizet's most inspired episodes in an opera whose cup runneth over with inspiration. Frasquita foresees fortune, Mercédès love, and Carmen? Death! ". . . me first, then him" in this fantastic trio incorporating Carmen's soliloquy on immutable destiny. Dancairo summons his troops to move on in execution of their plan, leaving behind Don José to guard their camp.

Micaela now appears in the mountain wilderness. Seeking José, she has been directed to this spot by a guide, who hastily departs. Micaela's *Air*, a most beautiful and profound aria, is an extraordinary contrast to the songs of Carmen. The young peasant girl gathers courage from prayer to confront the dangers of this remote place and, even more, her confrontation with the beautiful temptress for whom José has so thoroughly dishonored himself. She sees him and calls out but he does not hear. He is taking aim at an intruder. He fires and almost wings him. Micaela hides as Escamillo enters. His duet with José reveals they both love Carmen and will fight for her. Out come knives. With the calm bravado of one steeled in the bullring, the matador successfully has parried every thrust when he slips and falls. José is about to pounce on him to strike a mortal blow when he is restrained by Carmen, who has arrived at this critical moment. The fight, at least temporarily, is over. Dancairo separates the men and dismisses Escamillo, who, in parting, invites them to the bullfights in Seville. Looking only at Carmen he says, "Whoever loves me will come."

Remendado brings forth Micaela, whom he has discovered in hiding. She asks José to return home to his unhappy mother. Carmen says, "Go . . . our work is not for you." He refuses. In his mind, their fates are enmeshed until death. But when Micaela reveals his mother is dying he relents, promising to return to Carmen. As the voice of the bullfighter is heard from afar singing of those "two dark eyes promising love," Carmen tries to run to him but is thwarted by José, who then leaves with Micaela as the curtain falls.

Act IV

Because the fourth act is brief, twenty minutes or less, some performances present the opera in three acts with another ever so familiar entr'acte (music, usually instrumental, played between the acts) providing time for a change of scene. Every entr'acte in Carmen perfectly "sets the stage" for the action to follow. The more usual, and preferred presentation, plays the entr'acte as a prelude to the final, fourth act. The curtain opens on another square in Seville, showing the entrance to the bullring. Vendors hawk their wares to the milling crowd wherein Zuniga, Frasquita, and Mercédès converse. We learn Carmen is now attached to Escamillo and José is being hunted for arrest. Frasquita shudders for Carmen.

From beyond the square youthful shouts announce the arrival of the bullfighters. Led by the excited children, a grand procession enters the square. Bizet's music is so infectious that if you are not stirred, there simply is no hope at all for you and opera ever to be friends. Before they enter the stadium, Escamillo and Carmen profess their love. Frasquita and Mercédès, having spotted Don José hiding in the crowd, are gravely concerned for Carmen. They urge her to leave. She is not afraid. She will wait for José to tell him something.

The crowd follows the procession into the stadium. José appears before Carmen and pleads with her to return to him. Thus begins the great final duet. "It's over between us," she asserts. Cheers from within the stadium resound and Carmen attempts to leave. Stopping her, José begs her to go with him. She refuses, admitting she now loves Escamillo. José tries to force her to go with him. She won't, not even in the face of death. As victory shouts fill the air, in a violent gesture she throws at him the ring he had given her. It recalls the episode of the flower in the first act. José grabs Carmen and stabs her. She falls to the ground and dies. Cheers for the victorious matador ring out as José falls sobbing upon her body. As a refrain of the "Toreador Song," sung by all, tells of those "two dark eyes promising love," Escamillo enters the square surrounded by Zuniga, Frasquita, and Mercédès to look upon Carmen dead on the ground. Don José gets up.

> *Vous pouvez m'arrêter . . .*
> *C'est moi qui l'ai tuée!*
> *Ma Carmen adorée.*

> You can arrest me . . .
> I killed her!
> My beloved Carmen.

The curtain falls.

Two words are dominant in this opera. They are *love* and *death*. Not only are they inextricably linked in the drama, but they are also linked intimately, in the French language, by sound. *Love* in French, *l'amour*, is pronounced la-moo-er. *Death* in French, *la mort*, is pronounced la-more. You must listen carefully!

And now I have answered my own question, "How do I write about *Carmen*?" At great length. I cannot help it. I love this opera so much and I want you to love it as well. There are many good recordings and videos for you to start with, but my students of many generations, both graduate and undergraduate, enthusiastically recommend the 1984 film version with Julia Migenes as Carmen and Placido Domingo as Don José. It was shot on location in Andalusian Spain. In every way—scenically, theatrically, and musically—it is captivating. Lauren, my granddaughter, at age six, before she could read the subtitles, watched it nonstop.

Bizet wrote other operas before *Carmen*, *Les pêcheurs de perles (The Pearl Fishers)* being the most familiar. It has a fine tenor aria and the most beautiful duet for tenor and baritone in all opera: *Au fond du temple saint* ("In the Depths of the Holy Temple"), known as the "Friendship Duet." Great tenor/baritone combinations from the early gramophone days, Caruso and Scotti and McCormack and Sammarco, to the best singers of today make this duet a staple of their recordings. For me the standard by which all others must be measured was made in 1950 by Jussi Björling and Robert Merrill. I can hear the warmth of their close off-stage friendship when they portray friends on the stage. I know of those who consider this duet the supreme expression of Bizet's gift. For more than twenty-seven years, it has been the number one request on my "Saturday Afternoon at the Opera" on Vermont Public Radio. One is left to muse on what else might have come forth from Bizet's pen had he not died in his thirty-sixth year.

⁀

CAMILLE SAINT-SAËNS

SAMSON ET DALILA (1877)
Samson and Delilah

Camille Saint-Saëns perhaps had the longest musical career of all the great composers. Born in 1835, he died eighty-six years later in 1921 having composed almost two hundred works of an astonishing variety: symphonies, concerti for various instruments, symphonic poems, cantatas, oratorios, songs, choral works, a ballet, incidental music, piano and organ music, operettas, and operas. He was a child prodigy, playing the piano by his third year and composing his first little waltzes at five. Unlike those who became composers in spite of parental opposition, Saint-Saëns's mother wanted nothing more than that he become a great musician. His father, who had died when Camille was two months old, left sufficient funds to meet all family needs, a good musical education being paramount.

Saint-Saëns was ten when he first performed in public. He played a piano concerto by Mozart. At thirteen, he was enrolled in a music conservatory. I find my favorite story about him in the pages of Richard Wagner's autobiography. Wagner was immensely impressed by the skill and talent of this young musician, who, with a glance, could memorize a complicated orchestral score. Even more, Wagner's huge ego obviously must have been stroked when Saint-Saëns played music from his *Tristan und Isolde* on the piano by heart. Years later Saint-Saëns would say, in one of two of his most frequently quoted statements, that composing for him merely fulfilled a natural function in the same way an apple tree bears apples. The other, a pronouncement, I respect completely. He said that there is nothing more difficult than talking about music.

Saint-Saëns was not a reforming or revolutionary musician intent upon either correcting or altering the course of music history. Classical restraint was his trademark. For him, form was art. In this sense, his ultimate appeal would be to other musicians who were fully aware of his uncompromising mastery of basic musical structures. He had no interest in writing music of intense emotional content to bowl over an audience or to leave them limp under the effect of passionate outpourings. He sought elegance in his melodic lines, a variety of harmonious instrumental colors, and beautiful choral sequences expressed in perfectly constructed musical forms. Compared to his contemporaries, drunk with the elixir of romanticism, his music may seem cold and unemotional. I suggest, however, in a careful listening to *Samson et Dalila*—his only opera of thirteen to remain in repertory—you will hear precise characterizations of the two central characters, both intimate and angry, and the remarkable sensuality of the music as it authentically evokes exotic, Oriental moods and atmospheres so much in vogue with French composers of that time.

Samson et Dalila was begun in 1868 as an oratorio but ended six years later as an opera—perhaps because the surest way to fame and fortune for a composer in France of this time was to achieve an operatic success. The first performance was brought about, however, in Wiemar by the composer's friend Franz Liszt on December 2, 1877. Because of its biblical subject matter, the opera had been banned in Paris.

Operas based on biblical stories are rare: *Salome* by Richard Strauss, *Moses und Aron* by Schoenberg, and *Samson et Dalila* being the most familiar. The ban against Saint-Saëns's opera is interesting because Samson's story, as told in the Bible (Judg. 14–16), has limited significant Jewish or indeed any other religious content. He is a hero of early Hebrew folklore whose exploits are similar to pagan counterparts, the myths of Hercules and Gilgamesh, for example. The biblical myth of Samson contains elements of ancient solar mythology found in several cultures. Above all, his long hair, in which lies the secret of phenomenal strength, symbolic of the sun's rays, is common to other solar heroes of primitive times. Ferdinand Lemaire (you will not meet him again) made a good libretto out of the biblical story, Saint-Saëns made for it wonderful music of great appeal unto this day, and that's that. To approach this opera as if it were sacred music is to go astray, and to ban a production for religious reasons is to have missed the boat. Its religious implications are limited, far fewer than those of other operas that were never banned.

The opera is in three acts. The characters:

DALILA (Delilah), a beautiful Philistine woman, *mezzo-soprano*
SAMSON, a powerful Hebrew hero, *tenor*
High priest of Dagon, *baritone*
ABIMELECH, satrap of Gaza, *bass*

An old Hebrew, *bass*
Philistine messenger, *tenor*
Hebrews and Philistines

The setting is ancient Gaza.

The plot of *Samson and Delilah*, based on a biblical folktale, is neither complicated nor profound. The most terse synopsis I know is the popular Peter, Paul, and Mary recording of "If I Had My Way." The few bars (units of musical measure) heard before the curtain opens on the first act are an introduction to a remarkable behind-the-scenes choral lamentation. Suffering subjugation under the Philistines, voices of the Hebrews join with the orchestra in a prayer for pity to the God of Israel.

Act I
The curtains part on Scene 1. It's night in a public square in Gaza, Palestine, where Hebrews, Samson among them, have gathered to pray. Their prayers for the deliverance from enslavement by the Philistines have gone unanswered. They all despair except for Samson, who, in the aria *Arrêtez, ô mes frères!* ("O, cease, my brethren"), claims to have heard the promise of freedom from their god. The doubting Hebrews are not convinced. Samson reminds them of their past, most notably, the delivery through the Red Sea. Skepticism prevails, however, until he demands they faithfully implore God once more to rescue them. Becoming convinced that the Lord is working through him, the people agree to follow Samson.

Abimelech and Philistine soldiers enter, responding with annoyance to the commotion of rebellious slaves who think their god superior to the great god Dagon. An inspired Samson reveals his vision of deliverance through the wrath of the God of Israel. Abimelech, considering him a madman, orders him to stop but Samson persists and calls upon the Hebrews to rise up and break free of their shackles. With this, Abimelech lunges at Samson with his sword, but the fearless Hebrew grabs it and slays his foe, who, with his dying words, calls for help. (The part of Abimelech is a brief one: one aria and he is done for.) The Philistines join the fray. Samson fends them off and in the prevailing confusion the Hebrews escape.

The scene changes to the gates of the temple of Dagon. The high priest of Dagon rebukes the Philistines for allowing the escape and orders pursuit. The Philistines attempt to explain how some inexplicable force seemed to render them helpless against Samson and his followers. A messenger arrives to report a ravaging of the harvest by the Hebrews led, of course, by Samson. The infuriated high priest will have revenge in an aria of curses that includes, prophetically, a denunciation of ". . . the breast of the woman who gave him [Samson] life," followed by the hope that ultimately ". . . an infamous love may betray his love." The aria concludes with a curse upon the god of Israel, and he departs with the Philistine soldiers, who take with them the body of Abimelech.

Day is dawning as the Hebrews enter, now victorious over their enemy. As old men sing a joyful hymn, the warriors, with Samson leading them, arrive. Soon thereafter, from out of the temple, Delilah comes with an entourage of maidens carrying garlands to crown the victors. Her first aria is an intimate song to Samson of erotic invitations. She is there to celebrate the victory of "him who reigns in my heart" and he is invited to follow her to her dwelling for a feast of love. Her famous seduction has begun with her first words (interspersed with Samson's asides fearing capitulation and warnings to him from an old Hebrew man to avoid this woman at all costs). The French word *coeur* (heart) is central to the opera. Delilah just tempted Samson by telling him he "reigns in her heart" and in his first aside, reacting to her wiles, he begs God, "Close my eyes, shut my heart to the sweet voice tempting me." As Delilah persists, the old Hebrew's admonitions intensify but the hero's resolve is weakening. It is *la douce voix* ("the sweet voice") that is irresistible to Samson—and to us, too, when Delilah is sung by a mezzo-soprano with rich, evocative, and melodic tones (first to my mind are the recordings of Italians Ebe Stignani and Giulietta Simionato, the Belgian Rita Gorr, and Americans Rïse Stevens and Shirley Verrett). If ever a composer was able to translate exotic seductiveness into music, it was Saint-Saëns in the role he wrote for Delilah. This opera falls flat if the Delilah cannot deliver the goods.

For the pleasure of the Hebrew warriors, the Philistine girls dance enticingly, Delilah joining them. She aims a succession of seductive poses, one after the other, exclusively at Samson, who fails utterly in his attempt not to follow her every move. The act concludes with a bewitching aria, *Printemps qui commence* ("Spring that comes"), wherein Delilah promises to keep "a burning love" kindled for Samson. He says nothing but his entire attitude, his gestures and expressions, tell the whole story: He is under her spell when the curtain falls. What music!

Act II

During the first act, in which the imprisoned Hebrews successfully revolt and overwhelm the Philistines, night symbolically yields to day. When the Act II curtain rises on Delilah's house, set among luxurious liana vines in the Sorek Valley of Palestine, it is dusk. As the act plays symbolically, night will fall upon the seduction and betrayal of Samson. Night-and-day (dark-and-light) symbolism is a constant in many operas; indeed, it is in all art. Another demanding aria for Delilah follows the Act II prelude, yet another example of why this Philistine beauty must be portrayed by a singer with a rich, lusty mezzo-soprano voice. Alone, seated on a rock near her house, she muses on her intent to utilize her provocative feminine powers to subdue Samson's strength and to return him to fetters by dawn. She hates the man who has attacked both her people and her god. She expects him soon, for she knows he cannot banish her from his heart. She will have revenge. And he will yield, too; the strongest of the strong will be no match for her. This aria, *Amour! viens aider ma faiblesse* ("Love! Come to assist my frailty"), concludes with Delilah's low, penetrating chest tones on the words "he will succumb."

The high priest enters. Guided by Dagon to Delilah to convince her to use her seductive powers to entrap Samson, he finds her predisposed to do so. His visit serves only to increase her resolve. Their pact is proclaimed in a powerful duet. His last words to her before departing are "Strip from his heart the invulnerable shield and discover the hidden secret of his strength."

Alone and leaning against one of the pillars of her house in a dreamy, speculative posture, Delilah wonders why Samson has not come to her. Could it be that "love has lost its power over his heart"? As darkness intensifies and ominous, distant lightning streaks the sky, he arrives, hesitant and obviously agitated. In spite of himself he has returned to "this place that in my weakness I adore." Delilah runs to him with endearments. He utters a feeble attempt to resist. The long, famous duet of seduction and capitulation, the core of this act, has begun. The word *heart* again is pivotal. Let us follow its course.

Delilah asks why he repulsed her as she draws him close to her. He confesses that she remains "always dear to my heart." She asks if he could ever doubt her "heart." He tells her he has come only to say farewell because the God of Israel has chosen him to lead his people. She responds: "What does my disconsolate heart care for the glory of Israel?" He proclaims his love. (That was easy!) Lightning strikes. Delilah continues telling him that a god greater than his speaks to him through her mouth. It is her god, the god of love. She bids him recall to his heart the pleasures of their past. He is helpless. Lightning strikes closer as again he proclaims his love for her. Her reply is the most famous music of the score and one of the monuments in the literature of French opera:

> *Mon coeur s'ouvre à ta voix comme s'ouvrent les*
> *fleurs*
> *Aux baisers de l'aurore!*

> My heart opens to your voice as the flowers open
> To the kisses of dawn.

Will he stay with her fluttering heart? Their voices join ecstatically. With his kisses he wants to dry her tears and remove all concerns from her heart. Thunder and lightning. But she is unhappy. She wants proof. She is jealous of the hold his god has on him. She demands his trust. Nearer still, thunder and lightning. What does the sacred bond with his god, the secret hidden in his heart, matter to her, he wonders aloud. The storm strengthens. She implores. He won't yield; the thunderbolt is the voice of his god. Enraged, she despises his "loveless heart" and storms into her house as the other storm reaches its peak. Samson raises his arms to the sky, an apparent invocation. He starts to follow Delilah, hesitates, then races into her house after her as Philistine soldiers furtively approach and surround Delilah's home. Claps of thunder resound. She reappears and summons the soldiers. Samson's cry of *Trahison!* ("Betrayed!") prompts the closing of the curtain as the soldiers rush into the house.

Act III
The third act opens at night in the Gaza prison. A miserable, blinded Samson laboriously turns a millstone. His hair has been shorn. His self-reproach, "my guilty, wretched heart," for example, is expressed in a powerful aria: *Vois ma misère, hélas!* ("See my misery, alas"). He is joined by a chorus of Hebrew prisoners who blame him for their return to bondage. Philistine soldiers enter the prison and drag Samson away.

The scene changes to the interior of the temple of Dagon, a huge stone structure whose roof is supported by two giant columns. The high priest and Philistine princes enter, followed by Delilah leading maidens crowned with flowers and carrying goblets. Day dawns as the Philistines praise the power of love. Next, the orchestral interlude that anyone who knows the opera awaits with edge-of-his-seat anticipation. It is the celebrated Bacchanale heard in concert halls around the world and on countless recordings. It is music, once heard, that you will want to indulge in again and again. A highlight of the entire score, its intoxicating, evocative music is unlike any other opera music known to me, so marvelously expressive of the hedonistic indulgences portrayed.

As Samson is led in by a child, he is taunted as the "Judge of Israel" by the high priest, who summons Delilah to give her lover a cup of mead. All toast Samson, who, in an aside, calls upon his god to allow him to fulfill his destiny. Cup in hand, Delilah approaches Samson and sings triumphantly of her victory over him. Samson is contrite, the high priest persists in his scoffing, and the Philistines laugh at the blind, helpless man. Delilah and the high priest move to the altar to thank their gods and to praise Dagon. In an exotic scene, to riveting music, libations to their great god are poured upon the altar flame, which flares with each dose as the drama, rising to its pitch, culminates with the high priest instructing the child to take Samson to the middle of the temple where all can see him, there to offer, upon his knees, a cup to the mighty Dagon. The hero of Israel asks of his god not to be abandoned in this great moment, then asks the child to lead him to the marble pillars. As the Philistines, the high priest, and Delilah joyfully join in denouncing Israel, Samson, with a mighty effort, begins to rock the pillars, calls upon his god to restore his former strength for an instant, and with a single, final surge of power causes the pillars to fall. Cries of terror are silenced as all are crushed to death by the collapsed temple.

I try to be very careful about using the word *unique*, but here I can say that for me, *unique* perfectly describes the music of Saint-Saëns's *Samson et Dalila*. When I listen to this opera I do not hear influences of any other composers. It is a unique musical experience even though creating operas with an exotic, Oriental appeal was popular in France during Saint-Saëns's time.

❧

Léo Delibes

Léo Delibes, so famous for his ballets overflowing with one popular melody after the other, yielded to this appeal. His opera *Lakmé* was produced in Paris in 1883. Though outside the limits I have put on this book, I must note two excerpts that remain exceedingly popular. *Lakmé's* Act II "Bell Song," *Où va la jeune Hindoue* ("Where does the young Indian girl go?"), has remained for more than a century a coloratura staple. It is the most famous music in this opera. For me, the most beautiful music occurs soon after the curtain has risen on the first act. It is the duet of Lakmé and Mallika. *Dôme épais le jasmine* ("The dense jasmine dome") is sung as the two Indian girls float lazily in a little boat down a stream winding through their world of jungle flowers and *chirrup*ing birds.

I know of no duet for female voices more lovely than this. I have three recordings of this opera and this is the order in which I prefer them: Mado Robin (Lakmé) and Agnes Disney (Mallika); Mady Mesplé (Lakmé) and Danièle Millet (Mallika); Joan Sutherland (Lakmé) and Jane Berbié (Mallika). Mado Robin had the highest operatic voice I have ever heard. This in itself is not what appeals to me. High female voices that are shrill and oscillate irritate me, but every once in a while into the operatic world comes an exceedingly thrilling high voice, firm as a rock and pristine as a bell. Mado Robin is my Lakmé. Her brilliant songs died with her in her forty-second year. I select recordings to buy according to who is singing. The orchestra is important; so is the recording engineer and the acoustics. I have favorite conductors; but, ultimately, with an opera recording it is for the singers that I buy. What is opera if not great singing? And not all singing is wonderful. The more you listen, the more sophisticated your ear will become. You will begin to distinguish those singers who combine a beautiful voice with dramatic authenticity from those using effects to appeal to an audience or from those who simply do not yield great singing.

❧

JACQUES OFFENBACH

LES CONTES D'HOFFMANN (1881)
The Tales of Hoffmann

Les contes d'Hoffmann is the only serious opera of Jacques Offenbach, composer of almost one hundred operettas (yes, you read that correctly: almost 100 operettas) and you will meet him again in chapter 11. Both story and music of *The Tales of Hoffmann* are unusual. Years ago, I remember reading an opera expert who claimed that this work is unlike any other repertory opera. This requires explanation.

E.T.A. Hoffmann

Hoffmann was both the historical and literary source of Offenbach's opera. Today his international fame is that of one of the seminal authors of fiction during the Romantic Movement, even though he enjoyed abundant recognition during his lifetime for considerable achievements as a lawyer, as a composer of eleven operas and two symphonies, and as a conductor. Hoffmann is the central character in Offenbach's opera. He was a small man whose portraits reveal him to have been much less than a matinee idol. Nevertheless, it is recorded that he had an active and varied sex life cut short, perhaps, by other passions—to wit, alcohol and constant conviviality: He died in his forty-sixth year.

His famous stories, grotesque and fantastic conglomerations of real and supernatural events, anticipate Edgar Allan Poe's bizarre writings. Three of his stories provided incidents out of which the libretto of Offenbach's opera was made by Jules Barbier and Michel Carré (remember them from Gounod's *Faust*). Previously, they had adapted Hoffmann's stories for a stage play, and from it they prepared the libretto for an opera. Hoffmann also had written a significant Romantic interpretation of Mozart's *Don Giovanni* (a fragment of which, as I soon will explain, is quoted in *Les contes d'Hoffmann*). So great was Hoffmann's love and admiration of Mozart that he changed his own name of Ernst Theodore Wilhelm Hoffmann to Ernst Theodore Amadeus (Mozart's middle name) Hoffmann.

❧

As a boy, Offenbach would have been familiar with Hoffmann's stories because he was not a Frenchman but a German. Born in Cologne in 1811, he was the son of Isaac Eberst, a Jewish cantor and itinerant violinist who became known as *Der Offenbacher* (The Offenbacher) after his hometown, Offenbach. He gave to his sons Offenbach as their surname. Jakob (who would become Jacques when he settled in France) had extraordinary musical gifts easily recognized by his father, who, accordingly, took him to Paris to study. It was believed, and partially true, that one had to go to Paris to make it in music in the nineteenth century. There the boy studied, lived, worked, and became famous as Jacques Offenbach.

He was a prankster at heart who throughout his life possessed a sardonic wit, a penchant for satire, and a remarkable ability not to take life too seriously. He was a virtuoso cellist who had paid his dues, prior to becoming a famous composer, by playing in the orchestra of the comic opera. There he also paid fines for his tricks such as convincing a cellist friend that, as a joke, each should play every other note of their part.

He could have made a good living as a cellist but all he wanted to do was to compose comic operas. He wrote and was rejected, so he opened his own theater and in the following thirty-two years composed nearly one hundred operettas, influencing the entire course of light, comic music all the way to the present. Some of these operettas have been immortalized by generations of an adoring public (more about this in chapter 11). To obtain permission to marry the daughter of an English impresario, he had to become a Catholic, and so it was that the son of a Jewish cantor became a French Catholic. His unequaled triumph as a composer of comic opera was crowned by one serious work, *The Tales of Hoffmann*, written during his final years when he knew he was dying. His greatest wish was to complete this extraordinary work and see a performance before he died.

It was his bent, when composing comic operas, to work at the speed of light in the midst of partying friends or at a desk he had had specially made to fit into his carriage, thus allowing virtually every minute to be used. It was different with *The Tales of Hoffmann*. He progressed slowly, working in solitude and revising again and again what had been written.

He left the orchestration incomplete when he died in Paris on October 5, 1880, having lived and worked through the revolution of Louis-Napoléon, providing his empire with the sophisticated and fashionable music it desired. Ernest Guiraud, who wrote the orchestra recitatives for Bizet's *Carmen*, completed the orchestration, made some revisions, and saw the work premiered at the Opéra-Comique on February 10, 1881. Because Offenbach left his masterpiece incomplete, it has been given in many different forms in different places at different times: with spoken dialogue and with orchestral recitatives, with an inconsistent order for the three acts, and with cuts or with moving a scene from one act to another. Such, of course, has made a definitive production difficult, but major efforts have been made in the second half of the twentieth century to research Offenbach's intent and to show and record the opera with spoken dialogue and the acts in a set order so that they relate to one another as intended by the composer.

The opera opens with a prologue and concludes with an epilogue. Between are three acts, each about a different love of Hoffmann derived from his stories. The published score of the opera presents these loves in the following order: Olympia, Giulietta, and Antonia. It is now known, however, that Offenbach's intent was for the order to be Olympia (first act), Antonia (second act), and Giulietta (third act), and that is how I will present it.

What is so unusual about *The Tales of Hoffmann*? The music is wonderful, start to finish, but, of course, that is not unusual, for many of the operas in this book are musical treats from beginning to end. It is the story, or the stories, I should say, and the way Offenbach expresses and intensifies them with his music that is so unusual. There are so many characters enmeshed in such an astonishing variety of episodes that one easily can become lost. I can make it simple and clear for you by presenting only the central characters next and introducing the others as they enter into the series of events enacted upon the stage:

HOFFMANN, a poet, *tenor*
NICKLAUSSE, his young friend, *a mezzo-soprano breeches role in the original but today sometimes portrayed by a tenor or baritone*

The three heroines once loved by Hoffmann:
OLYMPIA (Act I), daughter of a physicist and inventor, *soprano*
ANTONIA (Act II), a girl, *soprano*
GIULIETTA (Act III), a Venetian courtesan, *soprano*

It is wonderful—and the ideal—when all three of Hoffmann's past loves are sung by the same superb soprano, but this does not happen often. Usually, each is portrayed by a different singer. This is both more costly and at a remove from the representation of Hoffmann's three different loves as a single supernatural incarnation of his beloved. After all, he is a poet. The four personifications of evil who act upon Hoffmann are:

> LINDORF (Prologue and Epilogue), a councilor, *baritone*
> DR. COPPÉLIUS (Act I), a spectacle-maker, *baritone*
> DR. MIRACLE (Act II), an evil physician, *baritone*
> DAPERTUTTO (Act III), an evil magician, *baritone*

Again, in the ideal presentation or recording, the evil manifestations would be sung by the same baritone. Finally, Stella, an opera singer, is, ironically, only a speaking part. She is Hoffmann's latest love. She is singing in Mozart's *Don Giovanni* in Nuremberg when the epilogue begins and it is for her that Hoffmann waits. Here is what happens in the opera.

Prologue

A few vigorous orchestral bars precede the first curtain. The prologue is set in a Nuremberg tavern located next to the opera house where Stella is singing. Luther is the innkeeper. It is night, and moonlight streams through the windows. "*Glug, glug . . .*" etcetera sing, in turn, the offstage spirits of wine, then beer.

Lindorf enters and asks Andrès (Stella's servant; tenor) if the letter he holds is a message from Stella to an admirer and he bargains to buy it. Andrès holds out until forty thalers is too much for him to refuse. Lindorf dismisses him and looks at the addressee to confirm his suspicion that it is intended for Hoffmann. Referring to the poet as a drunkard enslaved by women, he opens the letter, removes a little key, and reads aloud a declaration of love and an invitation to use the key to her dressing room. In a song, Lindorf discloses his plot to cheat Hoffmann out of the assignation with Stella:

> *Dans les rôles d'amoureux langouroux*
>
> In the role of a languishing lover

Luther, owner of the tavern, and his bustling waiters enter in anticipation of the animated drinking associated with the opera's intermission. Thirsty students are the first to arrive. They sing a splendid drinking song, rapping their glasses for wine. Then they toast the artistry of Stella and call for Hoffmann, who at that very moment happens to be arriving with Nicklausse. The two seat themselves, Hoffmann head in hands and Nicklausse humming *Notte e giorno faticar* ("Working night and day") from *Don Giovanni*, the first aria in Mozart's opera wherein the Don's servant, Leporello, complains of working endlessly for an unappreciative master: an ironic reference to his own companionship with the irritable, gloomy poet who curtly silences him. Hoffmann's philosophy is "Life is short . . . we must drink, sing, and laugh in this adventure." So he is coaxed into song, one of the most memorable tunes in the score, "The Legend of Kleinzach," with its onomatopoeic repetitions provided by a chorus of students.

As Hoffmann, describing the oddities of Kleinzach, contemplates his face, he is easily diverted into a reverie of the charming face of his love; he must be brought back to reality to conclude his song. Hoffmann spots Lindorf and the arch antagonists immediately commence a barrage of vituperous insults, each worse than the other until Nicklausse steps in to prevent a fight. Minor insults resume but the subject changes to women and Hoffmann confesses his love for Stella. She, to him, is three women in one: ". . . artist, young girl, and courtesan," the very embodiment of the three crazy love affairs of his past. He offers to tell their stories. In spite of Luther's call of "Curtain time," all prefer to remain, drinking, smoking their pipes, and listening to the tales of Hoffmann. The plotting Lindorf hopes drunkenness will prevail. Olympia was the first, Hoffmann begins, as the curtain falls.

Act I

The minuet was the only baroque dance step to survive the eighteenth century. An example of this elegant dance in three-quarter time is heard in a famous manifestation in Mozart's *Don Giovanni*, the very opera being passed up by those gathered about Hoffmann eager to hear of his loves. Is this why Offenbach opens the first act with his own minuet, though one hardly in the aristocratic and elegant vein characteristic of this dance's origin in the court of Louis XIV two hundred years before? Offenbach's minuet is pompous and bombastic. Perhaps it's a minuet mocking a minuet as a portent of things to come.

The opened curtain presents a room in Spalanzani's Parisian

quarters. He is an inventor (tenor), Olympia's "father" (the meaning of these quotation marks will become immediately obvious), and Hoffmann's tutor. Hoffmann enters, greets his master, then is left alone. He believes himself to be in love with Olympia without realizing that the object of his distant adoration is only a mechanical doll created by Spalanzani. He pulls back a curtain, gazes on what he assumes is her beautiful, sleeping form, and sings a love song, *Ah! vivre deux* ("Ah, to live together"), the first of our famous excerpts in this act. Nicklausse arrives and just barely stops short of disillusioning Hoffmann, who would not have heard anyway for his ears are deaf to all but Olympia.

Coppélius appears. He is an awful-looking character bearing, perhaps, a resemblance to Lindorf. He, too, is an inventor and as such is Spalanzani's rival. He dupes Hoffmann into buying a pair of "magic eyes" (spectacles) to see Olympia even better in his notable aria *J'ai des yeux* ("I have some eyes"). Spalanzani comes into the room and, out of Hoffmann's hearing, is approached by Coppélius, who asks for money owed to him for making Olympia's wondrous, lifelike eyes. (The historical Hoffmann in his bizarre stories did not miss a trick: One meaning of the Italian word *coppo*, consider Coppélius, is "eyesocket.") Spalanzani purposely passes to him a check he knows to be worthless.

Guests who have been invited to watch Olympia dance begin to arrive and Spalanzani leads her into the main room. Hoffmann is mesmerized and the guests comment upon her beautiful eyes, her prized figure, and her beautiful clothes. She sings the third hit tune of this first act and the first of the famous soprano arias in this opera: *Les oiseaux dans la charmille* ("The birds in the bower"). However, periodically, in this celebrated "Doll Song," Olympia's voice, after singing beautifully and normally, commences to slowly run down and fade out, sending Spalanzani to rewind her mechanism. All this, of course, is lost on the captivated Hoffmann, whose desire is to take her to supper after her song is done. All depart but Hoffmann and her father, who again rewinds her, seats her upon a chair, and tells Hoffmann to remain with her. Alone, the poet touches her shoulder and takes her hand. She rises, revolves about the room, and departs. Nicklausse, who has entered, is told by Hoffmann of his ecstasy: "She loves me." Hoffmann will not listen to Nicklausse. They depart.

The act's finale begins as Coppélius enters intent on revenge for having been given a worthless check. He hides in Olympia's room, off the main room. The guests return to dance—indeed, all have reassembled and Hoffmann is in pursuit of Olympia as his partner for a waltz (now known around the world). They dance with increasing intensity and vivid animation until, suddenly, Spalanzani stops them. Hoffmann falls in a swoon, his glasses shattering on the floor. As he regains consciousness, he hears the smashing of machinery from behind the curtain to Olympia's room. Spalanzani has destroyed his doll. Coppélius comes out of hiding, sardonic laughter resounding. He and his rival exchange insults as all join in the extraordinary conclusion by iterating and reiterating, "He was in love with an automaton!" The curtain falls.

Act II

Even though the recording you have bought or borrowed may represent Giulietta's story next, that was not Offenbach's intent, as explained previously, so it is to Munich and Antonia we go for Hoffmann's second love.

Chords sound ominous notes as the curtain parts on a room in Crespel's home. He is a councilor of Munich. Prominent on the wall is a portrait of a woman with violins hanging nearby. Stage right, his daughter Antonia is seated at a harpsichord and, as the ominous opening notes yield to a plaintive, engaging tune, she sings *Elle a fui, la tourterelle* ("She has flown away, the turtle-dove"), music well known by now to generations of those who love this opera. This music, now always anticipated, is the second famous aria for soprano voice in the score, its pristine, pensive tenderness quite a contrast to the mood established by those opening chords.

Her father (baritone) comes into the room. His concern is great. She had promised she would not sing anymore to avoid the emotional and physical strain on a disease afflicting her but, she explains, she was prompted to by the portrait of her mother. It was from her mother that she inherited her beautiful singing voice. Sadly, she again promises not to sing, and leaves an alarmed father alone, for he has seen in her face those dire streaks of color associated with her illness and he fears losing her. He blames her rapture on the poet Hoffmann, who has won her heart and from whom he has fled with his daughter to Munich.

Frantz (tenor), his servant, enters and is instructed to bar the door to any and every caller. Frantz is partially deaf, must be yelled at, and still tends to misconstrue what is being said. Crespel leaves and Frantz has center stage for a comic song. *Jour et nuit* ("Day and night") he works for this crotchety man but, at least, he can amuse himself with singing and dancing, neither of which, as his little performance aptly demonstrates, is accomplished faultlessly. Exhausted by his entertainment, Frantz slumps in a chair only to be aroused by Hoffmann, followed by Nicklausse, who has entered from the back. Frantz does not protest. In fact, he believes Crespel will be glad to see him, as he has misunderstood his master's injunction to admit no one. Hoffmann urges him to bring Antonia to him. She enters and Nicklausse departs, leaving the lovers alone to embrace, exchange loving words, and vow to be man and wife by the next day in an impassioned duet that concludes with a charming little love song these two used to sing together. And Antonia is not supposed to sing? Apparently, this Hoffmann does not know.

Their song completed, Antonia, hearing her father's approach, departs while Hoffmann hides. Soon after Crespel's appearance, Frantz enters to announce the arrival of Dr. Miracle. The very name stirs Crespel's wrath, for this "assassin" killed his wife and may try to kill his daughter, he claims. With demonic, snarling laughter the evil Dr. Miracle appears and proclaims he is certain he can cure Antonia of her illness. Hearing this, Crespel (and Hoffmann in hiding) expresses a fear that becomes intensified when the doctor miraculously proceeds to diagnose the absent Antonia as if she were present. Examining "her," he demands she sing and from afar, offstage, her brief, brilliant vocal flourish is heard. Then, as if led by some strange power, she appears. Crespel is furious and attempts to rid his house of the sorcerer but as soon as Dr. Miracle is driven out he returns, as if by magic, coming right through the walls.

Antonia, who briefly had left, now reappears. Hoffmann reveals himself and makes her promise, before departing, never again to risk her health with singing. She agrees.

But as Hoffmann departs, magically the evil doctor returns, scolds Antonia for wasting her precious natural gift, and berates her for missing out on the dazzling life it can bring her. His temptations are unnerving her and she protests, begging him to leave. After all, she just promised Hoffmann she will not sing. As she calls upon her mother's portrait for support, it becomes animate and her mother's spirit (mezzo-soprano) answers her. A most remarkable trio ensues, the spirit-voice, Antonia, and the doctor, also playing wildly on one of the violins that had hung on the wall, all singing with intense emotion until the girl falls dying. The portrait returns to normal, the evil doctor disappears, and

Crespel enters, grief-stricken to hear only his beloved daughter's last words. Hoffmann now is also on the scene. Crespel accuses him violently of causing all this. Hoffmann calls for a doctor and instantly, as if by a miracle, Dr. Miracle appears, takes the daughter's hands, and pronounces her dead as Crespel cries out "My daughter" and the despairing poet utters her name. The curtain falls.

Act III
In a tantalizing musical manner the entr'acte preceding the third act introduces the popular boat song and the curtain parts showing a magnificent room on the Grand Canal in Venice. As Nicklausse and Giulietta arrive at her palace by gondola, they sing one of the most familiar of operatic tunes. The guests, who have preceded them, join in the barcarolle:

> *Belle nuit, ô nuit d'amour*
> *Souris à nos ivresses!*
>
> Beautiful night, o night of love,
> Smile upon our _____!

The last word in the translation I left blank for additional consideration. Often it is translated as "revels," meaning merrymaking, and this fits the mood of most of the guests. The French word *ivresse*, however, means more than just having fun. It means drunk with an additional ingredient inspired by drunkenness: anger or ecstasy, or, in this case, more of E. T. A. Hoffmann's blend of inexplicable, malicious supernatural forces intervening in the love life of a poet who happens to have an uncontrollable weakness for pretty girls. "Smile upon our orgy" will do just fine. Offenbach borrowed his now celebrated Barcarolle from an earlier, unsuccessful opera. In fact, neither of the two most famous tunes in this act was composed for *The Tales of Hoffmann* but rather were lifted from operettas soon forgotten. More on that other tune in a few minutes.

Hoffmann answers the boat song with a lively drinking song in which the critical line is "To the devil with him who cries over two beautiful eyes." Guess what will happen to Hoffmann? Schlemil (baritone), Giulietta's companion of the moment, enters with his friend Pittichinaccio (tenor), also a great admirer of the seductive courtesan. They are introduced to Hoffmann by Giulietta, who then leads all her guests to the gambling tables—all, that is, except Hoffmann and Nicklausse, who warns his friend that he will be whisked away the moment he shows any sign of infatuation. One does not love a courtesan, protests Hoffmann, to which Nicklausse retorts, "Just be prepared, for the devil is cunning."

They go off and, speak of the devil, onto the scene comes Dapertutto (*dappertutto*, with two *p*'s, means "everywhere" in Italian), promising himself that Hoffmann will fall prey to Giulietta's irresistible eyes as did Schlemil. Dapertutto's song, another manifestation of Offenbach borrowing from himself, is a tour de force, not only a highlight of this score but also a real gem for the baritone voice. And speaking of a gem, that is what the *Scintille, diamant* ("Sparkle, diamond") aria is about. Prior to the first words of his song Dapertutto withdraws a large diamond ring from his finger. It sparkles brilliantly in the candlelit room. What woman could resist such a ring, he sings, and as if the ring had a huge magnetic force of its own, Giulietta returns and, curiously, greets Dapertutto as his servant. He puts the ring on her finger. It is a bribe, of course, to enact his will: Intoxicate Hoffmann with desire so we can steal his reflection from your mirror. He primes her by relating that Hoffmann has just denied he will capitulate before "two lovely eyes."

Hoffmann enters the room, bows to the courtesan, and, having lost all at gambling, proceeds to leave. Dapertutto kisses Giulietta's hand and departs. Hoffmann instantly becomes like putty as she feigns weeping over his proposed departure. Lyrically he confesses his love, and they sing an ecstatic duet in which Giulietta eventually produces her mirror and requests Hoffmann's reflection: It can disengage from her glass to lodge forever in her heart, she explains. At first, Hoffmann thinks this a strange madness but her persistence prevails and he agrees. Schlemil, followed by other central characters, enters. Dapertutto horrifies Hoffmann by holding up to him the mirror now devoid of any reflection. Nicklausse fails in attempting to lead Hoffmann out. The poet, now both loving and loathing the seductress, is totally possessed by her.

Here begins the opera's famous septet wherein Offenbach blends marvelously the differing thoughts of the central characters into magnificent music. Hoffmann curses the love consuming him, Dapertutto mocks the poor poet beguiled by a woman willing to give her kisses for a trinket, Giulietta allows she may adore Hoffmann but only as another momentary victim of her kisses, Nicklausse laments that poor Hoffmann's heart is soon to be broken again, a violently jealous Schlemil will have revenge by his sword, Pittichinaccio comments that Hoffmann's brain has gone soft if he thinks Giulietta really cares for him, and the wonderful chorus urges Hoffmann to try to calm his heart, for loving this courtesan will prove to be folly. And, of course, this splendid singing is the "voice" of the orchestra.

The music of this act, up to this point, has been, indeed, an orgy of remarkable sound. Offenbach, nearing death but at the absolute height of his tremendous lyrical powers, is at his masterful best. So, then, what does he do as the septet ends so dramatically? Softly, the lilting strain of the boat song returns to introduce a most innovative finale. It progresses to its culmination through spoken dialogue, except for the muted strains of the departing guests singing the boat song. Gondolas have arrived. The party is over. Giulietta and her guests depart. Hoffmann, mesmerized, stares after her as if in a trance. Nicklausse makes another attempt to bring him into reality but the poet, instead, demands of Schlemil the key to the courtesan's private apartment. Guarding it with his life, Schlemil threatens Hoffmann with his sword. Dapertutto arms the poet with his own, the poet kills his foe, takes the key, and races into Giulietta's quarters. Dapertutto sheathes his sword. As the boat song chorus fades off into the distance, Giulietta reappears in a gondola the moment Hoffmann bursts forth from her apartment claiming she is not there. She "abandons" the poet to the care of Dapertutto as Pittichinaccio gets into her boat, receiving there a passionate embrace. Hoffmann, now aware that he has been duped, curses her as Nicklausse drags him away. The curtain falls.

Did you notice that Giulietta, unlike Hoffmann's other loves, Olympia and Antonia, has no famous solo number? That her seductiveness is heard only in duets? First, the barcarolle and, second, her impassioned flirtation with Hoffmann wherein she steals his reflection?

Epilogue
Through an intermezzo, another version of the boat song, the audience is brought back to Luther's tavern in Nuremberg for the brief epilogue. Hoffmann has completed the tales of his three loves. Also finished is next door's performance of Mozart's *Don Giovanni*, a huge success for Stella, exclaims Luther. Lindorf, observing Hoffmann, is convinced he will be no threat to foil his

plan to possess Stella for himself. He departs as the poet utters her name. It is left to Nicklausse to divine the relevancy of what has transpired:

> I've got it!
> Three dramas in one:
> Olympia,
> Antonia,
> Giulietta
> are but the same woman—
> La Stella!

All drink again to La Stella except Hoffmann, who furiously smashes his glass upon the floor, then instantly recuperates, praising alcohol's ability to reduce all human folly to mere forgetfulness. All agree to get drunk and the vigorous drinking song of the prologue resounds again throughout the tavern as the students head outside.

A huge cask at the rear of the inn suddenly becomes luminous as a very drunk Hoffmann, deep in thought, refuses to answer Nicklausse, who simply accepts his friend's stupor. Fully illuminated, the cask reveals the haloed Muse of Poetry (speaking part), who begs that Hoffmann's passions may finally be stilled and that he may be reborn to her love. "Hoffmann be mine," she concludes and in an ecstatic, final outburst of song, before passing out, he will accept her love and return to her. Stella enters and, in spoken dialogue, asks why Hoffmann is asleep. Nicklausse, also speaking, replies that she is too late, for Hoffmann is dead drunk. Lindorf appears to escort Stella away. As she walks out, her gaze remains fixed on Hoffmann's inert form. The students again are heard calling for more drinks as the final curtain falls.

∾

I recall a literary scholar of E. T. A. Hoffmann's writings who claimed this opera to be a mere trivialization of Hoffmann's remarkable ability to blend seamlessly normal, everyday events and emotions with an extraterrestrial revelation of horrific ambiguities. This ingenious element within Hoffmann's writings certainly has not been completely and directly translated into the libretto of Barbier and Carré, but their work certainly was not trivial. With them Offenbach made an opera unlike any other I know.

Compare what goes on in *The Tales of Hoffmann*, for example, with operas also written in the 1880s now familiar to you from previous chapters: the abnegation of the will and redemption through sympathetic love in Wagner's *Parsifal* and *Otello*'s self-destructive jealousy. Offenbach's lyrical masterpiece probes in a significantly modern manner surrealistic considerations of conscious and unconscious behavior more in line with the twentieth century's preoccupation with psychological investigations. Perhaps that is why in my first encounters with this opera it was primarily the music that captivated me. It was not until later, after reading Hoffmann, that I became smitten by both the words and the music of this remarkable opera. When produced by those with an eye for innovative sets and legerdemain special effects of the miraculous, and when performed by those who have mastered the arts of singing and acting, it is, indeed, a unique theatrical experience. And if I have failed to isolate the several wonderful choral moments in the opera, it is only because they happen so naturally and spontaneously as to be part of what appears to be a seamless musical fabric. From the student drinking song to the reveling guests in Venice, those who join in the choruses sound precisely as you would expect them to. Finally, the image of the dead-drunk hero, his unconscious form sprawled on a tavern table next to his half-empty glass, as students call for another round of drinks with the fall of the final curtain, remains forcefully with me long after the applause has faded into the silence of an empty opera house.

JULES MASSENET

MANON (1884)

The last drama in our nineteenth-century French opera chapter is *Manon*, by Jules Massenet, based on a story by Abbé Prévost.

Antoine-François Prévost d'Exiles is known more simply as l'Abbé Prévost. This fascinating and complicated man is important to opera history because his most famous literary work, *Les Aventures du chevalier des Grieux et de Manon Lescaut (The Adventures of the Chevalier des Grieux and of Manon Lescaut)* became, more than one hundred and fifty years after it was published under a pseudonym in Paris in 1733, the subject of two of the most popular operas during the latter part of the nineteenth century to this day: *Manon* (1884), by Jules Massenet, and *Manon Lescaut* (1893), by Giocomo Puccini (Puccini's opera will be introduced in chapter 12).

This novel certainly contains autobiographical sources. Born in 1697, Prévost vacillated in his youth between a career in the army and one in the church, finally joining the Benedictine order after a second stint as a soldier and the end of an unhappy love affair. Eventually he took his vows, studied, taught, preached, and quickly tired of priestly life. Without proper leave granted by his abbey, he fled to London, where he pursued his passion for writing and where he even spent some prison time, perhaps for fraud. Returning to France, he was reconciled with his order and continued to write until his death in 1763.

His book about des Grieux and Manon immediately was immensely popular, even more so when it was banned in France. In this story, des Grieux suffers the loss of his beloved Manon to a wealthy man and decides to become a priest. Manon is arrested as a prostitute, briefly returns to des Grieux, and dies soon thereafter. The two exceedingly popular operas already cited are not the only musical versions of this love story. The once famous French composer Auber composed his *Manon Lescaut* in 1856, but it was soon almost totally forgotten, and in the twentieth century, Hans Werner Henze made his modern adaptation of this story. His *Boulevard Solitude* of 1952 has had some success and has been praised by critics. Nevertheless, it remains obscure to most operagoers.

Were it not for Massenet and Puccini, l'Abbé Prévost probably would not be remembered by many today, but these two operas, so faithful to the original story in strikingly differing manifestations, capture the mystery of Manon, thus endearing her to a public worldwide. It was perfectly normal that they should do so, for even though both worked in remarkably different operatic modes, both composers had a theatrical fixation for the young woman often caught up in circumstances and events beyond her control that ultimately are her undoing. In their respective musical scores, one hears their complete sympathy for Manon. But this is Massenet's chapter; more about Puccini later.

Massenet's *Manon*, the fifth of his more than two dozen now mostly forgotten operas, premiered in 1884 at the Opéra-Comique which, as now you know, does not mean it was a comedy (it certainly is not) but rather that it includes spoken dialogue. Massenet was, in his last years, as famous as any other opera composer then living. Today you will likely hear about only a few of his operas: *Herodiade* (1881), his version of the Salome story, has been almost totally eclipsed by Richard Strauss's notorious opera (see chapter 13); *Le Cid* (1885) still has periodic performances; *Esclarmonde* (1889) was Massenet's own favorite; *Werther* (1892) remains performed and recorded to this day and is a setting of the famous story by Goethe; and I'll have a brief word about *Thaïs* (1894) at the end of this chapter. An 1894 sequel to *Manon* was a flop, and if you can name many more than this, you should be writing this book.

Manon is unquestionably his masterpiece. One scholar writing about it has gone so far, in detailing Massenet's preoccupation with writing overtly sensuous music to stories about erotic women, to conclude that having heard *Manon* is to have heard all of Massenet—an unfair assessment, yet nevertheless one that points to this composer's limitations. His contemporary, the composer Vincent d'Indy agreed: It is almost impossible to read an article or a book about Massenet without encountering his now famous statement claiming that Massenet was able to produce effortlessly an endless supply of "discreet and semi-religious eroticism." Music of this sort had at this time a huge following in the opera houses of France. It made Massenet quite famous, but with his death in 1913, there came a virtual end to the *opera-comique* tradition. His works were too schmaltzy, perhaps, for a fin-de-siécle audience now being nurtured by the first powerful assaults of twentieth-century modernism, and they quickly fell into disfavor. They had to wait about fifty years for a significant revival. All, of course, except *Manon:* ever popular since the day it was born.

Though Massenet did not limit himself to writing opera, it is unlikely that you will hear much of the other music he wrote. He had learned piano as a child from his mother and quickly advanced to an early acceptance at the Paris Conservatory, where soon he was winning pianoforte first prizes. He progressed to study composition, winning major prizes in this field as well, and when some early works received the warm response of appreciative audiences, his composing career was under way. Massenet knew his audiences well, and appealed to both their religious and their sensual proclivities by making operas expressing both. Wagner's *Tannhäuser*, which nearly fifty years before had melded sacred and profane themes, was firmly established and well known to French musicians, and the German's influence on Massenet is evident not only in the mix of religious and sexual themes but also in the manner by which certain characters and their personality traits are represented in *Manon* by recurring musical motifs à la Wagner. But Massenet was no mere copycat. Wagner's overwhelmingly powerful influence was hard, if not all but impossible, for younger composers of this age to escape. Massenet, this influence notwithstanding, nevertheless developed his own musical vein, his own voice or idiom, as a composer. Had he not done so, his appeal would not have been pervasive. He appealed not only to operagoers but also to certain singers who were greatly attracted to the singable and often seductive melodies of the ill-fated lovers des Grieux and Manon Lescaut—and of characters in his other operas as well, especially the leading roles for women. Many great sopranos near the end of the nineteenth century were identified primarily by their Massenet roles.

Manon plays in five acts. The libretto is by Henri Meilhac (you remember him from *Carmen*) and Philippe Gille and except for the conclusion (Act V), which they invented, they were exceedingly faithful to Prévost's novel, even though it had to be reduced significantly. The characters and their voice ranges:

> CHEVALIER (a noble title) DES GRIEUX, *tenor*
> COUNT DES GRIEUX, his father, *bass*
> MANON LESCAUT, *soprano*
> LESCAUT, her cousin and a member of the Royal Guard, *baritone*
> GUILLOT DE MORFONTAINE, wealthy finance minister and an aged roué, *tenor*
> Poussette, Javotte, and Rosette, Guillot's mistresses, "actresses," *sopranos*
> DE BRÉTIGNY, a nobleman, *baritone*
> Chorus: citizens, travelers, gamblers, soldiers, vendors, etcetera

The story is set in France (Amiens, Paris, Le Havre) in 1721.

For many who become familiar with this opera, it is Manon's psychological development, through the music Massenet made for her, that is so fascinating. When the young lovers by chance do meet she is sixteen, des Grieux eighteen. On stage or video they are, of course, portrayed by mature adults with years of vocal lessons behind them. When you interpret their actions, her impetuousness and his inflexible resolve, it is helpful to remember that they are teenagers. Follow Manon through her famous arias, as she evolves from provincial, naive girl into a young woman made for pleasure and with an instinct for making her own way in the world. And, as she does so, Manon Lescaut acquires for herself a prominent place with other formidable heroines like Carmen, Tosca (chapter 12), and Elektra (chapter 13).

Act I

The brief prelude prior to the first curtain primarily is made of music associated with festivities in Act III, love music from Act IV, and the soldiers' music in the fifth act. The curtain opens on the courtyard of an inn at Amiens, busy with excitement and anticipation of the arrival of the stagecoach. Guillot, De Brétigny, and Guillot's three mistresses (called "actresses"), Poussette, Javotte, and Rosette, clamor for food and drink. Lescaut appears. He is to meet the coach transporting his young cousin, Manon, to a convent. They have never met. The coach arrives. Manon steps out and sings her entrance song: *Je suis encore tout étourdie* ("I am so bewildered"). The vivaciousness of this simple tune, so consistent with her youthful wonder over the many sights she has just seen on her first trip, is our introduction to Manon Lescaut. Lescaut greets her, they introduce themselves, and, in an aside, he exclaims how pretty she is. This, obviously, will be the understatement of the opera.

Strikingly beautiful, Manon instantly catches the eye of Guillot. De Brétigny, too, is stunned by her loveliness. Guillot leaves his party and is quite forward in making a pass at her, which is laughed off by Manon. He makes it clear to her, however, before returning to his friends, that he is placing his soon-to-arrive coach at her service should she change her mind. Lescaut, who had gone for her luggage, returns as Guillot departs. In an aria, he warns her not to heed any more flattery that may come her way, then excuses himself for the moment. Alone, Manon looks at the other young girls, Poussette, Javotte, and Rosette, noticing their fancy clothing and jewelry. They are having such a good time and Manon, in an arioso, sadly sings in a resigned manner that a world such as this is but an illusion soon to be left at the door of a convent.

The orchestra, an additional character in the opera, nobly introduces the arrival into the courtyard of the handsome Chevalier des Grieux. Abstractly musing, at first he does not even see Manon. Then, looking at her, he sees nothing else. He is dumbstruck. And he has not gone unnoticed by Manon. As he approaches her to offer an introduction, it obviously is love at first sight, musically developing in a splendid love duet as they get to know each other. Do not let this passionate music cause you to miss, first, her admission that often her family has said of her how she loves pleasure too much; second, that des Grieux is under the influence of an inexplicable cosmic force; and, last, Manon's line ". . . c'est là l'histoire de Manon Lescaut," the very same words she will utter when she dies. The lovers agree there will be no convent for Manon; des Grieux calls it a "living tomb." They will elope to Paris in, of course, the carriage Guillot placed at Manon's disposal.

When a performance ends the act with their departure, it is following an 1895 revision. In the original version Lescaut, finding on his return that Manon has fled in Guillot's coach, naturally assumes it to be the work of the wealthy old roué who soon is on the scene. With the facts before them (Manon ran off with a young man), Lescaut fears loss of family honor and Guillot vows he will have revenge on the lovers as the curtain falls.

Act II
The theme associated with the arrival of des Grieux into Manon's life in the courtyard briefly is heard prior to the Act II curtain, showing him writing at a little table in the Paris apartment where he and Manon live. Humble surroundings suggest he is not a young man of means. He is writing to his father seeking permission to marry Manon. We hear what a glowing letter it is when Manon, leaning over his shoulder, reads portions aloud. As des Grieux prepares to leave to post the letter, he notices fresh flowers in a vase and inquires who sent them. She replies that someone had thrown them through the window and she found them. This may pacify des Grieux, who denies any jealousy with an assertion of complete trust, but we should be leery of Manon's explanation.

A commotion is heard in the hallway and a servant girl enters to announce that two officers simultaneously are demanding admittance. One claims to be a relative of Manon, obviously Lescaut. The other, in an aside to Manon, informs her that it is her wealthy neighbor, de Brétigny, who adores her, disguised as a soldier. Lescaut's impetuous demand for satisfaction is defused when des Grieux shows him the letter of his honorable intent to marry Manon. During their exchanges, de Brétigny informs Manon that des Grieux Senior already is coming, with the intention of forcefully taking his son away from Manon. Furthermore, he suggests it would be folly for her to warn her lover. Were des Grieux to foil the abduction, the consequences for him would be harsh. Rather, she should live in luxury with him, especially because the Count des Grieux will never approve of her. She rejects his offer and sends him off, but have we detected some wavering?

Des Grieux departs to post the letter, leaving Manon alone with her confused emotions. She moves to their little table where they write, read, sit, and eat. It is the meager symbol of their love affair. *Adieu, notre petite table* ("Farewell, our little table"), she sings. She knows their idyll is over. It is her meditative, sensitive side we hear in this celebrated aria. When des Grieux returns he finds her sad and nervous, but she diverts him to supper. He relates a dream that came to him while mailing his letter. Thus begins the aria *Instant charmant* ("Charming moment") of reflections, wherein he relates how he envisioned them living happily together in an isolated woodland retreat.

As appealing and popular as Manon's arias are, I prefer those Massenet wrote for des Grieux, probably because I know them from countless playings of tenor Jussi Björling's recordings as a young boy, years before I heard a complete performance of the opera. I have three different versions of Björling singing "The Dream" *(La Rêve)*, as this aria is called. I grew up on the August 2, 1938, recording. A second is from a live radio broadcast performance of August 1951. The third version, with piano accompaniment, is from Björling's famous September 24, 1955, Carnegie Hall recital. In my ears I have never heard from Massenet music more exquisite than "The Dream," on the last notes of which des Grieux sings "O Manon," to me the most hauntingly beautiful in the entire opera.

Björling's singing is superb on each of the three versions but the second and third, the live performances, are marred by boorish dolts who commence their obnoxious clapping before the delicate, transparent "O Manon" dies away into the silence meant for it. Both audiences, sorry to say, are American. This insensitive, rude trait I hear constantly in American opera houses, where certain egos simply must burst forth to show everyone that they know the millisecond when the music ends. "Bravo," they shout, even when the aria has been sung by a woman (when it should be "Brava") as they pound their hands together. Please, never, ever ruin a beautiful performance by smothering it with applause, especially music lovely as this dying away with the subtlest pianissimo. Let five heartbeats go by with silence before you put your hands together.

Björling's incomparable voice continues to sell well on remastered compact discs more than forty years after his death. When you buy some of his recordings you will have added my favorite tenor to your collection. And when you buy them, look for those conducted by Björling's friend and colleague of countless collaborations, Nils Grevillius, who said, when learning of Björling's death, "During my fifty years as a musician I have never heard anything as wonderful—the infinite beauty of tone . . ." That says all.

Back to the story. After relating his dream, a knock on their door interrupts the lovers. Repeatedly, Manon implores him not to answer it. Des Grieux cannot comprehend why and goes out to the door. A brief struggle is heard. Then nothing. Des Grieux does not return. Manon rushes to the window sobbing his name as the curtain falls.

Act III

A minuet introduces the first scene of the third act, set in Cours la Reine (The Queens Way)—Manon will make something of this—a crowded, fashionable section of Paris where vendors hawk their wares, Poussette, Javotte, and Rosette enjoy themselves, and Lescaut buys some trinkets before departing. Guillot and de Brétigny, now living with Manon, enter. She appears soon thereafter, the admiration of all the men more than obvious. Pleased by their attentions to her natural beauty, now so elegantly attired and bejeweled, she sings first a little aria crowning herself the "Queen of Beauty," followed by music now as familiar as any other in the score: her famous gavotte *Profitons bien de la jeunesse* ("Make the most of youth"). Some of the Opéra-Comique recordings and performances substitute in its place another aria, little known to most, written by Massenet as an alternative to the gavotte. Why replace one of the highlights? Some producers consider the gavotte too hackneyed, too commonplace, too popular for their production. A sorry misapprehension.

As Manon moves about in the crowd after her songs are sung, Count des Grieux, now present, notices an old friend, de Brétigny, and they greet each other and begin to talk. Manon, returning, overhears something about des Grieux from his father, who is telling de Brétigny that the Chevalier des Grieux now is l'Abbé des Grieux at Saint-Sulpice, where tomorrow he will take his vows. Manon sends off de Brétigny to hunt for a bracelet for her, feigns to be a friend of the new abbé, and asks about him. She is startled to hear that des Grieux, according to his father, has learned the most important lesson for all men: how to "forget." He has recovered from a broken heart. De Brétigny, Lescaut, and Guillot join them. Guillot has arranged for the opera ballet to dance here as his attempt to impress Manon. He is still intent on having her for a mistress and hopes to win her away from de Brétigny. The audience always enjoys the ballet, but not Manon. She is distracted. Preoccupied with thoughts of des Grieux—"He *cannot* forget me"—she calls a carriage to take her to Saint-Sulpice.

There the second scene takes place. Des Grieux the younger has delivered an impressive sermon but his father expresses distaste for his son's new vocation, for he wishes he would marry some nice, proper young girl. He departs, having promised to send to the abbé the legacy left him by his mother. Alone, des Grieux sings another great aria for tenor voice, *Ah! fuyez, douce image* ("Ah! Fly from me, sweet image"). His attempt to put behind him all evidence of the profane world, primarily the memories of Manon Lescaut, Massenet has expressed in one of the most glorious soliloquys in French opera. An organ is heard marking the beginning of a service and des Grieux goes off. Manon arrives, sends a porter to bring him back, and soon they are together again. Des Grieux's resistance, at first impressive, eventually collapses beneath Manon's charms of tender words and touches. Massenet has represented well in this entire second scene of the third act the contrasting emotions of religious commitment and erotic urge for which he is so justly famous. With the unmistakable passion of their reconciliation, the curtain falls.

Act IV

The fourth act is set in a Parisian gambling hall. Guillot, his three "actresses," and Lescaut are there and entering is Manon with a reluctant des Grieux in tow. He is not a gambler, like the others, but Manon is persuasive that he should try his luck, and her enticing song of love for him and for flowers, gold, youth, and all the pleasures that sustain her convinces him. Guillot and des Grieux play, the latter beginning to win heavily until the wealthy old roué stops the game, accuses the other of cheating, and leaves, only to return with the police an instant thereafter. He charges des Grieux with cheating, fingers Manon as his accomplice, and relishes his revenge. Des Grieux strikes out at him but is restrained and then ashamed as his father appears. Various emotions are expressed in an ensemble: Guillot gloating, des Grieux asking for mercy, Manon fearing the future. As guards approach, des Grieux attempts to defend Manon with his life. He is disarmed, however, and she faints as the curtain falls upon their mutual despair.

Act V

The fourth act was not long; the fifth is even more brief. The setting is a deserted road heading to the port of Le Havre. Des Grieux is waiting. It is early evening. He has learned that Manon and other female criminals will pass here on their way to deportation to a penal colony. Count des Grieux has seen to his son's release but, of course, cared not a whit for Manon. Lescaut and des Grieux had plotted Manon's escape but their plan was foiled. Lescaut arrives just before the soldiers approach with their prisoners. He learns from the sergeant that one of them, Manon by name, is ill, exhausted, and nearly dead. Lescaut bribes him to let her go with him briefly. She appears, a pitiful ghost of her former self. Lescaut leaves her alone with des Grieux. Their duet is the major musical event of this brief, culminating act. He assures her that he will effect her escape but she clearly is too weak. She wants only to find comfort in his arms, where she recalls their past happiness. They express their love for each other. She becomes remorseful as she feels death near. Terrified, des Grieux can say only "Manon." She dies, having spoken what those who so love this work consider among the most pathetic words in any French opera: "This is the story of Manon Lescaut."

From its premiere to the present, Manon's several thousand performances, recordings, and videos have fascinated an ardent following of those for whom this is "the French opera." The attraction is not only Massenet's finest score but also Manon herself. She continues to provoke speculations. Was she a bad girl? Did she look out only for herself? Did she really love des Grieux? If so, how could she have used and abused him? If not, why return to him? I have never been intrigued by these questions. Manon is a good story with considerable admirable music. Her music tells me she was a hedonistic young woman drunk with the wonders of urban life and all that money can buy and it tells me her feelings for des Grieux were authentic. In his music I hear about an honorable young man who, once touched by Manon's love, could never again be whole without it. That is sufficient for me. Evidently, it also was sufficient for the great English conductor Sir Thomas Beecham, who preferred a good performance of *Manon* to all of Bach's Brandenburg concerti.

For Massenet, however, it was not *Manon* but rather *Esclarmonde* that he considered his best work. This most certainly was not an aesthetic judgment. It had to do with the attractive soprano from California who created the role, Sibyl Sanderson. Massenet adored her voice, and the rest of her as well. Soon the inevitable circulated. She also created the role of Thaïs, in an opera after a fine story by Anatole France. A monk concerned for the soul of an adventurous and beautiful courtesan, Thaïs, persuades her to change her ways and in the process becomes possessed by a passionate desire for her. The transformation that takes place in the life of Thaïs is known in the opera as "The Meditation of Thaïs." It is a violin solo with orchestra of remarkable beauty. If you do not have it, go buy Anne-Sophie Mutter's recording. Once you've heard it you'll wonder how you lived without it. (After *Manon*, Massenet's most familiar work, at least to American audiences, is his opera *Werther*, based on the famous story by Goethe.)

Jules Massenet certainly turned to exemplary literary works for his major operas: stories by l'Abbé Prévost, Anatole France, Goethe, Corneille *(Le Cid)*, and Cervantes for *Don Quichotte*, a great success with one of the most famous singers of the twentieth century creating the title role. But more about the colossal talent of Fyodor Chaliapin (also transliterated Shalyapin) in the following chapter.

Modest Mussorgsky

Peter Ilyich Tchaikovsky

19ᵀᴴ CENTURY SLAVIC OPERA: MUSSORGSKY AND TCHAIKOVSKY

A number of years ago I was invited to make an introduction to opera before a group of college students whose combined musical awareness was limited to the top-forty songs of the day. It was, therefore, suggested to me that a catchy title for my lecture, supplemented by musical examples, would be appropriate. I chose "Operatic Sex and Other Matters" and my opening remarks went something like this, with only a little bit of my tongue in my cheek:

> The operatic masterpiece of Modest Mussorgsky, *Boris Godunov*, is about people suffering in Russia during the period known historically as "the Time of Troubles" and Peter Tchaikovsky's opera *Eugene Onegin* is the only one I know where a beautiful young wife rejects the advances of a passionate, handsome pursuer in order to remain faithful to her adoring but aging husband. So much for the other matters. And now on to operatic sex.

We had a lively time with *Don Giovanni*, *Carmen*, *Manon*, and others of that ilk.

In opera houses beyond her native soil, Russia's two most well-known and appreciated operatic exports are *Boris Godunov* and *Eugene Onegin*. They are, therefore, the two Russian operas you are most likely to hear about and the two you should begin with. We anticipate their discussion by first meeting two important artists.

Fyodor Ivanovich Chaliapin (1873–1938)

The origins of genius can be quite humble, even grim, and such is the case of a boy born in the nineteenth century into a Russian peasant family headed by a drunken, impoverished father who beat his wife. At an early age this boy expressed a love for singing, and as soon as he was old enough he joined a church choir. A short time thereafter, having attended his first play, Fyodor became equally possessed by a passion for the theater. His life thus was set. In spite of a remarkable aptitude for languages, art, writing, and sports, all became subsumed by his dream to become a singing actor. That meant opera.

At seventeen he joined a traveling provincial opera company as a chorister, supplementing meager earnings—and at times no income—by doing anything he could get paid for: sweeping streets, toiling as a stevedore, or working as a porter. The move from the chorus to small parts and on to leading roles happened quickly, but starring in a regional opera company was not the fulfillment of his lofty dream. Hungry and impatient, he was rescued from despair by the goodwill of a talented singing teacher who gave lessons to the impoverished youth at no charge.

The lessons had two basic thrusts: to master the techniques of the art of singing and to master the actor's art of interpretation. For an operatic performer, this means becoming through one's voice, actions, expressions, gestures, and makeup the character portrayed. It was as a singing actor that this tall, well-built, agile youth would rise to fame unequaled in international opera theater. With his teacher, Chaliapin learned fourteen roles in less than six months. From provincial theater to the Imperial Opera to the Bolshoi, he was a sensation. The international career began at La Scala in 1901. London, Paris, and New York followed. While audiences were mesmerized and critics struggled for superlatives, the greatest praise came from his colleagues. The incomparable Lotte Lehmann, one of the finest singers of the last century, remarked that he transformed the operatic stage into reality. On the stage next to him, as he portrayed Mephistopheles, "I felt in the presence of the devil," she confessed.

Chaliapin's teacher also introduced him to the music of Modest

Mussorgsky, a composer who died when the singer was nine years old. Mussorgsky's masterpiece is the opera *Boris Godunov*. Primarily as Boris, but in other great bass parts as well, Chaliapin introduced Mussorgsky and, indeed, the magnificence of Russian opera, to Europe and America.

During his second Metropolitan Opera engagement, in 1921, my grandfather took my father to a production of *Boris Godunov* with Chaliapin in the title role. My father was merely a young boy, but the impression lasted a lifetime. Nothing he would experience in any opera house thereafter, he often told me, compared to having seen and heard Chaliapin as Boris. Above all, it was the death of Boris that he would recall in complete detail: the dying tsar advising his son and heir, the beautiful prayer to God for forgiveness, and the seizure catapulting him from his throne to tumble down six steps bumpty-bump to end in a prostrate heap center stage, his crown spiraling across the floor as the curtain slowly fell. (Those interested in acting will be intrigued to learn that Chaliapin was the living model from whom Stanislavsky developed his system of "method" acting.)

Those fortunate to have heard Chaliapin in recitals or, even more, to have seen him on the stage have left memorable accounts that condense into "there was nothing like him." I was not that lucky. Chaliapin's last opera performance was in the year I was born. I began collecting his recordings as a teen, first the 78 rpms, then those remastered onto long-playing records. One of these appeared in 1958 and a critic who often had attended Chaliapin's performances, reviewing it in *High Fidelity* magazine, wrote:

> Due to responsible selection and superb engineering, this is the first microgroove record that does justice to the art of Chaliapin, the greatest singing actor of the twentieth century . . . One of the towering stage figures of all time, Chaliapin also possessed a magnificent and sonorous voice with which he could play as a violin virtuoso with his bow. To have seen and heard Chaliapin as Boris was an experience capable of transcending and dwarfing one's theatrical memories . . .

And now a new generation can hear him on compact disc breathing life into music with his rare gift. When I listen to his 1922 recording of "The Song of the Volga Boatmen," I visualize what Chaliapin certainly saw repeatedly as a child in his home-town of Kazan on the banks of the Volga, where boat haulers walked along the riverbank pulling the heavily laden barges while chanting their monotonous "yo-heave-ho."

His influence remains to this day in the studies of young opera singers diligent in their efforts to learn the art of both singing and acting—young singers who, believe it or not, may never have listened to the recordings of Fyodor Chaliapin. Ultimately, he is best remembered for his portrayal of Boris, and it is no exaggeration to say he was initially responsible for Mussorgsky's fame circling the globe.

I cannot leave this introduction to Chaliapin without mentioning another Russian bass whom I discovered much later through associations with exceedingly knowledgeable record collectors. Mark Reizen's recordings now are available on remastered compact discs. I needn't elaborate. Reizen always avoided the excesses for which Chaliapin at times was criticized and his voice was an instrument of incredible beauty. He, too, was a famous Boris.

Alexander Pushkin (1799–1837)

Pushkin, considered their greatest writer by many Russians, once expressed in a letter to his wife exasperation over constantly being under the eye of censorship. He wrote, "Only the devil could have thought of having me born in Russia with a mind and talent." Born in Moscow in 1799, his father's family was of the nobility and through his mother he was descended from a minor Ethiopian chieftain of northern Abyssinia whose son was adopted by Peter the Great. This African blood gave Pushkin his dark coloring.

From an early age his passion was for words. He read constantly in his father's excellent library, both Russian and French authors, wrote poems in French, and read them for friends of his father, who offered him encouragement. He was twenty-one when he wrote his first major work, a long narrative poem entitled *Russlan and Ludmilla* (1820). Overnight he became recognized in Russia as a major poet. This same year he published "Ode to Liberty." This liberalism brought about exile to southern Russia, where he was introduced to the poetry of Lord Byron, mixed with secret, revolutionary societies, and wrote magnificently. Transferred to Odessa as a public servant, he was later dismissed from

his official position when a letter in defense of atheism was intercepted by his superior.

In 1825 he discovered, and was greatly influenced by, Shakespeare's historical dramas in blank verse. *Boris Godunov* (not published until 1831) was the result. Pushkin married, was pardoned
for his radical views, and received a new appointment. *Eugene
Onegin*, a long novel in verse, with clearly the Byron influence at
work, appeared in 1832. It remains his most famous poem. His
most well-known short story, *The Queen of Spades*, appeared in
1834. He died on January 29, 1837, from a wound incurred in a
duel. In a bizarre, life-is-stranger-than-fiction episode right out of
the pages of his own *Eugene Onegin*, Pushkin had challenged a
French baron who reportedly had become involved with his wife.

Ruslan and Ludmila, *Boris Godunov*, *Eugene Onegin*, and
Queen of Spades are four of Russia's most beloved and often performed operas. All are adaptations of Pushkin creations, placing
him within the center of Russian opera history. For your introduction to Russian opera, this book presents *Boris* and *Onegin*, as
they are often called. The first by Mussorgsky, the second by
Tchaikovsky, they are to non-Russian audiences the most familiar. They are strikingly different works primarily because the two
composers, though both Russian head to toe, had contrasting
approaches to writing music. Tchaikovsky was smitten with the
melodic and harmonic tradition of Western classical music as he
knew it and studied it in a conservatory. Mussorgsky, lacking
extensive formal study, was his own man and heard a more primitive and original Russian voice. His *Boris Godunov* has been performed in at least four versions and probably as many as five or
six. It is essential to know which one we are considering and why.
Strange as it is to write this, it is an extraordinary fact of opera history that Mussorgsky's masterpiece had to wait more than one
hundred years after the composer's death for authentic productions and recordings.

∾

MODEST MUSSORGSKY

BORIS GODUNOV (1874)

Modest Petrovich Mussorgsky (sometimes transliterated as Moussorgsky), born in 1839, began this opera in October 1868, worked on it assiduously, and completed his first version fourteen months later. He was both librettist and composer. He based his story on Pushkin's drama, which in turn owed much to Karamzin's monumental, eleven-volume history of Russia. Mussorgsky's use of Pushkin's work is a brilliant condensing, omitting, adding, and altering of twenty-three short scenes into seven scenes for his first version of the opera and nine scenes for his revised version. His literary reconstruction of Pushkin for his musical purposes is ingenious. The title character, Boris Godunov, is Mussorgsky's representation of an actual Russian tsar who ruled unofficially, and then officially, from the 1580s until his death in 1605.

Boris Godunov was the brother-in-law of Tsar Fyodor, eldest son of Ivan the Terrible, who had succeeded his father to the throne in 1584. Of weak mind, and thus a weak ruler, Fyodor quickly allowed Boris to become the power behind the throne. Another son of Ivan the Terrible, who eventually could have succeeded Fyodor, was the child Dmitri. In 1591, Dmitri died mysteriously in a monastery where he lived with his mother. The official investigation concluded that death was caused by "a self-inflicted throat wound during an epilectic fit." But one widespread theory purports that he was murdered by agents of Boris, thus making Boris's ascendancy to the throne clear sailing. Mussorgsky bought this theory for his drama from Pushkin, and though some historians have exonerated Boris of the crime, others, to this day, consider the matter an unresolved historical enigma. This was not the only suspicion that circulated. Another rumor that gained credence claimed the child Dmitri escaped, grew to manhood, and reappeared in 1603 as a pretender to the throne during the reign of Boris. Mussorgsky did not accept this. In our explication of the opera's plot, we will see that Mussorgsky's pretender is a runaway monk who pretends to be Dmitri.

The historical Boris became more than the power behind the throne. In 1598, he was elected tsar after Fyodor's death, and in several ways he was a good ruler. He was the first Russian tsar to import good foreign teachers and send talented young Russians abroad to be educated. He was the first tsar to allow Lutheran churches to be built, and he worked to secure Russia's borders. He was taking Russia out of the medieval world. There was, however, another side of Boris. Relentlessly, he persecuted those whom he deemed a threat or to him were suspicious. Ultimately, his definite talent for ruling was no match for the disorder inherited from Ivan the Terrible, for the constant political intrigues of the nobility, and especially for the famine and plague that began in 1601 and soon was afflicting and ravaging many thousands of sick, homeless, wandering people. When Boris died in 1605, chaos reigned.

I consider Mussorgsky's rendition of "The Death of Boris" one of the most magnificent and powerful scenes in all opera. The son of Boris ruled for only a few months before being murdered by enemies of his family. Dmitri, the pretender, whoever he really was, ascended but soon thereafter also was murdered. And so on and on it went during this terrible time in Russian history, the Time of Troubles.

The pretender's attempt to gain the throne is the central political event of Mussorgsky's opera. The central psychological event is the deterioration of Boris's mind as he goes mad from guilt over his part in the murder of the child Dmitri. The central dramatic event of *Boris Godunov*, culminating in the incomparable final scene of the opera, is the suffering of great Mother Russia and the anguish of her poor people during this period of political turmoil, famine, and plague.

Mussorgsky presented his opera to the management of the Imperial Theater in St. Petersburg. It was rejected in 1871 for various reasons. Mussorgsky had ignored traditional operatic conventions familiar to Russians through their brief flirtation with Italian operatic imports. (These would soon yield to the fast developing school of a homegrown opera tradition in which both Mussorgsky and Tchaikovsky were instrumental.) In Mussorgsky's first version, there was no prima donna role, no love interest, no big vocal ensembles, and no dances. Furthermore, the committee considering the work was under imperial orders and probably anticipated problems with the censors.

In 1871–2, Mussorgsky revised his opera, adding a love story with historical origins. Dmitri, the pretender, raised a sympathetic force of followers with which to challenge Boris with the backing of a local Polish ruler at Sandomierz Castle. This was solidified by the betrothal of Dmitri to Marina, daughter of the Polish ruler. This second incarnation was also rejected but it had gained sufficient support in some circles for several scenes to be presented in a concert version (a concert version of an opera is sung without costumes, staging, or action). A great success caused the theater management finally to accept the work.

Boris Godunov, in this second version, had its world premiere in 1874. Though the critics growled, it was appreciated by the audience and enjoyed twenty-five more performances during the following eight years before being withdrawn from repertory. Mussorgsky had died before the run was over, his mind and body, wrecked by alcohol, fits, and visions, having given up in his forty-second year. He left three other operas unfinished: *The Marriage, Khovanshchina*, and *The Fair at Sorochinsky*.

After his death, Mussorgsky's good friend, the great composer Rimsky-Korsakov, seeking to have the work returned to the stage, made a third version and then a fourth. Rimsky-Korsakov was a brilliant, schooled orchestrator. He was convinced that the score of his friend, who lacked a thorough conservatory training, needed revisions, cuts, additional music to bridge what he was cutting, and rescoring. This third revision appeared in 1896, and soon thereafter, the great Chaliapin was being heard in the title role. In the years from 1906 to 1908, Rimsky-Korsakov made his second and, now, the fourth version of the opera. It was first produced in Paris in 1908, then in Milan in 1909, and at the Metropolian Opera in New York in 1913. In each of these historic presentations, Chaliapin was Boris.

For his second revision of Mussorgsky's work, Rimsky-Korsakov both restored the cuts he had made in his first revision and retained his additions. Any attempt to represent these versions as mere tinkerings with the original is ludicrous. His hand invaded every page. Melodies were changed, and with them their harmonies. Tempos and dynamics were altered and the orchestration was made to be brighter, smoother, less stark, and more to conventional operatic taste.

It was in this fourth version of the opera that *Boris* was most often performed for many years. Thus it must be amended when one writes of Chaliapin having introduced the masterpiece of Mussorgsky to the world. The fact is that Chaliapin introduced to the world Rimsky-Korsakov's well-intentioned version of Mussorsky's masterpiece. Rimsky-Korsakov had failed to recognize the originality of *Boris Godunov*. He had failed to perceive the genius of his friend, who knew exactly what he was doing as well as his reasons why. Mussorgsky did not want a lush, brilliant score of flowing melodies to express his adaptation of immeasurable suffering during a terrible period in the history of his country. He did not choose to represent either the psychological disintegration of Boris or the misery of the Russian people through traditional operatic conventions. Quite consciously, he utilized and elaborated on aspects of Russian folk music, and rather than forcing words to fit lovely melodic lines, he employed the music he heard in the sounds, rhythms, and inflections of the Russian language. He did not force speech into music but instead heard music in speech. Mussorgsky wanted, and brilliantly achieved, a stark score to convey the horrors of political turmoil, Boris's disintegration, and the misery of a starving people floundering without leadership.

Mussorgsky's music, often harsh and brutal, is, nevertheless, uniquely powerful and dramatic. Always, when introducing this opera to my beginning students, I had to prepare them for this. Few were they who took to it immediately, who did not find Mussorgsky too dark and rough. But when, given a chance, the music gets to you and becomes part of your heartbeat and breath, you will know of the incomparable originality of Mussorgsky's genius. And for me, there was that special delight when for a rare student *Boris Godunov* was love at first listen.

It was not until 1928 that the first steps toward presenting a version of the score consistent with the composer's intentions were taken. Scholarly work finally was vindicating Mussorgsky. Nevertheless, *Boris Godunov*, for nearly fifty more years, continued to be performed in America and Europe in both Mussorgsky's and Rimsky-Korsakov's versions until a triumphant "pure Mussorgsky" production of the drama appeared in the 1970s. Did this now famous presentation finally put Rimsky-Korsakov's revisions to rest . . . forever, we hope? No, not yet, but Rimsky-Korsakov's own words recorded in *My Musical Life* may still prove to be prophetic:

> If ever the conclusion is arrived at that the original is better than my revision, then mine will be discarded, and *Boris Godunov* will be performed according to the original score.

But what version constitutes the original score?

This question of the original score of a "pure Mussorgsky" is not easily resolved because, remember, there are two decidedly different Mussorgsky versions. The total number of scenes in his first version is seven. His second version has nine. The relatively recent restoration of Mussorgsky's *Boris Godunov* solved the problem by making a composite of the original two versions. Those scenes appearing in both versions form the core of the drama. When the same scene has two versions, the better one is selected. To this core add those scenes that appear only in the second version and always honor Mussorgsky's most important change: the ending. "The Death of Boris" concluded the first version. In Mussorgsky's revision, Boris dies in the penultimate scene and the drama concludes with a chilling lament for the fate of Russia. The only cuts should be those that are either inconsistent or redundant.

The composite version of *Boris Godunov* presented here follows a wonderful 1977 recording featuring the splendid Finnish bass Martti Talvela in the title role. And for what follows, I am much indebted to an introduction by Arthur Jacobs that is included in the libretto accompanying this recording. Unless further research reveals something we do not know, or until new discoveries of now unknown sources alter what is known—and I think that unlikely—this will be as close to Mussorgsky's conceptions as we can get. Over this issue I have labored because it is important to me to present Mussorgsky's *Boris Godunov* to my students rather than versions prepared by Rimsky-Korsakov or by two other composers, Shostokovich and Rathaus. When you have an opportunity to hear a recording of this opera, or to watch a video, or best of all to attend a performance, I hope it will be important to you, too, to know what version you are experiencing. Emphatically I urge you, at least for your first encounter, to make it Mussorgsky's composite version.

The Mussorgsky composite version presented here is made from the following scenes:

Scene 1: The courtyard of the Novodievichy monastery, from the first version.

Scene 2: A square in the Moscow Kremlin; this "Coronation Scene" is the same in both versions.

Scene 3: A cell in the Chudov monastery, from the first version.

Scene 4: An inn near the Lithuanian border, the same in both versions.

Scene 5: The Imperial Apartments in the Moscow Kremlin, from the second version.

Scene 6: Marina's room at Sandomierz Castle, new to the second version.

Scene 7: The gardens of Sandomierz Castle, new to the second version.

Scene 8: Moscow: a square in front of St. Basil's Cathedral, from the first version.

Scene 9: A hall in the Moscow Kremlin, from the first version.

Scene 10: A clearing in a forest near Kromy, new to the second version.

The opera begins with a Prologue and Scenes 1 and 2. Act I comprises Scenes 3 and 4. Act II is Scene 5. Act III is Scenes 6 and 7 and Act IV consists of Scenes 8, 9, and 10.

The hardest part of introducing Mussorgsky's *Boris Godunov* is sorting out what, indeed, constitutes Mussorgsky's *Boris Godunov*. I hope I have done my homework correctly for you. With this completed, I can assure you that the action of the drama is far less complicated and its events are straightforward as they unfold scene by scene.

Here are the many characters and their voices:

BORIS GODUNOV, *bass*
FYODOR, his young son, *mezzo-soprano; a trouser role*
XENIA, his daughter, *soprano*
The nurse of these children, *contralto*
PRINCE SHUISKY, leader of the nobles, *tenor*
SHCHELKALOV, secretary of the council, *baritone*
PIMEN, an old monk and chronicler, *bass*

GRIGORY, who becomes Dmitri the pretender, *tenor*
MARINA, a Polish princess, *soprano*
RANGONI, her confessor, a Jesuit, *bass*
Two other Jesuits, *basses*
VARLAAM, vagabond monk, *bass*
MISSAIL, vagabond monk, *tenor*
Hostess of the inn, *mezzo-soprano*
Police officer, *baritone*
A simpleton, *tenor*
Chorus of Russian people, boyars, and Poles

The time is the reign of Boris Godunov, 1598–1605. The action transpires in Russia and Poland.

Prologue

After a brief, solemn, and somber orchestral prelude, the curtain rises for the first of two scenes of the Prologue. In the courtyard of the Novodievichy monastery near Moscow, a police officer orders a crowd to drop to their knees and pray loudly. "Why do you forsake us, our Father?" the crowd obediently responds. With the completion of their prayer, the bewildered populace asks why they have been summoned and forced to pray. The policeman returns, insists on more supplications, and then, as Shchelkalov, the secretary of the council, appears, he silences the crowd. "Boris will not yield," announces Shchelkalov. From offstage we hear a chorus of pilgrims before the officer says to the throng, "Go forth and meet the tsar." He dismisses them with an order to meet the next day at the Kremlin. Dismayed, the people do not comprehend why they were assembled, and the curtain falls on the first scene of the prologue.

It is a ruse, part of Boris's strategy to ascend to the throne. His henchmen, we will learn, murdered the child Dmitri, the legitimate heir. Now dwelling in the monastery, Boris has pretended to refuse the council's offer to become tsar. If a policeman, under his thumb, prods the multitude to pray and beg for his ascension, then will it not appear as if Boris, in eventually accepting the crown, is only capitulating to the will of the people?

The curtain opens on the second prologue scene, a square in the Kremlin on the following day. A ceremonial procession wends its way toward the cathedral: boyars, troops, children of the boyars, Prince Shuisky carrying a crown upon a cushion, Shchelkalov with the tsar's staff, more boyars and more troops, all heading for the cathedral.

"Long live Tsar Boris Feodorovich," Shuisky declares. "Long life and good health to you, Tsar and father," the masses respond.

Then, as Shuisky enters the cathedral, he demands glorification of Boris. The people obey. The grand ceremony, with its pealing bells and choral tributes, ceases when Boris appears. He asks God to bless his reign and concludes with an invitation to all to join in a feast. The curtain falls.

Throughout the prologue, approximately half an hour long, there is no operatic highlight in the normal sense of these words (a musical excerpt made quite familiar through numerous recordings and concert performances). The entirety of the two scenes is a highlight of powerful, original music. Individual voices are few: a policeman, several members of the crowd, Shchelkalov, Shuisky ever so briefly, and the response of Boris. It is the voice of the Russian people that is prominent in choral magnificence. Not, however, a lush or seductive magnificence. Mussorgsky's music is an economic and fitting expression of what is said. Paradoxically, this sparse, to-the-point, and matter-of-fact score is one of the richest and most emotional musical episodes in Russian opera—indeed, for me, in all opera! Especially glorious is the final chorus. Bells ring out, chimes play, and the orchestra swells as the multitude sings, *Sláva, Sláva, Sláva!* ("Glory! Glory! Glory!"). I cannot listen to this music without a rush of excitement and shivers.

Act I
Scene 1: The scene transpires in a cell of the Chudov monastery in the Kremlin. It is night. Pimen, an aged monk, writes by lamplight. He is only one story away from completing his chronicles—the history of Russia. Five years have passed since the coronation of Boris. Grigory, a young monk, lies asleep in the cell as Pimen writes, reflects, and then begins to compose his final episode, bringing his history to the present. As dawn nears, monks can be heard chanting lyrically offstage.

Grigory awakens with a start to complain that while Pimen writes peacefully, he has been plagued by a dream. After an exchange of respectful greetings, Grigory relates the evil dream he has now experienced for the third time. Tormented by the devil, he runs to the top of a tall tower in Moscow. Below, a jeering crowd taunts him as he looks down upon them. As he plummets toward them he awakens. He continues by lamenting that he never had the opportunity to experience the excitement of youth given to a soldier's life as did Pimen before becoming a monk. The old monk assures him it is better to have taken refuge from the temptations of the world, noting that even numerous tsars converted to the monk's cowl. Such a tsar as the good Fyodor, a man of peace, Pimen continues, but now God has inflicted us with terrible times because we have accepted as tsar "the murderer of a tsar." Grigory is prompted by this reference to ask about the death of Prince Dmitri because he knows Pimen was in Uglich at the time.

In a long monologue, perpetuated by questions from Grigory, Pimen relates the story that generations of great basses have made famous. It is the tale of how the tsarevich Dmitri was murdered by henchmen acting on orders from Boris Godunov. This is an excellent place to experience how Mussorgsky's restrained, stark orchestration brings to the fore the powerful music of the Russian language. With a libretto that includes a transliteration of the original Russian, as well as a translation into English, Pimen's account can be followed even if you do not know a single Russian word. Why follow it, then, word for word? It is to hear how the beauty and power of the music inherent in the words, Mussorgsky's fascination and great concern, dominates the story.

This murder took place twelve years ago. As the tale concludes, Pimen notes that had the Prince lived, he now would be Grigory's age and on the throne. Grigory does not miss this. During the telling of this terrible crime, Mussorgsky introduces a musical theme hereafter throughout the drama associated with either Prince Dmitri and his death or with Grigory, who soon will become Dmitri the pretender in spite of Pimen's hope that the young monk will be the one to whom he can pass along his chronicles for their continuation. His tale finished, Pimen rises, extinguishes his lamp, and listens to the offstage sound of the chanting monks: "Have mercy upon us, O Lord." Grigory, however, with great emotional intensity, vows Boris will not escape the judgment of both men and God. The curtain falls.

I just mentioned Mussorgsky's employment of a musical motif associated with Dmitri/Grigory. *Boris Godunov* is replete with many such themes, nearly fifty if not more. Those associated with individuals or the Russian people have been given names. Those who can read music, and who wish to undertake a far more thorough and intense study of the drama than what is presented here, can obtain a thematic guide. Utilizing themes as the building blocks of his orchestral score did, of course, prompt criticism of Mussorgsky as "a Wagnerian," a similar charge having been leveled at Verdi, in his later years, as well as other composers. Just because Wagner made operatic scores out of a network of commingled themes, no other composer thereafter is allowed to use this technique without condemnation? Just because one painter uses countless little dots of color to create an impression of something, or another painter uses vague, undefined bold strokes to do the same, no other painter is allowed to do so without censure? Just because one poet writes poems in lowercase free verse, no other poet should do the same? Isn't it too bad some critics have nothing better to do or nothing more insightful to say?

Scene 2: If you are counting, this is the fourth of the opera's ten scenes and it is a fascinating contrast to what heretofore has transpired, both musically and textually. The scene opens on the interior of an inn near the Lithuanian border after an orchestral prelude introduces themes to be employed later. While sewing the pocket of an old coat, the hostess of the inn sings a humorous song of double entendres. Musically, Mussorgsky creates an appealing, catchy little tune reminiscent of a folk song. Textually, the poem is about a drake that the hostess catches, the gist being that the drake is really a boy with whom she, a lonely widow, makes love. Voices outside the inn are heard in the distance. She pauses in her song, anticipating guests, hears them no more, and resumes singing. The voices are heard again, louder now; she opens the inn door, and two monks enter followed by a young peasant. The holy men, Varlaam and Missail, are vagabond monks who beg for alms to sustain themselves. The audience recognizes the young peasant as Grigory now in disguise. Having fled from his monastic existence, he is on his way to freedom in Lithuania. Certain unruly comments made when hastily departing have put the police on his trail.

The monks order drink and inform Grigory that he has arrived at the frontier. Wine arrives, both monks drink, Grigory abstains, and Varlaam, holding a bottle, sings a vigorous ballad—with pauses for swigs—telling the story of Tsar Ivan's defeat of the Tartars at Kazan. A long draft follows the conclusion of his song, always one of the highly appreciated excerpts from the opera. Grigory again refuses the offer of wine. Varlaam responds by proclaiming that it is the drunken man to whom the gate of heaven is opened and suggests to Missail that he join him in a toast to their hostess. The wine is working its wonders. Missail dozes while Varlaam sprawls on a tabletop.

Grigory asks the hostess if there are sentries at the border

with Lithuania. Policemen are checking all along the highway trying to find an escapee from Moscow who, she allows, could easily
avoid them by taking back roads whose whereabouts she just happens to disclose. No sooner said than knocks are heard on the inn
door. Answering, the hostess admits two policemen making their
rounds. As they question Grigory, who claims to be on his way
home after accompanying the monks to this inn, Varlaam and
Missail revive. The officers explain their mission: to apprehend
and hang an escaped heretical monk. They show Varlaam the
tsar's warrant and accuse him. He claims he lacks the wit to read
it and because all but Grigory are illiterate, it is left to Grigory to
read the warrant demanding the arrest of the monk Grigory
Otrepiev. As he does so, he amends the description of the wanted
monk to fit that of Varlaam in an attempt to frame him and save
himself, adding that nothing is written about hanging. As the officers attempt to hold Varlaam, he pushes them aside and seizes the
warrant, saying he can make some sense of it. As he elucidates a
perfect description of Grigory, the youth pulls a knife, leaps
through the window, and is gone as the first act concludes.

Act II

Act II, in one scene, begins with a domestic setting and ends with
one of the most powerful, hair-raising episodes in all opera. In it
Boris finally will come to the fore of the drama. With no orchestral introduction, the curtain opens on Xenia's pathetic lament for
her recently deceased betrothed as the nurse does needlepoint and
Prince Fyodor studies a map. To the left, in a corner of the opulent
interior, stands a chiming clock that has an important part in this
act. Fyodor tries to comfort his sister while the nurse, attempting
to divert the young girl's grief, sings a children's song about a gnat.
Fyodor, claiming it is too sad, sings another nursery song, the
nurse joining in. Boris enters as the song concludes. He comforts
his daughter, then excuses her, with the nurse, suggesting she will
feel better if she spends time with friends. Turning to Fyodor, who
is at his map, Boris says he is proud of how much geography the
boy knows and outlines for him the huge empire he will some day,
perhaps even soon, inherit. As Fyodor goes to the back of the stage
to study, the tsar, in profound consternation, delivers a famous
monologue beginning *Dostig ya v´yshey vlásti* ("I have attained
supreme power").

For almost six years I have ruled peacefully

And yet I am sad and my soul is tortured.

Nowhere has he been able to find happiness, neither in the praises of his people nor with the diversion of his daughter's great wedding festivity, aborted now because of the death of the groom. He feels the weight of guilt and attributes hints of a plot against him, plague and famine in Russia, and intrigues in Lithuania all to God's judgment upon him for his sin. From the deepest sleep, in the dark of night, he has awakened to visions of a bloodstained child. His cry for mercy remains unheeded. This dramatic monologue, after rising to a pitch, concludes solemnly as Boris all but collapses beneath the weight of such torment. There are two prominent musical themes, to be heard again: One relates to his guilt over the murdered child; the other will be associated with his own stupendous death scene.

Outside the apartment a disturbance is heard. As Fyodor exits to investigate, the chief boyar enters to inform Boris that Prince Shuisky has requested an audience. He adds that other boyars have met with Shuisky, who with them is in communication with some Poles. The boyar departs. Fyodor returns and entertains his father with a vivid account of the cause of the disturbance, a fracas involving nurses and a disobedient parrot. Boris praises his son's ability to tell a story. This is Fyodor's major musical contribution to the drama. Boris admonishes him not to choose disingenuous advisers like Shuisky when he becomes a tsar.

Shuisky enters. His obeisance is met with charges of treason from Boris. The Prince, however, dodges the accusations. He is there, he informs Boris, to let him know that a pretender has appeared in Poland who has the support of some nobles, the pope, and perhaps even the Russian people, should they believe him to be the tsarevich who disappeared mysteriously years ago. Boris inquires, "Under what name does he presume to take arms against us?" Shuisky replies, "By the resurrected name of Dmitri!" Fyodor is ordered by his father to leave the room. Boris then demands to know if Shuisky actually saw the dead child and could identify him as Dmitri. Shuisky's response is not reassuring, however, to Boris. He describes the child as appearing to be sleeping peacefully.

Boris can hear no more. He waves Shuisky out, grabs the arm of his chair, and slumps into it feeling as if he is suffocating. Though it is less than four minutes long, Boris's second great monologue of this act is both magnificent and chilling. As he gasps for air, the clock in the corner begins to chime. Its figures, animated by the striking, appear to the hallucinating tsar as the murdered tsarevich moving toward him under the protection of the people. He attempts several times to shoo away the child, then falls to the floor overwrought, praying to God to have mercy ". . . on the soul of the guilty Tsar Boris!", As said before, I am cautious about employing the overused, and often misused, word *unique*. The music Mussorgsky created for this culmination of Act I, minacious and threatening, is, indeed, unique. Hearing it, how could anyone, especially a gifted musician like Rimsky-Korsakov, ever doubt for a second that Mussorgsky knew precisely what he was doing every step of the way in creating this masterpiece?

The hysteria of Boris before the moving figures of the chiming clock often is referred to as "the Clock Scene," even though it is the brief conclusion to an act playing in a single scene. There are other celebrated scenes portraying the onset of madness in opera. They are, to cite the most well known, Lucia in *Lucia di Lammermoor* and Anna in *Anna Bolena*, both by Donzetti; Ophélie in the rarely performed opera *Hamlet*, by Thomas, and Imogen in Bellini's *Il pirata*. These scenes are madness with melody. There is no madness in music to compare with that composed by Mussorgsky for Tsar Boris losing his mind to a guilty conscience.

Act III

Scene 1: The maidens' chorus, opening the third act, is a delicate and lovely antithesis to the eerie insanity with which the previous act ended. This is the "Polish Act" in two scenes, the first set in Marina's dressing room in the castle at Sandomierz. Interrupting the maidens' song, praising nature's loveliness and the beauty of their mistress, Marina interjects a request that reveals all we need to know about her: "Pass me my diamond crown!" The maidens resume their flattery but Marina politely silences them, saying her preference is for songs of Polish victories in battle and of valiant, powerful Polish women. At this point in her long solo, she dismisses her attendants and then, as if daydreaming aloud to herself, reveals how she will overcome the tedium of her existence. Inspiring her beloved Dmitri to conquer Russia, she will obtain the power and glory she covets when sitting on the throne as tsarina (this woman is a megalomaniac!). Her long aria in a mazurka style (a mazurka is a Polish dance form) concludes in a laughing mockery of the Russian foe.

Rangoni appears, requesting to be heard. (The Jesuit priest is not to be found in Pushkin. Rangoni is Mussorgsky's invention.)

Holding sway over Marina, he commands her to employ all her feminine wiles to enslave Dmitri to do her will, or, I should say, to do Rangoni's will. It is his desire that the pretender Dmitri return victoriously to Russia and through his conquest Marina will ensure the restoration of the true faith over the infidels. At first she curses his deceitfulness of which she will have no part, but quickly capitulates before his threat of damnation. The curtain falls.

Scene 2: At midnight of a moonlit night, Dmitri exits the castle of Marina's family, enters the garden with its magnificent fountain, and sings a love song while waiting for his beloved. It is not Marina, however, who interrupts his reverie but rather the sinister, manipulative Jesuit. Having cast his spell over the Polish maid, next Rangoni will have his way with the pretender Dmitri, who is, of course, none other than the runaway monk Grigory (obviously you have figured this out already). His plan is to unite their Dmitri and Marina and, captivated by their love for each other, they will fall prey to his will. Rangoni quickly shoos away Dmitri as the garden suddenly fills with guests, Marina entering on the arm of an aged nobleman. The music, so appropriate for the Polish episode of the drama, is a polonaise (a Polish national dance, stately, festive, and associated with grand occasions). Dmitri frees himself from Rangoni, enters the garden, and goes to Marina. The guests depart. In a long scene, the two young people confess their love, but not without the Princess having made clear her ambitions for power and glory in Russia. As they embrace, Rangoni can be seen rejoicing silently in the distance as the curtain falls.

Act IV
Scene 1: A square before St. Basil's Cathedral in Moscow is crowded with impoverished, agitated people kept in line by milling police officers. It is announced that Grishka Otrepiev (Grigory, alias Dmitri) has been excommunicated and already is marching on Moscow, defeating the troops of Boris at every encounter. The focus shifts to the simpleton, who sings his song.

He is not what you may think. In old Russia, a simpleton (the Russian word is *yuródivy*) was not a dumbbell but rather one considered holy and blessed with powers to see into the future. These prophets wandered about naked (even in winter) except for a cloth covering their middle and chains hanging from their neck or waist. They were free to speak their mind without reproach.

Once his little song is sung, some boys taunt and tease him, then run off as he cries loudly. Boris, who has just exited the cathedral, stops and asks why he cries. When the simpleton replies it is because the boys stole his *kopeck* (a coin of Russian currency), Shuisky, accompanying Boris, wants "the fool" silenced. The tsar intercedes:

Do not touch him.
Pray for me, blessed one!

The simpleton refuses, calling him a Herod tsar, and he laments for the starving Russian people. This same provocative lament will end the opera. The curtain falls.

Scene 2: In a great hall in the Moscow Kremlin, the boyars have been summoned to vote on a proclamation issued by Boris against the pretender. It is approved. Shuisky reveals that Boris was seen attempting to ward off the ghost of the pretender and it is in this aberrant state that the tsar enters the hall. Quickly, however, he recovers his senses and agrees to see a holy man seeking an audience. It is Pimen. This famous part of the opera is known as "Pimen's Tale." The aged monk tells of a miracle cure for blindness that a shepherd received at the tomb of Dmitri and how the shepherd was spoken to by the voice of Dmitri, "son of the Tsar." Hearing this, Boris utters a cry, clutches his heart, and, knowing he now is dying, calls for his son and for a monk's habit. (It was a tradition of the tsars to be accepted into the church as a monk before dying.)

His son arrives. Boris dismisses the boyars. Here begins one of the most momentous events in all opera: the "Farewell, Prayer, and Death of Boris." Those who saw Chaliapin's enactment, as did my father, contend it had no dramatic equal in opera. All the music of this second scene of the fourth act is intense, resounding, and thoroughly masculine: Shchelkalov's baritone, the choral responses of the boyars, Shuisky's tenor, and Pimen's sonorous bass, all culminating with the last, gripping minutes in Boris's life.

I must remind you, however, that Mussorgsky's music is different from the classical restraint of Mozart, the soaring melodiousness of Puccini, the evocative orchestral power of Wagner, the hummable tunes of Verdi. Accordingly, you must listen differently. Listen for its chasteness, for the absence of anything extraneous, for its evocative power, and for the lack of calculated effects. With this music you are present in the great hall, part of Pimen's fantastic story, and then alone with the contrite tsar bidding his son farewell. The emotion is there but not, as is often heard in operatic culminations, in an extravagant manifestation. The word cogent comes to mind.

The "Farewell, Prayer, and Death of Boris," though a continuous episode of more than twelve minutes, is actually a sequence of subtly shifting emotions. After dismissing the boyars, Boris's monologue begins with somber, stately admonitions to Fyodor to fear the threat of the pretender, to distrust seditious boyars, and to show no mercy to those guilty of treachery. Boris appears to be talking to his son even though he sings to orchestral accompaniment. A more obvious melodic strain takes over in the orchestra as Boris urges his son to pursue justice, guard the true faith, and take care of his sister Xenia. Startling strings interrupt a pause following this counsel as the prayer portion begins with Boris begging the Lord (*Góspodi! Góspodi!*) to protect his son. And with the line "From thy inaccessible celestial height . . ." (*S górney nepristúpnoy . . .*) I hear one of the most subtle and beautiful melodic phrases I know. It is Mussorgsky at his best, never forcing words into music but with a craftsmanship so perfect that the music is drawn out of speech imperceptibly until the prayer's virtually inaudible conclusion as the tsar embraces his son.

An offstage bell tolling the death knell strikes such a contrast that one's heart jumps into one's throat. Also offstage, an ethereal choir anticipates the end as Boris calls for the monk's habit. Fyodor attempts to calm him but it is too late. As boyars and choristers almost surreptitiously fill the hall, the choir now lamenting Boris's unheeded plea for help, the dying tsar one more time asks the Lord if he is not to be forgiven for his sin. Then with a startling proclamation he exclaims, "I am still tsar." He clutches his heart, begs forgiveness, and acknowledges his heir before expiring. A long silence is broken by the voice of the orchestra as the boyars confirm that Boris Godunov is dead. The curtain falls.

Scene 3: The final scene dramatizes the disastrous consequences for innocent people when ambitious men vie for power. This opera ultimately is about turmoil and chaos in Russia. In a clearing of a forest near Kromy a crowd opposed to Boris, and unaware that the tsar has died, derides Khrushchov, a captured boyar. Dmitri has successfully marched into Russia, a country rampant with starving, pillaging people. The music of this final scene, start to finish, is a most appropriate evocation of the turbulent, desperate situation. Varlaam and Missail, arriving from Moscow, proclaim the guilt of Boris, thus inciting the mob to demand the death of the tsar and stirring them to follow Dmitri when he arrives.

Two Jesuits enter. They are supporters of the pretender but nevertheless are captured and dragged off because of their alien religion. A trumpet announces the arrival of Dmitri and his troops on their course to Moscow. They torch the woods as they depart. All follow him, clearing the stage, except for the simpleton, who in his haunting, pathetic song iterates his lament for the starving people. The poetry is as unforgettable as the music. Sitting on a stone in the deserted clearing and rocking back and forth in the glow of destructive brushfires, he sings:

> Flow, flow, O bitter tears,
> weep, O Christian soul,
> soon the enemy will come
> and darkness will fall,
> darkness, black and impenetrable.
> Woe, woe unto Russia,
> weep, weep, O Russian people.
> Hungry people.[†]

The simpleton shudders as slowly the curtain falls.

Mother Russia, and not Boris Godunov, obviously is the main character in Mussorgsky's masterpiece. The historical Boris Godunov died suddenly in 1605 in Moscow. Two months later the pretender triumphantly entered Moscow. Fyodor, son of Boris and the assumed successor, was murdered. Shuisky recognized the pretender as tsar even though Dmitri was never crowned. He did, nevertheless, bring Marina to Moscow, where they were married. One intrigue followed another. Dmitri was murdered in 1606. Shuisky, a turncoat, now denounced Dmitri as an imposter. He became tsar and reigned until 1610, when he was dispatched. History, almost but not irrefutably, has exonerated Boris Godunov of the crime for which he was made infamous in the opera. You can visit his tomb in Moscow.

[†] Modest Mussorgsky, *Boris Godunov* (EMI Records, Ltd., 1977), p. 46

PETER ILYICH TCHAIKOVSKY

EUGENE ONEGIN (1879)

Though contemporaries, Mussorgsky and Tchaikovsky, composers of Russia's two most famous operatic exports, were very different men. Accordingly, their music differs significantly. Mussorgsky, writing to his friend Rimsky-Korsakov, explains his concern for the relationship between words and music: "Whatever speech I hear, no matter who is speaking nor what he says, my mind is already working to find the musical statement for such speech." The mighty Russian language was the inspiration for Mussorgsky's music. His music has a fitting dramatic power—a primitive, ancient quality, a dramatic starkness without ever getting in the way of the words. Tchaikovsky, writing to his patroness Nadezhda von Meck, reveals the source of his music:

> If you had asked me whether I had ever found complete happiness in love, I should have replied no, and, again, no. Besides, I think the answer to this question is to be heard in my music. If, however, you ask me whether I have felt the whole power and inexpressible stress of love, I must reply, yes, yes, yes: for often I have striven to render in music all the anguish and the bliss of love.

With a confession like this, is it any wonder that scholars writing about Tchaikovsky have concluded that for him, musical composition was an emotional release for relentless sexual passions never satisfied in a fulfilling, loving relationship? Tchaikovsky's music is romantic and lyrical but his Russianness is filtered through the cosmopolitan tradition of western European conservatory training, with its emphasis on melody, harmony, form, and polish. In other words, the great classical composers of Germany and France were his models.

Though both he and Mussorgsky, for example, were profoundly attracted to their native musical folk idiom, Tchaikovsky's adaptations, unlike those of his contemporary, were not simple and barren of ornamentation, but rather lush and elegant. In comparing random passages from *Boris Godunov* and *Eugene Onegin* you will hear the differences: Mussorgsky more primitive and original, Tchaikovsky more traditionally under the influence of a long-established Western European approach to music making. This approach had made such inroads into the Slavic countries that by the middle of the nineteenth century some of the most significant Russian and Czech composers reacted by forging their own distinct national identity in their music. Mussorgsky was a member of the Russian group.

Tchaikovsky is incorrectly known to many Westerners as a composer of only instrumental music: famous concertos for piano, one for violin; six well-known symphonies; ballets; and songs and incidental pieces known the world over, such as "Marche Slav" and "The 1812 Overture." Tchaikovsky was ten years old when he saw Mozart's *Don Giovanni*. Instantly smitten and hooked, during his lifetime he would write ten operas. Perhaps others went into the fireplace. Two of them, *Eugene Onegin* (1879) and *The Queen of Spades* (1890), equally well known by the title *Pique Dame*, are exceedingly popular both in Russia and abroad. *Eugene Onegin* is considered the operatic masterpiece of Tchaikovsky who admitted he lacked the heroism required, like Johannes Brahms, *not* to write an opera.

Eugene Onegin, based on Pushkin's great narrative poem, is an opera in three acts about love ironically unrequited. The libretto is by the composer and K. S. Shilovsky (you do not meet him again in this book). This is an opera of set numbers (arias, duets, ensembles, and dances composed with an obvious beginning and end). The cast is as follows:

> MADAME LARINA, owner of a country estate, *mezzo-soprano*
> TATYANA and OLGA, her daughters, *soprano* and *contralto*
> FILIPEVNA, the daughters' old nurse, *mezzo-soprano*
> VLADIMIR LENSKY, Olga's fiancé, *tenor*
> EUGENE ONEGIN, his friend, *baritone*
> ZARETSKY, another friend of Lensky, *bass*
> PRINCE GREMIN, elderly, retired army officer and Onegin's cousin, *bass*
> A captain, *bass*
> TRIQUET, Frenchman and tutor, *tenor*

> The time is early nineteenth century and the action
> takes place on and about Madame Larina's country estate

located near St. Petersburg and in Prince Gremin's home in St. Petersburg.

Act I

Scene 1: The conductor's raised baton gives the downbeat and as if out of nowhere the brief musical introduction establishes a fitting mood for the world we are about to enter. The curtain rises. Madame Larina, in the garden of her estate, is making jam, Filipevna helping her. The large doors of the house that lead to the terrace behind the garden are open and we hear the voices of two girls singing wistfully of love. Their song prompts Madame Larina to reflect on her youth and the marriage her parents arranged for her. As Filipevna joins her mistress with her own reminiscences, the girls' duet has become a fascinating quartet expressing youthful aspirations and adaptations of age as the older women, with resignation, sing, "Habit is sent us from above in place of happiness."

In the distance, we hear the singing of peasants approaching the house. Their tune is one of my favorites in the opera, a lovely, simple, folklike melody of infectious lyricism. These are the workers who have come to present their benefactress with a decorated sheaf symbolizing the successful harvest. Gladly they respond to Madame Larina's request to sing for her while the peasant girls dance around the sheaf. Their fetching music has brought Olga and Tatyana onto the balcony to listen. When the latter comments on how such music makes her dream and float away into her own faraway world, her sister responds with a fine little song about how she is so different, preferring carefree fun to dreamy meditations.

The peasants leave with Filipevna, all having been offered wine by Madame Larina. Tatyana, who loves to read romances, sits and becomes lost in her book about the torments of young lovers until her mother brings her back to reality. Olga, hearing someone approach, bursts with excitement when she realizes it is her beloved Lensky, who comes with another. Filipevna announces the arrival of Lensky and a Mr. Onegin. Tatyana's nervous attempt to flee is restrained by her mother, and the gentlemen are shown in. Lensky introduces Onegin as a new neighbor. After exchanging formalities, Madame Larina—a wise mother—finds something to do in the house.

The men stand apart from the women and talk. Onegin asks which is Tatyana and wonders why Lensky would prefer the younger sister. To her sister Tatyana confesses, "My waiting is over." She has fallen in love at first sight. Olga is not surprised and we are into a second quartet as the men discuss the women and the sisters contemplate a suitor for Tatyana. The men approach the women and the couples pair, Olga and Lensky talking of their love, Tatyana and Onegin getting to know each other. Onegin wonders if she is bored living in the country. She says she reads and dreams. He says that is not enough and they stroll away, leaving Lensky, a poet, to declare again his passion for Olga in an ardent love song—one of the big solo numbers of the score.

As night begins to fall, Madame Larina and Filipevna return and encourage the sisters to invite the gentlemen for supper. The old nurse is suspicious that Tatyana, so terribly shy, nevertheless has become intrigued with the new young neighbor. Thus ends the first of three scenes in the opening act.

Scene 2: The curtain rises on Tatyana, in a white nightdress, who sits before a mirror in her room. She is lost in thought. Her nurse urges her to bed but Tatyana is not tired and asks Filipevna to relate for her the story of her love life when she was young. One did not talk of love in the old days, the nurse tells her, days when marriages were arranged by parents through a broker. Tatyana blurts out that she is consumed with longing, requests pen and paper, and asks to be left alone. For a few moments Tatyana, alone with her thoughts, remains motionless. The orchestra, with increasing intensity, tells us what is going on in those thoughts before Tatyana, in a state of excitement and determination, begins the greatest scene in the drama and one of the most romantically beautiful letter scenes in opera literature.

A favorite device in earlier opera history had a character read a letter delivered to him or her, and in some operas, characters actually write a letter (Mozart's *Le nozze di Figaro*), but so overwhelming is Tatyana's scene in which she writes Onegin to confess her love that it has become for many of us *the* operatic letter scene. This was the first music Tchaikovsky composed once he settled on Pushkin's poem as the subject for an opera. Unquestionably, this episode is the germinating factor of the whole drama, both dramatically and musically. It is well known that the hypersensitive Tchaikovsky fell in love with his Tatyana, giving to her some of the most exquisite music he ever wrote. He retained Pushkin's title, *Eugene Onegin*, but Tatyana is far and away the central character. This will be obvious once you hear the music he gives her.

Puskai pogibnu ya, no pryezhde ("Let me perish, but first let me summon, in dazzling hope, bliss as yet unknown"), the scene begins, her repressed emotions exploding with orchestral magnificence. Tatyana goes to her writing table, writes, reads what she has written, and, in an alternating series of reflections, writing, and reading aloud what she has written, pours out her love for Onegin in a letter. And, what the audience does not get in words is supplied by the orchestra. Tatyana is consumed, on fire, possessed.

I first learned to love this music from a 1943 recording in a German translation sung by the incomparable Tiana Lemnitz, then acquired her 1946 recording (also in German and available on CD), and eventually heard it in Russian on the 1951 recording with the thrilling voice of the Italian soprano Licia Albanese, with Leopold Stokowski conducting his orchestra. Years later, and knowing that Albanese does not speak Russian, I asked her how she managed the difficult Russian text. "Maestro Stokowski taught me phonetically, each and every sound," she told me. This recording is also on CD. I knew this music by heart long before I heard a complete performance of the opera. Good recent recordings are available both on video and CD.

By the time Tatyana has finished, signed, and sealed her letter, it is dawn as she opens the curtains. A shepherd's pipe is heard. Filipevna enters the room and Tatyana instructs her to have her grandson deliver the letter to Onegin. She then returns to sit at her table, once again becoming lost in thought as the curtain falls.

Scene 3: The final tableau of the first act takes place in another portion of the garden. As servant girls pick fruit they sing an enchanting song, another of those little gems Tchaikovsky seemed to produce effortlessly. The girls depart. Tatyana enters. Exhausted, she slumps onto a bench and reproaches herself for having confessed her passion in a letter. Onegin enters. Tatyana leaps to her feet, her head lowered. Politely and unemotionally, he tells her he will answer her letter now. Distraught and humiliated, she sinks back down onto the bench. Were he the marrying kind, he says, he would choose her for a bride, but he was not made for wedded bliss. He loves her with a brother's love and advises her to learn how to control her feelings. The servant girls can be heard again in the distance singing their song. Onegin offers Tatyana his arm. She looks long at him, rises stiffly with obvious mortification, and takes his arm. They depart slowly as the curtain falls.

In elementary school, I began what has remained a lifelong fascination: reading about the lives of great composers. Those who might share such a curiosity will be interested to learn that Tchaikovsky did not like Onegin, whom he considered insensitive and a boring show-off. So struck by Onegin's refusal of Tatyana's love, Tchaikovsky, struggling with his own homosexuality, would not have the heart to refuse the confession of love from a young woman he met while teaching at the Moscow Conservatory. Unwisely, he succumbed to a marriage that ended for him in a nervous breakdown. Ironically, it was while he was at work on this opera that Tchaikovsky received the woman's declaration of love.

Act II
Scene 1: This act plays in two scenes, the first in the ballroom of Madame Larina's house, where she is giving a party for Tatyana's birthday. A brief entr'acte gives way to a waltz, one of the most famous and beautiful Tchaikovsky ever wrote. When one remembers that he composed three of the most popular ballets in the world, *Nutcracker, Swan Lake,* and *The Sleeping Beauty,* that is a bold statement. As young people dance, Lensky with Olga and Tatyana with Onegin among them, they sing in praise of the wonderful party. Elderly people watch the festivities and chat. Focusing on Tatyana and Onegin, some women disparage the young man's drinking, gambling, and Freemasonry loudly enough for him to overhear. In an aside, angered by their gossipy babble, he blames Lensky for bringing him to such a parochial gathering and resolves to take revenge on his friend by openly dancing and flirting with Olga to make him jealous. Olga enjoys the attention and Lensky responds as predicted. He commences to argue with her. She cannot comprehend his jealousy and punishes him by accepting another Onegin invitation to dance. A scene is averted temporarily when young girls invite Monsieur Triquet to sing a song he wrote for Tatyana. He places her in the middle of a circle of the girls and sings his fulsome praises, in French, of course. This fine song is appreciated by all, those on stage and those in the audience, with applause.

Dancing resumes with the Cotillion, a portion of which Onegin dances with Olga as Lensky's fury mounts. Onegin goes to his friend and chides him for not joining in the fun. A quarrel begins and intensifies such that the party is interrupted. Aware of what has happened, Onegin attempts to ameliorate the situation but Lensky, raging, is too far gone. To the horror of all, he challenges

Onegin to a duel. The scene culminates in a remarkable ensemble, an amalgam of various emotions as Madame Larina, her daughters, Lensky, Onegin, and guests express deeply troubled feelings. Displeased with himself for the trouble he has caused, Onegin, nevertheless, is aware that his prank has evolved into an insanity from which there is no way out. He accepts the challenge. Lensky and Onegin rush out of the room. Olga, attempting to follow her lover, faints in her mother's arms as the curtain falls.

Scene 2: The curtain rises to show an old mill next to a stream in the woods. It is dawn of the following day. Lensky sits in the snow under a tree. His second, Zaretsky, paces in this desolate place awaiting the arrival of Onegin. Then, seeing the miller at his door, he goes over to strike up a conversation. Lensky has center stage for one of the most coveted tenor arias in Russian operatic literature: *Kuda, kuda, kuda vi udalilis, vesni moyei zlatiye dni* ("Where, oh where have you gone, golden days of my youth?"). Known simply as "Lensky's Farewell," his melancholy thoughts anticipating the possibility of dying are expressed in music of exquisite lyricism. I first heard this poignant aria on a recording made by the Swedish tenor Jussi Björling, who sang a Swedish translation (now remastered onto compact disc). I will not even attempt to find superlatives for this one!

Onegin arrives and introduces his manservant, who he calls his second, one Monsieur Guillot. While Zaretsky and Guillot withdraw to establish the conditions of the duel, Lensky and Onegin stand back to back, awaiting instructions. In a canon (a melody sung by one voice is imitated by a second voice soon after the first voice), they sing of their friendship and anger. Zaretsky and Guillot, in absolute silence, measure distances, load pistols, and position the antagonists. Zaretsky claps three times. The adversaries step forward, raise pistols, and fire. Lensky falls. The act ends with the spoken word *Ubit* ("Dead"). With irony stranger than his fiction, Alexander Pushkin was killed in a duel six years after writing this *Onegin* poem by a man he accused of sleeping with his wife.

Act III
Scene 1: For the first of two scenes in the final act, the story now several years later—has moved to St. Petersburg. As the curtain rises on the salon and ballroom of a nobleman's mansion, couples dance a polonaise, music as familiar to the concert hall and

recording studio as the celebrated waltz that opened the second act. Onegin, who was bored by the provincial life on and about Madame Larina's country estate, is bored here too, in the mix of urban high society. The dance ends and he laments his world-weariness in an aria of despair. He is twenty-six, aimless, idle, and consumed by guilt at having killed his best friend in a duel. He suffers the ennui and angst of a pointless existence. His cousin, Prince Gremin, enters with a young woman of supreme, serene beauty on his arm. He leads her to a sofa. Her arrival has stirred the guests to stare approvingly at a woman so wondrous. Onegin is stunned.

> Can that be Tatyana? Surely . . . no! . . .
> She bears herself like a queen!

Oh, how the tables have been turned since his rebuke of her as the first act ended.

From a distance Tatyana glances in his direction. Onegin is talking with Prince Gremin. She asks some guests, "Tell me, who is that . . . over there with my husband? I cannot see him very well." When told it is the melancholy Onegin returned from traveling abroad, she fears the tumult she instantly feels in her heart. Meanwhile, Onegin has questioned the Prince as to the identity of the beautiful woman across the room. The Prince says he will present him to her. She is "my wife" he says, confirming that the woman is, indeed, Tatyana.

The music of this act is varied and wonderful, the most memorable being Prince Gremin's song about his love for his wife. Perhaps you noticed with both *Boris Godunov* and *Eugene Onegin* that, unlike most all other operas you have now encountered, the tenor is generally not the major male voice. This often is true in Russian and Slavic opera literature, where the greatest music has been written for the bass. There is no finer example than Prince Gremin's aria sung to Onegin. Love, he says, ignores age. It made me young again. I love Tatyana to distraction. She is everything to me. And he leads Onegin to her for an introduction. Formally, and without apparent emotion, they greet each other and acknowledge they had met in the country years ago. Politely and briefly they exchange pleasantries before Tatyana, who is tired, leaves on Prince Gremin's arm.

Onegin is left staring. He cannot believe this magnificent woman is the same Tatyana he once coldly admonished, "Learn to control your feelings." In the matter of a few minutes in her presence his meaningless existence has been instantly transformed. He sees only her wherever he looks. The same love that restored the aging prince now rages passionately within Onegin. Instantly, he has become possessed with Tatyana. With his passionate confession, in an aria ingeniously utilizing musical themes from Tatyana's letter-writing scene, the curtain falls.

Scene 2: In her drawing room, Tatyana is holding a letter. It is morning and she is distressed. Onegin has reawakened her passion for him. He rushes in and falls at her feet. She asks him to rise so that she may speak frankly to him. To his utter anguish he is reminded of the severity with which he answered her love letter. So why does he pursue her now? Is it her social status, her wealth, her nobility? Tormented by this reproach, he tells her how hopelessly in love he is. Tatyana, weeping now, reminds him how close to happiness they once were, but those days are gone. He must leave. She is a married woman. Onegin drops to his knee, takes her hand, covers it with kisses, and pleads. She withdraws her hand and implores him to go. He cannot. Ceasing to pretend any longer, Tatyana admits that she does still love him and briefly they embrace. Her resolve returns. She frees herself and says she will be true to her husband always. While Onegin continues to plead, Tatyana's resolve stiffens, as Tchaikovsky pours intense music upon them both until with a "Farewell forever" she walks out of the room. Onegin blurts out his last words, "Oh, my pitiable fate!" and runs out of the house. The curtain falls.

Early in my teens I developed a passion for the music of Tchaikovsky, especially the piano concertos and the symphonies. Symphony No. 5 was a particular favorite and I played my recording over and over, immersed in its laments and theme of resignation before fate. Adult musical friends of the family, no longer intoxicated by Tchaikovsky's brooding lyricism, told me my fascination would pass. The great appeal of his music is to an adolescent head and heart, they assured me. They were partly right. In time I did hear passages that were too sentimental, too flamboyant, too shallow, no longer as nurturing. But they were partly wrong, too. A lot that Tchaikovsky composed has remained with me all my life. At the piano I still pick out favorite themes from the Fifth Symphony and I cannot live without *Eugene Onegin*. It is a masterpiece, one of the greatest romantic operas ever written.

During its composition, deeply disturbed by a profound depression, Tchaikovsky attempted suicide. Had he succeeded, our musical loss would be unthinkable: an incomplete *Eugene Onegin*; his tour de force violin concerto; the second piano concerto; Serenade for Strings; Symphonies 4, 5 and 6; *The Sleeping Beauty* and *Nutcracker* ballets, and five more operas of which *The Queen of Spades* is the most renowned, to cite only the most prominent compositions that come to mind. In St. Petersburg during the fall of 1893, feeling indisposed, Tchaikovsky unwisely drank a glass of unboiled water, developed cholera, and died a few days later. He was only fifty-three years old.

With the two most familiar of all Russian operas now within your ken, you may wish to explore more of the great Slavic tradition. Here are a few suggestions. Glinka's *A Life for the Tsar* (1836), also known as *Ivan Susanin*, is one of the earliest. Smetana's *The Bartered Bride* (1866) is unquestionably the national opera of the Czech people, and if you listen to classical music, you must have heard at least the ever popular overture and familiar dances from this tuneful spectacle. Borodin did not live to complete his *Prince Igor* (1890); Rimsky-Korsakov and Glazunov finished it after his death. He was a gifted scientist who also happened to write lovely music. The popular song "Strangers in Paradise" was made from one of his best melodies. Of course, other operas by Mussorgsky and Tchaikovsky await you, and when we reach twentieth-century opera, I will have more on the Slavic tradition. In fact, beyond the two master works introduced in this chapter, a vast and seemingly unconquerable world of Russian and Slavic opera is opened to you.

Now, to the melodious world of operetta.

Jacques Offenbach

Johann Strauss, Jr.

W.S. Gilbert

Arthur Sullivan

THE GREAT AGE OF OPERETTA

The original meaning of the word operetta is "little work" and, operatically speaking, for the seventeenth and eighteenth centuries it was used to designate a short opera, or a "little opera." During the nineteenth and twentieth centuries, the word came to mean a lighthearted and often sentimental theatrical piece of a musical style sometimes more simple than opera. That is the meaning presented here.

The story was advanced by spoken dialogue and embellished by songs and dances. Because it was thought to be less profound than opera and because its music was considered simpler and less demanding than operatic music (this, certainly, is not always true), operetta generally has had a history and following somewhat unto itself. There are those opera lovers who scorn it as trivial, unworthy of serious musical consideration. Furthermore, even though an opera, especially a comic opera, and an operetta can seem to have much in common, the operetta tradition has its individualities. For these reasons, and others, few books on opera treat the subject of operetta. Like opera buffa and singspiel, from which it derives, operetta relishes in mistaken identities, disguises, and shenanigans leading to seemingly impossible situations that are ultimately resolved happily. This book does not dismiss operetta—it is so closely related to opera history that to exclude it would be both an arbitrary and, to me, an unacceptable omission.

Franz von Suppé, an eccentric Viennese who reportedly chewed wineglasses and slept in the coffin he eventually was buried in, was one of the originators of nineteenth-century operetta. He was born in 1819 and between 1860 and 1895 wrote thirty of them. Unless you go looking, you are not likely to come upon anything of his except a charming, elegant tune or two. It is otherwise with Jacques Offenbach (1819–1880). You met him in chapter 9 as the composer of the masterpiece *The Tales of Hoffmann*, his one serious opera. Between 1855 and 1880, he composed more than ninety operettas, and who in the world has not heard his famous "Can-Can"? It was Johann Strauss the Younger, "the Waltz King," whose operettas swept Europe and America like wildfire. He lived from 1825 until 1899 and between 1871 and 1897 wrote about sixteen operettas, one of which, *Die Fledermaus (The Bat)*, is certainly the most well-known operetta in the world. His Viennese tradition was perpetuated by Franz Lehár (1870–1948), whose *Die lustige Witwe (The Merry Widow)* 1905 remains popular unto this day, its famous waltz having worldwide appeal. The so-called Savoy operas of Gilbert and Sullivan, called thus after the London theater where they had their premiere, are in reality operettas, the first noteworthy achievement in English dramatic music since the death of Purcell nearly two hundred years earlier. With Offenbach, Strauss, and Gilbert and Sullivan, the three foremost traditions of operetta were established: the French, the Viennese, and the English.

There is a fourth tradition, the American. Were we to follow its course, it would take us to a subject beyond the limits of this book: the American musical. Early in the twentieth century, the Irishman Victor Herbert and the Hungarian Sigmund Romberg, independently, brought to this country their brand of operetta. Herbert's *Naughty Marietta* and Romberg's *The Student Prince*, to cite only two of their numerous popular works, had huge success. These works were very much in the tradition of European operetta. During the 1920s, this European heritage began to be altered by a native impact. *Showboat* (1927) with music by Jerome Kern and lyrics by Oscar Hammerstein II, is the classic example. "Musical comedy" became the phrase for this type of theater whose great future lay in the string of successes by Rogers and Hammerstein, Lerner and Loewe, and others.

The American musical, a direct descendant of European opera, was born, and with it came one uninherited, distinguishing characteristic. Those who perform in traditional operetta must be able to sing. Many great singers who have performed and recorded both operas and operettas make no vocal distinctions in their work. They bring the same talent, the same highly trained, schooled voices to their work whatever it is. As the American musical developed, however, achieving in time huge popularity, some stars performed songs with a certain highly personal style or simply belted out a song, often with little or no regard for having mastered the art of singing. It is for this reason that the American musical goes beyond the subject of this book. Even though its origins are in European opera, this book is about masterful singing: opera and operetta.

The combined operetta output of Offenbach, Strauss, and Gilbert and Sullivan is about 125 different works but I know I am safe, when representing only one of each, to introduce their most enduringly popular work: Offenbach's *Orphée aux enfers (Orpheus in the Underworld)*; *Die Fledermaus* by Strauss; and *The Mikado* of Gilbert and Sullivan. These three masterpieces of the operetta stage have in common two basic ingredients: unforgettable music and humor. It is a truism of the stage that tragedy touches the emotions, the heart, while humor goes to the head. If you don't get the joke, you don't get the humor, but the music of all three works is so enticing that you can miss the humor and still fall in love with the operetta. The humor, however, because it is so good, makes something wonderful even better. Offenbach was addicted to parody, Strauss's *Die Fledermaus* has disguises and jokes, and Gilbert and Sullivan enjoyed satirizing the mores of Victorian England. Our introduction is limited to these three even though Karl Millöcker, Leo Fall, Emmerich Kalman, Franz Lehár, Rudolf Friml, and others wrote perfectly delightful operetta music that awaits you.

JACQUES OFFENBACH

ORPHÉE AUX ENFERS (1858 & 1874)
Orpheus in the Underworld

Why are there two dates? The original version in two acts, a parody of the Orpheus myth, brought Offenbach considerable notoriety for both the score he composed and the scandal he created. He was accused of a heretical abuse of a classic myth, of mocking the great composer Gluck, and, to the great delight of many in the audience, of making fun of French politics and morality. The original version was designated an opéra bouffe, a term for nineteenth-century satirical French operetta that derives, obviously, from the Italian opera buffa (comic opera). Ludovic Halévy, one of the *Carmen* librettists and son of the composer Fromental Halévy, who wrote the excellent and once popular opera *La Juive*, drafted a text for Offenbach from which Hector Cremieux (we do not meet him again) produced a libretto. The success of the 1858 version prompted Offenbach, needing some quick cash, to greatly expand the work into a four-act version in 1874. Invariably, this is the version that is produced and recorded today.

To appreciate Offenbach's parody of the Orpheus story it is necessary to know what is being parodied. In the nineteenth century, it could be assumed of educated people that they would be familiar with the myth. Not so today. If you need a reminder, go back to chapter 1, where it was presented as part of our introduction to another famous opera on the subject, Gluck's *Orfeo ed Euridice.*

The characters are:

Public Opinion, *mezzo-soprano*
ORPHEUS, a violinist, *tenor*
EURYDICE, his wife, *soprano*
JUPITER, King of the gods, *baritone*
PLUTO, god of the underworld who can appear in mortal guise as ARISTEUS, a beekeeper, *tenor*
JOHN STYX, Hades prison lackey, *baritone*
MERCURY, *tenor*
MARS, *bass*
MORPHEUS, *tenor*
DIANA, *soprano*
VENUS, *soprano*
CUPID, *soprano*
JUNO, *mezzo-soprano*

The time is antiquity. The setting: countryside near Thebes, Mount Olympus, boudoir of Pluto, and Hades.

Act I

Within the brief overture, we hear two of the most famous excerpts from the operetta—the violin solo and the celebrated Can-Can. When stage directions are honored, the curtain opens on a funny set representing a slice of Theban countryside. The background is a field of corn. Foreground left, a cottage wears a sign reading "Aristeus, honey manufacturer, wholesale and retail, Mount Hymettus warehouse." Foreground right there is another cottage bearing a sign as follows: "Orpheus, director of the Thebes male voice choral society, music lessons by the month or by the hour." The empty stage suddenly fills with shepherds and shepherdesses singing that it is time to go home followed by the pretentious members of the town council, who, while passing by, sing loftily of their self-importance. Next comes a monologue by Public Opinion admonishing woe unto any unfaithful wife or husband with a disclosing of potent *deus ex machina* resources to set things right within an instant. The stage clears as Eurydice enters gathering flowers and singing to herself. The flowers, she says ("Say nothing of this to my husband"), are for the handsome shepherd who has her emotions deeply stirred. As she hangs a wreath on the door of Aristeus, her back is to Orpheus as he enters with his violin. This ludicrous anachronism alone is worthy of a laugh even before the famous violin episode has begun.

Is the woman at the shepherd's door perhaps the lovely young nymph after whom he has been lusting, he wonders? He launches into a passionate phrase on his violin, the startled Eurydice spins around, and husband and wife confront each other in a compromising situation. At first, Eurydice feigns that she gathered the flowers for the wind but soon thereafter comes clean and admits her love for Aristeus. While at it, she tells Orpheus to go fiddle for the shepherdess he has been pursuing. Responding to his questions, she admits infidelity, her dislike of his musical career, and her hatred of the violin. Orpheus seeks immediate revenge for these insults. He will play her his latest concerto, which lasts one hour and fifteen minutes. Her pleadings fall on deaf ears and thus begins the opera's famous violin solo. There is no music in the entire score more enchanting than this, and as Eurydice and Orpheus add their squabbling voices, the poetry is both amusing and clever in its rhyme schemes. For example, she condemns the music as "deplorable" and he responds with "adorable." They part, each happy to be rid of the other.

A lovely pastoral ballet precedes the arrival of Aristeus, who then sings of bucolic pleasures. Eurydice enters and tells him that her husband knows all and that he has released poisonous snakes in the cornfield where they have made love. Aristeus, who really is the god of the Underworld, has no fear of the reptiles. Eurydice returns, however, is bitten and must go off to Hades with her lover. She finds dying intoxicating, and before departing leaves a note tacked to her husband's cottage door informing him she is leaving home because she is dead. Eurydice and Aristeus vanish. Orpheus returns and the tuneful finale of the first act is under way. Public Opinion, on the heels of Orpheus, demands he go after his wife. Orpheus, after remonstrating, relents, bids a sad farewell to his pupils, and follows Public Opinion as all agree that "honor comes before love." The curtain falls.

Act II

The curtain rises on a dark stage. In the clouds, slumbering gods wish only to sleep. Returning home, in succession, Venus, Cupid, and Mars join the others until the sound of Diana's hunting horn awakens her father, Jupiter, who rouses the other gods. Diana has returned home in a snit. In a little song, with its repetitive every other line being a "hey nonny nonny no" sort of refrain, she tells us she is distressed because she cannot find her beloved Acteon. Because you were making a fool of yourself with this young mortal, "I changed him into a stag," her father tells her. The humans have their eyes on us, and we must "keep up appearances." Diana censures her father for his endless infidelities; her mother, Juno, adds her two cents' worth. Mercury enters and sings a jaunty rondo (a playful musical form in which the major theme keeps returning) about all the duties given to him by Jupiter. "He will probably finish by putting me in a barometer to show the weather" is the little joke that ends the song.

Mercury informs the gods that Pluto has taken the pretty Eurydice from her husband, then Pluto, as if on cue, enters. He and Jupiter argue, the King of the gods demands silence, and in return, he gets a chorus of revolt from the other gods, who are bored by his tedious tyranny. (If I were to note for you every musical gem in the score, there would be no end to this introduction. When you listen to a complete recording you will hear one delightful tune after another, the "Uprising Chorus" being one of countless examples. All the music in this operetta is a "highlight." You are virtually propelled to sing along or at least to wave arms and tap feet.)

The gods have turned on Jupiter. Their diet of nectar and ambrosia is monotonous and Jupiter's behavior reproachable. They remind him of the numerous disguises he has employed for amorous activities on earth, but are interrupted when Mercury announces two strangers seeking an audience. Orpheus, followed by Public Opinion, is admitted. Here begins the great Act II finale. Pluto, who all along has denied having had anything to do with Eurydice, shows concern while Orpheus, urged on by Public Opinion, presents his case to Jupiter. "My Eurydice has been stolen from me," he sings to music, note for note, taken by Offenbach from Gluck's greatest scene, the *Che farò senza Euridice* lament of Orfeo in his masterpiece *Orfeo ed Euridice.* (Offenbach was scolded by some critics for this irreverent parody.) Pluto's infamy is revealed and Jupiter orders Eurydice restored to her husband. When he declares his intention to go to hell to see this done, all the other deities beg to be allowed to accompany him in order to have some fun. Jupiter consents and is praised by all, and they troop out behind the falling curtain.

Act III

Offenbach's music opening the second act in the realm of the bored, slumbering gods was subdued. The brief entr'acte making the connection from Mount Olympus to Hades, where the third act plays, is anything but. The curtain rises on Pluto's boudoir. Alone and bored to death, Eurydice sits waiting. In a song of memorable melody she ponders her fate: A once passionate love affair with Pluto has grown cold. He has left her alone with his servant John Styx, who is to keep her under lock and key. To her this man is a most odious character, especially when he sings about how once he was King of Boeotia. He is a fatuous little man, with music to fit him, and he confesses his adoration of Eurydice, who would, were he king again, be his queen. A commotion outside alerts them to Pluto's return, evidently with guests. According to orders, Eurydice is locked into a room at the back. She is furious. Jupiter enters first, with Pluto. Obviously, he is overly eager to meet the "pretty young woman" he has heard so much about and demands to know where she is. Still protesting his innocence, Pluto will be tried by the judges of hell. The judges, however, are in Pluto's pay. Their brief septet, barely two minutes long, is one of my favorite tunes of the endless series of little musical gems that pepper this extraordinary score.

Only with Cupid's help is Jupiter ever enabled to see Eurydice.

About two dozen police are called in to search. The round they sing is more of the same music you simply cannot get enough of. Cupid's waltz song tells Jupiter that were he to disguise himself as a fly, he could go through the keyhole of the door to the room where Eurydice is being kept. This metamorphosis is not easy for a director to realize but when it is done well, we have before us a most amusing episode. As the keyhole grows bigger and bigger before our eyes, Jupiter now as a fly, admits himself to Eurydice's boudoir. Instantly he is entranced with her, and she finds him a fine fly. In their duet he brushes against her, buzzing, while she praises such a lovely fly, catches it, and, covers it with kisses until, hocus-pocus, there is the full fat Jupiter before her. He promises to take her to Mount Olympus. They will escape during the party Pluto will be giving in honor of Jupiter's visit. They sidle off as Pluto enters looking for the fly. While a host of children, all dressed like John Styx, sing the King of Boeotia song, Cupid directs a swarm of flies at Pluto. (You will also love the singing of the flies.) They carry off Pluto as the curtain falls to Offenbach's marvelous parody of a galop (a popular dance of Offenbach's time with quick steps, jumps, and hops).

Act IV
When the curtain rises, we are in Hades next to the river Styx, where all the gods of heaven and hell are enjoying a magnificent feast. Flowers are everywhere and all are drinking copiously. In their "Infernal Chorus" they praise wine, Pluto, and hell . . . "the place where people know how to enjoy themselves." Cupid then bids Eurydice, who is disguised as a bacchante, to sing a hymn to Bacchus. She does. Jupiter follows by dancing a minuet, acclaimed by all, that becomes transformed into the most famous tune in the operetta. This, of course, is the Can-Can (also Cancan), a French dance of the later part of the nineteenth century that became notorious for its lascivious implications and its overt offending of what was considered "good taste," long before the suggestive gyrations of Elvis.

As Jupiter and Eurydice attempt to slip out, they are apprehended by Pluto, who finally admits he abducted the wife of Orpheus but regrets he ever did so: She made his life as miserable as that of her husband; furthermore, she, so to speak, made a hell-hole of Hades. Jupiter laughs but Pluto promises to have the last laugh. Eurydice will be returned not to him but to her husband. Orpheus, as always, is right on cue. His violin can be heard in the distance and getting closer and closer. Jupiter once again calls on Cupid for help. Cupid whispers a plan. Eurydice pleads with Jupiter to save her. Orpheus enters. Jupiter announces that he will return Eurydice to Orpheus conditionally. Orpheus is to lead his wife back to earth by walking several steps before her and never once looking back upon her. If he looks, he will lose her forever. Pluto's protest is quashed.

The finale begins. Public Opinion cautions Orpheus to fix his eyes firmly forward. Orpheus departs, Eurydice following behind. As they near earth, Public Opinion rejoices prematurely because Jupiter thrusts a thunderbolt that kicks Orpheus in the pants, spins him around, and leaves him face to face with Eurydice. He has lost her forever, but to neither Pluto nor Jupiter. Jupiter turns her into a bacchante. The operetta ends as Eurydice joyfully anticipates serving the god Bacchus in a brilliant coloratura display as the famous Can-Can, quietly and slowly at first, returns. As it swells to full force, all join in singing "La, la, la, la, la!" as the curtain falls. You have to love it!

I do. I love the endless wit, charm, and effervescence of Offenbach's music, which never lingers as it prances delightfully from one good tune to another. I love also the irreverence of the story. Always I am nurtured by good satire. Aristophanes, Chaucer, Rabelais, Shakespeare, Swift, Voltaire, Mark Twain—these are a few of my literary heroes who place our foibles before us as they mimic ludicrous religious, political, and moral conventions that govern so much of human behavior. From one generation to the next, on and on, we never seem to learn. *Orphée aux enfers* is another fine spoofing of we silly humans set to irresistible tunes.

JOHANN STRAUSS, JR.

Strauss (1825–1899) is the composer of our next operetta, *Die Fledermaus*. It is easy to become confused over composers with this same name, so briefly, let us sort them out. Four in one famous family were responsible for more than eleven hundred compositions, most of them waltzes. Johann Strauss, Sr. (1804–1849) was an orchestra leader and a composer of 150 waltzes and more than one hundred other dances. He conducted his orchestra while playing on his violin popular waltzes and other dances, many of which he had written. To prevent his sons from following in his musical career, he forbade them to study music.

His perceptive wife, recognizing in her eldest son, Johann, an extraordinary musical gift, secretly provided the future "Waltz King" with lessons. Johann Strauss, Jr. (known also as "the Younger" or as "the II"), against his father's wishes, left his job as a bank clerk to play his own music, and that of his father, with another orchestra. When his father died in his forty-fifth year, Johann Jr. succeeded him by merging the two orchestras. During his lifetime he would write more than four hundred waltzes, some of them the most popular ever written: "Blue Danube," "Vienna Woods," and "Vienna Blood," for example. He was greatly admired both by a music-loving populace and by great composers as diverse as Wagner and Verdi. Once Brahms signed an autograph beneath an inscription that read, "'The Blue Danube': unfortunately not by me." Of sixteen operettas written by Strauss *The Gypsy Baron* and *A Night in Venice* remain favorites while *Die Fledermaus* retains its rank as one of the most popular stage pieces ever written. Johann's brother Josef, a composer of 283 dances, succeeded him and he was, in turn, succeeded by the youngest Strauss son, Eduard, who composed some two hundred dances. Oscar Straus (notice there is only one *s*), also a Viennese, was not related. Two of his operettas once achieved immense popularity. They are *A Waltz Dream* and *The Chocolate Soldier*. Also not related was Richard Strauss, a composer of orchestral music, beautiful songs, and operas (see chapter 13).

DIE FLEDERMAUS (1874)
The Bat

Strauss was already quite famous when he began to compose operettas. On a trip to Paris he had met Offenbach, who encouraged him to try his hand in this genre. *Die Fledermaus* was his third attempt. It was politely, but not enthusiastically, applauded at its premiere on April 5, 1874. Soon, however, the waltzes caught on and the operetta was on its way to the place it holds today: one of the most popular and often performed works for the stage ever written. The libretto, by Haffner and Genée (we do not meet them again), two Viennese dramatists, is based on a play by Meilhac and Halévy. These two French playwrights (the librettists of Bizet's *Carmen*) had embellished a German play the title of which, in English, would be "The Prison." A German-speaking person would (or should) recognize immediately some fun in some of the names of this cast of characters in *Die Fledermaus*.

GABRIEL VON EISENSTEIN, a rich Viennese, *tenor*
ROSALINDE, his wife, *soprano*
ALFRED, her old flame, *tenor*
ADELE, maid of the Eisensteins, *soprano*
DR. FALKE, an old friend of Eisenstein's, *baritone*
DR. BLIND, Eisenstein's lawyer, *tenor*
FRANK, governor of the prison, *baritone*
PRINCE ORLOFSKY, a young, rich Russian, *mezzo-soprano or tenor*
FROSCH, the jailer, *speaking part*
IDA, Adele's sister, *speaking part*

Eisenstein is a compound of two German words, one meaning "iron" and the other meaning "stone," and he is no weakling. The name Rosalinde connotes beauty. The name Adele in German means aristocratic, of noble birth. Adele, though a servant, will prove to be a star in every act. The word *Falke* means falcon or hawk, quite a contrast to a bat (*Fledermaus*), which is how once he disguised himself for a costume party. The word *Blind*, like our blind, here implies false, without judgment, and he is the lawyer. *Frank* means open or free, an appropriate name for the governor of a prison. Finally, the name of the inebriated, stammering jailer, *Frosch*, means "frog" in German. I mention these connotations because in German they are too obvious to be missed. And yet, having just written that, I remember how once it had to be pointed out to me that the name Willy Loman, in *Death of a Salesman* characterizes a "low man" (How did I ever miss one as obvious as that?).

I once read an introduction to this operetta by an author who began by saying how complicated and difficult it is to follow the plot. In spite of ploys, disguises, and schemes, the plot actually is well constructed, and one need not get lost. Because I know it and you may not, it will help when you are told that the whole point of the story, we learn at the denouement, is the revenge of Dr. Falke upon his old friend Eisenstein, who once played a practical joke on him. Together they had gone to a costume party, Eisenstein dressed as a butterfly and Falke as a bat. Eisenstein got his friend drunk, by carriage took him to a forest outside the city, laid the sleeping "bat" under a tree, and went home alone. In the morning "the bat," to get home, had to go through the entire city dressed in his costume, to the great amusement of many, who thereafter referred to him as Dr. Bat.

The operetta is in three acts. The time is the late nineteenth century, the place Vienna: in other words, contemporaneous with those who attended the first performances in Vienna. *Die Fledermaus* is the only Strauss operetta set in Vienna, a city where at this time, some proper people who outwardly adhered to the generally accepted rules of decorum pursued sexual pleasure hidden by costumes or masks and promoted by excessive drinking.

Almost anyone who has heard some classical music, even if he or she is new to opera, must have heard the overture. It is made from melodies prominent in each of the three acts, the dominant one being the "Fledermaus Waltz" from the second act, one of the most recognizable waltzes in the world.

Act I

The curtain opens on an empty room in the Eisensteins' home. To one of my favorite melodies of this never-ending melodious score, Alfred's voice from outside is heard serenading his old lover, Rosalinde. He pleads with her to come to the window. It is Adele, however, who first enters the room, her voice soaring. Her sister, Ida, a ballet dancer, has written to inform her that the eccentric, wealthy Prince Orlofsky is giving a champagne party after her performance. She urges Adele to take some time off, "borrow" an elegant dress from her mistress, and attend. Rosalinde enters, looking for her husband. Sobbing, Adele asks for the night off to visit her aunt who is ill, but Rosalinde tells her such is impossible because her husband is about to begin a five-day jail sentence and Adele will be needed.

Alfred's seductive tenor voice is heard again and recognized by Rosalinde, who is startled by his pursuit of a married woman. Alfred enters through the window and proposes a rendezvous. He is unconcerned both that Rosalinde is married and that her husband may be home at any minute. A persistent Alfred agrees to leave only if she will promise to let him return while her husband is in jail. She agrees. Alfred leaves and Rosalinde admits to the irresistible power his voice has on her.

Outside, Eisenstein can be heard berating his lawyer before both enter the room. In a lively scene, Eisenstein blames his lawyer for not getting him off and the lawyer faults his client for hot-headed behavior resulting in a sentence increased to eight days. They call each other names. Blind leaves after their highly emotional trio; husband and wife accept their fate of an imminent, temporary separation; and Dr. Falke is announced by Adele. As Rosalinde goes to see about Gabriel's supper, she asks Falke to cheer up the poor prisoner. Falke suggests Eisenstein join him at a party being given for all the beautiful women of the ballet company. He can start his jail term in the morning; tonight is the night for another conquest.

Adele announces supper and is surprised to be given the night off by her mistress, who obviously is anticipating both her husband's departure for jail and Alfred's return. In one of the supreme highlights of this intoxicating score, she, joined by her husband and her maid, feign anguish over Gabriel's leaving for jail. Privately, of course, each is anticipating the many pleasures that await. Eisenstein and Adele leave the room, while Rosalinde is only slightly perplexed by her husband's seemingly frivolous reaction to going off to jail for eight days.

As soon as Eisenstein is out, Alfred is in. He dons Eisenstein's dressing gown and nightcap, anticipates the untouched supper, and offers they drink together in a song so captivating no woman could resist, especially one with such a weakness for a beautiful tenor voice. Together they join in singing a motto of Viennese upper-crust morality:

> Fortunate are they who forget
> what after all cannot be altered.

Rosalinde is concerned when she hears someone coming up the stairs. Frank has arrived to take her husband to jail. Alfred denies the assumption that he is Eisenstein and entreats Frank to join him, with a glass, in his drinking song. Rosalinde, however, will not be compromised and she convinces the prison governor that she is not the kind of woman who would be at a late supper in her home with a man in a dressing gown and cap who was not her husband. Frank, too, is going to a party and must get going. In another fine trio, Rosalinde urges along Alfred, who capitulates to his ascending honor while Frank hauls him away to jail. The curtain falls.

Act II

This act begins with a chorus of party guests, toasting and sampling the food and drink that servants are offering. Falke promises to amuse his host, Orlofsky, with a little drama of his own contriving entitled *The Revenge of the Bat*. Adele meets Ida, who denies having invited her sister but who is willing to pass her off as an actress, which, after all, is what Adele would rather be. She is introduced to Orlofsky as Olga, then goes off with her sister. Falke confides she is really only the maid of the hero of the drama, who has just arrived. It is Eisenstein pretending to be one Marquis Renard (*renard* is French for "fox"—a fox to be out-foxed by a falcon . . . that is, by Falke). Falke also divulges to Orlofsky that he has invited Eisenstein's wife to the party. Eisenstein joins his friend, who introduces him to their host. Orlofsky invites his guest to enjoy himself because he reserves the right to eject anyone who is not having a good time. This is Orlofsky's big aria that ends with the famous French phrase *Chacun à son goût!* ("Everyone to his own taste"). He then tells an unsuspecting Eisenstein that Dr. Falke has promised him a good time with a good laugh at his expense.

Ida and Adele return, the latter being introduced as Olga to the Marquis Renard, who thinks he sees in her a strong resemblance to a certain chambermaid. This slur creates quite a stir and all gather around to chastise the ungallant marquis, who is shaken by the similarity of Olga to Adele. Her response is a tour de force, perhaps the second most familiar music in the operetta (after the soon-to-be-heard waltz), *Mein Herr Marquis* ("My dear marquis"). She advises him to look more carefully to see that she is much too sophisticated and well dressed to be a servant and she laughs in his face. The Bat's revenge has only just begun.

Commonly known as "Adele's Laughing Song," this aria has had an unusual life outside the operetta. It was a favorite of Florence Foster Jenkins, who often sang it in concert and recorded it. She was a woman of huge musical ambitions, virtually no talent, and a grand inheritance. To fulfill her dreams, she gave an annual private recital for a select few friends and followers until October 1944, when she took the big step and, at great personal expense, rented Carnegie Hall for her recital. The concert sold out. The performance was a sensation, but only because she could not sing. Her voice was terrible. If you can find one of her recordings, you will know what I mean. And if you do locate the "Laughing Song," sneak it on as background music the next time you have a few friends over (I have had fun doing this).

In an aside, Falke informs Orlofsky of the arrival of another of his personae: The Chevalier Chagrin (French for "trouble" or "grief") is Frank, the prison warden. Orlofsky introduces the marquis to the chevalier, who says "I hope we will see each other often in the future." Falke, in one of the many little jokes missed by those who either do not know German or do not study the libretto, asserts it will be thus. Another special guest will soon arrive, Orlofsky says, a married Hungarian countess who must, accordingly, remain masked and whose disguise must be respected. All sing happily in praise of "amusement" as the countess enters.

Obviously, you know it is Rosalinde, who has been enticed by Falke to attend in order to view her husband in action. And her husband soon is at the side of this stunning Hungarian. His seduction commences with his tried-and-true modus operandi. He dangles before her his beautiful, chiming pocketwatch. With a plan of her own in mind, Rosalinde decides to play along as Eisenstein begins to flirt outrageously. He tries to get her to unmask. She refuses but claims his advances are making her heart pound. Would he please use his watch to count the beats? Gladly. Placing a hand upon her breast, he holds his watch as she begins to count. As his excitement mounts, she is able to swipe the watch and conceal it—guess where? (A wonderful video version of this seduction-scene duet always was a highlight for the freshman men and women in my Introduction to Opera courses.) Rosalinde thanks Eisenstein for the gift of the watch. He can only stammer.

Disrespecting Orlofsky's request, all join in begging this extraordinary woman to take off her mask. The Prince remonstrates but Ida questions her authenticity as a Hungarian. For proof, Rosalinde responds with a brilliant *czardas*, a nineteenth century Hungarian dance form. With this celebrated aria, a great soprano puts the audience in the palm of her hand. Everyone, on stage and in the audience, applauds Rosalinde. Orlofsky reminds Falke he promised to tell the story of the joke on the bat. Unaware that Falke is setting him up step by step, Eisenstein joins his friend in relating the prank he pulled on Die Fledermaus. Everyone laughs heartily. Orlofsky wonders why Falke has never had revenge. Tomorrow we will see who gets the last laugh, Falke assures him.

The finale of the second act begins with an exuberant praise of champagne, the king of all wines. Couples form and, to a beautiful, slow waltz (the music expresses perfectly the intoxicating

atmosphere of alcohol and sex), male and female, led by Eisenstein, pledge themselves to each other for eternity: *Brüderlein und
Schwesterlein* ("We brothers and we sisters"). The ballerinas perform, then rest while the others dance and sing the famous waltz,
Eisenstein continuing to fail in attempts both to unmask the Hungarian beauty and to regain his watch. A clock strikes six in the
morning, Frank and Eisenstein get their hats and coats and depart,
unaware that it is to the jail both are headed. A chorus of guests
expresses great delight with such a night as the curtain falls. If all
the music of this great finale does not have your heart singing,
then there is no hope for you and operetta!

Act III

It is in this act that too often a performance of *Die Fledermaus* can
go astray. The act opens, after a brief entr'acte, in Frank's office in
the prison. Frosch is there. His is a comic speaking part and some
directors give to it too much prominence by embellishing the role
and/or giving it to a noted comedian and allowing him considerable freedom to improvise, or "do his thing." Victor Borge, who
usually I think was extremely talented, once rolled his piano on to
the prison stage when he played Frosch. Dom Deluise has performed the part, and several unsuccessful attempts were made to
secure Danny Kaye for the role. Great comedians can be very
funny as Frosch, but some make too much of the part and thus
prolong the Bat's revenge, toward which all the action is supposed
to be moving. Furthermore, *Die Fledermaus* is a drama that provides a great temptation for tampering. Because the jokes are in
German and, in some cases, connected to a world of yesteryear,
Die Fledermaus is often given in translations in which rewritten
topical jokes replace the originals. I know of a recent production
where the time was altered to the twentieth century, the dialogue
was up-dated and spoken in English, and in some insane way Dr.
Falke becomes Sigmund Freud while all the music is sung in the
original German. Mishmashes such as this make me livid and are
insulting to you, the assumption being that you have neither the
time nor the intelligence to become familiar enough with the original to appreciate it as it is. A good translation certainly is acceptable, but ludicrous rewriting and updating are not.

With the following idiomatic performances, you cannot go
wrong: On CD, get Elisabeth Schwarzkopf and Nicolai Gedda as
Rosalinde and Eisenstein with Herbert von Karajan conducting;
on video get Gundula Janowitz and Eberhard Wächter (a baritone

for whom the tenor part has been transposed) in those roles with Karl Böhm conducting. If you have retained your record player, keep your eyes open when in used-records shops for the 1950 London long-playing recording with Julius Patzak as Eisenstein, Hilde Gueden as Rosalinde, and Anton Dermota as Alfred, Clemens Krauss conducting the Vienna Philharmonic Orchestra and the chorus of the Vienna State Opera, and you will have my all-time favorite recording of this operetta. Sometimes it is only the Viennese who can play a Strauss waltz with its unique, distinctive lilt, and *Die Fledermaus* is, in a way, one big, wonderful waltz.

Frosch is drunk—another temptation to some to overplay the part. He takes a swig of schnapps, claims it makes "another man of me," and then offers a swig to that other man. From cell no. 12, strains of his Rosalinde serenade can be heard as Alfred sings this as well as snatches of famous tenor arias from other operas in spite of Frosch's warnings that singing is forbidden. Suddenly, all is quiet and Frosch staggers off to investigate. Frank, also drunk, staggers in. Too much champagne! Babbling and stammering, he thinks of Olga and is impressed by the pledge of brotherhood with a real marquis. He whistles a bit of the famous waltz, babbles on, sings a few lines of the champagne song, yawns, stretches, whistles more of the waltz, and falls asleep.

Frosch returns and wakes him in order to make his morning report: the prisoner in no. 12 demanded a lawyer, so Dr. Blind has been summoned. The drunken jailer, attempting to say *Advokaten* (German for "lawyer") first blurts out the word *Affen* ("ape") in but one example of the jokes made in German. Frosch then announces that there are four ladies asking to see Frank. Obviously seeing double, he lets in only Ida and Olga (Adele). When Frank dismisses Frosch, the jailer retorts that two women are beyond his strength. Adele admits she is only a chambermaid and asks the favor of Frank helping her to become an actress. She puts on a little show for him to demonstrate her talent, portraying first an innocent country girl and then a flirtatious upper-class woman of Paris. Frank is charmed. And he should be. Remember I told you that Adele is one of the big stars. Frosch announces a Marquis Renard and the ladies are herded to another room.

Eisenstein reveals his true identity, thus baffling Frank, who tells him that only last night he himself took Eisenstein from his wife, after a prolonged good-bye kiss, and locked him up in cell no. 12, where he now resides. When Frosch announces still another lady, who will not give her name, Frank leaves to meet her. Dr.

Blind enters and asks Eisenstein why he sent for him. Eisenstein has a brainstorm. He disguises himself as a lawyer with Blind's hat, coat, wig, glasses, and briefcase and the two go out. Frosch brings in Alfred to see his lawyer and leaves. Rosalinde enters and, fearing her husband is soon to arrive, begs Alfred to go, however, Dr. Blind (Eisensein in disguise) enters. In a vehement cross-examination he learns not only what happened the preceding night between his wife and Alfred but also that Rosalinde knows all about her husband's deceitfulness. As the revelations unfold, tempers rise. Eisenstein especially demands revenge, in this extraordinary trio, until Rosalinde replies:

> You dare to reproach me when all the while I
> know what you've been up to. "Would you be
> good enough to count the beats of my heart, Herr
> Marquis?"

She dangles his watch before him. Falke enters, followed by all the party guests, who praise him for having gotten the best of Eisenstein with his revenge of "the Bat." Falke explains how he staged everything for an evening's entertainment. The tryst of Alfred and Rosalinde was not part of Falke's little drama, of course, but they take advantage of the situation and claim it was as all admit their role in the joke on Eisenstein. Frank invites Adele to stay with him and receive acting lessons and Orlofsky iterates his "each to his own taste" philosophy. When Eisenstein begs Rosalinde for forgiveness, her brief, brilliant final song puts all the blame on champagne, the king of wines. All join in praising champagne and the curtain falls.

When I was sixteen, I took my girlfriend of two years to her first opera, a touring Metropolitan Opera production of *Die Fledermaus*. Two teens at the opera on a school night must have been an unusual event in Cleveland, Ohio. Our picture was taken, we were asked some questions, and there we were in the next morning's paper. Six years later Joanne and I were married and many, many years later, when we listen to this operetta, we always hear a little something extra special.

∽

W.S. GILBERT AND
ARTHUR SULLIVAN

Together they created the first lasting works of musical theater in England since Purcell, two hundred years previously. Along with Mozart and da Ponte, and Strauss and von Hofmannsthal, they remain preeminent among the elite musician/poet teams. Even more than those others it is unthinkable—no, impossible—to refer to one of their operettas without naming both. Sir Arthur Sullivan was born in London in 1842 and died in 1900. Sir William Schwenk Gilbert (both were knighted but not at the same time) was born in 1836, also in London, and died in 1911. For those who like to read the stars, Gilbert was born in May, the month in which Sullivan died, and Sullivan was born in November, the month in which Gilbert died. (I don't get into this but some do.)

Each had achieved considerable recognition in his own field before fate brought together these opposite personalities to create what many rank to be far and away the finest musical comedies written in the English language. Furthermore, Gilbert is almost alone in having written libretti that are marvels even without music. Sullivan's primary professional desire was to compose what he considered "serious music" and Gilbert had little interest in music for its own sake. He wanted to be a successful dramatist. To others he appeared defiant, bitter, and, at times, misanthropic; Sullivan was considered sociable, easy to get along with, and, accordingly, quite popular. Their mutual genius transcended personal differences that precluded a deep, abiding friendship. In fact, their collaboration was not without several serious rifts that produced periods during which they refused to communicate with each other. The chemistry of their collaborations, however, was dynamic. Together they transcended every aspiration either ever had for success in his own field by making incomparable masterpieces of wit and music combined in a unique theatrical marriage.

In 1871, impresario John Hollingshead asked Sullivan to write the music to Gilbert's libretto *Thespis: or, The Gods Grown Old.* Sullivan accepted and "their first child was born." But had it not been for Richard D'Oyly Carte, a composer turned theater manager, there may never have been any more offspring. In 1875, Gilbert and Sullivan having gone their separate ways for three years,

D'Oyly Carte contracted Sullivan to write the music to Gilbert's little play *Trial by Jury* and herewith began the succession of triumphs by this remarkable triumvirate: D'Oyly Carte producing in his own theater the operettas of Gilbert and Sullivan. I know no one who has memorized portions of dialogue and all the words to numerous songs in operettas by Frimal, Lehár, Herbert, and others, except, of course, those who perform them. I have several friends, however, who have memorized massive amounts of Gilbert and Sullivan.

Barry Hawkins and Sam Sanders have worked with me in making radio programs. One day recently, we were involved in a conference call. Barry and Sam had not seen each other for many months. Right off the bat, without any pleasantries, Barry said, "Sam, I have something to say to you," and he sang perfectly every word and note of the first verse of a song from one of the G & S operettas (as they are affectionately known by those who love them). Without missing a beat, Sam did likewise, answering with the second verse and, without missing a beat, together they made a perfect duet of the third verse. And where was I in all this? Well, I could join them only in the chorus.

Gilbert's words are imperishable and no composer ever set the rhymes and rhythms of English speech with more joyfulness or humor than Sullivan. The humor of *Trial by Jury* abounds in both words and music as Gilbert satirizes an English institution and Sullivan musically mocks Italian opera finales. It was this wondrous little spoof that captivated another friend of mine Bob Grinnell. Years ago, when he was at Milton Academy, he attended a performance of *Trial by Jury* in Boston. Instantly, he was hooked for life. He, too, knew lengthy segments by heart, most certainly learned by repetitive playings of his complete collection of G & S performed by the D'Oyly Carte Opera Company. When Bob moved to an apartment some years ago, he made a gift of his collection to me: a treasured gift indeed.

D'Oyly, so impressed by the success of *Trial by Jury*, decided to form a company to produce the musicals of native Englishmen. He did so. Essentially, it became an opera company that performed Gilbert and Sullivan. *The Sorcerer* opened in November 1877. It was a success except for a few critics. Some went after Gilbert, accusing him of irreverently portraying a vicar and of being sacrilegious. Others taunted Sullivan, a composer of serious music, for stooping to compose superficial tunes for comic opera. Such critiques would stalk their entire collaboration. After the success of

The Sorcerer, D'Oyly Carte had little interest in any other drama-tist and composer. One of the greatest hits appeared in May 1878: *H. M. S. Pinafore*. I was an adult before I saw a production of *Pinafore* by the D'Oyly Carte Opera Company but I had known many of the songs since fourth grade. Have you ever heard anyone say something like "I never, never . . ." do or say this or that to which someone else responds with "What, never?" To this the first reacts with "No, never!" producing from the second another "What, never?" At this point the first replies with a "Well, hardly ever!" This comes from the well-known song "I am the Captain of the Pinafore" and is another example of how Gilbert's words have taken on a life of their own.

Pinafore, by 1879, was a sensation in America, and in London had a run of 675 performances. This means that for nearly two years it was all that played at D'Oyly Carte's theater, day after day, and while all of London was queuing for tickets, Gilbert and Sul-livan were at work on new operettas. In December 1880, *The Pirates of Penzance* opened and in April 1881 *Patience*. By this time so much money had been made by the G & S collaborations that D'Oyly Carte built a theater for their works. The Savoy was at that time a model opera house. *Iolanthe* opened in November 1882 and *Princess Ida* in January 1884. It was followed by one of their squabbles.

Sullivan threatened to set no more of Gilbert's texts wherein he consciously limited musical expression so that every word could be heard and understood. This, of course, is quite interest-ing to those attempting to resolve one of the original, elemental questions of operatic composition: What is more important, the music or the words? Sullivan had to have been unique as a com-poser to defer willingly to the art of the poet. Or at least he thought he was and now wanted to compose a serious, romantic work. He had had his fill of Gilbert's texts in which the improba-ble is made actual and supernatural events propel the outcome to its happy end. So Gilbert responded with a text to allow Sullivan's music to have some sway (as if this had not already happened again and again).

The result, *The Mikado*, opened at the Savoy in March 1885, and had a run of nearly two years. In fact, according to Deems Tay-lor, the American opera composer, once *The Mikado* was born, its "run" has never stopped. Taylor was convinced that at all times, somewhere in the world, a production of *The Mikado* was on a stage. *Ruddigore* followed in January 1887 and in October 1888

484 ™ W.S. GILBERT and ARTHUR SULLIVAN

The Yeoman of the Guard, a text giving Sullivan ample opportunities for romantic lyricism. Their last unqualified success, *The Gondoliers*, appeared in December 1889, Sullivan declaring then that the collaboration was over.

He went his own way to write his serious romantic opera *Ivanhoe* without a text by Gilbert. It had a brief and limited success and since has been forgotten. Gilbert wrote *The Mountebanks* without music by Sullivan. Its life also was short. They reconciled and wrote together, first, *Utopia, Limited* (1893), and, second, *The Grand Duke* (1896). Both had short runs. The magic was gone.

Sullivan died in London from heart trouble in 1900. He was fifty-nine. Gilbert died in his seventy-fourth year, also from a heart problem. Racing into a lake to rescue a young woman friend who had slipped into deep water, his heart gave out from exertion and he drowned.

Aside from collaborations, their most enduring contributions are two religious pieces by Sullivan, "The Lost Chord" and "Onward Christian Soldiers," and Gilbert's poetry collection, *The Bab Ballads*. If you encounter these ballads in an edition incorporating Gilbert's original illustrations, you will find he was also gifted at drawing.

THE MIKADO, or, THE TOWN OF TITIPU (1885)

The operetta, set in Japan, is in two acts. The characters of the story are:

THE MIKADO OF JAPAN
NANKI-POO, his son, disguised as a wandering minstrel in
  love with Yum-Yum
Ko-Ko, Lord High Executioner of Titipu
POOH-BAH, Lord High Everything Else
PISH-TUSH, a Noble Lord
YUM-YUM   ⎫
PITTI-SING   ⎬ three sisters, all wards of Ko-Ko
Peep-Bo   ⎭
KATISHA, an elderly woman in love with Nanki-Poo
Choruses of schoolgirls, nobles, guards, and coolies

The Mikado first was performed at the Savoy Theater, built by D'Oyly Carte exclusively for the Gilbert and Sullivan collaborations, on March 14, 1885. Received with thundering ovations, it began what would be the longest run of all G & S operettas and remains unto this day, worldwide, the most popular English operetta. Some Japanese, however, have been offended by the work, thinking it—erroneously—to be a satire on their culture. Because the dramatic personae have such ludicrous Japanese-like names and their story is so silly, this, on the surface, is not an unfair assumption.

This was not Gilbert's intent, however. In the much larger world of the 1880s, he employed the then remote Oriental culture as his means of poking fun at England and English institutions, always the object of his satire. His choice of subject matter was, in fact, a positive concession to the growing enthusiasm for everything Japanese spreading throughout England at this time. Rudyard Kipling notwithstanding, the "twain" of East and West was indeed beginning to meet.

As was often the case with the G & S premieres, Sullivan had left composing the overture for last. One week before the first performance he still had not written one. To a fellow musician, Hamilton Clarke, he gave the job of constructing an overture from prominent tunes in the operetta. Sullivan designated the tunes and how they were to be arranged and left the rest to Clarke. This now famous overture "by Sullivan" is one of several he, so to speak, did not exactly compose.

Act I

After the overture, the curtain rises on the courtyard of Ko-Ko's palace in Titipu. Noblemen standing or sitting in postures familiar to Japanese art sing "If You Want to Know Who We Are." An excited Nanki-Poo enters, a stringed instrument on his back and hands full of ballads, seeking Yum-Yum. Joined by the chorus of nobles, he sings "A Wandering Minstrel I," revealing his preparedness to provide a song for any occasion. The curtain has been up less than ten minutes and two of the most famous Gilbert and Sullivan numbers in their entire corpus have been sung!

But what does Nanki-Poo want with Yum-Yum? Pish-Tush queries. The minstrel explains that a year ago, they fell in love at first sight but because she was promised to her guardian, he fled. Then he heard Ko-Ko had been condemned to death for flirting (Gilbert obviously having sport with Victorian morality) and, accordingly, hastily has returned to press his suit. Pish-Tush, accompanied by the noblemen, enlightens Nanki-Poo to the present state of affairs: "Our Great Mikado, Virtuous Man." Ko-Ko was given a reprieve and elevated to the lofty rank of Lord High Executioner by the townspeople of Titipu. The Mikado had decreed that any unmarried man who flirts, leers, or winks at a woman shall ". . . forthwith be beheaded." This stern decree caused dismay and young men condemned to die ". . . usually objected." Executions followed the order in which men were condemned, but by elevating Ko-Ko to the highest rank obtainable by a citizen, all executions were brought to a halt: Ko-Ko, the next in line, could not execute another before dispatching himself.

Gilbert next takes a swipe at bluebloods as he has Pooh-Bah make a dissertation on his lofty genealogy. He explains how, in an effort to mortify his pride, he was the only noble who did not resign an important town office when the cheap ex-tailor Ko-Ko was elevated to the highest rank. Pooh-Bah, greedily, accepted all vacated posts, and the salaries associated with them, from treasurer to chief justice to commander-in-chief, etcetera, to become, in short, Lord High Everything Else. Nanki-Poo tips him in return for news of Yum-Yum and joins Pooh-Bah and Pish-Tush in a trio: "Young Man, Despair, Likewise Go To," in which he learns the heart-breaking news that this very day, when school is out, his beloved Yum-Yum will marry Ko-Ko. After the song, Pooh-Bah and Nanki-Poo exit.

Onto the set comes a chorus of nobles singing one of the operetta's hit tunes (actually, it seems as if every tune in *The Mikado* is a hit), "Behold the Lord High Executioner," introducing Ko-Ko at the end of their train, who has joined them in song and then sings his "As Some Day It May Happen." In this rumination he is foreshadowing events to come. It may happen that he needs someone to be a victim of his trade and he suggests examples of those society offenders who never would be missed: autograph seekers, those with flabby handshakes and noisome laughs, third persons spoiling têtes-à-têtes, and "people who eat peppermint and puff it in your face." His enticing list goes on.

Pooh-Bah returns and Ko-Ko consults him on how much to spend on his wedding ceremony because the town of Titipu is paying for it. From each of his various official positions Pooh-Bah answers differently, thus providing an awkward and unresolved situation. Ko-Ko is reassured that a considerable bribe would scare up an answer. They go off and Yum-Yum, Peep-Bo, and Pitti-Sing enter at the end of a procession of their fellow school maidens, all singing a perfectly wonderful tune: "Comes a Train of Little

Ladies." Ko-Ko and Pooh-Bah return and the groom-to-be, with permission from the Lord High Chamberlain, Pooh-Bah, of course, embraces his bride-to-be. Yum-Yum, glad to have that over with, sees Nanki-Poo and rushes to him. He is introduced to Ko-Ko, who appears to remain amenable when Nanki-Poo confesses he is in love with his ward. In an aside, however, he orders Pish-Tush to take away Nanki-Poo and they depart. Pooh-Bah, introduced to Ko-Ko's wards, agonizes over being ordered to bow to anyone of lower rank, especially when they are young women. Ko-Ko leaves and Pooh-Bah and the three sisters sing, with a female chorus, "So Please You, Sir, We Much Regret," after which all but Yum-Yum depart. Nanki-Poo, obviously, enters and wonders why Yum-Yum simply does not refuse to marry Ko-Ko. She explains that her position as his ward gives her no choice in the matter and, furthermore, a wandering minstrel who performs outside teahouses is hardly a fitting husband for one so intimately connected to the Lord High Executioner. Nanki-Poo responds by revealing his true identity. Refusing his father's order that he marry Katisha or die, he slipped into a marine band, disguised as a second trombone, and made his way to freedom. At first she rebuffs his suit, fearing the severe decree prohibiting an unmarried man to flirt, but his persistence prevails and they admit mutual affection in a love duet, of course: "Were You Not to Ko-Ko Plighted." Then they kiss—several times, in fact. Yum-Yum's response is not to be missed, G & S always ready to make fun of serious opera:

> To embrace you thus, *con fuoco* (with fire)
> Would distinctly be no *giuoco* (no joke) . . .

Don't forget we are in an operetta about Japan, written in English, and into which Gilbert inserts a little Italian joke. After their song, they leave the stage in opposite directions.

Ko-Ko returns followed soon after by Pooh-Bah and Pish-Tush, who bears a letter from his majesty the Mikado, expressing his anger over the dearth of executions in Titipu during the past year. If one more month passes without an execution, the letter says, the position of Lord High Executioner will be abolished and Titipu reduced to a mere village. They are confronted with a dilemma. Ko-Ko is next in line to be executed but how can he execute himself? To do so would be suicide, which is a "capital offense." What are they to do? In a significant trio, "I Am So Proud," they consider the situation. It is a masterful blend of words and music. Ko-

Ko's comrades depart but he remains to think over the matter. He is interrupted by Nanki-Poo, who enters with rope in hand. Suicide is preferable to life without Yum-Yum. An idea thus comes to Ko-Ko: Substitute Nanki-Poo for himself. That will give him another month to live. Nanki-Poo retorts with his own idea: Let me marry Yum-Yum for that month and then you can behead me. The bargain is struck.

The finale to the first act begins as all sing happily of the resolution, until peace is shattered by Katisha's unexpected, melodramatic entrance. She claims the right to Nanki-Poo. All raise their voices in an attempt to drown hers, Gilbert actually introducing Japanese words into the turmoil: "*O ni! bikkuri shakkuri to!*" Katisha, nevertheless, is not to be silenced. As the magnificent finale concludes, all of Titipu bids her to go away, but her voice is resolute:

> Prepare for woe,
> > Ye haughty lords,
> At once I go
> > Mikado-wards,
> My wrongs with vengeance shall
> > be crowned.

The curtain falls.

Act II

As the curtain parts, we see Yum-Yum looking into a mirror as her maidens arrange her hair and paint her face. Pitti-Sing, with the maidens, sings "Braid the Raven Hair," music of extraordinary loveliness. The maidens depart. Alone, Yum-Yum wonders aloud, as she continues to dwell upon her mirror image, why she is, indeed, more beautiful than anyone else in the world. She sings a solo: "The Sun, Whose Rays Are All Ablaze." Her sisters return and break the self-indulgent reverie as "the happiest girl in Japan" with sobering news. Nanki-Poo, her beloved husband-to-be, will be her husband for only one month, after which, in accordance with the deal he made with Ko-Ko, he will be beheaded. Nanki-Poo enters and attempts to assuage Yum-Yum's weeping by suggesting they "call a second a minute, each minute an hour—each hour a day—and each day a year," thus allowing them approximately thirty years of marital bliss. Joined by Yum-Yum's sisters, they force a melancholy laugh and sing a stately madrigal (originally Italian vocal music, usually of pastoral or amatory subject by both poetic and musical complexity). Gilbert and Sullivan, having fun, as always, nevertheless meet the challenge admirably and convincingly.

The lovers are in an embrace as Ko-Ko enters and acknowledges that he must get used to this sort of thing, but he adds a request. Would they proceed slowly: first, just an arm around the waist, then a head upon a shoulder? He comes bearing terrible news for all of them. By law of the Mikado, when a married man is beheaded his wife is buried alive. Acting as Ko-Ko's solicitor, Pooh-Bah explains the conditions. Ko-Ko adds that he consulted with the Attorney General, the Lord Chief Justice, the Master of the Rolls, the Judge Ordinary, and the Lord Chancellor (all Pooh-Bah, of course) and was dumbstruck by the unanimity of opinion. It's obvious to Ko-Ko, Nanki-Poo, and Yum-Yum that the three of them are in a fix, and they express as much in the celebrated brilliant trio "Here's a How-De-Do! If I Marry You." Yum-Yum exits.

Nanki-Poo and Ko-Ko attempt to sort out the problem. If Nanki-Poo cannot marry Yum-Yum this very day he will "perform the Happy Dispatch" (suicide) but Ko-Ko cannot allow this because then, in a month's time, he will have to be executed as by the Mikado's decree, as next on the list. So Nanki-Poo consents to be beheaded as planned but Ko-Ko, who has never killed a bluebottle, needs time to learn his trade. Then he has a brainstorm. He will bribe Pooh-Bah, in all his various capacities, to sign an affidavit that the execution took place and Nanki-Poo and Yum-Yum will have to go away never to return. Pooh-Bah fetches Yum-Yum and orders her to prepare for a quick wedding; the Mikado is coming.

A march signals the arrival of a grand procession heralding the Mikado and Katisha. To music with a decided Oriental flair, the choral procession sings Japanese words prior to a duet in which the two dignitaries proclaim their wills will be done. Immediately thereafter, with chorus, the Mikado sings his famous "A More Humane Mikado Never Did In Japan Exist" with its often quoted rime,

> My object all sublime
> I shall achieve in time—
> To let the punishment fit the crime—
> The punishment fit the crime . . .

and exemplified by this, one of several, clever verses:

> The billiard sharp whom any one catches
> His doom's extremely hard
> > He's made to dwell—
> > In a dungeon cell
> On a spot that's always barred.
> And there he plays extravagant matches
> > In fitless finger-stalls
> > On a cloth untrue,
> > With a twisted cue
> And elliptical billiard balls!

Pitti-Sing, Pooh-Bah, and Ko-Ko enter, the latter presenting the Mikado with certification that the execution has taken place. The lofty ruler regrets not having been "in time for the perform-ance" and asks for a description, duly given in song by the three aforementioned and the chorus: "The Criminal Cried as He Dropped Him Down," an undeniably graphic and ludicrous account of the imaginary beheading. According to Pooh-Bah,

> Now though you'd have said that head was dead
> > (For its owner dead was he)
> It stood on its neck, with a smile well bred,
> > And bowed three times to me!

The subject changes to Katisha's interest. She and the Mikado know Nanki-Poo is masquerading in Titipu. Ko-Ko claims he has gone abroad but Katisha, reading the death certificate, is stunned to see the victim's name is Nanki-Poo. The Mikado does not ques-tion Ko-Ko's judgment. After all, if his son, the heir to the throne of Japan, eluded the clutches of Katisha by disguising himself as a "Second Trombone" to escape in a marching band, he deserved what he got. Nevertheless, there is a punishment to fit the beheading of his heir. Ko-Ko will be executed after lunch, Gilbert putting a bit of his own cynicism into the ruler's mouth when he has him say, "I'm really sorry for you all, but it's an unjust world, and virtue is triumphant only in theatrical performances." This is, of course, also a presentiment of this story's eventual outcome, at this point unbeknownst to His Majesty. Pitti-Sing, Katisha, Ko-Ko, and Pooh-Bah now offer a brief glee (an eighteenth-century genre of English choral music traditionally unaccompanied, but not so here). The use of classical forms by G & S certainly would not have been lost on sophisticated members of their audiences.

This glee, "See How The Fates Their Gifts Allot," is less than two minutes of some of my favorite music in this score of one hit tune after another.

The Mikado and Katisha depart. What is to be done? Nanki-Poo must be brought to life again, and right on cue he enters with his new wife, prepared for their departure from Titipu forever. But what is to be done? Katisha has claimed him as her husband. Already married, Nanki-Poo recommends that Ko-Ko marry Katisha. Ko-Ko is appalled but joins Nanki-Poo, Pitti-Sing, and Pooh-Bah in a discussion of the concept in a song as well known as any other in the entire Gilbert and Sullivan canon: "The Flowers That Bloom in the Spring." All except Ko-Ko depart. Katisha enters and sings "Alone, and Yet Alive!" to lament the loss of the man she loves. To her astonishment, the one who killed her beloved now is before her, on his knees, professing his love for her first in prose, then in yet another song, "On a Tree by a River," with its "willow, titwillow, titwillow" refrains. Katisha's heart nearly breaks as she listens to the fate of a little tomtit who dies of unfulfilled love. She and Ko-Ko burst into a duet of their new-found and virtually instantaneous togetherness, "There is Beauty in the Bellow of the Blast." They exit.

Now commences the Act II finale. Enter the Mikado, Pish-Tush, and the court. His Majesty, having satisfied himself with a fine lunch, is now ready to enjoy the execution. Ko-Ko, Katisha, Pooh-Bah, and Pitti-Sing enter, throw themselves at the Mikado's feet, and beg for mercy. He is told that Katisha and Ko-Ko have married, that Nanki-Poo is alive, and, in fact, that the entire situation was a ruse. As all is forgiven and joyfulness reigns in a happy ending for everyone—especially for Gilbert and Sullivan, who, to repeat, in this spoof of Victorian morality and English institutions set to one memorable tune after the other crowned their collaboration with the most popular operetta they ever wrote.

ひ

Only twice in my opera-going life have I failed to really enjoy my first hearing of a drama. I was a young teen when my father took me to my first *Der Rosenkavalier (The Knight of the Rose)* by Richard Strauss and I recall getting lost and bored in the middle section of the opera. Next time around, a little more preparation solved that. The second time was a production of *The Mikado*. I was quite young when an aunt took me. It was my first G & S. I knew then only a couple of the tunes, the humor was over my head, and the Japanese facade was perplexing. Now, of course, I sing all the songs when I play one of my recordings. If you start with *The Mikado*, I guarantee you will not stop there. You will enter the wide intoxicating world of the pair's incomparable collaborations from *Trial by Jury* to *The Gondoliers*.

As you become increasingly familiar with their operettas, you will notice the unmistakable similarities in construction that run through them. A recipe of sorts naturally emerges as the audience anticipates new patter songs with a little dance at the end, tenor arias, often with string accompaniment, the brilliant trio vigorously applauded and encored, the contralto with the bellowing voice, the tuneful choruses, be they of Japanese gentlemen, pirates, or sailors, and the entire-company finales.

The English comedienne Anna Russell, whose masterpiece of hilarity is her analysis of Wagner's *The Ring of the Nibelung*, created a sensation with her "How to Write Your Own Gilbert and Sullivan Opera." Her career as an opera singer sputtered and expired, but her career as a humorist whose target was music brought her lasting international celebrity. I love my Wagner but I can laugh until my sides ache when Anna Russell mocks him, and she is no less cordial to G & S, her powerful voice, high to low, capable of spoofing any and every vocal style. Thus, would not my dinner guests, so in love with Gilbert and Sullivan that they would travel to London for performances, find Anna Russell's recipe for writing their own G & S operetta as ingenious as the originals? Not at all. As my Anna Russell recording played on, a pall descended on the after-dinner mood. This couple emitted not a single laugh. They worshiped at the shrine. Gilbert and Sullivan were not to be made fun of. Oh dear, how sad to be so serious.

If you become familiar with Gilbert and Sullivan through recordings made by the D'Oyly Carte Opera Company, which to aficionados is the only proper entrée to the music, you will hear some voices that lack the refinement or the elegance and beauty of voices that you have come to expect in Mozart or Verdi. This is true of this genre. Some D'Oyly Carte stars of yesteryear were more famous for their humorous characterizations than for having perfected the art of song. The G & S canon, in this manner, is similar to American musical theater (Broadway), where it is not always the great voice that immortalizes a role. It is in this way especially that the American musical is but a baby step away from operetta—indeed, a direct descendant of European opera individualized by a frontier temperament forged on the other side of the Atlantic.

Finally, I do understand how and why some Japanese find in *The Mikado* an exploitation of some of their customs and an overtly silly exaggeration of names. But Japan and the Japanese were the means, not the end, of Gilbert's satire on his native time and place, a small price, I hope, for witty, musical poetry perfectly wedded to innovative, matchless tunes, which, after all, is precisely what musical theater is all about.

And with that said, we return to the world of opera and that composer who just may be the most popular and beloved of them all: Giacomo Puccini.

Giacomo Puccini

THE INCOMPARABLE PUCCINI

When Verdi set down his pen after completing *Aïda* (1871), no one—not even the reigning king of all Italian opera himself—would have guessed two consummate masterpieces (*Otello*, 1887, and *Falstaff*, 1893) lay dormant within him. Having said no two or three times before agreeing to the *Aïda* commission, it could be assumed this was his last opera. Thus, it was a perfectly natural question that arose in operatic circles: "Who after Verdi?" Who would inherit his mantle? Could it be Amilcare Ponchielli, whose *La Gioconda* once was quite popular and still receives occasional revivals?

This opera, the only one of Ponchielli's to survive, premiered in 1876. Arrigo Boito, so indispensable to Verdi in the making of *Otello* and *Falstaff*, wrote the text for Ponchielli. The title, which means the merry or joy-filled girl, ironically is a tale with a dire ending. The most famous song, the aria for tenor *Cielo e mar* ("Sky and sea"), was made world famous by Enrico Caruso's recording, and few are the tenors in the Italian tradition today who do not offer it in their repertoire. Gioconda contemplates suicide in her most celebrated aria, *Suicidio!* and many great, dramatic sopranos have taken their turn with both performances and recordings, most notably, since the long-playing recordings, Montserrat Caballé, Zinka Milanov, and Renata Tebaldi, who much admired the recording of Maria Callas, her archrival. The

Callas portrayals of Gioconda, the ballad singer, are unforgettable and now can be heard in a complete recording on CD.

The most familiar music in the opera, made so by Walt Disney's celebrated film *Fantasia*, is the "Dance of the Hours." Those of my generation, when hearing this music, inevitably visualize dancing hippopotami adorned in tutus.

But Ponchielli, with one big dramatic hit, was not to be Verdi's heir. No other candidates seemed to loom before Puccini appeared as the primary successor. Nor would it be Mascagni nor Leoncavallo: But their one masterpiece each must have a place in this book.

PIETRO MASCAGNI AND RUGGIERO LEONCAVALLO

Pietro Mascagni's *Cavalleria rusticana (Rustic Chivalry)* was first performed in Rome in 1890. It was much admired by Verdi, who praised Mascagni for having invented a fascinating new operatic form, the little one-act opera that moves, start to finish, rapidly without a single delay or unnecessary episode. Immediately it was—and remains—exceedingly popular. Equally important to the form of the opera was the content. Mascagni's librettists based their text on a story with the same title by Giovanni Verga, written in 1880 and dramatized in 1884. Verga, from Sicily, was a leading figure in the *verismo* (truthful, realistic) movement in Italy that flourished late in the nineteenth century.

Verismo is a concept you must know. The *verismo* school maintained that art must not exclude representations of the real world and of the way ordinary people actually live their lives. Ugliness, vulgarity, the erotic, and the sadistic were not to be excluded from art. Art portraying only goodness, truth, and beauty falsifies life. So much for John Keats and his "Beauty is truth, truth beauty," and that is all one can know or needs to know while on this earth.

Verga's story of lust and infidelity culminating in a duel unto death is not a pretty one, though the music Mascagni provided to intensify an already tense drama is remarkable for its authenticity and memorable for its extraordinary melodic appeal. Soon thereafter, in 1892, Ruggiero Leoncavallo's opera *Pagliacci (Clowns)* premiered in Milan: Often you will find the title inauthentically given, even in books and on record jackets, as *I Pagli-acci (The Clowns)*. Leoncavallo's father, a magistrate, once presided over a court case that gave his son, who served as his own librettist, all the gory details he needed for his "truth is stranger than fiction" operatic portrayal of passionate infidelity and murderous revenge.

Both his work and Mascagni's speed to their culminations. Neither is long enough to provide a full evening of theater. The stories and their music, though unique, have much in common. What a perfect pair they make and thus it was that soon they were linked on the most popular double bill (two shorter dramas offered for the price of one to compose a single performance) in opera history. And with them, an important movement was born: *verismo*. These two operas are so important in opera history that our answering of the Verdi heir question must be delayed while they are considered in some detail.

Cavalleria rusticana and *Pagliacci*, perhaps because their pronunciations twist the English-speaking tongue and perhaps because they have become so overwhelmingly popular, commonly are known simply as "Cav and Pag." Such makes me cringe. I have heard radio announcers resort to this abomination, which is ludicrous to begin with because the *g* in *Pagliacci* is not a hard *g* as in *go*. In Italian *gli* is pronounced *lyee*, like the *lli* in the English word *million*. Please, do not ever let me hear you use this horrendous abbreviation when referring to two of my all-time favorite masterpieces. Learn the Italian. It's not difficult. If, for *Cavalleria rusticana* you can say CAH-vahl-a-REE-uh ROOS-tee-CON-uh and POL-lyee-AH-chee for *Pagliacci*—and surely you can—then you will be more than respectable.

Both Mascagni and Leoncavallo had conservatory training, though the former for a while was disowned by his father, who wanted his son to be a lawyer. Both had no initial success as composers and therefore had to eke out a living by giving piano lessons.

The world premiere of *Cavalleria rusticana* was given a tumultuous ovation and Mascagni awoke the following day a famous man. This was his first opera. *Pagliacci*, too, was an instantaneous hit and Leoncavallo overnight also went from obscurity to fame with his third opera. Both men wrote more than a dozen operatic works but only one from each achieved repertory status. Avid opera buffs can name a few of the other, more familiar operas of these two composers but the average operagoer knows each for his single sensation. Obviously, therefore, neither Mascagni nor Leoncavallo could be Verdi's heir, but their little masterpieces are so important in opera history that you must know them: Thus, the following digression from our central question is essential.

These operas have much in common. The characters are average people, Italian villagers, neither nobles nor heroes. Both plots have been called tawdry exploitations of sexual passion and infidelity bringing about death through revenge. The setting for both happens to be a religious holiday against which sadistic eroticism is portrayed. An unusual musical event occurs during the overture of each: In one, a famous tenor aria is sung behind the curtain; in the other, a famous baritone aria is sung as one of the characters steps out from behind the curtain. Both are superb theatrical touches. In each, also, as the plot thickens, a beautiful intermezzo (remember that the most recent and familiar use of this word, operatically, refers to a brief orchestral interlude often representing a brief passage of time between two scenes) separates the ultimate dissolution from the rapid unfolding of events preceding it. Finally, the musical cup of both of these operas runneth over with a brilliant tunefulness absolutely befitting the action, virtually the totality of both composers' greatest inspiration condensed into one work of little more than an hour. In the order in which they always are performed as a double bill, I will tell their stories and direct you to the most famous musical excerpts, even though I cannot think of either of these gems as excerptable, so perfect are they first note to last.

CAVALLERIA RUSTICANA (1890)
Rustic Chivalry

The opera is in one act. The characters of the drama, and their voice ranges:

TURIDDU, a young peasant, *tenor*
MAMMA LUCIA, his mother, an innkeeper, *contralto*
SANTUZZA, a young peasant girl in love with Turiddu, *soprano*
ALFIO, a carter, *baritone*
LOLA, his wife, *mezzo-soprano*
Villagers and peasants

The time is given as "the present" (meaning the latter part of the nineteenth century) on Easter Sunday and the place is a village in Sicily.

Offstage, while the prelude is played, the voice of Turiddu is heard. His lovely song praises the beauty of his lover, Lola, for whom he willingly would die, and all the action will speed to the fulfillment of this declaration. The prelude continues, and at its conclusion, the curtain rises on the empty village square.

Backstage, to the right, is the church and, to the left, the house and tavern of Mamma Lucia. Villagers enter, singing of love, labor, and springtime as they pass through the square or enter the church. Mamma Lucia comes out of her house and instantly is greeted by Santuzza, who asks for Turiddu. When told Turridu has gone to another village for wine, Santuzza responds that this cannot be for he was seen nearby last night in this village. The despairing tone of her voice reveals that she knows something. We hear a cracking whip in the distance, bells jingle, and soon Alfio, followed by men of the village, rides into the square behind his team singing of the joys of a carter's life, happy now to be returning home to his waiting, faithful wife. When he asks Mamma Lucia for a favorite wine, he is told that Turiddu has gone to a neighboring village to acquire some. But Alfio, unsuspectingly, also comments on having seen Turiddu this morning not far from his own house.

Santuzza quiets Mamma Lucia's curiosity before too many questions are asked at the very moment the Hallelujah is heard soaring out of the church. (The opera has numerous juxtapositions of the sacred and the profane as terrible events unfold on Easter day.) Alfio departs. Santuzza, explaining why she silenced her, tells Mamma Lucia that Turiddu pledged his love to Lola before soldiering. Finding her married to Alfio upon his return home, he and Santuzza became lovers, but while Lola's husband was away working, she and Turiddu again became involved. A stunned Mamma Lucia crosses the square and enters the church.

Turiddu arrives and claims he had gone for wine. Santuzza denounces him, calls him a liar, and says she saw him early this morning at Lola's door. They argue violently but soon Santuzza is pleading for his love. Lola interrupts them. She is looking for Alfio. The two women exchange some not-too-subtle insults before Lola goes to church. The confrontation is resumed and becomes even more heated, and Turiddu ends it by throwing Santuzza to the ground. He goes to the church. Santuzza furiously curses him and wastes no time, as Alfio returns, in spilling the beans:

> *Turiddu mi tolse l'onore*
> *E vostra moglie lui rapiva a me!*

> Turiddu has dishonored me
> And your wife has stolen him from me.

Before this day is over, an outraged Alfio will have revenge. He and Santuzza depart in separate directions, leaving the stage empty for what probably is the most beautiful and popular intermezzo in opera literature.

Mass has ended and the square fills with villagers. Mamma Lucia goes into her house and Lola is about to go home to find Alfio but is restrained by Turiddu, who proposes a toast to wine and love in his famous drinking song. All join the toast and drink. Alfio appears. Turiddu offers him a glass of wine. Alfio refuses it: "It would become poison in my heart," he says. Turiddu dashes it at Alfio's feet. Comprehending women herd Lola away and Turiddu, in true Sicilian fashion, embraces Alfio and gives his right ear a substantial bite. Mortal combat has been declared. Turiddu admits his guilt to Alfio but explains that now he must kill him in order not to leave Santuzza abandoned. Alfio leaves.

Mamma Lucia enters. Claiming to have had too many glasses of wine, Turiddu kisses her good-bye several times, asks her to promise to care for Santuzza, should he not return, and heads for the orchard. Mamma Lucia doesn't get it. Santuzza enters and embraces Mamma Lucia as distant voices cry out that Turiddu has been killed. With great speed the curtain falls.

This operatic version of Verga's violent story was enough of a shock to audiences at the end of the last century even with the duel taking place offstage. In the literary version, Verga describes how Alfio blinds Turiddu by throwing a handful of sand into his eyes and then stabs his helpless rival first in the stomach and then in the throat—much less decorous than the operatic version.

Newcomers to Mascagni's magnificent score should begin by becoming familiar with the most famous highlights, which include arias, duets, choruses, and instrumentals. Listen especially to how intense emotions are made more so by the way Mascagni offsets impassioned outbursts with episodes of extraordinary lyrical beauty: the happy choruses of the villagers, for example, and the glorious Easter Resurrection hymn. Notice, as well, how the superb libretto has characters converse without wasting a single word, thus allowing Mascagni to keep his music flowing, soaring, surging to its end. It never loiters because the terse libretto has not one verbose situation to be covered or filled by music.

Basic musical ingredients of the prelude include themes heard in the opera when Santuzza pleads with Turiddu for his love and when their emotions explode in their duet. The intensity of this is in contrast to the novel inclusion of an offstage aria within the famous prelude (Turiddu's serenade on the wonders of Lola). This is the renowned *Siciliana* (a traditional Sicilian dance form known for its lyrical, gentle, even pastoral expression), which concludes with ". . . if I were to die for you and go to paradise and did not find you there, then I would not stay."

Alfio's song, in praise of the life of a carter, wherein he is joined by a chorus, is quite popular. Santuzza's big solo aria is *Voi lo sapete, o mamma* ("You know so well, Mamma"), in which Mamma Lucia is told that Turiddu is betraying her by resuming his love affair with Lola. The great duet of Santuzza and Turiddu has two parts, the first rising to a pitch as Turiddu's voice soars with *Bada, Santuzza, schiavo non sono di questa vana tua gelosia* ("Listen, Santuzza, I will not be enslaved by your vain jealousy"). (When Jussi Björling performs this on my favorite recording of this opera, I know there has never been another Turiddu who can sing like this, and Zinka Milanov as his Santuzza is a perfect match.)

At this point Lola's voice is heard, first offstage and then onto the scene she comes. Her little aria, without naming him, is in praise of Turiddu, the fairest of them all. After she departs, the hostility of Turiddu and the pleading of Santuzza resume, becoming increasingly more dramatic. A number of years ago I attended a performance of this opera primarily because I had never heard in person the soprano portraying Santuzza but had admired her voice from recordings. In fact, both Santuzza and Turiddu had prominent voices, hers for its extraordinary power, his because it was almost nonexistent. During the most intense part of their duet, Turiddu's mouth was as open as it could be and he gestured dramatically, but all I could hear was a soprano overpowering even the orchestra.

The beautiful intermezzo, popular worldwide to millions who could not even name this opera, is less than four minutes long. It is also dramatic music played before an empty stage condensing so magnificently the emotions of the previous scene as well as anticipating the tragedy to come. Turiddu has the two final famous arias. The first is a catchy drinking song wherein he is joined by a chorus of villagers and last is the farewell to his mother.

PAGLIACCI (1892)
Clowns

Though not performed until two years after *Cavalleria rusticana,* *Pagliacci* also was completed by 1890. Leoncavallo wrote both the libretto and the music. I have already mentioned that the plot was drawn from a court case presided over by Leoncavallo's father when the composer was still a boy. All libretti by Leoncavallo, those he wrote for himself as well as those provided for other composers, reveal his gift for dramatic poetry. *Pagliacci* is a masterpiece.

The action is swift without a wasted word or contrived emotion. The device of performers enacting their own story in a play within a play obviously was not invented by Leoncavallo (recall, for example, Hamlet's "The play's the thing / wherein I'll catch the conscience of the king"). Nevertheless, nowhere is it more effective than in Act II of this opera, about a *commedia dell'arte* troupe of players moving from village to village. (In *commedia dell'arte* theater the performers improvise dialogue in accordance with a predetermined plot outline.) In the village of Montalto, in Calabria, where the action of the opera is set on the day of the Feast of the Assumption (August 15) about 1865, their comedy ends in tragedy. As a *commedia dell'arte improviso* (comedy improvised by professional actors) troupe, the characters in the opera have both real names and stage names. They are:

CANIO, head of the troupe, is Pagliaccio in their play, *tenor*
NEDDA, his wife, is Columbine in the play, *soprano*
BEPPE, one of the troupe, is the Arlecchino (Harlequin) in
   the play, *tenor*
TONIO, another of the troupe, is the clown Taddeo in the
   play, *baritone*
SILVIO, a villager and Nedda's lover, *baritone*
Villagers, peasants, and children

Before the curtains part, a prelude—built mainly from themes in the drama—musically introduces the story about to be portrayed. It is interrupted, however, by Tonio attired as Taddeo. He slips out from between the curtains and to the audience excuses himself for appearing alone. He is the Prologue, whose purpose it is to convey the author's intent: to paint a true picture of human emotions and behavior no matter how unpleasant. The credo of *verismo* opera could not be articulated more immediately or clearly than this. Again, this theatrical device of having a player appear in front of the curtain with a message before the play begins is an old one but Leoncavallo, like the play within a play, employs ancient devices with striking originality and effectiveness. Act I is ready.

Act I

The curtains part to show crossroads at the entrance to a village. A trumpet blares, a drum beats, and villagers hail the arrival of the players with unrestrained enthusiasm. Canio, in his Pagliaccio costume, urges everyone to attend their performance. At eleven o'clock at night they will witness how Pagliaccio gains his revenge through a well-laid trap. (In an old score, the hour is mistranslated as seven o'clock, and this error has been perpetuated in various libretti ever since. Also, in this same score Beppe is called Peppe. This, too, one occasionally encounters.)

As Nedda moves to descend from their wagon, Tonio, much in love with her, offers assistance. He is cuffed away by Canio, and when villagers jeer his gallant attempt, he, to himself, vows revenge. When a villager offers to buy drinks, Beppe and Canio prepare to go off but Tonio declines. Canio, teased that Tonio remains behind to woo Nedda, yields a slight smile, turns it into a frown, and declares that on stage if Pagliaccio surprises his wife, catching her with a lover, it is the stuff of comedy but in real life it would not be funny. Nedda is bothered by this until Canio adds that he has nothing to suspect. Bagpipes sound, vesper bells ring out, Canio removes his costume, and he departs with Beppe and the friendly villagers.

Alone, Nedda confesses fears should Canio be able to read her secret until the sounds of singing birds in flight divert her thoughts and she sings her brilliant "Bird Song." Tonio appears, and when Nedda's song is over, he confesses his love and moves to kiss her. He is thwarted by Nedda who grabs Beppe's whip and strikes him across the face. Within a few minutes both Canio and Nedda have humiliated Tonio and she too will pay. Tonio departs. Silvio enters and entices Nedda to give up her old husband and the tiresome theatrical life to run away with him. After wishy-washy resistance, she agrees and they embrace just as Tonio and Canio, sneaking on to the scene, are close enough to hear those evocative words of both the opera and the play within the play. To Silvio, Nedda says,

A stanotte, e per tua sarò.

Until tonight, when I'll be yours forever.

Hearing this, Canio utters "Oh!" Nedda exhorts her lover to run and Silvio leaps over the wall and is gone, Canio fast upon his heels. Tonio gives forth a cynical laugh. Nedda is disgusted by him. Canio returns, having failed to find Silvio. He demands that Nedda reveal her lover's name. Never; her lips are sealed. Canio threatens her with a knife but Beppe, returning just in time, wrests the stiletto from him. Settling this quarrel must wait, for they must ready themselves for their performance. Beppe pushes Nedda off to change, orders Tonio to go out and beat the drum, and, having restored order, at least temporarily, departs. A broken-hearted Canio is left alone to sing the most celebrated tenor aria in all opera as the act ends. It is *Vesti la giubba*.

Act II

The scene is the same except now it is night. Tonio urges spectators to enter, Beppe assists with seating, and within this exciting confusion Silvio and Nedda are able to exchange a few words to confirm their tryst. All is set and the curtain rises on the play within a play, showing a small room with a table and two chairs. Columbine (Nedda) paces anxiously. Her husband, Pagliaccio, is away. The voice of Arlecchino (Beppe) is heard serenading her in an offstage love song. Sitting with her back to the door, Columbine (Nedda) awaits the arrival of her lover. Unseen by her, it is Taddeo (Tonio) who enters, admires her ardently and, in a replica of events in the first act, confesses love and makes a pass. Of course, he is rebuffed. Arlecchino (Beppe) enters and kicks Taddeo (Tonio) about to the great delight of the applauding audience, until he goes off having agreed to serve as a lookout. The lovers sit at the table to eat and drink. Arlecchino (Beppe) gives Columbine (Nedda) a narcotic to administer to Pagliaccio that will knock him out, thus allowing them to run away together. An agitated Taddeo (Tonio) enters and warns that an enlightened Pagliaccio (Canio), with a weapon, is about to arrive.

Arrive he does, just after Arlecchino (Beppe) has jumped through the window. He recoils in pain as he hears Columbine's (Nedda) parting words, the very same words he overheard Nedda say to Silvio: "Until tonight, when I'll be yours forever." Attempting to play his part, he asks why two places have been set at the table. He is told one was for Taddeo (Tonio), who hastened away in fear. Taddeo (Tonio) is called in and he confirms the lie, but an unconvinced Pagliaccio (Canio) demands to know the name of her lover. Canio has by now emerged from Pagliaccio but Nedda continues her portrayal of Columbine. Refusing to answer, she addresses him as Pagliaccio. Canio can endure no more. With shattering emotion he cries, "No, I'm not Pagliaccio," and reminds Columbine (for Nedda still is playing her part) how he rescued her as an orphan, fed her, cared for her, and loved her.

Women in the audience are deeply touched by his powerful, heart-wrenching portrayal. "So true to life," they exclaim in an utterance of the creed of *verismo* opera.

Too much so for Silvio, who scarcely can contain himself. Canio continues. He gave her everything and now she has betrayed him. He condemns her. His brilliant performance is applauded. Again Canio demands the lover's name. Nedda's attempt to portray Columbine finally gives way as Canio rages uncontrollably. Murmurs of concern race through the crowd. A final time Canio demands she reveal the name of her lover and once more Nedda refuses. Canio draws his dagger and stabs her, demanding that she reveal the name with her dying breath. "Help . . . Silvio!" she cries. Silvio, rushing onto the stage, is greeted by Canio's knife. As Silvio falls dead next to Nedda, the astounded crowd cries out "Jesus and Mary" as Canio, now facing them, lets his knife fall upon the stage as he proclaims the most notorious spoken line in opera literature:

La commedia è finita!

The comedy is ended!

The curtains close.

In *Cavalleria rusticana* the drama progresses as musical episodes alternate in expressions of gaiety and intensity until the dreaded end occurs offstage. In *Pagliacci* the audience is carried directly toward a heart-sickening pitch of emotion that ends the first act, then is allowed to enjoy briefly the levity of the play within a play, all the while anticipating a tragic outcome. At last, the tempestuous finale explodes right in front of them. Similar yet different, these two dramas were made for each other.

The most famous numbers in the *Pagliacci* score begin with Tonio, as Taddeo, singing his famous Prologue before the curtains part. Few baritone arias in all Italian opera equal its undiminished popularity. Canio's cantabile, wherein he warns against anyone messing with his wife in real life, is followed by the lovely chorus of the bells as the villagers go to vespers. Nedda's hit tune is her famous "Bird Song," the *Ballatella*. The melody of this beautiful song imitates birds in flight. The love duet of Silvio and Nedda is one of few in Italian opera written for baritone and soprano. The first act ends with Canio's celebrated *Vesti la giubba* ("Put on your costume"). Canio must play the part of a clown while his heart is breaking. The drama of the last lines especially is a gold mine for a beautiful, powerful tenor voice:

> *Ridi Pagliaccio, sul tuo amore infranto!*
> *Ridi del duol che t'avvelena il cor!*

> Laugh, Pagliaccio, at your shattered love!
> Laugh at the grief that poisons your heart!

Leoncavallo put all the drama necessary in his words and music but some tenors sob and sob over the orchestral conclusion to this famous aria, under the assumption that this adds to the scene. Too often this is overdone. I can take a restrained sob or two, but I prefer the purity of Jussi Björling's approach. When asked why he did not cry at the end of the aria, the great Swedish tenor replied, "Because it is not in the score."

An intermezzo as beautiful as that heard in *Cavalleria rusticana* bridges the two acts. This music has never shared the popularity of the other; why, I do not know. Beppe, as Arlecchino, is given a classic serenade in Act II ingeniously composed in an earlier style to fit the harlequinade, which disintegrates when Canio denies he is Pagliaccio. This music of his denial, equaling the drama of his *Vesti la giubba*, charges forth from this moment to the terrifying end.

The world premiere was conducted by Arturo Toscanini, a musician of inexorable opinions, most of them sound. In 1908, when he came to the Metropolitan Opera, he immediately abolished the tradition of encores (acceptable in numerous houses in America and Europe): After a stupendous rendition of an aria, the singer responds to tremendous applause by singing it again, or at least part of it. Almost never again did a Metropolitan Opera encore occur. One of just a few exceptions took place while the company was on tour in Atlanta in 1930. The great American baritone Lawrence Tibbett's singing of the Prologue put the audience in a frenzy, so he sang the last part again beginning with the words *E voi . . .* where Tonio urges the audience not to be fooled by costumes, for they upon the stage are ordinary human beings with the same emotions as those in the audience. Elsewhere in this book I have mentioned both Tibbett's friendship with our family and my father's beautiful baritone. This aria was a favorite of both. It is in my blood. When a Tonio does it right, I am always moved.

In no way whatsoever should one assume that because these two operas are set on high holy days they are moralizing denunciations of infidelity. They are not dramas about a divine hand working behind the scenes to make certain sinners pay for their indiscretions. They are true-to-life tragedies. The victims, Turiddu, Nedda, and Silvio, however, are ordinary human beings and not great, noble personages whose characters are flawed by a single weakness. All three are good people who happen to follow their hearts, marriage vows notwithstanding. Sound familiar? Fortunately, their dire fates are not the rule for all love affairs.

Cavalleria rusticana and *Pagliacci* are two operas I could never do without. They are the quintessential *verismo* operas. I hope you will come to love them as much as I do.

GIACOMO PUCCINI

Now back to Verdi's heir.

On February 1, 1893, Giacomo Puccini's opera *Manon Lescaut* had its premiere. Soon thereafter, a music critic who used the pseudonym Corno di Bassetto predicted: "Puccini looks to me more like the heir of Verdi than any of his rivals." The critic was the young George Bernard Shaw and, as often would be the case, he was right. Puccini's first two operas, *Le villi (The Spirits)* and

Edgar, had produced limited impact. *Manon Lescaut* was the first of many successes. Verdi's final work, *Falstaff*, appeared a month after Puccini's first triumph. A new king was about to be crowned.

Puccini's musical lineage is impressive. His father was Michele Puccini, an important music teacher, an organist, a scholar of music history, and a composer. Michele's father was a composer of sacred music, as was *his* father, Antonio, who also was an organist. Antonio was the son of Giacomo, an organist and prolific composer of sacred music. Thus our Puccini, the famous opera composer, was the fifth generation of Puccini musicians, all born in Lucca.

Though their profession was sacred music, a passion for the theater seemed to course through their blood. This reached musical fulfillment with the fifth generation. The last of the line, born December 23, 1858, was appropriately christened Giacomo Antonio Domenico Michele Secundo Maria Puccini. As far as I know, he made only one attempt to write church music. *Messa di Gloria* was his conservatory graduation composition. It received one performance, which greatly pleased his proud mother, and was placed on a shelf. This extremely beautiful music, quite astonishing for an eighteen-year-old, was rediscovered in 1950, subsequently was performed and recorded, and continues to gain an enthusiastic following. After this one piece, the long line of Puccini sacred music composers came to an end. Giacomo knew opera was his calling.

Many years ago, when we were in graduate school together, a friend told me he did not like Puccini. Because he is very bright and knows his music, I was quite surprised. Many years later, I wanted him to hear some early, rare historic recordings of a great tenor. He melted away as several Puccini arias followed one another and, of course, I reminded him of his anti-Puccini position of years before. He smiled and said, "What did I know then?"

Puccini has had his detractors, his immense popularity notwithstanding. I have encountered these criticisms more than once: ". . . one-plot Puccini," "overtly melodramatic," and "too popular with the masses." Briefly, let's take these one by one.

There is no denying the repetitive predilection for women unlucky in love in Puccini's plots. In his first opera, *Le villi* (1884), Anna dies of a broken heart when deserted by her fiancé. In his second opera, *Edgar* (1889), a gypsy temptress not only lures away Fidelia's love but also, in the end, stabs her. In *Manon Lescaut*

(1893), Puccini's first unequivocal triumph and his third opera, Manon, ill and abandoned, dies in her lover's arms. Mimi, in *La bohème (The Bohemians)* staged in 1896, his fourth and most popular opera, loses love in dying from tuberculosis. The heroines of *Tosca* (1900) and *Madama Butterfly* (1903), operas five and six, respectively, commit suicide when love is lost. Audiences had to wait until Puccini's seventh opera in 1910, *La fanciulla del West (The Girl of the Golden West)*, before a woman gets her man: Minnie and Dick ride off into the sunset together. In *La rondine (The Swallow)* produced in 1917, the eighth, because she knows consent to marry will never be given to a woman of impure past, Magda walks out on the love of her life.

Puccini's ninth opera was actually three one-act operas presented together under the title *Il Trittico* (1918), which means "The Triptych." In the first drama, *Il tabarro (The Clock)*, Giorgetta's lover is murdered by her elderly husband. In the second, *Suor Angelica (Sister Angelica)*, which has no men in the cast, Sister Angelica, a nun who bore a son out of wedlock before taking holy orders, is told of the child's death, and she poisons herself. A subplot in the third drama, *Gianni Schicci*, brings Lauretta and her beloved happily together.

Puccini left his final opera, *Turandot* (1926), not quite finished when he died in 1924. This exceedingly gruesome tale ends with the imperious Turandot, opera's number one man hater, falling in love.

Seven of ten Puccini heroines not only are unlucky in love but also their misfortune is what drives the plot. Though there is some truth to the ". . . one-plot Puccini" criticism, this does nothing to diminish the riveting qualities of the differing stories of women consumed by love and how refreshing it is to find real, flesh-and-blood women who are not queens, princesses, or goddesses. Which women in all opera literature continue to captivate audiences of every generation more than Mimi, Tosca, and the little Japanese girl, Cio-Cio-San, known as Madama Butterfly?

"Overtly melodramatic" is not applicable when *melodrama* is used to mean, as often it is in literary criticism, a play whose form does not conform to the dramatic laws of cause and effect. Puccini was a master of the theater. The demands for perfection he placed upon his librettists and on himself have become operatic legend. Nothing extraneous or contrived was allowed. A story must move naturally, honestly, and speedily from start to finish. There was much of the *verismo* school in his artistic instincts.

The melodramatic critique aimed at Puccini refers to what some consider excessive sentimentality and emotional exaggeration. Sometimes Puccini's characters are driven more or moved more by feelings than by reason, but aren't we all at times? And I know of no passage in all of Puccini in which his music is superficially contrived to tug on the heart strings.

The problem is his gift for melody; and here, *gift* is an understatement. The beauty of Puccini's melodic inventions, especially in expressions of pathos, are second to none, and when our hearts are touched by them it is authentic emotion at work. There are those tough old birds or those of stiff upper lip—or, perhaps, of repressed feelings—for whom Puccini's music is too emotional: melodramatic, they would say. Through my many years, they have been very rare indeed. After many years of teaching introductory courses on opera, I was able to predict with precision that for the majority of students in a given class, their first favorite composer of opera would be Puccini. And for millions around the world, thus he remains. This brings up the third charge against him.

Puccini is "too popular" to those who must disassociate themselves from any and all art that appeals to multitudes. Now, there is considerable poetry, painting, music, and, of course, countless movies, that are just too sappy or shallow to be taken seriously. This is especially irritating when something shallow sells well and makes the progenitors rich and famous. Puccini never, ever could fit into this class. He was a serious artist through and through, a master craftsman with an uncanny sense of what worked on the stage. He is popular because the masses rise up to art and not because he has lowered himself to the masses. And speaking of masses, where, outside of some European exceptions, has opera ever had mass appeal anyway?

Puccini was not, however, on the cutting edge of the arts. We must remember that while he was making one opera after another that overflowed with glorious melodies and harmonies, Igor Stravinsky and Arnold Schoenberg were honing their music knives in preparation to reshape musical forms for the twentieth century (more on this in chapter 14). They were the "cutting edge" of modern music, whereas Puccini, a generation older, brought to its culmination several centuries of the supremacy of melody in Italian opera. Puccini, Verdi's heir, had no successor. He was the last of a long line of Italian opera geniuses. This is not to say there are no good Italian operas written after Puccini, but it is to say that the long tradition of Italian composers writing several masterpieces, one after the other, came to an end when he died. His popularity continues to grow more than seventy-five years after his death.

Only his first two operas are obscure. The first, *Le villi*, I love but because it is not yet a household word, we pass it by. The second, *Edgar*, was a flop due to a dismal libretto, and you are not likely to encounter it even though it also contains music I like. Everything he wrote thereafter, however, starting with *Manon Lescaut*, is so wonderful and popular that you must know about it or you do not know your Puccini.

MANON LESCAUT (1893)

It was a bold gesture of extraordinary self-confidence for young Puccini, not yet famous, to take up the Manon subject. Massenet's *Manon* (chapter 9) was almost ten years old, extremely popular, and soon to have its eight-hundredth performance. Both these composers have been called "eternal feminists" and they, of course, shared a literary source (Abbé Prévost's novel *The Story of Chevalier des Grieux and Manon Lescaut*).

There the similarity ends. Massenet's opera benefited from a fine libretto; Puccini's succeeded in spite of its having been patched together by six different writers (Ruggiero Leoncavallo was one of them). Massenet, sixteen years Puccini's senior, and with greater experience in the theater, created a far more subtle and polished work. His Manon unquestionably is French, tantalizing in her restraint and understatement, and even at times a little childlike. Here Gallic niceties and charm prevail. Puccini's Manon Lescaut is not in any way French and, at eighteen, neither is she childlike. Italian emotions are not hidden but instead surge through the music like a brook bursting its banks. Puccini's summary is the best. When repeatedly his publisher attempted to steer him away from the subject already made famous by Massenet, he replied, "Massenet has felt the subject as a Frenchman, with the powder and the minuets—I feel it as an Italian, with despairing passion."

Puccini's opera, which is in four acts, premiered quite successfully in Turin on February 1, 1893. I have read accounts of how the appreciative audience called the composer for repeated curtain calls. The characters and their voice ranges are:

MANON LESCAUT, a beautiful young woman, *soprano*
LESCAUT, her brother, a sergeant of the King's Guards,
   baritone
CHEVALIER DES GRIEUX, a student, *tenor*
EDMONDO, another student, *tenor*
GERONTE DI RAVOIR, treasurer-general, *bass*
Innkeeper, *bass*
Dancing master, *tenor*
Singer, *mezzo-soprano*
Lamplighter, *tenor*
Sergeant of the Royal Archers, *bass*
Naval captain, *bass*
Students, village girls, townspeople, singers, gentlemen,
   abbés, archers, and sailors

The time is the eighteenth century and the action moves
from Amiens to Paris to Le Havre to Louisiana.

Act I

A brief orchestral introduction, lively, youthful, melodic, and suggestive of gaiety and pleasure, is no more than an instrumental
preface to Edmondo's song. He is joined by a chorus of young people who have gathered in front of an inn at Amiens in anticipation
of the pleasures that come with the evening when youth is free
and willing and ready for love.

Des Grieux enters and Edmondo coaxes him to join the fun or,
perhaps, is he morose because he is consumed by some unattainable love? Des Grieux denies knowing anything about love but to
amuse his friends he approaches a group of girls and with gallant
teasing asks if there is one who will love him. *Tra voi, belle, brune
e bionde* . . . ("Among you beauties, brunette and blond, is there
one who waits for me?"). This is the first of numerous famous
arias in the score. When the girls realize Des Grieux is having
sport with them they are angry, students laugh, and all join in a
chorus in praise of seeking pleasure.

A carriage arrives and its occupants descend. Lescaut is followed
by Geronte and then Manon Lescaut. Des Grieux is struck dumb by
Manon's beauty. Servants bustle attending to luggage, the innkeeper
escorts the gentlemen into the inn, and Manon sits down to wait.

Des Grieux approaches her and requests her name. "My name
is Manon Lescaut," she answers. Asking forgiveness for speaking
so openly, he tells her he is mysteriously drawn to her. When told

she is headed for a convent, Des Grieux protests passionately and proposes that they meet later. For his kind concern she asks his name. (This would make a good opera trivia question, for who would ever know or suspect his first name is Renato.) Reluctant at first, eventually Manon is persuaded by his begging to meet him later, when it has grown darker, before running off to answer her brother's summons. Des Grieux gives brilliant expression of his love at first sight in the second famous aria in the score, *Donna non vidi mai simile a questa* ("Never have I seen a woman like this"). Notice, especially, his thrilling repetitions of her first words to him: "My name is Manon Lescaut." When other students tease him about being in love, he strides off while they assemble at tables to drink, flirt, and gamble with cards.

Geronte and Lescaut return together, their conversation revealing that they have yet to meet formally even though Lescaut has spoken about his displeasure at having to place his sister in a convent according to their parents' wishes. Introductions are exchanged and the wealth associated with Geronte's position certainly is not lost on Lescaut, while the old coot evidently is keenly interested in Manon's fate. Their dialogue is woven ingeniously through varied expressions of the reveling students. (Puccini was the absolute master at creating perfectly natural, lifelike crowd scenes on the operatic stage. You will encounter numerous others.) Lescaut becomes preoccupied with the card game and accepts an invitation to join while Geronte goes over to the innkeeper to hatch his scheme. Geronte orders a carriage with fast horses to be made ready for him behind the inn in one hour and buys silence with a purse of gold. An eavesdropping Edmondo, however, is now privy to the plot, which he shares with his friend Des Grieux.

Manon appears on the stairs. Cautiously she makes her way to Des Grieux and, with *Vedete? Io son fedele alla parola mia* ("You see! I am true to my word"), begins a duet that culminates in Des Grieux revealing Geronte's plan to abduct her, a confession of love, and, with a little urging from Edmondo, an agreement from the new young lovers to use the old man's carriage themselves both to foil the abduction and to refuse taking the veil. This great duet is reminiscent of the many attestations of love that will flow from Puccini's pen for thirty years to come.

Manon and Des Grieux steal away behind the inn. Seeing Lescaut absorbed in cards, Geronte is determined to seize this moment for his seduction of the beautiful woman but is stopped in his tracks when Edmondo reports that he is too late: Manon

already has fled in his carriage with another student. Pursuit
would be futile. Lescaut calms the old man with a promise to
help. His pleasure-loving sister quickly will exhaust a poor student's purse. Then and there, he will be of service (to this man of
considerable resources, he fails to add). After all, his sister is incapable of living without luxury. Together they enter the inn for
supper. To the laughter of the young people, the curtain falls.

Act II

The second act takes place in a luxurious salon in Geronte's house
in Paris. With two assistants attending to his every command,
Manon's hairdresser fusses over the many details of making her as
beautiful as possible. Her brother enters, admires his sister, and
congratulates himself for having rescued her from the poverty of
Des Grieux's humble abode and ensconcing her so lavishly in the
wealth of the General Cashier. The look in her eyes tells him
something is missing. Correctly he guesses that she wants news
of Des Grieux and sadly she sings, in one of the most beautiful
arias in Puccini's incomparable portfolio of melody, of what has
been lost. Amid all the wealth she is, in fact, freezing in a death-
ly silence: *In quelle trine morbide* ("In those soft silken curtains"). Lescaut, friend both of Geronte and of Des Grieux,
explains to her how long it took him to convince Des Grieux, who
constantly asked for her, that he did not know her whereabouts.
Des Grieux has taken to gambling madly in hopes of acquiring the
money to win her back. In a reverie, Manon admits that were he
to come, she could no longer resist. Her pensive mood evaporates
as she glimpses herself in a mirror and inquires of her brother as
to the fit of gown and wig as musicians enter. Irritated, she tells
Lescaut that Geronte composes madrigals praising her. Overtly
bored by the performance, she gives a purse to Lescaut to pay the
musicians. He pockets the purse, claiming it would be an insult to
art, and dismisses them. As the singers leave they are passed by
Geronte, accompanied by some elderly friends, who enter with
the dancing master—time for Manon's instruction in how to
dance the perfect minuet. Her boredom has affected Lescaut, who
surreptiously steals away to find Des Grieux. After Geronte's
toadies bow and scrape, gifting Manon with flowers and jewels,
the lesson begins. As she dances with Geronte, the overly serious
dancing master comments upon every step, her carriage, and her
gestures. Manon then flirts with Geronte in the aria *L'ora, o Tirsi,
è vaga e bella* ("The hour, O Tirus, is desirous and beautiful"),

after which all depart, she promising to join them soon. In this scene of formality, elegance, and superficiality, Puccini has established a mood of restraint to intensify all the more the passion about to explode.

Manon has a self-approving moment of readying herself in the mirror when, just as she is about to go out, Des Grieux appears at the door. *Tu, amore?* ("You, my love?") exclaims Manon, to begin a stupendous love duet. Des Grieux's reproaches for jilting him soon are overcome by her beauty and her seduction. Naturally, he yields. Tired of waiting, Geronte returns to see what is keeping Manon, and what he sees makes him irate. She offends him. He departs, with the promise to return . . . soon! She expresses exhilaration, believing herself free, while Des Grieux questions his fate in the hands of a woman who holds him so helplessly within her power: *Ah, Manon, mi tradisce il tuo folle pensier* ("Ah, Manon, your foolish thoughts betray me"). A great tenor can make mincemeat out of you with this one.

A breathless Lescaut bolts into the room with news that Geronte has denounced Manon and that police are on the way. The lovers must flee instantly, and Puccini's music so marvelously conveys the fright, chaos, and confusion of the moment. Manon, however, cannot leave her jewels. The delay is costly. Soldiers, followed by Geronte, stop her in her tracks. The jewels fall at her feet and scatter to the floor. She is arrested and dragged away. Des Grieux, who has been restrained by Lescaut, cries out in agony, "Oh, my Manon," as the curtain falls.

Act III

A lovely, plaintive intermezzo separates the second act from the third. It is a musical representation of the journey to Le Havre, where Manon and other prisoners have been taken for disembarkation to America. Des Grieux has followed her. The curtain opens on a square next to the harbor in Le Havre where a large boat is made fast to pilings. Lescaut and Des Grieux's scheme to rescue Manon fails, causing a commotion. Townspeople fill the square, another famous Puccini crowd scene in the making. Soldiers hold back the throng, sailors board the ship, and a sergeant calls the roll of the women being banished. For each one—Rosetta, Madelon, Manon, etcetera—the townspeople chatter and comment. Des Grieux works his way through the crowd until he is close enough to Manon to touch her hand. He will not leave her side, and as the captain comes forward to investigate the problem,

Des Grieux makes an impassioned plea from his knees to be taken on as a cabin boy, or anything, so that he does not have to leave her. The captain relents and the act ends. This scene spirals to its powerful dramatic climax. Hearing this music, it is no wonder that Shaw crowned Puccini to be Verdi's heir.

Act IV
This act, like Act III, is brief; each is twenty minutes or shorter. The final act has been criticized as one in which nothing happens. Well, not much by way of a story line, but Puccini knew too well what music could do. After the intensity of the third act the final curtain rises on an undulating, desolate plain in Louisiana. Night falls as Des Grieux attempts to support an obviously weak and exhausted Manon as they stumble along dressed in tatters. She stops, slumps to the ground, and faints. Reviving somewhat, she and Des Grieux lament the fate that has brought them to such an ignominious end. As her lover goes off to look for water and shelter, Manon, in her final aria, knows she is dying: *Sola, perdutta, abbandonata in landa desolata* ("Alone, lost, abandoned in this desolate land"). Having found nothing, Des Grieux returns. For the final time they express their love for each other, then she expires in his arms. The curtain falls. Puccini marvelously has transformed the passion of Manon and Des Grieux, which has dominated the first three acts, into a godless requiem for a love that will never die. That is how I hear this last act in which "nothing happens."

I have read critics who find fault with *Manon Lescaut*, claiming that it is an opera wherein the music attempts to compensate for characters incompletely drawn and disjointed dramatic action. In this youthful work of Puccini, the first outpouring of his genius, I do not encounter those issues in spite of the numerous problems he had with half a dozen librettists. The drama is all in the two central characters. They are not the least bit complex, yet nor are they inadequately drawn. Manon is young, beautiful, much tempted by luxury, but unquestionably as much in love with Des Grieux as he is with her. For him, once having seen Manon alight from a carriage, he sees nothing else. They are young and not without their shortcomings, but ultimately what matters is their limitless love for each other. The dramatic action of the four acts could not be more clear: Boy meets girl and they elope; girl briefly jilts boy for wealth but realizes she still loves him; boy follows his denounced, banished love to the ends of the earth, where she dies in his arms.

✧

The Royal Opera, Covent Garden, video with Placido Domingo as Des Grieux and Kiri Te Kanawa in the title role is a superb introduction, Maria Callas devotees cherish the recording she made with Giuseppe di Stefano as her lover, and my favorite is the 1954 recording made in Rome with Licia Albanese and Jussi Björling, absolutely chilling in its passion and beauty. The blood of Puccini's music surges through Madame Albanese's veins and here and there in this book, several times, it will emerge that when pushed into the "favorite tenor" discussion, I say that never have I heard a voice more beautiful than Björling's.

Several years ago, I was talking with Licia Albanese about making this recording with Björling. She told me that they, while singing together at the Met, had agreed to record *Manon Lescaut* in Rome, and that they had signed a contract with RCA. Suddenly Björling departed for Sweden, claiming he was ill. As often was the case, the great Swedish tenor was being difficult. His considerable fame notwithstanding, Björling was troubled by self-doubt, fears of not being perfect, worries about whether he could give his listeners their money's worth. Not only did he not arrive in Rome at the appointed time, he sent a telegram to say that he could not record because he was sick.

Albanese, the other musicians, and the recording staff were dumbfounded. RCA's attempts to engage another world-class tenor on a moment's notice were futile. What appeared to all as a hopeless situation was joyfully resolved when, out of the blue, a wire from Björling arrived: "Arriving tomorrow! Feeling much better!"

"Thank God," Licia exclaimed, and soon thereafter a brilliant *Manon Lescaut* had been taped. More than fifty years later, she still wistfully referred to it as "Oh, so very beautiful." At a dinner celebrating the completion of the recording, Björling revealed that his illness had been promptly cured by a telegram sent to him from Rome by RCA. The telegram, however, was not from anyone at RCA. Licia's husband, Joe, had taken it upon himself to get Björling to Rome pronto. Whatever the telegram said did the trick. And so we have a recording I cannot live without! If you will get to know *Manon Lescaut* through these recordings and then can honestly say you do not like this opera, you should be careful where and to whom you admit it.

LA BOHÈME
A Bohemian Life (1896)

Puccini's incomparable masterpiece, one of the most beloved and often performed operas in the world, *La bohème*, followed *Manon Lescaut*. Let us continue the discussion of recordings because there is more I want to say about *La bohème*. I introduced this opera in my preface, relating the tremendous emotional impact that a certain video of *La bohème* had upon several generations of my beginning opera students. It was the Metropolitan Opera production, directed by the brilliant Franco Zeffirelli, that stars José Carreras and Teresa Stratas. Part of the emotional impact, aside from the obvious beauty of the music, rests in the extraordinary camera work and the *verismo* acting of the central characters, every telling gesture so perfectly appropriate as called for by Zeffirelli. Before Mimi dies of tuberculosis, I would tell my students to focus carefully on the gripping portrayal of Teresa Stratas (as Mimi), who so well knew what she was doing; she suffered tuberculosis when she was a young woman. For a complete opera recording, if you can have only one, make certain it is the 1956 recording with Sir Thomas Beecham conducting. Victoria de los Angeles is Mimi and Jussi Björling is Rodolfo.

Now, before you conclude that I write this just because of Björling again, I must tell you this is a common conclusion in that little world of those who fastidiously fuss over finding the definitive recording of such and such. I know of three nice music experts who wrote a book (now out of date and out of print, so let's let it go at that) telling readers what recordings to buy. Invariably, on vocal music, I disagreed with them. Their singers rarely are mine. Under their *La bohème* entry, however, we are together. Basically they dismiss all other recordings before and since. The entire cast is superb and orchestra and chorus under Beecham's direction are flawless: Beecham studied the entire score with Puccini in London in 1920 even though they were not close friends, having knocked heads on other musical issues. This is the only complete opera recording Beecham ever made in the United States. All musicians, from far and near, were under a rigid deadline, with the consequence that start to finish the air of every recording session was electric with inspiration. You hear it in every note.

Sir Thomas Beecham marched only to an inner drumbeat. His ideas were his own and he had much to say about the greatness of Puccini before many others had yet to acknowledge him as one of the very best opera composers ever. Beecham conducted *Bohème* more than three hundred times. During the year of this famous recording, the music critic Irving Kolodin talked with Beecham about the opera and quoted him as follows in an article in the *Saturday Review* (August 25, 1956):

> I have made a practice wherever I go to ask intelligent amateurs or the better informed dilettanti, whether in my own country, or in Italy—where there are many more of them—who their favorite operatic composer is. Almost without exception, regardless of whether they are doctors or cab drivers or operators of a lift, they reply "Puccini." When I ask them to explain, they say in effect, though the words may differ: "He doesn't keep us waiting. He gets on with it." And that is one of the abiding attractions of an opera like *Bohème*. It doesn't keep us waiting. It does get on with it.

For two reasons *Bohème* fits the *verismo* label best of all Puccini's operas. First, it is a story of the ordinary life of ordinary people. Mimi is a seamstress and the bohemian friends are artists and teachers attempting to eke out a living. Mimi (and Musetta, too) is less "foreign," so to speak, than other famous Puccini heroines. For example, Tosca is an opera singer; Madama Butterfly, a Japanese geisha; Minnie owns a saloon in a mining camp; and Turandot is a Chinese princess. Second, *Bohème* is a *verismo* masterpiece in its extraordinary naturalism of expression, both in small ensembles and in the second-act crowd scene. Here we must comment on the score, the manner in which Puccini "gets on with it" and "doesn't keep us waiting."

Wagner's influence was pervasive. A composer writing in the final decades of the nineteenth century who employed the then passé technique of developing story lines through *recitative secco* and expressed emotion through arias isolated from the dramatic flow of action would have been shunned as a musical reactionary. The Wagnerian operatic orchestra did not simply provide an accompaniment for the songs of the singers. It had a voice of its own, commenting on the action, reminding the audience of past events, and anticipating things to come, all in one symphonic flow. Wagner called this—perhaps you remember from previous chapters—"endless melody."

Verdi's final works show Wagner's impact and Puccini, Verdi's heir in the tradition of glorious Italian melodies, is even more Wagnerian in his creation of a symphonic orchestral style wherein the music constantly moves along, often restating and developing themes already utilized. In no way did Puccini employ a gigantic system of Wagnerian leitmotifs: nevertheless, Wagner's influence can be heard as Puccini's orchestra also iterates and alters familiar themes as it sings along. It is more difficult to compose an operatic score in a symphonic style. There is no time to stop and start again after pauses for recitatives because there is no recitative of a traditional sort. The story develops through a conversational style that seems perfectly natural except, of course that the words are sung, not spoken. When an aria does come, it emerges as an intimate part in association with this conversational style. This conversational style commences in less than thirty seconds after the first note of the score is heard. In Puccini's *Bohème* the story often develops so fluently, naturally, and rapidly that even those for whom Italian is their native language must pay constant attention or they will miss something.

For the rest of us, to obtain the complete story and the full wonder of the libretto, it means much study beforehand. But even without assiduous preparation, one knowing only the bare bones of the plot (see my introduction, p. 1), and the characters will be swept away by Puccini's most fluent score. *La bohème* is considered by many musical experts to be Puccini's finest masterpiece. Indeed, more than this. With Sir Thomas Beecham, we can agree that in the huge literature of several hundred years of opera (*Bohème* premiered three hundred years after the first opera performance in Florence), this work of Puccini's is one of the best ever written. Obviously, it's the unforgettable music that prevails, yet while one is carried away by the unending beauty of Puccini's melodies, it is his perfect synthesis of words, music, and action that unconsciously captures us completely. No wonder my students left the room, eyes wet and red, without a word after watching Zeffirelli's film. The cast:

RODOLPHO, a poet, *tenor*
MARCELLO, a painter, *baritone*
COLLINE, a philosopher, *bass*
SCHAUNARD, a musician, *baritone*
BENOIT, their landlord, *bass*
MIMI, a seamstress, *soprano*

MUSETTA, a grisette, *soprano*
PARPIGNOL, an itinerant toy vendor, *tenor*
ALCINDORO, a state councilor and Musetta's admirer, *bass*
Customs-House Sergeant, *bass*

TOSCA (1900)

Puccini became familiar with and interested in Victorien Sardou's play *La Tosca* in 1889, eighteen months after it opened in Paris, but was unable to obtain the rights to make an opera from it: thus, *Manon Lescaut* (1893) and *La bohème* (1897). Sardou, in France a noted playwright, today is known only to a few English-speaking people. One of his most famous plays, *Madame Sans-Gêre*, written in collaboration with Emile Moreau, was made into an opera by Umberto Giordano. Were it not for Puccini's *Tosca*, outside of France Sardou would be a forgotten name.

While Puccini considered another subject, Luigi Illica turned Sardou's *La Tosca* into a book for an opera by another composer. Illica, you will remember, collaborated with Giuseppe Giacosa on the *La bohème* libretto and his was also one of the six hands attempting to give Puccini what he wanted in *Manon Lescaut*. These two men, Illica and Giacosa, will become familiar to you as the librettists of Puccini's three most well-known and often performed operas, *La bohème*, *Tosca*, and *Madama Butterfly*. After *La bohème*, Puccini gave cursory consideration to several other plots before becoming preoccupied by the *Tosca* story. He wanted it so much that he participated in a little conspiracy of talking the other composer into giving up his rights to Illica's *Tosca* book. A successful opera never could be made from such a brutal story was the ruse.

Puccini acquired the rights to the book and Giacosa put Illica's prose into poetry. The long play of five acts they condensed into three, focusing exclusively on the intrigue surrounding the famous singer Floria Tosca and her lover, the painter Mario Cavaradossi, and by de-emphasizing the intensity of the political and religious battles of the original. Sardou ultimately claimed the opera libretto was superior to his play. He was right. Today his *La Tosca* is forgotten while Puccini's *Tosca* is one of the world's most popular operas.

There was one important aspect of Illica's book that Puccini could not accept. In the last act, facing death by execution, Illica gave Cavaradossi a big speech, a heroic farewell to life and art. No, no, no, said Puccini. At this time Cavaradossi would think only of his beloved Tosca. He provided a draft along these lines and from it Illica and Giacosa made *E lucevan le stelle* ("And the stars shone"), now one of the most famous tenor arias ever written. Puccini knew best. He knew what he wanted and demanded it.

Both the opera and the play (more so the opera) tell a dire story of political crimes, sexual obsession, lies, cheating, and the violent deaths of the three central characters. In spite of this, Puccini always focused on finding within this dark drama the lyricism of love binding Tosca and Cavaradossi through the machinations of the evil baron Scarpia. Here is their story. The characters and their voice ranges:

> FLORIA TOSCA, a famous singer, *soprano*
> MARIO CAVARADOSSI, her lover, a painter, *tenor*
> BARON SCARPIA, chief of police, *baritone*
> CESARE ANGELOTTI, a political prisoner, *bass*
> A sacristan, *baritone*
> SPOLETTA, a police agent, *tenor*
> SCIARRONE, a police officer, *bass*
> A jailer, *bass*
> A shepherd, *(preferably a young boy's voice)*
> Choirboys, soldiers, policemen, ladies, nobles, citizens,
>   artisans, etcetera

All three acts are set in famous buildings in Rome during the month of June in 1800.

Act I

Tosca is a drama of three characters: Tosca and her lover and the sinister baron Scarpia. The forceful chords at the beginning of the opera will later be associated with his evilness. Again, the singing starts almost immediately as the curtain rises on the first of three famous architectural sites in Rome, the interior of the Church of Sant' Andrea Della Valle. A painter's scaffold, holding a large, covered painting, is stage left, the Attavanti Chapel is on the right. An obviously highly agitated Angelotti rushes in, says something about a hidden key, rummages here and there, finds it, unlocks the gate to the chapel, enters, closes the gate, and disappears. The sacristan enters with a bucket of paintbrushes, mutters about washing the filthy things, sets them down, and, as the Angelus is heard, kneels and prays. Cavaradossi comes in, climbs the scaffold, removes the cover from the painting, and goes to work on a large canvas portraying a blue-eyed Mary Magdalen with her glorious mass of golden hair. The sacristan comments on the likeness to a girl who, frequently of late, has come to pray. Cavaradossi acknowledges having used her as a model as she knelt through her long prayers. As he paints, the sacristan bustles about. Suddenly, Cavaradossi stops, removes from his pocket a miniature of Floria Tosca, and compares it to his painting. *Recondita armonia* ("Obscure harmony") is the first famous aria of the opera, barely five minutes old. "What is it about Puccini? He doesn't keep us waiting!"

While he paints the blonde beauty, Cavaradossi thinks only of his beloved Tosca, with her dark hair and dark eyes, blending in the mystery of art. Throughout the sublime lyricism of his meditation, the sacristan periodically grumbles reproachful comments, then, after a few more words to the painter, leaves him alone. Cavaradossi resumes his painting.

Assuming he is alone, Angelotti unlocks the gate, the sound causing the painter to turn around. They recognize in each other dissenters and sympathizers in the republican cause. Angelotti has escaped prison and Cavaradossi will aid him, but the voice of Tosca is heard. Angelotti is given a basket of food and told to hide. Calling "Mario, Mario," a jealous Tosca enters, convinced she has heard the hasty departure of another woman. Cavaradossi denies it. She prays, briefly, arranges a few flowers she has brought, and proposes another assignation after her concert that evening: *Non la sospiri la nostra casetta* ("Do you not long for our little house?"). Here begins one of Puccini's finest love duets. The wonder of it is that it is not one sustained declaration of mutual love but rather a series of differing events: their confession of passion, Cavaradossi's attempt to dismiss Tosca so he can aid Angelotti, and Tosca's concern over who modeled for the painting, her jealousy reignited. Cavaradossi explains and reassures her but Tosca is haunted by "those eyes!" "What eyes in the world can compare with your black and ardent eyes?" *(Quale occhio al mondo . . .)* he replies, with Puccini at his very best. Tosca capitulates but says, ". . . let her eyes be black ones!" The duet climaxes passionately, Cavaradossi disengaging her hair, until their presence in a church sobers them. Cavaradossi must get on with his work but once more before she goes Tosca implores, "But make the eyes black."

Angelotti comes out of hiding and Cavaradossi explains he has said nothing to Tosca. Angelotti's sister, the beautiful young woman now represented in the painting, has risked everything to help save her brother from the hideous Scarpia. She stashed a disguise of women's clothes under the altar. Cavaradossi offers to hide him in a secret room off the well at his villa. Gathering up the disguise, they hurriedly depart as the sound of a distant cannon signals the escape of a political prisoner.

A joyful sacristan returns, believing Bonaparte has been defeated. Priests and choristers flood the church. A *Te Deum* in honor of the victory will be sung and that night Floria Tosca will sing a cantata at a gala in the Farnese Palace. Scarpia strides in, followed by Spoletta and some policemen. Their search reveals only an empty food basket, a dropped fan—with the Attavanti crest—and the features of the marchesa represented in the painting of a saint. Scarpia learns from the sacristan that the painting is by Mario Cavaradossi, Tosca's lover and a suspected revolutionary. Scarpia factors all quickly: "Iago had a handkerchief, and I a fan." Iago and Scarpia: the apotheosis of operatic villainy.

Tosca appears in search of Mario. Instantly, Scarpia commences to inject his poison by insinuating that there's a love nest in the church for the painter and the woman in the painting. As evidence he produces the fan. His lust for her is as intense as Tosca's jealous fury. As she races out to catch the lovers in the act at Cavaradossi's villa, Scarpia orders Spoletta and his bloodhounds to follow wherever she goes. *Va, Tosca!* ("Go, Tosca!") begins the famous finale to the first act. Generally, it is known simply as the *Te Deum*, but it is much more than that. As the church fills during the sacred *Te Deum*, Scarpia sings a heretical soliloquy revealing his two utmost desires: the deaths of Angelotti and Cavaradossi and the passionate, sexual conquest of Tosca. What could be more astounding than a church filled by a glorious *Te Deum laudamus*, from the pen of one whose ancestors were famous for their sacred music, as Scarpia's demonic baritone thunders, *Tosca, mi fai dimenticare Iddio* ("Tosca, you make me forget God"). He makes the sign of the cross and sinks to his knees as the procession passes and the curtain falls.

The poet Giacosa, while turning Illica's book into verse, remarked that *Tosca* as a story was all plot and no poetry. I know how he felt as I retell it. *Tosca* is an opera of countless little details, considerable stage directions, significant gestures, and pregnant phrases, and one frets over leaving out something important.

Act II

The Act II curtain rises on the second famous bit of Roman archi-
tecture, an elegant apartment on the upper floor of the Farnese
Palace. Scarpia lives here. It is night and he sits before his dinner,
preoccupied. Has Tosca led his henchmen to Angelotti and
Cavaradossi? He rings for Sciarrone, writes a note, orders him to
give it to Tosca immediately when she arrives, and in another
monologue expands upon his plan to force her, through her love
for Mario, to submit to his lust.

I have read an essay about the opera by a critic who claims one
act ought not end and the next begin with monologues by the
same character. Who invents these ludicrous rules of dramaturgy,
anyway? Actually, the novelty here is quite effective as our
loathing of Scarpia's demonic nature is heightened just in case the
first intermission happened to divert your attention a bit.

Spoletta arrives to announce that he has arrested Cavaradossi
even though Angelotti could not be found. Charged with aiding a
prisoner of state, he is brought in and questioned. When he claims
to know nothing of the whereabouts of Angelotti, Scarpia threatens him with torture. Tosca appears; on seeing Mario, she runs to
him. In a quick aside he warns her to say nothing, then he is taken
to an adjoining room. Tosca informs Scarpia that her jealousy was
unfounded foolishness, for when she found Cavaradossi at his
villa, he was alone. Scarpia plays on this "alone." Alluding to the
terrible torture now already in progress, and vindicated by groans
from Cavaradossi, he informs Tosca that she could save her lover
from considerable pain. She is stunned. She asks to see Cavaradossi, who is brought in, refuses to talk, and is taken back, this time
the door to the torture room being left open. Tosca can endure no
more as the relentless inflicting of pain resumes. "In the well . . .
in the garden," she cries out. Scarpia stops the torture and has an
unconscious, bloody Cavaradossi carried in. Tosca goes to him. He
revives enough to learn that she revealed the hiding place. He
reproaches her. Sciarrone brings news of Bonaparte's victory at
Marengo and the agonized painter finds strength to shout "Victory! Victory!" Scarpia has him taken away and tells Tosca that only
she can save him, by yielding to his lust for her. Disgusted, she
recoils. Cavaradossi will die in an hour, Scarpia says.

Tosca responds with a controversial aria. Most find no fault
with the music of *Vissi d'arte, vissi d'amore* ("For art and for love
I have lived"). It is *Tosca's* most famous song. Common criticisms, however, claim it holds up the action, which has been rac-

ing toward a climax. Even Puccini briefly considered omitting it for this reason before his instincts prevailed. My opinion differs. Perhaps because I know one of opera's great dramatic scenes is about to happen (actually, anyone who knows the story also knows this), this pause of remarkable restrained lyricism is a welcome respite from the overwhelming drama of this second act. Tosca's reverie queries God why she, a good person, is thus repaid. She then beseeches Scarpia for help. He wants only her body for an instant in return for Cavaradossi's life. Spoletta interrupts to inform Scarpia that Angelotti has killed himself. "Hang him anyway" is the order, and then when Scarpia says, "The other prisoner?" Tosca's blood freezes. She nods assent, drops her head into her hands, weeping, collects herself, and demands an immediate pardon for Mario. Scarpia explains why he cannot pardon him and orders instead a mock execution before a firing squad, his insidious true intent hiding in the code words *Come facemmo del Conte Palmieri*, the meaning which Act III will reveal. This phrase is iterated and reiterated by the two men, its implication impossible to miss. Spoletta departs.

Scarpia is ready for his conquest but Tosca stops him. She demands a written safe-conduct for both her and Cavaradossi. As the villain writes, Tosca, to fortify herself, moves to the dinner table, takes a glass of wine, drinks, spies a long, sharp knife, and without ever taking her eyes from him manages to get it into her hand, which she puts behind her back. Scarpia finishes writing, turns with open arms, and rushes toward her. His ejaculation of joy, "Tosca, finally you are mine," ends with a shriek of anguish. She has plunged the knife into his heart while delivering one of the greatest lines in opera: *Questo è il bacio di Tosca* ("This is the kiss of Tosca!"). Stumbling and calling for help, Scarpia crashes to the floor, his death cries choked by blood as another great line comes from Tosca: "And killed by a woman!"

As he utters two more futile cries for help, she bends over him, knife still in hand, and insists "Die! Die! Die!" He does. But Tosca's inspired words continue as she concludes,

> He is dead! Now the pardon.
> And before him all Rome trembled!

The dumb show (pantomime) preceding the curtain is riveting. Here are the stage directions in the libretto, Puccini's fitting music having, of course, the last word.

Her eyes still fixed on the body, Tosca goes to the table, puts down the knife, takes a bottle of water, wets a napkin and washes her fingers. She then goes to the mirror to arrange her hair. Then she hunts for the safe-conduct pass on the desk, and not finding it there she turns and sees the paper in the clenched hand of the dead man. She takes it with a shudder and hides it in her bosom. She puts out the candle on the table and is about to leave when a scruple detains her. She returns to the desk and takes the candle there, using it to relight the other; and then places one to the right and the other to the left of Scarpia's head. She rises and looks about her and notices a crucifix hanging on the wall. She removes it with reverent care and returning to the dead man kneels at his side and places the crucifix on his breast. She rises, cautiously walks to the door, goes out and closes it behind her.[†]

Act III

The last act is the shortest and least complex of the three, and all its music is justly famous. The scene is the platform of Castle Sant' Angelo, the third historic architectural site of the opera. It is night but soon dawn will reveal the outlines of the Vatican and the Basilica of St. Peter's in the distance. Church bells toll matins. A perfectionist, Puccini studied the sounds of the actual bells in order to reproduce authentic representations. An orchestral introduction, establishing the somber quietude before daybreak, incorporates the mournful (offstage) song of a shepherd boy heard as he passes below with his flock.

Guards bring Cavaradossi before the jailer, who offers to call a priest for his last hour. Cavaradossi refuses, requesting instead he be allowed to write a letter to a loved one. For permission to do this, he gives the jailer a gold ring from his finger. He tries to write but, overcome by too many memories, pauses, looks at the stars shining, sings his farewell to Tosca, the beautiful aria *E lucevan le stelle* ("And the stars shone"), and sobs. Spoletta brings Tosca into

---

[†] Giacomo Puccini, *Tosca* (Angel Recording Libretto, 1963, translation by Winston Burdett) p. 20

the prison. She goes to Cavaradossi and lifts his head. Astonished to see her, he rises and reads the safe-conduct she has handed him. This is Scarpia's first act of clemency, he says. "And his last," Tosca replies and recounts how she plunged a knife into his heart. "With your own hands you killed him for me," Cavaradossi says, introducing for me a favorite portion of the drama. *O dolci mani mansuete e pure* ("O sweet hands tame and pure"), he sings, taking her hands in his own with loving care. Tosca explains that a mock execution will precede their passage to freedom. With the shots from the blank cartridges he must fall and lie still. In a cappella (without orchestral accompaniment) unison their rapture culminates as they sing ecstatically of the triumph of their love. This gets me every time.

Dawn has arrived and with it the executioners, their rhythmic, haunting, daunting steps so perfectly portrayed by the orchestra. Tosca, an actress, gives Mario final instructions on how to play his part, then fidgets nervously through what to her seems like an eternity of preparations. The shots ring out. Perfectly, he falls, lying still as a stone. His body is covered with a cloak and the executioners march out. From afar, Tosca urges him not to move, sees they are alone, and goes to him. Quickly, he must now get up. They have to go. She calls his name. He does not stir. She removes the cloak and shrieks, "Dead!" Scarpia's *Come Palmieri* to Spoletta was a code for the mock execution to be a real one, "like Palmieri." Even in death the villain has tricked her. Confused voices disclose that the corpse of Scarpia has been discovered as Spoletta and Sciarrone charge in to grab Tosca. She gives Spoletta, the first to arrive, a sudden, violent shove, races to the parapet, climbs up, and jumps to her death, proclaiming,

O Scarpia, avanti a Dio!

Oh Scarpia, before God!

Tosca, one of Puccini's greatest hits, for all its complexity of plot plays in less than two hours, more than fifteen minutes shorter than Act III of Wagner's *The Mastersingers of Nuremberg*. How should the title role be portrayed? Certainly not like a Hollywood star, self-confident and flaunting celebrity. Nor is Tosca a strong, independent, liberated woman. Unfortunately, I have seen her represented in both of these ways. Her words and music make irrefutable her kinship with other admirable, vulnerable, and thoroughly feminine Puccini heroines. Tosca is, so to speak, the sister of Manon Lescaut, Mimi, and Cio-Cio-San, all different and yet instantly recognizable women of Puccini. Just because she was capable of one heroic act does not mean Tosca should be played with a swaggering *bravata*. That is all wrong for her. For an entire generation of devotees, Maria Callas was Tosca and Tito Gobbi, Scarpia. Available but rare video footage tells why. Together they made two complete audio recordings, both still available, now on CD, and both with different but fine tenors. The first was with Guiseppe di Stefano; the second, with Carlo Bergonzi. A 1976 film version on location in Rome with Raina Kabaivanska and Placido Domingo as the ill-fated lovers remains popular.

Once, when in Rome leading an opera tour, I stared persistently at the parapet from which Floria Tosca leapt to her death. When asked by one in the group what I was doing, I explained. "But Tosca is only a story," said another. I said nothing. I knew that that poor soul wouldn't believe Sherlock Holmes was real, either!

Some last words on *Tosca*. Several times within this book, I have registered my extreme disapproval of directors who tamper with the intentions of the composer. It almost never, ever works for me when a director feels compelled, which is all too often the way it is today, to change the historical period and setting. *Tosca* is a common candidate for such mistreatment, probably because political dissent and execution never become dated and so are easily made contemporaneous, which is what some directors want to do. I know of several versions of *Tosca* (and unfortunately had to see one of them) by different well-known companies that have given *Tosca* a World War II stigma by moving the time of the drama into the 1940s and giving to Baron Scarpia a Benito Mussolini *Il Duce* aura administered to by his goose-stepping henchmen.

Here I bypass historical and aesthetic arguments as to why this is wrong and offensive and rest my case with one brief example. The beginning of Act III is magical as church bells toll matins and the beautiful offstage boy soprano of a shepherd passing with his flock beneath Castle Sant' Angelo floats through the fading darkness. It is 1800. In the modernized Mussolini versions it is the 1940s, when church bells and shepherd song (no room for a passing shepherd to graze sheep in urban Rome in 1940) would be obliterated by the roar of engines and the honking of cars, trucks, buses, and, probably, even the clatterings of tanks as the city awakens to a new day. And, as for the shining stars, could one even see them for the countless headlights and streetlights? The year 1800 fits *Tosca* and that is where the opera belongs. The Mussolini-inspired versions are just plain dumb!

MADAMA BUTTERFLY (1904)
Madame Butterfly

I have read that John Luther Long based his novelette about a Japanese girl and an American sailor on a true episode. From this story David Belasco made the play *Madame Butterfly*, which became quite popular both in London and in New York. In 1900, while visiting London, Puccini was urged by the stage manager at Covent Garden to attend a performance. A Japanese mode, promoted partially by the great popularity of *The Mikado*, still prevailed and Puccini, despite knowing almost no English, went to a performance and was able to follow the basics of the plot. He was profoundly moved. Belasco's play tells the story of a teenage geisha who marries an American naval officer stationed in Nagasaki. She is motivated by love, he by sex. Heartlessly, he deserts her, returns several years later with his American wife, and the Japanese girl kills herself.

Puccini obtained permission to use the play for his next opera and set to work with Illica and Giacosa, the threesome referred to by their publisher as the "Holy Trinity." Working fastidiously and revising constantly, it took Puccini three years to complete the score. Recovering from a car accident also may have delayed him. Puccini was fascinated with motor cars, drove with abandon, and in a mishap badly broke a leg, which took a long time to heal. He was knocked unconscious by the accident. A common story, and I was not there so I only pass it along, claims his first words on regaining consciousness were "Butterfly, my child." I mention the auto accident to jar you into realizing his *Madama Butterfly* is part of the modern world. All other twentieth-century operatic considerations in this book, except for Richard Strauss, make up the final chapter. Strauss and Puccini, the heirs of Wagner and Verdi, even though both were remarkably productive in that century, are so important that they must have chapters of their own.

Madama Butterfly had its first performance in Milan on February 17, 1904. In great anticipation, Puccini attended the performance thoroughly convinced this score represented his best work to date. The occasion has been well recorded in opera history as a failure—indeed, it was a fiasco. Jeers and howls, catcalls, whistles, and denunciations became so prevalent by the second act that the music was obliterated. The stunned soprano portraying Butterfly wanted to quit when her big aria was destroyed by hoots of derision. Was the ruination of this premiere due to faults in the score or was it the malicious objective of a scheme perpetrated by an envious anti-Puccini operatic faction? A little of the former and much of the latter, probably.

Puccini withdrew the opera before the second performance, made revisions, and presented it again, this time in Brescia, several months later. There, *Madama Butterfly* was a triumph. Puccini continued to revise in preparing the opera for a 1905 London production and his final revisions were made for the 1906 opening in Paris. This has become the definitive version. All the revisions, large and small, except one, improved the opera: I agree with those Italian productions that perform the opera in Puccini's original two-act version even though it makes for a long second act. To give his audience a break, Puccini interrupted Butterfly's vigil with an intermission in the Brescia revision. As the vigil commences at night, the curtain falls on the second act, as dawn breaks, the vigil concludes at the beginning of the third act. I gladly sit without a break in the two-act version so that this enchantingly beautiful scene is not interrupted. It is a rare performance in the United States that allows this, but there are always videos.

There are other reasons why there were problems with the premiere. The Milanese audience evidently was unable to adjust to the unfamiliar exoticism of sets and score. Ever the perfectionist, Puccini requested he be given some original Japanese tunes to adapt for local color. They were provided by the wife of the Japanese ambassador in Rome. Furthermore, the two Americans in the cast appeared in contemporaneous dress and Puccini made a musical point of utilizing snatches of "The Star-Spangled Banner." All of this, the first time around, just may have been too new for those nurtured on nineteenth-century Italian opera.

One of the highlights of the revised score is a memorable aria for tenor in the newly structured third act, and I know of no love scene in all of Italian opera more beautiful than the long duet (fifteen minutes is a long love duet in Italian opera) at the end of the first act of *Madama Butterfly*. In one way it may be too beautiful: The loveliness of the music perhaps causes us to overlook the fact that Butterfly's new husband is a creep, the biggest cad in all opera. (I said as much and elaborated at length in an opera course I was giving to adults a number of years ago, only to read my very words, without quotation marks and unacknowledged, in a synopsis published by one of the "students" who had been in the class. My memory of him is that he took copious notes.)

Much of the first act openly points toward the inevitable tragedy and a careful reading of the words of the love duet leaves little doubt as to where the drama is heading. Often it is otherwise in literature; it is not knowing how things will resolve that fixes one's attention on the story. With *Madama Butterfly*, when the libretto is carefully read, the eventual outcome materializes before the eyes line by line.

Because *Butterfly* in three acts now is common, that is how it will be represented here. The characters and their voice ranges are:

CIO-CIO-SAN ("Cho-Cho-San" in English), Madama Butterfly, *soprano*
SUZUKI, her servant, *mezzo-soprano*
LIEUTENANT B. F. PINKERTON, U.S. Navy, *tenor*
KATE PINKERTON, his American wife, *mezzo-soprano*
SHARPLESS, American Consul in Nagasaki, *baritone*
GORO, a marriage broker, *tenor*
The Imperial Commissioner, *bass*
The Bonze, a priest and Butterfly's uncle, *bass*
The Official Registrar, *baritone*
PRINCE YAMADORI, a wealthy Japanese, *tenor*
SORROW, Butterfly's little boy, *a voiceless part*
Butterfly's friends and relatives, servants, sailors

The action takes place in Nagasaki in the beginning of the twentieth century.

Act I

A brief orchestral prelude introduces Puccini's adaptation of a Japanese theme, which appears here and there during the first act, to establish an Oriental atmosphere.

The curtain opens on a Japanese house, with gardens, situated high on a hill overlooking Nagasaki's harbor. Goro is showing his client, an American naval officer, the house he has just rented. Pinkerton's first question, in a contemporary translation, would be ". . . and where is the marriage bed?" a good job by the librettists in wasting no time in delineating his self-indulgent character and his primary interest. The marriage broker claps for the three servants, who enter and kneel before their new master for introductions. Suzuki commences to chatter until they are dismissed by Goro, who assures Pinkerton that all preparations for the wedding have been completed. He is pleased with his client's praise.

Sharpless enters. Pinkerton informs him that he has rented this fine home for nine hundred and ninety-nine years with the right to cancel the contract during any month. Goro and two servants set a little table for refreshments. As he prepares two whiskeys, Pinkerton articulates his philosophy of life, reminiscent unto this day to many foreigners as that of "the ugly American." Simply put, it is this: All over the world the American, indifferent to any risks, seeks pleasure and profit and is content only if in each new place personal desires are satiated, especially sexual ones. Now, if you think I am making this up, consult the libretto beginning with Pinkerton's line *Dovunque al mondo lo Yankee vagabondo si gode e traffica*, which, by the way, is introduced by a snatch of "The Star-Spangled Banner."

Pinkerton's discourse concludes with his telling Sharpless that he, accordingly, is entering into a Japanese marriage for nine hundred and ninety-nine years with the right to become free during any month. "An easy creed," Sharpless acknowledges as they touch glasses in a toast to "America forever." Sharpless asks about the bride-to-be: Is she pretty? Is Pinkerton infatuated with her? "Be it love or a whim," the sailor responds, he is absolutely bewitched by this girl who is like a butterfly and whose fragile wings could be damaged by the mad passion burning within him. Sharpless shows concern. He knows that the girl who has agreed to Goro's arranged marriage has fallen in love with the naval officer. It would be a sin to hurt her. An oblivious Pinkerton scoffs at such a worry, refills their glasses, and toasts the day when he has a real marriage to an American wife. Within fifteen minutes of the first act, Pinkerton's blind, insensitive self-interest and Butterfly's fate are established before the innocent girl has even stepped on the stage.

Goro announces that the wedding party is wending its way up the hill and will arrive momentarily. Offstage, voices of excited girls blend with Butterfly's soaring expression of happiness; she's the happiest girl in the world. Few are the women who could manage the demanding vocal line of this entrance song, its melody to be heard again in the opera as her theme. This is her opera and there is no doubt about it as soon as she opens her mouth. The girls begin to appear on stage, followed by Butterfly, carrying resplendent parasols that they close before curtseying before

Lieutenant Pinkerton. Butterfly gives him an impressive compliment before conversing with Sharpless, who asks about her and her family. She explains she had to become a geisha (a Japanese girl trained as a singer, dancer, and companion to men) to support herself when her well-to-do Nagasaki family lost its wealth. Her childlike manner and forthright conversation already are arousing Pinkerton. She continues. She has no siblings, but has a fine mother, and her father is dead. When asked her age, she invites guesses before answering. Butterfly is fifteen years old. Others of the wedding party now arrive, the officials and Pinkerton's new relations, to him all a bizarre assortment—a laughing matter, he tells Sharpless. He is eager to get the formality accomplished.

In an extraordinary ensemble, another of Puccini's realistic crowd scenes, the relatives prattle to one another as they comment on Pinkerton's looks and affluence while a sozzled uncle stumbles about looking for more wine. Sharpless, much taken by Butterfly's beauty and innocent love, exhorts his friend to take his marriage contract seriously. Butterfly comes to Pinkerton and from within the huge sleeves of her kimono removes the few possessions she has brought to her new home to show him—handkerchiefs, pipe, sash, clasp, mirror, fan, rouge, and her most sacred possession, a long narrow case the contents of which, because there are too many people, she cannot disclose at this time. Goro, however, provides the answer as Butterfly takes away her possessions. The case contains a gift from the Mikado to her father inviting him to . . . and here Goro makes signs indicating that Butterfly's father committed hara-kiri.

Pinkerton rejoins Butterfly, who informs him of her renunciation of the faith of her ancestors to accept his god as her own. In the briefest possible ceremony they are married, the contracts are signed, and Sharpless prepares to leave. "I'll see you tomorrow," he says, to which Pinkerton replies, *A meraviglia*, which means, "splendid" or "wonderful," but I happen to have an old English libretto of *Madama Butterfly* from London and its translation makes Pinkerton respond with "Capital." Anxious to get rid of his new relatives as soon as possible, Pinkerton toasts the new bond. An angry Bonze, Butterfly's uncle, storms on to the scene at this moment and denounces Butterfly for having abandoned her faith. Pinkerton throws them all out.

Butterfly, feeling alone and rejected, is comforted by her husband. Suzuki chants her prayers, and Pinkerton begins the most sustained and beautiful love duet in all Italian opera: *Viene la sera*

("Night is falling"). Suzuki provides Butterfly with her night-clothes, bows low, and then departs. To herself Butterfly express-es embarrassment as she undresses while Pinkerton eyes her eagerly: "To think that this little plaything is my wife" (*giocàtto-lo* is Italian for "toy" or "plaything"). Ouch! This is why I warn you not to let the incredible beauty of the music in this long duet mesmerize you into believing it is an expression of true love. But-terfly's emotions are pure and there is no doubt about Pinkerton's intense desire, but it is not a mutual love setting him on fire.

"Butterfly renounced—renounced and happy," she repeats. As they come together on the terrace, she fears to say how much she loves him ". . . for fear of dying" at hearing these words. It is a fool-ish fear, he assures her, ". . . for love does not kill." Then love me, she responds, with ". . . a little love, a childlike love . . ." but when he calls her Butterfly she says she has heard how, far across the seas, there are those who put a pin into butterflies to stick them to a table. To keep them from flying away, he assures her, again, clasping her to him. "You are mine." Pinkerton wants to get on with it but Butterfly is overwhelmed by the beauty of the night. She looks on the innumerable stars, head and heart both lost in the ecstasy of love. Pinkerton's last words before the curtain are "Ah! Come! You are mine."

Puccini composed a wealth of the most beautiful music ever written, but he never wrote anything more exquisite than this duet. I had listened to it hundreds of times in my youth, swept away by the unbelievable flow of sound, before going over the text word for word. Only then does the subtle, powerful drama emerge in the music. Too much so, evidently, for some. One young woman in my freshman seminar several years ago, while still much in the thrall of the music, told me she wished I had not made Pinkerton's base perfidy so clear. Obviously, she held her own dreams of what a wedding night would be like.

Act II

Throughout this act Pinkerton is present without setting one foot on the stage. He has flown the coop. Three years have passed. But-terfly, now eighteen, has a small son. An adaptation of another Japanese tune introduces the parting curtains to reveal Suzuki praying before a statue of the Buddha even though her mistress deeply distrusts Japanese gods. Suzuki then shows Butterfly a few coins, all the money they have left, commenting that they will be in a bad way if Pinkerton does not soon return. Butterfly tells her:

"He will come back!" and she articulates her reasons. Unconvinced, Suzuki retorts with a question: Who ever heard of a foreign husband returning? Butterfly is livid. In the last conversation on the morning of his departure, she tells Suzuki, he said to me, and here her melodic line becomes one of a haunting, frail, and tender beauty . . .

> Oh, Butterfly, my little wife,
> I'll return with the roses
> in that fair season
> when the robin makes its nest . . .

and she orders Suzuki to say the words "He will return," but in repeating them her servant begins to cry. Butterfly chides her lack of faith and with absolute conviction enacts the long anticipated reunion of "one beautiful day." *Un bel dì* is Butterfly's most famous aria.

Goro and Sharpless arrive, the latter entering the house, the former remaining in the garden. Butterfly has yet to see Sharpless when he greets her as Madam Butterfly. She answers, "Madam Pinkerton, please," then turns, recognizes the consul, and along with pleasantries offers him a pipe or cigarettes. She, of course, has not divined the unpleasant business of a mission he wishes to complete as soon as possible. He informs her of a letter he has received from Lieutenant Benjamin Franklin Pinkerton. "When do robins make their nests in America?" she asks, arising happily. The befuddled consul does not know.

Goro enters with Yamadori, whose suit of Butterfly he has been nurturing. He knows Pinkerton will never return to her and knows, as well, that Butterfly's money is almost gone. She is polite but resolute in her refusal to entertain the wealthy, aged man's intentions. She is still married and the return of her husband is imminent. She remains blind to the true situation, known to both Goro and Sharpless, who, in particular, is deeply pained by her incredible naïveté. Indeed, Pinkerton is soon to arrive but with no intention of seeing Butterfly. When Yamadori leaves, Sharpless attempts to read the letter, the message of which is to disillusion her, but in the innocuous opening words Butterfly hears only hope and happiness. Exasperated, and cursing Pinkerton under his breath, he gives up before revealing the terrible news, shoves the letter into a pocket, and tries another tack by urging her to marry Prince Yamadori. Her first response is to dismiss him, but each retracts and an amicable mood returns. Perhaps some message is beginning to sink in. Sadly, Butterfly allows that Pinkerton may have forgotten her and she races out of the room, only to return in an instant holding her son. "Can he forget this as well?" she wonders aloud, knowing very well that Pinkerton, who left before the child was born, has no idea he is a father. Surely he will return when he finds out, and she asks Sharpless to write accordingly.

Dramatically, she sings to her child, now called Sorrow, whose name upon his father's return shall be Joy. I do not understand why so many libretti and opera books in English give the child's name as "Trouble." When Sharpless asks the child what his name is, Butterfly says to the boy,

> *Rispondi: Oggi il mio nome è Dolore.*
> *Però, dite al babbo,*
> *scrivendogli,*
> *che il giorno del suo ritorno*
> *Gioia, Gioia mia chiamerò.*

> Answer: Today my name is Sorrow. However, tell my father when you write him that the day he returns Joy, Joy will be my name.

Dolore is Italian for "sorrow." The Italian word for "trouble" is *disturbo* or *fastidio*. From Sorrow to Joy is a far more telling rendition of Butterfly's point than the more common Trouble to Joy.

Promising to inform Pinkerton, Sharpless kisses the child and leaves. This entire scene with the American consul, though not a famous excerpt, is terrific musical theater. Listen to the music as you follow the words of the libretto or watch a video with subtitles. Sharpless is a good man on a dire mission, and Butterfly confronts him with an arsenal of emotions too vast for any man to handle: inexorable faith, impenetrable naïveté, and a small child with his father's blue eyes and golden hair. It is all in the music.

Offstage, cursing is heard before Suzuki drags Goro onto the stage and Butterfly is told of the malicious rumor that this unconscionable entrepreneur spreads everywhere: No one knows who sired Butterfly's child. In a rage, Butterfly denounces him, threatening him with a dagger she has seized, and runs him out of the house.

The harbor cannon reverberates, signaling the arrival of a ship. Butterfly can see it is white and flying an American flag. Through binoculars, shaking from her excitement, she can discern the name. It is his ship, the *Abraham Lincoln*. In ecstasy, she rejoices over the confirmation of her faith. Believing her love triumphant, she runs onto the terrace and shakes a branch of the cherry tree. Thus begins the incomparable "Flower Duet" of Butterfly and Suzuki: *Scuoti quella fronda di ciliegio* ("Shake that branch of the cherry tree"). Every flower in the garden, Butterfly tells Suzuki, is to be gathered in honor of Pinkerton's return. Then she and her son are to be made ready, Butterfly attired in her wedding gown with a red poppy in her hair. Finally, she pokes three peepholes in the paper wall, one for herself, one for Suzuki, and one for her boy. Their vigil begins. Night closes in, the moon rises, and soon the baby, followed by Suzuki, drifts into sleep. Not Butterfly. Motionless, like a statue, her eyes fixed on the harbor and the path winding up to her house, she stands and waits, the lovely soft voices of the offstage humming chorus bringing the act to its end with a Pucciniesque stroke of pure musical magic.

But the act ought not end here. And in Puccini's original version it didn't. An orchestral interlude, representing the passing of night, follows this chorus and this is how the drama's vigil scene should be played—not with a curtain closing after the chorus for an intermission to destroy the mood, to be followed by another curtain opening on a third act with the dawn of the next day, Butterfly still standing where she was, waiting. For his orchestral vigil Puccini develops another Japanese tune with little fragments of themes reminiscent of the Act I love duet. I have been to a performance in two acts and found the unbroken drama far more gripping. So right was Puccini's original theater instinct.

The vocal technique producing this haunting, mesmerizing chorus is called, in Italian, *bocca chiusa*, which means "closed mouth." It is a form of singing without words; that is, humming. This chorus and an episode in the last act of Verdi's Rigoletto are the two most notable operatic examples of this technique, though, just to add a little opera trivia, Enrico Caruso used to learn the music of his roles by first "singing" them *bocca chiusa*.

As night gives way to the bright shining sun, Suzuki awakens and persuades Butterfly to get some sleep, promising to call her when Pinkerton arrives. "Poor Butterfly," she says sadly to herself.

Sharpless and Pinkerton arrive. Seeing the flowers and learning that Butterfly has waited three years, including an all-night vigil, Pinkerton is deeply disturbed. Suzuki sees another woman in the garden and is told about Pinkerton's American wife. She slumps to her knees and bows her head, despairing aloud for Butterfly. Sharpless begins an animated and captivating trio, *Io so che alle sue pene non ci sono conforti!* ("I know there is no consolation for her deep distress"), requesting Suzuki's assistance; Pinkerton, now aware of his crude behavior, paces and laments; Suzuki protests before agreeing to go to the other woman. Sharpless gives the remorseful Pinkerton a pointed "I told you so," prompting the naval officer to sing farewell *(Addio, fiorito asil di letizia e d'amor)* to what was once his flowery nest of happiness and love. (This is the aria added by Puccini to his revised score.) Tortured by the revelation of what he has done, Pinkerton, opera's number one cad, also is a coward. After he finishes his song, he admits as much and runs off, unable to face Butterfly.

Arriving from the garden with Kate Pinkerton, Suzuki assures her that Butterfly will be told that the American couple want to raise the little boy. Butterfly's offstage voice can be heard calling for Suzuki. Kate retreats to the garden and Butterfly enters in search of Pinkerton. She spots the woman in the garden. Suzuki begins to cry and Butterfly understands that Pinkerton is not coming. Sharpless confirms that the woman is, indeed, Pinkerton's wife. Instantly, Butterfly realizes that Pinkerton wants her son. Sharpless urges the sacrifice for "his sake" and Butterfly yields only if Pinkerton will come for the child. Kate and Sharpless are escorted out. Suzuki and Butterfly close the house, making it dark inside. Butterfly then orders Suzuki to go play with the child. Before the statue of the Buddha she prays. She goes for her father's knife, reads the inscription—"Death with honor for one who cannot live with honor" and puts the knife to her throat. Suzuki slides open the door with one hand and with the other gently pushes the little boy into the room. Butterfly goes to her son, embraces him fervently, and sings her powerful, dramatic farewell *Tu! Tu! Piccolo Iddio!* ("You? You? Little God!"). She places her son on a rug, blindfolds him, and, placing a doll in one hand and an American flag in the other, coaxes the child to play. Butterfly takes the knife, looks at the child, and goes behind the screen. There is the sound of a knife falling as her hand grabs a white veil from the screen, knocking it over, and she holds the veil to her neck while stumbling toward her boy. She kisses him and collapses at his side. The offstage voice of Pinkerton is heard crying "Butterfly! Butterfly! Butterfly!" Violently he shoves open the door and rushes into the room, followed closely by Sharpless. Butterfly points to the child and dies. Pinkerton drops to his knees, head in hands. Sharpless picks up the child and kisses him. The curtain falls.

⁂

A few final words on Puccini's Butterfly. His little Japanese heroine is one of several famous opera women who are difficult to cast. She is fifteen, tiny, like a porcelain doll, and must have a voice given by the gods and trained by the best teachers. Some of the greatest "Butterfly"s are in their thirties or forties before mastering the role, and not all are tiny. On the Hollywood screen, looks, as we all know so well, are everything. In the opera house, the voice is everything, and don't let anyone tell you otherwise. One must be forgiving in the opera house.

Also, do be careful in selecting a libretto. Sometimes (though this is happening less and less, fortunately) a recording will come with a libretto whose English translation is long out of date and you may get, for example, a Butterfly who says, during her Act I love duet, "Ah! Night of rapture! Stars unending! Never have I seen such glory!" when you should be reading "Oh, lovely night! So many stars! Never have I seen them so beautiful!" A good translation gives you the story and makes you feel the characters are real. A poor one, or one out of date, gives a silly or antiquated impression.

One of the most fascinating students I ever taught was a lovely young Japanese woman from Nagasaki. She was a candidate for a master's degree and, having taken an opera course with me, she honored me by asking me to be her thesis adviser. Her subject you easily will guess: Puccini's *Madama Butterfly*. Specifically, it was her intent to make a comprehensive comparison between two video versions of the opera, one with a Western cast directed by a European, the other starring a Japanese Butterfly directed by a Japanese. Ours was a fascinating collaboration and during her research and writing she showed me photographs taken in Nagasaki while she was home for a holiday. The pictures included statues and memorials to Nagasaki's most famous citizen—Butterfly, of course.

One of many intriguing insights in her thesis related to a specific event in the first act, the entrance of Butterfly. Referring to the European version and the manner in which Butterfly walked, gestured, and interrelated with her friends, my student wrote, "A Japanese woman would never do that." In this version the famous European soprano portraying Butterfly was placed at the head of the wedding entourage. Majestically and flamboyantly she makes her entrance, head held high and arms fully extended and swirling the gigantic sleeves of her kimono like billowing sails of a great schooner. The native Japanese version bore her out perfectly. In it a shy, demure Butterfly, hidden by a veil, walks slowly with tiny steps at the end of the wedding procession, preceded by her family and friends. All the women, Butterfly included, are much obscured by beautiful parasols that are being turned rhythmically and deliberately in unison above their heads as they enter.

During the two years we worked together on her thesis, this graduate student, at first as shy as Butterfly, became less formal and more relaxed with me. She eventually told me how astounded she was when she came to my office for our first meeting. "It was the dead of winter. I walked in and you got up, greeted me, helped me off with my coat, hung it up, and offered tea," she reminded me. "A Japanese professor would never do that!"

Today she is happily married to an American, a fate Madama Butterfly did not enjoy for long.

LA FANCIULLA DEL WEST (1910)
The Girl of the Golden West

I have tried a little experiment with friends who love opera and know their Puccini, meaning they could name and identify the famous arias and duets from the four operas heretofore represented. Then we come to *La fanciulla del West*, which is always translated as "The Girl of the Golden West" even though there is no equivalent of the word for "golden" in Puccini's title. Name the hits in this opera, I challenge them. Almost all know that the most famous tune is Dick Johnson's third-act aria *Ch'ella mi creda libero e lontano*, known to many Italians everywhere. Some, but not all, can identify the nostalgic *Che faranno i vecchi miei*, sung by Jake Wallace and his fellow gold miners. It gets more difficult when I ask for the big Act I aria of the title role, *Laggiù nel Soledad*, and almost never do I find one ready to add the aria *Minnie, dalla mia casa son partito*, sung by Jack Rance, immediately before it. There are substantial reasons why.

Even though the world premiere was a triumph, Puccini's *La fanciulla del West* never sustained the successful momentum of *La bohème*, *Tosca*, and *Madama Butterfly*. Critics picked at it and audiences, not hearing an endless succession of Puccini's long, soaring melodies to which they were accustomed and therefore expected, were not certain what to make of it. Recordings, video-tapes, and frequent performances during the last twenty-five years, however, immensely increased its stature and today the work is recognized as among Puccini's finest creations.

More important than the belated and deserved popularity is the giant step taken by Puccini in his development as a composer. Not only did he answer critics who had charged him with rewriting the same old tune, but he also produced something truly different. Obviously, he had said all he wanted to about vulnerable women in love whose lamentable youthful demise brings tears to the eyes.

Minnie, who is the Girl of the Golden West, through cunning, persistence, and the overwhelming love and respect accorded her by her friends, gets her man against formidable odds . . . with a pistol. Furthermore, in telling her story Puccini does not rely on a score wherein a host of intoxicating melodies, here and there, step forward and stop the show. But do not assume the famous touch for melody is not there. The music of *La fanciulla* is an ever-present, unbroken flow of sterling melodic content. The great tunes are here but they are interwoven ingeniously within the total orchestral fabric so as to give the impression of an opera made from one long, lovely melody. Also, in conjunction with this, both interesting and important is the brevity of the famous arias. Most often, and quite purposely, they are terse, over soon after they are under way. The famous song of Dick Johnson, the most overtly traditional Puccini showstopper, is two and three-quarter minutes; the nostalgic song of Jake Wallace, even with chorus included, is less than four minutes; Minnie's Act I aria is two and three-quarter minutes, following immediately upon the heels of the "big aria" of Jack Rance, less than two and one-half minutes; and so it is throughout the opera, one brief little gem linked almost imperceptibly to another, making it more difficult to isolate and identify each as a separate number. This, of course, since the revolution of Richard Wagner, more than ever had become the objective in operatic composing—the famous "endless melody," Wagner called it—and Puccini certainly was not oblivious to the pervasive influence. It did take awhile for it to become accepted in Italian opera, however, where the faithful wait to go bonkers over the big tunes. With repeated listenings to *La fanciulla*, you hear both the lovely melodies as well as the symphonic development of the score.

Some opera people have concluded that *La fanciulla* is an inferior work of Puccini's because they cannot, or, at least do not, go about humming and naming the tunes. This is balderdash. With this opera, Puccini's genius expresses itself anew in a captivating assertion of seemingly endless melodic fragments, sophisticated harmonies, and masterful orchestration. A melody, I am sure you know, is a simple horizontal line of tones, aptly demonstrated in the song "Do-Re-Mi" from *The Sound of Music*: "Doe, a deer, a female deer, ray, a drop of golden sun, me, a name I call myself . . ." etcetera. Harmony is the other aspect of a musical composition—the chords accompanying the melody. The harmonic accompaniment creates moods, musical colors, and an endless variety of expressions and feelings. The orchestration puts it all together and, depending on what instruments the composer selects—sumptuous strings expressing romance or a quacking, raspy oboe uttering some haunting fear—exhibits how well he or she can tell a story musically. In all of this Puccini's *La fanciulla del West* score excels. I cannot take seriously numerous articles written between the 1920s and 1960s in which scholars offer reasons why, then, *La fanciulla* was not as popular as the other great Puccini works. Their readers were edified with regard to the opera's weaknesses: The American Wild West subject matter was alien to Puccini, the masculinity of the story was unsuitable to his natural gift and inclination for sympathetic portrayals of fragile women, and a real-life domestic tragedy in his home temporarily impaired his creative powers significantly. (The latter refers to the suicide of Doria Manfredi, a servant girl employed in the Puccini household. Puccini's wife, Elvira, possessed by an aberrant jealousy, accused the young woman of having had an affair with her husband. Doria denied it, then took her life. This unpleasant situation ended in a sensational court case in which an autopsy proved Doria innocent and the judgment went against Elvira.) The terrible ordeal unquestionably stifled for a while Puccini's creative drive, but when it erupted again in *La fanciulla del West*, it did so with remarkable originality. Puccini scholars say this composer's "second phase" of operatic composition begins with *The Girl of the Golden West*.

Puccini was in New York City in January 1907 for an opera festival in his honor with *Madama Butterfly* the featured work. During his stay he attended several plays, one of which was *The*

Girl of the Golden West, by David Belasco. And so it was Belasco again, following the *Madama Butterfly* triumph, who provided Puccini with his next subject. (Because the title of Belasco's play is *The Girl of the Golden West*, Puccini's opera, derived from it, is always translated into those words even though *La fanciulla del West* translates literally as "The Girl of the West," as previously mentioned.)

Like *Tosca*, the action focuses on the desire of two men, enemies, for the same woman. Carlo Zangarini and Guelfo Civini (we do not encounter them again) provided the libretto, Puccini, as always, "suggesting" what would happen and how and inventing episodes or scenes to add to the original play. With authentic atmosphere always a Puccini priority, the composer's score includes use of a folklike American tune, as well as some ragtime, a cakewalk, and bolero. (Ragtime, a style of popular American music reaching its peak of appreciation around 1910 to 1915, would probably be an innocent anachronism in the opera; a cakewalk is a promenade of fancy steps or a march of American origin; and a bolero is a dance of Spanish origin involving brilliant, intricate steps.) Because of the American setting and subject matter, the California gold rush, the Metropolitan Opera was granted the world premiere, which took place on December 10, 1910, with an immortal cast: Emmy Destin sang the title role; Enrico Caruso portrayed her lover, Dick Johnson; and Pasquale Amato was the villainous Jack Rance. Arturo Toscanini conducted. There are historic photographs of some scenes, and all these famous musicians can be heard on antique, restored recordings.

The opera plays in three acts. The characters:

MINNIE, owner of the Polka saloon, *soprano*
DICK JOHNSON, a bandit known as Ramerrez, *tenor*
JACK RANCE, the sheriff, *baritone*
NICK, bartender at the Polka, *tenor*
Miners: TRIN, HARRY, JOE, *tenors*
Miners: SONORA, SID, HANDSOME, HAPPY, *baritones*
LARKENS, *bass*
ASHBY, Wells Fargo agent, *bass*
BILLY JACKRABBITT, an Indian, *bass*
WOWKLE, an Indian and servant to Minnie, *mezzo-soprano*
CASTRO, bandit member of Ramerrez gang, *bass*
Pony Express rider, *tenor*
JAKE WALLACE, itinerant minstrel, *baritone*

The settings are the saloon of a mining camp, Minnie's cabin, and a clearing in the woods. It is the height of the California gold rush of 1849–50.

Act I

A short orchestral prelude introduces the events of Act I in Minnie's saloon. Various hellos instantly set an American tone as miners greet one another while entering the Polka. A game of faro commences and drinks are ordered. Only Larkens, homesick for his beloved Cornwall, remains morbidly aloof. All are smitten with Minnie and when first Sonora and then Trin separately confide in Nick, the bartender tells each he is, of course, the favored one. Jake Wallace, singing a nostalgic song, the sad and lovely *Che faranno i vecchi miei* ("What will become of my old folks, far, far away"), enters and is joined by all the miners. This is too much for Larkens, who begins to sob. The miners contribute enough money to pay his fare home. He departs. The card game resumes and Sid is caught cheating. Sheriff Rance prevents an immediate lynching by suggesting that Sid be made to wear a card pinned over his heart to identify him as a cheater. They kick him out. Ashby arrives. He is hot on the trail of a notorious Spanish bandit. Sonora and Rance fight over which of them will win Minnie. Sonora draws a gun but his shot is sent wild by Trin, who knocks his arm as he fires. Minnie rushes in, grabs the gun, and restores order. One after the other, Joe, Sonora, and Harry sidle up to her to offer a little present. With a bag of gold, Sonora then settles his overdue account and Minnie gathers the miners about her for some "schooling." From the Psalms she reads about the pure of heart and love.

The Pony Express arrives with mail and newspapers. As the men read, Ashby informs Rance that Nina Micheltorena, the former girlfriend of Ramerrez, has disclosed the bandit's hideout. Nick announces he has seen a stranger outside who ordered whiskey with water. The miners, who drink theirs straight, mock the concoction. Even though he is married, Rance has managed to isolate himself with Minnie and tells her he loves her. With no success, she attempts to divert his declarations. He tells her, in one of the few clear-cut arias, that his lifelong cynicism has ended with her and he offers a fortune for just one kiss: *Minnie, dalla mia casa son partito* ("Minnie, when I left home"). With back-to-back arias she replies, *Laggiù nel Soledad*: She wants only that kind of love she saw her mother and father share when she was a little girl back in Soledad. In walks Dick Johnson, right on cue. He is the one who had ordered water with his whiskey. Minnie and the stranger suppress the surprise of mutual recognition. Rance attempts, briskly, to send the stranger on his way, then demands his name. The stranger is Johnson, from Sacramento. Briefly, he and Minnie manage a private moment to remember their first meeting, one, we learn, that left a strong impression on both of them. Rance butts in again, intent on causing trouble, but Minnie vouches for Johnson. He in return invites her into the dance hall for a waltz.

Ashby, with miners harshly escorting the half-breed bandit Castro, enters the saloon. Rance grabs the outlaw by the hair and exclaims the only operatic "You son-of-a-bitch" *(Figlio di cane)* I know. Castro is a member of the nefarious Ramerrez gang, but he tells his captors that he has left them. He would gladly lead them to the hideout, and even would sink a knife in the back of Ramerrez. Then he sees his boss dancing in the next room. When Ramerrez (Dick Johnson, of course) returns, Castro, in an aside to him, says that he has given away nothing, that the gang is nearby, and that a whistle will signal their readiness to steal the miners' gold. All Ramerrez has to do to set the robbery in motion is to whistle back when he is ready. Castro is taken away by the miners, Rance following, thus leaving Minnie and Johnson alone.

Through a long discourse, mostly small talk and a reminiscence of their first meeting, they begin to experience the awakening of love between them. Nick interrupts to say that he has spotted a suspicious-looking character outside. A whistle is heard. Johnson does not return it but says he must go. A stalwart Minnie says she must remain to guard the fortune of gold the miners stashed in her saloon, and she will do so with her life, but perhaps Johnson would come to her cabin later? He accepts the invitation declaring, as he picks up his saddle, "You've the face of an angel." He leaves, and she repeats the touching words as the curtain falls.

This act-ending love scene is almost exactly as long as the one with Pinkerton and Butterfly. Just because it is not as famous for lyrical enchantment, it should not be dismissed, or missed. It is of a different sort. It is more conversational than overtly lyrical. Two young people who once met briefly and who made a lasting impression each on the other have been brought together again by fate. Finding themselves alone and talking, getting to know each other better, they share the feeling of a strong attraction between them. The beauty of this scene is more subtle, the melodic appeal not as obvious as in the *Madama Butterfly* duet. It takes repeated, concentrated listenings, perhaps, for its undeniable appeal to assert itself fully, but it sure is there to be heard. It is the work of an older, more experienced, more sophisticated Puccini demanding more of his listeners, wearing his heart less obviously on his sleeve than in this opera's predecessors.

Act II

It is an hour later when the curtain, without orchestral prelude, rises on the interior of Minnie's cabin in the mountains. Wowkle is singing a lullaby to her baby as Billy Jackrabbitt, the child's father, comes in to tell the woman that Minnie has instructed him to marry her. Unfortunately, many "ughs" punctuate their dialogue, surely the work of Carlo Zangarini, the librettist, who knew English and enough about American culture to employ the stereotype. Even worse, some translators make Billy sound like Tonto: "What your father give for wedding?" Here it is best to rely on the Italian.

Minnie arrives home, sends Billy off, and asks Wowkle to prepare supper for two. Wowkle, again, is limited to many "ughs." Minnie dresses up and Johnson's voice is heard as he appears in the doorway. Not seeing Wowkle, his first impulse, after entering, is to make a little pass at Minnie, who diverts him with a few questions. Why did he come to the Polka? Did he miss the road to Nina Micheltorena's house? But she does not wait for answers as her thoughts wander into an expression of how much she loves her isolated life: *Oh, se sapeste* ("Oh, if you only knew"). Wowkle is dismissed and Minnie finally will yield to Johnson's persistent desire to kiss her. The wind begins to blow a heavy, swirling snow but the couple are oblivious in a declaration of love. Johnson prepares to leave but the snowstorm prompts Minnie to invite him to stay the night. Pistol shots ring out in the distance. Maybe it is Ramerrez, but "What do we care?" she says, "Stay here! It's fate!" Passionate feelings erupt as they promise eternal love.

Minnie next prepares a bed for him while Johnson denies knowing Nina Micheltorena. They are about to retire, separately, when Nick knocks and calls out. He and others, having spotted Ramerrez nearby, have come to protect Minnie. She hides Johnson and admits Nick, Rance, Ashby, and Sonora, who inform her that the man she thinks is Johnson is the bandit Ramerrez and that his intent was to rob the Polka. "But he didn't," Minnie retorts. They wonder if she has seen Johnson, for they have tracked his trail near her cabin and when Rance tells her Nina is the lover of Ramerrez, Minnie hides her emotions, sends them off, and confronts Johnson with his deceit. His sole defense, for he now admits he is a scoundrel, is instantly having changed his life upon falling in love with her. *Una parola sola* ("Just one word"). She tells him to leave. He does. A shot is heard. Johnson falls back against the cabin door. Minnie admits him, weeping, and hides him in the loft, repeating "I love you! I love you!"

Rance returns, searches the cabin, and, finding no Johnson, cannot resist the attempt of another seduction. As a repulsed Minnie orders him out, blood from the loft falls on his hand. Johnson is found and forced down, then faints. An inspired Minnie offers Rance the challenge of three hands of poker. If Rance wins two, he gets his prisoner and the satisfaction of his insatiable lust for Minnie. If she wins two, Minnie and Johnson go free. Burning with desire for her, Rance accepts and gives his word. They play. Minnie wins the first hand, Rance the second. In the critical game, Minnie diverts Rance, dupes him, cheats magnificently, and sends him on his way. She is laughing and weeping hysterically as the curtain falls.

Act III

Minnie is not the vulnerable Puccini heroine of previous creations—no luxury-loving teen rescued from a convent; no tubercular seamstress; no jealous opera singer; no shy and diminutive geisha. Minnie rules her wild western world but she is no less Pucciniesque than her traditionally more feminine sisters, and this unquestionably is her act.

A short, somber, brooding orchestral prelude establishes the early-morning mood just before dawn in the clearing of a California forest as the curtain opens on the brief final act. Ashby, his posse, and miners, who are closing in on Johnson—or Ramerrez, as he is known to most of them—sleep near their horses. Nick and Rance, awake and sitting by a fire, bemoan the ill effect on all their lives since Johnson's appearance. Rance especially laments Minnie's affection for the outlaw and looks forward to his capture, which surely must be imminent. Distant voices alert everyone. Do they have him? No! False alarm. Everyone is up and about, searching in all directions. Now do they have him? Again, not yet. The scurrying continues. Ashby insists that Ramerrez be taken alive. When caught, Rance says, Ramerrez will pay for all the agony he has caused him. This is another fine crowd scene from

Puccini's pen, as chorus and orchestra join in the chase.

Offstage, Johnson is caught. Cheers resound. Rance exults at the news. He kept his word but now it is over for Minnie and her lover. The miners insist on an immediate hanging. With a little bag of gold, Nick surreptiously bribes Billy Jackrabbitt to take his time preparing the noose. Johnson is hauled in. The men cheer, "Dooda-dooda-day" (but not Stephen Foster's!), and Ashby releases Johnson to Rance before riding off. Soon the outlaw will be swinging from a rope. The men curse Johnson and accuse him of various crimes, including murder. Never murder, Johnson insists, and he requests time for some final words about the woman he loves. Rance grants two minutes but it takes Johnson almost three to sing one of Puccini's most delectable and enduring arias, the most familiar music in the score. Johnson does not want Minnie to know of his ignominious end. "Let her believe me free and far away" *(Ch'ella mi creda libero e lontano)*. Scorned, Johnson is led to a tree and positioned for the lynching.

A woman's cry rises above the sound of galloping hooves. It is Minnie. She leaps from her horse, runs to Johnson, shields him with her body, and confronts Rance, drawing a pistol to hold all at bay. Rance demands justice and the miners close in. But Minnie will not budge, threatening to kill both Johnson and herself if they do not back off. Sonora breaks the tension by demanding that Minnie be left alone. She reminds them all of their life together, her sharing their troubles, her caring for them. She throws down her pistol and one by one appeals to the miners to let her have the only thing she ever asked them for, all that she has ever wanted, Dick Johnson. One by one they yield. Freeing Johnson, the miners are thanked by Minnie. They lament knowing that she is leaving, never to return to them again. As Minnie and Johnson bid the miners farewell, strains of the homesickness song are heard, representing now their departure together to a faraway home. As the lovers, arm-in-arm, walk away, waving their good-bye, the curtain falls.

LA RONDINE (1917)
The Swallow

The firm of G. Ricordi & Co. published all of Puccini's operas except *La rondine* (one can still come across its vocal scores at antiquarian book sales, and I count my 1897 *La bohème* as one of my treasures). Giulio Ricordi believed in Puccini, nurtured his work, and treated him as a member of his own family, like a son.

When Ricordi died in 1912 and his son, Tito, inherited the business, a rift developed. Tito and Puccini did not share a loving relationship. Among other differences, Tito judged Puccini's work as passé, a remnant of the nineteenth century, and he championed other composers now mostly forgotten. When the directors of a Vienna theater offered Puccini a considerable sum of money to write an operetta for them, he agreed only after defining the terms under which he would compose and only after finally getting an acceptable libretto.

La rondine (*The Swallow*), with text by Giuseppe Adami (who will return in our story of Puccini two more times), opened in Monte Carlo on March 27, 1917, to considerable appreciation. Since then it has traveled a rocky road, never achieving the favor of the works already discussed until the past twenty-five years, during which numerous recordings, both audio and video, and more and more performances are winning a new and larger audience. You should at least know the story and the most popular tunes. You will be missing something quite special if you don't in spite of what Mosco Carner, the eminent Puccini scholar, has to say. Several times he has claimed *La rondine* to be "the weakest of Puccini's works . . . and devoid of striking lyrical melody." Mr. Carner must have gone to a performance with cotton in his ears. My wife, Joanne, cannot listen to Kiri Te Kanawa or Renée Fleming sing "Doretta's Dream" from the first act without exclaiming, "I have never heard anything more beautiful than that," and the lilting waltz ensembles from the second act are irresistible.

Originally, *La rondine* was to have premiered in Vienna. The intent of the theater directors was to acquire an operetta composed in the Viennese style by Puccini. World War I got in the way, however—thus the Monte Carlo opening. *La rondine* certainly is not an operetta in the Viennese style, but its lovely music is lyrical and lighter in character, more of the Puccini before *La fanciulla del West*. This reversion, this step musically backward, so to speak, is deemed by some its elemental weakness. Phooey! And I pass on the issue of opera or operetta. This quibble simply does not interest me. *La rondine* certainly is a much better work than it has been made out to be for too long.

It plays in three acts. There are numerous characters, as follows:

MAGDA DE CIVERY, mistress of Rambaldo, *soprano*
RAMBALDO FERNANDEZ, a wealthy Parisian banker,
   baritone

RUGGERO LASTOUC, son of a friend of Rambaldo, *tenor*
LISETTE, Magda's maid, *soprano*
PRUNIER, a poet, *tenor*
YVETTE, BIANCA, SUZY, friends of Magda, *soprano,*
    soprano, mezzo-soprano
PÉRICHAUD, GOBIN, CRÉBILLON, friends of Rambaldo, *tenor,*
    baritone, bass
GEORGETTE, GABRIELLA, LOLETTE, grisettes, *soprano,*
    soprano, mezzo-soprano
RABONNIER, a painter, *bass*
Student *tenor*
Ladies and gentlemen, students, artists, grisettes,
    dancers, flower girls, and waiters

The action takes place during the Second Empire
(1852–70) in Paris and on the Riviera.

Act I

In Puccini's customary manner, he gives the orchestra a few
moments to introduce a mood as the curtains part on an elegantly furnished room in Magda's Paris house, where she and Rambaldo are entertaining friends. The poet Prunier has claimed that old-
fashioned, sentimental love is the new rage in Paris. All but
Magda find this quaint idea amusing. Prunier persists by insisting
on the power of such an emotion once unleashed within one's
heart and he goes to the piano to sing his latest song about his
heroine Doretta, who is thus afflicted. But the song, which tells
how Doretta one day was visited by a king, as yet has no ending.
Magda takes his place at the piano, sings, and completes the song
known as "Doretta's Dream" *(Chi il bel sogno di Doretta).*

Puccini obviously knew he had a hit (it far and away is the
most appreciated and well-known music in the opera) and must
have had a very good time spinning out this lovely, captivating
melody while Magda's friends interject their highest praise as she
sings. (Also, this is one of those rare episodes in which two
singers, first Prunier and then Magda, accompany themselves at
the piano on stage. One always awaits a performance where this
actually is done and not faked.)

The party continues. Rambaldo gives Magda an expensive
necklace and Lisette informs him that a young man has called
asking to see him. Magda and her friends remember days gone by
when they were girls out on the town seeking pleasure, going to

Bullier's café to dance, drink, and find love. Magda recalls a brief, bewitching, and ultimately chaste encounter she had there one night dancing with a stranger and looking deeply into his eyes. The subject changes, as Ruggero, son of a friend of Rambaldo, is introduced to the group as Prunier tells futures by reading palms. Magda, like a swallow, may migrate across the sea to a sun-filled land, there perhaps to find love.

Where should Ruggero go on his first night in Paris? After various speculations, all agree on Bullier's, in a marvelous ensemble, and the party ends. Lisette reminds Magda it is her night off. Prunier awaits Lisette, their on-again, off-again feisty relationship constituting the opera's subplot. Magda leaves. Lisette returns and flings herself into Prunier's arms, only to be told that her clothes are not quite right. She goes off, then returns elegantly attired, to Prunier's considerable satisfaction. They depart. Magda walks into the room. Remarkably transformed, she looks little like herself. Attired like a grisette (a French working girl), she takes a single red rose from a vase of flowers, fixes it carefully in her significantly revised hairdo, and, humming a fragment of "Doretta's Dream," goes out as the curtain falls.

Act II
This act plays in the Chez Bullier ballroom, teeming with men, women, students, artists, boys seeking girls, girls looking for boys, flower girls, and waiters all in a melodic hubbub of another masterful Puccini crowd scene. Ruggero, sitting alone at a table, ignores flirtatious attempts by numerous enticing young women to introduce him to the fun. Magda appears and when some young men try to pick her up, she claims to be meeting someone. Her eyes and Ruggero's meet across the room. The young men assume the obvious and escort her to his table. And so there she is reliving the enchantment of another night at Bullier's, for it takes but a few minutes for them to be waltzing about in each other's arms. The persistent waltz music is intoxicating, both to Magda and Ruggero, who quickly fall helplessly in love, and to anyone listening to what Puccini has produced throughout this act.

Prunier and Lisette now arrive. Lisette believes she recognizes her mistress, potentially an embarrassing moment for her who has adorned herself in Magda's clothes, but then seems to think otherwise when Ruggero introduces his partner as Paulette, the name she has given him. The pairs of lovers express their emotions in a quartet as other dancers and flower girls cover them with blos-

soms. Their exhilaration is sobered when Rambaldo is seen entering the ballroom. Prunier hastens Lisette and Ruggero away. Rambaldo invites Magda to go home with him. She is forthright in
refusing, confessing she has found love and is leaving him. Rambaldo is a gentleman both in receiving bad news and in departing
promptly. The act ends as Ruggero returns and leaves with Magda.

Act III

In Act III Madga and Ruggero are established in their love nest, a
small, lovely cottage on a hill overlooking the Côte d'Azur. As
their words and Puccini's music tell us, they are exquisitely
happy. It is late afternoon of a glorious spring day and as the lovers
converse over tea, Magda learns of Ruggero's intention to marry
her; he has written to his parents asking for consent. He is confident of their approval but she is anxious, knowing now that she
must inform him of how she has provided for herself by selling
herself. If Puccini was uninspired, as some critics maintain when
he composed *La rondine*, and simply responding to an offer so
lucrative that he could not say no, then I wonder where all this
lovely, light music came from.

The lovers depart, first Ruggero and then Magda. Prunier and
Lisette appear in a heated discussion over his failed attempt to
turn this maid, with whom he is infatuated, into an actress. Poor
Lisette was hissed off the boards in her first and last performance.
She is eager to come back to her old position and Magda, having
returned, is quite willing to take her on. Prunier then, in the face
of Magda's indignation, delivers a message from Paris, where one
awaits her. So hostile were the words between Prunier and Lisette
that we can only assume they are finished. They are, however, one
of those couples who squabble when together but are more miserable when apart. The first thing he asks, having claimed to be
through with her forever, is what time that night is she off duty.

Ruggero, beginning the intensely emotional finale, reappears
to show Magda a letter from his mother. Her heart breaks as she
reads it. Of course, she will be welcomed into the family as Ruggero's bride as long as he knows for certain that ". . . she is good,
mild, pure, and possesses all the virtues . . ." Magda does not
deceive him any longer, thus breaking the news that breaks their
hearts. She can love him but she cannot marry him. There is nothing virginal about her and his family could never accept her past.
Their idyll is over. They must part, he to the serenity of his family's home, she to "my swallow's flight and my pain." He slumps,

sobbing, as Lisette, having intuited the situation, leads her mistress away from the only old-fashioned, sentimental love she has ever known. Puccini's music is exquisite in its soft closing as the curtain falls.

Critics seldom fail to point out the copycat likeness between Lisette and Adele of *Die Fledermaus* dressing up in clothes of their mistress to go dancing. More pronounced are the complaints declaring *La rondine* little more than "a poor man's *La traviata* " (somewhere I have read those exact words), referring, of course, to the courtesan Violetta, who had to sacrifice her one true love because of the provincial moral beliefs of the family of the man she loved, echoing the plight of Magda. Ignore the comparison. In chapter 6, I stated clearly my love for *La traviata*, to me one of the definitive masterpieces of all opera literature and, on most days, my favorite Verdi. *La rondine* is its own self; it need not suffer from comparisons. Gustave Kobbé, in his great opera book, lists *La rondine* as a "lyric comedy" and that says it best except I must add that it is a damn good lyric comedy, overflowing with lovely melodies. It has taken the critics too long to recognize its worth and beauty. You give it a good listen and I'll bet you get the message right away.

IL TRITTICO (1918)
The Triptych

Il trittico means "the triptych" (which is a painting with three separate but connected panels). As the title of Puccini's next work it designates three separate but connected one-act operas, each lasting more than fifty minutes, and because of this connectedness they always should be performed together, as Puccini conceived them. When they weren't, while he was still living, it made him irate and rightfully so. His conception, based on a French model, was for three separate, dramatically different operas performed in a single evening to represent a *verismo* tragedy *(Il tabarro)*, a highly sentimental romance *(Suor Angelica)*, and a comedy *(Gianni Schicchi)*. To omit one of the works from a performance meant excluding an essential element of Puccini's conception. So why, then, are they not always performed as a unit? There are three interrelated reasons.

First, *Gianni Schicchi*, one of the greatest comic masterpieces in operatic literature, has always overshadowed the other two, *Il tabarro* eventually being recognized as a major work but *Suor Angelica* never quite catching on with either a large audience or theater managers and producers. Accordingly, some productions omit *Suor Angelica*, which is as wrong as leaving out the middle movement of a symphony, as Gustave Kobbé aptly pointed out. Second, a production of all three, with intermissions both before and after *Suor Angelica*, constitute for some people too long a night at the opera. More nonsense. Four hours for *Il trittico* is still much less of an evening out than Wagner's *Parsifal*—indeed, less than most any of Wagner's operas, or *Les Troyens*, by Berlioz. So that argument does not wash with me.

Last, managers and producers too often simply try to do something differently or to make a different double bill assuming it may be more financially beneficial. For this reason the matchless *Gianni Schicchi* will be found paired with who knows what other short opera.

I do wish managers and producers would mind their own business, which is to honor the intentions of the artist with the best possible production, rather than attempting to put a feather in their own cap by resorting to being "modern," "arty," or "different," none of these being a justification for altering an artist's creation. If one does not like something, then ignore it, leave it alone; don't tamper with it. Museum curators don't take a brush and change El Greco's colors, nor do publishers rewrite Byron's poems. Produce Puccini's *Il trittico* as he conceived it or put something else on the boards.

Finally, before we get to the operas, I have changed my mind significantly about *Il trittico* since hearing it for the first time so many years ago. Immediately, I loved *Gianni Schicchi* but considered *Il tabarro* only okay and just did not like *Suor Angelica* much at all. Today my admiration for *Gianni Schicchi* has only increased. Like Verdi's *Falstaff*, Puccini's comedy is his penultimate drama. It came toward the end of a remarkable career and, like *Falstaff*, it is a comic masterpiece in the buffa tradition. My admiration for the other two also has grown to the point where I love *Il tabarro* and very much enjoy *Suor Angelica*. As I experience a presentation of *The Triptych*, I appreciate the three different moods, from grisly reality to sentimental piousness to enjoying a hearty laugh over a good joke. Sometimes the appreciation of a work of art takes time.

IL TABARRO (1918)
The Cloak

This is the first opera of *The Triptych*. Based on a French play by Didier Gold, *La Houppelande*, the translation into Italian for the title of Puccini's opera is literal: "The Cloak." Giuseppe Adami (you will meet him again with Puccini's final work, *Turandot*) prepared the libretto. The characters are, their French names having been Italianized for Puccini's opera:

MICHELE, owner of the barge, age 50, *baritone*
GIORGETTA, his wife, age 25, *soprano*
LUIGI, a bargeman and lover of Giorgetta, age 20, *tenor*
IL TINCA, nickname of a bargeman, meaning "the Tench" (a freshwater game fish), *tenor*
IL TALPA, nickname of another bargeman, meaning "the Mole," *bass*
LA FRUGOLA, nickname of Talpa's wife, meaning "the Rummager," *mezzo-soprano*
A song-seller, two lovers, and a few others along the bank of the river

This *verismo* opera portrays a grim episode on a barge moored next to the bank on the Seine in Paris. The time is early in the twentieth century and all the characters are of the working class.

Opera experts will be able to isolate and identify specific arias in *Il tabarro* but most people who know and like the opera do not think of it as a drama wherein the action leads from one hit tune to another. Rather, the mood of the opera is established in the first bars of music and flows like a river to its end. Winston Churchill, an amateur painter, indicated that for him the hardest part of making a painting was to decide where and what the first brush-stroke would be. Once it was on the canvas he was under way. Puccini also knew the importance of those first few "strokes." Such is the *motivo di prima intenzione* (the intended primary theme), and all his operas begin accordingly, the audience instantly being immersed in the theme that establishes the primary mood or direction of the drama as it moves flawlessly from exposition through development to dénouement.

With *Il tabarro*, this first theme represents the rolling waters of the Seine, their wavy, ongoing motion obvious in the music, and this is how I listen to the opera: as a flow of music, like the flow of the river, moving on without interruption. My appreciation for this work grew considerably as I became more immersed in the text as it melds with the words. Puccini was committed to the concept of creating dramas wherein the action was so self-evident it could be comprehended even if one does not know the words or has not grasped their meaning. After all, such was his own experience when he saw Belasco's *Madame Butterfly* in London. And such, as well, was my early experiences with *Il tabarro*. I got the gist of the story, as anyone can, without focusing on all the words. This opera, however, really came alive for me once I worked on following the words closely. But if you attend a performance, do not pay for an expensive ticket to sit and read sub- or supra-titles. They can be helpful with a quick glance if you have carefully read the libretto ahead of time, this always being a good idea. No point to pay dearly to sit and read the story while missing all the action but you might be surprised to learn how often this is done. Here is the story of *The Cloak*.

In an unusual and effective beginning, the curtain rises before the rolling music of the ongoing river begins. Michele is watching the setting sun while Giorgetta busily attends to household chores on the barge. Bargemen can be heard working below and an auto horn sounds in the distance (actually written into the score by Puccini, who was fascinated by motor cars). Giorgetta suggests the toiling stevedores be given a refreshing drink. Before going to bring them topside, Michele affectionately moves toward his wife to kiss her. She offers a cheek in place of lips.

Luigi arrives first, then Il Tinca and Il Talpa, all gladly accepting Giorgetta's offer of wine. An organ grinder passes, then plays while Giorgetta and Il Tinca bungle through a few dance steps before Luigi steps in and she glides into his arms and over the deck. Michele appears, Luigi calls for the music to stop, and gives the organ grinder a coin. The stevedores return to work while Giorgetta asks her husband about their plans for departing, chatting idly as a passing song peddler attempts to sell his ballads by singing one. Playing a little harp, he sings *È la storia di Mimì* ("Mimi's story") as the orchestra, with a fun in-joke, quotes some music from *La bohème*. Some working girls buy the song and join in singing as Giorgetta admits to her husband that it is in Paris that she is most happy.

La Frugola arrives. She presents Giorgetta with a nice comb she found on this fine day, extols the wonders of her beloved cat, and, as Il Tinca returns, reproves him for drinking too much. Il Tinca's response demonstrates how numerous bits of down-to-earth philosophy emerge in the dialogue of this laboring class:

> So wonderful is wine . . .
> when I drink I do not think
> and when I think I do not laugh . . .

Luigi, interjecting, comments further in what is one of those arias known to the experts: *Hai ben ragione* ("You are right"), life is hard, put your head down, work and don't think. And drink, adds Il Tinca before leaving. Ever so aptly Puccini captures in his music the harshness of life evoked by Luigi. La Frugola sings of her dream, a quiet little cottage in the country. Giorgetta, in her reply, prefers the Paris suburb Belleville, home also once to Luigi, who joins in. La Frugola and Il Talpa leave. Luigi and Giorgetta are alone and, as we already know, they are lovers.

Fearing the imminent return of Michele, gently Giorgetta brushes aside Luigi's advances. Michele does return and is queried by Luigi, who is seeking a ride to Rouen. Michele declines, assuring him wages are better in Paris than Rouen. When Michele returns to the cabin of the barge, the lovers share an impassioned duet. Their wish is to be alone together and far away. Before Luigi leaves, he agrees to return later that night when Giorgetta lights a match to signal that the coast is clear.

Luigi departs and Michele, emerging from the cabin with a lighted lantern, seeks affection from his wife, who remains cold to him. He mentions their little boy, now deceased but she cannot talk about it. Michele recalls how he would gather together the three of them beneath his huge cloak to keep them all warm and close. He cannot comprehend what has happened to their love. She protests she still loves him but that things change as people get older. She claims to be headed for bed as she enters the cabin. Michele arranges the nightlights and allows expression to his repressed anger and suspicions in a great, powerful monologue. *Nulla!* . . . *Silenzio!* ("Nothing! . . . Silence!"), as sung by the incomparable Italian baritone Tito Gobbi on his 1955 recording, is the work of the consummate singing actor.

Listening next to the cabin entrance he hears nothing. He knows Giorgetta is there but neither has she undressed, nor is she sleeping. He concludes she is waiting for someone. Who? Luigi? He intends to find out. He will wait and see. He slumps down, takes out his pipe, strikes a match, and lights it. The waiting Luigi, seeing the signal, races up the gangplank and jumps onto the barge. Michele pounces and grabs him by the throat. And here is one of my favorite lines in the libretto, one of the reasons I so enjoy a close reading of all the words. As Michele throttles Luigi he says, "And so you wanted to go to Rouen, didn't you? Well, you'll get there, dead in the river." Such lines are so true to the character, which is what *verismo* is all about.

Michele forces him to confess that he is, indeed, Giorgetta's lover, and he strangles him. Michele hears Giorgetta heading for the deck. Quickly, he hides the corpse, which still is clinging to him in death, under his cloak. She has come to apologize for being hurtful to him. She wants forgiveness and to be close to him. "Under my cloak?" he asks. As he rises up, opening his cloak, Luigi's body spills out at her feet. Michele grabs Giorgetta and forces her face upon that of her dead lover as the curtain crashes

SUOR ANGELICA (1918)
Sister Angelica

Dramatically, in both senses of the word, I have changed my mind about this opera. *Sister Angelica* is a romance in that it is a narrative depicting heroic or marvelous achievements, and the first few times I heard it I allowed myself to be put off by two factors. First, the critical word was negative. *Sister Angelica* was declared to be the weak link in the triptych. An important opera book, significant for its thoroughness, declares the work has never been popular, offers an abrupt token synopsis, and isolates only one musical excerpt. Second, I did not give the story a fair chance, the overt sentimentality of this religious romance not appealing to me. Years later I reflected on the numerous other opera stories, ludicrous, silly, and bad, I never questioned because I liked the music. Had I then, as later I would do, simply ignored the criticism, given the story a chance, listened carefully to the music, and made up my own mind it would not have taken so long for me to like *Suor Angelica*. Not Puccini's best—I will not argue that—but certainly not a work to be dismissed, and what an extraordinary contrast, which, of course, is precisely what the composer intended, to *Il tabarro*.

After the gruff, sordid atmosphere of harsh life on a river

barge, culminating in murder, one stretches one's legs during an intermission, returns to one's seat, and in words and music is immediately taken into a totally different world. The text is by Giovacchino Forzano, who also authored *Gianni Schicchi*. The characters are, without a single male voice:

SUOR ANGELICA, a nun, *soprano*
Princess and Angelica's old aunt, *mezzo-soprano*
ABBESS, *mezzo-soprano*
Monitor, *mezzo-soprano*
Mistress of the novices, *mezzo-soprano*
SUOR GENOVIEFFA, a nun, *soprano*
SUOR OSMINA, a nun, *soprano*
SUOR DOLCINA, a nun, *mezzo-soprano*
Nursing sister, *mezzo-soprano*
Two alms sisters, *sopranos*
Two lay sisters, *soprano and mezzo-soprano*

The place is a convent and the time is the end of the seventeenth century.

Puccini, with his infallible theatrical instinct, musically leads the listener through three distinct episodes, the third being the musical event toward which the drama is constantly moving. First presented is a slice of life in the convent, the purpose of which is to distinguish Suor Angelica from the other nuns. Second, Angelica's aunt, the mean old Princess, brings devastating news to the repenting nun, who, for seven years, has been waiting to hear from her family. Finally, the death and miraculous salvation of Suor Angelica concludes the opera. Church bells and the singing of an *Ave Maria* set the mood of the first part, which, thereafter, is lighter and conversational. When the aunt arrives, Puccini draws a stark contrast between the haughty, insensitive old woman and the anxious, loving Angelica. With the departure of the aunt begins the most well-known music of the drama, melodically extending to the final curtain. If you will listen to the opera as the development from one to the other of those three events, Puccini's music will be more meaningful and more infectious.

The curtain rises on the interior of a convent, chapel, cloister, cemetery, and garden apparent. Voices singing can be heard from the chapel. When the service is over, the nuns file out. The monitor reprimands several sisters for small offences and Sister Genovieffa explains to the novices how the light from the setting sun has turned the fountain water into a golden flow, an event they experience for only three days a year every May. A recently deceased sister will have some golden water spattered upon her tomb. The sisters talk about having desires, knowing they ought to have none, but Genovieffa admits one: to see and hold a lamb again. She once was a shepherdess. When asked if she has any desires, Angelica is firm in her denial but all the sisters know this to be untrue. Not having heard a single word from her family during seven years in the convent, she prays and waits daily for some contact. The nursing sister, in an agitated state, interrupts and presses Angelica for a cure for a sister who has been stung by wasps. Knowing all about curative potions, Angelica makes a mixture from herbs. Alms sisters arrive with provisions on a donkey, and as they unload, one mentions having seen an elegant carriage arrive outside the convent. All hope the visitor may be Angelica's.

The abbess enters and summons Sister Angelica, and the other sisters head for the cemetery with golden water. The abbess announces the arrival of Angelica's aunt and leaves the two alone. The aunt is rigid and unfeeling, and will not even look at Angelica. Sternly and matter-of-factly, she explains she needs a signature by which Angelica will bequeath her significant inheritance to her younger sister, who is to be married. She shows Angelica not an ounce of understanding, kindness, or forgiveness, reminding her that bearing a child out of wedlock forever disgraced the family. Desperate for news, Angelica begs passionately for a word about her son. She is told the child died from a disease two years ago. This scene is extraordinary for the contrasting warmth of Angelica and the heartless iciness of her aunt. It is now dark. A sister leads in the abbess, who presents Angelica with a document to sign, which she does. Abbess and aunt depart. Angelica is alone.

With one of Puccini's greatest arias for soprano voice, the most famous music in *Suor Angelica*, the final portion of the story begins. *Senza mamma, o bimbo, tu sei morto*, Angelica sings ("Without his mama, my little boy died"), an aria expressing her desire to be united with her child. Returning from the cemetery, the other sisters surround Angelica, who, now in an ecstatic state, exclaims her happiness. The sisters retire to their cells, Angelica soon thereafter to reemerge. She makes a poisonous concoction from some flowers mixed with water from the fountain, accompanied by music of an extraordinary lyricism, and sings farewell to her sisters in a second significant aria, though certainly not the equal of the first one. She drinks the poison, lurches against a tree in the garden, and instantly is sobered by what she has done: Suicide is a damnable mortal sin. She drops to her knees to beg forgiveness from the Madonna.

Heavenly voices are heard as a miracle commences. The chapel floods with light and slowly the door opens to reveal a church filled with angels. The choir sings in Latin as Angelica, in Italian, continues to ask for mercy. The Blessed Virgin appears in the doorway with a small boy dressed all in white who is pushed by her toward his mother. As the vision of the child moves toward Angelica, she dies, the chorus singing *Sancta Maria*. The glowing miracle is dispersed by the closing of the curtain.

I would be made very happy if this little introduction to *Suor Angelica* in any way at all helps to undo its undeserved bad press. The more I hear the music, the more I love it. And remember: Always make it part of the triptych. That is its only proper place. If you listen carefully to the religious music sections of *Suor Angelica*, it will be evident that four generations of church composers were not lost, despite Puccini's calling to the theater rather than the cathedral.

Finally, as I finish writing my introduction to *Suor Angelica*, I think of a conversation I had with Licia Albanese, one of the greatest Puccini sopranos on record and today, even at age ninety, the head of The Puccini Foundation in New York City. Often singers are asked which of their recordings best represents their artistry—by which one would they wish their reputation to be measured: Without hesitation, when I put this question to Licia, she replied, *Senza mamma* from *Suor Angelica*.

GIANNI SCHICCHI (1918)

But the miracle that closes *Suor Angelica* continues, for how else can I describe one of the uncontested masterpieces of Italian comic opera, the last of an incomparable line going back through *Falstaff* and *Don Pasquale* to Bellini, Rossini, and Mozart. Parts One and Two of *Il trittico* have had a difficult time because the third part, *Gianni Schicchi*, instantly was and remains an overwhelming sensation. To experience it as such, remember that you have just seen *Suor Angelica*, which ends with an operatic representation of the supernatural. You have gone through the necessity of an intermission, you have returned to your seat, and now you are to be made to laugh. Puccini will treat you to a non-stop trip through some of his most inspired music, so unlike that of the two dramas preceding it. *Il trittico*, experienced as a unity, as it ought to be, makes his genius for authentic music theater obvious as the ghastly, the supernatural, and the comic are placed before you, one following the other and each with just the right touch.

Gianni Schicchi has only one world-famous aria. *O mio babbino caro* has been exploited by films, a TV commercial, and schmaltz renditions by the dozens. Millions who never have heard of *Gianni Schicchi* and countless others who can hum the music (but could not begin to identify the composer) love this heart-wrenching tune wherein a daughter appeals to her beloved father. So! If just one famous tune, then what is so masterful about the opera? Every note, first to last, perfectly captures every emotion expressed in the excellent libretto by Forzano. Gianni (the diminutive of Giovanni) Schicchi was a historical person. Do not be intimidated by his name. If you can say Johnnie Ski-key, not even an Italian will blanch! He lived in Florence in the thirteenth century and was immortalized, so to speak, by Dante, who wrote about him in Canto XXX of his Purgatory (Part One of *The Divine Comedy*). Gianni Schicchi is confined by Dante to that circle of hell reserved for "the falsifiers": those who impersonate another (falsifiers of persons), perjurers (falsifiers of words), and coiners (falsifiers of money). Gianni Schicchi impersonated Buoso Donati and dictated a will leaving the bulk of an inheritance to himself:

> lent his own false frame
> To Buoso de' Donati, and made a will
> In legal form, and forged it in his name.

This is both the historical and the literary source from which the opera is made. Already you know tragedy is aimed at the human heart; for example, Puccini followed the tragic story of Madame Butterfly in Belasco's play even though he knew no English. Comedy, however, is aimed at the head. If you do not understand the humor, you simply don't get it. To get *Gianni*

Schicchi, both the humor of the story and the remarkable skillfulness with which Puccini created a brilliant score wherein the music enormously enhances the drama, you need to read carefully every word of the libretto. A good video will do, but nothing will prepare you better than listening to a recording while you put one eye on the Italian, the other on the English translation, and both ears open to the music.

The characters of the opera:

GIANNI SCHICCHI, a recent resident of Florence, *baritone*
LAURETTA, his daughter, aged 21, *soprano*
ZITA *(La Vecchia)*, old woman and cousin of Buoso, *contralto*
RINUCCIO, her nephew, aged 24, *tenor*
GHERARDO, Buoso's nephew, *tenor*
NELLA, his wife, *soprano*
GHERARDINO, their little boy, aged 7, *alto or boy soprano*
BETTO, Buoso's impoverished brother-in-law from Signa, *bass*
SIMONE, aged cousin of Buoso, *bass*
MARCO, his son, *baritone*
LA CIESCA (the blind woman), his wife, *mezzo-soprano*
MAESTO SPINELLOCCIO, a doctor, *bass*
AMANTIO DI NICOLAO, a lawyer, *bass*
PINELLINO, a shoemaker and friend of Buoso, *baritone*
GUCCIO, a dyer and friend of Buoso, *bass*

The time of the story is the year 1299, the place is the bedroom of Buoso Donati's villa in Florence. Buoso has just died.

The opera starts with what you by now recognize as Puccini's formulaic opening: a few moments of music to establish mood, then the curtain, then the voices begin. The grieving relatives of Buoso Donati, gathered around his corpse, which is lying under a red blanket on his bed, weep, lament, and offer prayers. Sitting on the floor, with his back to everyone, little Gherardino obliviously plays marbles. It is nine o'clock in the morning and sunlight melds with candlelight surrounding the recently deceased Buoso. As the heartfelt mourning continues and the relatives prepare again to pray, Nella and Betto whisper in a corner. Rinuccio overhears the word *Signa* and asks what is being said in

Signa. The whisper tours one to the next until Betto lets all in on the secret. If Buoso croaks, so says the gossip in Signa, the monks will be happy because he is leaving everything to the monastery.

Remaining on their knees, but with no more thoughts of prayer, the shocked relations look at each other and then to Simone, the eldest, for advice. If Buoso's will already has gone to a lawyer, any hope they have for sharing in an inheritance vanishes. If it still is in the room, however, there may be something they can do. All leap to a frantic search of the room. Rinuccio, who first heard the rumor and exposed it, takes the next step in saving the day. After the relatives have turned the room inside out—Betto taking advantage of the commotion by stealing pieces of silver—Rinuccio finds the will in a cabinet at the top of the stairs. All bound toward him but are fended off. If they soon are to be rich, will Zita give Rinuccio, her nephew, consent to marry Lauretta, daughter of Gianni Schicchi? She says yes and Rinuccio, now certain his rich uncle's will benefits him, gives Gherardino two coins to fetch Schicchi and Lauretta immediately. More candles are lit to honor "poor Buoso" and as the will is opened, each desperately hopes he or she has been bequeathed the most coveted possessions, the house, the mills at Signa, and the mule. All gather around Zita, who holds the will, reading to themselves. They are stunned. It is true, Everything is left to the monastery. They mock and curse the monks.

The relatives can think of no way to circumvent the will until, once again, Rinuccio offers a solution: Gianni Schicchi. He is the only one who can advise them and perhaps even save them. Zita wants to hear no more about Schicchi and his daughter and she is joined by others who object to a country bumpkin, recently relocated in Florence, having been sent for by Rinuccio. Schicchi is crafty and shrewd and he knows codes and laws, Rinuccio retorts, bidding them to bury their petty prejudices. In his aria *Firenze è come un albero fiorito* ("Florence is like a flowering tree"), he explains that in all fields of endeavor, their city always has benefited from the talents of newcomers like Gianni Schicchi. Schicchi, knocks, then enters right on cue.

From the sorrowful looks on all the faces Schicchi concludes, aloud, that the ailing Buoso must be recovering but then realizes otherwise as he views the bed. Schicchi is told of the disinheritance and Zita retracts her consent, declaring that her nephew will not marry one with no dowry. In a distinguished ensemble Schicchi and Zita denounce each other while Lauretta and Rinuccio express love for each other but fear the worst, the relatives joining in. The insulted Schicchi is about to leave with his daughter but Rinuccio, driven by his intense desire to marry Lauretta, asks that Mister Giovanni stay for a moment and be given the will. He then pleads with Schicchi to help them. "For these people, no! no! no!" is Schicchi's response. No! until his daughter sings *O mio babbino caro*. "Oh, my dear daddy," she implores, "have pity," and no father in the world could resist this appeal, sung to what may be Puccini's most popular melody of all. "Give me the will!" is the unequivocal answer.

Rinuccio gives the will to Schicchi, who paces back and forth while intently reading, the anxious relatives following him first with their eyes but soon on their feet pacing in his footsteps. There is no way out of the will, he exclaims, dashing their hopes, but then a huge smile spreads across his face and he sends Lauretta out onto the terrace to feed birds. Schicchi makes certain no one but the relatives know Buoso has just died, then into motion he sets his scheme. The corpse must be moved to another room and candlesticks removed, and the bed made. Just as this is accomplished Buoso's doctor, Spinelloccio, knocks. Schicchi says he is not to be allowed to enter and hides behind the bed curtain. The doctor is told repeatedly that Buoso now is feeling better. This makes him all the more anxious to see his patient, but the relatives detain him at the door claiming the sick man needs his rest. Buoso's voice, perfectly imitated by Schicchi, confirms this. The doctor agrees to return later.

In a dramatic monologue, Schicchi explains his plan. They will request a lawyer to come immediately to Buoso, who is declining and wishes to dictate his will. He will pose as Buoso, in his bed and under his nightcap, in a partially darkened room, and will give the notary his last will and testament, again imitating Buoso's voice. The relatives rejoice, pay him homage, and send Rinuccio for the lawyer.

They agree that five lesser parts of the estate will be divided among Simone, Betto, Gherardo, Marco, and Zita, leaving the prizes of villa, mills, and mule unsettled. Of course, each wants them and they begin to quibble, but fall silent when a death knell tolls. What relief to learn it is not for Buoso! All agree to leave the allocation of the three most prized items to the integrity and good judgment of Schicchi, who, as he puts on his disguise, is separately approached by the five inheritors, who offer bribes for that which they most covet. Schicchi's "Okay" satisfies each in turn and he gets into Buoso's bed as the women sing a mock lullaby. He then reminds them all of the punishment for impersonating another as a means of falsifying a bequest: One's hand is chopped off before being exiled from Florence. "*Addio, Firenze, addio,*" he sings, waving the arm of an empty nightshirt at them. This farewell to Florence will soon play an evocative part as the drama unfolds because Schicchi has made it abundantly clear that the punishment applies to both impersonator and any and all accomplices.

The lawyer and two friends of Buoso, serving as witnesses, arrive. Amantio begins by reading a formal statement in Latin, to which Schicchi adds an annulment revoking any previous wills. The relatives are delighted at how ingeniously Schicchi is working on their behalf. Only five little lira are left to the monastery because, as "Buoso" explains, when large sums are left to religious orders it is assumed to be stolen money. All cash, divided equally, is left to the relatives, who are profuse with their appreciation. The property, except for villa, mills, and mule, is left to Zita and the four men exactly as they had predetermined. "Buoso" next leaves the best and most costly mule in all of Tuscany ". . . to my devoted friend—Gianni Schicchi." This jars the relatives. Simone tries to question why but is silenced by Schicchi, as other relations mutter, "Scoundrel." Their anguish mounts when the house in Florence is left " . . . to my dear, devoted, and affectionate friend Gianni Schicchi," but their protests are silenced by the notary, who demands respect for one making a will. Schicchi informs the notary that he will do as he pleases and if relatives scream, he will simply sing and as he leaves the mills at Signa to Gianni Schicchi the bequest is made with repeated strains of "Farewell, Florence," Schicchi waving a handless nightshirt as he bids the silenced relatives good-bye " . . . with this stump." The will has been dictated and Zita is ordered to pay the witnesses and the notary. The officials lament, fearing the passing of this fine man to be imminent. They depart.

Rinuccio runs onto the terrace to his beloved Lauretta, who had been sent there by her father while he orchestrated his little scheme. The outraged relatives of Buoso, screaming "Thief" and "Traitor," attack Schicchi, who stands on the bed in an attempt to defend himself. He then jumps to the floor, grabs Buoso's walking stick, and swings madly at the relations, who race about pillaging and creating chaos. Schicchi orders them out of "his" house and chases them downstairs and onto the street. Slowly the terrace doors swing open to reveal the young lovers embracing in the sunlight, the beauty of a Florence skyline behind them. They are blissfully happy to know they can afford to be married. They sing of their love. Heavily loaded with his own possessions, Schicchi comes back and sets his recaptured goods on the floor. He gazes at Rinuccio and Lauretta, turns, center stage, to the audience, and, in one of opera's supreme conclusions, addresses them, not in song, but with spoken words:

> Tell me, ladies and gentlemen,
> If Buoso's money
> could have been put to a better end.
> For this extravagance
> I have been thrust into hell,
> and so be it,
> but, with permission from the great father
> Dante,
> if this evening you have enjoyed yourself,
> allow me [and here Schicchi claps his hands]
> extenuating circumstances.

The curtain falls as the orchestra declares the end of the opera.

Such is the famous story of *Gianni Schicchi*, but to experience the wonder of the drama in all its brilliant richness you must hear the music—some of the best Puccini ever wrote!

TURANDOT (1926)

First of all, we must resolve the controversial issue of how to pronounce the name of this opera. You will hear both TOUR-an-dot and TOUR-an-doe. Recently, I'm hearing TOUR-an-dote and where that came from I don't know. Most of my American opera friends, but certainly not all, prefer the former, while English counterparts much prefer the latter. But this is not one of those English/American matters of pronunciation like saying CLARK for CLERK or PA-truh-nyz for PAY-truh-nyz. It is rather a matter of two different groups, both of whom are convinced they are right. Those who say TOUR-an-dot have a variety of recordings, audio and video, to support their claim but these tend to be recordings made in America and of a recent vintage, meaning within the last five to forty years. I, however, have a recording made in Italy almost fifty years ago with a one hundred percent Italian cast and throughout the opera, in every instance, they say or sing TOUR-an-doe. The importance of the old Italian recording is the honoring of a tradition claiming Puccini said TOUR-an-doe.

Is there any evidence for this? *Turandot* had its world premiere at La Scala on April 25, 1926, with the Polish soprano Rosa Raisa creating the title role. In an interview late in her life (she died in 1963), she corrected the interviewer when he said TOUR-an-dot. Puccini, who had been dead for almost a year and a half when she sang the first performance, insisted on the TOUR-an-doe pronunciation, she explained. Of course he did. Is not the correct pronunciation in the poetic rhyme scheme of the libretto? The second act opens on a pavilion where three of Turandot's (how did you just pronounce her name to yourself?) ministers are recalling better times of days gone by:

> *Tutto andava secondo*
> *l'antichissima regola del mondo . . .*
> *Poi nacque Turandot . . .*

> Everything went along
> according to the ancient laws of the world . . .
> Then was born Turandot . . .

The rhyme scheme of the librettists, Giuseppe Adami *(La rondine* and *Il tabarro)* and Renato Simoni is both impeccable and incontrovertible:

> . . . *secondo*
> . . . *del mondo*
> . . . TOUR-an-doe

Puccini, who knew his libretti better than those who wrote them, would have leapt out of his skin if he were to hear

> . . . *secondo*
> . . . *del mondo*
> . . . TOUR-an-dot . . .

I have always said TOUR-an-doe and when I do so on my radio broadcasts sometimes I get letters, once from an opera-loving professor of Italian, attempting to correct me. Until they can come forth with something new that I don't know, I'll continue to say TOUR-an-doe and I hope you will, too. Whenever the name Turandot is utilized in either an internal or an external rhyme scheme in the libretto, no fewer than fourteen times, the rhyme always is with the sound DOE; never once is it a DOT rhyme. This internal evidence of a poem Puccini sweated over, created parts of by himself, and knew by heart is conclusive for me, so let's have no more of this TOUR-an-dot business!

⁓

The eminent Arturo Toscanini conducted the first performance of *Turandot*. He and the composer were friends, but not without some reservations. Put two unrelenting, unforgiving men of musical genius in the same room and there can be a difference of opinion. Toscanini had conducted the world premiere of *La bohème*. Perhaps a note of discord was struck when Toscanini, in 1922, also conducted the first performance of an opera by Pizzetti, a composer now so forgotten (or neglected) that his music would stump even the experts. Pizzetti was part of an exceedingly vocal movement (it included musicians and critics, among others) who considered Puccini a throwback to an earlier age, unaware of modern musical trends and developments, and committed exclusively to opera as a means of making money.

To whatever extent there was a Puccini/Toscanini rift, spat, or period of silence, the friendship was repaired. When Puccini, almost having completed *Turandot* after several years of frustration and intense work on the score, was in Brussels awaiting treatment for throat cancer, he was visited by Toscanini. Together they went over the score. Toscanini was much impressed. This was during the first week of November in 1924. Though the treatment was considered successful, Puccini's heart failed on November 29. His body was returned to Milan and temporarily was buried in the family tomb of the Toscanini family.

Puccini had written everything except the final scene of the opera, a great love duet for which he left notes and sketches. Under Toscanini's guidance, the young composer Franco Alfano completed the opera utilizing the material Puccini left outlined at his death. An ordinary listener experiencing a performance will not notice that the music was not written by Puccini. Alfano did a fine job of integrating Puccini's sketches and imitating his style in completing the opera. What is regrettable, and what we will never hear, is the musical metamorphosis, in the final scene, of the icy princess, Turandot, into a warm, loving woman through the bold, forthright love of Prince Calaf. We do know Puccini intended to make this scene the crowning achievement of his career. We all know so well those lines from Longfellow's poem "Maud Miller":

> For of all sad words of tongue or pen,
> The saddest are these: "It might have been."

During the world premiere, just before the final scene, when Toscanini reached the last notes written by Puccini, he stopped the performance, put down his baton, and, turning to the audience, said, "It is at this point that Puccini laid down his pen." The curtains closed. Thereafter he always conducted the complete opera with Alfano's ending and that is how it is performed and recorded today.

Puccini did not answer his critics publically. Probably *Turandot* was to be his response. He had stated it was time to move away from what he had done and to seek a new direction. He decided to have a libretto made from Carlo Gozzi's play *Turandotte*, a mix of ancient improbable legend and authentic human emotions operating within a story at once both ghastly and redemptive. Unlike *Tosca* or *Butterfly*, for example, in which both stories are stripped of all excess and speed to their tragic conclusions, *Turandot* ultimately ends happily, after an execution and a suicide are countered by several comic episodes that bounce our emotions back and forth. *Turandot* is Puccini's version of grand opera or, at least, it is grander, more exalted, and more elaborate than anything heretofore conceived by him. There are critics, scholars, and opera lovers who consider it his ultimate masterpiece. The characters are:

TURANDOT, a Chinese Princess, *soprano*
EMPEROR ALTOUM, her father, *tenor*
TIMUR, blind exiled King of Tartar, *bass*
CALAF, his son, the Unknown Prince, *tenor*
LIÙ, a young slave woman who cares for Timur, *soprano*

PING, Grand Chancellor of China, *baritone*
PANG, Supreme Lord of Provisions, *tenor*
PONG, Supreme Lord of the Imperial Kitchen, *tenor*
A mandarin, *baritone*
Chorus of soldiers, attendants, children, priests, mandarins, and others

The story takes place in Peking during a legendary antiquity.

Act I

Notice that I have listed the chorus as one of the "characters." The chorus in *Turandot*, unlike other Puccini crowd scenes, does not merely lend color, atmosphere, and a *verismo* dimension to the drama. In *Turandot* the chorus is a central character, a protagonist, willful in its vacillating moods. This is especially so in the magnificent first act, dominated by the chorus except for two famous back-to-back arias. After a typical concise but nonetheless evocative mood-setting orchestral introduction of a few moments, the curtain opens on the walls of the Imperial City of Peking. Under a sculptured portico hangs a huge bronze gong. Stuck on tall poles about the bastions are the decapitated heads of recent suitors of Princess Turandot, who, failing to answer correctly her three riddles, have been executed. The sun has just set and to a huge gathered throng a mandarin reads a proclamation:

> People of Peking!
> This is the law: Turandot the Pure
> will be the bride of the man of royal blood
> who can solve her three riddles.
> However, should he fail her test he
> must submit his haughty head to an ax.

The Prince of Persia, the mandarin continues, was fated to fail and with the rising of the moon he will lose his head. As guards constrain an agitated, bloodthirsty crowd, eager to witness the spectacle of still another execution, the voice of a young woman is heard calling for help. It is Liù. Her blind, aged master, the exiled King of Tartar, has fallen in the bustling turmoil. The Unknown Prince rushes to their aid and amid this turmoil Calaf finds that fate has reunited a separated father and son, both in hiding and both seeking the other. He helps his father to his feet. They must be careful. If their identity is discovered, they will be killed. When Calaf is told by Timur how Liù has lovingly cared for him and guided him, he asks her why has she suffered so much for them. "Because one day in the palace you smiled at me," she replies, quite simply.

Liù, the most loving, warm, and human character in the drama, was Puccini's creation. She is not to be found in the play from which the opera was made. Liù, her words and music will reveal, is a sister of other Puccini women who gave all for love, their lives included: Manon Lescaut, Mimi, Tosca, Butterfly.

Throughout the surrepetitious reunion of father and son, the rabble calls for the executioner and the honing of his ax. "The riddles are three, death is one," they chant, imploring the moon to hurry and show itself, and as soon as its first faint, ghostly white glimmer spreads across the sky, their voices ring out for the executioner by name: Pu-Tin-Pao.

In *Madama Butterfly*, Puccini integrated several Japanese melodies into his score. At this point, in *Turandot*, we hear an authentic Chinese tune of remarkable beauty sung by some little boys. They introduce into this gory atmosphere an appeal for the world once again to be brilliant with flowers and, as the executioner, his men, mandarins, and dignitaries, followed by the young, graceful Prince of Persia, appear, the mood of the mob suddenly changes to one of begging for mercy. They call for their *principessa* to grant a reprieve but Turandot has not yet even been seen on the stage of "her" opera. They repeat their appeal, Calaf joining in. He wishes to see and curse the cruel princess. High on a covered imperial loggia she appears. The crowd prostrate themselves. Calaf is benumbed by her beauty. The imperious Princess makes a quick gesture indicating death, the Prince of Persia is led off, and as suddenly as she appeared, Turandot, without a word, is gone. All but Timur, Liù, and Calaf disperse to attend the execution. Calaf is in another world. Devastated by Turandot's beauty, from one quick glimpse, he is immune to appeals from his father and Liù to flee this awful country. He begins to rush toward the gong to declare himself a candidate to attempt answering the riddles, shouting "Turandot" just as the distant voice of the Prince of Persia declares her name with his last breath. He is restrained, however, by Timur. Again he tries to move to the gong, overcome with desire for the beautiful Turandot, this time stopped by the emperor's three ministers, Ping, Pang, and Pong.

Through their words and exaggerated gestures, embellished

by lighthearted, jocund music, to which they move about in dancelike fashion, a comic dimension is introduced into the austere plot. They admonish the Unknown Prince to return whence he came. He is acting like a fool and Peking already has a surplus of those. Calaf persists in trying to reach the gong. Why, they query? Turandot is just a woman. Take off her clothes and all there is is flesh—not even good to eat. Ping advises him to take a hundred wives and enjoy many arms and legs and sweet bosoms.

Handmaidens of Turandot appear to still the chattering. The Princess is resting. The ministers resume their plea but Calaf is deaf and delirious with desire. Ghosts of decapitated suitors appear on the ramparts singing of their love for Turandot. No, proclaims Calaf. He alone will love her. As the ministers persist and Calaf desists, the executioner can be seen in the distance carrying the severed head of the Prince of Persia. Timur tries to dissuade his son, then Liù, in a magnificent aria, *Signore, ascolta* ("My lord, listen"), appeals. Calaf replies in the second of these two famous back-to-back Act I arias: *Non piangere, Liù* ("Do not weep, Liù"). If he fails, he asks, please continue to care for Timur.

With these two superb arias the stupendous climax to the first act is under way. The ministers join Timur and Liù in an attempt to deter Calaf. They are joined by the crowd, all bolstered by the power of a full orchestra in one of Puccini's greatest crowd scenes. In a frenzy the resolute Calaf frees himself, rushes to the gong, and strikes it three times while calling out the name of the forbidding Princess. Above the din the sounds of Ping, Pang, and Pong laughing are heard as the curtain falls.

Act II

I was a young man when I attended my first performance of *Turandot* and only half of me liked the first scene of the second act. The other half was keen to get on with the story: Calaf's attempt to answer Turandot's enigmatic riddles. Because some critics also questioned the importance of the scene, I felt aligned with opera experts. Today, much older and, I hope, a little wiser, I anticipate it eagerly. Puccini, of course, the master of theatrical technique, through instinct, insight, or both, knew that his audience needed a lull after the tremendous energy of the Act I finale.

What is this scene? Before a huge curtain, decorated with

Chinese figures, Ping, Pong, and Pang converse. Will they need red lanterns for a festivity or white lanterns for a funeral? They recall ancient days when all life in China was lived peacefully in accordance with time-honored rules of the world, but then with Turandot came the relentless turmoil of gongs, riddles, decapitations, and burials. To one of the loveliest melodies of the score, Ping commences a nostalgic recollection of days of happiness in his house in Honan by a little pond *(Ho una casa nell' Honan)*. Pong has beautiful forests near Tsiang and Pang has a garden near Kiù, and together they lament their absence from the place they love. What madness Turandot's beauty provokes. They recall the dire fate of different princes, the terrible carnage of one execution after another. Oh, how they long for a victor: to prepare a bridal couch, to fill the air with perfume, to light the way with lanterns for the bridal pair, and they fantasize the day when their princess lies powerless in the arms of a husband. Then love will restore peace to China. Activity stirring within the palace breaks the reverie of the three ministers and, cynically, they depart to enjoy still another execution.

The curtains of their pavilion disappear and for the second scene of the second act we are within a vast square in front of the palace. Onto a landing, high above the gathering crowd, come mandarins and eight wise men bearing scrolls. An impressive staircase with three landings connects the square to the palace. Clouds of incense disperse to reveal the aged emperor seated on his throne at the top of the stairs. The crowd pays homage and he, in a high thin voice, reveals that it is a terrible oath binding him to the cruel ritual of the riddles and he has had enough. He urges Calaf to go, several times, and each time Calaf begs for a chance to solve the riddles. The mandarin steps forth and repeats the same proclamation we heard at the beginning of the opera. Offstage ethereal voices of boys offer again the beautiful Chinese melody and they repeat their hope for a shining world as Turandot approaches the throne dressed in a gold gown with a seemingly endless train.

What an unusual title character she is. Her entire opera is not quite two hours. During the first act she allowed us a momentary glimpse of herself, she does not appear in the first scene of the second act, and she has yet to sing a note. But now she does, standing stiff and regal, and looking coldly down at the Unknown Prince. *In questa Reggia* ("Within this palace"), her first words of the drama, commence a masterful, tour de force aria for dramatic soprano. Addressing her suitor, she explains that thousands of years ago her ruling ancestress, in a time of war, was conquered, ravaged, and murdered ". . . by a man like you, a stranger." That is why she takes revenge on men through her inscrutable enigmas. No man will ever possess her. Hers is an "I hate men" aria. She warns the Unknown Prince not to tempt fate: "The riddles are three and death is one." With confidence, Calaf responds, "No, no! The riddles are three, life is one." And so the stage is set for one of the oldest and most intriguing theatrical devices, the testing of someone by asking questions or posing riddles, the consequence of failure being dire indeed.

Turandot poses the first question: What dies every day in every human heart only to be reborn again each night? Calaf breezes through this one. It is "hope" *(la speranza)*, he tells her. The wise men, unrolling the first scroll, confirm that he is correct. Before posing the second riddle, Turandot walks halfway down the staircase toward the Prince, her golden gown trailing behind her.

What, she asks, is like a flame but is not a flame, can grow cold, or, with dreams of conquest, can flare like the setting sun? Calaf does not respond as quickly this time, thus prompting encouragement from the emperor, the crowd, and Liù. When his answer comes, "Blood" *(Il sangue)*, it is verified by the wise men. One more correct answer and the reign of death will be over. The excited crowd now is on the side of the Prince, causing Turandot to order her guards to quell them. She hurries to the bottom of the staircase and stands over the Unknown Prince, who, accordingly, falls to his knees.

Turandot delivers the final riddle, her proud, steadfast voice unwavering, Puccini's music uttering tantalizing fragments of sound: "What is the ice that sets you on fire?" Absolute silence increases the tension. She urges him to hurry. More silence and more tension. Again she urges him to answer, confident that she has him stumped, and repeats the question. Still the Prince is silent. Only eerie chords struck by the orchestra can be heard until, all of a sudden, Calaf jumps to his feet, exclaiming the certainty of victory. "My fire will thaw you: 'Turandot'!" and the wise men confirm that the final answer is, indeed, the name of the princess. Calaf has won.

As the crowd exults, Turandot ascends the stairs and appeals to her father to release her from her commitment, but he is bound to the oath. She refuses, nevertheless, to accept the stranger and with intense derision tells him so. All proclaim that the oath is sacred but the inexorable Turandot will not relent and she asks the Prince if he will take her against her will. Only through love will he have her, he replies, never by force. He will turn the tables. He will give her only one riddle. If she can tell him his name before dawn, he is ready to die. Turandot nods agreement, the emperor expresses hope soon to have a son, and the crowd praises him as the act ends.

Act III

The first scene of the final act plays in the garden of the palace, where Calaf listens to the distant voices of heralds announcing Turandot's royal edict throughout the city: "No one shall sleep tonight in Peking." In the most anticipated music of the opera, *Nessun dorma* ("No one shall sleep"), Calaf speculates that the Princess also is not sleeping as his secret lies hidden in his heart. Tomorrow, he is certain, will bring her to him. (You already know this music if you have watched television presentations of the first concert of the "Three Tenors," José Carreras, Placido Domingo, and Luciano Pavarotti. At the end of their concert all three sing it together making an unfortunate circus-act travesty of this magnificent aria for tenor voice.)

Turandot has threatened death if the name of the Unknown Prince is not discovered before dawn. An anxious Ping, Pong, and Pang steal into the garden, followed by other shadowy figures. They attempt to lure Calaf into releasing Turandot from her commitment. First they offer him a bevy of beautiful girls and from behind bushes some emerge, dressed scantily, to dance around him. He is unfazed. Next they proffer riches and Calaf is shown caskets of gold and gems. These, too, are refused. When the offer of glory also is rejected, the situation seems hopeless. The three ministers beg and a crowd, which by this time is filling the garden, threaten him with knives, all fearing the consequences of Turandot's wrath. The Unknown Prince will not budge. He will have her.

Offstage shouts declare that they have the name and into the garden come soldiers dragging Liù and Timur, "bruised, exhausted, and bleeding," the libretto states. Even though Calaf asserts they do not know his name, the three ministers call for Turandot. Torture will make them talk. Liù, to save Timur, confesses she alone knows the secret and no amount of torture can make her reveal it. Calaf moves to protect Liù but is restrained by soldiers. Liù is tortured until she sinks to the ground, but she will not yield Calaf's name. Turandot asks Liù what gives her such strength and courage. Love, she answers, and through her silence Liù will give the Unknown Prince, whom she loves, the love of Turandot. The heartless Princess calls for more torture, Ping sends for the executioner, and the crowd approves. Liù, fearing she can bear no more, insists upon approaching Turandot to speak to her. Her aria, one of the most sublime Puccini ever wrote, unequivocally presents her as the heroine of the drama. *Tu che di gel sei cinta* ("You, who are encased in ice") will love him before dawn after "I shall close my tired eyes, never again to see him!"

Liù grabs a dagger from a soldier's girth, stabs herself, falters toward Calaf, and drops at his feet, the secret of his name dying with her. Timur kneels next to her, mourning, while the crowd, constant in its vacillating emotions, now repents. Liù's body is lifted and carried away, Timur walking beside his beloved companion, holding her hand. All except Calaf and Turandot follow in a procession to a dirge, the last music Puccini composed. The fickleness of the crowd in this opera, calling for blood one minute and begging for mercy the next, recalls Pascal, who noted with what ease the emotions of a mob can be swayed this way or that. Puccini's choral music in Turandot always is the perfect expression of such vacillations.

Alone together for the first time, Calaf scolds Turandot for her cruelty and tears from her face a covering veil. She is furious. He threatens to kiss her. She repulses him but Calaf persists, seizes her, and kisses her passionately. Instantly her will dissolves. Distant voices of men, women, and boys, offstage, greet the dawn of a new day. Turandot cries her first ever tears and admits she feared the Unknown Prince the first moment she saw him. In his eyes she saw the certainty of his victory, both hating and loving him for it. Now that he has conquered her, she bids him to go and take his secret with him. No! He will have her and into her hands he places his life: "I am Calaf, son of Timur." (Calaf, by the way, now that the pronunciation of the title character has been resolved, is not pronounced KAY-luff but rather CAL-ahf.)

The scene changes. Outside the imperial palace, high on a staircase, the emperor is seen with his court, a huge crowd standing below. Turandot addresses him:

Noble Father,
I know the name of the stranger!

(and looking directly at Calaf only)

His name . . . is Love!

Calaf rushes to her, they embrace, and the happy crowd rejoices to a refrain from the famous *Nessun dorma* aria, just as Puccini had sketched it before he died, as they cover the lovers with flowers. The curtains close.

ᔐ

I know I will be criticized by sophisticated opera people for giving so much attention to Puccini. After all, isn't Verdi the greatest of all Italian opera composers? So why did I introduce only six operas by Verdi, who wrote more than two dozen, while representing ten of Puccini's twelve operas? And how do I justify including merely three operas by Rossini, a composer of gigantic genius, who wrote more than three dozen?

There are several reasons. First, I included those works of Rossini and Verdi you are most likely to initially encounter, all masterworks. Second, two wonderful operas of Puccini too often have suffered bad or unfavorable press. Both *The Girl of the Golden West* and *La rondine* are good, accessible, and entertaining operas, much, much better than the considerable nonsense I have seen written about them, including an article by one scholar who judged both "failures." I want you to give them a chance and to love them as much as I do. Nor do I want you to be misled by what you may read about *Suor Angelica*. Give it a chance as an essential ingredient within an ingenious triptych. I did not, at first, and I do not want you making my mistake. Again, I want you to like it as much as I do, my original coolness now long gone, all of which brings me to the most important reason for including almost all the Puccini operatic corpus.

During many years of introducing opera to students in my classes, and in producing more than fifteen hundred radio opera broadcasts, I know it is Puccini, more than any other composer, who repeatedly lures the neophyte into the incomparable world of opera, and that, above everything else, is what this book is about. All my life opera has nurtured and sustained me. It is a compulsion of mine to share it with you. I will do anything I can to eradicate misconceptions, to break down barriers, to eliminate any and all intimidations, and to entice you into its world of virtually endless marvels. I do not want you to live your life without opera. It is my intent and hope to convert you. Opera is one of the greatest and most emotional of all art forms and it is an art anyone who will give it a chance can enjoy. I want everyone to experience its wonder and I know, if armed with Puccini, I can make this happen. A rarity is one who can resist the master of operatic melody. And once within his grasp, the rest of the huge world of opera beckons.

Richard Strauss

GERMAN OPERA AFTER WAGNER: RICHARD STRAUSS

With the "Who after Verdi?" question resolved, it is time to ask after the other of the two most towering figures of nineteenth-century opera: "Who after Wagner?" When Wagner died in February 1883, Richard Strauss, the son of a famous horn player, was nineteen years old and a decade away from composing his first opera and, at this time, much too young and inexperienced with operatic composition ever to have assumed it would be he who would take the great tradition of German opera into the twentieth century.

There is no unanimity regarding the reputation of Richard Strauss as an opera composer. No one reasonably could doubt or seriously disagree over *Salome*, *Elektra*, and *Der Rosenkavalier (The Knight of the Rose)*, the three operas introduced in this chapter, which premiered one after the other beginning with *Salome* in 1905, and each is a masterpiece. But Strauss composed ten more operas after these early works and two before them, fifteen in all. There are eminent musicians and musicologists who claim few, if any, developments of either inventiveness or maturation are to be heard after *Der Rosenkavalier* in the operas written during the last thirty years of his life. Others, like the splendid conductor Wolfgang Sawallisch, consider Strauss the greatest opera composer of the twentieth century. Sawallisch finds throughout the operatic corpus of Strauss, as he has stated, "an eternal mystery in the opera scores of Strauss," and I am with Sawallisch. Richard Strauss fully perceived the controversy surrounding his work and his legendary response is one of music's most familiar tongue-in-cheek quotations: "I may not be a first-rate composer but I am a first-rate second-rate composer." Strauss, who lived eighty-five years, also said of himself, late in his life, that he had lived long enough to have been regarded a rebel as a young musician and a classic in his later years.

His father, Franz Strauss, was a prominent hornplayer, a conservative traditionalist, and an anti-Wagnerian. He played Wagner under this composer's directing but told him he did not like his music. In the Wagner-Brahms controversy (see chapter 7) he stood with Brahms, and it was in this classical vein that his musically precocious son was trained. Richard began piano lessons at age four and had written his first music at six. As a young man he, like his father, favored Brahms and teenage compositions reflect the influence. But then, while studying at the University of Munich in the early 1880s, he discovered Wagner and became infatuated with *Tristan und Isolde*.

His career was given a huge boost when Wagner's friend and disciple Hans von Bülow hired him as his assistant conductor. Von Bülow is credited with one of opera lore's most humorous anecdotes. As Richard Strauss's compositions developed from a Brahmsian influence through a Wagnerian impact unto the discovery of their own voice, at first often harsh and dissonant, von Bülow offered this opinion: "When it comes to Richard, I prefer Wagner and when it comes to Strauss, I prefer Johann."

The greatest single influence on his musical development, Strauss emphatically recognized, came from another Wagnerian, Alexander Ritter, a violinist married to Wagner's niece. In the tradition of Berlioz, Liszt, and Wagner, Ritter argued persuasively, "music is expression," and, as such, at times must express emotions and dramatic elements that are not beautiful. The purpose of music is not simply to shelter the listener from the realities of life by enclosing him in a cocoon of beautiful sound. Music must express the totality of the human experience from, one is tempted to say, its ecstasies to its agonies. And this Strauss explored in a series of masterful tone poems written during the decade between 1889 and 1899. They made him famous—and infamous. There is in this music great beauty and considerable inventiveness. Also to be heard are moments of what one hundred years ago struck uninitiated ears as painfully cacophonous, and critics protested.

Strauss's belief in music as an expression of reality, to cite but one example, prompted him to employ, in the orchestra, a wind machine to simulate the sound of windmills in his tone poem *Don Quixote*. And in this same composition he contrived, to the extreme displeasure of some listeners and the bemused delight of others, musical sounds to mimic sheep bleating. With the arrival of the twentieth century, Strauss was recognized as the most formidable force in contemporary music, and he had yet to compose the first of the three operatic masterpieces that would ensure his immortality.

Just as Puccini inherited the mantle of Italian opera from Verdi, Richard Strauss upheld the Wagnerian tradition in German opera. What did Strauss take from Wagner? The three basics were a commitment to the concept of music as a dramatic expression; the making of music from themes, or motifs, woven together and iterated and reiterated throughout an operatic score; and the employment of a gigantic orchestra capable of expressing diverse thoughts and feelings through a huge tapestry of sound. Strauss's first opera, *Guntram* (1894), was a failure and his second, *Feuersnot (The Need for Fire)*, fared only a little better in 1901. Then, on December 5, 1905, in Dresden, came *Salome*, one of the greatest, and most intensely loved and hated operas of the twentieth century, but unquestionably a masterpiece.

SALOME (1905)

Salome created an even greater storm of controversy around Strauss than did his tone poems. English censors forbade a production in their country, soon after the premiere, on the grounds of its "immorality," and at the Metropolitan Opera in 1907 the work was withdrawn after one performance, its licentiousness having created a scandal. More than twenty-five years would pass before the second Met performance greeted the opera's return with applause and the once controversial subject matter with nonchalance. Today we, hardened by a century permitting virtually anything in the arts (including much having no artistic merit at all), find there is little, if anything, in *Salome* to shock or even mildly faze us. But in 1905 its overt neurotic sexuality stunned many, and puritans, in particular, maligned the composer—thus, as anyone could have predicted, vastly increasing both his notoriety and an interest in the opera.

In 1901, while in Berlin, Strauss had seen a production of

Oscar Wilde's play *Salomé* and instantaneously felt called to set it to music. Strauss used a translation into German (by Hedwig Lachmann) of Wilde's play for his libretto. His dramatic, powerful, sensuous, chilling music, in spite of English and American prudery, made the work a quick sensation in Germany and Austria. Wilde merely used the terse story of the beheading of John the Baptist (see Matt. xiv. 3ff and Mark vi. 17ff) as a starting point for embellishing biblical bare bones into a sordid tale of libidinous sexual desire and murder. This amending of scripture, this tampering with "biblical truth," enraged the faithful.

The events of the Bible's story are quite brief. King Herod married Herodias, the wife of his dead brother. John the Baptist accused Herod of incest, and Herodias deeply resented this. She retaliated by demanding that Herod imprison John and then kill him. Herod refused. During a birthday celebration for Herod, the daughter of Herodias, by her first husband, dances for the King in return for whatever she wants. The girl consults with her mother and to Herod's horror asks for the head of John the Baptist. Reluctant, yet bound by his oath, the King orders the execution, and the decapitated head is presented to the girl on a platter. She gives it to her mother.

The biblical account does not refer to the girl as Salome, but we will not enter into exegesis here. Salome she is in both play and opera and Wilde, in his play of 1893, alters her dramatically. In the Bible the girl is merely the instrument of her mother's revenge. In Wilde's play Salomé is possessed by sexual desire for the imprisoned John the Baptist and Herod is possessed by lust for his alluring stepdaughter. When the Evangel refuses Salome's advances, she uses Herod's lust for her as the means of her own revenge on John. Wilde wrote his play in French; thus, his Salomé is pronounced sal-oh-MAY. Strauss's opera is in German; thus his Salome is pronounced TZAL-oh-may.

The characters are:

HEROD ANTIPAS, Tetrarch of Judea, *tenor*
HERODIAS, wife of Herod, *mezzo-soprano*
SALOME, her daughter by her first husband, brother of Herod killed by his command to appease Herodias, *soprano*
JOKANAAN—the Greek name used by Wilde for John the Baptist, *baritone*

NARRABOTH, young captain of the guard who is in love
   with Salome, *tenor*
A Cappadocian, *bass*
A slave, *soprano or tenor*
Five Jews, *four tenors and one bass*
Two Nazarenes, *tenor and bass*
Two soldiers, *basses*
Page for Herodias, *contralto*

The time of the drama is about 30 AD and it takes place
in the palace of King Herod in Galilee.

The opera plays in one uninterrupted act of about one hour and
forty-five minutes, with the events of the drama appearing to transpire in real time. There are four scenes. I think of them as "The
Prophet;" "Salome;" "Salome and the Prophet;" and "The
Dance."

Without orchestral introduction, the curtain opens on a terrace
adjacent to the palace of King Herod, whose birthday is being celebrated by guests with much gaiety. A large cistern can be seen at
the back of the terrace. It is the middle of the night and all is lit
by a beautiful full moon. Narraboth, possessed by the beautiful
Salome (and we should think of her as still in her teens), stares at
her from afar. She is not yet on stage when the page comments on
the moon and then admonishes Narraboth to cease looking at the
young princess: "Something terrible may happen." And there we
have it, within the first few lines of dialogue!
   Two soldiers join them in commenting on what is taking place
in the banquet hall when, from the cistern, the resonant voice of
Jokanaan proclaims the coming of the Messiah. One soldier wants
to silence his ludicrous rantings but the other is fond of the holy
man, who hails from the desert and now is contained in the cistern by the Tetrarch with strict orders forbidding anyone to see
him. Narraboth, his gaze still on Salome, notices she has left the
table and is walking toward the terrace. Again, the page begs him
to cease staring.
   The second scene begins as an agitated Salome enters. She has
left the banquet table annoyed by crafty Egyptians, loathsome
Romans, and Jews bickering over theological matters. Perhaps,
above all, she is distressed because the Tetrarch, her mother's hus-

band, will not take his eyes from her. Nor can Narraboth, and once again, fearing something terrible will happen, the page gives his warning. Salome comments on the beautiful, chaste moon, then hears the voice of Jokanaan proclaim the coming of the Messiah. When she asks about the voice, she is told it is that of the prophet Jokanaan. Salome says the Tetrarch is afraid of this holy man who denounces her mother and she asks if he is an old man. A soldier informs her of the prophet's youthfulness and again the voice cries out speaking in an arcane manner. Intrigued, Salome asks to speak with him but the soldiers insist it has been forbidden by the Tetrarch for anyone to see or talk with the prophet. Her curiosity will not be quelled. She approaches the cistern, peers into its intimidating blackness, and, wildly, demands to see the prophet. When the soldiers refuse, and the page reiterates foreboding, Salome prevails upon Narraboth's preoccupation with her until he relents and orders Jokanaan be brought forth from the cistern. With the arrival of the prophet, the third scene begins.

Strauss's music, to this point of the drama, has been wonderfully expressive and descriptive of what has been said by the characters. There has not yet been heard, however, what one would call a famous excerpt or highlight. Like the Wagnerian dramas he so much admired, Strauss has not created what could be called set numbers; the music flows without stop and start. In this third scene, the encounter of the princess with the prophet is a prolonged, tremendously captivating duet and one of extraordinary musical contrasts. Salome's music tends toward an angular sharpness of edges while Jokanaan's is resonant and round. Rather consistently throughout the drama, the music associated with Salome, her mother, and her stepfather has a fractured, frenetic quality contrasting with the solid, sustained accompaniments to the prophet's proclamations.

As he climbs out of the cistern, as the third scene begins, the prophet abstractly castigates first a man and then a woman, taken by Salome to be her mother. Salome looks at him and finds him both terrible and fascinating. His eyes, she thinks, are like black caves in which dragons dwell and his body, tall and thin, like an ivory statue, seems chaste as the moon. Her preoccupation with the prophet is upsetting Narraboth, who begs her to depart. Now, however, she draws even closer to Jokanaan, who demands she be taken away. Salome tells him who she is and he curses this daughter of Babylon and her wanton mother. Salome, transfixed by his voice, asks him what she should do and is told to cover her face with a veil and to seek the Son of Man in the desert. The evocative duet of this scene intensifies as Salome openly acknowledges "Jokanaan! I am in love with your body," and, rapturously, she describes how wonderfully appealing it is. When Jokanaan responds by repulsing her, ordering her not to speak to him, she angrily denounces his body as hideous. It is his hair she loves and an exotic description of it, hanging like black grapes, then follows, ending with her request to touch his hair. A second time he repulses her and she retorts by telling him his hair is horrible. It is his mouth she desires. Her description, both sensuous and erotic, culminates with the embodying words of the entire drama:

Lass mich ihn küssen deinen Mund.

Let me kiss your mouth.

With a soft, horrified whisper he protests "Never!" Well, we'll see. This is a girl with a fixation. Twice she repeats herself, "I will kiss your mouth, Jokanaan." All this being too much for Narraboth, he inserts himself between princess and prophet and stabs himself to death. As Jokanaan continues to denounce and curse Salome, she says nothing other than that she will kiss his mouth, reiterated nine times in all before the disgusted prophet descends back into his cistern. With his exit the third scene, or episode, is over.

Salome's celebrated "Dance of the Seven Veils," both musically and dramatically, propels the drama to its gruesome conclusion. An orchestral interlude connects the third and fourth scenes. Herod, followed by his guests, has come onto the terrace in search of Salome, who ignored his command to return to the banquet. He finds her and Herodias rebukes her husband for his preoccupation with her daughter. He gazes at the moon, commenting on how it has the look of a madwoman. Herodias suggests they go back inside but Herod, who has decided to move the party outdoors, refuses, slips in the blood of Narraboth, and orders the corpse be removed. He begins to hear things like the beating of vast wings in the wind. Herodias hears nothing. Thinking him ill, again, she bids them go inside. Herod says he's fine. It is Salome, whom he notes is pale, who looks ill. Herodias repeats her demand not to look constantly at her daughter. Herod, ignoring her, calls for wine and commences to woo his stepdaughter, first offering her wine, then fruit, and finally inviting her to take her mother's seat next to him. By polite terse replies, with each bidding, Salome informs him she lacks thirst, hunger, and wishes not to sit.

The prophet's voice rings out. Herodias, taking his words as a personal insult, wants him silenced and taunts her husband for being afraid of his prisoner. Herod denies fear of any man. Herodias wants her husband to give Jokanaan to the Jews. Herod refuses. Jokanaan is a prophet, a holy man who has seen God.

This comment stimulates a curious and intriguing segment in the drama, a hiatus in the action, wherein five Jews enter into an investigation as to who or what is a prophet. Their quibbling annoys Herodias, who wants them silenced, but Herod perpetuates the discussion, all taking place to an ingenious musical accompaniment. Again the voice of Jokanaan announces the arrival of the savior of the world. When Herod questions what this means, a Nazarene emphatically proclaims the Messiah has come, evidence being in the many miracles this savior has accomplished. Jokanaan's voice denounces the daughter of Babylon and a riled Herodias assumes he means her. She demands her husband silence the voice from the cistern. Herod changes the subject with a critical request: *Tanz für mich, Salome* ("Dance for me, Salome").

Herodias will not let her daughter dance, nor does Salome desire to do so. Herod, possessed by the girl's beauty, persists in offering her anything she wants if she will dance for him. Salome becomes interested and asks Herod if he will swear an oath to give her whatever she requests. This he vows upon his life, his crown, and his gods. Ignoring her mother's injunctions, Salome consents. Her "Dance of the Seven Veils," the only operatic striptease I know of, is the most popular music in the entire score, often removed without the choreography to the concert hall. During the nearly ten minutes of this lavish, erotic music, Salome dances before Herod enticingly removing one veil after another. When the opera was still young, some Salomes would slip into the gathered guests to hide while a professional dancer performed. A tradition eventually developed in which some sopranos portraying Salome would do the dance. The vocal demands given to Butterfly by Puccini far exceed the ability and training of most every teenage soprano and so it is with Salome, another teen, who after her demanding dance must deliver one of the greatest monologues in opera. Hers is a taxing role. Vocal stamina is essential and how many sopranos can really dance? And how many sopranos have the figure to bring Herod to feverish lust as the veils are removed? In fact, I know of only a few performances where all seven veils are totally removed.

One of them is a performance in 2004 that achieved significant attention because the Finnish soprano Karita Mattila is magnificent. The production, however, is absurd in moving the biblical setting forward to the 1930's and dressing Salome, for her celebrated dance, in a Marlene Dietrich look-alike pants suit that,
along with its accoutrements, needs the assistance of supernu-
meraries to remove. If contemporary producers think this is the
only way to fill seats in an opera house I gladly yield mine. Such
travesties make me livid. I agree with conductors Herbert von
Karajan and Erich Leinsdorf who could not tolerate the prevalent
tendencies to modernize operas. Such tampering often completely destroys the intended meaning of a work of art. The best book
on the subject that I know is *Opera and Its Symbols* by Robert
Donington where, among numerous other perceptive insights, he
writes

> A director who claims that the work in question
> is no more than the raw material for his own self-
> expression is the victim of a narcissistic delusion
> . . . Experimental productions on some occasions,
> yes, perhaps; but not to the exclusion of ordinary
> productions. I am all in favor of a lunatic fringe,
> but not of a lunatic core. There is altogether too
> much of this fashionable gimmickry going on at
> present for my piece of mind. It is, I fancy just a
> little sick. †

Donington's book was published in 1990 and regretfully the sick-
ness has spread. It is critically important that one's first experience with an opera be with an "ordinary production" and not one
of the "lunatic fringe."

Consider the Salome of the American soprano Maria Ewing. An
exceedingly attractive singer, actress and dancer, she gives a brilliant performance of *Salome* on the 1992 video of a live performance with the Royal Opera Covent Garden in England, by the way
the first to ban the opera in its early years. To choreography by
Elizabeth Keen, Ewing performs an intoxicating dance to Strauss's

---

† Robert Donington, *Opera & Its Symbols* (New Haven: Yale University Press,
1990), p. 16

music taunting both the occupant of the cistern, if he dare look up at her, and the lascivious Tetrarch. The dance ends with the removal of the seventh veil as Salome stands, arms stretching above her head, beneath the moon before falling to the floor and rolling over to Herod's feet. Maria Ewing is one hundred percent in her birthday suit as the dance concludes, and a magnificent suit it is, too! Herod concurs. "Ah! Magnificent!" are his first words, then he asks Salome what it is she desires.

On a silver platter she wants brought to her

Den Kopf des Jochanaan.

The head of Jokanaan.

Herod is horrified; Herodias is pleased. Herod thinks Salome has asked this as revenge for her mother. Salome makes it clear she desires the prophet's head for her own pleasure and she reminds Herod of his oath. Nevertheless, he makes attempts to lure her into accepting anything else up to " . . . half of my kingdom." Herod offers Salome the largest emerald in the world, his flock of prized peacocks, and, finally, jewels galore. In each instance Salome wears him down, refusing with a terse and emphatic "Give me the head of Jokanaan." Beaten, Herod reluctantly capitulates and the executioner descends into the cistern.

Here begins the famous and chilling culmination of the drama, the episode in which Salomes make it or break it. Through the years, numerous great sopranos have put themselves into the history books with their portrayal of the deranged and sexually obsessed princess. To cite only a few—Olive Fremsted, Ljuba Welitch, Birgit Nilsson, and Maria Ewing—I know does an injustice to many others omitted.

As Herodias congratulates her daughter and Herod utters a fear of misfortune Salome creeps over to the cistern and listens. Hearing nothing, she fears the executioner has lost his will and she summons the page to get soldiers to do as she has asked. As she demands the prophet's head for the eighth time, the powerful arm of the executioner rises above the top of the cistern to deliver the severed head upon a silver shield. Salome seizes it. She is ecstatic:

You would not let me kiss your mouth, Jokanaan!
Well, I will kiss it now . . .

and, fondling the head as she sings to it, Salome repeats the very same themes of her first meeting with the prophet: the "terrible eyes" but now they are shut, "the voice" saying nothing now, the once ivory body, and the black, black hair. But her passion is for the "red mouth" and she will, as she has repeatedly vowed, kiss it. She does. Herod is disgusted, Herodias proud, and Salome, noting a bitter taste, assumes it is the prophet's blood. Triumphantly she declares, "Jokanaan, I have kissed your mouth." As moonbeams cover Salome in chaste, white light, Herod orders to his soldiers, "Kill that woman!" They obey by rushing to Salome and crushing her to death beneath their shields as the curtain falls.

In 1905, *Salome* was both shocking and intriguing. Dramatic realism had never reached an operatic presentation as evocative as this. Strauss had made a masterpiece with his third opera in setting Wilde's grim exploration of unnatural desires, or, perhaps, as both the play and the opera intimate, those passions and urges our conscious minds deem unnatural while, in fact, they fester below the surface within us all. As so often is the case, it is the artists who are the prophets of a new age, and Wilde's play and Strauss's opera were in the forefront of the growing fascination with human psychology, the First International Congress of Psycho-Analysis with Adler, Freud, Jung and others being held in 1908.

In his next musical drama, *Elektra* (1909), Richard Strauss would take another giant step into exploring psychological realities often expressed in weird, eerie, and dissonant sounds, nonetheless powerful and convincing. On this occasion the text, after the ancient Greek story, is by the gifted poet Hugo von Hofmannsthal. It was the first of six remarkable collaborations. Theirs would become one of the supreme associations of poet and musician in opera history.

ELEKTRA (1909)

At the dawn of the twentieth century, Puccini and Strauss were the dominant figures of operatic composition. It is fascinating to experience the vast difference between them, Puccini hanging on to the long and beloved tradition of Italian opera as melody and Strauss, at least in *Salome* and *Elektra*, pushing traditional Western music to the limits of avant-garde expressionism. If you would like to hear the difference, compare scores of theirs premiering about the same time: Puccini's *Madama Butterfly* (1904) with

Strauss's *Salome* (1905) and Puccini's *Girl of the Golden West* (1910) with Strauss's *Elektra* (1909). The contrast is not only extraordinary but also indicative of problems some people have in listening to new music.

These two works of Strauss, both brutal, evocative musical portrayals of human heads and hearts possessed by abnormal desires, lack the captivating melodic surge of Puccini's scores. Accordingly, opera neophytes, and, indeed, even many seasoned opera lovers, much prefer Puccini's operas over those of Strauss. Many ears simply are not accustomed to his new, often cacophonous sounds.

With Strauss you have reached the other end of the operatic musical spectrum. Recall how I said, many pages ago in chapter 1, that ears unacquainted with early operatic composition may find seventeenth-century music sterile, unemotional, and even boring. It is a matter of getting accustomed to unfamiliar sounds, and the only way to do this is to listen, to give the music a chance. And so it is with these demanding works of Richard Strauss. They must be given a chance and, who knows, you may be one of those who become smitten, counting *Salome* and *Elektra* among your favorite works. I happen to like twentieth-century music. The dissonance does not bother me. In fact, often I like to sit at our piano just to play with all different kinds of sounds, some melodic and harmonious, others harsh and discordant. My ears enjoy this. And my ears were enthralled, first note to last, when I heard my first broadcast of *Elektra* many, many years ago. I was driving with my wife from Boston to Ohio to visit relatives. It was the Saturday afternoon of a Metropolitan Opera broadcast. I knew a famous excerpt from Kirsten Flagstad's famous recording of *Elektra's* recognition scene but had never heard a complete performance of this opera. As we drove along the highway, I was mesmerized by the dramatic power of this music, which ended moments before our arrival. I was exhausted—not from driving, but from intense listening.

The opera *Elektra* tells of an event in the ancient Greek myth of the House of Atreus, rulers in Mycenae over the kingdom of Argos. This doomed family could not rid itself of a divine curse as one disaster followed another. For example, Agamemnon was King when the Trojan War began and as he sailed toward Troy his fleet was becalmed by the goddess Artemis who had a bone to pick with the King. Agamemnon learned his only hope lay in sacrificing his daughter Iphigenia to the goddess, a terrible act for which his wife, Clytemnestra, would never forgive him. While he was at war, she took a lover, Aegistheus. Together, they killed Agamemnon in his bath just after his return home.

Agamemnon and Clytemnestra had other children: the sisters Elektra and Chrysothemis and their brother, Orestes, whose fate it was to avenge his father's murder. The opera is about the sisters, subjugated by their mother, awaiting the revenge on her by their brother.

All three of the great Greek tragedians, Aeschylus, Sophocles, and Euripides, made plays out of the Atreus myth but it was the drama of Sophocles, in which mental depravity is most intense, that appealed to Hofmannsthal when he was invited to make a modern adaptation. Strauss, who had met the poet once, saw a performance of Hofmannsthal's version on a trip to Berlin and obtained the rights for an opera. Their first collaboration premiered on January 25, 1909, in Dresden.

Both *Salome* and *Elektra* are in one long act of an hour and three quarters. Salome's four scenes represent four major events in the drama, but the scenes play without an intervening curtain. *Elektra* has no scenes designated in the libretto but scholars have long agreed it is a play consisting of seven distinct segments or episodes. They are:

1. We meet Elektra and learn of the reason for her wrath.
2. We meet her sister, Chrysothemis, who is quite different.
3. We meet Clytemnestra and learn of her torment.
4. Elektra contemplates revenge with Chrysothemis.
5. Orestes arrives.
6. The famous recognition scene occurs.
7. Revenge is exacted.

The characters and their vocal ranges are:

ELEKTRA, daughter of Clytemnestra, *soprano*
CHRYSOTHEMIS, her sister, *soprano*
ORESTES, their brother, *baritone*
Tutor of Orestes, *bass*
CLYTEMNESTRA, widow of Agamemnon, *mezzo-soprano*
Confidant of Clytemnestra, *soprano*
Trainbearer of Clytemnestra, *soprano*
AEGISTHEUS, lover of Clytemnestra, *tenor*

Young servant, *tenor*
Old servant, *bass*
Overseer, *soprano*
Five maidservants, *one contralto, two mezzo-sopranos,*
   and two sopranos

The story takes place in Mycenae, Greece, in ancient
times. It will be elucidated in accord with the seven basic
episodes as outlined above.

1. Elektra's Wrath

The orchestra declares a somber mood with a handful of notes and
within fifteen seconds of the opening curtain the singing begins as
the five maids, in the inner court of the palace of Mycenae, are
gathering water from the well. Elektra is the subject of their conversation. They wonder where she is and when she will commence to wail for her father. Elektra appears, bounding like an
animal in a hallway, and the maids comment on how like a wild
beast she is. She is hated and pitied, in turn, by the maids except
for the fifth one. She loves Elektra, who has been reduced by her
mother and her lover to live, eat, and howl with the dogs. The
overseer enters, adds a few disparaging comments regarding Elektra's deranged behavior, and conducts the maids into the house,
where, it can be heard, four of them beat the fifth because of her
compassion.

Elektra emerges from the house into the empty court. Her first
words, *Allein! Weh, ganz allein!* ("Alone, O woe is me, all alone"),
begin a powerful monologue lamenting the murder of her father,
which she recounts in graphic detail, by her mother and her lover,
who now sleep together in the royal bed. She speaks, in this great
scene, to her father, Agamemnon, promising him his three children will avenge the crime of his death by sending Clytemnestra
and Aegistheus to their graves. Only then will they dance the
dance of royal triumph around his grave.

2. Chrysothemis Is Not Like Her Sister

Chrysothemis appears and awakens her sister from her vengeful
reverie. She has the more dominant vocal part in this episode,
which consists primarily of a dialogue between Agamemnon's
daughters. Elektra is intent on revenge; the more moderate
Chrysothemis warns that other terrible events will occur if they
do not desist. Chrysothemis feels, within her breast, the heat of

love, the desire for husband and children, and she cannot continue to endure the living death of being possessed, like her sister, by the need for revenge. A commotion within the house alerts both to the probability of Clytemnestra's arrival in the courtyard. Chrysothemis has heard that her mother has been tormented by a dream, and she wants no part in hearing it. She urges her sister to join her in departing, but Elektra is intent on confronting their mother.

3. The Torment of Clytemnestra

The orchestral tumult introducing Clytemnestra throbs with weird, dissonant sounds, not as jolting to our ears, conditioned by nearly a century of "modern" music, but surely testing to those reared on the melodies and harmonies of the nineteenth century. The superstar who created the role of Clytemnestra was such a one who had her sincere doubts. She was the incomparable Austrian (and later American) contralto Ernestine Schumann-Heink, famous for her Wagnerian roles but remarkably impressive in roles by Verdi and Donizetti, among others. You may hear her rich, powerful, deep voice on historic recordings mastered onto compact discs. Her dominating stage presence lasted into her seventies. She sang the role of Clytemnestra at the premiere but afterward said, "Never again." She believed Wagner had taken the human singing voice to its absolute limits, and with Elektra, Strauss had gone too far. "I will never sing the role again. It was frightful. We were a set of madwomen." Today, of course, with the softening of time passing, there are dramatic mezzo-sopranos and contraltos who would kill to get an opportunity to portray Clytemnestra in a major house with a great orchestra.

I have mentioned Strauss's love affair with the soprano voice. Clytemnestra can be portrayed by a mezzo-soprano (more common today) or by a contralto. In either case, it is the dominance of the female voice continuing as mother and daughter face each other.

Clytemnestra knows her daughter hates her. The feeling is mutual except Clytemnestra also is afraid of Elektra. Before Clytemnestra enters she can be seen through a window approaching the courtyard. In spite of flamboyant clothes and jewelry, she looks pale, tired, tortured. To the approval of her confidante and trainbearer, she deplores Elektra's treatment of her, then, wishing to hear no more from her underlings, dismisses them to stand face to face in the courtyard with her animal-like daughter. She now needs Elektra, who, perhaps, is the only one who can provide a remedy for the bad dreams tormenting her nights. She wants to know who sends the terrible dreams, whose blood must flow to rid her of such anguish. Elektra answers ambiguously: "When the appointed victim falls under the ax, then you will dream no more!" Clytemnestra interprets this to mean a consecrated beast must be sacrificed. Elektra corrects her. It will be "a woman." Perhaps one of her maids, or a child, or a virgin? Clytemnestra speculates, but we know.

Next, she wonders how she is to make the sacrifice. Elektra tells her only a man can do it. "Aegistheus?" Clytemnestra wonders, and in the only joke of this grim drama, Elektra answers, laughing, "I said a man!" Clytemnestra presses on and is told the man will be a stranger but also one from the household.

She completely misses the point of her daughter's riddles even when Elektra follows with a critical question, "Will you let my brother come home?" Clytemnestra reminds her she is forbidden to speak of her brother; nevertheless, Elektra accuses her mother of sending money to those caring for Orestes as payment for killing him. Furthermore, she declares her mother lives in dread of the return of Orestes, who is alive and, she predicts, is going to come home. Clytemnestra claims not to be worried; she has armed guards enough to protect her. Once more she attempts to learn from Elektra whose blood must flow to release her from nightmares. Like a wild animal, Elektra springs at her mother.

> What blood? Blood from your own neck . . .

and she recites a description of the murder of Clytemnestra, who, terrified, attempts to run off but is held fast by the ranting Elektra:

> Then you will dream no more . . .

Eye to eye they stand, Elektra intoxicated with hatred, Clytemnestra horrified until the spell is broken as her confidante comes to her and maids with torches light the darkened courtyard. Into her ear alone the confidante gives a message that brings immediately unto Clytemnestra relief and joy. She rushes into the house with her entourage.

4. The Sisters Contemplate Revenge
For only a moment is Elektra left alone in the courtyard before

Chrysothemis, howling in agony, rushes in to exclaim, "Orestes is dead!" Elektra will not accept this at first, yet it seems as if her sister knows how and where the horses of Orestes dragged him to his death, news apparently confirmed by the voice of a young servant demanding a mount so he may ride out to the field to inform Aegistheus. Accordingly, Elektra calls on her sister to help her attain revenge. Alone, she is not strong enough. With the ax by which their father was murdered, together they, this very day or night, will kill their mother and her husband. Elektra praises the strength of her sister but Chrysothemis begs Elektra to use her wits to help them escape this dreadful house. Elektra demands that her sister swear to help her. Chrysothemis cannot. She runs into the house, away from Elektra's curses.

5. The Arrival of Orestes

Alone again in the courtyard Elektra, on all fours, digs about like an animal. She then notices, in the last rays of sunlight, the figure of a stranger standing by the courtyard gate. It is a man. He enters the courtyard. Elektra tries to dismiss him but he declares he must wait to deliver to the lady of the house the message of the death of her son, Orestes. The tender feelings expressed by Elektra alert the stranger to ask who she is; could her emotions derive from being of the same blood as the deceased father and son? Indeed, she responds, "Elektra is my name." The stranger now is willing to reveal the truth: Orestes is alive. Who is this man? Elektra wonders, and asks just before male servants run in, drop down, and kiss his hands and feet. "The dogs in the yard know me but my sister does not?" says Orestes.

6. The Recognition Scene

One reason it can be exhausting to experience this drama is that there is so little relief from intensity. The vocal score associated with threatening events quite understandably expresses terror, horror, and hostility. To this point the loving, lyrical voice has been absent. Thus, all the more lovely it is when we finally hear it. Elektra recognizes her long lost brother. "Orestes!" she repeats four times, beginning the tremendous release of feelings in the glorious recognition scene. She realizes he must be stunned by her changed appearance, the mere shadow of what once she was, and together they recognize what must be done by himself alone as ordained. Orestes makes it clear to her. Elektra is overcome with happiness as the old tutor of Orestes steps into the courtyard to tell him the time has come. Elektra's monologue of recognition is the most famous music in the opera.

7. Revenge
Once again Elektra is left alone as Orestes and the tutor enter the house. Excited almost beyond restraint, she awaits the shriek that will tell her Clytemnestra has been slaughtered. It comes, piercing the walls of the house to resound in the courtyard. Maids, alarmed by the scream, race to get men to help them but Elektra bars the door. Then, hearing and fearing the voice of Aegistheus, they scatter. Elektra runs up to him with a torch to light his way. He wonders where are the men bearing news of the death of Orestes; can such good news really be true? Elektra dances about as she lights his way to the door, bidding he enter to be with those looking for him.

He goes in. Silence at first, then noises, then Aegistheus screaming for help at the window. "Can no one hear me?" he cries out. "Agamemnon hears you!" Elektra replies as he is pulled from sight. Chrysothemis runs into the courtyard to Elektra exclaiming the revenge wrought by their brother. Voices rejoice and proclaim his return as Elektra now dances in unrestrained jubilation, her swirling becoming more and more wild in an increasingly uninhibited madness until her wracked body and spirit can endure no more. She collapses. Chrysothemis rushes to her, then realizes her sister is dead. Calling "Orestes! Orestes!" she runs to the palace door and pounds on it.

The orchestra has the last word as the curtain falls on one of the most overwhelming scenes in opera.

Strauss would go no further into the world of avant-garde music. Indeed, with his next opera, *Der Rosenkavalier*, he and Hofmannsthal would re-create the world of Vienna in the mid-eighteenth century with glorious lyricism and lilting waltzes. That opera remains their most popular collaboration and one of the most endearing and enduring composed in the twentieth century.

DER ROSENKAVALIER (1911)
The Knight of the Rose

Almost a year after the premiere of *Elektra*, Hofmannsthal wrote to Strauss about an idea for a completely original libretto. It would become *Der Rosenkavalier*, a libretto so astonishingly creative and brilliant it would work convincingly without music. But when Strauss first saw the draft for Act I he was ecstatic. *Der Rosenkavalier* became their unequivocal masterpiece. Strauss's only concern, in the early stages, was whether the story was "a little too subtle, perhaps, for the general public . . ." Hofmannsthal was not worried. He wrote back, "Your fear lest the work should prove too subtle does not disturb me. The progress of the action is simple and intelligible enough for even the most unsophisticated public . . . "

Well, not so for me—not, at least, when I was eleven years old and saw *Der Rosenkavalier* for the first time. The subtlety in this story of a grotesque, fat old suitor for the hand of a beautiful young girl who loses her to the young gentleman he appoints to deliver a silver rose to her on his behalf was missed by me. I recall liking aspects of the first act, then becoming lost and not getting back into the opera until near the end. In short, *Der Rosenkavalier* was one of two operas that did not work magic on me when first I saw it (*The Mikado* was the other, as was already mentioned in chapter 11).

The magic soon was forthcoming, however, and never as a teacher did I offer an opera course without including *Der Rosenkavalier*. In one such course I recall a student who at first also had her reservations about the opera. She was in my freshman seminar, an introduction to opera for college students who knew nothing about the subject but who wanted to learn. This lovely young woman from a conservative family and community in the American heartland was, to employ the vernacular of college students, "grossed out" by an opera opening in the boudoir of a married, thirty-year-old woman deeply involved in passionate love-making with a teenage boy. I was barely able to keep her enough involved with the opera to go through it once. I suggested she study the drama toward the end of producing a paper on what was wrong with the story and why. Reluctantly, she went to work. The opera won her over, or, I should say, the Marschallin (the wife of a field marshal), the woman having the affair with the youth, won her over. To her surprise and mine, the student's paper was entirely sympathetic to the Marschallin and supported her less than conventional behavior.

Hofmannsthal's Marschallin, one of the most intriguing women in all opera, cannot fail to gain the heart of anyone who reflects with empathy on the ephemeral nature of the human condition. What is there about this woman who could inspire the empathy of a student whose upbringing did not brook a married women having an affair, especially with a teenage boy? The answer is in the music Strauss found for Hofmannsthal's telling poetry, even though its most intriguing character, the Marschallin, after dominating the first act, does not appear in Act II or in the first part of the third act.

The drama is in three acts. The characters and their voice ranges are:

> PRINCESS VON WERDENBERG (the Feldmarschallin), known
>   as the Marschallin, *soprano*
> OCTAVIAN, a young nobleman of the Rofrano family,
>   *mezzo-soprano*
> BARON OCHS AUF LERCHENAU, relative of the Marschallin, *bass*
> HERR VON FANINAL, a wealthy parvenu, *baritone*
> SOPHIE, his daughter, *soprano*
> MARIANNE LEITMETZERIN, Sophie's duenna, *soprano*
> VALZACCHI, an Italian intriguer, *tenor*
> ANNINA, his partner, *contralto*
> Police officer, *bass*
> MARSCHALLIN'S MAJOR-DOMO, *tenor*
> FANINAL'S MAJOR-DOMO, *tenor*
> Lawyer, *bass*
> Innkeeper, *tenor*
> Italian tenor, *tenor*
> Four children, *sopranos*
> Four waiters, *one tenor and three basses*
> Four servants of the Marschallin, *two tenors and two*
>   *basses*
> Dressmaker, *soprano*
> Animal seller, *tenor*
>
> *Nonspeaking Parts*
> MAHOMET, the Marschallin's page
> Flute player
> Hairdresser
> Scholar
> A noble widow

It takes place in Vienna during the reign of Maria Theresia, about the middle of the eighteenth century.

Most of the characters in the large cast have minor parts. The orchestra required for the score also is very large and plays a major role. Because *Der Rosenkavalier* is a comedy, much of the humor is in the words. Accordingly, the orchestra cannot obliterate them and yet, at other times, the score calls for a full, rich, lush sound. The conductor, therefore, must be attuned to all such nuances. Richard Strauss, also a famous maestro, often conducted his own operas but rarely did he do so with *Der Rosenkavalier*. When a music critic asked him why, Strauss quipped: "It is very difficult to conduct." The libretto also has its demands because it is replete with extensive stage directions and considerable dialogue. You can acquire the basics of the plot of *Der Rosenkavalier* and then give in to the music to do the rest. This is the most common approach. To experience the humor, the subtlety, and the remarkable way words and music work together to tell their story demands you take the time to study the libretto by reading it carefully. A good video with subtitles is an excellent preparation. You will be greatly rewarded for your homework.

Act I

Always I think of the brief orchestral introduction preceding the opening of the Act I curtain as an instrumental love song conveying in its luscious phrases the aftermath of a passionate night of lovemaking but, of course, surely this is because I know the story so well. What this music would suggest to one hearing it in the abstract, knowing nothing of the opera, I do not know but I would imagine cozy, warm, and romantic feelings are likely. Scholars have written about the two major musical themes. One, they claim, represents Octavian's boyish fervor, the other the full-bodied and full-blooded sensuousness of the much experienced Marschallin.

Whatever was intended by Strauss, the music perfectly suits the erotic scene greeting us as the curtain opens in her boudoir. She is lolling on her bed in the quiet bliss of a consummated love affair while her husband is away. Octavian kneels at her bedside. His is a trouser role: A mezzo-soprano female is portraying a boy about seventeen years old. Trouser roles are unusual in twentieth-century opera and I recall showing a video of this scene to a class, some members of which instantly misinterpreted what they were seeing as a sophisticated, contemporary opera on lesbian love.

Touching tenderly, Octavian and the Marschallin talk of their love for each other, using private, endearing nicknames. Sunlight pours through an open window and Octavian, with words reminiscent of Wagner's *Tristan und Isolde*, praises night and condemns daytime, when he must then share his beloved with others. He closes the window and draws shut the curtains. A tinkling sound is heard. Octavian hides sword and self as Mahomet, a black page with silver bells on his attire, enters with a salver, sets it on a table, bows to the Marschallin, and dances out, all without a word. Octavian emerges from hiding and sits next to the Marschallin, and they take their breakfast. Her concern drifts to thoughts of her husband and his return, which, she fears, is imminent as she hears a disturbance in the antechamber. Octavian hides behind the curtains as the Marschallin goes to listen at her door, there to discover the voice she has heard is not her husband's but rather that of her cousin Baron Ochs auf Lerchenau.

Octavian reappears disguised as a chambermaid in an interesting turn of events—a woman disguised to portray a man now is a "man" disguised as a woman. No wonder Hofmannsthal's original description of his libretto was "a comedy for music." The Marschallin wants Octavian to slip out, but before he can do so, the ill-mannered baron bursts into the room unannounced, bumping into the chambermaid. Octavian busies "herself" with making the bed while Baron Ochs divides his attention between ogling and flirting with the maid and informing the Marschallin of his impending marriage to the beautiful young daughter, and only child, of the extremely wealthy and not too healthy Herr von Faninal. In a matter of moments, Ochs has revealed himself as a boorish fortune hunter with eyes for every pretty face and figure crossing his path. He is aptly named. *Ochs* is German for an ox, a bull, or a bullock and, figuratively, a duffer, or blockhead. If anyone is to be made a fool of during the course of the drama, he is a likely candidate.

As Mariandel (Octavian) serves Ochs chocolates, the baron propositions her, alternately talking to the Marschallin about whom he should depute as his ambassador to present, according to the noble aristocratic custom, a silver rose to his bride-to-be. They are interrupted by the major-domo, who announces a long list of those waiting to see the Marschallin, as Ochs continues his overt pursuit of the chambermaid. When mildly rebuked by the Marschallin for behavior unbecoming a man about to be married, Ochs boasts of his constant quest in a monologue and then asks the Marschallin to give him the pretty chambermaid as a servant for his wife-to-be. The Marschallin orders Mariandel to show the baron a miniature of Octavian, and asks if such a one would make a suitable ambassador for the presentation of the rose. The baron agrees, noting instantly the similarity between the face in the miniature, that of the Marschallin's young cousin Count Octavian, and that of the chambermaid.

Mariandel is dismissed and the long parade of callers is finally admitted. They are the attorney, the chef with his kitchen boy, a milliner, a scholar, a pet salesman with miniature dogs and a monkey, Valzacchi and Annina, a needy aristocratic mother and her three fatherless daughters, and, a tenor and a flautist. They, of course, all want something: The chef needs menus, the milliner attempts to sell hats, the pet salesman shows off some animals, Valzacchi reads trashy news items from a scandal sheet, the fatherless children need money, etcetera. The flautist plays a cadenza, the Marschallin's hairdresser, with assistant, enters and sets up shop, and, finally, the Italian tenor sings an aria, *Di rigori armato*, about how he was captivated by love. It is one of the most anticipated hits of the entire score. (With this one glorious aria, the part of the Italian tenor is over. He arrives, sings, and soon thereafter is gone. The famous tenor Luciano Pavarotti has made cameo appearances portraying the Italian tenor, always to the great delight of the audience.)

Meanwhile, Baron Ochs discusses his marriage contract with the attorney. The flautist steps forth and offers another cadenza. The tenor counters with another verse about love, which is interrupted by the baron shouting his demands. The Marschallin can endure these trivialities no more. She asks the major-domo to dismiss them all. Valzacchi and Annina, however, linger, sidle up to the baron, and ingratiate themselves to his desire to employ their help in his lust for Mariandel. Ochs leaves the silver rose with the Marschallin and leaves. All now have gone.

The Marschallin, alone briefly, reflects on the ways of the world and the transience of life. She picks up her hand mirror. Soon she will be old, and she cannot bear the agony of watching herself age. She, too, like Ochs's bride-to-be, once was a girl forced into a loveless marriage of convenience. The pensive and evocative finale to the first act has begun, a profound contrast in mood to the mundane madness preceding it. The dignity of the Marschallin, a woman of extraordinary introspection and humanity, has begun to change drastically the mind and emotions of my student whose off-the-cuff reaction to the story was harsh and insensitive. Octavian returns to find his beloved in a sad, contemplative mood. He attempts to cheer her with an embrace. "Do not hug too much," she exhorts him, moving away. "He who embraces too often holds nothing for long." She admonishes him to be gentle and good and not like all men, men like the field marshal and Baron Ochs. Octavian persists in his attempt to hold and comfort her but again the Marschallin frees herself:

> *Oh, sei Er gut, Quinquin . . .*

> Oh, be good, Quinquin [her loving nickname for him],
> I am in the mood when I perceive the weakness of
> all temporal things . . .

Hofmannsthal's poetry, vivid and terse, is too abstract for the teenager: Octavian does not comprehend. He now believes the Marschallin is rejecting him when she continues

> . . . Unto the bottom of my heart
> I know how one should hold nothing,
> how one can seize nothing,
> how all runs between the fingers,
> how all we grasp breaks apart,
> everything dwindling away like
> haze and dreams . . .

She realizes she must console this youth, who does not fathom that soon it will be he who leaves her. She comforts him in a great monologue, *Die Zeit im Grunde, Quinquin* ("Time in the long run, Quinquin"). She explains how we all live heedless of time passing quickly until, all of a sudden, we become aware of nothing else. Hofmannsthal's penetrating poetry and the perfect fit of the music provided by Strauss always make me shiver. "Often I get up in the middle of the night to stop all the clocks," concludes the Marschallin, in a role coveted and interpreted by numerous great sopranos. For me, however, nothing compares to the 1933 recording by Lotte Lehmann. Her unequivocal musical greatness, the incomparable beauty of voice, and her utter pathos remain the measure for all others, before and after.

When told he will be the one who gives her up for a younger and more beautiful woman, Octavian remonstrates. She tells him he now must go. It is time for her to attend church and then call on an aged relative, an invalid nourished by her visits. He departs. Realizing she has forgotten to kiss him good-bye, the Marschallin sends her footmen to retrieve him, but Octavian has fled all too quickly. She calls for her page and instructs him to deliver the case containing Ochs's silver rose to Octavian. Placing her head deep in her hands, the curtain falls. Who in the audience cannot foresee the consequences when her seventeen-year-old lover presents the silver rose to the beautiful fifteen-year-old bride-to-be of the grotesque, middle-aged Baron Ochs?

Act II

The second act opens in a salon of Faninal's house. Both recently wealthy and ennobled, Faninal anticipates an even greater increase in his social status through the marriage of his daughter to Baron Ochs auf Lerchenau, with his aristocratic lineage of many generations. Faninal is leaving to get Ochs, who will be brought to meet Sophie after the presentation of the silver rose by the groom's ambassador. Decorum decrees that neither the father nor the groom is to be present when the bearer of the rose arrives. Lovely as all this sounds, the tradition of the presentation of a silver rose was pure invention by Hofmannsthal.

Sophie prays for humility as she awaits marriage into a distinguished noble family. Marianne, the duenna, spots the arrival of Octavian's carriage and is fascinated with the pomp, while Sophie is overcome by the beauty of the ceremony unfolding before her, especially when Octavian, dressed in silver and white, followed by his servants, enters with a silver rose. With halting speech, he presents it to Sophie on behalf of her future husband as a gift of love. She receives it and thanks him, and as they begin to converse formally, both seem to drift off into an intoxicating, timeless state in which each is aware only of the other. They sit down, and their conversation becomes more personal as they get acquainted. This rapidly growing mutual fascination is dashed on the rocks of reality when Faninal enters to introduce his daughter to her future husband.

Ochs is as ill-mannered as he was in barging into the Marschallin's boudoir. His presence infuriates Octavian and repulses Sophie, though Marianne attempts to assuage her. Ochs tries to place Sophie on his lap. She draws away. Ochs persists, Sophie rebuffs him, and Octavian fears doing something rash. Unflustered by such willfulness, which he deems is a good trait, Ochs sings of her eventual capitulation. This waltz, his signature tune, is one of the most familiar in the score (Richard Strauss has some fun with his namesake, Johann Strauss Jr., the celebrated Waltz King, in an imitation of his nineteenth-century Viennese waltz style anachronistically set one hundred years earlier). Oblivious to Sophie's disgust, the baron excuses himself to meet with the attorney, who has now arrived, over the real import of the marriage: the goods. He willingly leaves her in the company of Octavian, who immediately is asked for help. Sophie has determined not to marry Ochs under any circumstances. When the baron's servants start to flirt with Faninal's servant girls, they provoke a commotion, which empties the room. Now alone and overcome by mutual desire, Sophie and Octavian embrace and sing of their happiness. Their love duet is the most lyrical music of the second act.

During the duet, Valzacchi and Annina steal into the room to spy on the lovers. With the last note of their declarations, the pair leap from behind chairs and seize the couple while shouting for the baron. Now in his service, they, of course, expect a fee for what they now can reveal about his future wife. Ochs enters. Octavian informs him of Sophie's refusal. The baron, who will not accept this, attempts to take Sophie away. Octavian intervenes, showers insults—he calls the baron an unscrupulous fortune seeker—and challenges him to a duel. The baron laughs this off, dismissing Octavian as a spirited teenager, but, nevertheless, whistles for his servants. Again he attempts to shuttle Sophie away. Octavian advances toward him, sword drawn. Reluctantly the Baron unsheathes his and in a tiny skirmish is nicked. He howls and calls for a doctor and the police.

An ensemble commences. Sophie notes how everything seems to be going wrong, Faninal's servants ask countless questions about the fracas, Marianne notes it is, indeed, an unlucky day, Octavian holds Lerchenau's servants at bay, and thus turns their attention to calling for bandages, and the baron fears the sight of his own blood. Faninal enters. He becomes greatly distressed as he discovers what has happened to Ochs, and becomes more so when Sophie declares she will not be married to such an oaf. Faninal is furious. He calls Sophie names, threatens to send her to a convent, and has a fine wine brought to Ochs, who vows he will avenge the wound delivered by Octavian.

As the wine gradually begins to restore better feelings, he muses positively on the joy engendered by Sophie's rebellion, for he finds it has had a most stimulating effect. He now is alone with servants and the doctor. Another glass of wine, and he begins to hum his favorite waltz. Annina, disgusted with his parsimonious recompense for her factotum services, has switched allegiance to Octavian, who is not yet finished with the baron. Producing a letter addressed to Ochs, she teases him with its contents before reading it. The letter from Mariandel proposes a tryst. Restored, he delights in the good luck of the Lerchenaus, dismisses Annina without a gratuity, and, to his lilting tune, with bravado sings of his forthcoming erotic assignation as slowly the curtain falls: "With me, with me, with me no night is too long."

I have mentioned how Wagner undid an age-old operatic tradition of set numbers interspersed with dialogue by composing in a style he designated "endless melody." Also noted was the symphonic, conversational aspect in the scores of Puccini, where dialogue and arias seem to flow in and out of one another. Strauss and Hofmannsthal also create a miracle blend of words and music in *Der Rosenkavalier*, and because of the comic nature of the piece, the words are especially important. Strauss is careful, his gigantic orchestra notwithstanding, to allow them to be heard without being swallowed by the music.

Der Rosenkavalier is more than a comedy, however. The humorous episode of the Marschallin's Act I levee was followed by her moving contemplation of the nature of the human condition, especially its brevity, and the Act III light-hearted joke, a farce perpetrated upon the baron, a "Viennese masquerade," she will call it, will be followed by another serious occasion: one of the most ethereal operatic conclusions ever created.

Der Rosenkavalier is not an opera in which hit tunes cascade one after the other. Much of the long drama transpires within the aforementioned format of conversations heightened and embellished by music. Herein lies the source of trouble I had when, as a boy, I attended my first performance of this opera. As mentioned before, I knew the basics of the story. So much more, though—for example, gestures, innuendos, and subtle intrigues—are an integral mix within this witty conversational flow and blend of words and music. These I missed and, therefore, responded with excitement only to the obvious famous segments of the drama. Each act does have these serene moments, none more supreme than those awaiting us after Octavian's joke played on the baron is exposed. This jest, which comprises most of the third and final act, is both long and complicated. I will condense its essentials as well as I can.

Act III

An energetic, brilliant orchestral introduction accompanies a pantomime in which a private room in an inn is being made ready for its clients, the many alternating happy moods of this music all anticipating the frivolity about to transpire. The room contains an alcove and bed as well as trapdoors in the floor. Valzacchi and Annina help Octavian, attired as Mariandel, to prepare the prank. When all is ready, Mariandel leaves, then returns on the arm of Ochs as dance music is heard in the distance. Ochs orders candles extinguished and, when satisfied that the room is dark enough, dismisses Valzacchi, the waiters, and the landlord. He leads Mariandel to a table and offers wine, step one of his seduction attempt. Mariandel refuses, rises, as if preparing to leave, comments inquisitively on seeing a huge bed, and is led back to the table by Ochs, who nearly succeeds in kissing his date before being jolted by "her" uncanny likeness to his despised rival.

The sight of a face retracting behind a trapdoor startles him. As dinner is served, more mysterious faces—none seen by Mariandel, of course—begin to terrify Ochs, who believes he is being besieged by ghosts. Annina, disguised, comes into the room and claims Ochs as her husband. When he denies this, four children bound into the room calling him "Papa." Landlord and waiters are shocked. A police commissioner, obviously engaged by Octavian, enters and demands to know the identity of the girl beside the baron. He introduces her as his fiancée, Sophie von Faninal. Faninal then enters and deeply resents Ochs's misuse of his daughter's name.

Sophie is next to arrive, having been sent for by her father, who, humiliated by the behavior of Ochs, swoons. He is carried out, Sophie following. The police remove all but the baron, Mariandel, Annina, and the children. Ochs attempts to escort Mariandel home but "she" refuses to leave and goes into a recess of the room. There "she" hides behind a curtain where, one by one, items of women's clothing are cast into the room. The Marschallin, absent from the drama since the end of Act I, arrives. A servant of the baron had sent for her, hoping she might be able to resolve the predicament. Octavian, now as Octavian, appears, as does Sophie, who is quick to inform the baron that her father forbids him ever to visit their house again. The Marschallin explains the entire episode to the police as nothing more than a prank, a "Viennese masquerade." The trapdoor people show themselves, Annina removes her disguise, and Valzacchi ushers in his accomplices. Ochs, stunned, is willing to forgive and forget until the Marschallin finally gets it into his head that all contacts with the Faninals are now forever finished. When the landlord presents him with a huge bill, Ochs is quite willing to worm his way through the now assembled swarm of bystanders to disappear into the night.

All but the Marschallin, Sophie, and Octavian disperse. The glorious finale, the most astonishing manifestation of Strauss's life-long love affair with the soprano voice, begins. Seeing Octavian with the Marschallin, Sophie fears she means nothing to him after all. Octavian, between the two women, is visibly embarrassed. With magnanimity, the Marschallin understands the time has come for her to surrender Octavian to the younger woman: "Go to her quickly and tell her what your heart is saying." He does so. Sophie, confused and uncertain of his love, suggests he return to the Marschallin, who, recognizing their bewilderment, intervenes and unites them. In the most beautiful trio for soprano voices in opera history, each shares the private thoughts and emotions swirling within: the Marschallin, knowing such an affair would be ephemeral, did not think, however, it would end so abruptly; Octavian's emotions genuinely are divided between the two women who have so completely captivated him, and Sophie, aware of the sacrifice taking place, also experiences a mix of emotions.

The Marschallin quietly walks out, virtually unnoticed by the lovers, who inch together, embrace, and sing a tranquil love duet of unearthly beauty: *Ist ein Traum* ("'Tis a dream"). The Marschallin, who had gone to boost the spirits of Faninal, recovering from the evening's turmoil in the adjacent room, returns holding his arm. The lovers respectfully bow to their elders, who respond with the most famous lines in the entire lengthy drama. "They are like that, the young ones," says Faninal, to which the Marschallin responds with only "Ja, ja" (Yes, yes), but spoken with so much poignancy its meaning is unmistakable. They walk out. The love duet resumes. Octavian and Sophie then embrace, kiss, and run out, her handkerchief falling unnoticed to the floor. The little page trots in. With a lighted candle he looks for it, finds it, picks it up, and trips out. Quickly the curtain falls.

Emphatically, at this chapter's beginning, I disagreed with those critics who claim that after *Der Rosenkavalier*, Strauss's creative powers declined, leaving him doomed to repeat himself. More wonderful operas, virtually all of them demonstrating his love affair with the soprano voice, were to follow and thus await your consideration, *Ariadne auf Naxos (Ariadne on Naxos)*, *Die Frau ohne Schatten (The Woman without a Shadow)*, and *Arabella* being a good way to start. *Capriccio*, his last opera, is a fascinating dramatic exploration of the ageless question in musical theater: Words or music; which is the more important? The French composer Claude Debussy will make this the central issue of his opera aesthetics when composing his only opera *Pelléas et Mélisande*, the first masterwork of our next, and final, chapter.

ॐ

Nothing proves that Strauss never lost his creativity more than his ultimate composition, written just before his death: *Vier letzte Lieder* ("Four Last Songs"). His settings of three poems by Hermann Hesse and one by Joseph von Eichendorf constitute an obvious premonition of death in one of the most emotional farewells ever composed. I have more than half a dozen recordings of this ineffable music. No recording of these magnificent songs is more dear to me than one by Elly Ameling but it is not commercially available. It was a gift to me from Elly out of her private collection for use on a special program that we did together. Her voice of incomparable beauty and consummate artistry can, nevertheless, be heard on numerous recordings. For many years she was one of the world's supreme singers of songs. Start your collection with the 1961 recording of Elisabeth Schwarzkopf, which also contains her incomparable interpretations of a collection of Strauss's finest songs. This recording should be owned and played by anyone who loves magnificent music beautifully performed. Next, get the recording with Jessye Norman. Then, that with Gundula Janowitz. Then you are on your own.

ॐ

The Strauss and Hofmannsthal collaboration, as historic as Mozart's with da Ponte and Gilbert's with Sullivan, was conducted mostly through letters. Their collection of correspondence makes fascinating reading for those curious about how their dramas were made.

Strauss and von Hofmannsthal were an odd artistic couple. Strauss, his musical and literary sophistication notwithstanding, was bourgeois in both tastes and behavior. Hofmannsthal was elegant and urbane. They never would become close friends. They seldom met in person, and when they did, Hofmannsthal was often unnerved both by Strauss's middle-class manners and by his wife's brusque, outspoken, temperamental behavior. Hofmannsthal's son committed suicide just as poet and musician put the finishing polish on *Arabella*, his sixth and last collaboration with Strauss. Before the funeral, Hofmannsthal died of a stroke. Strauss did not attend the funeral of his collaborator and publicly it was discussed as evidence of the lack of closeness between them. The truth is otherwise. So devastated was Strauss that he could not even think of Hofmannsthal or utter his name without becoming despondent. Attending the funeral, irrefutable evidence of the end of a most productive association, was unthinkable for him.

Strauss died in 1949 and with him the great line of German opera was over. There has been no one to carry on this tradition. It was the same with Italian opera when Puccini died. Our story of opera in the twentieth century after Puccini and Strauss, without the dominance of the Italian and Germanic traditions, consequently will be interesting. As Strauss lay dying he said to a friend, *"Grüss mir die Welt."* These words, "Greet everyone for me," are spoken by Isolde to Brangäne in the first act of Wagner's *Tristan und Isolde* as she contemplates her own end. What a fitting farewell from Strauss, who had inherited from Wagner the mantle of German opera.

Claude Debussy

Béla Bartók

Alban Berg

Leoš Janáček

George Gershwin

Benjamin Britten

OPERA IN THE 20TH CENTURY:
SIX MAJOR DRAMAS

Puccini and Richard Strauss are the two most important opera composers of the twentieth century, so much so that already we have met them in chapters of their own. Their dominance, nevertheless, is certainly not the whole story in this period of opera history. Thus, you will want to ask, What other twentieth-century operas and their composers should I know about?

In chronological order, they are *Pelléas et Mélisande* (1902), the only completed opera by the French composer Claude Debussy; *Bluebeard's Castle* (1918), the only opera by the Hungarian composer Béla Bartók; *The Cunning Little Vixen* (1924), one of several important operas by the Czech Leoš Janáček, so I will have to defend my choice on this one; *Wozzeck* (1925), the most important of two operas (the second left unfinished at his death) by the Austrian Alban Berg; *Porgy and Bess* (1935), the only opera by George and Ira Gershwin, though they did write numerous musicals; and *Peter Grimes* (1945), the most well known of many operas by Benjamin Britten.

Please do not conclude, though, that opera composition thereafter came to an end. Noteworthy works have been written during the last six decades, but no triumphs or masterpieces provoking universal praise and acceptance. You already have learned that often it can take time for a work to become established in the repertory of major opera houses. From the above list, only two composers, Janáček and Britten, made operatic composition a major focus of their work; the total number of operas by the four other composers is a mere five. This means, except for Berg's second and incomplete opera, *Lulu*, four of the six masterworks of this chapter are the only venture into operatic composition by these men.

Before considering these operas, it is essential for me to mention some other composers whose operas have made a mark in the twentieth century. This will not be an exhaustive list; rather, it amounts to an invitation to go on from here when the work of this chapter is done.

French Opera

Gustave Charpentier (not to be confused with Marc-Antoine Charpentier, a famous French composer of the seventeenth century) wrote *Louise* (1900), an opera of liberal social views long before the onset of the women's liberation movement. It contains an aria no great soprano can afford to do without, the ever-popular *Depuis le jour* ("Since the day"), known to millions who have never heard another note of the opera. I have at least a dozen different recordings of this aria and am still collecting.

Maurice Ravel, composer of *Bolero*, one of the twentieth century's most frequently played compositions, wrote an opera of considerable musical interest as well as youthful appeal because of its story about a naughty child cast under the spell of a talking teacup and a spate of equally loquacious creatures: cat, owl, and squirrel among them. This is the short opera *L'enfant et les sortilèges (The Child and the Magic Spell)* of 1925.

Francis Poulenc wrote several operas, and they have a sophisticated following. His masterwork is *Dialogues des Carmélites* (1957), a drama based on the murder of nuns during the horrors of the French Revolution. Its final scene is spell-binding. A recent production by the Metropolitan Opera elicited different responses to my "How did you like Poulenc's opera?" by two musically sophisticated friends who just happened to be at the same performance. They do not know each other and are about the same age. One is a professor, a male, the other a female who teaches piano and organ. I knew this was their first encounter with *Dialogues of the Carmélites*. I happened to see the professor first. "Peter, I just loved the opera," he said, "but it certainly is a difficult work. I think it must be seen to be understood and appreciated. One must experience the drama by focusing on the action and in doing so the music creeps inside you virtually without your knowing it." Soon thereafter, I spoke with the music teacher, who lives nearby, and her response was, "I have become completely possessed by Poulenc's music and I love the opera but I couldn't watch it. The visuals distracted me; they diverted my attention from the amazing and totally captivating music. I had to close my eyes, listen to the words [She is fluent in French] and music, and let the drama transpire in my head, in my imagination." But they both loved it, and that's all I wanted to hear.

English Opera

Frederick Delius wrote several operas, the best known being *A Village Romeo and Juliet* (1907), in which his highly unusual musical style prevails start to finish and reaches its greatest appeal in the now famous orchestral interlude "The Walk to the Paradise Garden."

Ralph Vaughan Williams wrote *Riders to the Sea* (1937) to a text from J. M. Synge's play about a woman on the isle of Aran, off the west coast of Ireland, who loses her husband and four sons in a series of unrelated accidents at sea.

Benjamin Britten, who composed numerous operas beside *Peter Grimes*, awaits your judicious investigation as, later in this chapter, you consider his *Billy Budd* (1951) after Melville's story, *The Turn of the Screw* (1954) after Henry James, and *Death in Venice* (1973) based on a Thomas Mann story. They represent the most well known of his more than one dozen works for the stage. His many significant works are taking awhile to become more accessible to a large body of operagoers because of his difficult musical style.

German Opera

Arnold Schoenberg indisputably is one of the most influential composers of the twentieth century. Even though I have not selected any of his operas for inclusion in this chapter, I will in some detail consider his huge role in the history of twentieth-century music when discussing *Wozzeck*, by his famous student Alban Berg.

Brecht and Weill are as famous to Germans as Rodgers and Hammerstein are to Americans. Of the several collaborations of the poet Bertold Brecht and the composer Kurt Weill, two works remain ever popular. *Die Dreigroschenoper (The Threepenny Opera)* in 1928 is their modern adaptation of Gay's *The Beggar's*

Opera (see chapter 1). Their song "The Ballad of Mack the Knife," heard near the beginning of this songspiel (song play, as they described it), has achieved worldwide popularity in numerous languages and countless renditions. *Aufstieg und Fall der Stadt Mahagonny (Rise and Fall of the City Mahagonny)* in 1930 contains another well-known song, now frequently heard in popular musical circles: the haunting "Alabama Song." *Die tote Stadt (The Dead City)*, 1920, by Erich Korngold, has much expressive music, a rich mix of his own melodic voice with hints of Richard Strauss and Puccini to some ears. "Marietta's Song" *(Glück, das mir verblieb)* is haunting, beautiful music and a constant favorite with many listeners to my opera program.

Czech Opera

Bedřich Smetana wrote half a dozen works much appreciated by his fellow countrymen. In particular, if his most well-known work, *Prodaná Nevěsta (The Bartered Bride)* in 1866, was as popular beyond the borders of his native land, I would gladly have found an important place for it in a previous chapter. The music is wonderful.

Aside from Janáček, soon to be considered, Antonín Dvořák is the composer of the most important twentieth-century Czech opera. His *Rusalka* premiered in 1901 in the National Theater, Prague. A few years ago, I had the opportunity to take one of my opera tour groups to a performance of this opera in this very theater. *Rusalka* is second only to *The Bartered Bride* with Czech audiences. *Rusalka's* love song sung to the moon, in Act I, is of infinite beauty and I treasure my 1956 recording of "O Lovely Moon" made by Jarmila Novotna. This once private recording eventually made it into the marketplace, but I have others sent to me by Madame Novotna from her private collection that are worth more than gold to me. It was my great pleasure to become a friend of this great Czech singer long after she retired from the stage and even longer after one Saturday-afternoon Metropolitan Opera broadcast so many, many years ago when my father cautioned me to listen carefully to this true vocal aristocrat. To round out family sentiments on this matter, Dvořák far and away is the favorite composer of my wife, Joanne. Outside the Czech Republic his instrumental and chamber compositions are better known and more often played than any of his operas.

Russian Opera

Stravinsky, Prokofiev, and Shostakovich are the giants of twentieth-century Russian music, and all three wrote important operas.
These three famous—to some less oriented ears, infamous—composers contributed enormously to the development of what is
called "modern music" (I'll have more to say about this vague,
elusive, and relative concept in this chapter).

Igor Stravinsky's best-known operas are *Oedipus Rex* (1927)
with text after Sophocles by Jean Cocteau (translated into Latin
for the opera) and *The Rake's Progress* (1951), to which the poet W.
H. Auden contributed much to the libretto. Sergei Prokofiev's
most successful opera appeared in 1921. It is *Lyubov k trem
Apelsinam (The Love for Three Oranges)*, and it was written for
the Lyric Opera of Chicago when the composer left Russia after
the revolution. Dmitri Shostakovich's *Nos (The Nose)*, which premiered in 1930, is a bizarre drama based on a story by Gogol about
a major who awakens one morning to find that his nose has disappeared. It soon is discovered in a loaf of bread belonging to his barber. *The Lady Macbeth of Mtsensk* (later retitled *Katerina
Izmaylova* after he revised it), also by Shostakovich, had, in 1934,
a triumphant premiere in Leningrad. When Stalin saw a performance months later, however, he stalked out after the satire on the
police in the third act. Two days later *Pravda* denounced the opera
as disgusting and depraved. Of late it has been catching on, especially in the United States—its sexual explicitness and savage conclusion apparently more tolerable to our age and place. For me this
opera is a mad and marvelous mixture of dissonance and beauty.

Italian Opera

Even though no Italian composer has contributed a string of triumphs after Puccini, Cilèa, Busoni, Wolf-Ferrari, Montemezzi,
Zandonai, and Menotti are names you may encounter. Francesco
Cilèa's *Adriana Lecouvreur* (1902) has remained on the boards of
opera houses, and the aria in the fourth act, *Poveri fiori* ("Poor
flowers"), as recorded by Maria Callas, is at the heart of record col-
lections for those who esteem her above all other twentieth-century sopranos. Ferruccio Busoni certainly has fans, but his two
most prominent works, *Turandot* and *Doktor Faust*, have been
greatly overshadowed by other operas on these subjects. Ermanno
Wolf-Ferrari's *The Secret of Susanna* (she smoked cigarettes a hundred years ago), Italo Montemezzi's *The Love of Three Kings*, and

Riccardo Zandonai's *Francesca da Rimini* have periodic revivals. Puccini, however, was twentieth-century Italian opera.

Gian Carlo Menotti is actually an American composer of Italian birth. Though he has composed many successes, the most famous being *Amahl and the Night Visitors* because of frequent TV presentations at Christmastime, there really are no masterpieces. His best work sounds like an imitation of Puccini.

American Opera

Maybe my comments on Menotti belong here, for it is in this country that he has had his career. Homegrown American operas, other than *Porgy and Bess*, which took a long time to be accepted as a full-fledged operatic work, that have achieved international recognition and repertory status are few indeed. The American musical is the triumph of this country. I am quite fond, however, of Scott Joplin's *Treemonisha* (1911), which is getting a long overdue hearing. In spite of great premiere performances by the famous singing actor Lawrence Tibbett, *The King's Henchman* by Deems Taylor, and *Merry Mount* by Howard Hanson, have fallen into oblivion. Works by Virgil Thompson and Marc Blitzstein have done much better. John Adams, Jack Beeson, and Phillip Glass have their following, while *Vanessa* by Samuel Barber, and *Candide* by Leonard Bernstein, have achieved significant popularity. Carlisle Floyd's *Susannah* continues to gain a wider audience and the incomparable importance of Arnold Schoenberg will be noted later in this chapter.

For the most part, nevertheless, opera in the United States is imported, not exported, though we must never overlook the huge contribution of our great orchestras, conductors, and many singers who have shared their supreme talents at home and abroad for over a century. I also have reason to be quite optimistic about the future of American operatic composition and other forms of serious music if my area of Vermont, a rich pocket of creativity, is an indication of what is occurring. Not far from my home, in all directions, live American composers whose music has been heard with considerable appreciation on my Vermont Public Radio programs as well as elsewhere throughout the country in live performances and on recordings. To cite only three of numerous examples, they are the award winning opera *A Death in the Family*, based on James Agee's novel, by William Mayer; *A Fleeting Animal*, an opera about Vermont by composer Erik Nielsen and librettist David Budbill; and a ballet, choral works, and a cantata

The Jolly Beggars, based on the poetry of Robert Burns, by Robert De Cormier.

Spanish Opera

Spain, like the United States, enjoys its reputation for producing a host of famous opera singers (two of the celebrated "Three Tenors" are Spaniards) but boasts few internationally accepted operas. *La vida breve (The Brief Life)*, by Manuel de Falla, premiered in 1913. It has been criticized for its weak plot, but so have many other operas that were rescued by wonderful music. After a slow start, this short opera of about one hour acquired a devoted following in the 1950s and sixties among those who witnessed performances with one of the greatest soprano voices of that period singing the part of Salud, a young gypsy girl who dies brokenhearted when jilted by her lover. The performance I saw with Victoria de los Angeles remains as vivid today in memory as when I saw it nearly fifty years ago. I could not do without her recording, and you should not either if you want the most authentic Spanish opera in your house.

"Modern" Music

The composers of this chapter's master works, Debussy, Bartók, Janáček, Berg, Gershwin, and Britten, all would be called "modern" musicians. In the last chapter, I hinted at problems associated with using this imprecise concept. *Modern* means belonging to the present or no more than the recent past, yet this word is used in writing or speaking about his place in music history for each of the above composers, none of whom is still living, and none of whom was alive in the recent past. All were dead before 1950 except Britten, the most recent of the group, who died in 1976. So what, then, is "modern music"?

Unfortunately, unlike the terms *romantic music* and *baroque music*, which can be defined with a certain meat and potatoes, *modern music* is a concept used in so many differing and vague ways by a battalion of writers and speakers that its meaning remains indecisive. Some use the phrase to mean music written only by those still living. Others mean twentieth-century music that has a new, "modern" sound: that jarring, discordant quality distinguishing it from the melodic and harmonious music of previous centuries. More specifically, the concept often is used to refer to an identifiable trend in music, occurring during the last decade of the nineteenth century and the early decades of the twentieth, wherein old, honored rules of composition were seen going out the window. Already we mentioned Richard Strauss as a part of this new trend, and no one more so than Claude Debussy. Both—and they were not alone—produced music sufficiently individualistic in style, construction, content, character, and sound as to be considered by many as the beginning of a new age in the continually developing history of Western music.

One can write about twentieth-century music with greater precision by avoiding the elusive phrase "modern music," which too often is used to describe music many people do not like, as in the comment, "Oh, I love classical and romantic music but I simply cannot stand modern music." That is a common way of saying "I like the music of the last half of the eighteenth century and the music of most of the nineteenth century but not that of the twentieth century" and thereafter. If we use words and concepts such as *impressionistic* or *expressionistic* music and *atonal* music in discussing music written during the last one hundred years or more, meanings will be much clearer. But this is so, of course, only if such terms are carefully defined.

I begin with *impressionism*, the term most often used to describe the music of Debussy, who, by the way, just happens to be called the composer who "began modern music" in a book I read recently.

CLAUDE DEBUSSY

Impressionism in music was an adaptation by Debussy of what Monet, Manet, Degas, Renoir, Pissarro, and Cézanne sought to achieve in painting and what Verlaine, Mallarmé, and Baudelaire sought in poetry. Words often were used by the poets more to convey a mood than to articulate a precise meaning, and these painters did not attempt to achieve reproductions of reality indistinguishable from a photograph. Their paintings captured a mood often more a representation of their feelings while painting something rather than a realistic representation of what was being painted. Painting and poetry of this type did not boldly represent or state something. Rather, they merely hinted at something:

They created an atmosphere, at times dreamy, vague, and imprecise. It offered an impression of something.

This new direction in art was decidedly French and, with Debussy and music, was especially a reaction against the Germanic influence, namely Wagner. It was impossible to be a western European composer at the end of the nineteenth century and remain impervious to Wagner's influence. Early in his career Debussy had fallen under Wagner's spell. He would soon strike out on his own unique musical course, but, by his own admission, no matter how hard he tried to turn away from Wagner, he would never totally escape the influence. More on this shortly.

Debussy was born into a French bourgeois family of no special musical interest. His extraordinary talent did not begin to show itself until he was ten years old, and his long association with the Paris Conservatory as a student, though eventually he would win prizes, was more memorable for the musical rules he broke than for those mastered. This intensely retiring man, who even at the height of his considerable fame rarely was seen in public and who virtually never performed his own works either at the piano or on the podium, was a rebel. He followed his own star wherever his genius led him. This he had in common with Wagner and also Mussorgsky, whom he greatly admired. Mussorgsky, who had very little musical training, followed his musical instincts, breaking right and left long accepted rules of musical composition. This, too, was the direction Debussy was to follow as he sat for hours at his piano tinkering with sounds pleasing to his ears even though their construction, sequences, and relationships were forbidden by the rules of academic composition. The result was a small but unquestionably remarkable corpus of impressionistic masterpieces: *Prélude à l'après-midi d'un faune* ("Prelude to the Afternoon of a Fawn"), the nocturnes for orchestra, *La Mer* ("The Sea"), *Images*, *Préludes*, and his opera *Pelléas et Mélisande*, to list only the most famous.

PELLÉAS ET MÉLISANDE (1902)

Wagner was for Debussy the summation of an age. One must go forward from Wagner, not back to him. Nevertheless, two Wagnerianisms constitute the musical foundation of Debussy's only opera. (I must be more careful about saying "his only opera." Another, called *Rodrigue and Chimène*, long thought to have been destroyed, apparently exists somewhere; however, I know nothing about it and know no one who does.) Even though he wrote about the inappropriateness of using musical motifs to identify and represent characters in an opera, as Wagner did, Debussy's three central characters in *Pelléas et Mélisande* have musical themes linked to them throughout the drama that by any other name remain what Wagnerians call *Leitmotifs* (leading musical motifs). Debussy, however, would employ such themes in a manner unacceptable to Wagner.

An explanation of such technicalities is not needed here. What you do need to know is that in listening to the opera, you will hear certain musical themes used again and again. This is especially important because *Pelléas et Mélisande* contains no arias or ensembles. It is not an opera of famous highlights that you find on a recording featuring beloved excerpts. Like Wagner, Debussy would not interrupt the flow of the drama by creating set pieces. This is what Wagner called "endless melody" but what in Debussy's opera might better be called "endless harmony." Melody, as you know, is the tune that can be hummed or sung. The direction melodies travel is horizontal, one note after another. Music that embellishes a melody, giving it a mood and coloring it, is called harmony. Harmony has a more vertical direction as clusters of notes, called chords, are sounded beneath the melody as it moves along. For years, strict rules of harmony governed what a composer could and could not do in harmonizing a melody. In breaking these rules Debussy created a new world of harmonic sounds and hues that became influential throughout the twentieth century. This, and not singable songs, is the predominant feature of *Pelléas et Mélisande*, a masterpiece of harmonic sounds and impressions: an operatic kaleidoscope of ever-changing colors.

Years before he had encountered the *Pelléas* subject, Debussy knew precisely what kind of an opera he would write, should he do so. He explained his plan to his teacher, Ernest Guiraud (who added recitatives to Bizet's *Carmen* and completed the orchestration of Offenbach's *Les contes d'Hoffmann*; see chapter 9). He would select a libretto that does no more than "hint at what is to be said," but the words, no matter how elusive, would be given the primary role. With a comment aimed directly at Wagner, he continued, ". . . music in opera is far too prominent."

Unlike Rossini, for whom the human voice was at the center of opera, Debussy believed that the "voice should blossom into true song only when this is called for . . . there should be no musical development just for development's sake." Words are to be served by music and should not be obliterated by it. "In the opera house," Debussy said, "they sing too much." By this he meant opera is not just an exercise in beautiful singing accompanied by an orchestra, but rather a dramatic impression created by a story told in both words and music, the words alluding to thoughts and feelings often difficult to express, and supporting these words in a rich tapestry of impressions is music.

This was clear to Debussy before he found his libretto, so it was instantly equally clear to him as soon as he experienced the play *Pelléas et Mélisande*, by Maurice Maeterlinck, that the perfect libretto had been found. Debussy sought and received permission to use the play for his opera, and used it virtually intact.

The intensely spiritual Maeterlinck, born the same year as Debussy, in all his writings, poetry and prose, was preoccupied with an attempt to express mysteries of life seemingly always just beyond the reach of ordinary human comprehension. Maeterlinck was a symbolist: In his poetry, words were used to represent more than their ordinary meaning. A common, mundane example would be the use of the word *autumn* to suggest the last "season" of life. Dead dried leaves could symbolize the end of life, and the aimless swirling of dead dried leaves, for a poet, could represent the pointless brevity of the human experience.

Maeterlinck's play, and Debussy's opera made from it, is about the thoughts and feelings of the three central characters: They do not always speak directly; often questions are left unanswered; often they change the subject. This hinting at something held great appeal for Debussy. The action is more mental than physical.

The three characters are the handsome young Pelléas, who falls in love with Mélisande, the beautiful young wife of his much older half brother, Golaud. In a jealous rage, Golaud kills Pelléas. Mélisande dies soon thereafter. There—you have the plot in three short sentences!

In the drama, time and space are blurred in a story where little of an external nature transpires. The drama takes place in the minds and emotions of the central characters, who move and speak in a dreamlike atmosphere. One of the few critics who did not like Debussy's masterpiece claimed *Pelléas et Mélisande* to be a long opera wherein absolutely nothing happens. His attempt at a disparaging remark probably would not have fazed Debussy had he been around to hear it. The worst attack came from Maeterlinck just prior to the world premiere in Paris on April 30, 1902. In granting permission to Debussy for his play to be made into an opera, the playwright assumed his mistress would be given the role of Mélisande. Debussy, having met by chance the unique Scottish singing actress Mary Garden, would have none other. Maeterlinck was furious. He called at Debussy's home with a stick in hand to beat him; he attempted, but failed, to win an injunction preventing the performance; and he published a letter in the major Paris newspaper hoping for a failure. It was accorded a triumph. Maeterlinck, who had vowed never to attend a performance, in time capitulated. Eventually he forgave Debussy and wrote to Mary Garden, who created the role of Mélisande, "For the first time I have understood my play, and because of you."

The opera is in five acts with a total of twelve scenes. Between most of the scenes are connecting orchestral interludes. These interludes both unify the story and allow time for scene changes. The characters and their voice ranges are:

ARKEL, King of Allemonde, *bass*
GENEVIÈVE, mother of Golaud and Pelléas, *contralto*
GOLAUD, her oldest son, *baritone*
PELLÉAS, Golaud's half brother, *tenor*
MÉLISANDE, marries Golaud but loves Pelléas, *soprano*
YNIOLD, Golaud's son by his first marriage, *soprano or boy soprano*
SHEPHERD, *baritone*
Doctor, *bass*

The opera takes place during medieval times in the imaginary kingdom of Allemonde.

Act I

The prevailing symbol of the opera is darkness. To comprehend the drama, to participate in the interrelationship of its words and music, you must allow yourself to become part of the dim, shadowy atmosphere, the gloom and obscurity dominating virtually every scene from the forest, to the cave, to the dusky gardens, as well as to rooms of the castle. The first notes, preceding the curtain, emerging with a slow unfolding, as if escaping from a subterranean world, tell us this.

The curtain opens on a dense forest. Night is approaching. Golaud, tracking a beast while hunting, has become lost. He hears crying, sees a girl by the edge of a pool, and approaches. "Don't touch me!" are the first words of Mélisande. Golaud's first impression is of how beautiful she is. He asks if someone has hurt her and she replies, "Yes . . . everyone!" Golaud urges Mélisande to come with him; the night will be dark and cold. She wonders where he is going. He does not know: "I also am lost," he says. That is the first scene of the first act. It establishes the vague, murky mood of the rest of the story.

Do not come to *Pelléas et Mélisande* as you would an opera by, for example, Mozart or Verdi, wherein you wait for the parade of hit tunes. This opera does not play like that. Its music is a constant counterpart to words in conversations; the music, indeed, is a conversational handmaiden. Its presence and its appeal are subtle. Rather than going for the jugular, so to speak, it tiptoes about behind you. You must listen to it over and over as you follow the words. Then, when you know the story well, listen again and visualize what is taking place until the music seeps inside you and becomes part of you. For most people, *Pelléas et Mélisande* lacks the immediate appeal of Puccini's melodic operas. It takes work. But, oh, is it ever worth the effort!

The second scene of Act I is in an apartment within the castle. Geneviève reads to the nearly blind Arkel a letter written by Golaud to Pelléas in which he relates how he found, rescued, and married Mélisande, all the while remaining ignorant of who she is or where she is from. He fears Arkel's displeasure, for he knows the old man wished him to honor his choice when remarrying. Arkel, however, philosophically accepts Golaud's choice. Pelléas enters the room with news from another letter. A dying friend requests he come to him. Here Arkel protests, telling Pelléas his first obligation is to his sick father, who lies seriously ill upstairs. Geneviève tells Pelléas to light the turret lamp to welcome Golaud and his new wife.

The final scene of the first act is set in a garden in front of the castle. Debussy's beautiful, quiet interlude has painted the picture. Mélisande and Geneviève comment on the utter darkness of the world they inhabit and the older woman suggests they look toward the sea, whence may come some light. Pelléas enters and forecasts a storm during the night. Distant voices are heard coming from the harbor. Soon a ship will leave. As it sails away, Mélisande recognizes it as the one she came on. Voices of sailors drift across the water up to them. Geneviève must go to attend to Yniold. She urges Pelléas to lead Mélisande home. "Will you give me your hand?" he asks. "You can see they are full of flowers," she replies. "I will take your arm," he says, "the path is steep and it is very dark. Perhaps I will be leaving tomorrow." "Oh, why will you be going away?" she wonders. These are the last words of the first act.

Act II

The curtains part on the first scene of the second act. Pelléas has taken Mélisande to a fountain in the park. To avoid the intense heat of the day, they loll in the shade. Fascinated by the water, Mélisande lies on some marble to peer deeply into the fountain. She wants to put her hands in the water. Pelléas fears she will lean too far and fall in and warns her to be careful. She continues to reach, however, but is unable to touch the water. Her long blond hair cascades into the fountain. Pelléas says: "He also found you next to water." Mélisande replies yes in one of many excellent examples of the obscure dialogue created by Maeterlinck:

> *Pelléas*: What did he say to you?
> *Mélisande*: Nothing; I don't remember.
> *Pelléas*: Was he near you?
> *Mélisande*: Yes, he wanted to kiss me.
> *Pelléas*: And you did not want him to?
> *Mélisande*: No.
> *Pelléas*: Why did you not want him to?
> *Mélisande*: Oh, oh, I saw something move at the
>   bottom of the pool.

Mélisande, playing with the ring given to her by Golaud, fumbles it and drops it into the seemingly bottomless waters. She worries about what to do now. Pelléas tells her not to be concerned. They will come looking for it another day but the clock has struck twelve and they must go. "What shall we tell Golaud if he asks where it is?" Pelléas responds, "The truth! The truth!" End of first scene.

Another lovely orchestral interlude connects scenes, the curtain opening now on an apartment of the castle where Golaud lies on his bed, Mélisande at his side. He was mildly injured when thrown from his horse. In an explanation replete with symbolism he tells his wife how precisely on the striking of the twelfth chime of midday his horse bolted, galloped into a tree, and fell on him: ". . . it felt as though the entire forest had landed on my chest. I believed my heart had been torn out of me." Ring lost and Golaud unseated at the stroke of twelve.

Mélisande, trying to care for him, suddenly starts to cry. She confesses her unhappiness. Golaud assumes someone has harmed her but she says it is not that, but she cannot seem to put her sense of foreboding into words. She would like to leave this place with Golaud. It is so gloomy. There is no light; she never sees the sky. Attempting to comfort her, he takes her hand. He notices the ring is gone and inquires about it. She lost it but she knows where it is: ". . . the cave by the sea," she lies. Golaud insists she ask Pelléas to take her there to find the ring. She cannot believe he is making her do this in the dark of night. She repeats her vast unhappiness. The scene ends.

A brooding, somber, speculative interlude takes us to the third and final scene of the second act, showing the entrance to a dark cave by the sea. Pelléas suggests he and Mélisande wait for the moon to give some light before they enter the cave. Mélisande must see the interior in case Golaud demands she describe the place where she reported losing the ring. Inside they come upon three old vagabonds asleep. Have they been driven to the cave for shelter by a famine in the land? It is eerie. Mélisande wants to leave. She discourages an offer of help from Pelléas. She prefers to walk by herself. Pelléas tells her they will return another day. The whole scene takes less than five minutes but it feels longer and the impression lingers.

Act III

It is night as the third act opens on one of the castle towers where Mélisande can be seen combing her extremely long hair. She sings to herself a little song. Mary Garden, the small Scotswoman who mesmerized audiences with her interpretation of Mélisande, made a historic recording of this song with Debussy at the piano. Even though they worked closely together in creating the role, she would reveal many years later, in a New York City lecture/demonstration, "Debussy was not easy to know. He was intensely timid and unsociable. I have never observed in his nature any real exuberant expression for anyone or anything. It was quite impossible for him to reveal his inner self to anyone. He was mystery itself." Sounds like Debussy was a character in his own opera. I have some of Mary Garden's recordings made in

1911–12. Hers was a good voice but not a great one, and the gramophone, still in its infancy, was not kind to her. Her greatness was as a singing actress. Of her it was written by an adoring observer that she could not act without singing or sing without acting. Mélisande, perhaps, was her most famous role—this or her Salome, which was so pleasing to Richard Strauss.

Pelléas approaches on a path beneath Mélisande's window. The beauty of the night and of Mélisande finally achieves speech as Pelléas tells her how lovely she is and bids her to lean out of her window to be closer to him. Climbing and reaching as high as he can, he asks for her hand and tells her again he is leaving the next day. He wants to touch his lips to her hand but she will not agree if he is going to leave. He promises to wait. As she leans as far as she can, her hair falls down. Pelléas holds it in his hands and puts it to his mouth. Her hair envelops him and snags upon some twigs. They are connected by her hair. He kisses it. They fear they will be caught. Someone is heard approaching. It is Golaud. He tells them it is late, that Mélisande must be careful not to fall, and goes off with Pelléas, having scolded them to stop behaving like children.

We have witnessed a unique love scene, hinted at in words and fully articulated in the music of Debussy. Every time I encounter this scene of the long, tangled hair I think of a graduate student in one of my opera classes who became, in a positive and productive manner, obsessed with the opera *Pelléas et Mélisande*. She wrote her term paper on it, bought a complete recording, and listened to it again and again. Beginning students rarely fall in love with unique, sophisticated masterpieces like *Boris Godunov* and *Pelléas et Mélisande*. Does it surprise you to be told that this particular young woman had the longest, thickest mane of blond hair I have ever seen?

In the brief second scene of the third act, Golaud and Pelléas descend into the utter darkness of the castle vaults with one small light. There is little air and the odor of a stagnant pool is most offensive. As Pelléas leans over a chasm, held by Golaud, he is stifled by the stink, a smell his older brother associates with death. They agree to leave, then depart silently. Now, what do you make of this scene in Maeterlinck's symbolism?

Another interlude and now we see a terrace outside the vaults. Pelléas, restored by fresh air from the sea, reflects on the hideous experience of being in the vaults. It is midday. He sees his mother, children heading to the beach for a swim, and, high in a tower window, Mélisande. Golaud, referring to the child's play he stumbled on the previous night, demands that it not happen again. Soon Mélisande may be a mother. It was not the first time he noticed that something between Pelléas and Mélisande may be going on. He informs his brother to avoid Mélisande as much as possible without being obvious about it.

After another interlude, brief and moody in the woodwinds, the final scene of the third act takes place beneath Mélisande's window. Golaud and Yniold, a son by his first wife, sit on the lawn. Golaud interrogates the boy about the behavior of his uncle Pelléas and Mélisande when he is alone with them. What do they talk about? Do they talk about me? Do they ask you to go out and play? Do they kiss? Golaud bribes the boy with the promise of a gift of a bow and arrows to keep the dialogue going, then he lifts Yniold up onto the ledge to spy on Pelléas and Mélisande in her room, clearly lighted by a lamp. Yniold reports: They are not close together; they are not talking; they are looking at the light. Yniold has had it. He will cry out if his father does not take him down Golaud yields.

Act IV

Act IV opens on a room in the castle. Pelléas tells Mélisande he must see her this evening. His father has recuperated and, seeing Pelléas, has told him he has the face of one who has not long to live and that he must travel. Pelléas and Mélisande agree to meet by the fountain for their last rendezvous. As Pelléas goes out one door, Arkel enters through another. He hopes the recovery of the father of Pelléas bodes the arrival of happier times. He has felt sorry for Mélisande, a beautiful young woman in such a gloomy environment. Golaud enters and announces the imminent departure of Pelléas. He begins to speak incoherently. He takes her hand, then seizes her hair, forcing her upon her knees, and drags her left to right, back and forth, up and down: "Ah! Ah! Finally your long hair is good for something." Arkel puts a stop to Golaud's raging. Golaud leaves. Arkel asks Mélisande if he is drunk. "No, no, but he does not love me any more . . . I am not happy," she says. The first scene ends as Arkel's resonating bass voice, with the insight of a prophet, proclaims, "If I were God, I would have pity on the human heart."

The first portion of the next scene, again connected by an interlude, has Yniold attempting to move a big stone entrapping a ball. He is in the park by the fountain where Pelléas and

Mélisande have vowed to meet. A shepherd passes by with his sheep. Yniold wonders why they do not bleat. Because it is not the way to the stable, explains the shepherd. Perhaps they are on the road to be slaughtered. Yniold runs in from the dark. Pelléas arrives. He is aware of what has been going on. He knows he will never see Mélisande again. She comes. No longer can they deny their love. Sheltered by the beauty of the night, they embrace.

If this forbidden love, in the protection of night, recalls for you the love scene of *Tristan and Isolde,* you are doing well—Debussy, in his conscious attempt to avoid anything Wagnerian, must have had the German master in mind when he made his scene, similar in form, so different in its content. Unlike the declaration of love by Tristan and Isolde, the longest and most intoxicatingly erotic love duet in any opera I know, Pelléas and Mélisande are simple and brief. They get right to the point and the music stops as Pelléas says, "I love you" *(Je t'aime)* and Mélisande replies, "I love you, too" *(Je t'aime aussi).* It is so natural and happens so quickly that you will miss it if you do not know it is coming. Mélisande hears the rustle of leaves and assumes they are not alone. She sees Golaud in the shadows. Pelléas sees him too and urges her to flee. She will not. They don't care. They are everything to each other. Golaud rushes to them and kills Pelléas with his sword. The curtain falls.

Act V
The final act plays in a room of the castle. Mélisande lies in a bed, asleep. In a corner stand Arkel, Golaud, and a doctor. Golaud is remorseful. Mélisande awakens and says she feels fine, but admits she really does not know what she is saying. Golaud asks to be alone with his wife. He is miserable. He feels responsible for all the unhappiness suffered by Mélisande and asks forgiveness. She forgives him but is lost to another world. Golaud must, however, have the truth. He asks if she loved Pelléas. She admits it. But what Golaud really is after is the nature of their love. Was it a forbidden love? Are they guilty? She replies it was not. He accuses her of lying while at death's door. She seems unaware that she is dying. Golaud persists in demanding the truth but Mélisande no longer is with him. Arkel and the doctor return. Mélisande feels and fears the cold of winter approaching. She is told by Arkel of having given birth to a daughter but is too weak to hold her. Servants enter and sink to their knees as Mélisande dies. Arkel leads Golaud out. Mélisande is dead. She needs silence now. It is the

turn of the newborn child to live. The curtains close to the gentle, final strains of Debussy's incomparable score.

With Debussy's impressionistic masterpiece, we have taken a giant step toward giving substance to the nebulous phrase *modern music* and with Béla Bartók's *Bluebeard's Castle* we take another step, but one not so easily measured.

BÉLA BARTÓK

Bartók eludes labels. On him they do not stick like impressionism to Debussy. Every bit the innovator of a Stravinsky or a Schoenberg, with his fascination with intricate rhythms and complex tonalities (I will define *tonal, atonal,* and *polytonal* music when we discuss Alban Berg next), Bartók, if you must label him, ultimately was a nationalist whose committed collecting of Hungarian folk music affected his own compositions in ingenious ways.

Born in 1881, Béla Bartók was accomplished at the piano by his sixth year, was composing by nine, and gave his first public performance at ten. He was eighteen when he entered the Royal Hungarian Academy of Music as a gifted student in both piano and composition. Talented and impressionable, he was drawn first to the romanticism of Brahms and the music of fellow countryman Franz Liszt, but when he heard the tone poems of Richard Strauss, which affected him profoundly, he would be under the sway of a new idol for several years while his own unique voice was still formulating.

When that voice developed and was heard, it was not popular. His riotous rhythms and savage sounds were appreciated by a small circle of musicians and critics who recognized Bartók's unusual originality. His was a new Hungarian voice, deeply influenced by Magyar folk tunes. Bartók traveled extensively throughout Hungary for years collecting folk songs passed along by oral tradition from one generation to the next. Numerous other composers have used the folk music of their native land in their compositions, usually quoting tunes directly or by creating a set of variations from a folk tune.

Folk music, as distinguished from art music composed by trained musicians, usually is rural and anonymous in origin, generally is transmitted orally rather than being written, and, accordingly, is subject to constant modifications. Bartók collected and preserved thousands of these songs of a working class, often somber expressions of despair found in the lives of hardworking and deep-suffering laborers. But Bartók did not simply reuse the tunes he collected. They influenced his writing in a subtle, complicated way. The brooding asperity of many Magyar folk songs influenced Bartók's own compositions in which harsh and sober moods remain, but gone are hummable tunes. Bartók collected and used authentic folk songs of native Magyars, which filled his head and heart, not the far more familiar gypsy airs of nomads popularized by the Hungarian dances of Brahms and the Hungarian rhapsodies of Liszt.

BLUEBEARD'S CASTLE (1918)

Bartók's *Bluebeard's Castle*, known also as *Duke Bluebeard's Castle*, despite certain similarities of names, multiple wives, and locked doors, is not a setting of Charles Perrault's well-known fairy tale of the monster Bluebeard, who murdered wives and hid their remains behind locked doors. That Bluebeard is part of widespread folklore and was operatically represented in a rarely performed work by Paul Dukas. Bartók's opera sets a text by Béla Balázs about an idealistic, suffering man, a loner much like Bartók. Perhaps the opera is about the Bluebeard dwelling within us all. As the spoken prologue preceding the first curtain makes abundantly clear, the opera takes place in the imagination of each listener and it is the story of each and every one of us.

Bartók finished his only opera in 1911. His choice of subject may have been influenced by the dark, meditative, introspective world of *Pelléas et Mélisande* but the music is his own. Zoltán Kodály, Bartók's friend and collaborator in the collection of Magyar folk music, said *Bluebeard's Castle* was a "musical volcano erupting for sixty minutes of tragic intensity." Seldom during his lifetime was Bartók to experience the warm acceptance of his music. When he submitted his opera in 1911 to a competition for the best opera of the year, the commission rejected it as incapable of being performed. Seven years later, it received a successful premiere at the National Opera in Budapest, but only as recently as during the second half of the twentieth century has it been received by an operagoing public as the masterpiece unquestionably it is.

There are two characters:

DUKE BLUEBEARD, *bass*
JUDITH, his wife, *mezzo-soprano; sometimes soprano*

The bard who steps before the curtain to deliver the prologue informs the audience that even though the story they are about to see takes place in legendary times and is about Bluebeard and his wives, it has a new moral and new meanings, because "our story is about you." The hour long drama plays with virtually no action. The two characters, male and female, converse with limited movement. The gestures they do make—an embrace, holding hands, opening a door—thus are all the more important.

The curtain rises on a huge empty Gothic hall. Stage left, steep stairs lead to a small iron door. To its right are seven enormous doors. All doors are closed. There are no windows, no furniture, no light; the empty hall, the stage directions inform us, is "like a cave hewn in the heart of solid rock." It is so dark one can barely make out the set. The orchestra paints the forbidding scene suddenly altered when the small iron door to the left quickly opens and framed in brilliant white light stand the silhouetted figures of Bluebeard and Judith. They enter the hall. Bluebeard speaks first. He tells his young bride their journey is over, for they have reached Bluebeard's Castle. The home she left to be with him, he knows, was brighter. Is she still with him? "Lead me, loved one, I will follow," she assures him. They embrace on the stairs. The small iron door closes and in near total darkness only the outlines of the two figures and the seven huge doors remain visible.

The action of the drama is in the music, but not in the form of arias, duets, and excerpts now famous. Continuously and inseparable from it, the conversation of Bluebeard and his young wife is elucidated and intensified in the orchestra. To experience the magnificence of Bartók's score requires more than a casual acquaintance with the plot. It requires paying attention to how and why Bluebeard and his bride enter his castle hand in hand— she having given up everything to follow him—and embrace, only to become involved in a divisive conversation, the consequences of which ultimately leave them isolated, silent, and completely alone in their estrangement.

As Judith fumbles along the giant wall, holding Bluebeard's hand, she comments on the lack of windows in his castle and the impenetrable, foreboding darkness. He tells her darkness and sorrow will always pervade his castle after she has asked for warmth and light. She pushes on, stops before the first of the huge doors, and, insisting on the end of the reign of darkness, demands the doors be opened. Bluebeard, having told her they are kept locked so no eye may look behind them, is frightened by her persistence. She rests her head on his shoulder to reassure him. Together, bound by their love, they will open the doors. Pay attention to the differing musical moments associated with the opening of the doors. In the darkness, the clinking of keys can be heard as he gives her one. Moaning issues from behind the door, but she unlocks it and a streak of horrid red light, like a gaping bloody wound, is cast across the floor to the dominance of violins and flutes.

The originality, beauty, power, and appropriateness of the music, inspired by the eerie story, constitute the core of the drama wherein little else happens beyond two people talking and doors opening. Lighting, to alter and contrast darkness, also is critical. The red is representative of Bluebeard's blood and it will appear everywhere as a symbol of his constant suffering. The first door reveals his torture chamber. The walls are wet with blood but Judith tells him she is not afraid. She moves on to the second door and asks for the key, telling Bluebeard it is her love for him that demands all the doors be opened. He warns her, for the sake of them both, of danger as he yields the second key. She unlocks the door. Noiselessly it swings ajar and through the opening streaks a garish reddish yellow light. This is the door of his armory, containing the ghastly tools of war covered with blood.

When Bluebeard asks if she is frightened, Judith replies by demanding the rest of the keys. For her the opening of doors allows streams of sunlight to flood into the cold, dark, dank hall. Bluebeard's inclination is to keep his past hidden under lock and key. Judith wants no secrets. Enlightenment must overtake this obscure world she has entered.

Judith asks for all the remaining keys. Bluebeard gives her only three with the admonition to question nothing of what she sees. As the third door opens, a streak of golden light shines across the hall. It is his treasury and the incalculable riches are hers, she is told, but Judith recoils when she sees blood on his treasures and on the crown of diamonds offered to her.

The fourth door is opened. A harp and strings sing out as a

bluish green light falls across the floor. Judith exults over the beauty of Bluebeard's secret garden until she discovers blood seeping beneath the lilies and roses. She asks the blood's source but her forbidden question is rebuked.

No music in the drama is more magnificent than the resounding of the entire orchestra as the fifth door is opened and a brilliant white light floods the hall. Through the door, stretching endlessly in every direction, lies Bluebeard's huge kingdom. He tells her all of it is hers in its vast and varied richness. But she sees clouds tinged with blood. Bluebeard opens his arms to her. The room is full of light. He wants to embrace her and call it a day. Judith's concern, however, is for two doors as yet unopened.

Bluebeard drops his arms. Has she not enough light? She wants the remaining doors unlocked and opened. He begs her to desist but she demands they be opened. He says he will give to her only one more key. She takes the key and as she turns it in the lock a frightening moan is heard. She backs away. Bluebeard asks her to leave the door closed. Her determination prevails. She opens it. Shadows of darkness invade the hall and through the door appears a watery world—teardrops from weeping, he explains, and the music is the sound of sorrow. They embrace. Judith asks if he truly loves her. She is everything to him, he tells her, and he asks for her trust: "Kiss me, trust me, ask me nothing." But she asks: "Tell me, Bluebeard, were there others who possessed your love before me?" Nothing he can say will persuade her to accept his love and ask no questions.

Separating from him, she suspects behind the seventh and last door will be the source of all the blood, his murdered wives, just as the rumors have proclaimed. Bluebeard, as he yields the key, warns her she will see his former wives. The door is opened and Judith backs away, dumbfounded by the beauty of three women dressed in a crown, mantle, and jewels. Bluebeard drops reverently before them. Judith moves into line with them. Bluebeard reveals they are the wives of the morning, noon, and twilight of his life, all beautiful, to be sure, but now it is Judith, the fairest of all, the fourth and final wife, the wife of his nighttime. He crowns her, puts a mantle over her shoulders, and places jewels upon her as the other doors quietly close and darkness begins to fill the hall, Judith protesting as he does so in the only duet in the opera. She then follows the path of the other three wives through the seventh door. It closes after her.

Bluebeard, alone as total darkness covers the stage, utters his last words, "Now, nothing but darkness, endless darkness," as the curtains close.

The music of this drama does not have those catchy, lilting melodies of Italian opera easily hummed or whistled almost instantly after first hearing them. The music expressing the desire of two people to be together as they face the ultimate isolation and loneliness of all human beings is continuously melodic in a powerful, probing, hauntingly different way.

Béla Bartók was an exceedingly private man. We all have our secrets and Bartók, like Bluebeard, preferred silence to their ever being told.

There is much in this little story to invite imaginative interpretations of the opera's exceedingly rich symbolism from audiences, performers, directors, conductors, critics, and scholars. Considerable controversy has been stirred. Judith has been made into a villain with an overactive curiosity and Bluebeard into the strong but too-silent male with all the accompanying feminine and masculine stereotypes. Is this a drama about the inability of people to truly communicate with one another and how ultimately each and every human being is alone?

Interpretations must not be limited to working only with the words of the libretto, however. What Bartók had to "say," and this, as far as the opera is concerned, is of the utmost importance, he put into marvelous music. It warrants careful and repeated listenings. In this music I hear both darkness and light, mutual love and individual differences, and the suffering and the joy of human existence. Above all, however, I hear the extraordinary beauty of Bartók's unique music.

LEOŠ JANÁČEK

Janáček was a Czech composer (1854–1928) who, for sixty of his seventy-four years, was almost unknown outside his Moravian homeland. Then, in 1916, his third opera, *Jenůfa* (1904), achieved notable success in Prague. This marked the beginning of his fame and intensified operatic creativity. He wrote nine operas, seven of them in the twentieth century. Today, with Smetana and Dvořák, Janáček resides in the pantheon reserved for only the greatest of the Czech masters.

Janáček was a contemporary of Puccini. He much admired the Italian's operatic genius and studied his methods, but what flowed out of Janáček's pen in no way was an imitation of an Italian gift for and preoccupation with heart-wrenching melodies. The masterworks of Leoš Janáček, with very few exceptions, were composed during the last decade of his life and, in spite of his romantic roots, a dedicated nationalism, and an abiding interest in the folk music of his native land, belong to modern music. Four of his nine operas have become quite well known: *Jenůfa* (1904), *Kátya Kabanová* (1921), *The Cunning Little Vixen* (1924), and *The Makropulos Affair* (1926). To choose among them was not easy, and there will be those who dispute my choice of *The Cunning Little Vixen* as the opera with which to introduce Janáček. I can't fret that. With charming and immediately accessible music, this opera about talking animals, insects, birds, and humans irresistibly probes the cycles of life and death in the natural world. Janáček would not be displeased to learn this is your introduction to his work as both librettist and composer, as often was the case, in his operatic career.

As early as 1897, Janáček developed his theory of "speech melody." It remained with him until the end of his life and greatly influenced his composing. During a lecture he attended, for example, he made notes of how moods and emotions are sounded. He noted pitches and melodies of words and phrases, and most of all his ears always were attuned to the varying rhythms of speech, both in formal situations, such as lectures, and in ordinary conversations. He was fascinated by the songs and noises of birds, made notes of these while walking in the woods, and incorporated this study with that of human speech toward the goal of creating unique musical rhythms and an authentic vocal style derived from nature. Janáček was smitten with Russia, for reasons cultural and political, and in the realm of operatic composition had much in common with Mussorgsky. He knew it, but did not like to admit it.

There was not an abundance of happiness in Janáček's life. Though he remained with the woman he had married before her sixteenth birthday, theirs was not a blissful union. Rifts emerged early, they parted temporarily, and both of their children would die, one as a child, the other as a young adult. Janáček, always a hard worker, immersed himself in teaching and composing, but recognition was slow in coming. He found diversion in love affairs, once with a woman who starred in one of his operas. His wife attempted suicide. Finally, they managed an accommodation. It is not surprising, with a long life of stingy rewards, to find gloom in the stories of many Janáček operas: The illegitimate child of Jenůfa is drowned in a brook *(Jenůfa)*; an unmarried woman, guilty of infidelity, drowns herself in the Volga *(Kátya Kabanová)*, and another woman, kept alive by an elixir for 337 years, longs for death *(The Makropoulos Affair)*, to give three examples. *The Cunning Little Vixen* is the happiest of his operas but it, too, is not without moments of sadness.

Most all of Janáček's music, including the instrumental pieces, is programmatic in origin (*program music* is inspired by a nonmusical idea, which the music attempts to express, often stated in the title, subtitle, or notes of the composer, and it is in marked contrast to *absolute music*, where no extra-musical conceptions, historical, poetic, or pictorial, are part of the creative process). A definite erotic impulse often was a motivating force in Janáček's creative process, especially in his operas, so notable for being clear, terse, well paced, and beautifully made. In fact, the erotic origin of his greatest works was Kamila Stöslova. She was the wife of an antique dealer, thirty-eight years younger than Janáček. His infatuation soon became an obsession. He kept her picture on his writing table, wrote her, and then waited for what seemed an eternity for her reply. She insisted he burn her letters. Theirs must have been somewhat of a lopsided love affair, yet when Janáček was seventy-four and more in love with her than ever, she visited him with her eleven-year-old son. The boy became temporarily lost in the woods. Frantically, Janáček searched in inclement weather, contracted pneumonia, and died soon thereafter. He identified several of the heroines of his great operas with Kamila. This prompts me to wonder, while leaving the answer up to you, if somehow, somewhere she is in *The Cunning Little Vixen?*

THE CUNNING LITTLE VIXEN (1924)

The Czech title *Příhody Lišky Bystroušky* literally means "The Adventures of the Vixen Bystrouska." The most common translations into English are "The Cunning Little Vixen" and "The Adventures of Fox Sharp-Ears." The origin of this unique opera is fascinating. The story, by Rudolf Tešnohlídek, was published both as a novel and as a serial in a newspaper with accompanying cartoon drawings. It tells of a vixen who is caught and raised by a forester and eventually escapes back to the wild. Janáček was intrigued by the tale, especially as it moved in and out of the animal and human worlds, the animals talking and behaving like humans. The longtime maid in the Janáček household, in her memoirs, gives herself credit for having introduced Janáček to the comic strip and for having suggested its appropriateness for operatic treatment—spurious, perhaps, but a good story.

Janáček wrote both libretto and music. As he took up the subject, he wrote to his beloved Kamila: It is a "merry thing with a sad end and I am taking up a place at that sad end myself." The story is about the passing of time, resulting changes, growing old, and nature's cycles of renewal. The sad end, wherein Janáček sees himself having a place, obviously is his own part in the aging process. He was nearing seventy at this time; Kamila had just turned thirty.

The characters and their vocal ranges:

BYSTROUŠKA, the vixen, *soprano*
The fox, *soprano*
LAPÁK, the dachshund, *mezzo-soprano*
The cock, *soprano*
CHOCHOLKA, the hen, *soprano*
The badger
The priest } *bass*
The screech owl
The forester's wife } *contralto*
The woodpecker, *soprano*
The forester, *bass baritone*
PEPÍK, the forester's son, *soprano*
FRANTÍK, Pepík's friend, *soprano*
PÁSEK, the innkeeper, *tenor*
The innkeeper's wife, *soprano*
HARAŠTA, the poacher, *bass*
A cricket, a caterpillar, a mosquito, a frog, a jay, and
    fox cubs

The opera is in three acts and seven scenes. Janáček did not number the scenes, however. Rather, he gave to them names (or most of them, at least) based on the actions of the vixen. Did you notice that Janáček designated two instances where a person plays two different parts? In some performances, the roles of the fox and the dog have been transposed for tenors. I do not know what Janáček would think of this but I can guess.

The opera is written in a rural Czech dialect unfamiliar even to inhabitants of Prague, and far, far beyond the little Czech I once learned. (Because of this, I made no attempt to work with the original text. All translations of Janáček's libretto into English I have taken from the published version made by Yveta Synek Graff and Robert T. Jones.) Learning to sing an opera by Smetana or Dvořák in Czech is hard enough for those who do not speak the language. I can imagine how the dialect could provide almost insurmountable difficulty to those confronting Czech for the first time. This is one reason why this opera is not more well known. I have a wonderful recording in Czech by native singers and another of a version in English. I like it but I can imagine what Janáček, who compiled copious notes on the sounds, pitches, rhythms, and music of human speech, would think of a translation.

The three acts of the opera, less than an hour and a half long, are balanced and beautifully made. The work moves rapidly in a most captivating manner among the characters and from event to event. In short, it never drags. But the music is so inextricably bound to the story and so perfectly expressive of it that you will miss the fun, joy, humor, and pathos if you do not follow the words closely.

Act I

The orchestral preludes, introducing the acts, and the interludes between the scenes have an immediate appeal and are important in establishing a mood. As the first notes of music are heard, the curtains part as the orchestral prelude perfectly depicts a shady spot in the woods on a warm summer afternoon. A lazy badger, puffing drowsily on his pipe, lolls in a ray of sun as it passes through the trees. Insects buzz annoyingly about him as a blue dragonfly dances. Janáček titled this scene "How Sharp-Ears [the vixen's name] was caught." With a shotgun on his shoulder, the forester comes through the woods and picks the shady spot as the perfect place to rest. He is as tired as he was after the first time he and his wife made love. He sits and hugs his shotgun, his "best mistress," void of fussing and nagging. A cricket and a grasshopper enter and, while the forester snoozes, they decide to dance to "good old-fashioned tunes." Also on the scene is a frog attempting to catch an intoxicated mosquito: Janáček having merely the first of several pertinent jokes in the construction of his most worthy libretto. The pursued mosquito tells off the frog, ". . . stop it now, go home! Go to hell!" A vixen runs onto the scene and frightens the frog, who jumps and lands on the forester, thus awakening him. The vixen, preoccupied with the tentative meal represented by the frog, is snatched up and held tight by the forester and the first scene ends as the ensnared vixen is carted off under his firm grip while the orchestra plays for a pantomime wherein the blue dragonfly reappears and searches for the fox.

It is, you will realize, a funny story as well as a probing and sad one and it is, even though undeniably anthropomorphic, true to nature: the story of each and every one of us. Eventually, we all, as Homer wrote, must give way to the next generation in the endless cycle of life. That is where this story is headed, and as you experience it do not listen for this or that excerpt. Listen to the whole. Listen to the skillful manner in which Janáček evokes a forest scene of insects, animals, and humans. It has taken more than half a century for the general public to become aware of the operatic mastery of Leos Janáček but at least—unlike Bizet—he did not die thinking himself a failure. What is sadder than a great artist who has given his or her life to creative work and dies thinking it a failure, especially when masterworks have been produced? For Janáček, recognition came to him, however briefly, before he died.

To a lovely orchestral interlude depicting a fading sun casting its light on an autumn afternoon, the second scene of the first act, titled "Sharp-Ears at the forester's lakeside farmyard," begins. The forester's dog and the vixen lie side by side. As the forester's wife pours milk into the vixen's bowl, her husband comments on how much the fox has grown. As the vixen laps milk, the dog, Lapák, confesses never having known what love is. The vixen has never been taught how to make love but she has learned about it by listening to the sparrows who live in the tree over the house. Her response is a classic mockery of human behavior.

> They made an awful racket, yelling, screaming,
> calling each other nasty and indecent and
> immoral names. The old one has his girl friends
> always hanging around . . . Everyone knew it.
> And then, one Saturday night he got so drunk

that the hawk and the raven came and then they
beat him up. Anyway, not one of the children
was any better. One of them ran off with a cuck-
oo bird, then started sleeping around with all his
neighbors. One of the sparrows had to give her
hazelnuts as alimony payments. The sparrow's
stepdaughter, oh! she was an ugly creature, was
the forest nymphomaniac.

The dog makes a pass at the vixen and is rejected. Pepík and
Frantík, teasing the young fox with sticks, nearly are nipped, and
the forester's wife, fed up with raising a fox, mumbles repudia-
tions. The forester responds by tying up Sharp-Ears. The dog sidles
away, the boys run off, and the forester and his wife go into the
house.

The interlude connecting with the final scene of the first act
is glorious. No music in the entire opera is more beautiful. The
afternoon wanes and turns to dusk. The despondent vixen appears
transformed as a young girl crying in her sleep. Is this remarkable
musical episode Janáček's depiction of the inseparable oneness of
all nature, of the unity of animals and humans? As dawn breaks,
the vixen is herself again.

"Sharp-Ears as a politician; Sharp-Ears runs away" is the title
of the final scene of Act I. The dog admonishes the vixen to curb
her temper. The rooster, strutting, comments on her now being
tied up and urges his hens to lay eggs. The hens comply. The chief
hen taunts the vixen, who leaps up and invites the sisterhood of
hens to organize, to reject all men, and to build a better world than
one in which a single rooster is well kept by humans to enjoy the
pleasures of using their bodies and eating all of the best food. "No
more rooster," chant the hens, until the cock convinces them to
be wary of a fox trying to trick them so she can catch and eat
them.

The vixen feigns dejection and pretends to bury herself alive.
When the birds get too close, to see if really she is dead, the vixen
kills the rooster and commences to slaughter the hens, then
laughs while the forester's wife furiously rushes onto the scene
and the chief hen cackles despairingly. The forester arrives and
starts beating the fox with a club. The vixen bites through the
rope, then bolts into the forester, knocking him down, and escapes
into the woods. This entire melee is captured by the music.

Act II

Scene 1: "Sharp-Ears expropriates a home." It is late afternoon in the forest. Janáček continues to have his fun. The vixen disturbs the drowsy badger by peering into his den and exclaiming, "Look at that badger lying there like a capitalist . . . He's got a house big enough for three." Thus begins an exchange of acrimony, iterated by flies buzzing about, between the two animals. The badger strikes the vixen and threatens, first a lawsuit if immediately she does not leave his premises and second, to have her arrested. Arching her tail, the vixen pisses on the badger and trots several yards away. Picking up his pipe, the affronted badger, who can stand no more of these indignities, vacates his den and saunters off into the woods. The vixen returns and makes the empty den her own.

A brief interlude accompanies the scene change to Pásek's inn, where the schoolmaster and forester play cards. The priest, smoking a pipe exactly like the badger's, is watching. The forester teases the schoolmaster about being too old to be interested in courting, the priest mumbles his Latin, *Non des mulieri corpus tuum* ("Do not give your body to a woman"), and the schoolmaster retorts by asking the forester if he and his vixen "are a happy couple." The forester curses the vixen and the repartee continues briefly. The schoolmaster leaves, then the priest. The forester would like to sit quietly and drink beer but Pásek also wants to know about the vixen. The forester snubs his questions, finishes his drink, and departs.

During another brief interlude, the scene changes to the forest. It is night. A full moon shows a steep path, a fence next to it, and sunflowers. Behind one of them hides the vixen. Bumbling along, supporting himself on his walking stick, the tipsy schoolmaster laments having drunk the night away. He falls and finds himself face to face with that sunflower. In his stupor he mistakes it for Terynka, the seductive gypsy girl for whom he yearns. The vixen, darting off, causes the sunflower to become animated. The schoolmaster reaches for it and is spilled by the fence. He hides behind it as the priest now approaches, attempting to identify the line of Greek he has been reciting as he bitterly recalls the episode that forever turned him away from all women. As the vixen runs across the stage, gunshots set the frightened priest and schoolmaster racing off in opposite directions. From offstage can be heard the voice of the forester. Surely, he had spotted the vixen.

The final scene of the second act, "The courtship, love, and marriage of Sharp-Ears," is introduced by one of my favorite orchestral interludes, this one with wordless voices of the forest, in the entire opera. Laying in front of her den, the vixen becomes mesmerized by a handsome fox who appears and then approaches. He begins to converse and soon the vixen is telling the story of her life even before formal introductions. Learning how much the vixen loves rabbit, the fox runs off, catches one, and returns to her, but their love at first sight has ignited a diffcrent appetite. Their emotions are poured out in a good old-fashioned love duet. One of the sublime features of the entire score, its humor will be lost on you if you do not know the words (unless, of course, you are listening to a version in English translation). In the culmination of the fox's declaration of love he sings, "I love you, not just your body, but your soul ever more. Novels will be inspired by you, operas will be sung about you . . ." After the duet, fox and vixen retire into her den as the dragonfly, owl, and jay gossip. At dawn the vixen and fox emerge from the den, she whispers some facts of life into his ear, and the woodpecker performs a quick wedding, which is celebrated by dancing and a wordless hymn of all the forest voices as the act ends.

Act III
The third and final act is in three scenes, the first being "Sharp-Ears outwits Harašta and Sharp-Ears' death." Midday, in autumn, at the forest's edge, Harašta wanders about singing a song. He spies the dead rabbit left by the fox and is about to poach it when he sees the forester coming. They chat. Harašta tells the forester he soon will marry Terynka and, as he departs, that he did not kill or poach the rabbit at his feet. Meanwhile, the forester sets a trap for the vixen with the dead rabbit and leaves in the opposite direction of Harašta. Fox cubs fill the stage dancing and singing to music I wish would go on for hours instead of two minutes. Instantly upon arriving, the vixen is suspicious about the dead rabbit. The fox appears soon thereafter. Cubs and parents all avoid the trap so obvious to them. The cubs scamper off and a conversation about having more children is interrupted when Harašta returns. The fox hides but not the vixen. She taunts the poacher by limping about, then makes a dash for his basket and steals a chicken. Harašta takes his gun and discharges it without even aiming. By pure chance, the vixen is struck. She dies.

With an orchestral interlude, the scene changes to the garden of the inn. Sitting with the schoolmaster, the forester is served a beer by the wife of the innkeeper. Time has passed. Things have changed. The forester is out of sorts. Hiking in the woods, he had found the vixen's den deserted; he never got for his wife the fox-fur muff. The schoolmaster also is sad as he mentions that Terynka is to be married this very morning and, adds the innkeeper's wife, it is this bride-to-be who will be sporting a new fur muff. Life must go on for the old men, who learn that their friend the priest is lonely and unhappy away in his new parish. Though still early, the men are no longer lively and young. The forester leaves.

"The young Sharp-Ears is the spitting image of her mother," the opera's last scene, is introduced by the final orchestral interlude. This is the great scene of the forester. It is springtime and, in a sense, the opera has come full circle, for the forester finds himself in exactly the same place in the forest where, so many years ago, he caught the vixen. But the music is not the same because the forester is not the same. (Janáček, who was his own librettist, asked Tešnohlídek, the author of the story, to compose the words of the forester's song and it was this music that Janáček requested be played at his funeral.) The old forester sits and reminisces about his youth, courtship, and marriage. It is a springtime hymn to love, to flowers—indeed, to the rebirth of life in the seasonal cycle. He falls into slumber. All the animals, just as in the first scene, appear. The forester, dreaming, sits up and looks about, but sees no vixen. Then a vixen cub enters:

> I see her! There she is. Baby Sharp-Ears! Little devil! Like a twinkle in her mother's eye! Hey there! Wait till I catch you, just like your mother! But I'll treat you better, that's for sure. Maybe then they won't try to make our lives into an opera.

He reaches out to catch the vixen but catches a frog instead. He thinks it is the same old frog of long ago. Stammering, the frightened frog exclaims "Tha-that was my Granddaddy!" The opera is over.

∾

You will have noticed that it was difficult for me to isolate excerpts or highlights from the score. There are reasons for this. Throughout the opera there are wonderful little moments, but often they pass on to something else almost as soon as they have begun. Let me say this differently: Throughout Janáček's ingenious magical uniting of human and animal worlds, his unique blend of dance and song becomes an unbroken musical continuum discouraging any thought of extracting highlights.

At the beginning of this section, I implied the possibility that some might quibble over my choice of this opera from Janáček's corpus as equally famous works also attract a following. I stand by my choice. This opera is not just one of the best of the twentieth century; it is an operatic masterpiece for any age. It is amazing to me that even almost three quarters of a century after his death the music of Janáček is unfamiliar to so many opera buffs. Get to know it well and you will have a lot to tell others who think they know so much about opera. And tell them, also, that Janáček was not only a great composer but a visionary as well, for he was among the first of the few to champion Berg's *Wozzeck*, another twentieth-century masterpiece whose recognition was slow in coming.

Atonal Music

In this section, I'll discuss what you need to know about modern music in order to understand Berg's *Wozzeck*. With Richard Strauss's avant-garde operas, Debussy's impressionism, Janáček's "speech-melody," and Bartók now opening the door to atonal music, "modern music" no longer is new to you. But Alban Berg constitutes a giant step into this new world. Berg was the disciple of Arnold Schoenberg, the revolutionary who introduced what commonly is called atonal music into the Western tradition. Schoenberg disliked the word *atonal* to describe the type of music he devised. *Atonal* implies without tones. He preferred the word *pan-tonal* (all tones), and *polytonal* (many tones) will do just as well. However, because the word *atonal* has become commonplace in the vocabulary of modern music to describe Schoenberg's system and that of his disciples, we will use it here.

Recall that when writing about Bartók, I said I would define *tonal*, *atonal*, and *polytonal* music when we came to Alban Berg. With the exception of Bartók's *Bluebeard's Castle*, which flirts with atonality, all the operas heretofore discussed in this book are tonal compositions. At least, they are by composers who, unlike Schoenberg, did not consciously create a system of atonal music even though traditional tonality was disappearing in Wagner's later work and in that of Debussy. Because the step from tonal music to atonal music is such a big one, and because Alban Berg, who composed our next opera, *Wozzeck*, was a disciple of Schoenberg, who took atonality to its extreme with his twelve-tone system, the following digression is necessary—especially because Berg often employed both tonality and atonality in his music, sometimes within the same piece. The concept of tonality and atonality constitutes a huge, complicated part of music history, the subject of volumes teeming with a most sophisticated vocabulary. I can do no more than to present a basic difference in ordinary language that will help you to understand what is transpiring when you hear music created with the intention of abolishing tonality.

Before a revolutionary development occurred early in the twentieth century, virtually all music composed between the sixteenth and twentieth centuries we Westerners would be likely to have heard, from classical to popular to folk, would be tonal music. In tonal music, all the notes are not of equal importance. In fact, one note, generally, which is called the *key note* or *tonic*, is much more important than all the other notes, so much so that all the other notes relate to it and are even determined by it. In composing tonal music, a preference is given to a tone, the *tonic*, which becomes the tonal center to which all other tones are related. A full-fledged explanation of how this works would be both a lengthy and complicated sojourn into music theory. Fortunately, I can give you a brief and uncomplicated example to make this concept simpler to comprehend. Sing aloud the first verse of "Mary Had a Little Lamb" and feel how the music of the last line, ". . . that lamb was sure to go," just pulls you to a resolution on the word *go*. A *resolution* in tonal music is a satisfying sound, the right sound; you just know the music has to end there to sound right. It is the tonic, the key note, the tonal center pulling the tune to a comfortable, satisfying conclusion. Now, sing the verse again and this time on the last note instead of going down to the resolution on the word *go*, raise your voice several notes. What happens? It simply does not sound right; the music does not resolve. Tonal music resolves; it feels good; it sounds right. That is why we like it.

Obviously, or literally, atonal means music composed without a tonic—that is, without a tonal center determining an ultimate resolution in the music. To most uninitiated ears, atonal music does not sound right. It is not satisfying. It lacks the comforting pull toward an end where everything relaxes and resolves. In atonal music there seem to be loose ends and unresolved tensions.

The breakdown of tonal music began in the nineteenth century with Richard Wagner, the most powerful force of change in the music of his age. Wagner's music is tonal, but much less so than that of his hero Beethoven, because Wagner begins with one key note (one tonic) but then subtly his music modulates (changes from one key note to another, from one tonic to another). This makes it more and more difficult to anticipate where the all-important resolution would be or should be. Wagner's mature music could go on and on, seemingly forever, without resolving, and this is one reason why it has been described as "endless melody." The opera *Tristan und Isolde* is a good example of Wagner's constantly modulating music.

ARNOLD SCHOENBERG

Wagner, and especially *Tristan und Isolde*, had a profound influence on Arnold Schoenberg, who would develop atonal music to its absolute limits. Schoenberg, however, as already noted, did not like the negativity implied in the word *atonal*: an absence of tone. *Pan-tonality* for him better described music composed without a tonal center. As Schoenberg strove to eliminate all aspects of traditional tonality in his compositions, as years went by, he concluded that without some rules, some structure, atonality unleashed chaos in music. To restore order he developed his twelve-tone system (also called *dodecaphonic* and *serial music*). Each of the twelve tones out of which all our Western music is made is of equal importance. To ensure this, Schoenberg's twelve-tone system is based on a rule: no note of the twelve tones can be repeated until the other eleven have been used in a series. Though composers other than Schoenberg were experimenting with similar concepts, his system became the most pervasive and influential in abolishing traditional tonality and its resolution of all tension. Without a tonal center, there is no resolution.

Schoenberg (1874–1951) composed some remarkable music but more than fifty years after his death there are many who know and love classical music who still consider his compositions too harsh and unsatisfying. This is so, at least in part, because one cannot listen to atonal music, especially in its serial music manifestations, and judge it by the standards of tonal music. This leads us to reject it because the music does not resolve comfortably in the manner we expect it, in the way our ears have been trained to expect. There is no question about his only opera, *Moses and Aaron*, being a seminal work in the history of twentieth-century opera. Not only is it one of the few operas written on a biblical subject, but also it was composed in the twelve-tone system Schoenberg devised.

Look at the keyboard of any piano and you will see the notes are arranged in a precise, repetitive pattern. There are twelve notes in each pattern. They are named sequentially by a letter of the alphabet.

This is the pattern from which all Western music is made. Notice the sign ♯ that is part of the name of the black notes. This sign, meaning "sharp," designates a note whose sound is a half tone different from that of the white note to its left and the white note to its right.

Consider C♯ as an example. The sound of C♯ is higher than that of C but lower than that of D; it is halfway between. This holds true throughout the keyboard. The twelve notes comprise the pattern that is repeated. Invariably the manufacturer of the piano places its name in the middle of a board behind the keyboard. The C in the middle of the keyboard is thus called *middle C*. As you go up the keyboard—that is, to the right—the notes sound higher. The C above middle C is called high C, the note that sends shivers up your spine when the tenor hits it gloriously in his big aria. As you go down the keyboard, to the left, the notes sound lower. But all Gs sound the same tone except higher or lower, and it is the same with all other notes.

The arbitrary rule Schoenberg made for his twelve-tone system is this: In composing music, all twelve tones must be used in some sort of a series before any one tone can be repeated. In this way, all musical tones in Schoenberg's system are equal. No one tone has any more say than another. This seems to be an extremely rigid and inflexible mathematical system completely at odds with the man who devised it: Schoenberg believed an artist is one who "feels as if what he does were dictated to him" from beyond, an idea utterly consistent with the ancient classical poet, who considered himself merely an amanuensis of a Muse, one taking, so to speak, dictation from some immortal power. Is it any wonder that some find it difficult to reconcile Schoenberg's seemingly mathematical system with his mystical vision of the artist as one who in some miraculous way is in an association with an ultimate power far beyond mere mortal perceptions?

Though I have chosen not to make Schoenberg's only opera a significant part of this chapter (because I think you will profit more by starting with Berg's *Wozzeck*), I cannot conclude these comments on Schoenberg without a few observations on *Moses und Aron*. Schoenberg wrote the libretto for his opera, and for those who know something about his life, it is tempting to make of it an autobiographical interpretation. Does he use the biblical story to express the dilemma of his own creative life? Schoenberg is both the idealistic Moses dwelling without compromise in his ivory tower and the practical Aron, who lives in the real world and must relate to other human beings. Melding words and music, Schoenberg contrasts what he deems are the two opposing worlds of the human condition, one bright and luxurious, the other dark and bleak. Schoenberg opposed the sterile view of science as the ultimate faith for modern times even though his inner struggle was that of mystical yearnings colliding with one of the most advanced and highly rational minds of his age.

The avant-garde nature of his music notwithstanding, ultimately Arnold Schoenberg reveals himself in his only opera as a throwback to religious Romanticism. Did he leave the work unfinished because within himself he could not resolve warring rational and mystical forces? Or did he not complete the work because he—like Moses in the story—struggles, yet fails, in his attempt to communicate the unspeakable, lofty word of God?

I saw the first performance of this opera in the Western hemisphere and am sorely tempted to introduce my understanding of this work to you. In the more than half a century of its existence, however, it has failed to achieve public acceptance beyond a small but growing circle of enthusiasts. Because of its limited cult following among some musicians and connoisseurs, I present instead the opera *Wozzeck*, the masterwork of Schoenberg's disciple Alban Berg.

ALBAN BERG

Both men were born in Vienna. Though Schoenberg was only eleven years older than Berg, he influenced his student profoundly—so much so that Berg acknowledged it by dedicating his other opera, *Lulu*, also an unfinished work, to his mentor.

Lulu was composed in the twelve-tone system. Many years ago, Joanne and I attended one of the early performances of this revolutionary work about a woman who winds up in London as a prostitute and an eventual victim of Jack the Ripper. We were in graduate school and bought the least expensive tickets way up in the peanut heaven section of the balcony. Both the story and the demanding music of the new, unfamiliar twelve-tone system took its toll on the audience. Half the house did not return after the first intermission and, having anticipated this (we saw coats going on), hurriedly my wife and I made a dash for two fine empty seats in the orchestra section on the main floor. Half of those remaining departed during the second intermission and we enjoyed the next act sitting in the two middle seats of the first row. Today we would not be so lucky: *Lulu* has gained quite a following due, in part, to worldwide acceptance of its predecessor, *Wozzeck*, as a modern masterpiece.

WOZZECK (1925)

Impressionism was the critical concept providing us an entrée to Debussy's *Pelleás et Mélisande*. For *Wozzeck* the critical concept is expressionism. Debussy's impressionism, borrowed from the impressionistic painters, you will recall, implies a music that hints at something rather than giving a total and objective representation. It is a vague, dreamy style of music full of changing colors and moods, a music of imprecise atmosphere. Expressionism in music is also a term borrowed from the visual arts. Schoenberg, himself a talented painter, befriended the great expressionistic painters of Germany and Austria—for example, Nolde, Kirchner, and Kokoschka, who worked in Munich, Berlin, and Vienna during the first quarter of the twentieth century. Expressionism goes beyond a painter's representation of what reality looks like on the surface to depict the artist's subjective interpretation of reality or a reaction to it. Thus expressionism represents the psychological and emotional aspects of a subject and therefore is highly introspective. Usually, this resulted in distortions, exaggerations, and complicated symbolism. Expressionism, in both painting and musical composition, is the opposite of impressionism. Both, nevertheless, are equally important to the development of modern art and music.

Schoenberg, and his disciple Berg, as expressionists, employed music without tonal centers to express their subjective interpretation of the world as they found it. This world, as we know so well, is not always pretty. Hatred, evil, and injustice are visually forced upon us when we view the paintings and drawings of the expressionists, who often found life ugly and unpleasant. In the music of Schoenberg and Berg, we hear that life is not always a comfortable resolution. This is one basic reason why atonal music is so dissonant: because for its composers, real life was dissonant.

For some, the purpose of art is to present the good, the true, and the beautiful. Especially in the twentieth century, this is not true for many great artists who in what they paint, write, or compose tell it like it is. This often is the case for two reasons: The artist must express his or her vision of reality both for own needs and to wake slumbering multitudes all too willing to live their own little lives completely insensitive to what is going on around them. The opera *Wozzeck* is an example of this. And what is so remarkable about it is that the riveting story is not a product of a twentieth-century dramatist placing the absurdities of contemporary life on a stage before us, but rather the product of remarkable insights into our modern age by a revolutionary man of the theater who died before his twenty-fifth birthday.

Wozzeck, a dramatic fragment of twenty-seven scenes was written by Georg Büchner who was born in Darmstadt in 1813 the same year in which Wagner and Verdi were born. He was blessed with extraordinary abilities in both science and poetry and because of an overt liberal posture had to flee his conservative hometown, as would Wagner years later, taking refuge in a more democratic Switzerland. By the time he reached the Swiss border he had completed *Danton's Death*, a major play. He was in his early twenties. At Zürich University, he earned a doctorate in natural science and was appointed to a lectureship in comparative anatomy. There he divided his time between science and poetry and within a few months, three more plays had come from his pen. One of them, *Woyzeck*, was found in a barely legible manuscript by his parents when this brilliant young man succumbed to the typhus epidemic in the winter of 1837.

This dramatic fragment fortunately was saved, and for nearly half a century it more than gathered dust. With age the pages darkened to virtually unreadable, but in 1879 they were made decipherable through the application of a chemical process.

Perhaps it was at this stage of attempting to salvage the work when *Woyzeck* became the *Wozzeck* that so captured the imagination of Alban Berg when he saw a production in Vienna in May 1914—in fact, not just one production, for so mesmerized was Berg by Büchner's revolutionary drama that he returned to the theater several times, instinctively knowing he wanted to make from it an opera. This morality play was drawn from the terrible life of Johann Christian Woyzeck. In 1924 this German soldier and barber, in a moment of insane jealousy, killed the woman he loved.

Berg faced what to others appeared to be two insurmountable problems: how to create a dramatic unity for a text from the twenty-three of Büchner's twenty-seven fragments available to him at the time and then how to give an opera musical unity having abandoned the traditional, time-honored technique of composing tonal music in which the music resolves and ties together into a unified whole its songs, dances, and orchestral episodes. Berg was advised not only by friends but also by his revered teacher Schoenberg to forget the project. Büchner's play, loosely cast in fragments and articulated in an innovative use of language and dialogue, simply could not be set to music. But it was. And Berg's achievement, though he never intended as much, amounted to a revolution in operatic composition.

A brief elucidation of how he solved these two problems provides the operagoer with an insight into one of the most powerful and influential music dramas of the twentieth century. To solve the problem of nearly two dozen dramatic fragments left by Büchner without any reference to their sequence, Berg recast them into three acts, each with five scenes. This alone provided significant dramatic unity. He gave a title to each act. The first act is the Exposition, wherein we meet Wozzeck and those whose behavior will torment him: his army captain; Marie, the mother of his child and the woman he loves; a doctor; and a drum major. Act II is the Denouement, wherein Wozzeck and Marie become estranged, he follows her helplessly, then is beaten up by the drum major. The third act is the Catastrophe: Marie, revealed as a sinner is killed by Wozzeck who then drowns, leaving their uncomprehending child an orphan at play with other children.

Through the dramatic unity Berg made of Büchner's fragments

it is easy to see in *Wozzeck* not just the terrible fate of one poor, unfortunate soul but also, in a mythic sense, the fate of all good human beings who love, who wish to be good and do good, but who are driven to self-destruction by those in an unjust social order who are incapable of living for more than their own private ends. Wozzeck's story, ultimately, is not about him, the murder of Marie, and his subsequent suicide but rather about how the pitiable fate of this one man is the transcending means to comprehending what terrible horrors an insensitive, unjust social order can create.

To solve the problem of giving his opera musical unity, Berg created—or, better said, in numerous instances—re-created distinct musical forms for each of the fifteen scenes. He connected them by a series of musical interludes serving a variety of purposes: providing a scene with an obvious ending, making a transition to another scene, or making a definite introduction to even another scene. I cannot overemphasize the importance of these orchestral interludes. Through Berg's ingenious use of them, the five separate scenes of each act achieve a seamless entity; furthermore, they constitute some of the most remarkable music in the score. Act I is composed of five character sketches. The corresponding music is a suite, a rhapsody, a march and cradle song, a passacaglia, and an andante. Act II, wherein Wozzeck becomes convinced of Marie's infidelity is set to a symphony in five movements: sonata form, fantasy and fugue, largo, scherzo, and rondo martiale. Act III, in which Wozzeck murders Marie and then atones through suicide, is accompanied by six inventions: invention on a theme, invention on a tone, invention on a rhythm, invention on a six-tone chord, an instrumental interlude with closed curtain, and invention on a persistent rhythm *(perpetuum mobile)*. There is no need to be intimidated by the above. Taken step by step, understanding will be a piece of cake. Furthermore, this schema outlining the dramatic and musical unity of Berg's *Wozzeck* was prepared by Willi Reich, the composer's biographer, and is available as part of the libretto with most of the audio recordings of the opera.

Finally, having thus provided an extraordinary and innovative musical unity for his opera, Berg quite reasonably exhorts his listener to ignore these specific forms and simply to listen to the music as the drama unfolds. That is precisely what you should do. Nevertheless, in the following synopsis I do remind you of what musical idea accompanies each section in Berg's meticulous arrangement, if for no other reason than that nothing like it ever before appeared in opera history. And, as you listen, it will be immediately apparent how something else you have not as yet encountered takes place.

The first words of the drama are declaimed by the captain in a form of expression called *Sprechgesang* (German for "speech-song"), a mode of vocalization in which the composer indicates the notes of the pitch but the actual delivery is neither singing nor speaking in a normal, natural manner. Just as the word indicates, it is a form of expression lying between talking and singing. It was first devised for operatic use by the composer of the opera *Hansel and Gretel*, Engelbert Humperdinck (the real one, not the pop star who adopted his name). Arnold Schoenberg significantly developed and used this mode of declamation, too, but he preferred to describe it as *Spechstimme* (German for "speech-voice") by which he meant "musically defined speech." Unlike singing, where the performer is to sing words precisely according to how the music is written, speech-song allows the performer certain liberties as to how his or her voice rises and falls after intoning the pitch prescribed by the composer. It also makes words much more easily understood, and by now you know so well that ever since opera's origins, the question of what is more important, the words or the music, simply will not go away. Different performers therefore can offer quite different interpretations of the same character.

The characters of the drama and their voice ranges are:

WOZZECK, a thirty-year-old soldier of low rank who is the servant of the captain, *baritone*
ANDRES, a soldier and friend of Wozzeck, *lyric tenor*
MARIE, Wozzeck's lover and mother of their child, *soprano*
Their child, *treble*
The captain, *tenor*
The doctor, *bass*
Drum major, *heroic tenor*
First apprentice, *deep bass*
Second apprentice, *high baritone or tenor*
MARGRET, neighbor of Marie, *contralto*
An idiot, *tenor*
Other soldiers and apprentices, *tenors, baritones, basses*
Servant girls and wenches, *sopranos and contraltos*
Group of children

Act I

Within a few notes of music, the first scene of the first act, denot-
ed Exposition, is under way. It occurs in a room of the captain,
who sits before a mirror. It is early morning and Wozzeck is shav-
ing him. The captain orders him to proceed more slowly and speculates abstractly on time and eternity, to which Wozzeck replies
tersely with no more than "Yes, indeed, Captain." The captain
inquires about the weather, then declares that even though
Wozzeck is a good man, he has no morality because of his illegitimate child. Wozzeck answers that he is one of the unfortunate
poor who cannot afford morality; furthermore, his child will not
be spurned by the good Lord who said, "Suffer the children to
come to me." The captain dismisses Wozzeck. The music of this
brief scene is a suite (originally Baroque instrumental music of a
number of movements in differing dance forms) of very short
pieces perfectly appropriate to the captain's lack of humanity and
Wozzeck's frustration and poverty.

Berg calls the music accompanying the second scene a rhapsody (a word used differently by different composers but usually
designating music with an emphasis on freedom of form; Berg
confines it to a strict structure and includes within it a hunting
song). It is now late afternoon and Wozzeck and Andres are in a
field outside the town where they are cutting sticks. Andres passes the time by singing of the joy of the huntsman but Wozzeck,
frightened by shadows cast by the setting sun, is plagued by eerie
visions and condemns the place as accursed. Andres attempts to
calm his terrified friend until he, too, commences to waver before
Wozzeck's description of what he sees. Night has fallen and the
two men depart. Berg's music for the uncanny hallucinations is a
perfect fit.

Even though Berg designated distinct labels for his musical
building blocks associated with each scene, they are mortared
together and given unity by the musical interludes connecting the
scenes. Thus, quite naturally, and without interruption, we are
taken to Marie's room, where she, her child in her arms, stands at
her window watching the approach of the military band. It is led
by the drum major, who struts to the military march. (I love this
little episode of the marching soldiers.) Margret, through the window, comments on what a hunk the drum major is and notices
that he and Marie have greeted each other. This leads to some
unpleasant slandering between the two women. Marie slams her
window and in the silence of her room sings a lullaby to her son

as she rocks him in her arms. It is one of the most beautiful melodies of the opera, an extraordinary example of how lovely atonal music can be. As her child sleeps, Marie is jolted frightfully from a reverie by a knocking on her window. It is Wozzeck, whom she addresses as Franz (Johann Franz Wozzeck is his full name). He has no time to come in. He must report. He does, however, pause long enough to relate, first mysteriously and then fretting with excitement, his fearful visions. Marie tries to calm him. She holds their son before him to see but he turns his eyes away and runs off. Her concern for the pained, distracted Wozzeck becomes her own anguish, heard in the music, for their situation. "Ah, we poor people," she says. "I can endure no more. It terrifies me." She runs to the door.

Berg's music for the fourth scene—he designates it a passacaglia (originally moderately slow Baroque music of continuous variations)—consists of twenty-one variations on a theme of twelve tones. The atonal music here becomes strictly twelve-tone serial music. Remember, in atonal music there is no one all-important note influencing the others and pulling them to that satisfying resolution your ears have been trained to expect. Schoenberg's twelve-tone system can place even greater demands on the listener. For the scene of Wozzeck's visit to the doctor, Berg states a twelve-tone theme and from it makes twenty one variations. Unless you are a sophisticated musician, variations on a theme, even in tonal music, can be exceedingly difficult to follow as the composer turns the motif around, upside down, and inside out. Don't even think about trying to decipher Berg's variations. I mention them only so you can be aware of hearing an example of the revolutionary technique in musical composition that attracted a school of exceedingly gifted followers, who altered the direction of musical composition in the twentieth century.

The doctor is a repugnant, conceited man who pays the impoverished Wozzeck, who is ill and needs a doctor, a pittance to come to him daily as the subject of his scientific dietetics experiment through which he hopes to win fame, fortune, and immortality. The scene is of a sunny afternoon in the doctor's study. The doctor chastises Wozzeck, who is increasingly confused. He reveals he hears terrifying voices; ultimately, Wozzeck becomes incoherent. As he speculates on how famous he will be due to this experiment, the doctor becomes ecstatic. Then, suddenly quite calmly, he asks Wozzeck to show him his tongue and the scene ends.

With an increasing intensity, the orchestral interlude connects us to the final scene of the first act. Of the five it is the shortest, which also is the case with the culminating scenes of the second and third acts. Its terseness notwithstanding, it is a scene of critical importance to the plot. In the street passing before her door, Marie stands with the drum major admiring his robust masculinity: "He has a chest like a bull and a beard like a lion," she says, proud to have captured his attention. He brags, in reply, that he will be even more resplendent in his Sunday attire. Marie haltingly rebukes his first attempt to embrace her but yields philosophically on the second: "Have your way with me, then. It's all the same." Together they enter the house. A resounding crescendo with a rapid tremolo floods the empty stage and we know what is happening behind her closed door as the curtain falls on the first act.

Act II

Act II, the Denouement, also plays in five scenes connected by orchestral interludes. For the first of them, the curtain rises to reveal Marie's room. It is a sunny morning as she, with her son asleep on her lap, studies herself in a fragment of a mirror. She admires her new earrings, a gift from the drum major we presume. Were she not so wretchedly poor, could she be like rich, noble women, looking as she does? she wonders. The boy stirs and sits up. She attempts to subdue him back into sleep by causing the mirror to cast flickers across the wall and telling him that it is the Sandman. Wozzeck enters and notices the earrings. She claims to have found them, but he does not believe her. Changing the subject, he comments on how the child always sleeps—indeed, now perspires in his slumber—because the days of the poor are passed in endless toil, even when they sleep. "We poor people," the core of Büchner and Berg's social criticism, is reiterated.

In a different mood, Wozzeck gives wages earned from serving the captain and the doctor to Marie. She thanks him, he leaves, and Marie condemns herself for bad behavior in noting how the whole world goes to the devil—man, wife, and child. The music of the entire second act Berg designated as a symphony in five movements (A symphony within an opera? What novelty.) For this first scene he composed music in a sonata form (generally three sections with different tempos, the first stating a theme, the second developing it, and the third repeating it with variations) based on three themes, presumably one associated with each of the three characters, Marie, Wozzeck, and their child, linking them as a family.

Scene 2 likewise has three characters, but they are not nicely linked in either word or music, for the doctor and his friend, the captain, could not be more unkind to Wozzeck. It is daytime. The two friends greet each other on the street and commence walking together but the captain lags behind. The doctor comments on the inevitable consequences of being overweight, thus alarming the captain. Wozzeck salutes as he hastens past but is summoned to turn back and together captain and doctor taunt him with merciless, humorous allusions to Marie's infidelity with the drum major until his face turns "white as chalk." Without asking their leave, Wozzeck rushes away from this bothersome twosome.

For this section of the symphony, Berg made what he calls a fantasy (a free flight of musical fancy) and a fugue (a strict musical form wherein one voice begins and others follow it), built once again out of three themes. The task of a musicological exegesis of this opera's various themes, however, like the countless musical motifs out of which Wagner made his music, lies well beyond the confines of this book.

The music accompanying the third scene is a largo, a slow movement. On a dull day, Marie stands before her door and greets Wozzeck as he hurries to her. She parries his obtuse accusations with nebulous replies until finally, having lost control, he suddenly asserts "you with him." "So what," she answers, as he rushes at her but she demands he not touch her: "Better a knife in my belly than a hand on me." She disappears indoors and Wozzeck, whispering a repeat of her extreme and unwittingly all too prophetic words, feels as if he is falling into an abyss.

As he leaves the stage a *ländler* (an Austrian dance like a slow waltz) introduces the scherzo (light, rapid, playful music) marked for the fourth scene. It is not, however, an old-fashioned typical *ländler*, but rather one distorted to fit the drunken atmosphere of a tavern late at night. Apprentices, soldiers, and servant girls crowd the scene, some dancing and others watching and still others milling about. Wozzeck enters and seeing Marie dancing with the drum major, seats himself in a rage on a bench. A chorus of apprentices and soldiers perform a hunting song. Andres, having borrowed a guitar from the band, leads them. After the song he and Wozzeck converse briefly, a drunk apprentice climbs on a table and preaches, and the fool sidles up next to Wozzeck, again alone. "It smells, it smells of blood," says the fool. Thrice

Wozzeck repeats the word *blood* as Marie and the drum major dance by him. The scene ends as he envisions a red mist enveloping the twisting figures whirling past him.

The little symphony concludes in a rondo with an introduction to this final scene of the second act. It is night in the barracks. A deep-breathing chorus of sleeping soldiers is heard as the scene begins. Wozzeck moans and awakens, tormented by visions of Marie with the drum major. He consults Andres, who suggests sleep. A fragment of the sleeping chorus is repeated and then shattered by the bombastic entry of a very drunk drum major, who is bragging about his prowess and conquest. Wozzeck refuses his offer of a drink and the two of them fight. In a remarkably telling musical repetition, Berg uses the same music for their fight as that which accompanied the drum major's grabbing and embracing of Marie in the culminating scene of the second act. The drum major wins and goes out. All the soldiers lie back down and return to sleep except for the exhausted, wretched Wozzeck, who sits on the edge of his bed staring blankly into space as the curtain drops.

It seems like a lot of opera to speak of three acts, each with five scenes. In fact, these two acts together consume merely a little more than an hour, and the entire drama lasts not even an hour and a half. Quite methodically, the scenes each last about five minutes. There is no fat, no waste, that could be done away with. Berg's terse condensation of Büchner's drama is set to a score tight and unalterable, perfect.

Act III

The first scene of the final act, the Catastrophe, returns to Marie's room. Alone with her child, she thumbs through pages of her Bible and reads snatches. When she happens to come upon "Wherefore the Pharisees had taken and brought to Him an adulterous woman, Jesus said to her: 'Thus condemned shall you not be. Go forth . . . in peace and sin no more,' " she covers her face in her hands. She becomes indecisive with her boy, pushing him away and drawing him close. Her eyes fall upon a passage about a child and she reads:

> And once there was a poor weë child . . .
> and he had no father, nor any mother . . .
> for all was dead, there was no-one in
> the world, therefore did hunger and

did weep . . . day and night . . . Since he
had no-one else left in the world . . .

Little does she know. She frets over the absence of Wozzeck,
who has not come to them. She begs the Lord for mercy. The
music of the entire third act consists of a series of intricate inventions (in music *invention* is a rarely used term but a familiar one,
because J. S. Bach used it as the title for several of his compositions, even though his reason for doing so remains historically
obscure; as for Berg's use, take it at face value to mean inventing
music from a theme, tone, or chord, etcetera). Berg's six inventions are a flawless fit for the drama's conclusion.

In Scene 2, dusk is falling on a path in the woods where Marie
and Wozzeck are walking toward town. Marie wants to hurry on
but Wozzeck bids her sit with him for a while. He asks how long
they have been together and when she replies that it is nearly
three years, he asks how long they will go on. When Marie jumps
up to leave, he pulls her down again, kisses her, and, as they note
that the moon has risen red, Wozzeck seizes her and plunges a
knife into her throat. Bending over her as she dies, he then proclaims her dead and rushes off.

In the third scene apprentices and girls, Margret among them,
dance a fast and furious polka in a dimly lit tavern. It is night.
Wozzeck, sitting alone at a table, damns the dancers and shouts at
the pianist. He grabs Margret and pulls her on to his lap and then
attempts to seduce her. As they begin to sing together, she
remarks that Wozzeck has blood on him. To the inquisitive gathering crowd, Wozzeck says that he cut his hand. Then, wonders
Margret, why does the blood cover his elbow? A flustered
Wozzeck rushes out of the tavern as Margret and the others agree
with certainty that it had the smell of human blood.

The fourth scene returns to the forest path, again by moonlight. There Wozzeck moves about, stops, and searches for the
knife. Dazed, crazed, and sick with guilt, he finds the knife and
throws it in a nearby pool. It lands too close to the shore—it will
be found. Wozzeck wades in after it. To him the moon appears red
as blood, as does the water with which he attempts to cleanse
himself of Marie's blood. He steps out too far, then sinks under the
water's surface and drowns. Passing by, the captain and the doctor
have heard but not seen what they conclude is someone floundering in the water. They scurry off.

When Wozzeck murders Marie, Berg's music is woven from a tapestry of themes associated with her. In the prolonged orchestral interlude following the death of Wozzeck, Berg employs the same technique. The curtain falls.

For the final scene, the curtain rises on the street in front of Marie's door. It is morning. Children shout and play and sing. Marie's son rides a hobbyhorse. One of the children says to him, "Hey, you, your mother is dead." Incapable of comprehending, the child continues his ride while the other children run off toward the forest to look. In an ending that gets me right in the gut every time, Marie's child is heard saying "Hop, hop! Hop, hop! Hop, hop!" as he rides off after the other children. The final curtain falls.

Knowing and loving this opera as I do, I cannot imagine it having been done any other way, first note to last. Some famous operas have been successfully set by more than one composer (*Manon* and *Manon Lescaut* are one isolated example). I could not possibly conceive of anyone attempting another *Wozzeck*.

The Bible plays an important role in *Wozzeck* in two differing ways. First, Wozzeck makes references to Scripture, several times quoting directly, and Marie, quite by chance, comes across passages applicable to her own situation as she thumbs through her Bible. The most provocative is the forecasting of the fate of her own child, though she cannot perceive it at the time, of course. Second, the use of the Bible is ironic. The theme of the drama, both in words and in music, is *Wir arme Laut* ("We poor people"). It appears again and again. The Bible says, "Blessed are the poor, for they shall inherit the earth." In the drama, the poor are neither blessed, nor do they "inherit the earth." As Marie aptly proclaims, they go to the devil. That is the message of the opera.

There exist several fine recordings of *Wozzeck*. Always I return to the historic 1951 Carnegie Hall concert performance with Dimitri Metropoulos conducting the New York Philharmonic because I came to it first and it got into my bones. It is especially interesting to me because in the cast there is not one native-speaking German in an opera so thoroughly German. Let me suggest starting with a video, for this important reason: Berg's atonal music, following the course set by his beloved teacher, is not easy for most people in the early stages of learning about opera. For some, all opera, even operas filled with song and flowing with melody, can be a giant step. Imagine the size of the step into the world of atonality. That is why I concentrated on the essential differences between tonal and atonal music as a preparation. With a video, you will become absorbed with the action and in reading subtitles (unless you are fluent in German) and the music will surreptiously sneak into your opera system without you realizing it. At least, this is my hope, and precisely what Berg intended when he urged his listeners to disregard all the various, tightly knit musical forms comprising the opera's music.

GEORGE GERSHWIN

PORGY AND BESS (1935)

Even if you are not familiar with the opera *Porgy and Bess*, you cannot have escaped its most famous songs: "Summertime" (of which hundreds of arrangements have been made, many doing an extraordinary injustice to the beautiful music), "A Woman Is a Sometime Thing," "It Ain't Necessarily So," among others.

Of all the operas in this book, my relationship to *Porgy and Bess* is unique for several reasons. It is the only opera introduced so far to have been premiered after I was born, and not long thereafter I heard the now famous songs, when they were brand new, being sung in our home. In New York City, the great American baritone Lawrence Tibbett, with another Metropolitan Opera star, Helen Jepson, had recorded the lovely duet "Bess, You Is My Woman Now" a few days after the world premiere in Boston on September 30, 1935. Tibbett was a friend of our family, as I mentioned earlier, and through him my father, a superb amateur baritone, learned of the marvelous score and obtained the sheet music (still in my little collection of memorabilia). Again and again I heard Porgy's songs as he learned them.

Also, through my life in music, it has been my good fortune to meet and work with a host of extraordinary people, Noble Sissle and Eubie Blake being two of them. Blake was one of the first to recognize the remarkable musical abilities of George Gershwin, who had so much impressed some of the best black musicians with his piano artistry while still in his teens. Blake was more than willing to explain and demonstrate several keyboard techniques mastered by the young Gershwin that would find their place in his own compositions. Eleanor Steber, the superb American soprano, made for many of us what remains the recording of "Summertime" by which all others must be measured. Miss Steber and I had made plans to do a radio broadcast, with this recording and her recollections as a central part of the interview. She died suddenly in 1990 before our program happened, one of my great regrets.

In still another way, *Porgy and Bess* has special personal connections. A friend of many years, Margo Melton Nutt, daughter of the famous American tenor James Melton, has shared with me many recordings of her father, including songs from *Porgy and Bess*, from her large, wonderful collection. Her father and Gershwin were on a tour together, she told me, while Gershwin was composing a portion of his opera, Melton leaning over his shoulder singing the tunes as soon as they appeared.

And finally, soprano Clamma Dale, who portrayed Bess in the now famous 1976 Houston Grand Opera recording of *Porgy and Bess*, met with me years ago to plan a special radio program. Naturally, Gershwin's opera and her considerable involvement with it constituted an important part of our considerations. This opera, throughout my life, has held a most special place.

Major operatic innovations of "modern music" come with each of the operas presented in this chapter: the impressionistic harmonic innovations of Debussy, Bartók's fascination with native folk music as an inspiration for his unique musical expression, Janáček's fastidious study of rhythms in nature and human speech, Berg's expressionistic abandonment of traditional tonalities, and now, with George Gershwin's *Porgy and Bess*, an opera featuring distinct influences from the music of black culture: blues, jazz, and spirituals.

Gershwin, a New Yorker, heard the music of black people as they migrated from the South and settled in Harlem. He was intrigued by the inventive improvisations of black musicians and their innovative, intoxicating rhythms. Theirs was the influence that so greatly shaped his own music. His opera features the musical styles of blues, jazz, and spirituals adopted from black musical traditions. Blues (a type of popular American music, both vocal and instrumental) evolved from spirituals, the religious songs of black people. However, they have three basic differences. Spirituals were originally sung by a group of people, and without instrumental accompaniment. They tended to be of a highly emotional or dynamic nature, often reaching a rapid tempo of expression. Blues, in contrast, were performed by the solo voice but with an instrument or instruments having an important accompanying role. Blues, furthermore, normally were of a slower tempo than spirituals and employed more subdued dynamics. Blues begin the opera. As the curtain rises on the first act, after the orchestral prelude, Jasbo Brown is seen sitting at his piano playing "Jasbo Brown Blues." Perhaps Thomas "Fats" Waller or Art Tatum, both of whom Gershwin enormously admired and heard many times, inspired this image of the black man's virtuosity at the piano. The unmistakable style of a spiritual is heard in the second scene of the first act as a chorus sings the hauntingly beautiful "Gone, Gone, Gone."

Jazz has a prominent place in Gershwin's score. It attracted the attention of numerous composers who wrote for the opera house and concert hall, those who composed what is called serious music or art music as opposed to popular music, which jazz is. Debussy, Stravinsky, Milhaud, and Krenek are a few who came to jazz from this tradition and incorporated their versions of it into their compositions.

George Gershwin arrived at stardom in the concert hall and opera house from an entirely different direction. He began writing songs for Tin Pan Alley but by the time of his premature death, at the age of thirty-eight, on July 11, 1937, this great talent had written the most popular American opera ever as well as classics for the concert hall, the celebrated *Rhapsody in Blue, An American in Paris, Three Preludes*, and the *Concerto in F* for piano and orchestra. In all of them one hears the influence of jazz.

Although the origin of the word *jazz* is lost in obscurity, the musical origins are easily delineated. Jazz derived from nineteenth-century minstrel shows, brass-band music, ragtime, blues, and early-twentieth-century Tin Pan Alley songs. Jazz was music for dancing during its early years, and for many was indistinguishable from ragtime, with its inexorable, regular beat for the dance steps and its captivating melody. Syncopation (the deliberate altering of an expected normal rhythm) is its most distinguishing characteristic. By the 1920s—seminal and formative years in Gershwin's all too brief career—the "Jazz Age" was the rage in dance halls, on the radio, and in recording studios. Jazz was big business crowned, perhaps, by Paul Whiteman's famous 1924 jazz concert in contemporary American music in New York City's Aeolian

Hall. The unquestioned triumph of the long, hot evening was Gershwin's *Rhapsody in Blue*, the composer at the piano and Whiteman conducting his orchestra.

Jazz, of course, has many elements and in its subsequent history, unto this day, has moved in several directions, some of them noted for their exceedingly rich and complex musical innovations. Accordingly, a comprehensive, airtight definition of *jazz* simply does not exist. Whereas some speak of a jazz composition, others—the old masters of Dixieland jazz—would not acknowledge as such any music not improvised on the spot. Thus any music written down, read, and, God forbid, conducted, was not jazz. Perhaps we should best leave it with the words of Fats Waller, whose keyboard mastery had so mesmerized the young George Gershwin: "If you gotta ask what it is, you'll never know."

In 1926, George Gershwin read the novel *Porgy*, by Edwin DuBose Heyward. Immediately he knew he wanted this story as the basis for an opera. In a letter to Heyward he expressed his interest, but soon thereafter Heyward and his wife, Dorothy, busied themselves at turning the novel into a successful play. In 1932, Gershwin wrote again, this time obtaining rights for an opera, but he backed off on learning that Jerome Kern and Oscar Hammerstein II were contemplating making the story into a musical to feature Al Jolson, who had made Gershwin's song "Swanee" so famous. When their interest waned, much to the delight of Heyward, Gershwin commenced working on his opera. He negotiated with Heyward for his brother Ira, a lyricist, to coauthor the lyrics. At one point George Gershwin lived for five weeks in Charleston, South Carolina, the setting of Heyward's story, to absorb all aspects of black culture. On August 23, 1935, Gershwin noted FIN-ISHED on the manuscript.

The opera opened to mixed reviews in Boston on September 30 of that year and 124 performances followed in New York City. In America, for a new opera, 124 is a sensational number of performances but on Broadway, to which it then moved, it constituted a financial failure. Many critics condemned the work as a hodgepodge of alien styles; others said it was no more than a string of songs stuck to a story. Gershwin defended his work. Verdi's operas, he pointed out, also present one hit song after another. History has shown once again a batch of critics talking folderol through their hats. *Porgy and Bess* has finally been recognized worldwide as a superb opera, its magical and memorable tunes consolidated, one after the other, by a brilliant symphonic score.

Like Janáček's *Cunning Little Vixen*, Heyward's *Porgy and Bess* had its impetus from the newspaper. Heyward, a native of Charleston, had seen an article about a maimed black man, Samuel Smalls, known as "Goat Sammy," who failed in his attempt to escape the police in his goat cart after assaulting a woman. Heyward's imagination soared with memories of life on Catfish Row, a once elegant section along the waterfront that became a black tenement, and also, in particular, of the 1911 hurricane. Porgy's story was born. It is interesting how the story's end changes from the novel to the opera. In the end of the book Porgy is an old man left all alone. In the opera, with the inexorable resolve of innocence, he sets out in his cart to find Bess, who is a thousand miles away in New York City. Perhaps Heyward and the Gershwin brothers agreed on the altered conclusion as more theatrically effective.

The opera is in three acts. The characters and their voice ranges are:

PORGY, a crippled beggar, *baritone or bass-baritone*
BESS, *soprano*
CROWN, a stevedore, *baritone*
SPORTIN' LIFE, a dope peddler, *tenor*
JAKE, a fisherman, *baritone*
CLARA, his wife, *soprano*
ROBBINS, an inhabitant of Catfish Row, *tenor*
SERENA, his wife, *soprano*
MARIA, keeper of the cook shop, *contralto*
MINGO, *tenor*
PETER, the honey man, *tenor*
LILY, his wife, *mezzo-soprano*
Strawberry Woman, *mezzo-soprano*
FRAZIER, a "lawyer," *baritone*
MR. ARCHDALE, a real lawyer, a white man, *speaking part*
ANNIE, *mezzo-soprano*
JIM, a cotton picker, *baritone*
Undertaker, *baritone*
NELSON, *tenor*
Crab Man, *tenor*
Detective, *speaking part*
Policeman, *speaking part*
Coroner, *speaking part*

SCIPIO, a small boy, *speaking part*
JASBO BROWN, the piano man, *mute*
Residents of Catfish Row: fishermen, children, stevedores,
etcetera

The action is set in and about Charleston, South Carolina,
in the 1930s.

George Gershwin's will and an inflexible rule of the Gershwin
estate stated that English-speaking countries may perform the
opera only with the predominantly black cast portrayed by blacks.
The language of the libretto is a mix of authentic black speech and
black stereotypes, which some contemporary performances tone
down. A standard audio recording of the complete opera is the
1976 production of the Houston Grand Opera, and a popular video
is the Glyndebourne Festival Opera production featuring Willard
White and Cynthia Haymon in the title roles. Because the opera is
in English, its story is more accessible. Therefore, the following
synopsis is less detailed.

Act I
Even though the audience is introduced to both Porgy and Bess in
the first act, its central event is the murder of Robbins by a drunk-
en Crown. There are two scenes in this act. After a short, vigorous
musical prelude, the curtain rises on the courtyard of Catfish Row.
It is a summer evening and as Jasbo Brown sits at a piano playing
his blues, there is much dancing and singing. The music is captivating in its lilting rhythms and mesmerizing "da-doo-da" lyrics. Clara
sings "Summertime" to her baby. This beautiful lullaby has
become the most famous song in the score. As the men gather to
shoot craps, Serena begs her husband, Robbins, not to play but he
enters the game nevertheless. Jake takes their baby from Clara,
claiming he can put him to sleep. His version of a lullaby is the lively and cynical "A Woman Is a Sometime Thing." Porgy arrives and
enters the game. Soon thereafter, Crown arrives with his woman,
Bess. She is disdained by the other women for her wanton ways.

With the entrance of Crown into the game, the mood becomes
increasingly tense. The huge, inebriated stevedore provokes an
argument with Robbins. They fight and Crown kills Robbins with
a cotton hook. The manner in which Gershwin's music portrays
an argument intensified into a fight and culminating in a sense-
less murder is masterful.

Knowing he must flee, Crown tells Bess he will return: Any other man she takes up with will be "temporary." He runs off. The residents scatter. Bess, shaking with fright, asks Sportin' Life for some "happy dust." He provides it and tries to entice her to go to New York with him. She refuses. He disappears. As Bess starts to run away, she is stopped short by the sound of a police whistle. Frantically, she races door to door looking for a place to hide. All remain closed to her except the door on the corner. It is Porgy's door. Bess goes in, leaving the courtyard empty except for Serena, who has collapsed over her husband's body.

The second scene of the first act is set in Serena's room on the following night. Robbins is laid out with a saucer on his chest onto which mourning friends and neighbors contribute money toward his burial. Obviously, Porgy has taken up with Bess, for they are there together. The mourners sing the moving "Gone, Gone, Gone." A policeman and a detective enter. They warn Serena that the body must be buried by the next day or it goes to medical students, and they then frighten Peter to confess that he saw Crown murder Robbins. Peter is taken off as a witness. Serena sings her powerful aria "My Man's Gone Now." A humane undertaker agrees to bury Robbins when Serena promises she will make up the difference between his fee and what's in the saucer. Bess, perhaps now partially accepted by the group, leads the singing of the emotional "Leavin' for the Promise' Lan' " and with this fifth famous song the curtain falls on the first act. Some of the dialogue is delivered recitativo style and some is normal speech.

Act II

The long second act, in four scenes, opens on Catfish Row a month later. As others sit about, Jake and some fishermen repair nets in preparation for an expedition while singing "It Takes a Long Pull to Get There." It is the hurricane season and in a similar vein to Serena's warning to Robbins not to enter the craps game, Clara begs Jake not to go, but he explains that he must earn money for their son's college education. Porgy enters the courtyard singing his famous "I Got Plenty o' Nothin'," the first music of the opera I ever heard. Hearing my father sing it so often, I knew it by heart as a very young child.

Porgy articulates his simple, easygoing philosophy in this lilting, catchy song. He's got Bess, the "Lawd," and a song. He needs nothing more. Sportin' Life saunters over to Maria's table. Instantly she grabs his hand and blows white powder to the wind. He can get the boys drunk on cheap whiskey, she says, "but nobody ain' gonna peddle happy dust roun' my shop." When he suggests they be friends, Maria grabs him by the throat with one hand, picks up a carving knife with the other, and delivers one of the superb mini-treats—it is barely a minute long—of the score as she threatens his life in an incomparable mix of words and music. Don't miss any of "I Hates Yo' Struttin' Style."

Sportin' Life races away and "Lawyer" Frazier enters. He has come to take advantage of poor Porgy by selling him a divorce for Bess even though she and Crown were never married. Porgy is duped. A white man, Mr. Archdale, also looking for Porgy, enters. He brings good news. He will put up Peter's bond because Peter's folks once belonged to the Archdale family. This good news is quickly tempered by Porgy, who has just seen a buzzard flying low over the rooftops. He sings "The Buzzard Song." A buzzard landing on a roof, it was believed, was a bad omen for the inhabitants and Porgy desperately fears losing his newfound happiness.

As the residents of Catfish Row ready themselves for the Kittiwah Island Lodge picnic, Sportin' Life, who has reappeared, slithers over to Bess with an offer of happy dust. She refuses and Porgy, who surreptitiously has observed this, limps forth and with his powerful grasp seizes the dope peddler by the wrist with a promise to break his neck if he does not leave Bess alone. Sportin' Life departs. Porgy and Bess are alone—the perfect setting for a love duet—and they share what in my ears always has been one of the loveliest and most tender declarations of affection in opera literature: "Bess, You Is My Woman Now." As the duet concludes, the stage suddenly becomes crowded as residents of Catfish Row now are ready to leave for the boat to Kittiwah Island. Full of anticipation for the picnic outing, they sing the rousing chorus "Oh, I Can't Sit Down." Bess intends to stay home with Porgy but Maria urges her to go and Porgy, who wants Bess to have fun, tells her to do so. As Bess leaves, her voice fading away with iterations of "Good-bye, Porgy," he begins a refrain of "I Got Plenty o' Nothin'," but as the scene ends we are left wondering how enduring will be his happiness.

The second scene, the Kittiwah Island picnic, opens with dancing, singing, and the playing of combs, bones, and mouth organs. Two hit tunes are heard one after the other, the chorus "I Ain't Got No Shame" and Sportin' Life's cynical sermon, with choral accompaniment, "It Ain't Necessarily So." This world-famous number always is one of the most anticipated and appreciated in the score and must be the most unoperatic aria in opera. It is a triumph of jazziness with brilliant rhyming lyrics such as

> Dey tells all you chillun
> de debbil's a villun
> but 'tain't necessarily so.

Serena spoils the gaiety by denouncing them all as sinners and announcing that it's time for the boat to leave. Bess, lagging behind the others, suddenly is confronted by Crown, who emerges from the thicket where he has been hiding. He reminds her he will be coming for her soon. She tells him she is happy with Porgy and tries to convince him to seek another, younger woman, "What You Want Wid Bess?" but Crown wants Bess. Her resistance evaporates, they repair into the woods, and the boat leaves without her.

It is a week later, moments before dawn, on Catfish Row when the curtain rises on the third scene of the second act. As Jake and the fishermen depart, the delirious voice of Bess can be heard ranting from Porgy's house. Peter returns and Maria informs him that Bess became lost, found her way back, and lies incoherent in Porgy's room. Serena prays for Bess and predicts her imminent recovery. The Strawberry Woman, the Honey Man, and the Crab Man hawk their wares, and the offstage voice of Bess reveals she is becoming herself again. She enters the courtyard, confesses her affair with Crown to Porgy, and begs him to help her resist when Crown returns for her: "I Loves You, Porgy." He promises her he will make Crown's return his business. The scene ends with Clara becoming increasingly frightened by the weather. Maria's attempts to reassure her become meaningless as the hurricane bell reverberates through the howling wind.

Scene 4, the hurricane scene, opens at dawn of the following day. As the storm rages, all have gathered in Serena's room. Huddled together, they sing prayers, pleading with God to pity them and be merciful, but lightning flashes, thunder roars, and when knocking is heard on the door they assume Death is there. It is Crown. He has risked his life to return for Bess, but as he goes for her she pulls away. Porgy moves to defend her but the big stevedore throws the cripple to the floor. Crown then struts his stuff singing his bragging, jazzy "A Red-Headed Woman," claiming no one can make a fool of him. Clara, fixated next the window, screams. Bess hurries to her. Clara hands her the baby and rushes out into the storm. Is there no man here who will help her? Crown, after deriding Porgy and promising Bess he will return, goes after Clara. Bess and the baby go to Porgy and all resume singing a prayer as the second act ends.

Act III
The third act plays in three scenes, all in the courtyard of Catfish Row. The first takes place the next night and a chorus of residents, assuming both Clara and Crown have also been lost in the storm, sing the somber "Clara, Clara." Maria reproaches Sportin' Life, who has not taken a man's death seriously; after all, he reports, there still remain plenty of good men for a woman to choose from. In fact, he implies, hinting that Crown may, indeed, not be dead, Bess may have the problem of two men to choose from and the inevitable subsequent encounter may leave one dead, the other in jail, and thus no man at all. Maria goes into her shop and Sportin' Life departs. Bess, singing a snatch of "Summertime," comes out of her house with Clara's baby and then returns inside. For the rest of the scene, the orchestra takes over. Crown enters and looks around the empty courtyard. He does not see Porgy, who has lifted himself onto the roof of his house. As Crown advances toward Porgy's door, the crippled man falls upon the stevedore, knocking both to the ground. After wrestling fiercely, Porgy, with his powerful arms and grip of steel, strangles Crown. He calls Bess, who runs out and screams, exulting "You got a man now, you got Porgy!"

Scene 2 and it is the afternoon of the next day. Police, with coroner, enter the court seeking information pertaining to the murder of Crown. When Serena, Lily, Annie, and other women fix themselves behind an inexorable facade of "We ain' seen nothin', Boss," Porgy is summoned from his house. Bess, holding Clara's baby, follows and Sportin' Life, unobserved, slithers into the court to eavesdrop on the proceedings. Porgy is told he must identify Crown's body because he knew him. His instantaneous terror intensifies when Sportin' Life comes forth and informs him the corpse will commence to bleed the moment it is viewed by the man who killed him. Bess advises Porgy merely to pretend to look before the wretched man is dragged off. Alone with Bess, Sportin' Life perpetrates his evil scheme. He tells Bess that Porgy will be locked up for at least a year, maybe two, or—and here he gestures a hanging before offering her some happy dust. Bess refuses it, denouncing him as "nigger." He, nevertheless, persists to taunt her by waving a packet in her face and all but forcing her to submit. Bess relents. She takes the "dust," inhales it, and commences to shake as he sings "There's a boat dat's leaving soon for New York," in which he envisions them living the high life in a Fifth Avenue mansion and strutting about in the finest clothes. Bess responds by telling the "little snake" to go away. He gives her another packet of dope. She throws it to the ground and goes into the house. Sportin' Life retrieves the packet and tosses it into her room. As he slowly walks away, Bess reappears. She now is totally drugged. Together they walk away from Catfish Row.

The final scene takes place on the morning of a week later. Neighbors greet one another, children play, and a happy Porgy comes home. While jailed for contempt of court, he refused to look at Crown, won money shooting craps, and with it bought presents for his friends and a new dress for Bess. Eager to avoid the inevitable crash of Porgy's high spirits, the residents begin to slip away and when Porgy sees Serena with Clara's baby he begins to wonder. Crawling to his room, he opens the door, calls for Bess, and is nearly frantic on discovering she is not there. Now only Serena and Maria remain. In a great trio, "Oh, Bess, Oh Where's My Bess?" Porgy questions the two women and learns of Sportin' Life's villainy. Ecstatic that Bess is alive, Porgy calls for his goat cart. He is going to look for Bess. Again the court fills with his friends, all of whom fail in various attempts to dissuade him. As he sets out singing the jubilant "Oh, Lawd, I'm on My Way" all join him as his goat cart carries him out of Catfish Row and the curtain falls.

"Does Porgy ever find Bess?" I would ask my father when I was very small. Always I wanted to know, especially when he and soprano Beverly Dame sang together the songs of *Porgy and Bess* in our music room. The opera, of course, does not resolve my question of long ago so I provided my own answer, but I'm sorry, you'll have to decide for yourself.

✏

In reading elsewhere about *Porgy and Bess* you may encounter sophisticated psychological interpretations of the opera: a tri-part Bess embodying, through her three men, all aspects of the female, each man representing and fulfilling different needs. Bess likes pretty clothes and the high life. This is Sportin' Life. She also is a sensual woman and much aware of her ultimate helplessness in the presence of Crown's awesome sexuality. Bess, finally, longs for a home and the security of a man who will love and care for her; this is Porgy. I am not aware that the Heywards and the Gershwin brothers were entreating their audience to probe either the novel, the play, or the opera accordingly. My experience with *Porgy and Bess* is on a far more loving and literal level. I'll leave it at that.

So many of the songs of *Porgy and Bess* have become universally popular in countless versions (some quite terrible, I am quick to add) that there are critics who reduce the opera to no more than a string of catchy tunes barely held together by the story. Not so, neither dramatically nor musically. Follow the words, both dialogue and songs, always with an ear to what the orchestra is saying, and you will experience a powerful, tightly knit drama, sometimes funny, at times sad, and ultimately bursting with an optimism for life as worth living.

To experience a great live production, nevertheless, is not common. Gershwin's will and estate allow performances only by black casts and the numerous roles demand excellent singing actors. Outside the United States, Gershwin's intent has not been respected. A production in Switzerland, some years ago, presented the cast in masks of blue and black colors and introduced into a bizarre interpretation of the opera Woton, Baron Ochs, and Peter Grimes, all characters from other operas. In the world of opera, nothing is more infuriating to me than directors whose motivation it is to make a name for themselves through "newness," doing something different just to be doing something different, with no regard for the composer's intentions and often oblivious to what the music demands. All opera must emerge from the music: the sets, costumes, and the way the singers move, each and every gesture. If the director is not a musician, he or she at least ought to know music and be sensitive to what it is saying. Today there are directors who are ignorant of music and force upon it their ludicrous novel conceptions rather than letting the music determine the entire production. And thus it is that their innovative absurdities remove *The Magic Flute* from ancient Egypt to the Los Angeles Freeway and *Madama Butterfly* from Nagasaki into a European brothel. *Carmen* has been played as part of the Spanish Civil War, *Rheingold* reset next to a French canal, and I could fill this page with an unending list of similar blasphemies. Directors who do this should be shot! Please don't support their outrageous gimmicks. As you so well know, in *Porgy and Bess* there is neither Woton (chapter 7) nor Baron Ochs (chapter 13) and there certainly is no Peter Grimes.

BENJAMIN BRITTEN

In town, 'twas plain, men took him for a thief.
The sailors' wives would stop him on the street,
And say, "Now, Peter, thou'st no boy to beat."
Infants at play, when they perceived him, ran,
Warning each other—"That's a wicked man!"
He growled an oath, and in an angry tone
Cursed the whole place and wishes to be alone.[†]

That's Peter Grimes, at least the Peter Grimes of George Crabbe's poem that so caught the imagination of Benjamin Britten, who made from it an opera. It was his first, and to this day it remains of the fourteen he composed the most familiar, the most approachable, and the most often performed. When it premiered in 1945, it was a sensation. In the past few years other operas by Britten have begun to gain a bigger audience; *Billy Budd*, for example, *A Death in Venice*, and always I enjoyed teaching *The Turn of the Screw* in my opera course for advanced-degree students. Immediately apparent is Britten's commitment to first-rate literature. *Peter Grimes*, as just noted, is based on a significant poem by George Crabbe; Melville wrote the short novel *Billy Budd*; *A Death in Venice* derives from a Thomas Mann novella; and *The Turn of the Screw* is a famous short novel of Henry James Jr. Britten's operatic corpus also includes an operetta, *Paul Bunyan*, from American folk legend; a church opera, *Noye's Fludde*, a setting of an English miracle play; *Albert Herring*, after a Guy de Maupassant short story; and *A Midsummer Night's Dream*, out of Shakespeare. This chapter, and our book, concludes with Britten's

---

[†] *The Norton Anthology of Poetry*, Third Edition (New York: W.W. Norton & Company, 1970) George Crabbe, The Borough: Letter XXII, Peter Grimes, p. 489

Peter Grimes. Surely, some other opera written within the last half century will also catch the public's fancy and become familiar, even a favorite, but it will have to be the subject of another book, by someone else.

Benjamin Britten greatly admired Alban Berg, especially the opera *Wozzeck.* Both Wozzeck and Grimes have been described as an "anti-hero," an unfortunate use of words suggesting his opposition to a hero. In neither opera is there a hero. What is meant is *misfit.* Both Wozzeck and Grimes are men incapable of living comfortably within his social order. They are outcasts. Wozzeck does not understand his situation and by frustration is driven to murder Marie. Grimes, though more comprehending, openly is rebellious. Both die by drowning: Wozzeck a victim of circumstances or, perhaps, by a conscious suicidal atonement, while Grimes clearly is the author of his own fate. The Peter Grimes of Britten's opera is, however, a softer version than Crabbe's original.

Unlike Goldsmith's "Deserted Village" and Gray's "Elegy Written in a Country Churchyard," both romanticized poetic visions of rural life, Crabbe's poem portrays what he, a common man, remembers of life in a seaside village. With a passion for truthfulness, he tells of lust, crimes, and horrible brutality. Though much admired by intellectuals and other literary figures, Crabbe's poem never became a popular favorite, most certainly because it was not an uplifting panegyric to goodness and beauty or a sentimental portrayal of life in a village. Crabbe's Peter Grimes is a villain, a sadistic loner suffering from delusions. A rigid and unpleasant man, he is appropriately named Peter Grimes. (The name Peter comes from the Greek word for stone and *grime* is self-evident.) In the opera he is not a villain but rather a nonconformist, a social outcast, incapable of living harmoniously within the society of a village on England's coast.

Britten became attached to the Peter Grimes story through an article on George Crabbe by E. M. Forster. Both Britten and his partner, English tenor Peter Pears, read the article while visiting the West Coast of the United States in 1941. The idea for a Peter Grimes opera was immediate and together they drafted a plot for the drama. George Crabbe was from Aldeburgh, a town in Suffolk, England, and it was there that Britten and Pears made their home on returning to England. How they must have identified with the outcast Peter Grimes! As pacifists and homosexuals, Britten and Pears lived in seclusion while German bombs fell on nearby London during the Second World War. Britten was, indeed, attracted to well-intentioned literary characters whose nonconformity left them living in isolation from society. Because of his homosexuality, it is easy to read it into his operas. Was that why Peter Grimes would not marry Ellen? Was his relationship with his apprentices "improper"? These are not the type of speculations I intend to consider here, even though the homosexual theme is overt by the time Britten got to his last opera, *A Death in Venice*.

Probably the best way to characterize Benjamin Britten's music— he is the last of our so-called modern composers—is eclectic. I have mentioned earlier that England has not grown and exported famous opera composers. In the seventeenth century there was Purcell and in the nineteenth century the operettas of Gilbert and Sullivan, and now Britten, who had no homegrown tradition of dramatic music to develop from. He studied with English composers Frank Bridges and John Ireland but it would take a most sophisticated musical ear to hear an influence.

Britten, a prolific composer in a variety of genres, began writing quite young—he wrote an oratorio at age nine. Britten's music for some is too taut, too terse, "so thorny," as one of my insightful colleagues once described it. His music is tonal but demanding. It must be given a chance. Like much "modern" music, it may take some getting used to. Rarely does it leap out and grab you instantaneously on first hearing, except, perhaps, for *Peter Grimes*, whose popularity never has been questioned, the famous "Sea Interludes" being an example of immediately accessible music.

I used the word *eclectic* to imply Britten's openness to many different sources and traditions. Without becoming a copycat, he was able to digest them and eventually come forth with his own voice with music quite unlike any other I know. The music of *Peter Grimes* is especially engaging. It surges ever onward without stalling and fits the story wonderfully. I know of no better place to begin an association with the music of Benjamin Britten than with *Peter Grimes*. As mentioned above, the opera was an immediate sensation at its premiere and remains exceedingly popular. So much so, it may have thwarted a wider acceptance to Britten's many more operas that were to follow.

PETER GRIMES (1945)

The opera has a prologue, an epilogue, and three acts. Montagu Slater was the librettist who adapted Crabbe's poem for Britten. The characters of the drama, and their voice ranges, are:

PETER GRIMES, a fisherman, *tenor*
JOHN, his apprentice, *silent role*
ELLEN ORFORD, a widow and schoolmistress of the
    Borough, *soprano*
CAPTAIN BALSTRODE, retired merchant skipper, *baritone*
AUNTIE, landlady of the Boar Inn, *contralto*
Auntie's two nieces, significant attractions at the Boar
    Inn, *sopranos*
BOB BOLES, a fisherman and a Methodist, *tenor*
SWALLOW, a lawyer and coroner, *bass*
MRS. (NABOB) SEDLEY, a rentier widow of an East India
    Company's factory, *mezzo-soprano*
REV. HORACE ADAMS, the rector, *tenor*
NED KEENE, an apothecary and a quack, *baritone*
DR. THORP, *silent role*
HOBSON, a carrier, *bass*
Chorus of townspeople and fisherfolk

The drama is set in the Borough, a fishing village on the east coast of England about 1830.

Prologue

Simultaneously with agitated notes in the orchestra, the curtain opens on the prologue showing a crowded Moot Hall. There an inquest is in session to investigate the death of young William Spode, the boy apprentice to Peter Grimes. Swallow calls on Peter Grimes to give evidence and swears him in. Grimes tells his story. Sailing toward London to deliver a substantial catch, he and his apprentice were blown off course for three days. They ran out of drinking water, the boy died of exposure, the dead fish were thrown overboard, and Grimes returned home and called for help. One by one, briefly, the main characters of the drama are asked to respond by telling what they saw or know. There is a noisy mocking and accusatory uneasiness throughout the spectators, for Grimes—as Swallow makes quite clear—is not a popular man in the village. With no evidence against him, however, it is concluded that William Spode died of accidental causes. This is, nevertheless, Swallow exhorts, "the kind of thing people are apt to remember." He suggests the next apprentice hired by Grimes be a man capable of fending for himself. Popular sentiment is against Grimes and he knows it. The session over, the crowd disperses.

Peter and Ellen are left alone. They have a brief duet. Ellen attempts to console him promising his name will be restored. Peter responds cynically. They sing in different keys (a *key note* is the main note of a section of music, its tonal center around which the other notes relate and ultimately resolve in tonal music). By singing in different keys, their divergent points of view are made obvious, especially so when, as the duet ends, they join together now in the same key, her key, to the words

> My/your voice out of the pain,
> is like a hand
> That I/you can feel and know:
> Here is a friend.

Together they walk away as the curtain falls, and we hear the first of the famous Sea Interludes.

There are six interludes, one at the beginning of each act and the others between scenes (music written to be heard before a closed curtain while scenery is being changed is sometimes referred to as "curtain music"). These interludes present remarkably engaging musical seascapes depicting their various moods as the psychological dimensions of the drama unfold. Often four of the six interludes are recorded independently from the opera or are given in a concert version. When thus presented, these four interludes—"Dawn," "Sunday Morning," "Moonlight," and "Storm" —are not played in the order heard in an operatic performance. "Storm" is the curtain music connecting the two scenes of the first act. As the stage director rehearsed the production for the world premiere, he realized the duration of this interlude did not allow sufficient time to change scenes. He asked Britten to extend it by a minute and a half. The composer, who musically had said what he wanted to say about natural and human turbulence, was not amused but, getting his feet wet (excuse the pun) as a man of the theater, he acquiesced.

Act I

The interlude "Dawn," bridging the Prologue and Scene 1 of the

first act, is a calm depiction of a gray sea in the morning as fishermen prepare their nets. The parting curtains reveal a Borough
street scene, the Moot Hall facade, next the Boar, farther on the
apothecary shop, and then breakwaters running out into the sea.
The interlude becomes a fine chorus about toiling on the sea and
longing for rest in pubs warmed by fiery drink. Some answer Auntie's call by going into the Boar, ignoring the protestations of the
righteous Boles. Working women continue to sing as Balstrode,
gazing through his eyeglass, predicts a storm. By now all the village
notables are milling about, commenting, chatting, and going about
their business: the doctor, Mrs. Sedley, the rector, Ned Keene,
Swallow, the nieces, and so on.

Peter Grimes calls for help in hauling his boat and is ignored
by all until Balstrode and Ned come to give him a hand as Bob
Boles comments to Auntie, "the lost soul of a fisherman must be
shunned by respectable society." In this seemingly casual observation resides the heart of the drama: man against society. That is
the story of Peter Grimes and, as often is the case in good theater,
the audience will dislike the protagonist and yet pity him and
identify with him.

If the words of the libretto are responsible in part for this
dichotomy, it ultimately is the authenticity of Britten's music, its
inventive expression of human longings and loneliness and overwhelming rejection, that does the trick. It is in the unusual harmonies that Britten's music becomes most captivating and not
simply this melody or that one. The harmonies, as noted previously, are the chord structures, the vertical textures of sounds playing
beneath the ongoing linear horizontal direction of the melodies. In
the harmonies are the varying colors, hues, emotions, and moods
of the music, and this was Britten's most striking achievement in
Peter Grimes. As the conversation of the characters jumps here
and there, telling the story, the story's most articulate evocation
is in Britten's unique continuous weaving of an innovative tapestry of sound. Follow the words to get the plot, but concentrate on
the music and what it is "saying."

Now, back to the story. Ned informs Grimes that he has hired
for him a new apprentice and Hobson is asked to fetch the boy
from the workhouse. Hobson is disinclined to take on the responsibility alone but agrees when the charitable Ellen, now on the
scene, offers to go with him and care for the boy. Ignoring the
warning of the crowd not to sully herself by associating with Peter

Grimes, Ellen answers with what actually is the first aria, in the traditional sense, of the opera now almost half an hour old: "Let her among you without fault cast the first stone." In words and music her compassion for others and her refusal to capitulate to public opinion, both consistent identifying traits of her character, are expressed.

Ellen and Hobson depart, Mrs. Sedley approaches Ned requesting her laudanum (with Bess and Mrs. Sedley, the issue of drugs has entered twentieth-century opera) and Balstrode, the retired captain, his eye ever on the sea through his telescope, announces the near arrival of a gale force wind. All the villagers join in one of the most spirited choruses of the score as they ready themselves for the blow before taking refuge in the Boar or heading home. Balstrode hesitates at the door of the pub to converse with Peter Grimes, who has made no effort to get out of the impending storm.

Balstrode asks him why always he stays so much to himself. Living alone has become my habit, Peter answers. You might be better off moving away and starting anew, Balstrode says but Grimes replies that he cannot for he is rooted here despite not being accepted. When Balstrode tells Grimes that public opinion will always be against him because of the way he treats his apprentices, Peter tells him what it was like to have his youthful helper die at sea. Furthermore, he will remain in the Borough and he will silence the gossips. He has his dreams to win over the people. He will "fish the sea dry," he says, become a wealthy merchant, and marry Ellen.

Then ask her now, Balstrode suggests, anticipating her acceptance. Not yet: Grimes does not want her to accept him out of pity. Balstrode fails in his attempt to get Peter to listen to him and, the storm now having arrived, the old captain is driven indoors. Peter, musing on life with Ellen, remains steadfast, "as if leaning against the wind." As the curtains close, the tempest arrives full force in the orchestra. The famous "Storm" interlude connects the two scenes of the first act.

Is nature's storm an omen of an impending storm in human relations? That Peter's dream of happiness is not to be? The storm dominates the events of the second scene through an interesting theatrical device: repetitions of the forceful closing of the door against the strong wind as different characters seek refuge in the Boar. The contrast between the external storm and the internal coziness will diminish, however, as human tensions rise with the appearance of Peter Grimes, who awaits the arrival of Ellen with his new apprentice.

Even though it is closing time, comfort from the storm is being sought in the Boar by residents of the Borough. Mrs. Sedley is the first to enter. The storm now is a hurricane and it takes both her and Auntie to push the door closed. She is there waiting for Ned, who promised the arrival of her drugs by Hobson the carrier. Balstrode and some fishermen are next and after them Bob Boles and other fishermen. From the second floor, bouncing down the stairs in nightclothes, come the nieces, who behave much in unison as if each were merely half the other. Usually they sing together, too. The women censure Balstrode for what they deem his rudeness. More fishermen and women struggle with the door, close it, and inform all of a landslide up the coast. A drunken Boles (the pious Methodist who earlier remonstrated against alcohol—a clever little touch in the libretto) makes an insistent pass at one of the nieces but is contained by Balstrode, who declares the eternal moral of "keep your hands to yourself" and "live and let live." Ned arrives, struggles with the door, then announces the effects of the storm: A cliff is down near the hut of Peter Grimes and badly flooded roads are detaining Hobson's delivery of Mrs. Sedley's pills. The door again, this time Peter Grimes without oilskins and with his wild hair soaked with rain. Mrs. Sedley faints and the others retreat, singing. "Talk of the devil and there he is and a devil he is . . ." Silence falls.

Grimes, awaiting his new apprentice, breaks the silence and, as if alone there, sings a haunting, reflective monologue of philosophical introspection. The villagers think him drunk or mad. Boles moves toward Grimes as if to eject him but is thrust easily aside. Boles picks up a bottle with which to whack Grimes on the head and denounces him as a killer of boys but is thwarted again by Balstrode. Auntie calls for the restoration of peace and Ned Keene begins to sing a round, a pleasant little ditty about fishermen. All join in, but Grimes takes it up in his own version of threatening lyrics. As the chorus attempts to drown him out, Hobson, Ellen, and a boy, all three of them soaked, muddy, and chilled, enter. The bridge is out. They had to swim. Women attempt to attend to Ellen and the boy but not for long. Grimes calls for his new helper. Lovingly, Ellen leads the boy to Grimes with the assurance that "Peter will take you home." As Grimes and the boy head out into the storm, a chorus asks "Home? Do you call that a home?" The curtain falls.

Act II

It is several weeks later when the curtains part for Act II on the same street scene as Act I after the "Sunday Morning" interlude. The first part of this first of two scenes is exceptionally innovative. Villagers hustle into church for a service. Ellen and the new apprentice of Grimes, John, enter but do not go to church. They sit between a boat and the breakwater and Ellen commences to knit and talk. Remember, John's part is a silent role. The intricate dialogue that transpires is between Ellen and what can be heard coming from the church. As parishioners sing about God keeping children free from harm, Ellen talks to John about his life, her role as a teacher, Peter's past, and the new start they are making together. During the confession, Ellen notices torn clothing around John's neck. As the rector and choir implore God for salvation, she finds a bruise on the boy's neck.

Grimes arrives. He needs the boy's help. The intriguing juxtaposition between the words of the service and the tiff between Peter and Ellen, who reminds him of his promise to give the boy a day of rest, continues until she claims they have failed. He strikes her as the service ends with an "Amen." The boy runs off, Grimes following, but the quarrel has been overheard by Auntie, Keene, and Boles, the first to exit the church. They reproach Grimes and, joined by the others, overpower Ellen's attempt to explain how she and Grimes agreed to care for the boy. She now is associated with the evil Grimes in the mind of popular opinion. Against attempts by Balstrode to calm the growing frenzy, the rector and Swallow form a party to go to the hut of Peter Grimes and investigate. Hobson beats his drum to call a mob of men together and off they march singing a threatening tune. The nieces, Auntie, and Ellen remain behind to sing a calming trio (remember, the singing of the two nieces mostly is in unison), contrasting the violent emotions preceding it.

This is wonderful music. Do not approach *Peter Grimes* with an anticipation for big, emotional arias sung in turn by the central characters. It is not that kind of opera. The wonder of the music is in the orchestra and with the ensemble singing and how it surges on and on with a variety of moods and captivating emotional contrasts. The ending of the first scene of this second act is an exemplar of this. A brilliant melding of words and music connect the act's second scene by an interlude of extraordinary importance. Britten titled it "Passacaglia" (originally moderately slow Baroque music of continuous variations). Recall how Alban Berg, so much admired by

Britten, utilized his version of a passacaglia as one of the musical forms giving structure to *Wozzeck*.

The second scene takes place in an isolated, walled-in, overturned boat. It is the hut of Peter Grimes. The boy is there, crying silently. Grimes rages. He gets the boy's fishing clothes and throws them at him. Seeing the sea teeming with fish, he muses on his dream of life with Ellen and remembers the sad fate of his last apprentice. The boy continues to weep. Peter gives him a shove, saying they must be off to sea, and concludes his reflective monologue without noticing the sound of Hobson's drumbeats in the distance. As the mob comes into sight of the door facing the road, however, Peter sees them and accuses John of having lied about him, thus causing the intervention. In a chorus, the mob iterates its threat:

> Bring the branding iron and knife:
> What's done now is done for life.

Hurriedly, Peter urges the boy out the back door next to the steep cliff. John falls, screams, and plunges downward. Peter scurries after him. The rector, Swallow, Keene, and Balstrode enter the hut, find it neat and clean, and conclude that its occupants have gone fishing. Assuming all is well, they decide to return to their wives and put an end to the gossipmongering. They lead away the mob, all except for Balstrode, who happened to notice the boy's Sunday clothes in a heap near the open door above the precipice. He steps out and begins to descend the cliff as the curtain falls.

Act III

"Moonlight," the fifth of six orchestral interludes, plays before the curtain parts on Act III a few days later. The scene is the same as Act I, it is a summer evening, and both Moot Hall, where a dance is in session, and the pub are brightly lighted. A polka is playing. The stage is empty until squealing nieces dash down the Moot Hall stairs, Swallow chasing them. He is pursuing the first niece but they find security in numbers. Swallow enters the pub and the nieces hide from Ned, who appears looking for niece two. Now begins a slow waltz as Mrs. Sedley stops him, reports that she has not seen the apprentice of Grimes for two days, and accuses Peter of murder. Ned dismisses her as a mad troublemaker or, perhaps, the victim of too much laudanum. Ned, too, goes into the Boar and Mrs. Sedley hides herself in the shadows of the boats. A hornpipe plays as

Burgess, the doctor, and the rector come out of the hall and have a thorough "Good Night" in an extended ensemble. Mrs. Sedley, preoccupied with crime, remains hidden to overhear Ellen and Balstrode returning from the beach. They know Peter's boat is in but his whereabouts are not known. Ellen shows Balstrode a jersey she found in the tide. It is John's, the one she embroidered for him. Thus begins one of the few major arias in a score where ensemble singing and chorales, the forte of Britten, dominate the music. This act soon will culminate in another powerful manifestation of this. Ellen and Balstrode agree to help Peter Grimes in his darkest moment.

They depart and Mrs. Sedley, out of the shadows, races to the pub in search of lawyer Swallow. What a magnificent musical episode this finale is. Grimes is back, she reveals, and that is enough. Hobson quickly assembles another posse and off they go, much to Mrs. Sedley's satisfaction. The pub and hall are empty and the dance music fades away as the great chorus ends this first scene of the final act:

> Him who despises us
> We'll destroy . . .
>
> . . . Peter Grimes! Peter Grimes!

His name is repeated again and again as they scatter in all directions before the closing curtain.

The brief final interlude connects the bombastic madness of the crowd to the mad scene of a deranged Peter Grimes by his boat on the waterfront. A distant foghorn and offstage voices continually intone "Peter Grimes" and he, too, in his delusion, repeats his own name. Ellen and Balstrode appear. Ellen goes to Peter and tells him they have come to take him home. There is a silence. The foghorn and chorus are quiet. Balstrode, in a speaking voice, tells Peter he will help him with the boat. To Ellen's "No" he tells Peter to sail out of sight and sink his boat. Together they push the boat to the sea and Balstrode waves good-bye. He returns to a sobbing Ellen, comforts her, and leads her toward home.

Epilogue

Dawn breaks and the normal sights and sounds of the Borough, with its various inhabitants, begin a new day. Swallow comments on the sinking of a boat at sea, too far out to be saved. Fishermen look at it through glasses but nothing can be discerned. The people go about their business singing

> In ceaseless motion comes and goes the tide.
> Flowing it fills the channel broad and wide;
> Then back to sea with strong majestic sweep
> it rolls in ebb yet terrible and deep . . .

to music sounding the flow of water rolling off into silence as the curtains slowly close on Benjamin Britten's masterpiece.

He was to write many more operas but to this day *Peter Grimes* remains his most often performed and appreciated drama. With it he accomplished what Wagner and Verdi, quite independently, agreed was the ultimate goal of operatic composition: to produce an unbroken blend of story and music in a seamless tapestry of sound. A good performance of this opera transforms the stage into a reality where dramatic characters, for better and for worse, seem no longer to act but rather to mirror the impenetrable vicissitudes of our human condition.

∾

Now, as we come to the end of this long operatic journey, I have a most telling confession to make. No opera lovers known to me love every opera of every composer simply because it is opera. It is no different with me. I knew when I prepared an outline of the chapters for this book that it must end with Britten's *Peter Grimes*. More than any other opera written during the past half-century or so, its considerable appeal has become solidly established. Nevertheless, I did not look forward to *Peter Grimes* as the end to this endeavor. Though I often introduced Britten to my opera students, his music heretofore had not one hundred percent captured me. Other than the "Sea Interludes," rarely would I listen to music from *Peter Grimes* on my own even though I knew well its importance.

All this changed as I disciplined myself to study the opera again for this presentation. Without realizing it, the music had gotten under my skin and become a part of me in the same way that countless other operas have over so many years. I learned something important about myself and in so doing relearned an important lesson of the arts. I had never given *Peter Grimes* a sporting chance. I had found the music of Britten difficult, deemed it always to be so, and was superficial in my considerations. Forced by this book to give it a fair chance, I was won over and swept away and so have added another masterpiece to my collection of operas I cannot live without. If I who know something about opera can have my difficult moments, then you can too.

The importance of my confession is obvious. Give opera a chance, especially when the music is new, modern, and contemporary. Anyone with a heart immediately can be touched by Puccini's sensuous melodies but the composers of this final chapter, those of "modern music," they especially need to be given a fair shake.

As Benjamin Britten said, "The musical experience needs three human beings at least. It requires a composer, a performer, and a listener; and unless these three take part together there is no musical experience."

This statement both is true and false. When you recall the objective of this book, for opera to become an indispensable part of your life, this quotation is true. You, the listener, have been introduced to the great composers of opera, their most notable dramas and superb performers, and now, we hope, incomparable musical experiences are yours. Britten's assertion, however, is false in missing another dimension of the musical experience that is also of critical importance. Wondrous musical experiences transpire in the presence of only one human being in what can be one of the most satisfying pleasures of musical companionship—indeed, of life itself. Think of the lonely shepherd, high on a hill, improvising on a pipe as sheep or goats graze, or of those who through the ages have filled lonesome hours making happy and mournful melodies on simple flutes. How many strings have been plucked, strummed, or bowed, how many keyboards extemporaneously played upon by those who, as Stephen Foster wrote, "dream the happy hours away"?

This other, oh so private musical story probably is one I will never write even though constantly I am nourished by musical moments such as these in a way quite different from listening to a great artist perform wonderful music. But were I ever to tell this story, I would begin by crowning myself "King of the World" and my first and everlasting decree would be, "Now and forever more do-re-mi will be as integral a part of every child's education as ABC and 1, 2, 3." Thus, early in every life, music would become a good, true, and indispensable friend. One cannot do better than that.

AFTERWORD

Vividly I recall Licia Albanese's exclamation at the end of the first opera program we did together years ago. Before a rapt audience at the Austrian Forum in New York City, I was asking this famous Puccini heroine and star of The Metropolitan Opera about her career as we shared some of her famous recordings. The program was being taped for a soon-to-be-heard broadcast and at its conclusion she said, "Oh, dear! Over already? There is so much more that I want to tell this man."

This is precisely how I feel. We have reached the end of the book and there is so much more I want to tell you—especially about the operas space did not allow me to include. Also, in the preceding pages, I was able to mention only a few of my favorite singers: There are so many great artists past and present whose countless wondrous recordings fill my study and our home to overflowing. And there are more stories about those who compose, conduct, and perform operatic music with whom I have had the good fortune to work and call my friends.

Perhaps I feel compelled to keep going hoping by doing so it will counter the disturbing trend of a declining interest in classical music. There is some truth to this and yet also true is the encouraging growth of operatic activity throughout the country and I want to be counted as part of it. Small, regional companies are spreading across the land, sustained by committed supporters so appreciative of their efforts to present unfamiliar works along with the classics. New operas, also, are being written and performed before a widening audience that includes more and more young people. Gifted young singers studiously work to master their art and with them resides the promise of thrilling new voices for the future. Attending their master classes prior to discovery always is a huge treat for me. I do not fear for the future of opera.

ᴥ

If you came to this book as an experienced and sophisticated opera lover I hope somewhere within its pages you found your knowledge expanded and your interest intensified. If a newcomer, I hope you discovered opera's magical powers and now will go forth to acquire recordings, attend performances, discover your own favorite operas and singers, and be vigorous in spreading the word of your enthusiasm.

Spreading the word is how it always has been with me. I was raised in a home where opera was heard constantly and even when quite young I wanted to share the music that brought me so much happiness. After playing football or baseball with friends I invited them to my home to hear arias played from our collection of RCA Victor Red Seal Records. I would start with the voice of the Swedish tenor Jussi Björling, so often mentioned in this book, because his was the first operatic voice that so mesmerized me every recording of his had to be acquired. Today, it could be Renée Fleming and tomorrow, who knows? Obviously, my radio program, my opera courses, and this book are an extension of this desire to share a love of music. For me, music always is more than one of life's most enjoyable pleasures. Like food and drink and sleep music fulfills an elemental human need.

GETTING STARTED WITH CDS

The following is a list of CD recordings of immediate and lasting appeal for generations of my students as well as countless listeners to my opera radio program.

AÏDA (Verdi) Price, Domingo (RCA 6198)
IL BARBIERE DI SIVIGLIA (Rossini) Prey, Berganza (DG 415695-2)
THE BEGGAR'S OPERA (Gay and Pepusch) Bryson, Caddy (Hyperion 66591)
BLUEBEARD'S CASTLE (Bartók) Ramey, Marton (Sony 44523)
LA BOHÈME (Puccini) de los Angeles, Björling (EMI 47235)
BORIS GODUNOV (Mussorgsky) Talvela, Gedda (EMI 54377)
CARMEN (Bizet) Stevens, Pierce (RCA 7981)
CAVALLERIA RUSTICANA (Mascagni) Callas, di Stefano (EMI 56827)
LA CENERENTOLA (Rossini) Bartoli, Dara (London 436902)
LA CLEMENZA DI TITO (Mozart) Johnson, McNair (Archiv 431806-2)
LES CONTES D'HOFFMANN (Offenbach) Domingo, Sutherland
  (London 417363)
COSÌ FAN TUTTE (Mozart) Caballé, Baker (Philips 422542)
THE CUNNING LITTLE VIXEN (Janáček) Watson, Allen (EMI 54212)
LA DAMNATION DE FAUST (Berlioz) Bakcr, Gedda (EMI 68583)
DIDO AND AENEAS (Purcell) Norman, Allen (Philips 416299)
DIE ZAUBERFLÖTE (Mozart) Dermota, Seefried (EMI 69631)
DON GIOVANNI (Mozart) Siepi, Grümmer (EMI 63860)
DON PASQUALE (Donizetti) Badini, Schipa (Opera D'Oro 1224)
ELEKTRA (Richard Strauss) Behrens, Ludwig (Philips 422574)
L'ELISIR D'AMORE (Donizetti) Battle, Pavarotti (DG 429744)
DIE ENTFÜHRUNG AUS DEM SERAIL (Mozart) Marshall, Simoneau
  (EMI 63715)

EUGENE ONEGIN (Tschaikovsky) Hvorostovsky, Focile (Philips 438235)
FALSTAFF (Verdi) Gobbi, Moffo (EMI 49668)
LA FANCIULLA DEL WEST (Puccini) Neblett, Domingo (DG 419640)
FAUST (Gounod) Gedda, de los Angeles (EMI 69983)
LA FAVOLA D'ORFEO (Monteverdi) Johnson, von Otter (Archiv 419250)
FIDELIO (Beethoven) Janowitz, Kollo (DG 419436)
DIE FLEDERMAUS (Johann Strauss, Jr.) Gueden, Patzak (Preiser 90491)
DER FLIEGENDE HOLLÄNDER (Wagner) Estes, Balsler (Philips 434599)
DER FREISCHÜTZ (Weber) Schreier, Janowitz (DG 415432)
GUILLAUME TELL (Rossini) Bacquier, Caballé (EMI 69951)
IDOMENEO (Mozart) Araiza, Hendricks (Philips 422537)
L'INCORONAZIONE DI POPPEA (Monteverdi) Auger, Jones
   (Virgin Classics 90775)
LOHENGRIN (Wagner) Hofmann, Armstrong (Sony 38594)
LUCIA DI LAMMERMOOR (Donizetti) Callas, Tagliavini (EMI 47440)
MADAMA BUTTERFLY (Puccini) de los Angeles, Björling (EMI 63634)
MANON (Massenet) de los Angeles, Legay (EMI 63499)
MANON LESCAUT (Puccini) Albanese, Björling (RCA 60573)
MEFISTOFELE (Boito) Siepi, Tebaldi (London 440054)
DIE MEISTERSINGER VON NÜRNBERG (Wagner) Edelmann, Schwarzkopf
   (EMI 63500)
THE MIKADO (Gilbert and Sullivan) Bottone, Rees (Sony 5884)
NORMA (Bellini) Callas, Filippeschi (EMI 47303)
LE NOZZE DI FIGARO (Mozart) Kunz, Schwarzkopf (EMI 69639)
ORFEO ED EURIDICE (Gluck) McNair, Ragin (Philips 434093)
ORPHÉE AUX ENFERS (Offenbach) Sénéchal, Mesplé (EMI 49647)
OTELLO (Verdi) Vickers, Rysanek (RCA 1969)
PAGLIACCI (Leoncavallo) Björling, de los Angeles (EMI 49503)
PARSIFAL (Wagner) Domingo, Norman (DG 437501)
PELLÉAS ET MÉLISANDE (Debussy) Henry, Alliot-Lugaz (London 430502)
PETER GRIMES (Britten) Johnson, Lott (EMI 54832)
PORGY AND BESS (Gershwin) White, Haymon (EMI 56220)
I PURITANI (Bellini) Callas, di Stefano (EMI 56275)
RIGOLETTO (Verdi) Merrill, Peters (RCA 60172)
THE RING (Wagner) Nilsson, Flagstad (London 455555)
LA RONDINE (Puccini) Te Kanawa, Domingo (Sony 37852)
DER ROSENKAVALIER (Richard Strauss) Jurinac, Reining (London 467111)
SALOME (Richard Strauss) Norman, Morris (Philips 432153)
SAMSON ET DALILA (Saint-Saëns) Domingo, Obraztsova (DG 413297)
SEMELE (Handel) Battle, Ramey (DG 435782-2)
LA SONNAMBULA (Bellini) Callas, Cossotto (EMI 47377)
TANNHÄUSER (Wagner) Hopf, Grümmer (EMI 63214)
TOSCA (Puccini) Callas, Gobbi (EMI 47174)
LA TRAVIATA (Verdi) Te Kanawa, Kraus (Philips 438238)
TRISTAN UND ISOLDE (Wagner) Kollo, Price (DG 413315)
IL TRITTICO (Puccini) de los Angeles, Gobbi (EMI 64165)
IL TROVATORE (Verdi) Björling, Milanov (RCA 6643)
TURANDOT (Puccini) Marton, Heppner (RCA 60898)
WOZZECK (Berg) Harrell, Farrell (Sony 62759)

BIBLIOGRAPHY

Though it is not possible to cite all books and articles on opera read throughout more than half a century, this book could not have been written without the following.

Books, Articles, and Reference Works

APEL, WILLI. *Harvard Dictionary of Music*, Cambridge, MA: Belknap Press, 1969.

ARNOLD, DENIS. *Monteverdi*, London: J.M. Dent & Sons, LTD, 1975.

BEKKER, PAUL. *Richard Wagner: His Life and Work*, New York: W.W. Norton & Co., 1931.

BUDDEN, JULIAN. *The Operas of Verdi*, 3 vols. New York: Oxford University Press, 1978.

CALVOCORESSI, M.D. *Mussorgsky*, London: J.M. Dent & Sons, LTD, 1974.

CHUSID, MARTIN and WILLIAM WEAVER, eds. *The Verdi Companion*, New York: W.W. Norton & Co., 1979.

COLLES, H.C., ed. *Grove's Dictionary of Music and Musicians*, New York: MacMillan Co., 1940.

DAVENPORT, MARCIA. *Mozart*, New York: Avon Books, 1979.

DAVIS, PETER G. *The American Opera Singer*, New York: Doubleday, 1997.

DEAN, WINTON. *Bizet*, London: J.M. Dent & Sons, LTD, 1974.

DENT, EDWARD J. *Mozart's Operas*, London: Oxford University Press, 1947.

DONINGTON, ROBERT. *Opera and Its Symbols*, New Haven: Yale University Press, 1990.

Encyclopaedia Britannica, Chicago: Encyclopaedia Britannica, Inc., 1946.

EWEN, DAVID. *20th Century Composers*, New York: Thomas Y. Crowell Co., 1937.

GARDEN, EDWARD. *Tchaikovsky*, London: J.M. Dent & Sons LTD, 1976.

GILBERT, W. S. *Plays and Poems of W.S. Gilbert*, New York: Random House, 1935.

GOSSETT, PHILIP ET AL. *Masters of Italian Opera*, New York: W.W. Norton & Co., 1983.

HANSLICK. EDUARD. *The Beautiful in Music*, New York: The Bobbs-Merrill Company, Inc., 1957.

HILDESHEIMER, WOLFGANG. *Mozart*, New York: Vintage Books, 1983.

HOWARD, JOHN TASKER and JAMES LYONS. *Modern Music*, New York: New American Library, 1963.

JACOBS, ARTHUR. *An Introduction to Boris Godunov*, London: EMI Records Ltd., 1977.

JACOBS, ARTHUR and STANLEY SADIE. *The Pan Book of Opera*, London: Pan Books, 1964.

JOHN, NICHOLAS, ed. *English National Opera Guides*, London: John Calder, 1981.

KOBBÉ, GUSTAV; Earl of Harewood, ed. *The Definitive Kobbé's Opera Book*, New York: G.P. Putnam, 1987.

MAREK, GEORGE R. *The Riddle of Turandot*, New York: RCA, 1960.

MORDDEN, ETHAN. *Opera Anecdotes*, Oxford: Oxford University Press, 1985.

NEWMAN, ERNEST. *The Wagner Operas*, New York: Alfred A. Knopf, 1963.

———. *The Life of Richard Wagner*, 4 vols. New York: Alfred A. Knopf, 1933-1946.

NICHOLS, ROGER and RICHARD LANGHAM SMITH, eds. *Claude Debussy: Pelléas et Mélisande*, New York: Cambridge University Press, 1989.

Opera Libretto Library, 3 vols. New York: Avenel Books, 1980.

ORREY, LESLIE. *A Concise History of Opera*, New York: Charles Scribner's Sons, 1972.

PAYNE, NICHOLAS. *An Introduction to William Tell*, Middlesex, England: 1973.

ROBB, STEWART. *Tristan and Isolde*. New York: E.P. Dutton & Co., Inc., 1965.

SADIE, STANLEY et al. *The New Grove's Dictionary of Opera*, 4 vols. New York: Grove's Dictionaries of Music, 1992.

SADIE, STANLEY. *The New Grove Mozart*, New York: W.W. Norton & Co., 1986.

SCHUMANN, KARL. *The History of Opera*, Alleur, The Netherlands: Philips Classics, 1993.

SEEGER, HORST. *Opern Lexikcon*, Berlin: Heinrichshofen's Verlag, 1978.

SHAW, BERNARD. *Shaw on Music*, New York: Doubleday & Co., Inc., 1955.

STEIN, JACK M. *Richard Wagner and the Synthesis of the Arts*, Detroit: Wayne State University Press, 1960.

TASSART, MAURICE. *Orphée aux Enfers*, Middlesex, England: EMI Classics, 1979.

TYRRELL, JOHN. *On the Cunning Little Vixen*, Middlesex, England: EMI Records, Ltd., 1991.

Victor Book of Opera, 4th ed., Camden, New Jersey: Victor Talking Machine Co., 1912.

WAGNER, GOTTFRIED. *Twlight of the Wagners*, New York: Picador, 2000.

WAGNER, RICHARD. *My Life*, New York: Dodd, Mead & Co., 1911.

WARRACK, JOHN and EWAN WEST. *The Concise Oxford Dictionary of Opera*, Oxford: Oxford University Press, 1996.

WEINSTOCK, HERBERT. *Rossini*, New York: Alfred A. Knopf, 1968.

Webster's Biographical Dictionary, Springfield, MA: G. & C. Merriam Co., 1961.

Libretti

Many of the libretti consulted were included with long playing opera recordings, some regrettably out of print, in my collection. Others are from CD boxed sets still available. For Italian, French, and German operas occasionally I used (and documented) a standard translation. Often I consulted several versions of the same opera and tinkered with the translations by taking the liberty to alter them, I hope, to read better and more naturally in accord with modern usage. In a significant number of cases, however, I made my own translations with no intention to render the words for singing. For the operas in Russian, Czech, and Hungarian I had to rely on long accepted translations. I know how difficult it is to make an intelligent and readable translation and thus am much indebted to all of the following:

AÏDA/Dale McAdoo/RCA Records
THE BARBER OF SEVILLE/Edward J. Dent
LA BOHÈME/William Weaver
BLUEBEARD'S CASTLE/Chester Kallman
BORIS GODUNOV/David Lloyd-Jones/EMI Records
CARMEN/ Nell and John Moody
LA CENERENTOLA/Cetra-Soria Records
COSÌ FAN TUTTE/Rev. Marmaduke Brown
THE CUNNING LITTLE VIXEN/Yveta Synek Graft and Robert T. Jones
LA DAMNATION DE FAUST/Deutsche Grammophon
DON GIOVANNI/Edward J. Dent, Norman Platt and Laura Sarti,
    William Weaver
ELEKTRA/G.M. Holland and Ken Chalmers
L'ELISIR D'AMORE/Arthur Jacobs
EUGENE ONEGIN/Peggy Cochrane
LA FANCIULLA DEL WEST/Gwyn Morris
FALSTAFF/Vincent Sheean
FAUST/B. Vienne
FIDELIO/Lionel Salter
DIE FLEDERMAUS/Edward Cushing, Paul Kerby
THE FLYING DUTCHMAN/Ulric Kaskell, Ernest Newman
DER FREISCHÜTZ/William Mann
LOHENGRIN/Michael Danner, Richard Hockaday
LUCIA DI LAMMERMOOR/Robert Bagar
MADAMA BUTTERFLY/William Weaver
THE MASTERSINGERS/Peter Branscomb, Frederick Jameson
MANON LESCAUT/Mowbray Marras
NORMA/Dale McAdoo, Herbert Weinstock
LE NOZZE DI FIGARO/William R. Gann, Edward J. Dent

ORPHÉE AUX ENFERS/EMI Classics
OTELLO/Avril Bardoni
PARSIFAL/Lionel Salter
PELLÉAS ET MÉLISANDE/Decca Record Company
IL PURITANI/William Weaver
RIGOLETTO/RCA Records Libretto
THE RING CYCLE/E.M. Holland, Peggy Cochrane, Andrew Porter,
   Stewart Robb, William Mann
LA RONDINE/CBS Recordings
DER ROSENKAVALIER/Walter Legge
SALOME/Lord Alfred Douglas
SAMSON ET DALILA/EMI Records
LA SONNAMBULA/William Weaver
TANNHÄUSER/William R. Gann
THE TALES OF HOFFMANN/Michael Kaye
LA TRAVIATA/Edmund Tracey, Alice Berezomsky, Dale McAdoo
TRISTAN AND ISOLDE/Stewart Robb
IL TRITTICO/Kenneth Chalmer
IL TROVATORE/Dale McAdoo
TOSCA/Joseph Machlis
TURANDOT/Decca Record Company
WILLIAM TELL/Decca Record Company
WOZZECK/Gary Bramall

INDEX